D1031854

West's Law School Advisory Board

CASES AND MATERIALS ON

INTERNATIONAL LITIGATION AND ARBITRATION

By

Thomas E. Carbonneau
Orlando Distinguished Professor of Law
Pennsylvania State University

AMERICAN CASEBOOK SERIES®

Mat #40347708

610 Opperman Drive
P.O. Box 64526
St. Paul, MN 55164–0526
1–800–328–9352

Printed in the United States of America

ISBN 0–314–15976–2

In memory of my father and mother:

Adrien J. and Lucille C. (Sirois) Carbonneau

*

Acknowledgements

Jeanette Jaeggi, Esq. and Kimberly Koko, Esq. provided invaluable editing, proof-reading, and indexing services. The students in my International Commercial Litigation course (Fall 2004) at Penn State Dickinson also provided proof-reading assistance. Professor Pat K. Chew of the University of Pittsburgh School of Law read the manuscript and supplied useful comments.

Publications Permissions Were Granted By:

The author gratefully acknowledges the copyright permissions granted by the following organizations:

1. The American Law Institute (ALI) and the International Institute for the Unification of Private Law (UNIDROIT) to reprint excerpts of PRINCIPLES AND RULES ON TRANSNATIONAL CIVIL PROCEDURE 30–35 (Proposed Final Draft 2004) (all rights reserved).

2. The Texas International Law Journal to reprint excerpts from Westbrook, *Theories of Parent Liability and the Prospects for an International Settlement,* 20 TEX. INT'L L.J. 321 (1985); Galanter, *Legal Torpor: Why So Little Has Happened in India After the Bhopal Tragedy,* 20 TEX. INT'L L.J. 273 (1985); Dhavan, *For Whom? And For What? Reflections on the Legal Aftermath of Bhopal,* 20 TEX. INT'L L.J. 295 (1985); Weinberg, *Insights and Ironies: The American Bhopal Cases,* 20 TEX. INT'L L.J. 307 (1985).

3. The American Journal of International Law to reprint excerpts from Leigh, Judicial Decisions: *International Land Boundary Delimitation—Principle of UTI Possidetis—Distinction Between Determination of a Land Boundary and Delimitation of Continental Shelf,* 81 AM. J. INT'L L. 411 (1987).

4. Juris Publishing, Inc. to reprint excerpts from T. CARBONNEAU, CASES AND MATERIALS ON THE LAW AND PRACTICE OF ARBITRATION (Rev. 3d ed. 2003); T. CARBONNEAU, THE LAW AND PRACTICE OF ARBITRATION (2004); Ball, *Probity Deconstructed—How Helpful, Really, are the New International Bar Association Guidelines on*

Conflicts of Interest in International Arbitration?, 15 WORLD ARB. & MEDIATION REP. 333 (2004).

5. The author and the Cleveland State Law Review to reprint excerpts from Przeracki, *"Working It Out": A Japanese Alternative To Fighting It Out,* 37 CLEV. ST. L. REV. 149 (1989).

6. The author and the Asian-Pacific Law and Policy Journal to reprint excerpts from Lin, *A Quiet Revolution: An Overview of China's Judicial Reform,* 4 ASIAN-PAC. L. & POL'Y J. 9 (2003).

7. The Tulsa Journal of Comparative and International Law to reprint excerpts from Zhang & Zwier, *Burden of Proof: Developments in Modern Chinese Evidence Rules,* 10 TULSA J. COMP. & INT'L L. 419 (2003).

8. The Hastings International and Comparative Law Review to reprint excerpts from Carbonneau, *The French Exequatur Proceedings: The Exorbitant Jurisdictional Rules of Articles 14 and 15 (Code Civil) as Obstacles to the Enforcement of Foreign Judgments in France,* 2 HASTINGS INT'L & COMP. L. REV. 307 (1979).

9. The Houston Journal of International Law to reprint excerpts from Staff & Lewis, *Arbitration Under NAFTA Chapter 11: Past, Present, And Future,* 25 HOUSTON J. INT'L L. 301 (2003).

10. Baker & McKenzie, L.L.P. to reprint Newman & Zaslowsky, *Cultural Predictability in International Arbitration* (2004).

11. Foundation Press to reprint excerpts from *H. Steiner & D. Vagts, Transnational Legal Problems* (2d ed. 1976).

Summary of Contents

*

Table of Contents

*

Table of Cases

References are to pages.

*

CASES AND MATERIALS ON

INTERNATIONAL LITIGATION AND ARBITRATION

*

Introduction

1. The Global Marketplace

Globalization, a phenomenon envisaged after WWII but begun in earnest in the 1990s after the fall of communism, confounds the traditionally domestic pursuit and regulation of business. Further, it ignores the long-standing national character of economic organization and political authority. As the emergence of the EU (European Union), NAFTA (North American Free Trade Agreement), and MERCOSUR (the attempt to create a common market between Argentina, Brazil, Paraguay, and Uruguay) demonstrates, globalization at a minimum demands that governments adopt a regional perspective on the regulation of business. The Internet and the computer revolution have contributed to the "denationalization" of commerce. Along with other technologies, they have eclipsed national boundaries by providing instantaneous access to people, events, and places throughout the world. International and local commerce are increasingly linked and becoming indistinguishable. It is commonplace to make deals, sell goods and services, or create business organizations in transborder circumstances. Companies look beyond borders to enter lucrative markets, benefit from cheaper labor, and find more accommodating regulatory policies.

The sputtering efforts toward globalization in the 1950s and 1960s were largely based upon American economic and military hegemony. Truly worldwide commerce did not develop because of disproportionalities in growth and resources and ideological warfare. In the next few decades, a powerful Japanese economy began to dominate world commerce. With the dissolution of the communist bloc, genuinely global economic activity flourished. The triumph of capitalism resulted in the formation of regional trading groups. From a historical perspective, however, these developments were merely spokes on the wheel of economic cycles. Global trade was certainly not new. Transborder commerce existed in the ancient world and in the feudal age. Medieval trade fairs, for example, relied on a global law of commerce, the would-be *lex mercatoria*, to resolve mercantile disputes anywhere business was transacted. The rules and practices that govern maritime relationships between shipowners, charters, buyers and sellers of cargo, sailors, and port workers date back to *les rôles d'Oléron*. Commercial activity has always been a centerpiece of human society, and commerce always seeks to grow and expand. New markets mean greater profits and provide consumers with access to a wide variety of goods at competitive prices.

Governments sometimes perceive disadvantage in unregulated non-domestic commercial activity. "Free" trade can devastate enterprises or make them thrive. Constituencies, therefore, pressure political leaders to engage in protectionism by establishing tariffs and duties against foreign goods and services. Such measures not only create barriers to trade, but they also falsify the dynamic and the positioning of actors within the marketplace. They insulate domestic businesses from the reality of commercial competition. The objective is to promote domestic commerce at all costs even if it means closing domestic markets to all foreign products. Trade unionism supports protectionist practices by demanding that domestic employment not be subject to external economic forces. The edifice of protectionism is built upon the misapprehension that self-sufficiency is possible through unilateralism and can create prosperous societies. It reflects the rule of fear rather than the positive ethic of autonomy. Nonetheless, economic protectionism, sometimes bordering on xenophobia, has been the basic State practice in terms of global trade. The World Trade Organization (WTO) and its predecessor, the GATT (General Agreement on Tariffs and Trade), are an exception to the rule of economic isolationism and the parochial safeguarding of national interest. The movement to globalization attempts to restore economic vitality to national economies by having them participate in a regime of economic competition.

2. The Impact on Law Practice

The doing-of-business across national boundaries creates special challenges for and has altered the practice of law. For litigators, the "front-end" problems of the trial process are exacerbated—service of process, jurisdiction and venue, as well as discovery and other record-building activities. The "back-end" factor of enforcement also is made more precarious. For office lawyers, contracts are more difficult to negotiate and write. The parties are separated by cultural and national diversity; miscommunications and misunderstandings are more likely; and it is unclear how transactional problems are to be resolved. When foreign parties and countries are implicated, diplomatic and political considerations emerge. The role of lawyers and courts varies from country to country. In fact, legality itself may be transformed when a border is crossed. National political and juridical institutions exercise sovereign authority only within national boundaries. The very concept of litigation and of the contract may change with venue. Foreign lawyers, trained according to civil law principles or who participate in religious or regional legal traditions, may not understand U.S. lawyers and, in fact, may exhibit hostility to an "alien" approach to law.

U.S. lawyers who engage in transborder practice must not only be well versed in the law, they must also develop diplomatic skills and refine their sense of juridical and cultural sociology. In addition to tolerating travel, they must learn to adjust to foreign circumstances and situations. Serious misunderstandings can arise when familiar assumptions are made about language, social and professional roles, and patterns of behavior. Different people think and behave differently. Although English may have become the language of international business, the ability to communicate in a foreign language remains a valuable asset and translations usually do not capture the cultural and other perceptions that underlie statements and conduct.

While it is a premier export, U.S. legal training and education are not universal commodities. European, Latin American, and African lawyers are not molded in the same way as their American counterparts. Most non-U.S. academic law programs are part of an undergraduate university curriculum. They do not lead to the award of a professional degree. Graduates have a standard bachelor's degree, in most cases. Generally, foreign law schools, known as faculties, do not provide the extra-curriculars—law review, moot court, legal writing, clinical or internship experiences. Codified law deplaces case law as the central source of legal rules. Lectures are substituted for discussions and dialogues. If they are to be effective and to influence their circumstances, U.S. lawyers must develop the skills necessary to deal with foreign-trained attorneys. There obviously must be reciprocity and mutuality between all of the implicated parties as well. It should be underscored, however, that tolerance of professional diversity is rare and that the differences between legal traditions and systems have sometimes generated the type of acrimony that can fuel a religious war.

3. The Diversity of Legal Systems and Concepts

The idea of contract illustrates the gap that can exist between legal systems and methods. In the United States, lawyers and courts revere the contract. It establishes the law between the parties—their rights and obligations. The contract must be written and is the final expression of the parties' intent. Unless the document fails to express the parties' basic agreement, the courts must not supplement or supplant it.

Civil law lawyers have a different assessment of how to craft a contract and establish its contents. Prior to the new surge toward globalization, they saw the detail and complexity of contracts drafted by U.S. lawyers as unnecessary and counterproductive. To lawyers trained in codified law, these American common law instruments lacked an essential elegance and synthetic quality. Moreover, rather than anchor transactions in a foundation of predictability, they encouraged lawsuits. In their view, the principle of the good faith performance of contractual undertakings constituted a sufficient basis for policing the enforcement of private bargains. Ponderous, air-tight documents were not a substitute for the intellectual discipline and certainty of the rule of law founded in the code.

To Asian lawyers, the contract has minor significance. It is neither a bible nor a literary work of art. It is nothing more than a relatively perfunctory documentary reflection of the parties' commercial relationship. In Japan, issues within the parties' relationship are resolved by reference to an established social hierarchy and patterned social practices. Moreover, government bureaucracy—and not courts—perform the oracular function in Japanese society. Lawyers, courts, and contracts are not as sacrosanct in Japan as they are in the United States. When economic circumstances demand it, Japanese merchants will abide by

Western commercial practices and engage in sophisticated contracting. These practices, however, are external and imposed. In China, where Asian cultural patterns are combined with the politics of totalitarianism, statist considerations can readily dominate all aspects of commercial transactions. The "people's imperative" can overwhelm private agreements and eliminate any reference to and the function of judicial or arbitral discretion.

The garb of juridical civilization, therefore, can differ radically between countries and systems. Even the notion of due process of law—instrumental to the constitutional legitimacy of legal or governmental action in the United States—is not necessarily recognized or applicable in other legal systems. Fairness can have many different structural expressions and definitions. Civil jury trials, for example, occur nearly exclusively in the United States. Adversarial representation is not the sole dialogue for the trial. In civil law systems, civil servant judges—not the parties' attorneys—have substantial authority in the conduct of trial proceedings. The very concept of the trial has a number of manifestations. Juridical civilization sports a variety of regional costumes.

Yet, U.S. lawyers must represent clients who want to do business abroad or with foreign parties. These lawyers, therefore, must confront a number of questions: Whether they can enter foreign jurisdictions for purposes of legal representation and, if so, on the basis of what status and under what restrictions; whether they can retain and work with local counsel in foreign jurisdictions, and what ethical rules apply in these circumstances; whether foreign courts in the host country are functional and impartial, especially in litigation involving non-domestic parties; and whether the host legal system recognizes or has articulated concepts of private international law and is hospitable to the application of non-national law and the enforcement of foreign judicial orders or judgments. Such lawyers must also be able to read the underlying cultural attitude of the prospective country of investment and be able to detect and assess the risk that might attend the transactions.

In these circumstances, prior experience and cultural affinity on the part of the U.S. lawyer are invaluable. Also, U.S. lawyers must strike some balance between providing "zealous representation" to the client according to U.S. standards and "over lawyering" the transaction. In situations in which foreign law and jurisdiction apply, foreign perceptions and cultural stereotyping can become significant obstacles to effective representation. Differences can breed antagonisms and offense. Simply following domestic training and practice is likely to lead to a situation of having deaf people shouting at each other (*le dialogue des sourds*). Skillfully adjusting to cultural dispositions while maintaining core representational protections appears to be the order of the day. The objective is not to cower to foreign practices, but rather effectively to deal with them.

* * * *

T. CARBONNEAU, ALTERNATIVE DISPUTE RESOLUTION 23–39 (1989)
[excerpted and footnotes omitted]

...There is a multiplicity of views on how world legal systems with their diverse juridical cultures should be classified. The proposed grouping is based upon how each legal system goes about establishing its substantive epistemology of law: What the system identifies as the primary source of substantive legal rules. The four principal juridical traditions that respond to the classification—the civil law, common law, soviet-socialist, and Scandinavian systems—represent divergent intellectual assumptions, methods, and processes about how the truth of legality should be integrated into society.

The distinction between the source of law in civil law and common law systems can be illustrated by the way in which lawyers in each system approach the discovery of governing legal principles. For example, in a legal action brought by divorcing parents over the custody of children, a civilian lawyer would typically refer to the codified law for guidance. By training and disposition, the civil-law lawyer is inclined to believe in and be persuaded by general rules that proceed from an organic, intellectually cohesive text of law. Accordingly, the Civil Code articulates the governing rule—be it a regime of sole custody, maternal preference, joint custody, or the caretaker parent standard—and the courts simply read the specific facts of each case and reach a determination in light of the Code's general answer to the problem. The civil-law lawyer is guided by the belief that the Code's general directives are sufficiently universal to provide answers to the resolution of particular controversies.

A lawyer trained in the common-law tradition has a much different evaluation of the legal significance and meaning of a general statutory statement of applicable law. The controlling directive on child custody matters would be of dubious adjudicatory merit until it had been implemented and refined in the context of specific cases. Succinctly stated, common-law lawyers view legislative answers, the "solemn expression of the legislative will" in civil-law systems, with considerable skepticism. Common-law systems do not fashion governing legal rules by initial and final reference to a codified text of law, but rather through the progressive elaboration of legal principles in judicial decisions. The heart of the common-law enterprise resides in a vision of the law as emerging in an evolutive context in which factually similar cases gradually yield a controlling rule of law, a precedent applying in subsequent, factually analogous litigation.

This basic difference between the two systems is operative primarily at the general level of systemic abstraction. It separates the systems and the actors within those systems on intellectual grounds and in terms of [how they] ascertain[] the truth of law. Yet, despite the [differences] in conceptual methodology, courts in each system tend to reach similar, sometimes identical, adjudicatory results. Moreover, civil-law systems, to some extent, do recognize the binding force of prior decisional law; in any event, they do not ignore the importance of facts and the specificity of factual patterns in reaching adjudicatory determinations. By the same token, the accumulation of precedent in common-law systems, especially in England, in conjunction with the growing enactment of and reference to statutes, does yield controlling and generalized principles of law, tending to moderate the skepticism about codified law.

Despite their affinity to the civil-law pattern, socialist legal systems espouse a unique epistemology of law—one that differs from its counterparts in all other juridical cultures. Under socialist organization, law is relegated to the status of an ancillary social force. Its content and scope are dominated by the political and historical dynamic that propels the evolution of the state. Laws are mere instruments for the expression of a higher political truth embodied in the tenets of Marxist–Leninist ideology. Accordingly, legal rules and principles are temporary vehicles in the quest toward a perfected communist society. Once the collective and individual consciousness have united in the ultimate socialist ideal, law will no longer be necessary. The truth of socialist law, therefore, is inextricably bound to the convictions of a political ideology that seeks to redeem humanity from its alleged historical and social corruption. Grounded upon absolute beliefs about humanity and the purpose of social organization, and bent upon transposing that creed into a social order, socialist legal systems and their truth resemble legal orders and systems founded upon religious teachings and beliefs.

Like socialist legal regimes, Scandinavian legal systems also are an offshoot of the civil-law paradigm. Although these systems have some form of codified law, continuous legislative enactments are the primary source of law. Legislative revision provides the social organization with the legal truthfulness necessary to its viability. With some national variations on the basic pattern, the intellectual disposition of Scandinavian lawyers is to look to the specificity and responsiveness of contemporary legislation for the content of their substantive legal epistemology. It has been said that "Swedish lawyers tend to think and argue in terms of legislative rulings and to regard statute law as the most important source of law."

The identification of a primary source of substantive law is, however, only part of the epistemology of legal systems. While the various systemic approaches reflect a diversity of intellectual foundations for establishing core legal principles and the truth of legality, civil codes, case law, political ideology, or statutes, by themselves, provide little guidance in evaluating how justice is finally achieved in a particular system. The sources of law also fail to proffer an adequate basis for appraising whether and how greater truthfulness might be introduced into legal systems. A comparison of the approaches merely indicates that the systems adopt a variable knowledge predicate for their eventual assertion of what is legally truthful.

[. . .]

The received wisdom of the comparative study of law is that the various legal systems can be further classified according to their adjudicatory methodologies. Moreover, this further basis for distinction corresponds to, and reinforces the classification of, legal systems according to their technique for discovering substantive law.

There are two basic methods of adjudicatory truth-seeking among legal systems: the inquisitorial and the adversarial models of adjudication. Typically, civil-law systems are reputed to espouse the inquisitorial method of adjudication because it better accommodates their central concern for the primacy of codified law and their general tendency to attribute subordinate importance to procedural law. Accordingly, adjudication through inquisition is an attempt to ascertain legal truth in disputes through oligarchical judicial control that places foremost value on the integrity of the substantive law. Discounting confrontational debate as a means of discovering the truth of disputed circumstances, it attributes significant weight to written evidence, an active role to the judge in the discovery of facts, and a central authority to the court in the conduct of the proceedings. The characterizing element of the process is that professionally trained judges, not the advocates or the parties, are invested with public adjudicatory authority and responsibility. Concomitantly, the truth of adjudication and legality should arise from the knowledge of law that proceeds from judicial expertise and experience.

The adversarial ethic is said to epitomize the common-law approach to the adjudication of civil disputes. At first blush at least, the adversarial methodology to legal truth-seeking appears to contrast sharply with the characteristics of inquisitorial justice. In adversarial adjudication, the parties do combat and are the prime movers of the proceedings. Judges assume an "umpireal" role, and juries—at least according to the general theory—perform a vital decision-making function in the civil trial process. The adversarial methodology, therefore, attributes predominant responsibility to the parties, in their confrontation for the discovery of facts and for the evolution of the proceeding. It also places significant importance upon the intricacies of procedure. Finally, it democratizes determinations by making the jury, the voice of community standards, the essential means of arriving at legally truthful results.

[. . .]

In England, there appears to have been a gradual evolution toward a judge-centered, *albeit* adversarial, trial process, accompanied by a decline in the importance of procedural requirements in judicial proceedings. Reliance upon legal expertise and specialized skills seems to characterize most stages of the English civil adjudicatory process. Under the bifurcated structure of the English legal profession, solicitors undertake to establish the evidence relevant to a client's case, including a summary of the client's statements and documents as well as interviews with other parties who have information pertaining to the matter. Barristers traditionally are distant from, and have little authority in, the fact-finding phase of the process, and limit their involvement to consultations with the solicitor.

[. . .]

As in the United States, the trial in England is an event, a dramatization of the parties' controversy, their opposing interests, and their positions on the law. Intended to be an uninterrupted, single occurrence, the trial proceeding is a highly concentrated, predominantly oral process that emphasizes the barrister's advocacy skills. That most, if not all, of the relevant documentation, including judicial precedent and statutes, are read aloud in court underscores the fundamentally oral character of the trial proceeding. Working from the documents supplied by the solicitor, the barristers call and examine witnesses (whose testimony may sometimes diverge from documentary accounts), debate the probative value of evidence, and argue pertinent points of law. The relatively rigid demarcation of professional duties among barristers and solicitors prevents staging the proceeding with prepared witnesses or with a stock presentation of the case. The oral, spontaneous discourse with its attendant element of surprise places a premium upon quick understanding and response in the dialogue among the barristers, the court, and the witnesses.

By comparison to their American analogue, the English rules of evidence, especially when the judge is sitting on the case alone, are quite relaxed. Judges usually take an active part in the questioning of witnesses and in developing their testimony. "Evidence precluded in the United States often is admitted unchallenged in an English proceeding, and a barrister is more hesitant in objecting to a line of inquiry presented by the judge than by opposing counsel." English judges, who are probably more revered than their American counterparts, also rule upon evidentiary and other procedural matters that arise during the trial and generally have the responsibility of supervising the proceedings to maintain fairness and efficiency.

[. . .]

In light of these basic differences, grouping Anglo–American common-law systems under the general rubric of adversarial adjudicatory systems is a misleading oversimplification of the reality. English and American civil procedure do share a number of core traits. Both involve a trial proceeding that is a single, concentrated, and oral episode. Their affinity lapses, however, by their eventual adoption and implementation of different epistemologies for ascertaining the truth of legality. Contemporary civil litigation in England places foremost reliance upon the knowledge that arises from legal expertise and experience to discover how disputes can be truthfully resolved. Adversarial debate and jousting appear simply to be other parts of the process, limited to the dialogue that takes place among the barristers and the court. The institution of the civil jury—which arose as an element of civilization in early common law, replacing the trial by ordeal as the means of ascertaining the factual truth of controversies—has a very limited significance in defining the truth of legality in the resolution of current private law controversies in England.

In the United States, the right to a civil trial by jury, an integral part of constitutional guarantees, gives the adversarial ethic a much greater imprint upon the process of civil adjudication. The presence of a civil jury in American proceedings attributes a much wider scope to the drama and possible distortion that can accompany adversarial legal dialogue. It makes complex procedural evidentiary rules necessary. Perhaps most significantly, civil trial by jury in the United States by comparison to England dislodges the expert reference to substantive law in the resolution of private law disputes, allowing in many instances procedural considerations and tactical maneuvering to dictate the rule of law. With the jury as the central decision-maker, mere adversarial posturing can sometimes be mistaken for the truth of a particular situation. The lack of a strict system of binding precedent among courts further encourages the recourse to this essentially *ad hoc* epistemology and emphasis upon procedural regularity as the central ingredient of justice.

The virtual elimination of the civil jury trial and the concomitant integration of a judge-centered feature to the trial proceeding brings the English process closer to some of the principal characteristics of the so-called inquisitorial prototype, in which substantive, expert determinations appear to have a greater hold. The English and American systems of civil adjudication, therefore, seek and achieve a markedly different form of legal truth.

The commonly held perception that civil adjudicatory procedures in civil-law systems are inquisitorial in character is also mistaken. Although an inquisitorial procedural framework—referring to the judge's active part and controlling authority in the conduct of the proceedings and in the discovery of facts—does govern criminal law procedures, civil proceedings in most romanist legal systems contain distinctly adversarial elements despite their judge-centered characteristics. The parties' right to be heard, known in French law as *le contradictoire*, attributes an essential adversarial aspect to the trial and is an indispensable element of the civilian concept of procedural due process. According to article 16 of the French Code of civil Procedure, "the judge must in all situations ensure that the principle that both sides must be heard be observed and must himself observe it."

In civil trials, civil-law judges—like their English counterparts—take an active role in questioning witnesses and developing the evidence and testimony presented by counsel. In both the English and French systems, the parties initiate the litigation and define its content through their statements of facts, allegations, and contentions. The court generally supervises and participates in these aspects of the process and is responsible for evaluating the issues generated by the dispute in reference to the controlling law. In England, the court decides the controversy in keeping with binding precedent and rules on the weight of the evidence according to flexible exclusionary rules. Similarly, in civil-law systems like France, the probative value of submitted evidence is subject to the court's free evaluation. Moreover, according to article 12 of the

French Code of Civil Procedure, the court has the ultimate authority to provide a legal ruling on the matter, provided the principle of *le contradictoire* (basically, adversarial representation) has been observed: "The judge decides the dispute in accordance with the applicable rules of law. He must give or restore the[] correct classification to the facts and [conduct] in dispute, not accepting the characterizations proposed by the parties. He may not raise pure points of law on his own motion without having previously invited the parties to submit their views."

[. . .]

Notes and Questions

1. The reading makes the basic point that the world of law is a complex place and consists of some radically different approaches to the making and administration of legal rules. Diversity creates interesting and rich distinctions, but it also generates challenges and dilemmas. Providing legal counseling and representation requires a good sense of identity and a capacity for tolerance, as well as the ability to adjust. The attempt to impose different foreign standards into a local legal setting always will lead to animosity and substantial problems of communication. The breakdown of a transaction can be very costly to the client.

2. If you could paint with words, what type of image would you create of the continental European civil law lawyer? Would it resemble the Dickens-like caricatures of 19th century lawyers that sometimes adorn U.S. law school walls? Is the more modern European lawyer different? Easier to approach and to do business with? Do you believe that European lawyers see themselves primarily as business counselors? Are they as "well-trained" as a U.S. attorney?

3. Can you extend your foray into cultural professional types to Latin American, Asian, and African lawyers? What do you really know about any of them? There are superficial views, but isn't it likely that their actual reality is much more complex? How should a U.S. attorney proceed to establish a working relationship with foreign lawyers? What requirements are absolutely necessary and which should be avoided at all costs?

4. When would you consider hiring a foreign lawyer? How would you proceed? What are the essential elements of the relationship?

5. Is it fair to say that continental European justice systems are bureaucratic? If that characterization is accurate, does it mean that they are somehow inferior? What are the elements of bureaucratic justice? Are European legal proceedings different from administrative law proceedings? Does it astound you that European civil law systems have "judge schools" and that their graduates begin to function as judges upon graduation, usually in their mid-to late twenties? Does it make any difference that the judge schools have highly competitive entrance requirements?

6. Is the American trial process better? Is it fair to say that, while the European trial relies on expertise and professional experience, its U.S. counterpart focuses upon theatrics and the staging of the proceeding? Is

there virtue to democracy in this setting? Is one model more truthful than the other? More reliable and predictable?

7. What intellectual dispositions underlie the European and American trials? How do each of them fashion rules of law and apply them? Are the would-be differences a matter of style? Is there an essential equivalence between the systems?

8. Formerly, socialist legal systems were unique in the central presence they attributed to politics in the administration of justice. Trial proceedings testified to socialist ideology and were effective instruments for promoting repression. What does the U.S. legal system and legal service industry attest to? Law appears central (sometimes begrudgingly) to American society and law firms, courts, and law schools are sophisticated enterprises. Strength, centrality, and adaptability are the watchwords of American law. Is it accurate to say that the U.S. system sets the global standard in law? That it has become not only a unique, but also universal process of law?

9. The possible global ascendancy of the U.S. legal system needs to take into account the drawbacks of its trial process. Apart from its appealing rigor, it has enormous foibles that relate to untrained jurors, exorbitant damages, enormous costs, and protracted delays. What reformation might be undertaken?

10. Would a composite system be possible that would consist of the best features of each legal tradition? What form might such a system take? How might you foster its transnational acceptability?

4. Characteristic Disputes

Tort and contract are the primary source of disputes that engender private international litigation. Of the two areas, contract historically has produced the majority of transborder claims. Typical circumstances involve the buying and selling and the transport of commodities: For example, Company USA seeks to diversify its holdings and—to that end—acquires a candy manufacturer in Michigan. The candy manufacturer, however, has not been realizing a substantial return on its investment of time, money, and assets in the last several quarters. The new CEO decides to cut costs in order to make her division of the parent company more profitable. She discovers that she can cut costs substantially by purchasing sugar from a Brazilian company. The company owns a number of farming collectives in an agricultural province that produce sugar cane. It also owns a number of processing plants that convert the sugar cane into refined sugar. The company has a long history in Brazil, but recently has been partially privatized. Its new managers are seeking to develop an international market for their product. They are offering to discount the market price of sugar by 35% provided the buyer accepts responsibility for the transport of the goods from Brazil to their ultimate destination.

The U.S. candy manufacturer sees the circumstance as a means of increasing its profitability by reducing the costs of production. It agrees to buy 50,000 metric tons of sugar from the Brazilian company. It also enters into a contract with a transportation company, headquartered in

Montréal, Québec, Canada, to haul the commodity from the port in Brazil to a company plant in Ann Arbor, Michigan. The sales contract states a purchase price of $10 million USD and provides that the sugar will be ready for transport by a given date. The Brazilian company also undertakes "to exercise its best efforts to secure the necessary government permissions and licenses to effectuate the sale." The contract further states that it is governed by Brazilian law to the extent that the law "conforms to the essential commercial usages of customary international commercial law."

The agreement with the transportation company stipulates a price for the service that is to be provided. The transaction involves the rental of a cargo ship through a charter party agreement. There is a "hold harmless" clause in the standard contract for delays due to *force majeure* events and other uncontrollable, irresistible, and unforeseeable external circumstances. The crew is the exclusive responsibility of the transportation company. The latter insists that the contract be governed by French law.

The sugar is produced and refined and ready for transport. The ship has been dispatched to the designated Brazilian port and is about to arrive. On the eve of its arrival, however, the Brazilian government decides to address a long-standing gasoline shortage by prohibiting indefinitely any export of sugar cane or sugar cane products. The license to effectuate the shipment is cancelled. Covering on the open market is a very expensive proposition. The additional cost and delay generated by the transaction, plus the problems with the transportation company, convince the parent company to liquidate the candy manufacturer.

The foregoing circumstances depict a typical transaction with equally typical transactional issues and problems. International transactions are froth with risk; risk accounts for their profitability and their potential for failure. Risk is greater because the transactions take place outside the known and familiar domestic context. The contract is a primary source of law in these circumstances. It is also a means of tempering the risks of the transaction.

Transactions that involve direct foreign investment are contractual in nature, but present a special set of counseling considerations. Establishing or buying a foreign company or entity demands attention to a variety of issues: Government permissions, language skills, familiarity with local business practices, tax regulations, labor law, social security, health benefits, other employment regulations, transportation, customs, import-export duties, tariffs, and product liability laws. Each of these issues is likely to differ substantially from its American counterpart and could be a critical factor to the success of the investment. They constitute the invisible overhead of foreign investment. Effective local guidance is essential; it must be both well-informed and accurately understood by the foreign investor.

Personal injury suffered abroad or (although less likely) at home through foreign products or parties also generate international litigation. In this setting, dispute resolution alternatives or other adapted devices are less plausible because usually there is no actual relationship between the parties prior to the causation of injury and, therefore, no opportunity to agree to particular processes or procedures in the event of harm. For this reason, court litigation is the most probable form of recourse. Much of the litigation is likely to arise from the presence of U.S. nationals on foreign soil. U.S. military personnel stationed abroad, business people, students, or tourists, all can suffer serious bodily injury or death abroad because of negligence or other lapses of duty. Personal injury litigation, which is quite ordinary in a purely domestic setting, can become extraordinary and exceedingly complex litigation when it involves transborder circumstances.

For example, a U.S. national travels to Mexico City on business. He picks up his rental car at the airport; the reservation was made through his company's travel agent. He uses the car for both business and recreational purposes, the latter with his company's express permission. While touring the countryside, the businessman's car breaks down; he brings it to a garage so he can eventually return to his hotel. He pays for the car repairs with the company credit card; the servicing includes an adjustment to the braking system. The car is a Mexican-made Japanese car which is part of the inventory of a Mexican subsidiary of a U.S. car rental agency. On the way back to the city, while driving on a poorly maintained public road, the businessman is hit head-on by a drunk driver and by a Japanese businessman who was speeding and driving a rental car from a local Mexican company. The drunk driver was a Mexican national.

5. The Basic Issues

These circumstances, hardly unrealistic or unimaginable, raise obdurately complicated threshold issues of jurisdiction and law applicable. Where can or should suit be brought? Does one forum have exclusive jurisdiction? Is jurisdiction to be defined by the place of the occurrence of the accident or by the parties' nationality or by the manufacturer's place of incorporation or domicile? Of the possibly affected jurisdictions, which national law will control the resolution of liability issues? Does Mexico have a federal tort law or would the law of a Mexican state govern? Are there special rules on damages or insurance?

Because the injuries occurred on Mexican territory, Mexican courts could use a traditional basis for asserting jurisdiction over the actions that are filed. The place of the tort has always been seen as a proper venue for litigating tort claims presumably for reasons of territorial sovereignty, because the evidence is accessible, and given the potential impact upon local interests. United States and Japanese courts also could serve as a proper forum for bringing tort claims on the basis of nationality, place of incorporation, or domicile. The location of the parent rental company or of the car manufacturer could be a factor in determining proper jurisdiction. The garage owner or the maker of alcohol might be defendants in any tort action that is undertaken.

Resolving the question of jurisdiction is not an idle academic exercise. It can have a significant impact upon the parties' rights and their ability to lodge a cause of action. There are important reasons to forum shop. Bringing an action before Mexican or Japanese courts will favor the interests of the corporate entities because both liability and damages are judge-determined in these courts. Moreover, Japan did not have a product liability law until quite recently. Therefore, personal injury litigation is not well-developed in the Japanese legal process. The court systems in these countries either do not favor tort litigation or do not see tort law as a solution to the problem of accidents in society. U.S. courts and the U.S. personal injury bar favor plaintiff actions because of extensive discovery techniques, the civil jury, and the availability of intangible relief and insurance. Liability is more readily admitted and damages are more generous and reflect a U.S. standard of living. Enforcement problems and other conflicts may develop during and at the end of the litigation.

Such cases do not create problems with facile solutions. There is no self-evident answer to whether courts in Mexico or the United States, on the one hand, or Mexico, the United States, or Japan, on the other hand, should assert jurisdiction. The selection of a forum can have an "outcome-determinative" effect. The variability of outcomes is inherently unfair, but it is protected by the rule of absolute national sovereignty. These difficulties result from the lack of an international tribunal for the adjudication of civil disputes, but that deficiency is not likely to be resolved at any time soon.

6. Purpose of the Text

Accordingly, these teaching materials introduce readers to private international disputes and to the remedies by which they can be addressed and resolved. The materials highlight established and "new era" remedies and assert that culture plays a vital role in the generation and resolution of international disputes. The challenge of diversity—legal, cultural, and national—is nowhere more evident than in the international setting. The international body politic and global marketplace are imbued with diversity. Their many points of light sometimes loose their twinkle when differences create conflict and render solutions inaccessible or approximative. The objective of the materials is to prepare prospective legal, political, and business counselors to respond creatively, knowledgably, and effectively to the transborder disputes of today and tomorrow.

The volume addresses international commercial litigation. In doing so, it emphasizes the utility and functionality of arbitration in achieving effective adjudicatory results. The readings depict the litigation of transborder contract and tort claims before national courts, describing the difficulties of jurisdiction, the problems of enforcement, and generally the limitations of national courts in processing such claims. The inventory of disabilities is overwhelming and commands the conclusion that the transborder use of domestic courts is ineffective and counterproductive. By contrast, arbitration provides a workable adjudicatory process for resolving transborder civil disputes. Offshoots of the arbitral process also supply a means by which to resolve transborder trade and regulatory law conflicts.

Chapter 1

LAW AND COMMERCE IN A TRANSBORDER SETTING

Table of Sections

---

§ 1. THE INTERNATIONAL CONTRACT

There are many types of international contracts, the contents of which in most cases is standardized. The provisions of maritime charter party agreements, for example, have been well-settled for a long time. The most common contemporary international contracts relate to joint ventures, franchising, licensing, and construction.

Beyond establishing the basic exchange and the respective rights and obligations of the parties (a definition of terms; a statement of warranties, providing for intellectual property protection; recognizing possible defenses to certain conducts; waivers of liability; the application of confidentiality to the transaction; how the cost of taxes, advertising, and insurance is to be apportioned; among other topics), a functional international contract must of necessity address matters that give it its distinctive international legal character. These matters—each of which highlights a feature of international contracting—include: choice and conflict of language questions; choice-of-law and governing law issues; jurisdiction and venue; choice-of-forum; dispute resolution alternatives, such as party negotiation, mediation, and arbitration; gap-filling; the purchase of political risk and other forms of insurance; currency stabilization provisions; the application of local, regional, or foreign regulatory law; the effect upon the transaction of full or partial sovereign status; specific defenses to nonperformance, such as *force majeure* and the effect of changed circumstances; and the enforceability of adjudicated outcomes.

As always, the language of the contract should constitute a limpid, fully transparent expression of the parties' intent. Reality, however, rarely allows for an ideal configuration of circumstances or for executed perfection. The content of the contract will reflect the difficulty of the bargain. Most exchanges involve some level of miscommunication (intended and unintended), complications in the prospective performance of the agreement, and the need to rely on third parties or external solutions. The contract codifies rights and obligations, but it also serves to identify and moderate transactional risk. It is impossible to know the future. Therefore, contracts are approximate transnational prophecies, especially in transborder circumstances where risk and uncertainty are greater. They represent a necessary attempt to envision the unknown.

Usually, longer contracts evidence the parties' ability to understand the complexity of their prospective undertaking. Complex agreements demonstrate that the parties are neither naïve nor ignorant and/or that they disagree and distrust each other. Attempting to anticipate every contingency is foolhardy, however. Moreover, such contracts require greater time and money, and reflect the possibility that the transaction could collapse before it begins. Lengthy agreements make for substantial "front-end" or threshold costs and may be impossible to implement. Shorter contracts bespeak ready but perhaps facile understandings between the parties. The confidence that pragmatism will prevail and that problems can be worked out is strongest at the outset of a transaction before difficulties arise. That confidence can dissipate when an actual dispute materializes. Shorter contracts, therefore, can betoken illusory agreements that engender later lengthy and costly litigation. Experience and judgment thus are valuable commodities in the drafting of international commercial agreements.

The lawyer's primary professional role in negotiating and writing a contract is to safeguard the client's rights and interests. Risk avoidance is central to the accomplishment of that goal. Risk seeps into every phase and facet of the transaction. Lawyers must get clients to focus upon and be mindful of transactional risk and, to some extent, ignore the deal's profit potential. When problems materialize, commercial parties must have a "bail out" or dispute resolution strategy that allows them to reduce their losses and salvage, if possible, the transaction. The agreement must provide for a process by which difficulties and conflicts can be addressed and misunderstandings repaired. When time, the circumstances, and attempts to compromise have failed to remedy the problem, the parties must pursue either judicial or nonjudicial adjudicatory relief.

§ 2. RESOLVING INTERNATIONAL CONTRACT CLAIMS BEFORE MUNICIPAL COURTS

Municipal legal systems are ill-suited to respond to the problems of transborder commercial litigation. Over the years, the processing of international commercial claims through national courts has resulted in a clash of jurisdictions, the creation of Byzantine legal rules, and conflicts in procedure. The system makes evident the profound limitations of legal methodology. It is a process created and operated by, and which, therefore, works for, lawyers and judges—not the clients who must have recourse to it and pay its costs.

Transborder commercial litigation before municipal courts is complex, difficult, and inefficient. It portrays the legal system at its theoretical best and practical worst. The ethic of administrative pragmatism succumbs to the darkness of systemic sectarianism. The practical goals of litigation are dissolved by the antics of forum-shopping. After pursuing remedial strategies, judgments are likely to conflict and to be ineffective. The diversity of legal systems and the quest for litigious advantage confound the functionality of the process. The expenditure of time and money is enormous and outcomes often are inconclusive. This legal consternation develops simply because domestic boundaries have been crossed and other legal cultures are implicated.

The problems with transborder litigation begin at the outset of the process. Private transborder lawsuits are riddled with jurisdictional issues. Whether a court has a lawful basis for asserting its authority over a dispute and the parties is generally determined by reference to the court's national law. Because there is no coordination among national laws on the question of court jurisdiction, the same lawsuit, however, can be brought in several different countries. These different laws provide for inconsistent results on the basis of different rationales. Even in those rare instances in which national prescriptions converge, the convergence is achieved on the basis of contradistinctive interpretations of the law. The standard situation: Parallel proceedings in different jurisdictions with an exchange of anti-suit injunctions between the venues, with each of them claiming to be the place with exclusively proper jurisdiction for the litigation. U.S. courts and courts from other common law jurisdictions benefit from the additional possibility of resorting to the *forum non conveniens* doctrine, under which they may refuse—for both practical and policy reasons—to exercise their constituted jurisdictional authority. Civil law courts, however, cannot abstain from exercising their authority to adjudicate once it is commanded by the law. The hapless U.S. national and California resident who goes to Tokyo, Japan to appear in commercial ads and is involved in a car accident there will get lost between the two trial systems as well as in the translation. Each affected venue will seek to impose its own brand of justice upon the case and will thereby contribute to a situation in which no useful result is reached.

* * * *

Since the end of WWII, there have been efforts to unify the law of nations in order to promote the international rule of law and to avoid the types of conflicts and inconsistencies that undermine the operation of legal systems. In keeping with these efforts, the American Law Institute (ALI) and the International Institute for the Unification of Private Law (UNIDROIT) have proposed the following uniform rule on jurisdiction in their PRINCIPLES AND RULES ON TRANSNATIONAL CIVIL PROCEDURE 30–35 (Proposed Final Draft 2004). [Principles and Rules of Transnational Civil Procedure (Proposed Final Draft). Copyright 2004 by the ALI and, for the "Principles" sections, also the UNIDROIT. Reprinted with Permission. All rights reserved. The complete and final work in ALI/UNIDROIT is scheduled for publication by Cambridge University Press in 2005.]

[. . .]

2. Jurisdiction Over Parties

2.1 Jurisdiction over a party may be exercised:

2.1.1 By consent of the parties to submit the dispute to the tribunal, subject to restrictions of forum law or international treaty;

2.1.2 When there is a substantial connection between the forum state and the party or the transaction or occurrence in dispute. A substantial connection exists when a significant part of the transaction or occurrence occurred in the forum state, when a defendant is a habitual resident of the forum, or when property to which the dispute relates is located in the forum.

2.2 Exceptionally, jurisdiction may be exercised, when no other forum is reasonably available, on the basis of the defendant's presence or nationally in the forum state, or presence in the forum state of the defendant's property whether or not the dispute relates to the property.

2.3 A court may grant provisional measures with respect to a person or to property in the territory of the forum, even if it has no jurisdiction over the controversy.

2.4 Exercise of jurisdiction may properly be declined when the parties have previously agreed that some other tribunal have exclusive jurisdiction, or declined or suspended when the court is manifestly inappropriate relative to another more appropriate court that could exercise jurisdiction.

2.5 The court may decline to hear the case, or schedule the proceeding in deference to another court, if the same dispute is pending in an appropriate forum.

Comment:

P–2A Subject to restrictions on the court's jurisdiction under the law of the forum and subject to restrictions arising in customary or conventional international law, ordinarily a court may exercise jurisdiction upon the parties' consent. In the absence of the parties' consent, and subject to the parties' agreement that some other tribunal or forum has exclusive jurisdiction, ordinarily a court may exercise jurisdiction only if the court is the defendant's home court or if the dispute is substantially connected to transactions or events that have occurred in the territory of the forum.

P–2B The standard of "substantial connection" has been generally accepted for international legal disputes. That standard excludes mere physical presence, which within the United States is colloquially called "tag jurisdiction." Mere physical presence as a basis of jurisdiction within the American federation has historical justification that is inapposite in modern international disputes. The concept of "substantial connection" may be specified and elaborated in international conventions and in national laws. The scope of this expression might not be the same in all systems.

P–2C Principle 2.2 covers the concept of "*forum necessitatis*"—the forum of necessity whereby a court may properly exercise jurisdiction when the plaintiff cannot reasonably be expected to assert the claim elsewhere.

P–2D Principle 2.3 recognizes that a state may exercise jurisdiction by sequestration or attachment of locally situated property, for example to secure a potential judgment, even though the property is not the object or the subject of the dispute. The procedure is called "*quasi in rem* jurisdiction" in some legal systems. Principle 2.3 contemplates that, in such a case, the merits of the underlying dispute might be adjudicated in some other form.

P–2E The concept recognized in Principle 2.4 is comparable to the common-law rule of *forum non conveniens*. In some civil-law systems, the concept is that of preventing abuse of the forum. This principle can be given effect by suspending the forum proceeding in deference to another tribunal. The existence of a more convenient forum is necessary for application of this Principle. This Principle should be interpreted in connection with the Principle of Procedural Equality of the Parties, which prohibits any kind of discrimination on the basis of nationality or residence....

Notes and Questions

1. Does the proposed formulation strike you as helpful and clear? Would it allow you to address the jurisdictional question with confidence for a client? Does it achieve a reconciliation of the differing approaches of the various legal systems to jurisdiction? Is synthesis or paring down a better description?

2. Does the proposed formulation satisfy the requirements of due process? Should it? Why is that consideration important?

3. Note the specific issues upon which the common law and civil law tradition appear to differ. Are these differences likely to be divisive and

disruptive of the international legal order and international judicial cooperation and assistance? Can you articulate a better uniform formulation?

4. In the PRINCIPLES, ALI/UNIDROIT has also proposed standards for defining international due process and establishing the legitimacy of the legal process:

1. Independence, Impartiality, and Competence of the Court

1.1 The court should have judicial independence to decide the dispute according to the facts and the law, including freedom from improper internal or external influence.

1.2 The judges should have reasonable tenure in office. Nonprofessional members of the court should be designated by a procedure assuring their independence from the parties, the dispute, and other persons interested in the resolution.

1.3 The court should be impartial. There should be a fair and effective procedure for addressing reasonable contentions of judicial bias.

1.4 The court should not accept communications about the case from a party in the absence of other parties, except for communications concerning proceedings without notice and for routine procedural administration.

1.5 Judges should have substantial legal experience and legal knowledge.

[. . .]

3. Procedural Equality of the Parties

3.1 The court should ensure equal treatment and reasonable opportunity for litigants to assert or defend their rights.

3.2 The right to equal treatment includes avoidance of any kind of illegitimate discrimination, particularly on the basis of nationality or residence.

3.3 A person should not be required to provide security for costs, or security for liability for pursuing provisional measures, solely because that person is not a national or resident of the forum state.

3.4 Whenever possible, venue rules should not impose an unreasonable burden of access to court on a person who is not a habitual resident of the forum.

[. . .]

4. Right to Assistance of Counsel

4.1 A party has the right to employ assistance of legal counsel of the party's choice, both representation by counsel admitted to practice in the forum and assistance before the court of counsel admitted to practice elsewhere.

4.2 The professional independence of legal counsel should be respected. Counsel should be permitted to fulfill the duty of loyalty to a client and the responsibility to maintain client confidences.

[. . .]

5. Due Notice and Right to Be Heard

5.1 At the commencement of a proceeding, notice, provided by means that are reasonably likely to be effective, should be directed to parties other than the plaintiff. The notice must be in the language of the forum and either in the language of the person to whom the notice is addressed, if known, or in the language or languages in which the transaction in dispute was conducted.

5.2 The initial notice should be accompanied by a copy of the complaint or otherwise include the allegations of the complaint and specification of the relief sought by plaintiff. Other parties should give similar notice of their defenses and other contentions and requests for relief. A defendant should be informed of the procedure for response and the possibility of default judgment upon failure to make a timely response.

5.3 After commencement of the proceeding, all parties should be provided prompt notice of initiatives of the court or other parties and rulings by the court.

5.4 The parties have the right to submit relevant contentions of fact and law and to offer evidence.

5.5 A party should have a fair opportunity and reasonably adequate time to respond to contentions of fact and law and to evidence presented by another party.

5.6 The court should consider all contentions of the parties and address those concerning a dispositive issue.

5.7 The parties may, by agreement and with approval of the court, employ expedited means of communication, such as telecommunication.

5.8 An order affecting a party's interests may be made and enforced without giving prior notice to that party only upon proof of urgent necessity and preponderance of considerations of fairness. An *ex parte* order should be proportionate to the interests that the applicant seeks to protect. As soon as practicable, the affected party should receive notice of the order and of the matters relied upon to support it, and should have the right to apply for an immediate full reconsideration by the court.

[. . .]

Is this a sensible protocol for due process? Is it complete? What would you add or eliminate? Can you provide the commentary or rationale for each group of principles? Does uniformity create too much dilution, making the proposed rules truly bastardized? Diversity creates the richness of individual personality, but it also generates conflicts and the sense that one prevails or dies in the competition. What might you suggest for achieving a workable international or transborder legal order?

* * * *

Much more lies in wait after the jurisdictional and due process preliminaries. The choice of a governing law, for example, can prime advocates into interminable debates. Legal systems have concocted recondite frameworks for choosing (or not) an applicable law for the litigation. After examining a legion of localization factors and concluding that it ought to rule pursuant to a foreign law, the court and the litigants must confront the problem of proving or establishing that foreign law. The presiding judge may not even read the relevant language or have any training in comparative law. This circumstance necessitates the hiring of experts—at least one for each side in the U.S. system—to discover what the law provides and to explain the findings to a judge (or, worse yet, to a jury) that has little or no training in foreign law or any real desire to learn it. Given the obstacles, the process—once culminated—usually ends, directly or indirectly, in the application of the only law that the presiding judge (or jury) knows and understands: The local law.

As the process evolves, the problem of identifying, gathering, and admitting evidence emerges. When transborder litigation is conducted in the United States especially, the gathering and admission of evidence creates special problems. The Federal Rules of Civil Procedure (Rule 28) authorize the federal courts to command the production of evidence and the Rules of Evidence (Rule 804[b][1]) impose relatively stringent standards for the admissibility of evidence. Orders for the production of evidence and subpoenas for testimony or documents sent to foreign jurisdictions often are met with local resistance and "blocking" statutes that express the foreign State's unwillingness to compromise or surrender its national legal sovereignty and dignity. The Hague conventions were drafted to enhance transborder service of process and evidence-gathering. The Hague framework, however, has been of limited utility. Despite their stated goals, the conventions fail even to approximate the promised reconciliation of common law and civil law trial differences. The bureaucratization of transborder service of process and evidence-gathering through national central authorities has not increased accessibility—there is now, in fact, greater delay, more political positioning, and less control over the quality of the evidence. Local obfuscation has not been eliminated; it simply has been given another means of expression. Moreover, the Federal Rules do not guarantee the admissibility of evidence gathered abroad under the Hague mechanism, nor do they warrant that foreign courts will assist U.S. parties in collecting usable evidence abroad.

The enormous differences in trial procedures among legal systems create even more difficulties. The adversarial and inquisitorial trials differ markedly; they represent different religions of law. Proponents see their approach as uniquely and exclusively right. The role of the judge, the function of experts, the means of establishing a record, the importance of oral testimony and written evidence, the function of party representation, and the availability of appeal are all dissimilar. Therefore, the measure of justice—the protection of rights and the availability of remedies—varies from national jurisdiction to national jurisdiction. The choice of forum can often give effect to or foreclose the parties' cause of action. Given the disparities between national legal systems, the lack of uniform trial procedures, and the competition between litigating parties, international litigators resort to forum-shopping strategies to neutralize and damage the other side. The attempt to maximize the client's position by going to a favorable forum, however, generally results in fleeting advantage. Both parties can and do engage in the procedural warfare. Their respective efforts usually cancel each other out.

It should be noted that transborder litigation is not unique to the United States. Although few, if any, States have enacted legislation to regulate international litigation, many countries have served as venues for such litigation. Generally, courts adapt the provisions of domestic law to this form of litigation. Therefore, not only is international litigation commonplace, but it also is plagued universally by the same problems. Foreign judicial systems, in fact, may be less hospitable to transborder litigation than their U.S. counterpart. Delays in foreign jurisdictions may be more considerable than before U.S. courts. In some countries, the national supreme court may have original jurisdiction in some aspects (especially, the enforcement of foreign judgments) of foreign litigation—a circumstance that can prolong the procedures inordinately. Also, juridical quality varies from country to country as does the influence of external political or religious beliefs. Finally, corruption and bribery can become factors in the process.

The final phase of transborder litigation involves the enforcement of foreign court judgments. In many ways, the "back end" issue of enforcement restates the "front end" problem of jurisdiction. The enforceability of the court's ruling, obviously critical to the successful resolution of the dispute, can depend upon whether the court of rendition had proper jurisdiction initially. Moreover, it is imperative that the judgment be enforceable in a jurisdiction in which the defendant has sufficient assets to satisfy the terms of the foreign court decision. Some legal systems impose a "reciprocity" or mutual guarantee requirement that must be satisfied before a foreign court judgment can be considered for enforcement. In effect, the reciprocity requirement asks whether courts in the country of rendition enforce the requested State's court judgments and other juridical acts. The concept of reciprocity can be as difficult of definition as the notion of the reasonable person. It can involve assessing the foreign courts' general policy on enforcement or ascertaining whether they give effect to specific types of judgments. In effect, what constitutes the requisite *quid pro quo* is a matter of judicial interpretation, judgment, and choice in the circumstances of each case.

Once reciprocity is established, foreign judgments are evaluated on the basis of various factors, *e.g.*, whether they are final in the place of rendition; whether the court of rendition had proper domestic and international jurisdiction under the law of the requested State; whether the judgment debtor had adequate notice of the proceeding and a reasonable opportunity to defend; whether the judgment is free of fraud; and whether enforcement violates the requested State's public policy or standards of natural justice. A merits review or *révision au fond* is generally excluded. The exclusion of a merits review represents an advancement in transborder legal cooperation and civilization. In some jurisdictions, enforcement can be resisted if the court of rendition applied the wrong choice-of-law or if the outcome of the litigation is not available under the law of the requested State. Although judgments from like-minded or aligned States could be deemed to be presumptively enforceable, except in the EU setting (The Brussels Convention, the Lugano Convention, and Council Regulation No. 44/2001), there is no functional multilateral treaty on jurisdiction and the enforcement of foreign judgments. *See* 29 I.L.M. 1413 (1990); 28 I.L.M. 620 (1989); OJ L 012, 1. The question is so divisive on cultural and systemic grounds that even the United States and the United Kingdom have been unable to agree to a bilateral framework (despite serious diplomatic attempts to do so). *See* 16 I.L.M. 71 (1977). Moreover, the work of the Hague Conference on Private International Law on a multilateral convention on jurisdiction and judgments, begun in 1992, is making slow, barely visible progress. *See, e.g.*, Burbank, *Jurisdictional Equilibration, The Proposed Hague Convention And Progress In National Law*, 49 Am. J. Comp. L. 203 (2001). Therefore, not only can the results of litigation in different venues conflict, but they may also be enforceable only in the place of rendition—and not where the judgment debtor has assets.

Some States (*e.g.*, Brazil, Switzerland, and France) require that the national against whom the judgment was rendered have clearly submitted to the jurisdiction of the foreign court of rendition. Other States, like the Netherlands and Saudi Arabia, will not recognize a foreign judgment unless the requested and requesting States are parties to a bilateral judgments convention. Many States view U.S. jury awards, punitive damages, and long-arm statutes as contrary to their public policy. Basic due process rights and fundamental fairness, moreover, must have been respected in the foreign proceeding. This generally means that reasonably effective notice be given and an opportunity to defend be provided. The parties must be treated fairly and equally.

In general, transborder commercial litigation before national courts produces unsatisfactory results. Enormous sums can be expended and clients left without an enforceable solution. Professional fees in such circumstances can be difficult to collect. Conflicts render a transborder rule of law extremely difficult of achievement. Diversity in the rule of law engenders disharmony and insecurity. The mere tolerance of these differences can be seen as a surrender of national authority and, as a consequence, a defeat. Even complete dysfunctionality is preferable to defeat. The key to transborder success, however, is precisely the need to sublimate national legal and political authority in a higher design that mandates a relinquishment of national sovereignty as a first and fundamental step to resolution.

§ 3. THE ARBITRAL SOLUTION

Arbitration appears to have tamed some aspects of transborder litigation. The characteristics of arbitration respond well to the exigencies of establishing a workable transborder adjudicatory process for transborder commercial disputes. In some respects, arbitration has achieved the monumental inroad of reducing the impact of national sovereignty on international commercial relations. It has done so indirectly by enticing States to participate in international arbitral proceedings under the rules of the ICC (the International Chamber of Commerce) or ICSID (International Center for the Settlement of Investment Disputes or World Bank Arbitration) to resolve the commercial conflicts that proceed from foreign investment and the State's marketplace activities. More directly, the NAFTA arbitral framework allows aggrieved individuals to sue directly a NAFTA State and also allows arbitrators to assess the transborder commercial liability of domestic political regulations. NAFTA arbitration, therefore, embodies a genuinely restrictive theory of sovereign immunity from suit and execution and gives the FSIA's (Foreign Sovereign Immunities Act of 1976) commercial activities exception its strongest expression.

States have also moderated their sovereign prerogatives by ratifying the New York Arbitration Convention and the ICSID Convention. Both instruments are popular among the nations of the international community and symbolize a commitment to the enforcement of international arbitral awards and to holding governments accountable for their transborder commercial conduct. In some respects, the need to develop world trade and commerce—to spread the benefits of economic development more widely—has broadened national perspectives and enabled an international common interest to triumph over the insularity that ordinarily accompanies diversity. Participation in transborder commerce is perceived as an effective means of stimulating domestic economic activity and achieving national prosperity. Arbitration is essential to the pursuit of global commerce. Therefore, the acceptance of and recourse to arbitration are a necessary pre-condition to entry into the international marketplace.

In many respects, it is inaccurate and unfair to criticize international arbitration as a "Northern" mechanism that silences or muffles the diversity of the world community. Transborder arbitration has reconciled a number of geo-political and systemic conflicts and erected from the reconciliation a global system of adjudication. At the outset, international commercial arbitration was a European procedure, reflecting the adjudicatory practices of continental civil law systems and—for that reason in part—was shunned by the United States. It eventually became the basis for the conduct of business between North America and Europe and a battleground for the competition between the American adversarial trial system and the European approach to litigation. During the cold war era, it also made East–West trade possible through East–West arbitrations conducted in Sweden. It is now a springboard for global commerce in Latin America, Asia, and—increasingly—Africa.

Arbitration both embraces and transforms global diversity when it fosters uniform law-making by nongovernmental international organizations, States, and arbitrators. It is beyond cavil that there is—both emerged and emerging—a world law of arbitration. The two international instruments referred to earlier attest to a transborder consensus on arbitration. The New York Arbitration Convention, in particular, symbolizes the State recognition of the international utility and necessity of arbitration. The Convention supplies the critical element of enforceability to the process. It is reinforced by other UNCITRAL (United Nations Commission on International Trade Law) instruments in the form of a Model Law on International Commercial Arbitration and Model Rules of Arbitration. The Model Law is particularly significant because it embodies those principles of arbitration law that experts worldwide believed in the mid–1980s were the core elements of the law of arbitration. The Model Law establishes the basic substantive rules for regulating arbitration, while the Model Rules supply the framework for the conduct of an arbitral proceeding.

UNCITRAL has recently undertaken to collect and catalogue all of the judicial opinions on the New York Arbitration Convention. This information will allow practitioners to gauge more accurately the prospects for enforcement in specific jurisdictions. It will also permit commentators to evaluate more lucidly the depth of the world consensus on arbitration—to distinguish between promotional rhetoric and meaningful reality. In addition, the UNCITRAL Model Law has played its role in an increasing number of national jurisdictions. It was designed to provide States with a highly advanced statutory framework of arbitration law—in effect, to make it possible, especially for developing States, to become instantly supportive of arbitration and thereby able to participate in transborder commerce. Numerous Latin American jurisdictions have adopted the Model Law as has Germany and nearly twenty U.S. states. The UNCITRAL framework, with the recent publication of the Model Law on International Conciliation, establishes a self-contained system of international commercial dispute resolution. It is an architecture of law that transcends national and regional differences and codifies a truly global approach to international commercial dispute resolution. The system is not without its flaws and idiosyncrasies; it even has some noticeable disabilities; it nevertheless has significantly advanced international uniformity and unity in matters of arbitration.

As with other developments in private international law, arbitration law relies heavily upon contract principles to establish its content. In fact, freedom of contract (*pacta sunt servanda* or party autonomy) is instrumental to the law of arbitration. Parties must agree to submit their disputes to arbitration; once they have entered into a valid agreement to arbitrate, they must have recourse to arbitration (unless they mutually rescind or disavow the agreement). The parties have the contractual right to forgo judicial relief at the time of entering into the contract and prior to the emergence of a dispute. Also, modern laws on arbitration provide for the presumptive enforceability of arbitration agreements and awards. The parties' decision to arbitrate is not subject to unilateral reconsideration and courts must uphold awards unless they transgress fundamental fairness. In any event, the substance of the arbitral ruling cannot be revisited or revised by a court. The controlling legislation requires courts to cooperate with and sustain the arbitral process. Actual court supervision of the procedures and results is extremely circumscribed. As stated recently by the U.S. Supreme Court in *Green Tree v. Bazzle*, 539 U.S. 444, 123 S.Ct. 2402, 156 L.Ed.2d 414 (2003), once the courts identify an enforceable contract of arbitration, the arbitrator assumes decisional sovereignty over the process and the eventual substantive determination.

A good portion of the content of the world law on arbitration is settled—*e.g.*, the application of separability and *kompetenz-kompetenz* doctrines, the use of the setting aside procedure at the place of arbitration, and the effect of the *functus officio* doctrine. Parts of the law, however, are still in evolution, indicating that the regulation of arbitration is dynamic and constantly in-the-making. Adapting the law by developing new rules revitalizes both the law and the arbitral process. Adaptative evolution avoids stagnation and obsolescence. To illustrate: Two issues of contemporary arbitration law not only challenge the foundational principles of the process, but also demonstrate that it must continually respond to change.

First, the topic of arbitrator neutrality has generated recent debate. The central focus has been upon the impartiality of party-designated arbitrators. Should party-appointed arbitrators be required or presumed to be neutral? How should arbitrator neutrality be achieved? If by a duty of disclosure, how far should the duty extend? Arbitrator neutrality clearly can affect the legitimacy of arbitration as an adjudicatory mechanism. Second, there is discussion among courts and commentators about whether parties have the contractual right to modify the statutory standards by which arbitral awards are confirmed, vacated, nullified, or set aside. In particular, can parties require the court of enforcement to review an award on the merits despite the prohibition against the merits review of awards in the applicable statute? Courts and commentators are divided on the question. Nonetheless, it tests the contractual foundation of arbitration by challenging the effectiveness of the principle of freedom of contract. Moreover, can arbitrators be asked or required to clarify an award? Does the "clarified" award replace or compete with the initial award?

The rule of law in transborder arbitration can be substantially influenced by private arbitral institutions. The most prominent among them include: The International Chamber of Commerce (ICC); the London Court of International Arbitration (LCIA); the Stockholm Chamber of Commerce and the Institute of Arbitration; the Chartered Institute of Arbitrators; the World Intellectual Property Organization (WIPO); the American Arbitration Association (AAA); and the National Arbitration Forum (NAF). A number of these institutions—vigilant about maintaining the fairness of arbitral procedures and the legitimacy of the process—spearheaded developments relating to arbitrator neutrality. For instance, the International Bar Association (IBA) recently released its *Guidelines* on arbitrator conflicts, neutrality, and disclosure. The ABA (American Bar Association) recently revised its standards on arbitrator ethics.

Further, the service providers, along with other parties, developed the practice of fast-track arbitration in order to respond more fully to the needs of the users of the arbitral process. Fast-track procedures attribute greater powers to the arbitrator and use time constraints to maximize the efficiency of arbitral proceedings. Arbitral institutions have also integrated mediation into their menu of services in an effort to respond more effectively to actual client needs. Finally, these organizations administer and supervise arbitral procedures to maintain their functionality, fairness, and finality.

Arbitration is no longer relegated to specialty fields; it is becoming the primary process of civil litigation within the United States. It also addresses regulatory and statutory claims. Furthermore, it provides transborder merchants with a stable and effective process of adjudication and is beginning to fashion—or at least to participate in the making of—an international law of commerce and international contracts. Arbitration, therefore, fills gaps, supplies access to adjudication, and develops workable substantive norms for transnational commerce and the primary subject areas of domestic civil litigation.

§ 4. REPRESENTATIONAL IMPACT

The critical objective for international lawyers is to understand the complexity of legal representation in their field and to assess properly and comprehensively the available remedies in various circumstances. The remedial options are, in reality, three in number: judicial litigation, arbitration, and mediation. The utility of self-help remedies probably expired with the retention of attorneys, although they can sometimes act as facilitators in this context. Mediation is a possible remedy, but it has not yet caught on in the international setting perhaps because of cultural differences or its lack of finality. It is especially important to understand the limitations and pitfalls of the municipal litigation of international contract claims. In many respect, it is difficult to imagine a more ill-suited system for resolving transborder commercial problems. An understanding of municipal litigation can allow clients to benefit from the limitations of the judicial process when they need to and can allow counsel to advise them on why it should be avoided in favor of international arbitration in most circumstances. This strategy is workable in the setting of transactions where privity of contract exists between the parties. It is much less likely to be effective in the context of transborder personal injury between strangers. Educating clients to these realities is a fundamental part of effective legal representation.

§ 5. THE INTERNATIONAL LAW FIRM

Global law practice is now well-established. Firms that began as a single office in a major commercial city grew offices, branches, or associations in other urban commercial centers. Baker & McKenzie, Clifford Chance, Linkletter, Sherman & Sterling, and Freshfields are excellent examples of the international law firm. The operation can be structured as a central partnership with satellite organizations or as a loose grouping of nearly autonomous offices or any degree of intermediary organization. The firm can have operations throughout the world—from London to New York, Paris, and Bogota to Singapore and Moscow. It can consist of hundreds, if not thousands, of lawyers and a large number of nationalities (U.S., French, Polish, Russian, German, Dutch, and Spanish), languages, and legal trainings. The clients literally span the globe and involve the production of hundreds of millions of dollars of revenue. The practice can be simultaneously local and international. It involves diverse commercial matters: mergers and acquisitions, tax, finance, trade and investment, intellectual property, distribution and agency networks, joint ventures, communications law, and real estate law. It includes both litigation and arbitration.

The competition for legal business can be fierce, especially in emerging and re-emerging markets. The development of business footholds, however, involves confronting substantial risk. The entry of Big Eight accounting firms into the legal services market, in particular, in Eastern European capitals, heightened competition. Whether large law firms are allowed to implant themselves into national markets and the conditions of that implantation are determined by national governments and bar associations. Establishing nationality-driven barriers to law practice can constitute a violation of trade treaty obligations or constitutional strictures in the United States.

Admission to the bar is controlled by state supreme courts and state bar associations in the United States. State bar associations are notoriously inhospitable to the admission of foreign-trained attorneys. More than half of the states (31 of them) provide that a foreign law degree is insufficient to qualify a candidate merely to take the bar examination. An even greater number of states (44 of them) provide that obtaining an LL.M. degree at an ABA-approved U.S. law school by a graduate of a foreign law school is not enough of an educational credential to allow a candidate to sit for the state bar examination. Only five state bar associations "recognize with regularity the sufficiency of a legal education received" at a foreign law school.

New York, California, and Texas—three very significant states for purposes of both domestic and international law practice—are on the more tolerant side of the ledger on these matters. Both New York and California recognize the status of legal consultant, under which foreign-trained lawyers are allowed to give advice on their national law and international law. They need not take the state bar examination to obtain this status, but must be admitted in and have practiced for some time in their home jurisdiction.

There are evident economic reasons for refusing state bar access to foreign-trained lawyers and for requiring that all test-takers have a J.D. degree from an ABA-accredited U.S. law school. Are there other reasons for the policy of general exclusion? Is U.S. legal education unique? Should the policy continue to stand if the prospective test-taker is a graduate of the law faculty at McGill University, the University of Toronto, Cambridge, or Oxford? What is a "law faculty"? How does it differ from a U.S. law school? Why isn't earning an LL.M. degree from an ABA-accredited U.S. law school sufficient—in conjunction with a foreign law degree—to allow a prospective candidate to sit for the state bar examination? The candidate still must pass the examination itself to become a member of the bar. Are there any advantages to allowing foreign-trained attorneys to become members of the state bar association?

In the early 1990s, France appeared to take a step backwards in terms of the international practice of law. In the aftermath of WWII, in the 1950s and 1960s, Paris became a haven for ex-patriot Americans who wanted to practice law in Europe. Law firms and various associations were established that allowed U.S. attorneys to practice as *conseils juridiques*. Like the legal consultant, this status allowed foreign attorneys to provide advice on matters of foreign and international law without becoming a member of the French bar. The *conseils* could not appear in French court or advise on matters of French law. The *conseil* status actually was a precursor to the legal consultant status in New York and California. It arose from the revolutionary ideology of the late eighteenth century France under which all citizens were presumed to know the law. After three years of probationary professional activity in France, the foreign lawyer could register as a *conseil juridique*. The status made possible a thriving international legal practice in Paris.

The law of December 31, 1990, however, did away with the *conseil juridique* status. Once the law came into force on January 1, 1992, there was only the single professional category of the lawyer—the *avocat(e)*. Existing *conseils juridiques* who were duly registered either were grandfathered into the French legal profession or given the title of *avocat(e)*. The single professional category of *avocat(e)* also applied to the *avoué* or solicitor, who became known as *avocat(e)* as well. The purpose of the reform was to modernize the French legal profession and make it more competitive and functional in contemporary circumstances. It had the effect of severely restricting access to French law practice by non-EU nationals, especially U.S. attorneys. In order to engage in international legal practice in France, the latter needed to pass a series of examinations on French law, provided their home jurisdiction allowed French lawyers to engage in the practice of law. Admission to the New York bar satisfied the latter requirement because French authorities came to regard the New York state bar as an "international bar." The testing on French law involved a year-long series of courses and trainings on French law subjects and demanded sufficient fluency in French to pass both written and oral examinations.

How do you evaluate the French "reform"? Don't its negative effects outweigh any positive ones? Isn't the legal consultant status an ideal compromise between all of the competing forces and interests in this setting? Can the age of globalization tolerate the parochial attitude of bar associations?

When France surrendered the legal consultant status, Japan adopted it in an attempt to open its legal services market to transborder legal practice by foreign (especially U.S.) lawyers. Despite a distrust of things foreign and a preference for the nonadjudicatory settlement of disputes, Japan enacted a foreign lawyer law in 1986 partially in response to pressure from the U.S. Trade Representative. Law Number 66 of 1986, entitled "Special Measures Law Concerning the Handling of Legal Business by Foreign Lawyers," allowed U.S. and other foreign lawyers to assist foreign company investment in Japan and Japanese companies to enter the international marketplace. The law, however, placed numerous restrictions upon the conduct of registered foreign lawyers—for example, they could not enter into partnerships with or hire Japanese attorneys and they could not use the name of their home firm (only the senior partner's name) in their professional dealings in Japan. In a word, the Japanese legal open-door policy was fledgling, reluctant, and hesitant. The reform was itself reformed to achieve the original intended objective.

The Japanese foreign lawyer law was amended in 1994, 1996, and 1998. These amendments liberalized the law. For example, the law as amended now allows a special association between Japanese lawyers and the foreign law firm known as a "specific joint enterprise." In particular, the 1996 Special Measures Law permits foreign lawyers to act as arbitrators or represent clients in international arbitral proceedings held in Japan. According to the Japan Commercial Arbitration Association, under Law Number 65 of June 12, 1996,

> A foreign lawyer practicing outside of Japan may represent a party to the proceedings of an arbitration case in regard to civil affairs where the place of arbitration is located in Japan and all or part of the parties have [a] domicile. . . or principal place of business in a foreign country. A foreign law solicitor [] registered in Japan. . . may also represent a party in the above-mentioned case. The long pending issue of whether foreign lawyers may represent a party in international arbitral proceedings conducted in Japan in relation to conflicts with the Japan's [foreign] lawyer's law is considered to have been eventually settled.

It should be noted that Japan has many fewer practicing attorneys than the United States. In the United States, there are 308 attorneys per 100,000 people, whereas the number in Japan is 12 attorneys per 100,000 people. To become a *bengoshi*, a student must be admitted to the Legal Training & Research Institute, a government-operated school. The school admits only 2% of the 35,000 applicants. There are only 16,000 lawyers in Japan, whereas the United States has more than a million.

§ 6. THE MULTINATIONAL ENTERPRISE (MNE)

(i)

An American Judicial and a Japanese View of the MNE

BULOVA WATCH CO. v. K. HATTORI & CO.

508 F.Supp. 1322 (1981).

[. . .]

2. MULTINATIONAL OPERATIONS IN GENERAL

When Cardozo enunciated the standard for doing business in New York, *Tauza v. Susquehanna Coal Co.*, 220 N.Y. 259, 267, 115 N.E. 915, 917 (1917), there would have been little need to consider how, or whether, a foreign-based multinational enterprise would be found to be doing business in New York. For one thing, the term "multinational firm," so common in today's parlance, was first used only in 1960. Aharoni, *On the Definition of a Multinational Corporation*, in *The Multinational Enterprise in Transition* 4 (A. Kapoor and P. Grub, eds. 1972). For another, it was not until after World War II that the phenomenon of the multinational enterprise, as we now know it, became a major factor in the world scene. P. Buckley & M. Casson, *The Future of the Multinational Enterprise* 1 (1976). Since then, tens of thousands of subsidiaries have been created or acquired by parent enterprises located in other countries. R. Vernon, *The Economic Environment of International Business* 200 (1972). By 1972, it was estimated that in a world that produced about $3,000 billion of goods and services a year, something like one-eighth of the output moved across international boundaries. *Id.* at 3. In that same year the value of American investments abroad was $94 billion. N. Fatemi & G. Williams, *Multinational Corporations: The Problems and the Prospects* 20 (1975).

After the Second World War, investment in the United States by foreign parent companies also expanded tremendously so that by the early 1970s non-United States corporations owned more than seven hundred "major manufacturing enterprises" in this country. R. Barnet & R. Muller, *Global Reach* 27 (1974). Direct foreign investment, defined as ownership by foreign parents of at least ten percent of the equity of an American enterprise, was $3.4 billion at the start of the 1950s, $6.6 billion in 1959, and $26.5 billion by 1974. U.S. Department of Commerce, *Foreign Direct Investment in the United States* 4, 11 (1976). Total assets of foreign-owned affiliates in the United States in 1974 were $174.3 billion, of which more than one-fifth was Japanese-owned. *Id.* at xiii. These trends have accelerated.

The vehicles of this modern international economic growth were and are the multinational enterprises. Their size is often awesome: the annual sales of General Motors exceed the gross national products of Switzerland, Pakistan, or South Africa. R. Barnet & R. Muller, *Global Reach* 15 (1974).

The phenomenon of penetration into the economies of distant areas can be traced through artifacts back into pre-history. But the current situation is in many respects quite different in the sophisticated organizational and legal techniques utilized from even that of earlier periods in American history when foreign financing made so much of our industrial and commercial expansion possible and when American companies like Singer, the American sewing machine company, established manufacturing plants abroad. M. Wilkins, *The Emergence of Multinational Enterprise: American Business Abroad from the Colonial Era to 1914*, 37 ff. (1970); R. Vernon, *The Economic Environment of Business* 203 (1972). Aside from their magnitude, today's multinationals are unique in the way vast investments in myriad locations are made to serve the interests of a single organization. Large advantages lie in the possibility of making centralized management and investment decisions on the basis of the situations and opportunities prevailing in various host countries. R. Hellmann, *Transnational Control of Multinational Corporations* 6 (1977); Hadari, *The Structure of the Private Multinational Enterprise*, 71 MICH. L. REV. 729, 749 (1973); Vagts, *The Multinational Enterprise: A New Challenge for Transnational Law*, 83 HARV. L. REV. 739, 746 (1970). Such an organization has the resources and scope to plan and to utilize world-wide markets and resources. N. Fatemi & G. Williams, *Multinational Corporations: The Problems and the Prospects* 58 (1975).

The profit motivation for international expansion is common to multinationals.... Nevertheless, the means by which the multinational exercises control over its far-flung elements vary. The degree and nature of control may depend upon the nationality of the corporate parent.... The formal structure of the parent's form of ownership also has control implications. Choice among the various corporate modes of entering a market, *e.g.*, by means of licensing arrangement, joint venture, minority-, majority-or wholly-owned subsidiary, has very significant implications for the control exercised by the parent. R. Vernon, *The Economic Environment of International Business* 214 (1972). Utilization of a wholly-owned marketing-based subsidiary is found where "the...retention of unambiguous control of foreign operations is critical to the firm's strategy." J. Stopford & L. Wells, Jr., *Managing the Multinational Enterprise: Organization of the Firm and Ownership of Subsidiaries* 107 (1972) (most of the sales subsidiaries of the multinationals were wholly-owned in 1966). The decision of marketing-oriented firms to choose wholly-owned subsidiaries means that they can exercise more control over their foreign operation in subtle, indirect ways, as well as directly. *Id.* at 112.

Another criterion that will determine the "corporate intimacy" joining a parent and its subsidiary, *Marantis v. Dolphin Aviation, Inc.*, 453 F. Supp. 803, 805 (S.D.N.Y. 1978), is the type and range of products being sold. Enterprises with narrow product lines tend to organize their operations on a highly integrated basis, linking production and marketing into tight strategic patterns. R. Vernon, *The Economic Environment of International Business* 231 (1972)....

Thus, sales subsidiaries tend to be under especially close control where a company produces a limited number of products. In such a case the company has

> a higher stake in the maintenance of quality standards, a higher sense of risk in sharing its technology with others, a higher need for a centralized marketing strategy.... The strategy of [these] firms, therefore, requires relatively tight controls.

R. Vernon, *The Economic Environment of International Business* 219 (1972).

Finally, a crucial factor in the degree of control over the subsidiary is the age of the subsidiary and the extent to which the subsidiary has been able to develop independently of its parent. A leading scholar of international trade distinguishes multinational firms from national firms with foreign operations: "A multinational firm starts out like a national firm with foreign operations, but after time each national operation takes on a life of its own." C. Kindleberger, *American Business Abroad* 183 (1969). The history of modern international business enterprise is largely the history of just this development from a national firm with foreign sales operations, to the truly multinational firm with quasi-independent component entities. *See* M. Wilkins, *The Maturing of Multinational Enterprise: American Business Abroad from 1914 to 1970*, 411–439 (1974).

An important question in assessing presence for jurisdictional purposes is whether a multinational has reached a state in its evolution when it can be said that its sales and marketing subsidiaries truly have a "life of their own." C. Kindleberger, *American Business Abroad* 183 (1969). Although such an organization can generally be defined as "an enterprise which owns and controls activities in different countries," P. Buckley & M. Casson, *The Future of the Multinational Enterprises* 1 (1976), it is clear that

> [T]here are distinct differences between a company like Unilever, with many manufacturing subsidiaries in dozens of countries; a company like Trans World Airlines, which also operates in dozens of countries but with distinctly different operations; a company like Bethlehem Steel, with mining operations in seven countries, all supporting the company's manufacturing activities in the United States; a company like Gulf Oil Company, which owns and operates oil fields in several countries and transports and markets oil; and a company like Rolls Royce or Omega watches, with manufacturing operations in one country, but export network and sales and services outlets all over the world. Whether or not we wish to call all these companies multinational, there are notable differences. . . .

Aharoni, *On the Definition of a Multinational Corporation*, in *The Multinational Enterprise in Transition* 15–16 (A. Kapoor & P. Grub, eds. 1972).

The expanding multinational generally traverses a number of stages. At first it exports its goods to markets abroad, next it establishes sales organizations abroad, then it may license the use of its patents, and finally it may establish foreign manufacturing facilities. At a later stage, it may "multinationalize its management and, ultimately, multinationalize the ownership of its stock." Jacoby, *The Multinational Corporation*, in *The Multinational Enterprise in Transition* 22 (A. Kapoor and P. Grub, eds. 1972). While many thousands of corporations are at the first, export stage, only a handful have developed into advanced multinational enterprises each of whose elements can be said to be significant in its own right.

After World War II, foreign companies gained familiarity with the United States market "by first exporting to this country; then, after achieving acceptance for their products, foreign firms set up manufacturing or assembly plants here." U.S. Department of Commerce, *Foreign Direct Investment in the United States* 100 (1976). As these later stages were reached, the businesses established came to have lives of their own. The "monocentric" enterprise gradually gave way to a polycentric one, with more autonomy in the different elements. Wilkins detects three stages: in the first stage, the firm "reached out to sell or to obtain and in doing so felt the necessity or saw the opportunity to cross over domestic boundaries." M. Wilkins, *The Maturing of Multinational Enterprise: American Business Abroad from 1914 to 1970*, 416 (1974). The relationship was "monocentric" with the center of operations clearly in the parent's home country. The external activities in a monocentric relationship were "spokes on a wheel, with the parent company at the hub." *Id.* In stage two, the functions of the branches broadened. There might, for example, be investment by the subsidiary in a plant for local production or the subsidiary might sell products in third-country markets. "What characterizes stage two is the presence of foreign units that have developed their own separate histories and their own satellite activities." *Id.* at 417. The final, third, stage is characteristic of the most advanced of these entities:

> It garbles any chart's attempt to delineate international trade and control lines. The parent company comes to have a number of foreign multifunctional centers, serving overlapping geographical areas with various products. Supply and market lines cross international boundaries in . . . chaotic confusion. . . .

Id. at 419.

> Over time, certain foreign subsidiaries and affiliates have become full-fledged, fully integrated, multiprocess, multiproduct enterprises, with engineering, product planning and research staffs, with a continuity of employee, supplier, dealer, consumer and banking relationships, with their own prominent role in foreign industries, with their own dealings with foreign governments and with their own third-country investments.

Id. at 420–421. At this final stage, complicated, multi-faceted relationships have replaced simple bilateral connections. *Id.* at 421.

3. Japanese Multinationals in General

Hattori, like many Japanese export-based multinationals, remains in large part a monocentric organization so far as involves the United States. It is only in the past decade that Japanese firms have invested in manufacturing and other non-marketing investments in this country. M. Yoshino, *Japan's Multinational Enterprises* 1 (1976); R. Tindall, *Multinational Enterprises* 36 (1972) ("prior to 1970 there was little talk about Japanese companies as multinational enterprises"). This relative lateness results from several causes.

Although in the 1930s Japan began to develop a thriving trade in Asia and ranked fourth worldwide in volume of export, G. Allen, *Japan's Economic Expansion* 227 (1965), the Second World War crippled Japan's foreign trade. It was the late 1950s before pre-war trade levels were again attained. *Id.* at 233. . . .

Another reason that the Japanese multinationals have been monocentric in focus is that they were the great Zaibatsu trading companies that traditionally functioned as commission distributors of merchandise. It was only in the 1960s that the large Japanese manufacturers first began to market their own products. K. Haitani, *The Japanese Economic System: An Institutional Overview* 129 (1976). Foreign direct investment by Japan in the West was historically late in coming and was generally restricted to sales and marketing activities. . . .

The boom in Japanese exports after the post-World War II recovery brought with it the incorporation of hundreds of sales subsidiaries abroad. Whereas prior to the War exports to the United States were largely commodities such as silk, tea, fish and textiles, after the Japanese recovery exports included highly sophisticated manufactured goods. G. Allen, *Japan's Economic Expansion* 236 (1965). These goods needed the kind of marketing and service apparatus that the huge trading companies were not able to provide. M. Yoshino, *Japan's Multinational Enterprises* 118 (1976). As a result, between 1952 and 1973, fifty leading firms dealing in automobiles, motorcycles, electrical machinery, precision instruments, non-electrical machinery, and other products established over three hundred sales subsidiaries in major export markets to perform marketing and technical tasks. In view of the requirement for close control over marketing and technical activities as well as for frequent communication between the local unit and headquarters, it is not surprising that nearly 71% of these subsidiaries were wholly-owned. *Id.* at 19. Activities of these Japanese-controlled sales and marketing affiliates accounted for approximately ten billion dollars of trade between the United States and Japan in 1974. U.S. Department of Commerce, *Foreign Direct Investment in the United States* 39 (1976). Japanese exports to the United States in calendar year 1979 were well over twenty-six billion dollars and they continued to increase in 1980. . . .

4. Japanese Hierarchical Structures

Significant in terms of cultural considerations that seem to affect real economic power relationships relevant to jurisdiction is the widely-noted hierarchical structure that joins the Japanese subsidiary to its parent, and the Japanese employee to his or her employer. In Japan subsidiaries are commonly referred to as *ko-gaisha* (child company) in relation to *oya-gaisha* (parent). "The use of the words 'parent' and 'child' suggests the existence of a familial relationship of control and dependency." . . . Thus, quite apart from the matter of one hundred percent stock ownership, a Japanese parent may expect to exert control over any of its child companies.

The sense of hierarchy is apparently to be found in typical employee-employer relations as well. An inferior in Japanese social organization is "conditioned to attribute authority to the wishes of his superior. . . . The subordinate is extremely conscious of his standing in the group." K. Haitani, *The Japanese Economic System: An Institutional Overview* 92 (1976). Although the precise systems of control may differ from those found in Western organizations. . .this cannot mean that control is any the less pervasive:

> Those reared in the tradition of American corporate culture cannot help wondering how Japanese organizations maintain their vigor and productivity in the absence of a formal control mechanism and an explicit system of performance evaluation supported by immediate financial reward. The answer is that the Japanese corporation relies on—and consciously fosters—emotional commitment to the organization by the employee at every level.

M. Yoshino, *Japan's Multinational Enterprises* 166 (1976). Decision-making is often done on a group basis; this strengthens, not weakens, the sense of employee loyalty to his employer. *See generally*, E. Vogel, *Japan as Number One* 146 (1979). Decision-making is also apparently widely diffused, rather than decentralized, throughout the organization. M. Yoshino, *Japan's Managerial System: Tradition and Innovation* 258 (1968).

The Japanese corporate employer reinforces the loyalty of its employees by the "implicit guarantee of lifetime security"; this ensures not only his technical and professional loyalty, "but more important, his emotional tie to the firm." M. Yoshino, *Japan's Multinational Enterprises* 163 (1976). Under the *shukko* system, an employee may be assigned to another employer or to a subsidiary. While on external assignment the employee keeps his "security in and identity with" his original employer. K. Haitani, *The Japanese Economic System: An Institutional Overview* 46 (1976). Thus, for example, new government agencies in Japan may be staffed with employees of another agency. However, "until the home-grown careermen rise through the ranks, the key positions in the new agency are monopolized by the *shukko* 'colonists,' and the agency is subjected to external controls exerted through them." *Id.* at 46–47.

[. . .]

Notes and Questions

The foregoing materials suggest that there is considerable complexity to the activities of the MNE and to its legal regulation. You should isolate the basic attributes of a characteristic multinational corporate organization and think about a suitable legal regime of governance and about the question of asserting judicial jurisdiction over the entity or part of it or over the entity through its parts. Should a binding mechanism of international regulation be instituted, and, if so, how might that be accomplished? Is it more realistic to depend upon individual national laws for effectuating the necessary control? Does such reliance eliminate any possibility of uniformity and harmonization? Or even basic coordination? As to problems of jurisdiction, the following materials on the *Bhopal incident* illustrate the difficulties to which multinational corporate activities can give rise in the host environment and within implicated legal systems.

(ii)

International Liability of the MNE

IN RE UNION CARBIDE CORP. GAS PLANT DISASTER AT BHOPAL, INDIA

634 F.Supp. 842, 844 (S.D.N.Y. 1986).

[. . .]

"On the night of December 2–3, 1984, the most tragic industrial disaster in history occurred in the city of Bhopal, state of Madhya Pradesh, Union of India. Located there was a chemical plant, owned and operated by Union Carbide India Limited ("UCIL"). The plant, situated in the northern sector of the city, was occupied by impoverished squatters. UCIL manufactured the pesticides Sevin and Temik at the Bhopal plant at the request of, and with the approval of, the Government of India.... Methyl Isocyanate (MIC), a highly toxic gas, is an ingredient in the production of both Sevin and Temik. On the night of the tragedy, MIC leaked from the plant in substantial quantities for reasons not yet determined.

"The prevailing winds on the early morning of December 3, 1984 were from Northwest to Southeast. They blew the deadly gas into the overpopulated hutments adjacent to the plant and into the most densely occupied parts of the city. The results were horrendous. Estimates of death directly attributable to the leak range as high as 2,100. No one is sure exactly how many perished. Over 200,000 people suffered injuries—some serious and permanent—some mild and temporary. Livestock were killed and crops damaged. Businesses were interrupted."

* * * *

In the wake of the tragedy, many questions were raised concerning culpability and responsibility for the accident. To evaluate these questions fully, the corporate structure of Union Carbide must be examined. Carbide U.S. has a wholly-owned subsidiary called Union Carbide Eastern, Inc., which is another United States company. This subsidiary in turn owns several foreign enterprises, including Carbide India. Carbide U.S. owns 50.9% of Carbide India because of a special exemption from Indian control regulations. Public investors in India own the minority interest in this company which in turn owns twelve other chemical plants throughout India.

In the weeks following the disaster, 145 actions were filed in U.S. federal courts, most seeking to assert claims against Carbide U.S. as well as its Indian subsidiary. In *Theories of Parent Company Liability and the Prospects for an International Settlement*, 20 TEX. INT'L L.J. 321 (1985) (reprinted with permission), Westbrook discussed possible theories of liability against Carbide U.S.

Westbrook proposed three theories of direct liability: 1) the traditional "piercing the corporate veil"; 2) a concept of worldwide financial responsibility for multinationals, regardless of corporate forms; and 3) a multinational's "duty to manage responsibly," derived perhaps from evolving multinational codes.

The concept of "piercing the corporate veil" can be invoked "to avoid corporate liability limitations when a showing can be made that the owner of the offending corporation previously had ignored or abused the corporate form and thus should be treated as if the limited liability shield had never been erected." 20 TEX. INT'L. L. J. at 323. Thus, the theory is most apposite in cases in which a parent corporation maintains control of the subsidiary in spite of a "paper" separation.

Westbrook's second theory, that of worldwide financial responsibility, entails a "vindication" of limited liability policies for MNEs especially those investing in emerging nations lacking a well-developed regulatory infrastructure. This theory, which largely ignores corporate form, was upheld by the U.S. Supreme Court in *Container Corp. of America v. Franchise Tax Board*, 463 U.S. 159 (1983). "In that case, California applied a 'unitary' treatment to the income of [a] multinational. Instead of taxing income attributable to the California corporation's or to the multinational's California operations, the state allocated the corporation's worldwide income on the basis of the proportion of its activities in California as measured by payrolls, amount of sales, and similar factors.... The rationale for permitting unitary treatment was in large part the risk that a multinational might otherwise manipulate its financial affairs and financial reporting to avoid income fairly taxable by California." *Id.* at 324–25. The shortcoming of applying this theory in developing nations is that it would act to discourage MNEs from investing in those countries.

The theory of "multinational management responsibility" involves the idea of imposing a "legal duty upon multinationals to manage their subsidiaries—at least those in emerging countries—in accordance with some standard of responsible international investment and management. The duty would include responsibility for training and supervising local management and providing regularly updated technology, at least that technology which is related to safety." *Id.* at 326. Existing international codes, however, do not address questions of management and safety directly and, therefore, offer only limited assistance in determining an appropriate standard.

Even if all three theories of direct liability failed, courts still had to determine whether the worldwide assets of the parent company could be made available to settle claims against the Indian company. "At the end of 1983, Carbide India had a net worth of 27 million dollars—by all accounts, insufficient to meet pending claims. One approach that might be fruitful for the victims would be a lawsuit by Carbide India against Carbide U.S. based on breaches of express and implied warranties in the technology licensing agreement between parent and subsidiary. While there has been no public revelation of the existence of such an agreement, it would be surprising if one did not exist. Even if such an agreement does not exist, or if an existing agreement is silent about a duty in Carbide U.S. to update technology and provide training, such covenants could probably be implied from ordinary commercial usage. Indeed, such an agreement might be read in conjunction with any duties of the same sort assumed by Carbide U.S. in its investment agreements with the Government of India." *Id.* at 328.

Westbrook, thus, was searching for a possible theory of liability that would place accountability upon Carbide U.S. Implicit in his discussion is the assumption that U.S. courts will decide the question of liability. *In re Bhopal*, however, presents a two-tier problem, the first tier being the appropriate forum and the second tier being the measure of liability.

Several factors contributed to the attractiveness of U.S. federal courts as the forum for the case: (1) the inadequacy of the Indian legal system in dealing with tort law; (2) the American propensity for aggressive tort litigation; (3) the availability in the United States of a civil jury trial and a contingent fee arrangement; and (4) the American lawyer himself.

India has a long history of restraining litigation through *ad valorem* court fees. These fees, while providing a major source of revenue for the state governments, also act to suppress litigation and to divert claims into requests for specific relief and into criminal complaints. *See* Galanter, *Legal Torpor: Why So Little Has Happened in India After the Bhopal Tragedy*, 20 TEX. INT'L L.J. 274–75 (1985) (reprinted with permission). Because of this impediment upon civil litigation, Indian courts have not been innovative or creative in dealing with civil claims—especially tort cases. "Because there are few Indian tort cases, the applicable law for the most part is the common law of England, even today. Although Torts is a required course in law colleges, legal professionals do not perceive it as a major component of the legal system." 20 TEX. INT'L L.J. at 75–76. "Basically, Indian tort law is balanced in favor of the defendant. The amounts awarded are low. A very low premium is placed on injury and death. If the tort claims for personal injury and death have not been advanced in Indian courts, it is because it hardly seems worth it to fight for a sum of compensation which is roughly equal to—and, in most instances, lower than—the amount given to victims and their relatives as a result of governmental handouts." *See* Dhavan, *For Whom? And for What? Reflections on the Legal Aftermath of Bhopal*, 20 TEX. INT'L L.J. 301 (1985) (reprinted with permission). In addition to a policy that discourages tort litigation, the Indian court system is plagued by a tremendous backlog of cases; it often takes years to obtain a final judgment. 20 TEX. INT'L L.J. at 297. Accordingly, India was not seen as a propitious forum for litigating the claims of the Bhopal victims.

The U.S. legal system, on the other hand, has a highly developed process for addressing personal injury litigation. The fact that so many cases were filed in U.S. courts did a great deal to further the cause of those victims. "[N]o more effective mechanism has yet been devised for obtaining an 'out-of-court' settlement, as promptly as the defendant's resolve will allow, than filing a class action in this country." *See* Winberg, *Insights and Ironies: The American Bhopal Cases*, 20 TEX. INT'L L. J. 307–08 (1985) (reprinted with permission). Tort cases in the United States, however, are governed by state law rather than federal law. "So in the end, the United States parent's liability, if any, under state law, will probably have to turn on its acts or omissions affecting the Bhopal plant that can be found tortuous in themselves, rather than violative of federal environmental standards.... The only way in which American courts can vindicate a national interest here, as opposed to a West Virginia or Connecticut or New York interest, if any, appears to be to make themselves accessible to the aliens suits...." 20 TEX. INT'L L.J. at 311.

"Interestingly, current proposals of the American Law Institute seem to lend weight, by way of analogy, to the argument that access to this country's tribunals should be afforded the Bhopal claimants. Under these proposals, in cases of transfrontier pollution, a duty to make reparation arises as against the country in which the polluting activity occurred, in favor of an aggrieved country. In such cases, the Institute would allow that duty to be satisfied by the responsible country's giving access to its tribunals to private citizens of the aggrieved country who have been injured by the pollution." *Id.* at 311–12.

Another factor enhancing the desirability of an American forum was the contingent fee arrangement that was not permitted in India. Although widely criticized and prohibited elsewhere in the world, the contingency fee device "gives access to justice to those who almost everywhere else, including India, could not afford their day in court." *Id.* at 317. U.S. lawyers could provide legal advice to victims who might otherwise go unrepresented.

U.S. lawyers would be more effective instruments for obtaining satisfactory compensation for the Bhopal victims than their Indian counterparts. In the Indian legal system, environmental torts are relatively unknown. "The Indian lawyer has thus remained locked into a restricted professional role. The roles of investigator, intermediary, negotiator, trustee, planner, advisor, and spokesman that might have gravitated to the lawyer are performed, if at all, by others—clerks and touts, village notables and businessmen, politicians, and administrators." *See* Galanter, *Legal Trooper*, *supra*, 20 TEX. INT'L L.J. at 279. U.S. personal injury lawyers, although criticized for being "ambulance chasers," raised consciousness about tort injury and created bargaining leverage for victims. "Their [the American lawyers'] public recital of alternative theories of liability and of claims for damages of a magnitude unknown in India, made palpable to all the possibility of pursuing a remedy in the United States—and thus reinforced the neglect of the possibilities in India. The suits they brought constituted a formidable threat to Union Carbide and both a goad to and constraint on the Government of India, simultaneously increasing its leverage while decreasing its room for maneuver. Whether the true victims will ever receive any compensation remains far from certain. But it seems fair to say that the possibilities of a sizable recovery—or any recovery for that matter—have enhanced by the intervention of the American negligence lawyers. As one prominent Indian lawyer told an American reporter: 'But for the American lawyer there wouldn't be any litigation against Union Carbide. I say God bless them. They deserve to be thanked by the Indian nation.' " *Id.* at 292.

Thus, U.S. courts appeared to be a better forum for deciding the *Bhopal* case. The central question before the courts was the *forum non conveniens* issue. Some commentators believed that deciding in favor of dismissal would be tantamount to deciding the merits in favor of Union Carbide:

> Will the United States courts entertain the private litigation filed by the United States lawyers on behalf of the Bhopal victims? One of the defendant's first moves in these cases will be motions to dismiss on the basis of *forum non conveniens*. That doctrine permits a trial judge to determine—by reference to an amorphous and open-ended set of factors loosely tied to the convenience of the litigants, witnesses, and the court—that a case properly within the court's jurisdiction should nevertheless be dismissed because trial in a foreign forum would be greatly more appropriate. The determination is committed to the trial judge's discretion and appellate review is accordingly limited. Our federal district courts grant *forum non conveniens* dismissal in dozens of transnational tort cases each year and deny such motions in dozens of others. These decisions are rarely reversed. There is almost no predictability. A number of court of appeals judges have deplored the lack of consistency and predictability and called for reformulation of this body of law.
>
> When a federal court in the United States dismisses a case on the basis of *forum non conveniens*, it ordinarily conditions that dismissal on the defendant's undertaking to submit to the jurisdiction of the foreign tribunal, to waive any statute of limitations that may have accrued in that forum during the pendency of the United States proceeding, to make all available evidence accessible to plaintiff, and to abide by any judgment rendered against it in the foreign tribunal. Further, the dismissal is ordinarily without prejudice to plaintiff's returning to the United States court should it prove impossible to get the case heard abroad. This conditional dismissal technique is seen as a safety net, mitigating the harshness of dismissing an action concededly properly before the court. But the safety net is more formal than functional. Typically, the transnational tort plaintiff who has lost his access to the United States forum either gives up altogether or manages to settle the case for a very small fraction of its value. The conditional dismissal technique overestimates the resources and stamina of personal injury plaintiff. Ordinarily, the United States lawyer, retained on contingency fee basis, will not remain active in the case after it is barred from our courts. The plaintiff may well not be able to pay a lawyer, and many systems put him at risk of having to pay the defendant's lawyers as well should the case result in judgment for the defendant. Further,

> many foreign litigation systems resemble India's in requiring the prepayment of substantial filing fees. In sum, judges may derive comfort from the conditional dismissal technique, but tort plaintiffs usually do not; the *forum non conveniens* dismissal is often tantamount to a decision for defendant on the merits of the case.

Robertson, *Introduction to the Bhopal Symposium*, 20 TEX. INT'L L.J. 270–72 (1985) (reprinted with permission).

* * * *

On May 12, 1986, the U.S. District Court for the Southern District of New York decided the issue of *forum non conveniens* in favor of Union Carbide's motion for removal of the action to Indian courts. The district court relied primarily on two cases cited by the defendant: *Gulf Oil Corp. v. Gilbert*, 330 U.S. 501 (1947), and *Piper Aircraft Co. v. Reyno*, 454 U.S. 235 (1981). "*Piper* teaches a straightforward formulation of the doctrine of *forum non conveniens*. A district court is advised to determine first whether the proposed alternative forum is 'adequate.'... Then, as a matter within its 'sound discretion,' *Piper*, 454 U.S. at 257, the district court should consider relevant public and private interest factors, and reasonably balance those factors, in order to determine whether dismissal is favored. This court will approach the various concerns in the same direct manner in which *Piper* and *Gilbert* set them out." *Union Carbide*, 634 F. Supp. at 845.

The first issue the court considered was the adequacy of an alternative forum, a factor dependent upon the defendant's amenability to process in another forum. Once the defendant exhibited a willingness to undergo trial in the alternative forum, the court examined the availability of relief in that forum. Although the court acknowledged the inherent delays and backlog of cases in Indian courts, it cited the Bhopal Act as indicative of the Indian government's commitment to a speedy resolution of the victims' claims. The court further discounted plaintiffs' assertions that Indian law firms were inadequate to represent the victims, that filing fees impaired access to the courts, that Indian pretrial discovery was inadequate, and that Indian tort law was not sufficiently developed to accommodate the Bhopal claims. *Id.* at 847–51. "To sum up the discussion to this point, the Court determines that the Indian legal system provides an adequate alternative forum for the Bhopal litigation. Far from exhibiting a tendency to be so 'inadequate or unsatisfactory' as to provide 'no remedy at all,' the courts of India appear to be well up to the task of handling this case. Any unfavorable change in law for plaintiffs which might be suffered upon transfer to the Indian courts will, by the rule of *Piper*, not be given 'substantial weight.' Differences between the two legal systems, even if they inure to plaintiffs' detriment, do not suggest that India is not an adequate alternative forum." *Id.* at 852.

Another factor considered by the court in deciding the *forum non conveniens* issue was private interest concerns. "The first example of a private interest consideration discussed in *Gilbert* is 'relative ease of access to sources of proof.' As stated, the analysis of this issue must hinge on the facts." *Id.* at 853. The court held that most of the relevant proof was to be found in India in UCIL records and through interviews with UCIL employees, the overwhelming majority of whom were Indian nationals:

> In the aggregate, it appears to the Court that most of the documentary evidence concerning design, training, safety and start-up, in other words, matters bearing on liability, is to be found in India. Much of the material may be held by the Indian CBI. Material located in this country, such as process design packages and training records of the 40 UCIL employees trained at Institute, constitutes a smaller portion of the bulk of the pertinent data than that found in India. Moreover, while records in this country are in English, a language understood in the courts in India, certain of the records in India are in Hindi or other Indian languages, as well as in English.... It is evident to the Court that records concerning the design, manufacture and operation of the Bhopal plant are relatively more accessible in India than in the United States, and that fewer translation problems would face an Indian court than an American court. Since Union Carbide has been directed to submit to discovery in India pursuant to the liberal grant of the American Federal Rules of Civil Procedure, and this opinion is conditioned upon such submission, any records sought by plaintiffs must be made available to them in India. The private interest factor of relative ease of access to source of proof bearing on liability favors dismissal of the consolidated case. *Id.* at 858.

The second private interest concern proposed by the *Gilbert* court and adopted by the district court in *Union Carbide* was the accessibility of witnesses. The court held that, if the case were heard in the United States, Union Carbide could be deprived of testimony from certain witnesses whereas, if the case were heard in India, all relevant witnesses could be questioned because the vast majority were Indian nationals and the few who where located in American could travel to India.

The third concern addressed was the ease of arranging a viewing of the disaster site. Although the court did not place much emphasis on this factor, it nevertheless recognized the possibility that a viewing might be necessary later in the litigation.

"The *Gilbert* court articulated certain factors which affected the interests of non-parties to a litigation to be considered in the context of the doctrine of *forum non conveniens*. These public interest concerns were held to be relevant to a court's determination of whether to dismiss on these grounds." *Id.* at 870. The first of these factors was administrative difficulties. The court held that both forum court systems were overburdened with heavy caseloads and that, in light of the appropriateness of the Indian forum with respect to the other factors, the United States courts should not be burdened with the tremendous resource demands of the *Bhopal* litigation. "The substantial administrative weight of this case should be centered on a court with the most significant contacts with the event. Thus, a court in Bhopal, rather than New York, should bear the load." *Id.* at 873.

"The Court concludes that the public interest of India in this litigation far outweighs the public interest of the United States. This litigation offers a developing nation the opportunity to vindicate the suffering of its own people within the framework of a legitimate legal system. This interest is of paramount importance." *Id.* at 865–66.

The District Court's Conclusion

[. . .]

"It is difficult to imagine how a greater tragedy could occur to a peacetime population than the deadly gas leak in Bhopal on the night of December 2–3, 1984. The survivors of the dead victims, the injured and others who suffered, or may in the future suffer due to the disaster, are entitled to compensation. This Court is firmly convinced that the Indian legal system is in a far better position than the American courts to determine the cause of the tragic event and thereby fix liability. Further, the Indian courts have greater access to all the information needed to arrive at the amount of the compensation to be awarded the victims.

"The presence in India of the overwhelming majority of the witnesses and evidence, both documentary and real, would by itself suggest that India is the most convenient forum for this consolidated case. The additional presence in India of all but the less than handful of claimants underscores the convenience of holding trial in India. All of the private interest factors described in *Piper* and *Gilbert* weigh heavily toward dismissal of this case on the grounds of *forum non conveniens*.

"The public interest factors set forth in *Piper* and *Gilbert* also favor dismissal. The administrative burden of this immense litigation would unfairly tax this or any American tribunal. The cost to American taxpayers of supporting the litigation in the United States would be excessive. When another, adequate and more convenient forum so clearly exists, there is no reason to press the United States judiciary to the limits of its capacity. No American interest in the outcome of this litigation outweighs the interest of India in applying Indian law and Indian values to resolving this case.

"The Bhopal plant was regulated by Indian agencies. The Union of India has a very strong interest in the aftermath of the accident which affected its citizens on its own soil. Perhaps Indian regulations were ignored or contravened. India may wish to determine whether the regulations imposed on the chemical industry within its boundaries were sufficiently stringent. The Indian interests far outweigh the interests of citizens of the United States in the litigation.

"Plaintiffs, including the Union of India, have argued that the courts of India are not up to the task of conducting the Bhopal litigation. They assert that the Indian judiciary has yet to reach full maturity due to the restraints placed upon it by British colonial rulers who shaped the

Indian legal system to meet their own ends. Plaintiffs allege that the Indian justice system has not yet cast off the burden of colonialism to meet the emerging needs of a democratic people.

"The Court thus finds itself faced with a paradox. In the Court's view, to retain the litigation in this forum, as plaintiffs request, would be yet another example of imperialism, another situation in which an established sovereign inflicted its rules, its standards and values on a developing nation. This Court declines to play such a role. The Union of India is a world power in 1986, and its courts have the proven capacity to mete out fair and equal justice. To deprive the Indian judiciary of this opportunity to stand tall before the world and to pass judgment on behalf of its own people would be to revive a history of subservience and subjugation from which India has emerged. India and its people can and must vindicate their claims before the independent and legitimate judiciary created there since the Independence of 1947.

"This Court defers to the adequacy and ability of the courts of India. Their interest in the sad events of December 2–3, 1984 at the UCIL plant in the City of Bhopal, State of Madhya Pradesh, Union of India, is not subject to question or challenge. The availability of the probative, relevant, material and necessary evidence to Indian courts is obvious and has been demonstrated in this opinion.

"Therefore, the consolidated case is dismissed on the grounds of *forum non conveniens* under the following conditions:

1. Union Carbide shall consent to submit to the jurisdiction of the courts of India, and shall continue to waive defenses based upon the statute of limitations;

2. Union Carbide shall agree to satisfy any judgment rendered by an Indian court, and if applicable, upheld by an appellate court in that country where such judgment and affirmance comport with the minimal requirements of due process;

3. Union Carbide shall be subject to discovery under the model of the United States Federal Rules of Civil Procedure after appropriate demand by plaintiffs. *Id.* at 866–67."

* * * *

M.C. MEHTA & ANR. v. UNION OF INDIA & ORS.

Civil Writ Petition N. 12739 of 1985, at 29–30 (Sup. Ct. India).
(Decided Dec. 20, 1986).

[. . .]

Law has to grow in order to satisfy the needs of the fast changing society and keep abreast with the economic developments taking place in the country. As new situations arise the law has to be evolved in order to meet the challenge of such new situations. Law cannot afford to remain static. We have to evolve new principles and lay down new norms which would adequately deal with the new problems which arise in a highly industrialized economy. We cannot allow our judicial thinking to be constricted by reference to the law as it prevails in England or for the matter of that in any other foreign country. We no longer need the crutches of a foreign legal order. We are certainly prepared to receive light from whatever source it comes but we have to build upon our jurisprudence and we cannot countenance an argument that merely because the new law does not recognize the rule of strict and absolute liability in cases of hazardous or dangerous liability or the rule as laid down in *Ryland v. Fletcher* as is developed in England recognizes certain limitations and responsibilities. We in India cannot hold our hands back and I venture to evolve a new principle of liability which English courts have not done. We have to develop our own law and if we find that it is necessary to construct a new principle of liability to deal with an unusual situation which has arisen and which is likely to arise in [the] future on account of hazardous or inherently dangerous industries which are concomitant to an industrial economy, there is no reason why we should hesitate to evolve such principle of liability merely because it has not been so done in England. We are of the view that an enterprise which is engaged in a hazardous or inherently dangerous industry which poses a potential threat to the health and safety of the persons working in the factory and residing in the surrounding areas owes an absolute and non-delegable duty to the community to ensure that no harm results to anyone on account of [the] hazardous or inherently dangerous nature of the activity which it has undertaken. The enterprises must be held to be under an obligation to provide that the hazardous or inherently dangerous activity in which it is engaged must be conducted with the highest standards of safety and if any harm results on account of such activity and it should be no answer to the enterprise to say that it had taken all reasonable care and that the harm occurred without any negligence on its part.

[. . .]

* * * *

Subsequent U.S. Developments in the Bhopal Matter

MONROE LEIGH, JUDICIAL DECISIONS

81 AM. J. INT'L. L. 411, 415 (1987).
(Reprinted with permission).

(footnotes omitted)

[. . .]

Appellants, several Indian plaintiffs in consolidated proceedings against Union Carbide Corporation, a New York corporation, appealed from a district court order dismissing the action on grounds of *forum non conveniens*. In June 1986, the District Court for the Southern District of New York granted Union Carbide's motion to dismiss and entered its order after Union Carbide, while expressly reserving its right to appeal, agreed to certain conditions. The U.S. Court of Appeals for the Second Circuit...eliminated two of the conditions imposed by the trial court, affirmed the order as modified, and *held*: that the court below had not abused its discretion in dismissing the action.

In its review of the decision below, the appellate court relied on the standard set forth by the U.S. Supreme Court in *Piper Aircraft Co. v. Reyno*, a seminal *forum non conveniens* decision that had also provided the framework for the trial court's analysis. The appellate court found that the trial court had reasonably considered and balanced all applicable factors and that under the given circumstances it would have been an abuse of discretion had the case not been dismissed. In particular, the appellate court rejected appellants' contentions that the trial court should have paid more deference to the plaintiffs' choice of forum and appellants' ongoing settlement negotiations with Union Carbide. According to the court, such deference would have been especially unwarranted because the Indian Government representing all but a few Indian plaintiffs, had ultimately decided to support the *forum non conveniens* dismissal and because it opposed as inadequate a $350 million settlement proposal which American counsel for appellants apparently would have been prepared to accept.

With respect to the conditions of the dismissal, the appellate court noted that it is not unusual to condition a *forum non conveniens* order on the moving defendant's consent to submit to the jurisdiction of foreign courts and its waiver of any statute of limitations defense in order to ensure that the case could be heard in the more convenient forum. But the appellate court found that it was inappropriate for the trial court to require Union Carbide to agree to satisfy any final judgment of an Indian court that "comport[s] with the minimal requirements of due process." The appellate court found that the district court had misread the applicable law when it assumed that an Indian judgment might not be enforceable against Union Carbide in the United States without Union Carbide's consent. In this respect, the appellate court referred to New York state law which provides concise rules for the recognition and enforcement of foreign money judgments. Under these rules, a foreign judgment would not be enforced if, among other clearly defined instances in which courts could decline enforcement, it "was rendered under a system which does not provide impartial tribunals or procedures compatible with the requirements of due process of law." While the district court might have intended to incorporate this concept in its order, the appellate court pointed out that the language used in the order may give rise to misunderstandings; in particular, the reference to "the minimum requirements of due process" could be understood to lower the otherwise applicable statutory standard. For these reasons, the appellate court decided to delete the condition in its entirety.

The court also addressed the argument (which is attributed to counsel for Union Carbide) that the due process language of the district court order suggested that U.S. courts could retain jurisdiction "to monitor the Indian court proceedings" and be "on call to rectify" any infringement of the Union Carbide's due process rights. It emphatically rejected the concept of parallel jurisdiction of courts in several countries: "[Such a proposition] is not only impractical but evidences an abysmal ignorance of basic jurisdictional principles, so much so that it borders on the frivolous." It reasoned that a court relinquished its jurisdiction when it granted dismissal for *forum non conveniens*. A party alleging shortcomings of the proceedings before a foreign court could raise them in a U.S. court only if and when enforcement of a resulting foreign judgment is sought against it in the United States.

Finally, the court deleted the condition requiring Union Carbide to provide discovery to the Indian Government pursuant to the U.S. Federal Rules of Civil Procedure even though no corresponding duty existed on the part of the Indian Government. While noting that in some instances it may be appropriate to require only one party to provide discovery, *e.g.*, if such party unqualifiedly consented or if the other party were believed to have no relevant discoverable materials, the court held that "[b]asic justice dictates that both sides be treated equally, without having equal access to the evidence in the possession or under the control of the other."

By deleting two of the conditions of dismissal, the court of appeals cured the few troubling aspects of the otherwise well-reasoned district court opinion. The *Union Carbide* case is a convincing example of the exercise of judicial restraint on the part of U.S. courts in application of the time-honored doctrine of *forum non conveniens*.

Notes and Questions

1. The readings indicate substantial complexity in the MNEs' corporate structure and organization. Do such economic entities owe allegiance to any particular country? Is Nestlé only a Swiss company or a company of any nation in which it does business or does a substantial business? Should the nationality of shareholders be considered relevant to the assertion of jurisdiction by courts and the legislative regulation of companies? If economic interest or impact is germane, how is it to be measured and when is there enough of it to be relevant? Should corporate formalities, as established by legislation in the jurisdiction, be dispositive of the jurisdiction question?

2. Is it fair to say that both predictability and economic complexity dictate a conservative approach to the assertion of jurisdiction over companies? Is it systemically sound to ignore and undermine the effects of incorporation? Should any judicial disregard of corporate structures be justified only by the company's clear abuse of position or avoidance of accountability?

3. Do the circumstances of emerging and re-emerging countries call for a different rule? Should the assets of corporate parents always be made available to subsidize the liability resources of foreign subsidiaries? Why? To what extent? What if the host government specifically immunizes the parent

from any exposure to liability because of the existence and activities of a subsidiary?

4. Is the corporate parent, located in the United States, liable in U.S. courts for the conduct of a separate company abroad? Or, is a foreign company liable abroad for its local conduct but to the extent of the assets of its absentee parent? What about the public investors in *Bhopal*? Who are they and why are they automatically immunized from liability? Doesn't the reasoning displayed by various authors in the Texas Symposium issue simply assume that U.S. legal liability standards should apply throughout the world? What concept of responsibility or liability underlies such a simple-minded and possibly biased view? What motivates it?

5. Attempt to establish a Code of Conduct for MNEs. Address jurisdiction, law applicable, liability, and nationality. How do you effectively regulate such corporate structures? What is the public interest here?

6. Is the U.S. District Court opinion in *Bhopal* political? Legal? Juridical? What does it tell you about client representation? Of MNEs? Of foreign tort plaintiffs?

§ 7. EXTENDING NATIONAL REGULATORY LAW

General Considerations

Extraterritoriality is a significant factor in private international litigation. Municipal courts can extend their jurisdiction beyond the political boundaries of the country in which they sit and that invested them with their authority to rule. Courts engage in extraterritoriality by asserting jurisdiction over foreign parties and/or conduct that occurred abroad. The jurisdictional assertion may or may not be effective. Affected countries generally resist such actions because they perceive them as a trespass to sovereignty and an infringement of national autonomy. The end result usually is a stalement. Each side ends up assuming an uncompromising unilateral position. Moreover, commanding that foreign parties appear in U.S. courts or that foreign conduct implicates the U.S. legal system is a means of exporting U.S. juridical standards and giving them a *de facto* universal standing.

U.S. regulatory legislation also can be given extraterritorial effect by being applied to conduct done abroad either by U.S. or foreign parties. Courts can decide to engage in this practice in individual cases as long as the controlling legislation states expressly or can be construed to state that it applies to conduct done abroad. In a recent controversial case, an environmental group brought suit in the federal Fifth Circuit against Freeport McMoran for its conduct in Indonesia. The corporate headquarters of Freeport McMoran is located in the Fifth Circuit's territorial jurisdiction (New Orleans). The "public interest" plaintiffs claimed that Freeport McMoran's mining activities in Indonesia violated U.S. environmental laws. The litigation raised a number of critical issues: For instance, whether U.S. environmental laws followed a U.S. company to foreign jurisdictions and dislodged the application of local laws? Moreover, could conduct deemed legal in the country where it takes place be considered unlawful in the country of the actor's origin or nationality? Does nationality or place of incorporation serve as a proper basis for the global application of domestic law and jurisdiction against an MNE?

There are many variations on the theme of extraterritoriality. It can create substantial problems for international commercial transactions. The core problems are related to the lack of a supranational mechanism or framework for addressing the issues of law applicable and jurisdiction assertion and their various manifestations. Nationalistic sovereign control over the matter is unlikely to be ceded or surrendered. Therefore, the only plausibly effective recourse is to insert relevant provisions into the parties' contract.

(i)

Antiboycott and Anti–Corruption Legislation

Several U.S. statutes have broad extraterritorial effect. There are two U.S. antiboycott statutes; one is administered by the Department of Commerce—Section 8 of the Export Administration Act (EAA), 15 C.F.R. Part 769—and the other is administered by the Treasury Department—the "Ribicoff Amendment," Section 999 of the Internal Revenue Code. The statutes apply to foreign boycotts generally, but they are directed to the Arab League boycott of Israel. Section 8 of the EAA is more complex and comprehensive than Section 999; it is also more confusing and contradictory. It involves civil and criminal penalties, while Section 999 involves the denial of tax credits and benefits. Both statutes can reach the activities of U.S. foreign subsidiaries. They prohibit companies from supplying boycott-related information—for example, the company's business relationship with Israel or Israeli companies or identifying their owners or shareholders. The information issue can arise when a company seeks to register to do business in a boycotting country. The statutes prohibit U.S. companies from having a third party undertake the prohibited conduct for them. The regulations prohibit agreements to refuse to do business with or in a boycotted country, with a boycotted country business, with a boycotted country national or resident, or with any other person for boycott-related purposes.

The Foreign Corrupt Practices Act (FCPA), 15 U.S.C. § 78dd–1(a), 2(a), is a criminal statute that prohibits payments to foreign government officials to obtain or retain business or to direct business to particular individuals. Maximum fines for violations of the antibribery provisions of the Act range from $100,000 for individuals to $2,000,000 for corporations. The maximum prison sentence is five years. The FCPA applies only to "domestic concerns," meaning U.S. citizens and residents, businesses incorporated or having their principal place of business in the United States, and the officers, directors, employees, and shareholders of these entities. It, therefore, covers foreign branches, employees who work abroad, but not foreign subsidiaries. The FCPA is most likely to be violated in circumstances that involve competing to secure a government contract. Commonplace promotional activities, such as entertainment, gifts, and samples can become highly suspect. Moreover, the actions of a foreign agent can be imputed to the U.S. principal. Under the FCPA, a company will be said to "know" of an improper payment by an agent if it is aware that there is a "high probability" of an illicit payment.

(ii)

Title VII and U.S. Employees Abroad

Title VII was passed as part of the Civil Rights Act of 1964 in an effort to eliminate discrimination based on race, color, sex, religion, or national origin in the workplace. In *EEOC v. Aramco*, 499 U.S. 244, 111 S.Ct. 1227, 113 L.Ed.2d 274 (1991), the U.S. Supreme Court held that Title VII did not apply extraterritorially. As a result, U.S. employees working abroad for U.S. companies had no statutory recourse against illegal discriminatory conduct. They lost the protection of their rights once they crossed national boundaries.

Ali Bourselan, a naturalized U.S. citizen of Lebanese descent, was employed as an engineer by the Arabian American Oil Company (Aramco), a Saudi Arabian Corporation licensed to do business in Texas. Bourselan became the subject of persistent racial, ethnic, and religious harassment by his supervisor shortly after he was transferred to the Aramco Saudi Arabian office. He was dismissed three and one half years later.

Boureslan subsequently filed charges with the Equal Employment Opportunity Commission (EEOC) and brought a civil suit in the U.S. District Court for the Southern District of Texas under Title VII and state law. Aramco moved to dismiss for lack of subject matter jurisdiction on the grounds that Title VII did not apply extraterritorially. The court ruled in favor of Aramco and dismissed the suit, noting that the legislative history and language of Title VII were ambiguous about an intent to have the statute apply abroad. *Boureslan v. Aramco*, 653 F.Supp. 629, 630 (S.D. Tex. 1987). The court found: "At a minimum, the absence of a clearly expressed intent creates a presumption that Congress did not intend extraterritorial application. It is doubtful that Congress reserved the question of Title VII's application for the courts to decide. It is much more likely that Congress never considered the issue."

The Fifth Circuit affirmed the district court ruling. Citing additional policy considerations, the court expressed the concern that:

> The religious and social customs practiced in many countries are wholly at odds with those of this country. Requiring American employers to comply with Title VII in such a country could well leave American corporations the difficult choice of refusing to employ United States citizens in the country or discontinuing business.

Boureslan v. Aramco, 857 F.2d 1014, 1020 (5th Cir. 1988). The Fifth Circuit reheard the case *en banc* and again affirmed the lower court decision: 892 F.2d 1271 (5th Cir. 1990). The *en banc* majority held that the presumption should be against such extraterritorial application in light of the lack of clear congressional intent to the contrary.

By a 6 to 3 vote, the U.S. Supreme Court affirmed the Fifth Circuit, holding that Title VII of the Civil Rights Act did not extend to American companies and their employees overseas. Chief Justice Rehnquist, writing for the majority, explained that the Court would not endorse a "policy which would raise difficult issues of international law by imposing this country's employment discrimination regime upon foreign corporations operating in foreign commerce" without clear congressional intent to do so. He observed that Congress was free to amend Title VII to authorize extraterritorial application.

In 1991, the U.S. Congress did amend the 1964 Civil Rights Act, 105 Stat. 1077. Read the amended language below and determine how it modifies the scope of the civil rights legislation. Do you agree with the change? With the U.S. Supreme Court's assessment of the circumstances? How should the extraterritorial application of U.S. civil rights law be taken into account in contract provisions?

Civil Rights Act of 1991

Sec. 109. Protection of Extraterritorial Employment.

(a) **Definition of Employee**—Section 701(f) of the Civil Rights Act of 1964 (42 U.S.C. 2000e(f)) and section 101(4) of the Americans with Disabilities Act of 1990 (42 U.S.C. 12111(4)) are each amended by adding at the end the following: "With respect to employment in a foreign country, such term includes an individual who is a citizen of the United States.".

(b) Exemption—

(1) **Civil rights act of 1964.**—Section 702 of the Civil Rights Act of 1964 (42 U.S.C. 2000e–1) is amended—

(A) by inserting "(a)" after "Sec. 702."; and

(B) by adding at the end the following:

"(b) It shall not be unlawful under section 703 or 704 for an employer (or a corporation controlled by an employer), labor organization, employment agency, or joint labor-management committee controlling apprenticeship or other training or retraining (including on-the-job training programs) to take any action otherwise prohibited by such section, with respect to an employee in a workplace in a foreign country if compliance with such section would cause such employer (or such corporation), such organization, such agency, or such committee to violate the law of the foreign country in which such workplace is located.

"(c)(1) If an employer controls a corporation whose place of incorporation is a foreign country, any practice prohibited by section 703 or 704 engaged in by such corporation shall be presumed to be engaged in by such employer.

"(2) Sections 703 and 704 shall not apply with respect to foreign operations of an employer that is a foreign person not controlled by an American employer.

"(3) For purposes of this subsection, the determination of whether an employer controls a corporation shall be based on—

"(A) the interrelation of operations;

"(B) the common management;

"(C) the centralized control of labor relations; and

"(D) the common ownership or financial control, of the employer and the corporation."

(2) **Americans with disabilities act of 1990**—Section 102 of the Americans with Disabilities Act of 1990 (42 U.S.C. 12112) is amended—

(A) by redesignating subsection (c) as subsection (d); and

(B) by inserting after subsection (b) the following new subsection:

"(c) Covered Entities in Foreign Countries—

"(1) In general.—It shall not be unlawful under this section for a covered entity to take any action that constitutes discrimination under this section with respect to an employee in a workplace in a foreign country if compliance with this section would cause such covered entity to violate the law of the foreign county in which such workplace is located.

"(2) Control of corporation.—

"(A) Presumption.—If an employer controls a corporation whose place of incorporation is a foreign country, any practice that constitutes discrimination under this section and is engaged in by such corporation shall be presumed to be engaged in by such employer.

"(B) Exception.—This section shall not apply with respect to the foreign operations of an employer that is a foreign person not controlled by an American employer.

"(C) Determination.—For purposes of this paragraph, the determination of whether an employer controls a corporation shall be based on—

"(i) the interrelation of operations;

"(ii) the common management;

"(iii) the centralized control of labor relations; and

"(iv) the common ownership or financial control, of the employer and the corporation."

(c) **Application of Amendments**.—The amendments made by this section shall not apply with respect to conduct occurring before the date of the enactment of this Act.

(iii)

U.S. Antitrust Laws and Extraterritoriality

The Sherman Act provides for the application U.S. antitrust laws to foreign anticompetitive conduct. Section One of the Sherman Act states that "Every contract, combination in the form of trust. . . or conspiracy in restraint of trade or commerce among the several states, or with foreign nations, is hereby declared to be illegal.'' Section Two of the Sherman Act adds that, ''Every person who shall monopolize, attempt to monopolize or combine or conspire with any other person or persons to monopolize any part of the trade or commerce among the several states, or with foreign nations shall be deemed guilty of a felony....''

To bring suit against a foreign defendant, the U.S. government or private plaintiff must demonstrate the existence of subject matter, prescriptive, and personal jurisdiction. Subject matter jurisdiction refers to a court's authority to adjudicate a particular category of disputes. Prescriptive jurisdiction describes a state's authority to enact laws. The Sherman Act furnishes the statutory basis for subject matter and prescriptive jurisdiction over foreign anticompetitive behavior. The plaintiff must also establish that the U.S. court has personal jurisdiction over the foreign national. The due process clause of the U.S. Constitution requires that the defendant have minimum contacts with the United States and that the exercise of jurisdiction comport with principles of fairness and substantial justice. The exercise of personal jurisdiction is proper if the foreign defendant's conduct and connection with the United States are such that he could reasonably anticipate being haled into a U.S. court.

Early case law, in particular *American Banana Co. v. United Fruit Co.*, 213 U.S. 347, 29 S.Ct. 511, 53 L.Ed. 826 (1909), did not recognize the principle of extraterritoriality. In *American Banana*, Justice Holmes stated, ''But the general and almost universal rule is that the character of an act as lawful or unlawful must be determined wholly by the law of the country where the act is done.... For another jurisdiction, if it should happen to lay hold of the actor, to treat him according to its own notions rather than those of the place where he did the acts, not only would be unjust, but would be an interference with the authority of another sovereign, contrary to the comity of nations, which the other state concerned justly might resent.'' *Id.* at 356. The Court thereby limited U.S. antitrust prosecution to those cases in which the offending act was committed within the United States.

As U.S. participation in international business grew, so did the Court's willingness to distinguish *American Banana* from subsequent cases and to allow the prosecution of antitrust violations extraterritorially. The trend culminated in *United States v. Aluminum Company of America (Alcoa)*, 148 F.2d 416 (2d Cir.1945), in which the Court extended the reach of antitrust jurisdiction beyond U.S. borders to include those violations that had an ''effect'' upon U.S. commerce.

The controversial approach adopted in *Alcoa* was modified by more recent cases:

> That American law covers some conduct beyond this nation's borders does not mean that it embraces all, however. Extraterritorial application is understandably a matter of concern for the other countries involved. Those nations have sometimes resented and protested, as excessive intrusions into their own spheres, broad

assertions of authority by American courts.... In any event, it is evident that at some point the interests of the United States are too weak and the foreign harmony incentive for restraint too strong to justify an extraterritorial assertion of jurisdiction.

[...]

The effects test by itself, is incomplete because it fails to consider other nations' interests.... Nor does it expressly take into account the full nature of the relationship between the actors and this country.

[...]

A tripartite analysis seems to be indicated. As acknowledged above, the antitrust laws require in the first instance that there be some effect—actual or intended—on American foreign commerce before the federal courts may legitimately exercise subject matter jurisdiction under those statutes. Second, a greater showing of burden or restraints may be necessary to demonstrate that the effect is sufficiently large to present a cognizable injury to the plaintiffs and therefore, a civil violation of the antitrust laws.... Third, there is the additional question which is unique to the international setting of whether the interests of, and links to, the United States—including the magnitude of the effect on American foreign commerce—are sufficiently strong, vis-à-vis those of other nations, to justify an assertion of extraterritorial authority.

Timberlane Lumber Co. v. Bank of America, 549 F.2d 597, 609–13 (9th Cir. 1976).

The balancing test proposed by the *Timberlane* court was endorsed by the Third Circuit in *Mannington Mills, Inc. v. Congoleum Corp.*, 595 F.2d 1287 (3d Cir. 1979):

In *Timberlane Lumber Co. v. Bank of America* ... the Court of Appeals for the Ninth Circuit adopted a balancing process in determining whether extraterritorial jurisdiction should be exercised, an approach with which we find ourselves in substantial agreement. The factors we believe should be considered include:

1. Degree of conflict with foreign law or policy;

2. Nationality of the parties;

3. Relative importance of the alleged violation of conduct here compared to that abroad;

4. Availability of a remedy abroad and the pendency of litigation there;

5. Existence of intent to harm or affect American commerce and its foreseeability;

6. Possible effect upon foreign relations if the court exercises jurisdiction and grants relief;

7. If relief is granted, whether a party will be placed in the position of being forced to perform an act illegal in either country or be under conflicting requirements by both countries;

8. Whether the court can make its order effective;

9. Whether an order for relief would be acceptable in this country if made by the foreign nation under similar circumstances;

10. Whether a treaty with the affected nations has addressed the issue.

595 F.2d at 1297–98.

The *Mannington Mills* court further recognized that "[w]hen foreign nations are involved . . . it is unwise to ignore the fact that foreign policy, reciprocity, comity, and limitations of judicial power are considerations that should have a bearing on the decision to exercise or decline jurisdiction." 595 F.2d at 1296.

The *Restatement (Second) of Foreign Relations Law of the United States* §§ 17 and 18 reflects this view, advancing the need for a balanced application of U.S. antitrust law:

§ 17

A state has jurisdiction to prescribe a rule of law

(a) attaching legal consequences to conduct that occurs within its territory, whether or not such consequences are determined by the effects of the conduct outside the territory, and

(b) relating to a thing located, or a status or other interest localized, in its territory.

§ 18

A state has jurisdiction to prescribe a rule of law attaching legal consequences to conduct that occurs outside its territory and causes an effect within its territory, if either

(a) the conduct and its effect are generally recognized as constituent elements of a crime or tort under the law of states that have reasonably developed legal systems, or

(b) (i) the conduct and its effect are constituent elements of activity to which the rule applies; (ii) the effect within the territory is substantial; (iii) it occurs as a direct and foreseeable result of the conduct outside the territory; and (iv) the rule is not inconsistent with the principles of justice generally recognized by states that have reasonably developed legal systems.

A return to a more aggressive enforcement policy, however, was announced in *In re Uranium Antitrust Litigation*, 617 F.2d 1248 (7th Cir. 1980). The Seventh Circuit in *In re Uranium Antitrust Litigation* held that the *Timberlane* decision was not comprehensive enough to undermine the viability of the *Alcoa* test for determining whether to assert jurisdiction over foreign anticompetitive conduct. Also, in *Laker*

Airways v. Sabena, 731 F.2d 909 (D.C. Cir. 1984), the D.C. Circuit rejected the balancing of interests approach and maintained that the *Timberlane* doctrine on how to decide whether to exercise extraterritorial antitrust jurisdiction did not necessarily advance international comity.

Commanding the integration of U.S. principles of commercial regulation into international markets created tension between the United States and its major trading partners. Foreign countries perceived the practice as an unwarranted intrusion on State sovereignty. National laws and regulatory policies differed; they harbored incompatible concepts of fair trade and were in different stages of development. Conduct prohibited under U.S. laws could be condoned or even encouraged under European and Japanese laws.

Foreign States objected strenuously to having lawful domestic conduct declared illegal under U.S. standards. They retaliated in three ways: (1) by enacting blocking statutes that created barriers to pre-trial discovery by U.S. plaintiffs seeking to impose U.S. antitrust laws extraterritorially on foreign defendants; (2) by enacting clawback provisions that enabled foreign defendants to recover some or all of the U.S. treble damages awarded to successful private plaintiffs; and (3) by refusing to enforce U.S. antitrust judgments.

Blocking statutes prevent the extraterritorial application of U.S. antitrust laws by disabling attempts at local discovery. Antitrust litigation requires extensive discovery. The United Kingdom, for example, enacted the Protection of Trading Interests Act (PTIA) to block the extraterritorial application of U.S. antitrust laws. It imposed fines on companies that complied with U.S. discovery requests. The legislation converged effectively with the doctrine of foreign sovereign compulsion, under which a foreign defendant served with a U.S. court order for discovery has a valid defense for noncompliance if compliance would subject the party to criminal penalties in the State of residence.

Clawback provisions allow foreign defendants to recover the punitive damages awarded to private plaintiffs in U.S. litigation. The award of treble damages is contrary to the policies of most other countries, including those with stringent antitrust laws. The United Kingdom, Australia, and Canada have clawback provisions. Finally, national laws can prohibit the recognition and enforcement of foreign judgments that contain exemplary relief.

The United States took steps to alleviate foreign concerns through international agreements. It concluded bilateral agreements with Australia, Canada, and Germany to promote cooperation and coordination in the application and enforcement of antitrust laws. The United States also encouraged international antitrust cooperation through mutual legal assistance treaties (MLATs). MLATs are treaties in which U.S. and foreign authorities agree to provide assistance and facilitate foreign discovery on a reciprocal basis in criminal antitrust investigations.

In 1991, the United States entered into an executive agreement with the European Community regarding competition laws. *See* 30 I.L.M.

1487. The agreement was designed to introduce certainty in enforcement practice and generally prevent conflicts which were previously addressed on an *ad hoc* basis. The agreement originated from recommendations developed by the Council of the Organization for Economic Cooperation and Development (OECD). The OECD recommendations were meant to alleviate the international disharmony that attended the application of U.S. antitrust laws. The agreement introduced the novel concept of positive comity, under which one Member State could request another Member State to institute an enforcement action against anticompetitive conduct occurring in its territory.

Hartford Fire Insurance Co. v. California, 509 U.S. 764, 113 S.Ct. 2891, 125 L.Ed.2d 612 (1993), represents an important recent ruling by the U.S. Supreme Court in this area. There, the plaintiff alleged that Lloyd's of London conspired to change the terms of general liability insurance policies in violation of the Section One of the Sherman Act. The conduct took place in London. In a 5 to 4 decision, the Court found that the London reinsurers engaged in unlawful conspiracies that produced a substantial effect on U.S. commerce. Lloyd's had contended that English law contained a comprehensive regulatory regime for reinsurance and that its conduct was consistent with British law and policy. Under the principle of international comity, Lloyd's maintained, U.S. courts should not exercise jurisdiction. Writing for the majority, Justice Souter stated: "[T]he fact that conduct is lawful in the state in which it took place will not, of itself, bar application of the United States antitrust laws even where one state has a strong policy to permit or encourage an activity which another state prohibits." Under *Hartford Fire*, international comity would prevent the assertion of judicial jurisdiction only if there is a clear conflict between the laws of foreign States. Even if the prohibited conduct is lawful in the foreign State, no conflict exists for the purpose of the applicable comity analysis if the actor can comply with the laws of both countries.

Justice Scalia issued a strong dissent, arguing that the majority fundamentally misinterpreted the provision of the *Restatement (Third) of Foreign Relations Law*. According to Section 403, a State may not exercise jurisdiction over foreign conduct when it would be unreasonable to do so. The majority failed to determine whether U.S. antitrust jurisdiction was reasonable. Justice Scalia explained: "[C]ustomary international law includes limitations on a nation's exercise of its jurisdiction to prescribe." The reasonableness factors in the *Restatement* provided that U.S. courts should not exercise jurisdiction because the United Kingdom had a comprehensive antitrust regulatory scheme and an important interest in regulating the activities of the reinsurers. "Rarely would these factors point more clearly against application of United States law." Justice Scalia also contended that the majority's concept of comity was too narrow. It blurred the distinction between comity and the defense of foreign sovereign compulsion and eviscerated the comity principle by considering only the conflict factor of the balancing of interests test. Finally, the ruling was at odds with the U.S.-EU executive agreement.

The Department of Justice and Federal Trade Commission Antitrust Enforcement Guidelines for International Operations reflect the approach propounded by the U.S. Supreme Court in *Hartford Fire*. The 1995 *Guidelines* endorse the *Hartford Fire* definition of international comity and demonstrate a renewed dedication to enforcing U.S. antitrust laws against foreign conduct that harms U.S. exports. They signal the U.S. government's intention to protect more vigorously U.S. markets and exporting opportunities from foreign restraints on trade.

Unilateral U.S. antitrust actions antagonize foreign countries, aggravating foreign relations and discouraging international cooperation on competition matters. Foreign States perceive U.S. policy as a political attempt to remove foreign trade barriers and open markets to U.S. exports. The application of the policy is likely to be met by defensive measures. Foreign States may even retaliate by challenging the conduct of U.S. companies that operate overseas.

The extraterritorial application of antitrust laws represents a departure from traditional antitrust principles. The purpose of U.S. antitrust legislation has been to promote competitive markets and protect U.S. consumers. It is not intended to promote certain businesses in the international marketplace or to protect U.S. exporting companies. The antitrust laws are a blunt instrument for defining foreign trade policy. Trade agreements and negotiation may be more effective means to counter foreign anticompetitive conduct.

Notes and Questions

1. "Extraterritoriality" is an ugly word in the conduct of private international relations. It smacks of unilateralism and imperialism. It disregards the cultural and political autonomy of sovereign States. It offends like any trespass and causes acrimony and the type of venomous squabbling that poisons relationships. Why does the otherwise "internationalist" U.S. Supreme Court endorse such a practice? Isn't this having transborder commercial regulation exclusively "on our terms," an effect prohibited by the Court in *The Bremen* (*infra* at 112)?

2. The other side to the discussion might argue that there is a transnational void in antitrust regulation. It is better to have U.S. law than no law at all. The choice is to have no regime or our regime. Do you agree? Is the statement accurate?

3. Is antitrust regulation part of U.S. international public policy? Is *Alcoa* the right way to express that concept?

4. What do you tell clients about extraterritoriality and how do you protect their interests in light of it?

Chapter 2

U.S. JURISDICTIONAL CONCEPTS IN TRANSBORDER LITIGATION

Table of sections

§ 1. BASIC CONSIDERATIONS

The judicial authority to rule is a significant threshold consideration in most cases of transborder litigation. The court must have both subject matter and *in personam* jurisdiction. Legislation generally defines a court's power to rule on particular types of disputes. The court's right to exercise its authority over the defendant is established either by the defendant's presence before the court or through the substitute means of contacts, service, and notice. Physical presence within the ruling court's territory or the filing of suit against the defendant at the defendant's domicile is the most ironclad way for judicial jurisdiction to be established. The devices that substitute for the primary mechanisms (contacts, service, and notice) place the defendant before the court in an abstract sense. Their purpose is to facilitate jurisdictional assertion and thereby provide for greater amenability to suit and accountability.

It is not surprising to discover that different legal systems approach the question of jurisdiction differently. Civil law systems have a more traditional and conservative framework for determining judicial jurisdiction than U.S. common law courts. The basic civil law rules on jurisdiction are well-settled: Place of the tort, place of contract formation or performance, or the defendant's domicile. Unlike most civilian counterparts, U.S. court jurisdiction is governed by more fluid and more aggressive rules in part because they function in a federal system that creates contests for jurisdiction and in which federal law needs to prevail on a national level. The would-be litigation crisis has tempered some of the competition and the aggressive use of authority. Much of this at the behest of the U.S. Supreme Court. Problems in administering civil justice systems have also modified the view of jurisdiction in civil law countries. Rigid systemic roles have become more malleable and adaptive. Fairness and functionality appear to have tempered formal juridical rectitude.

The critical concern for purposes of transborder litigation is which standard is likely to dominate in the inevitable clash of court jurisdiction. The battle between civil law and common law concepts is long-standing and fully in evidence in the jurisdictional battle. What is fair and for whom? Is systemic integrity a viable consideration or a rhetorical device? Should there be a judicial rule of reason on the jurisdiction question that eliminates the possibility of conflicts? From what source would such a rule spring? What would it provide? What exceptions would be admissible?

§ 2. THE FIRST STAGE

The U.S. law on the question has progressed through a number of historical changes that implicitly tracked the character of U.S. foreign policy and the fortunes of the U.S. economy. There was firstly an exuberant stage in which American courts appeared willing to serve as the courts for global litigation. They unhesitatingly applied the U.S. legal concepts of due process, minimum contacts, and corporate veil-piercing to foreign parties and interests. These concepts are uniquely American and their application was likely to and, indeed did, generate conflicts and animosity. The U.S. judicial practice reflected, to some degree, the overwhelming economic strength of the United States, its leadership of Western political and military policy, and the transformation of U.S. companies into multinational corporations.

Assess the nearly messianic quality of this stage in the historical transformation of U.S. transborder jurisdiction in light of the following case. Do you agree with the court's approach, rationale, and result? What aspects of the opinion are unquestionably correct and what aspects are completely wrong? Why? Outline the analytical elements of the controlling test for jurisdiction. Does it make logical or practical sense? Is there a better way?

TACA INT'L AIRLINES v. ROLLS-ROYCE OF ENGLAND, LTD.

15 N.Y.2d 97, 256 N.Y.S.2d 129, 204 N.E.2d 329 (1965).

CHIEF JUDGE DESMOND.

[. . .]

It is clear and now apparently conceded that the issue is as to jurisdiction *in personam* only, which resolves itself into an inquiry as to whether defendant, Ltd. [Rolls–Royce of England, a British Corporation], was doing business in New York through Inc. [Rolls–Royce, Inc, is located in New York City], as its separately incorporated department or instrumentality, so that service of the summons on an officer of Inc. suffices as service on the British corporation Ltd. Inc., a Delaware corporation, has an office and officers in New York City and is authorized to do business in this State. Ltd. has no office or officers in this State and is not so authorized.

To keep the casting straight: plaintiff, TACA, is a corporation of El Salvador suing for damages done to its airplane in Nicaragua and allegedly caused by [the] negligence of the several defendants. The defendant, Ltd., alone moves to set aside service of summons. We need not talk about the nonappealing defendants Capital and United. We must, however, mention Rolls–Royce of Canada, Ltd. (hereafter called Canada, Ltd.), not a party here but part of the picture because all of the stock of appellant Inc., the American subsidiary and defendant, is owned by Canada, Ltd., and all the latter's stock is owned by the parent English company Ltd. It was the theory of the service-vacatur motion made by Ltd. that it does no business at all in New York State and that Inc. is a distinctly separate corporate entity. Plaintiff, upholding the service, agrees that Inc. is a mere incorporated division or arm of Ltd. acting solely as the American sales and service department of Ltd.

Special Term, confirming a Referee's report after trial before the latter, held that Ltd. was not doing business in this State and that Inc. was not for purposes of service of summons an appropriate representative of Ltd. The court accordingly granted the motion of Ltd. and vacated the service as to it.

The Appellate Division majority held that the American subsidiary Inc., though nominally independent, actually functioned as a department of its British parent, Ltd. The majority stated that the claimed independence of Inc. was illusory and that despite form and appearance Inc. was a mere sales agent of Ltd. The sole dissenter expressed the view that on the facts the Special Term finding was justified, that is, that Inc., although a subsidiary of Ltd., maintained "complete separateness and independence" from and of Ltd. Among the cases cited by the Appellate Division majority is *Rabinowitz v. Kaiser–Frazer Corp.* (198 Misc. 707, *aff'd.*, 278 A.D. 584, *aff'd.*, 302 N.Y. 892). *Rabinowitz*, we hold, is a controlling authority for affirmance here.

The Appellate Division's majority opinion contains this accurate summary of the undisputed facts:

"Rolls–Royce, Ltd., manufactures and sells motor cars and airplane engines. It also sells parts and gives service to its customers. These products are sold practically world-wide and customers can get service at many places. Rolls–Royce, Ltd., owns all the stock of Rolls–Royce of Canada, Ltd., a Canadian corporation, and this company owns all the stock of Rolls–Royce, Inc. The business of Rolls–Royce, Inc., is solely in the sale of products manufactured by Rolls–Royce, Ltd., and the servicing of the purchasers of these products. The three mentioned companies have some directors in common, and key executive personnel in Rolls–Royce, Inc., were former executives of either the English or Canadian company and were assigned to their positions by the parent English company. There are frequent conferences among executives of the three companies at which the policies of Rolls–Royce, Inc., are determined. Rolls–Royce, Inc., employees who require technical training are given it by Rolls–Royce, Ltd., in England. All sales literature used by Rolls–Royce, Inc., is written and published by Rolls–Royce, Ltd. Rolls–Royce, Inc., gets its income in several ways. It owns no automobiles, and when a sale is made to a customer it buys a car from Rolls–Royce, Ltd., in England and imports it. The sale is at a fixed price which is lower than the price to the ultimate purchaser. Rolls–Royce, Ltd., gives a warranty directly to the purchaser which Rolls–Royce, Inc., delivers with the car. Rolls–Royce, Ltd., pays Rolls–Royce, Inc., a fixed annual fee for services rendered to customers in connection with these warranties. As to airplane engines, the compensation for service is paid by Rolls–Royce of Canada and this payment is measured by the price of the spare parts sold by Rolls–Royce, Inc.

"All of the net income of Rolls–Royce, Inc., goes to Rolls–Royce of Canada and appears in that company's balance sheet. As affected by the other operations of the Canadian company it then appears in the balance sheet of Rolls–Royce, Ltd."

To that statement, we add a few other items of fact. Rolls–Royce's manufacturing in England, plus the distribution, sales[,] and servicing of its famous automobiles and aero engines throughout the world, is carried out by the English parent company and 16 subsidiaries, including those in Canada and the United States. These scattered subsidiary companies are all wholly owned by the English corporation, all are set up like the English company in auto and aero divisions, all are controlled from England, all are in major part staffed from England, and important policies are arrived at in frequent conferences in England, New York[,] and elsewhere attended by various officials of the various corporations. One of the active American administrators is Thomson who was here serviced [sic] [served] with this summons. Inc. sells some aero engines but such transactions are usually handled from England or Canada. Inc. does sell autos and does perform on aero engines the operations required by Rolls–Royce warranties. The latter services are paid for to Inc. by $6,000,000 worth a year of Rolls–Royce autos and auto parts. The principal personnel of Inc. or most of them are former Ltd. employees, and key employees are exchanged both ways between New York and England and considered part of the Rolls–Royce employee "group." All operations of Inc. are reported to Ltd. and Canada, Ltd., and all American business appears in the consolidated earnings statements and profit and loss statements of Ltd. Personnel of Inc. are trained by Ltd. in England. As against all this, appellant Ltd. points to these facts only: that Thomson, who was actually served, was not an employee or officer of Ltd.; that Ltd. has no office, officer, bank account, or telephone or directory listing in New York; that Ltd. and Inc. have entered into contracts whereby the latter gets a fixed percentage on its sales of cars and parts and is compensated for other services to Rolls–Royce customers.

Decision of this appeal does not require us to decide whether, under modern Federal and New York law, Ltd., treated as a corporation separate from Inc., has substantial enough contacts with our State to allow our State to subject Ltd. to a judgment *in personam* (see *Simonson v. International Bank*, 14 N.Y.2d 281). Our question is more nearly a factual one: was Inc. a really independent entity or a mere department of Ltd.? If the latter, then obviously Ltd. was doing extensive business in our State through its local department separately incorporated as Inc. The affirmative answer is compelled by our 1951 case of *Rabinowitz v. Kaiser–Frazer Corp.* (302 N.Y. 892, *supra*) decided on facts remarkably similar to those before us in the present case.

Since the motion here made was no more or less than one to vacate service, we pass on no other question.

The order would be affirmed, with the costs, and the certified question answered in the affirmative.

Notes and Questions

1. Is the assertion of jurisdiction in the circumstances of this case truly extraordinary and, in fact, exorbitant? In effect, a company in El Salvador, probably government-owned, sues in New York an English manufacturer, which does business on a worldwide basis, because of an accident in Nicaragua. What is the basis for the U.S. court's assertion of jurisdiction in these circumstances?

2. TACA is engaging, it would seem, in international forum-shopping. What are the advantages of suing for an aircraft disaster in the United States instead of England (defendant's domicile), Nicaragua (place of the tort), or El Salvador (place of contract performance)?

3. Is forum-shopping an evil? When should it be permitted? When should it be prohibited? How might it be regulated? By whom?

4. Isn't Rolls–Royce (UK) an English company and Rolls–Royce (U.S.) a United States corporation? Why should one entity be responsible—legally and financially—for the conduct of the other? Is the insufficiency of assets the only justification for the blurring of lines between separate companies?

Of what legal and business significance is the act of incorporation? Should that significance be maintained in all or most circumstances?

5. What if, as was likely, the exorbitant jurisdictional result could not be achieved under the laws of the other affected States (the United Kingdom, Canada, El Salvador, and Nicaragua)? Should that factor have altered the result reached under U.S. law? In what way?

6. Can the opinion be given contradistinctive interpretations? On the one hand, it can be said to reflect American hegemony and imperialism and, on the other, it can be said to exemplify American outreach and the provision of access to a neutral and effective adjudicatory process on a worldwide basis. U.S. resources are expended for the benefit and detriment of foreign parties. Do you agree with the dual characterization? Which of the versions is more persuasive to you? Why? Are there other constructions?

7. What practical impact is the determination in *TACA International* likely to have on the U.S. court system? Is the impact desirable? Is it necessary and unavoidable?

8. How could a contract provision guard against the exorbitant assertion of judicial jurisdiction?

* * * *

The next case addresses the same issue of transborder corporate liability, but exclusively from the perspective of personal injury. In *TACA International*, Rolls–Royce's liability was based upon the alleged commercial failure of its product, as well as the attendant personal injury generated by the defects of the product. In *Frummer*, the financial consequences of a slip-and-fall in the UK Hilton are laid at the feet of Hilton USA and Hilton International and are to be determined according to U.S. economic standards and through the U.S. judicial process. The most salient difference is that, unlike the parties in *TACA International*, the plaintiff is a U.S. national. This circumstance raises the question of whether the nationality of the plaintiff is a sufficient basis for the assertion of judicial jurisdiction over an accident that occurred abroad and whether nationality should be able to trump jurisdiction in the place of the tort?

FRUMMER v. HILTON HOTELS INT'L, INC.

19 N.Y.2d 533, 281 N.Y.S.2d 41,
227 N.E.2d 851 (1967).

[. . .]

FULD, CHIEF JUDGE.

This appeal calls upon us to determine whether jurisdiction was validly acquired over one of the defendants, Hilton Hotels (U.K.) Ltd., a British corporation (hereafter referred to as Hilton [U.K.]).

The plaintiff alleges that in 1963 when he was on a visit to England he fell and was injured in his room at the London Hilton Hotel while attempting to take a shower in an "ovular," modernistic type bathtub. He seeks $150,000 in damages not only from the defendant Hilton

(U.K.), but also from the defendants Hilton Hotels Corporation and Hilton Hotels International, both of which are Delaware corporations doing business in New York. The defendant Hilton (U.K.), which is the lessee and operator of the London Hilton Hotel, has moved. . .for an order dismissing the complaint against it on the ground that the court lacks jurisdiction of the defendant's person.

Both parties argue that "the applicable statute" is CPLR 302 (subd. [a], par. 1) which authorizes our courts to exercise personal jurisdiction over a foreign corporation if it "transacts any business within the state" and the cause of action asserted against it is one "arising from" the transaction of such business. . . . However, the plaintiff does not allege that he had any dealings at all with the British corporate defendant or its agents in this State. Therefore, it may not be said that his cause of action *arose* from the British corporation's transaction of any business here, and he is not entitled to avail himself of CPLR 302 (subd. [a], par. 1) in order to bring the defendant within the jurisdiction of our courts. . . .

Jurisdiction was, however, properly acquired over Hilton (U.K.) because the record discloses that it was "doing business" here in the *traditional* sense. . . . As we have frequently observed, a foreign corporation is amenable to suit in our courts if it is "engaged" in such a continuous and systematic course of 'doing business' here as to warrant a finding of its 'presence' in this jurisdiction. . . . Although "mere solicitation" of business for an out-of-state concern is not enough to constitute doing business. . .due process requirements are satisfied if the defendant foreign corporation has "certain minimum contracts with [the State] such that the maintenance of the suit does not offend 'traditional notions of fair play and substantial justice.' "

In *Bryant v. Finnish Nat'l. Airline*, 15 N.Y.2d 426, 432. . .the court declared that the "test for 'doing business'. . .should be a simple pragmatic one," and, applying that test, went on to hold that the requisite minimum contacts with New York were made out when it appears that the defendant foreign corporation, an airline, "has a lease on a New York office. . .employs several people and. . .has a bank account here. . .does public relations and publicity work for defendant here including maintaining contacts with other airlines and travel agencies. . .transmits requests for space to defendant in Europe and helps to generate business."

In the case before us, these same services are provided for the defendant Hilton (U.K.) by the Hilton Reservation Service which has a New York office, as well as a New York bank account and telephone number. The Service advertises that it was "established to provide the closest possible liaison with Travel Agents across the country," that lodging "rates for certified wholesalers and/or tour operators [could] be obtained [from the Service] on request," and that it could "confirm availabilities immediately. . .and without charge" at any Hilton hotel including the London Hilton. Thus, it does "public relations and publicity work'' for the defendant Hilton (U.K.), including ''maintaining contacts with...travel agents'' and tour directors; and it most certainly ''helps to generate business'' here for the London Hilton—which, indeed, was the very purpose for which it was established. Moreover, unlike the *Bryant* case...where the defendant's New York office did not make reservations or sell tickets, the Hilton Reservation Service both accepts and confirms room reservations at the London Hilton. In short—and this is the significant and pivotal factor—the Service does all the business which Hilton (U.K.) could do were it here by [sic] [through] its own officials.

[...]

It is to be borne in mind, contrary to certain intimations in the dissenting opinion, that this appeal deals with the jurisdiction of our courts over a foreign corporation rather than the liability of a parent company for the acts of a wholly owned subsidiary.... The ''presence'' of Hilton (U.K.) in New York, for purposes of jurisdiction, is established by the activities conducted here on its behalf by its agent, the Hilton Reservation Service, and the fact that the two are commonly owned is significant only because it gives rise to a valid inference as to the broad scope of the agency in the absence of an express agency agreement....

We are not unmindful that litigation in a foreign jurisdiction is a burdensome inconvenience for any company. However, it is part of the price which may properly be demanded of those who extensively engage in international trade. When their activities abroad, either directly or through an agent, become as widespread and energetic as the activities in New York conducted by Hilton (U.K.), they receive considerable benefits from such foreign business and may not be heard to complain about the burdens.

Since, then, Hilton (U.K.) was ''doing business'' in New York in the traditional sense and was validly served with process in London, as provided by statute (CPLR 313), our courts acquired ''personal jurisdiction over the corporation for any cause of action asserted against it, no matter where the events occurred which gives rise to the cause of action.''...

The order of the Appellate Division should be affirmed, with costs, and the certified question answered in the affirmative.

BREITEL, JUDGE (dissenting).

The court is in agreement that personal jurisdiction cannot be extended over the defendant, Hilton Hotels (U.K.), Limited, a British corporation, under the provisions of New York's long-arm statute (CPLR 302, subd. [a], par. 1). Disagreement arises only over whether personal jurisdiction may be extended under ''traditional'' concepts of doing business in the State or by reason of the foreign corporation's ''presence'' in the State (CPLR 301). The difference in application of the two statutes determines whether judicial jurisdiction may be extended over a nondomiciliary to causes of action which arose outside the State as distinguished from those which arose in the State. The present case involves a tort which occurred outside the State.

[. . .]

The occasion for disagreement in this case is the extension of personal jurisdiction over a foreign corporation simply because of its relationship with subsidiary or affiliated corporations of a parent corporation. Moreover, such jurisdiction is extended in the absence of fraud, misrepresentation, or intermingling of activities of separate corporations. Before considering the particular facts of this case it should be observed that important policy and commercial considerations are involved in preventing or allowing [a] business enterprise to limit liability, suability, and exposure to governmental regulation, by the creation of truly separate corporate entities, with or without separate ownership structures, but especially where the ownership is not identical. These considerations are particularly important for a company engaged in world-wide trade and investment, often in the less developed countries of the world, because of the encouragement or discouragement to risk capital and the exposure to reciprocal treatment of jurisdictional bases in foreign countries.

The personal injury negligence tort of which plaintiff complains occurred in an English hotel in London resulting from a fall in the bathtub. Plaintiff is a New York resident who was then on tour in England. The hotel is operated by a British corporation, Hilton Hotels (U.K.), Limited, all but one of the shares of which are owned by Hilton Hotels International, Inc. International is a Delaware corporation owning directly or through subsidiaries a large number of hotels in countries outside the United States mainland. The stock of International is owned in part by Hilton Hotels Corporation, the American parent of the widespread Hilton Hotels enterprises. Both Hilton Hotels and International, although affiliated, have somewhat different stock ownership, with shares in each listed and available on public stock exchanges. Associated with this complex is an affiliate, Hilton Credit Corporation, providing credit card financing and distribution and a hotel reservation service, in New York and elsewhere. This latter corporation is jointly owned by Hilton Hotels Corporation and International.

There is no claim by plaintiff that the Hilton complex or any of its components is used to defraud, deceive, or mislead those who deal with it, or that there has been any failure in the operation and management of the several corporations to keep their internal affairs and management separate and distinct. It is contended, and it is undisputed, that the advertising and soliciting for business by the Hilton enterprises is done by offering the several respective services of the affiliated corporations, reservations services and credit card facilities, in common advertising.

The pivotal, but disputed, assertion upon which the present decision depends is that the Hilton Credit Corporation in handling reservations for the British corporation "does all the business which Hilton (U.K.) could do were it here by its own officials."

As recognized, the solicitation or mere promotion of business for an out-of-State enterprise does not constitute the doing of business in the State.... This is traditional law and there is no avowed intention to change it. On the other hand, the maintenance of localized activities in the State has, of course, been the basis for asserting personal jurisdiction.... The majority bridges the gap between these two rules by finding that separate but affiliated corporations perform the localized services, albeit local services of the narrowest scope, on behalf of the foreign corporation and, therefore, the foreign corporation is performing the localized services here, thus subjecting it to personal jurisdiction. This, of course, is a *non sequitur*, unless there is no power or privilege on the part of business enterprises to limit and segregate their assets, liabilities, and suability, if done, in fact, and if done without fraud or deception, by the utilization of separate adequately financed corporations, either subsidiary or affiliated.

[...]

On this analysis, the present case extends the "doing business" rule well beyond the existing principles or precedents. And the effect on the flexibility and promotion of world-wide business enterprises would be drastic and unhealthy. Those who have sought to liberalize and broaden the bases for jurisdiction have not considered any such drastic extension, although the occasion would be an obvious one....

Nor in private international law can there be found in this or other countries a jurisdictional reach as extensive as this.

It is well established in this country that a foreign parent corporation will not be subjected to the judicial jurisdiction of a State merely because of its ownership of a subsidiary corporation doing business within the State, if the parent diligently maintains the formal separateness of the subsidiary entity....

Similarly, courts in the United Kingdom evidently will not assert jurisdiction over a foreign corporation merely because it maintains a subsidiary in Britain.... Liberal Canadian jurisdictional statutes likewise do not recognize such a basis of jurisdiction.... The same is probably true in Australia....

In Civil Law and other code countries, the recognized basis of personal jurisdiction over foreign corporations admits of the assertion of such jurisdiction only on the existence of a specially designated office, situs of headquarters, or what is described as "domicile" in a special sense.... In some countries it has been held that a foreign corporation is not subject to personal jurisdiction even if it maintains branches in the country, through which it actually does business....

These are striking limitations in the code countries. They suggest very strongly that the extension of personal jurisdiction projected in this case would hardly be tolerated. The influence in the code countries of domiciliary jurisdiction (in the Anglo–American sense) is much too great, and the equivalent "presence" doctrine much more restrictive than here.

There is not the slightest suggestion in these materials that a formally separate foreign corporation could be brought before a foreign forum because of some intercorporate relationship, however intimate, with a local corporation.

These limitations elsewhere, and in the past, bespeak caution for the future, and especially when one considers the salutary purpose served by permitting enterprises to limit and segregate their activities as they are extended into other and frequently less developed parts of the world. Of great significance, of course, is what was also mentioned earlier, that harmful extensions of doctrine in this area will easily lend themselves to reciprocal manipulation against American enterprises operating through subsidiaries or affiliates in other countries.

While the circumstances in this case are not as serious in their effect in permitting personal jurisdiction, because plaintiff is indeed a New York resident, and the Hilton enterprises looked at in the large as a layman would view them are so much "present," the rules applied will not stay so limited. Under such grossly extended rules, nonresidents would also be able to sue in New York, where tort verdicts are regarded as very high; and there are other categories in which jurisdiction might be invoked under circumstances much less appealing than here. Again, it is pointed out that this case does not involve a cause of action which arose here, but one that arose in another country across the seas.

Accordingly, I dissent and vote to reverse and grant the motion to dismiss the complaint against Hilton Hotels (U.K.), Limited.

Notes and Questions

1. A question that arises in *Frummer* and which is a central consideration for all phases of transborder litigation is why domestic laws tailored to domestic concerns and circumstances are applied to litigation involving foreign parties and interests. Do you find that circumstance objectionable? If so, how might the situation be rectified? If not, why not?

2. What "burden" is associated with transborder litigation for defendants? Is this still a factor in the 21st century? Are there other, more real and substantial burdens?

3. Assess in your own words the majority's statement "that this appeal deals with the jurisdiction of our courts over a foreign corporation rather than the liability of a parent for the acts of a wholly owned subsidiary." What distinction is the majority making? How does it implicate the dissenting opinion?

4. At the end of the court's opinion, does the majority establish a rule of worldwide accountability before U.S. courts for companies that transact business in the United States? Is this a feasible position to assume? Does it take a legal doctrine to an unacceptable logical extreme and absurdity?

5. A critical part of the *Frummer* opinion is Judge Breitel's dissenting objections to the exorbitant assertion of judicial jurisdiction. Breitel writes an eloquent brief supporting the maintenance of the integrity of the formali-

ties of incorporation. He also compares the U.S. rule on jurisdiction to the approach adopted in other legal systems, thereby providing the essential comparative law basis for a rule of transborder litigation. His approach supercedes the mechanical application of domestic law rules to international transactions.

6. Is there an unavowed purpose by the majority to change traditional law? Why should the formalities of incorporation prevail?

7. What teachings does Judge Breitel distill from his analysis of foreign and international law? Why should an international consensus prevail over the tried-and-true technique of municipal law? Why should a foreign approach modify or prevail over a U.S. approach?

8. Judge Breitel raises large systemic concerns; the majority mechanically applies the domestic rule of jurisdiction to the case without any attempt to adjust it to the circumstances of the actual case; and the plaintiff's objective is to secure a jury-imposed American-styled recovery for his injury. Which perspective, in your view, should govern? Why?

9. In *Frummer*, because Hilton Hotels does business on a broad global basis and part of its corporate network extends to the United States, a U.S. national—injured in a Hilton establishment in London, England—has the right to sue for the injury in his home forum, benefit from U.S. trial procedures, and still retain the advantages of English tort law. In connection with the latter, the subsequent litigation of the matter before a New York state court raised an interesting choice-of-law issue. New York state tort law at this time gave the defense of contributory negligence an absolute preclusive effect: If the plaintiff had indeed been injured by the defendant's negligence, but the injuries also resulted in part from the plaintiff's substandard conduct, the plaintiff could not recover because of "unclean hands." England had already modernized its tort law. Under English law, the plaintiff's contributory negligence reduced but did not eliminate the recovery of damages.

The question before the court, therefore, was whether New York or English law governed the merits of the litigation. Ordinarily, because all other aspects of the litigation but for the place where the tort occurred were governed by U.S. law, it would seem sensible to have the merits decided according to New York law. Introducing English legal standards into the litigation would increase costs in the form of expert fees, create greater delays, and might confuse the jury or even the court. Moreover, the plaintiff and several defendants were U.S. nationals and, given the plaintiff's New York residence, the interests of the State of New York, rather than the United Kingdom, were directly implicated.

The court, however, decided otherwise. In reasoning that barely provided a fig leaf for the opinion's naked calculations in favor of the plaintiff, the court held that English tort law governed. Although the opinion is of little utility on this score, what factors should be applied or considered in deciding upon the governing law in transborder litigation? Nationality? Of the defendant or of the plaintiff? Place of the litigation, the tort, or contract performance? The law of the jurisdiction most substantially affected by or interested in the outcome of the litigation? A rule of administrative efficiency and effectiveness to be considered is that national courts should not apply foreign law in any circumstance. If parties choose or even if they are forced to have recourse to a given national court, that court should exclusively apply the law it knows and understands, namely its own law.

* * * *

The excerpts below demonstrate the state court's approach to the foregoing questions. It appears to be tendencious and anchored in other than juridical concerns. After reading the excerpts, articulate your assessment of the court's methodology, reasoning, and conclusion.

FRUMMER v. HILTON HOTELS INT'L, INC.

60 Misc.2d 840, 304 N.Y.S.2d 335 (1969).

On June 9, 1963, plaintiff registered as a guest at the Hilton Hotel in London, England. That night, upon returning to his room, he took a bath. The following night he followed the same procedure. On the third day of his visit, however, he came back to his room late and decided to go to bed immediately. The next morning, June 12, when he arose, he took a shower. While soaping himself he slipped in the bathtub, fell and sustained serious injuries.

At the trial[,] plaintiff sought to charge the defendant with liability on three separate bases: (1) failing to provide a rubber shower mat even after it had been specifically requested; (2) failing to install grab bars on the wall immediately adjacent to the overhead shower; and (3) not constructing the base of the tub so as to minimize the risk of a person losing his footing. Hilton Limited's position was that it had acted properly in providing all necessary safety devices and that in any case it was plaintiff's own carelessness that was the true cause of the accident. Evidence was offered by the plaintiff to establish each of his theories of liability, while Hilton countered with expert evidence tending to support its position that it had done all that reasonable care required. It may fairly be said that the evidence presented an issue of fact which was for the jury to resolve and which it has—in defendant's favor.

[. . .]

We turn then to the first point raised here, the contention that the court's charge on the Occupiers' Liability Act of 1957 was inadequate. In the charge, the court made no explicit reference to the statute's provisions. The charge contained a general statement of the responsibilities of an innkeeper. From the charge as a whole[,] the jury was informed that the failure of the defendant to provide mats, to install grab bars, or to construct the base of the tub differently, might be held by the jury to constitute negligence. The court felt then and after further research is still of the opinion that no difference is to be found in the duty of an innkeeper under English law than under the common law of New York. . . . The duty is the same in both jurisdictions—the exercise of reasonable care.

Since the court's charge did treat the defendant as owing the degree of care required by common law to an invitee, plaintiff's claim that the Occupiers' Liability Act increased the defendant's responsibility is without merit. Consequently, the moving papers do not establish any basis for the granting of the relief requested. Nevertheless, this discussion cannot terminate here.

During the course of the court's research on the Occupiers' Liability Act, the court became aware of an issue raised by plaintiff's counsel. It is that contributory negligence is not a defense to this action under English Law.

Here the jury was charged in accordance with established New York law, that any negligence on the part of the plaintiff contributing to the accident required a verdict for the defendant. Three questions are thus raised: (1) Assuming that the English statute applies, was the failure to charge the provisions of that statute prejudicial? (2) If the answer to the first question is affirmative, then is the English law the proper controlling rule? (3) Again, if the answer to the latter question be in the affirmative, does plaintiff's failure to bring the matter to the court's attention preclude relief?

As the use of the New York's contributory negligence rule rather than England's comparative negligence law was in all likelihood the determining factor, it must be decided which rule properly applies here. . . .

[. . .]

England's rejection of the all or nothing approach of the common law rule reflects a view that a person who is principally responsible for injuries to another should not escape liability completely because the injured party was also in part at fault. There is no doubt that the principal motive for change in the law in England is the harsh lack of proportion. . . in a rule which denies an injured person all compensation although his responsibility for the accident and for the resulting injuries may be minor.

[We now]. . . seek to determine whether either or both jurisdictions have any interest in the application of its domestic rule to the facts of this case, and if both are found to have some interest, then which jurisdiction has the paramount interest?

As we have already noted, the contributory negligence rule was principally meant to be a device to limit the liability exposure of a defendant. Since the defendant here is not a New York resident, New York would have no interest in seeing its liability-limiting doctrine applied in favor of a non-resident. If anything, New York might well be interested in seeing the application of English law. Were the plaintiff permanently disabled[,] he might well become a burden on New York's public and private facilities if his contributory negligence barred all recovery.

The problem of runaway juries does not require the application of New York law. New York courts have an adequate mechanism to control any such difficulty—the power of this court and the Appellate Division to set aside a verdict on the ground of excessiveness or to demand a remittitur. Our courts apply a comparative negligence rule in a Federal Employers' Liability Act case. Also, to avoid confusion, the special verdict procedure may be employed. Thus applying England's law would have no adverse effect on the administration of our court system.... Additionally, the power of our courts to control the size of a jury's verdict will protect the defendant.

To the extent that the English rule seeks to affect the conduct of persons within its borders, it has a significant interest in the application of its law. Candor, however, requires an acknowledgement that the contributory fault rule has little conduct-regulating function. With regard to the compensating policy of the comparative negligence statute, it may be contended that, since the plaintiff is a New York resident, England might well prefer New York law, which would benefit its domiciliary in this case. But it is difficult to conceive of England having such a parochial viewpoint. The statute by its language is not limited to any particular class of plaintiffs. Its enactment was in part brought about by a feeling that the common law rule was inconsistent with modern notions of justice. The problem is no different from the situation where the courts of this state hold a New York owner responsible for the negligence of a driver operating his car with his consent, even where the injured party is a resident of a foreign jurisdiction.

Moreover, all persons injured in England, even if not English residents, may have to be cared for by England. "Serious injuries may require treatment in [English] homes or hospitals by [English] doctors." In any event, the court concludes that the application of New York law here would not serve any legitimate interest of New York, but would defeat a legitimate interest of England (cf., *Intercontinental Planning Limited v. Daystrom, Inc.*, 24 N.Y.2d 372, 385, 300 N.Y.S.2d 817, 828, 248 N.E.2d 576. 583), and therefore England's comparative negligence rule ought to apply here. To do so, does not impose a greater liability on this defendant than it would have in England, and the application of the law of defendant's own country cannot be the grounds for any complaint.

* * * *

It is difficult to envisage the court's reasoning as anything but transparently calculated to achieve a particular practical end. Do you agree? Is the court's possible supervision of the quantum of damages awarded by the jury of any real comfort to the English defendant? Does the Hilton UK need to revise its insurance policy? Does England have any real interest in the actual circumstances or outcome of the case? Isn't England's concerns directed to matters of policy? Can the court's judgment be enforced in England? What objections might be made?

§ 3. EXCEPTIONS TO OR AMBIGUITIES IN THE RULE

The exuberant approach to jurisdiction did not always control judicial determinations. There were instances in which the courts did not privilege the factor of nationality or apply the concept of jurisdictional contacts in a loose and undemanding fashion to reach a foregone conclusion. *Delagi* illustrates a less accommodating approach to jurisdictional expansiveness and the espousal of a more rigorous and disciplined result.

DELAGI v. VOLKSWAGENWERK AG

29 N.Y.2d 426, 328 N.Y.S.2d 653,
278 N.E.2d 895 (1972).

[. . .]

JASEN, J. This action, based on negligence and breach of warranty, comes to us in the pleadings stage for a determination as to whether jurisdiction was validly acquired over the defendant, Volkswagenwerk AG of Wolfsburg, Germany, a German corporation, hereinafter referred to as VWAG.

The plaintiff in his complaint alleges that, in 1965, he purchased a Volkswagen automobile from an authorized Volkswagen dealer in Germany. While operating said vehicle in Germany, plaintiff claims that "the front wheel suspension and its appurtenant parts broke and collapsed, causing the front wheels to cave in and the motor vehicle to run out of control and hit a bridge abutment with such force as to cause [him] serious injuries."

Upon his return to the United States, plaintiff brought suit in New York against VWAG, alleging that "the defendant transacted sufficient of its business within the State of New York to subject itself to the jurisdiction of the courts of this State." Service of process was made on the defendant, pursuant to CPLR 313, in Germany.

The following facts are not in dispute. Defendant, VWAG, a German corporation, manufactures and sells, in Germany, Volkswagen automobiles and parts. VWAG has never qualified to do business in New York and has no office or place of business here. VWAG exports its automobiles into the United States through Volkswagen of America, Inc. (VWoA), a New Jersey corporation, which is a wholly owned subsidiary of VWAG and the exclusive American importer of Volkswagen automobiles. Likewise, VWoA has never qualified to do business in New York and has no office or place of business here. After these cars arrive in the United States at various ports, none of which are in New York, they are resold to 14 wholesale distributors franchised by VWoA. These distributors take title to the vehicles at the delivery point and, in turn, reship the cars to local independent franchised dealers. In New York State, the franchised wholesale distributor is World–Wide Volkswagen Corp. (World–Wide). The entire capital stock of World–Wide and its New York franchised dealer is owned by United States investors unrelated to either VWoA or VWAG.

Plaintiff does not claim that his cause of action arose from the German corporation's direct transaction of any business in New York in order to bring the defendant within the jurisdiction of our courts. . . but argues that jurisdiction was properly acquired over the defendant VWAG because it is "engaged in a systemic and regular course of business" in New York which subjects it to our jurisdiction. . . .

Our most recent pronouncement in this area of the law, *Frummer v. Hilton Hotels International*. . . reiterated the rule that a foreign corporation is amenable to suit in our courts if it is engaged in such a continuous and systemic course of "doing business" in New York as to warrant a finding of its "presence" in this jurisdiction. *Frummer* held that Hilton (U.K.) was "doing business" in New York in the "traditional sense" because of services performed—specifically publicity work and the making of final room reservations—by the Hilton Reservation Service as agent for Hilton (U.K.). The affiliate relationship existing between the Reservation Service and Hilton (U.K.) was significant only as it gave rise to an inference of an agency relationship. This "valid inference" may not, however, extend the actual scope of the agency. "The 'presence' of Hilton (U.K.) in New York," Chief Judge Fuld wrote, "for purposes of jurisdiction, is established by the activities conducted here on its behalf by its agent, the Hilton Reservation Service, and the fact that the two are commonly owned is significant only because it gives rise to a valid inference as to the broad scope of the agency in the absence of an express agency agreement. . . ."

In the case before us, however, the undisputed facts do not give rise to a valid inference of agency. Concededly, World–Wide is an independently owned corporation, in no way directly related to VWAG, and related to VWoA only by way of a "Distributor Agreement." Under this agreement, World–Wide purchases Volkswagen automobiles and parts outright from VWoA, takes possession at dock in Newark, New Jersey, and resells same to local Volkswagen dealers in its franchise area of New York, New Jersey[,] and Connecticut. Where, as here, there exists truly separate corporate entities, not commonly owned, a valid inference of agency cannot be sustained.

One point remains—whether jurisdiction was properly acquired over VWAG by reason of the "control" the foreign corporation exerts over World–Wide and the franchise dealers in the State. Specifically, plaintiff asserts that VWAG maintains a rigid control over World–Wide and its dealers by requiring: (1) sale of each dealer of a minimum number of automobiles upon penalty of forfeiture of their dealer franchise; (2) uniform design for dealer service departments; (3) service personnel to be trained in Germany; (4) uniform purchase and sales prices; and (5) prior approval of prospective dealers. In substance, plaintiff asserts that such control by the defendant manufacturer over its representatives in the State constitutes "doing business" sufficient to warrant the inference of "presence."

Aside from the fact that these assertions are seriously disputed by the foreign corporation, this court has never held a foreign corporation present on the basis of control, unless there was in existence at least a parent-subsidiary relationship. Even if World–Wide were a subsidiary of VWAG, which it is not, the alleged control activities of VWAG would not be sufficient to make World–Wide a mere department of VWAG.... We would only add that mere sales of a manufacturer's product in New York, however substantial, have never made the foreign corporation manufacturer amenable to suit in this jurisdiction. Thus, we conclude that VWAG was not "doing business" in New York in the traditional sense and, therefore, our courts did not acquire personal jurisdiction over the foreign corporation.

Notes and Questions

1. Can the use of minimum contacts, doing business, and corporate veil-piercing in *Frummer* and *Delagi* be reconciled? What elements are missing in *Delagi* that were present and so telling in *Frummer*?

2. Does *Delagi* reflect an application of the Breitel principles and reasoning? Does *Delagi*, then, alter your assessment of Judge Breitel's dissent in *Frummer*?

3. Does the result in *Delagi* amount to a denial of justice to the plaintiff?

4. What test for jurisdiction emerges from the *Delagi* court's reasoning? Do you agree that the factor of the German manufacturer's alleged control of the U.S. dealerships was not sufficient to establish agency? Why aren't sales enough? What about the element of nationality? Does the plaintiff have any real recourse?

5. What contract provisions might implement or defend against the holding in *Delagi*?

6. In *Sunrise Toyota, Ltd. v. Toyota Motor Co.*, 55 F.R.D. 519 (S.D.N.Y. 1972), the district court made the following statements regarding the rule in *Delagi*:

[...]

B. Jurisdictional Facts

Factory is a publicly held Japanese corporation which sells all of its products to Sales. Together these Japanese corporations own all—each owning 50%—of Importer, a California corporation, which in turn owns all of Distributor. Although the corporations maintain separate identities and keep independent records, there is significant overlap in the boards of directors and chief executive officers.

Importer orders cars from Japan, receiving title when they are loaded by Sales on ships in Japanese ports. Cars to the New York Region are shipped to the Port of Newark. In this area, Distributor contracts with independent dealers in the New York Region to provide for the service and sale of Toyota vehicles. Distributor's employees enter New York to promote the sale of Toyota vehicles and parts, service them, and attend to various problems that may arise. Neither Factory nor Sales deals directly with persons in New York State.

Under the franchising agreements with the independent dealers, the terms of sales and prices are fixed by Distributor for cars ordered but not yet shipped by either Distributor or Factory.

The Joint 1969 Annual Report for Factory and Sales indicates that Factory and Sales view their sales system as one part of an integral operation. It states: "With the steady buildup of overseas markets, Toyota launched programs to widen and strengthen its sales network. Along with these projects, Toyota is placing its Distributor–Dealer–Subdealer network throughout the world on a firmly organized footing." In the New York City telephone directory[,] there is a listing for "Toyota Motor Sales" with a Lyndhurst, New Jersey, telephone number. No attempt is made in the telephone listing to distinguish this as Importer or Distributor and not Sales.

The record also demonstrates communications between Importer and the parent Japanese corporations on important matters such as this litigation. Following imposition of the August 1971 ten percent import surtax, the independent dealers received a cable stating that statements on the tax "must come" from Sales and that "at this time" Importer "has received no instructions from either the parent company or any U.S. government agencies."

C. Discussion of Jurisdiction

Appling the relevant tests to these facts, we find that both Factory and Sales are doing business in New York through their agents, Distributor and its parent Importer.

1. Section 301 Jurisdiction

The threshold question is whether the Japanese parent corporations are present in New York under the traditional tests of "doing business" here according to § 301 of the New York Civil Practice Law and Rules. Delineation of the limits of *in personam* jurisdiction under the "doing business" test is still evolving. As recently as January 11, 1972, the Court of Appeals for this Circuit observed:

> "It appears that the New York Court of Appeals has sustained *in personam* jurisdiction under N.Y. CPLR. § 301 over foreign corporation each time it has considered the issue in the past decade. . . ."

Within a fortnight of that observation, the New York Court of Appeals handed down its significant decision in *Delagi v. Volkswagenwerk A.G. of Wolsburg, Germany*. . . holding for the first time since the line of cases expanding jurisdiction began that a foreign corporation "was not 'doing business' in New York in the traditional sense and, therefore, our courts did not acquire personal jurisdiction over the foreign corporation."

As restated in *Delagi*, there are two theories by which the Japanese parent corporations here may be found to be "present" in New York: (a) if the relationship between the foreign parents and local subsidiaries gives rise to a "valid inference" of "an agency relationship"; and (b) if control by the parent of the subsidiary is "so complete that the subsidiary is, in fact, merely a department of the parent."

Here the record is not sufficient to establish that Factory and Sales so control their American subsidiaries as to make them "one and the same corporation" such that "realistically no basis for distinguishing between them" exists for jurisdictional purposes....

[...]

In the instant case, Toyota Motor Sales ships Toyota vehicles throughout the world. Aside from its own network of offices, it and Factory own one subsidiary in Europe and one in the United States (*i.e.*, Importer, which in turn owns Distributor). Factory and Sales speak of "the steady buildup of overseas markets" and boldly state that "Toyota is placing its Distributor–Dealer–Subdealer network *throughout the world* on a firmly organized footing." (Emphasis added.)

The record is clear, however, that the American corporations are operating as agents for the Japanese parents, doing "all the business" which Factory and Sales "could do were [they] here by [their] own officials."...

When Factory and Sales created their American subsidiary[,] they used the name "Toyota Motor Sales U.S.A.," the same as the parent Sales. The use of this name—and the telephone listing without the suffix "U.S.A."—strongly connote the same entity. While this might be of no moment were the corporations entirely distinct and separately held by different public shareholders, that is not the case.

Unlike *Delagi*, where an entirely new and separate corporation assumed control of all distribution and servicing of the foreign automobiles in New York, here through a series of wholly-owned subsidiaries[,] Factory and Sales structured and monitored distribution of vehicles in New York. Only when the independent franchised dealer purchases the cars does a separate corporation, as in *Delagi*, enter the picture.

In sum, the Japanese parents have created wholly-owned subsidiaries solely to serve their interests. Whatever the advantages of limited liability or taxation this structure may have, under New York law[,] it does not insulate the parent from suit, for the parent is doing business here through its agents. Finding Factory and Sales present here through agents under § 301 of the N.Y. CPLR also satisfies the venue and personal jurisdiction provisions of 28 U.S.C. §§ 1391 and 1332(a)....

With as many contacts as the record evidences, it is clear that the exercise of jurisdiction *in personam* does not offend the constitutional standards of *International Shoe Co. v. State of Washington, Office of Unemployment Compensation and Placement*, 326 U.S. 310, 66 S.Ct. 154, 90 L.Ed. 95 (1945), and its progeny.

* * * *

Does the reasoning in *Sunrise Toyota* indicate an unintended bias or prejudicial effect against Japanese corporations and multinational organizations? Does it implicitly demonstrate that the court is trying to remedy what it perceives to be unfair trading practices by subjecting Japanese companies readily to U.S. liability standards and damages? Is the court's distinction between its case and *Delagi* persuasive? Why or why not? What is the test for jurisdiction now in light of *Sunrise Toyota*?

§ 4. CONTACTS JURISDICTION

The basis for asserting jurisdiction under the theory of minimum contacts resulted from state long-arm jurisdictional statutes and the federal constitutional standard established by the U.S. Supreme Court in *International Shoe Co. v. Washington*, 326 U.S. 310, 66 S.Ct. 154, 90 L.Ed. 95 (1945). The excerpts that follow from *Product Promotions, Inc. v. Cousteau*, 495 F.2d 483 (5th Cir. 1974), depict the basic elements of the test for contacts jurisdiction and its general application by courts.

PRODUCT PROMOTIONS, INC. v. COUSTEAU

495 F.2d 483 (5th Cir. 1974).

GOLDBERG, CIRCUIT JUDGE:

In this diversity case we are asked to gauge the reach of the Texas "long-arm" statute as limited by federal constitutional requirements of due process in order to determine whether the district court properly granted nonresident defendants-appellees' motion to dismiss for lack of jurisdiction over the person. . . .

[. . .]

II.

The power of a federal court entertaining a suit based on diversity of citizenship to exercise jurisdiction over [the] persons of non-resident defendants turns on two independent considerations. The law of the state in which the federal court sits must confer jurisdiction over the persons of the defendants, and[,] if it does, the exercise of jurisdiction under state law must comport with basic due process requirements of the United States Constitution.

[. . .]

The Federal Rules of Civil Procedure abolished the technical distinction between general and special appearances. . . . In all federal courts, including those exercising diversity jurisdiction, the principal method for attaching the court's jurisdiction over the person of a defendant, and the one used in the case at bar, is a Rule 12(b)(2) motion. It is by now well-settled that the party seeking to invoke the jurisdiction of a federal court has the burden of establishing that jurisdiction exists, and the burden may not be shifted to the party challenging the jurisdiction. . . . We find no merit in appellant's ingenious attempts to avoid this principle by characterizing its appearance in earlier decisions as *dicta*; nor do we agree that in [prior] decisions . . . this Court was really speaking of jurisdiction over the subject matter.

Recognition that appellant had the burden of establishing the district court's jurisdiction over the appellees' persons does not quite end the debate in the case at bar, for the parties also disagree over the weight of the burden to be shouldered.... [A]ppellees argue that appellant had to establish a *prima facie* cause of action. Appellant retorts that assuming *arguendo* it had the burden of proof, the task required only a *prima facie* showing of the facts on which jurisdiction was predicated, not a *prima facie* demonstration of the existence of a cause of action. We find the appellant's formulation of the burden it had to carry to be more accurate.

...The Texas Long–Arm Statute provides that a nonresident defendant who "engages in business" in the State is amenable to process "in any action, suit or proceedings arising out of such business done in" the State.... Section four of the Statute defines "doing business":

> For the purpose of this Act, and without including other acts that may constitute doing business, any foreign corporation, joint stock company, association, partnership, or non-resident natural person shall be deemed doing business in this State by entering into contract by mail or otherwise with a resident of Texas to be performed in whole or in part by either party in this State, or the committing of any tort in whole or in part in this State.

Because the plaintiffs in *Jetco Electronic Industries* relied on the commission of a tort to establish the court's personal jurisdiction over the defendant, they were obliged to make a *prima facie* showing that a tort had occurred in whole or in part in Texas. Thus the duty to make a *prima facie* showing of the facts on which jurisdiction was predicated required some reference to the facts alleged as a basis for relief.

What appellees overlook is that[,] although appellant initially pleaded several tort causes of action, counsel for appellant concentrated both at the hearing before the district judge and in this appeal on the breach of contract claim. In order to make a *prima facie* showing of the facts on which jurisdiction was predicated under the contract portion of the statute, appellant did not have to show *prima facie* evidence of a breach of contract. Rather, appellant had to present *prima facie* evidence that (1) a contract to be performed in whole or in part within Texas existed between itself and appellees and (2) the present suit arose out of the contractual arrangement. With this explanation of appellant's burden in mind, we proceed to our review of appellant's performance of the jurisdictional task.

III.

A. STATUTORY CONSIDERATIONS—JACQUES COUSTEAU AND THE COUSTEAU GROUP COMPANIES

This court has recognized that Article 2031b represents an effort by Texas to reach as far as federal constitutional requirements of due process will permit in exercising jurisdiction over the persons of nonresident defendants.... This means that many, if not most, challenges to *in personam* jurisdiction by nonresident defendants, whether in federal or State court will turn on constitutional considerations.... Nevertheless, a plaintiff must always look first to the statutory requirements lest a court conclude that the nonresident defendant stands beyond the grasp of Article 2031b....

The case *sub judice* illustrates the difference between deciding that the Texas Long Arm Statute will by its own terms reach far enough to cover a nonresident defendant and determining whether the statutory stretch must be hamstrung by federal constitutional limitations. We think it is beyond serious dispute that defendant CEMA [*Centre d'Etudes Marines Avancées*] was within the literal grasp of Article 2031b. The correspondence between Ross of Product Promotions and Caillart of CEMA, the course of conduct by both parties thereafter, and Ross's testimony at the 12(b)(2) hearing clearly establish the existence of a contract between Product Promotions and CEMA, performed at least in part in Texas through delivery of the films and reports to appellant in Dallas. And this proceeding has obviously arisen out of that contractual arrangement. Thus the district court had jurisdiction over the person of CEMA if the operation of the statute would not offend constitutional requirements.

Jacques Cousteau and the other corporate defendants, however, stand on [a] different ground. Since the contract was between CEMA and Product Promotions, counsel for appellant relies on an agency theory to establish the other defendants' amenability to process under the statute. According to this theory, in the negotiations and contractual relationship with appellant, CEMA was acting for, on behalf of, and as the agent of Cousteau individually and as agent or subsidiary for the Cousteau Group Companies. Thus these others are also parties to the contract and engaged in business within the State. We detect no particular flaw in this argument abstractly stated. Courts and commentators have recognized that an agency relationship may justify finding that a parent corporation "does business" in a jurisdiction through its subsidiary's local activities.... Moreover, an agent may in some circumstances itself be a party to an agreement between its disclosed principal and a third party....

Under this theory the alleged agency and parent-subsidiary relationships were facts on which jurisdiction was predicated, and appellant had the burden of making a *prima facie* showing of their existence. It is here that appellant founders from the confusion surrounding the identity of and relationship between the parties defendant. We can find no evidence in the record before us that CEMA was, as appellant argues, a subsidiary of the "Cousteau Group Companies," even assuming such a separate corporate entity existed. And even were we to assume the existence of a parent-subsidiary relationship, we can find no evidence that the parent exercised the type of control necessary to ascribe to it the activities of the subsidiary. Nor can we find any support for the assertion that the Cousteau Group Companies, either individually or collectively, were the "alter-egos" of Jacques Cousteau. Certainly[,] the hearsay testimony regarding Horton's statement to Ross that Cousteau does business through the Cousteau Group Companies does not suffice. We concede that the evidence in the record shows that the so-called Cousteau Group Companies were, at least at the time this contract was executed, related in some ways to each other and to Jacques Cousteau. Unfortunately, that is not enough; it was for appellant to sort out those business relationships, and the failure to do so is jurisdictionally fatal.

We are likewise convinced that appellant failed to carry the burden of establishing by *prima facie* evidence the existence of any agency relationship between CEMA and the other defendants other than that based on parent-subsidiary or alter-ego status. Under well-settled principles of law, appellant had to make a *prima facie* showing that in this contractual dealing CEMA acted with either actual or apparent authority on behalf of the others. Both types of authority depend for their creation on some manifestations, written or spoken words or conduct, by the principal, communicated whether to the agent (actual authority) or to the third party (apparent authority).... It is certainly true that "the entire transaction between Plaintiff and Defendant C.E.M.A. was permeated with references to Defendants Jacques Cousteau and the Cousteau Group Companies." Brief for Appellant at 16. Yet none of these references rises to the level of "manifestations" that Cousteau individually or the other companies were willing for CEMA to act on their behalf in contracting with appellant. More importantly, assuming *arguendo* that we could find such manifestations, they all came, not from the putative principals, but from the alleged agent CEMA. That appellant's president thought he was in effect dealing with Cousteau himself and an entity called the "Cousteau Group" is simply not enough on these facts to establish a *prima facie* case that he was in fact doing so.

We hold that appellant failed to present *prima facie* evidence that CEMA was clothed with the agent's authority to contract with Product Promotions on behalf of either Cousteau individually or the other Cousteau Group Companies, individually or collectively. Appellant having failed to carry its burden of bringing these other appellees within the reach of the Texas Long–Arm Statute, the able trial judge correctly dismissed the suit against them for want of personal jurisdiction.

B. Constitutional Considerations—CEMA

We turn to the questions whether the district court's exercise of jurisdiction over the person of CEMA, authorized by the Statute, would comport with constitutional requirements. We answer affirmatively, and hold, therefore, that the district court erred in dismissing the suit against defendant CEMA.

In reaching this conclusion[,] we work within the familiar framework provided by a series of [U.S.] Supreme Court decisions that rendered much of the learning on *in personam* jurisdiction obsolete.... Thus the decisions "set up a dual test for determining whether a court may take jurisdiction without depriving a defendant of due process of law." First, "there must be some minimum contact with the state which results from an affirmative act of the defendant." Secondly, "it must be fair and reasonable to require the defendant to come into the state and defend the action."...

In applying the first of these two tests in the case at bar, we emphasize that the number of the defendant's contacts with the forum state is not, of itself controlling. "[V]ery little purposeful activity with a state is necessary to satisfy the minimum contacts requirements," although "we have...unequivocally required *some* activity by the defendant...." ...As important as the existence of some contacts with the forum is that those contacts support an inference that the nonresident defendant purposefully availed himself of the benefits of conducting business in the forum....

Appellee CEMA insists that its contacts with the State of Texas were insufficient to meet the constitutional requirement. It had no local advertising, listings, or bank accounts; it solicited no business there, and did none aside from that with appellant; it sent no representatives there; and in fact it performed no physical act of any sort there. The contract was initiated by appellant when Ross visited France, and all of the negotiations occurred in France. Moreover, all of the studies and reports, which were prepared in French and translated into English, as well as the photographs and film were made along the Mediterranean coast, thousands of miles away. And all payments by appellant were to be made in Marseilles. In fact, CEMA concludes, its only contacts with Texas resulted from the performance of its contractual obligation to send the reports and film to Dallas, which admittedly required several deliveries.

We think appellee has understated both the number and the importance of its contacts with Texas. In the first place, we believe CEMA has incorrectly placed the essential locus of its contract with Product Promotions. Although the contract is silent regarding the law to be applied to it, it is generally recognized that "the place of the contract is the place where the last act necessary to the completion of the contract was done, that is where the contract first creates a legal obligation."...Under that principle, Ross's letter of February 7, 1972, accepting CEMA's offer, an acceptance which was effective on dispatch in Dallas, made Texas the place of the contract. Moreover, that most of CEMA's substantive work was done in the Mediterranean area does not alter the fact that an integral, essential portion of CEMA's performance, delivery of the results in satisfactory form, had to take place in Dallas. In any event, the [U.S.] Supreme Court in *McGee v. International Life Insurance Co.*, 355 U.S. 220, 78 S. Ct. 199, 2 L.Ed 2d 223 (1957), made it clear that neither the defendant nor the defendant's agents need have been physically within the State—contact by mail alone can be sufficient. And even if the defendant performs no physical act within the State, activities outside the state can provide adequate contacts if they have reasonably foreseeable consequences within the State.

Aside from their number, appellee's contacts are also adequate to support the inference of an affirmative, purposeful decision by CEMA to avail itself of the privilege of conducting some business in Texas. As a careful study of the [U.S.] Supreme Court decisions suggests, this requirement should not be read too literally; thus, for example, the nonresident defendant need not have agreed that suits on the contract will be heard in the forum state. Instead, the requirement reflects the Court's Conclusion that "[t]he unilateral activity of those who claim some relationship with a nonresident defendant cannot satisfy the requirement of contact with the forum State." *Hanson v. Denckla*, 357 U.S. 235, 253, 78 S. Ct. 1228, 1239, 2 L.Ed. 2d 1283, 1298. The operative consideration is that the defendant's contacts with the forum were deliberate, rather than fortuitous, so that the possible need to invoke the benefits and protections of the forum's laws was reasonably foreseeable, if not foreseen, rather than a surprise.

It is clear to us that this case rests on more than the unilateral activity of a Texas plaintiff claiming some relationship with a nonresident defendant. The cause of action for breach of contract arose out of a transaction between the parties that was consummated in Texas. Moreover, though CEMA may not have planned ever to come to Texas, we cannot say that CEMA's contacts with the State were purely fortuitous or accidental. CEMA entered a contract that required some performance in Texas; that it did not contemplate breaching its own contractual obligations does not make it unreasonable to foresee that those obligations might be tested in Texas. And since the contract was made in Texas, CEMA had reason to foresee that enforcement and protection of its own rights under the contract might depend on the laws of Texas. In short, CEMA voluntarily entered a transaction with one it knew to be a Texas resident, a transaction which had a substantial connection with Texas and which CEMA had reason to know could have consequences in Texas.

A second test must also be satisfied if a court's exercise of personal jurisdiction over a nonresident defendant is to be consistent with due process. Simply stated, it must not be unfair or unreasonable to require the nonresident to defend the suit in the forum. Although no particular factor controls our answer, this test requires us to consider such things as the interest of the state in providing a forum for the suit, the relative conveniences and inconveniences to the parties, and the basic equities. We conclude that the case *sub judice* meets the requirement of this second test.

We base this conclusion on several considerations. In the first place, Texas certainly has a legitimate and reasonable interest in providing a forum for this suit. The plaintiff is a Texas resident, the contract was made in Texas, and Texas law will surely be of some relevance in resolving the suit. In other words, we see a rational nexus between this lawsuit and a Texas forum. Measuring the convenience to one party against the inconvenience to the other results in something of a standoff, *Atwood Hatcheries, supra*, 357 F.2d at 854 n. 23. Obviously it is more convenient for appellant to litigate in Texas and more convenient for CEMA to do so elsewhere. Nevertheless, the important thing is that we are unable to conclude that any hardship or inconvenience to CEMA from having to defend the suit in Texas rises to the level of a denial of due process. Finally, CEMA has pointed to no particular inequity that might result if a court in Texas exercises jurisdiction over CEMA's person in this suit, and we can find none. The maintenance of this suit against CEMA in Texas will not "offend 'traditional notions of fair play and substantial justice.'" *International Shoe Co. v. Washington*, 326 U.S. 310, 316, 66 S. Ct. 154, 158, 90 L.Ed. 95 (1945).

[. . .]

Notes and Questions

How would you formulate the test for contacts jurisdiction? What law controls? Which law acts as the foundation? Does the opinion reverse prior decisions on the establishing of agency and subordination? Does the opinion represent a judicial rule of reason? What constitutes constitutional fairness in terms of contacts jurisdiction? Does almost any contact suffice? Doesn't that ultimately disfavor U.S. companies in the marketplace? Where is the center of the Product Promotions transaction with CEMA? Can it be really be Dallas? What does purposeful availment mean? When are contacts fortuitous? Deliberate? Is subjecting a French company to litigation in Texas on these facts really fair in any sense?

§ 5. THE NEW DOMESTIC STANDARD: *WOODSON* REJECTS *SHOE*

The U.S. Supreme Court eventually modified the *International Shoe* standard and adjusted it to the new realities of an overburdened legal system and a political administration that was more sympathetic to corporate interests. International litigation demanded substantial expertise and consumed an inordinate amount of judicial time. It created additional pressure on a system that was cracking under the weight of individualized due process. The advocacy that had created a customized system of justice was threatening to undo legal civilization itself. From a purely domestic vantage point, the nationwide accountability of companies expanded liability exposure and made damage assessments unpredictable, but likely to favor plaintiffs. Also, companies were subject to the sometimes variegated rules and practices of state legal systems. The prospect of hidden pitfalls increased the time and money being dedicated to legal representation and made companies more susceptible to settlements that favored the plaintiff. The following case demonstrates the Court's new approach to jurisdiction and its implied reversal of position.

WORLD-WIDE VOLKSWAGEN v. WOODSON

444 U.S. 286, 62 L.Ed.2d 490,
100 S.Ct. 559 (1980).

[. . .]

I.

Respondents Harry and Kay Robinson purchased a new Audi automobile from petitioner Seaway Volkswagen, Inc. (Seaway), in Massena, N.Y., in 1976. The following year the Robinson family, who resided in New York, left that State for a new home in Arizona. As they passed through the State of Oklahoma, another car struck their Audi in the rear, causing a fire which severely burned Kay Robinson and her two children.

The Robinsons subsequently brought a products-liability action in the District Court for Creek County, Okla. claiming that their injuries resulted from [the] defective design and placement of the Audi's gas tank and fuel system. They joined as defendants the automobile's manufacturer, Audi NSU Auto Union Aktiengesellschaft (Audi); its importer, Volkswagen of America, Inc. (Volkswagen); its regional distributor, petitioner World–Wide Volkswagen Corp. (World–Wide); and its retail dealer, petitioner Seaway. Seaway and World–Wide entered special appearances claiming that Oklahoma's exercise of jurisdiction over them would offend the limitations on the State's jurisdiction imposed by the Due Process Clause of the Fourteenth Amendment.

The facts presented to the District Court showed that World–Wide is incorporated and has its business office in New York. It distributes vehicles, parts[,] and accessories, under contract with Volkswagen, to retail dealers in New York, New Jersey, and Connecticut. Seaway, one of these retail dealers, is incorporated and has its place of business in New York. Insofar as the record reveals, Seaway and World–Wide are fully independent corporations whose relations with each other and with Volkswagen and Audi are contractual only. Respondents adduced no evidence that either World–Wide or Seaway does any business in Oklahoma, ships or sells any products to or in that State, has an agent to receive process there, or purchases advertisement in any media calculated to reach Oklahoma. In fact, as respondents' counsel conceded at oral argument. . .there was no showing that any automobile sold by World–Wide or Seaway has ever entered Oklahoma with the single exception of the vehicle involved in the present case.

Despite the apparent paucity of contacts between petitioners and Oklahoma, the District Court rejected their constitutional claim and reaffirmed that ruling in denying petitioner's motion for reconsideration. Petitioners then sought a writ of prohibition in the Supreme Court of Oklahoma to restrain the District Judge, respondent Charles S. Woodson from exercising *in personam* jurisdiction over them. They renewed their contention that, because they had no "minimal contacts". . .with the

State of Oklahoma the actions of the District Judge were in violation of their rights under the Due Process Clause.

The Supreme Court of Oklahoma denied the writ, 585 P.2d 351 (1978), holding that personal jurisdiction over petitioners was authorized by Oklahoma's "long-arm" statute, Okla. Stat. Tit. 12, § 1701.03(a)(4) (1971). Although the court noted that the proper approach was to test jurisdiction against both statutory and constitutional standards, its analysis did not distinguish these questions, probably because § 1701.03(a)(4) has been interpreted as conferring jurisdiction to the limits permitted by the United States Constitution. The court's rationale was contained in the following paragraph, 585 P.2d, at 354:

> "In the case before us, the product being sold and distributed by the petitioners is by its very design and purpose so mobile that petitioners can foresee its possible use in Oklahoma. This is especially true of the distributor, who has the exclusive right to distribute such automobiles in New York, New Jersey[,] and Connecticut. The evidence presented below demonstrated that goods sold and distributed by the petitioners were used in the State of Oklahoma, and under the facts we believe it reasonable to infer, given the retail value of the automobile, that the petitioners derive substantial income from automobiles which from time to time are used in the State of Oklahoma. This being the case, we hold that under the facts presented, the trial court was justified in concluding that the petitioners derive substantial revenue from goods used or consumed in this State."

We granted *certiorari*, 440 U.S. 907 (1979), to consider an important constitutional question with respect to state court jurisdiction and to resolve a conflict between the Supreme Court of Oklahoma and the highest courts of at least four other states. We reverse.

II.

As has long been settled, and as we reaffirm today, a state court may exercise personal jurisdiction over a nonresident defendant only so long as there exist "minimum contacts" between the defendant and the forum State. *International Shoe Co. v. Washington*.... The concept of minimum contacts, in turn, can be seen to perform two related but distinguishable functions. It protects the defendant against the burdens of litigating in a distant or inconvenient forum. And it acts to ensure that the States, through their courts, do not reach out beyond the limits imposed on them by their status as coequal sovereigns in a federal system.

The protection against inconvenient litigation is typically described in terms of "reasonableness" or "fairness." We have said that the defendant's contacts with the forum State must be such that maintenance of the suit "does not offend 'traditional notions of fair play and substantial justice.' "... The relationship between the defendant and the forum must be such that it is "reasonable...to require the corporation to defend the particular suit which is brought there."... Implicit in this emphasis on reasonableness is the understanding that the burden on the defendant, while always a primary concern, will in an appropriate case be considered in light of other relevant factors, including the forum State's interest in adjudicating the dispute...; the plaintiff's interest in obtaining convenient and effective relief...at least when that interest is not adequately protected by the plaintiff's power to choose the forum...; the interstate judicial system's interest in obtaining the most efficient resolution of controversies; and the shared interest of the several States in furthering fundamental substantive social policies....

The limits imposed on state jurisdiction by the Due Process Clause, in its role as a guarantor against inconvenient litigation, have been substantially relaxed over the years. As we noted in *McGee v. International Life Ins., Co.*...this trend is largely attributable to a fundamental transformation in the American economy:

> "Today many commercial transactions touch two or more States and may involve parties separated by the full continent. With this increasing nationalization of commerce has come a great increase in the amount of business conducted by mail across state lines. At the same time[,] modern transportation and communication have made it much less burdensome for a party sued to defend himself in a State where he engages in economic activity."

The historical developments noted in *McGee*, of course, have only accelerated in the generation since that case was decided.

Nevertheless, we have never accepted the proposition that state lines are irrelevant for jurisdictional purposes, nor could we, and remain faithful to the principles of interstate federalism embodied in the Constitution. The economic interdependence of the States was foreseen and desired by the Framers. In the Commerce Clause, they provided that the Nation was to be a common market, a "free trade unit" in which the States are debarred from acting as separable economic entities.... But the Framers also intended that the States retain many essential attributes of sovereignty, including, in particular, the sovereign power to try causes in their courts. The sovereignty of each State, in turn, implied a limitation on the sovereignty of all of its sister States—a limitation express or implicit in both the original scheme of the Constitution and the Fourteenth Amendment.

Hence, even while abandoning the shibboleth that "[t]he authority of every tribunal is necessarily restricted by the territorial limits of the State in which it is established,"...we emphasized that the reasonableness of asserting jurisdiction over the defendant must be assessed "in the context of our federal system of government,"...and stressed that the Due Process Clause ensures not only fairness, but also the "orderly administration of the laws".... As we noted in *Hanson v. Denckla*, 357 U.S. 235, 250–51 (1958):

> "As technological progress has increased the flow of commerce between the States, the need for jurisdiction over nonresidents has

undergone a similar increase. At the same time, progress in communications and transportation has made the defense of a suit in a foreign tribunal less burdensome. In response to these changes, the requirements for personal jurisdiction over nonresidents have evolved from the rigid rule of *Pennoyer v. Neff*, 95 U.S. 714, to the flexible standard of *International Shoe Co. v. Washington*, 326 U.S. 310. But it is a mistake to assume that this trend heralds the eventual demise of all restrictions on the personal jurisdiction of state courts. [Citation omitted.] Those restrictions are more than a guarantee of immunity from inconvenient or distant litigation. They are a consequence of territorial limitations on the power of the respective States."

Thus, the Due Process Clause "does not contemplate that a state may make binding a judgment *in personam* against an individual or corporate defendant with which the state has no contacts, ties, or relations." *International Shoe Co. v. Washington*.... Even if the defendant would suffer minimal or no inconvenience from being forced to litigate before the tribunals of another State; even if the forum State has a strong interest in applying its law to the controversy; even if the forum State is the most convenient location for litigation, the Due Process Clause, acting as an instrument of interstate federalism, may sometimes act to divest the State of its power to render a valid judgment....

III.

Applying these principles to the case at hand, we find in the record before us a total absence of those affiliating circumstances that are a necessary predicate to any exercise of state-court jurisdiction. Petitioners carry on no activity whatsoever in Oklahoma. They close no sales and perform no services there. They avail themselves of none of the privileges and benefits of Oklahoma law. They solicit no business there either through salespersons or through advertising reasonably calculated to reach the State. Nor does the record show that they regularly sell cars at wholesale or retail to Oklahoma customers or residents or that they indirectly, through others, serve or seek to serve the Oklahoma market. In short, respondents seek to base jurisdiction on one, isolated occurrence and whatever inferences can be drawn therefrom: the fortuitous circumstance that a single Audi automobile, sold in New York to New York residents, happened to suffer an accident while passing through Oklahoma.

It is argued, however, that because an automobile is mobile by its very design and purpose it was "foreseeable" that the Robinsons' Audi would cause injury in Oklahoma. Yet "foreseeability" alone has never been a sufficient benchmark for personal jurisdiction under the Due Process Clause. In *Hanson v. Denckla, supra*, it was no doubt foreseeable that the settler of a Delaware trust would subsequently move to Florida and seek to exercise a power of appointment there; yet we held that Florida courts could not constitutionally exercise jurisdiction over a Delaware trustee that had no other contact with the forum State. In

Kulko v. California Superior Court, 436 U.S. 84 (1978), it was surely "foreseeable" that a divorced wife would move to California from New York, the domicile of the marriage, and that a minor daughter would live with the mother. Yet we held that California could not exercise jurisdiction in a child-support action over the former husband who had remained in New York.

This is not to say, of course, that foreseeability is wholly irrelevant. But the foreseeability that is critical to due process analysis is not the mere likelihood that a product will find its way into the forum State. Rather, it is that the defendant's conduct and connection with the forum State are such that he should reasonably anticipate being hailed into court there.... The Due Process Clause, by ensuring the "orderly administration of the laws"...gives a degree of predictability to the legal system that allows potential defendants to structure their primary conduct with some minimum assurance as to where that conduct will and will not render them liable to suit.

When a corporation "purposefully avails itself of the privilege of conducting activities within the forum State,"...it has clear notice that it is subject to suit there, and can act to alleviate the risk of burdensome litigation by procuring insurance, passing the expected costs on the customers or, if the risks are too great, severing its connection with the State. Hence if the sale of a product of a manufacturer or distributor such as Audi or Volkswagen is not simply an isolated occurrence, but arises from the efforts of the manufacturer or distributor to serve, directly or indirectly, the market for its product in other States, it is not unreasonable to subject it to suit in one of those States if its allegedly defective merchandise has there been the source of injury to its owner or to others. The forum State does not exceed its powers under the Due Process Clause if it asserts personal jurisdiction over a corporation that delivers its products into the stream of commerce with the expectation that they will be purchased by consumers in the forum State....

But there is no such or similar basis for Oklahoma jurisdiction over World–Wide or Seaway in this case. Seaway's sales are made in Massena, NY. World–Wide's market, although substantially larger, is limited to dealers in New York, New Jersey[,] and Connecticut. There is no evidence of record that any automobiles distributed by World–Wide are sold to retail customers outside this tristate area. It is foreseeable that the purchasers of automobiles sold by World–Wide and Seaway may take them to Oklahoma. But the mere "unilateral activity of those who claim some relationship with a nonresident defendant cannot satisfy the requirement of contact with the forum State"....

In a variant on the previous argument, it is contended that jurisdiction can be supported by the fact that petitioners earn substantial revenue from goods used in Oklahoma. The Oklahoma Supreme Court so found, 585 P.2d, at 354–355, drawing the inference that because one automobile sold by petitioners had been used in Oklahoma, others might have been used there also. While this inference seems less than compelling on the facts of the instant case, we need not question the court's factual findings in order to reject its reasoning.

This argument seems to make the point that the purchase of automobiles in New York, from which the petitioners earn substantial revenue, would not occur but for the fact that the automobiles are capable of use in distant States like Oklahoma. Respondents observe that the very purpose of an automobile is to travel, and that travel of automobiles sold by petitioners is facilitated by an extensive chain of Volkswagen service centers throughout the country, including some in Oklahoma. However, financial benefits accruing to the defendant from a collateral relation to the forum State will not support jurisdiction if they do not stem from a constitutionally cognizable contact with that State. . . . In our view, whatever marginal revenues petitioners may receive by virtue of the fact that their products are capable of use in Oklahoma is far too attenuated a contact to justify that State's exercise of *in personam* jurisdiction over them.

Because we find that petitioners have no "contacts, ties, or relations" with the State of Oklahoma, *International Shoe Co. v. Washington*, *supra*, at 319, the judgment of the Supreme Court of Oklahoma is *Reversed*.

MR. JUSTICE BRENNAN, Dissenting.

The Court holds that the Due Process Clause of the Fourteenth Amendment bars the States from asserting jurisdiction over the defendants in these two cases. In each case[,] the Court so decides because it fails to find the "minimum contacts" that have been required since *International Shoe Co. v. Washington*, 326 U.S. 310, 316 (1945). Because I believe that the Court reads *International Shoe* and its progeny too narrowly, and because I believe that the standards enunciated by those cases may already be obsolete as constitutional boundaries, I dissent.

I.

The Court's opinions focus tightly on the existence of contacts between the forum and the defendant. In so doing, they accord too little weight to the strength of the forum State's interest in the case and fail to explore whether there would be any actual inconvenience to the defendant. The essential inquiry in locating the constitutional limits on state-court jurisdiction over absent defendants is whether the particular exercise of jurisdiction offends "traditional notions of fair play and substantial justice." *International Shoe*, *supra* at 316 quoting *Milliken v. Meyer*, 311 U.S. 457, 463 (1940). The clear focus in *International Shoe* was on fairness and reasonableness. *Kulko v. California Superior Court*, 436 U.S. 84, 92 (1978). The Court specifically declined to establish a mechanical test based on the quantum of contacts between a State and the defendant:

> Whether due process is satisfied must depend rather upon the quality and nature of the activity *in relation to the fair and orderly administration of the laws which it was the purpose of the due*

> *process clause to insure*. That clause does not contemplate that a state may make binding a judgment *in personam* against an individual or corporate defendant with which the state has *no* contacts, ties or relations. 326 U.S., at 319 (emphasis added).

The existence of contacts, so long as there were some, was merely one way to giving content to the determination of fairness and reasonableness.

Surely *International Shoe* contemplated that the significance of the contacts necessary to support jurisdiction would diminish if some other consideration helped establish that jurisdiction would be fair and reasonable. The interests of the State and other parties in proceeding with the case in a particular forum are such considerations. *McGee v. International Life Ins. Co.*, 355 U.S. 220, 223 (1957), for instance, accorded great importance to a State's "manifest interest in providing effective means of redress" for its citizens. *See also Kulko v. California Superior Court*, *supra*, at 92; *Shaffer v. Heitner*, 433 U.S. 186, 208 (1977); *Mullane v. Central Hanover Trust Co.*, 339 U.S. 306, 313 (1950).

Another consideration is the actual burden a defendant must bear in defending the suit in the forum. *McGee*, *supra*. Because lesser burdens reduce the unfairness to the defendant, jurisdiction may be justified despite less significant contacts. The burden, of course, must be of constitutional dimension. Due process limits on jurisdiction do not protect a defendant from all inconvenience of travel, *McGee*, *supra*, at 224, and it would not be sensible to make the constitutional rule turn solely on the number of miles the defendant must travel to the courtroom. Instead, the constitutionally significant "burden" to be analyzed relates to the mobility of the defendant's defense. For instance, if having to travel to a foreign forum would hamper the defense because witnesses or evidence or the defendant himself were immobile, or if there were a disproportionately large number of witnesses or amount of evidence that would have to be transported at the defendant's expense, or if being away from home for the duration of the trial would work some special hardship on the defendant, the Constitution would require special consideration for the defendant's interests.

That considerations other than contact between the forum and the defendant are relevant necessarily means that the Constitution does not require that trial be held in the State which has the "best contacts" with the defendant. *See Shaffer v. Heitner*, *supra*, at 228 (Brennan, J. dissenting). The defendant has no constitutional entitlement to the best forum or, for that matter, to any particular forum. Under even the most restrictive view of *International Shoe*, several States could have jurisdiction over a particular cause of action. We need only determine whether the forum States in these cases satisfy the constitutional minimum.

II.

In each of these cases, I would find that the forum State has an interest in permitting the litigation to go forward, the litigation is connected to the forum, the defendant is linked to the forum, and the burden of defending is not unreasonable. Accordingly, I would hold that it is neither unfair nor unreasonable to require these defendants to defend in the forum State.

B.

In No. 78–1078, the interest of the forum State and its connection to the litigation is [sic] [are] strong. The automobile accident underlying the litigation occurred in Oklahoma. The plaintiffs were hospitalized in Oklahoma when they brought suit. Essential witnesses and evidence were in Oklahoma. *See Shaffer v. Heitner*, 433 U.S. at 208. The state has a legitimate interest in enforcing its laws designed to keep its highway system safe, and the trial can proceed at least as efficiently in Oklahoma as anywhere else.

The petitioners are not unconnected with the forum. Although both sell automobiles within limited sales territories, each sold the automobile which in fact was driven to Oklahoma where it was involved in an accident. It may be true, as the Court suggests, that each sincerely intended to limit its commercial impact to the limited territory, and that each intended to accept the benefits and protection of the laws only of those States within the territory. But obviously these were unrealistic hopes that cannot be treated as an automatic constitutional shield.

An automobile simply is not a stationary item or one designed to be used in one place. An automobile is *intended* to be moved around. Someone in the business of selling large numbers of automobiles can hardly plead ignorance of their mobility or pretend that the automobiles stay put after they are sold. It is not merely that a dealer in automobiles foresees that they will move.... The dealer actually intends that the purchasers will use the automobiles to travel to distant States where the dealer does not directly "do business." The sale of an automobile does purposefully inject the vehicle into the stream of interstate commerce so that it can travel to distant States. *See Kulko*, 436 U.S. at 94; *Hanson v. Denckla*, 357 U.S. 235, 253 (1958).

[...]

Thus, the Court errs in its conclusion...that "petitioners have *no* 'contacts, ties, or relations' " (emphasis added) with Oklahoma. There obviously are contacts, and, given Oklahoma's connection to the litigation, the contacts are sufficiently significant to make it fair and reasonable for the petitioners to submit to Oklahoma's jurisdiction.

III.

It may be that affirmance of the judgments in these cases would approach the outer limits of *International Shoe*'s jurisdictional principle. But that principle, with its almost exclusive focus on the rights of defendants, may be outdated. As MR. JUSTICE MARSHALL wrote in *Shaffer v. Heitner*, 433 U.S. at 212: " '[T]raditional notions of fair play and substantial justice' can be as readily offended by the perpetuation of ancient forms that are no longer justified as by the adoption of new procedures...."

International Shoe inherited its defendant focus from *Pennoyer v. Neff*, 95 U.S. 714 (1878), and represented the last major step this Court has taken in the long process of liberalizing the doctrine of personal jurisdiction. Though its flexible approach represented a major advance, the structure of our society has changed in many significant ways since *International Shoe* was decided in 1945. Mr. Justice Black, writing for the Court in *McGee v. International Life Ins. Co.*, 355 U.S. 220, 222 (1957), recognized that "a trend is clearly discernible toward expanding the permissible scope of state jurisdiction over foreign corporations and other nonresidents." He explained this trend as follows:

> In part, this is attributable to the fundamental transformation of our national economy over the years. Today many commercial transactions touch two or more States and may involve parties separated by the full continent. With this increasing nationalization of commerce has come a great increase in the amount of business conducted by mail across state lines. At the same time[,] modern transportation and communication have made it much less burdensome for a party sued to defend himself in a State where he engages in economic activity. *Id.* at 222–223.

As the Court acknowledges...both the nationalization of Commerce and the ease of transportation and communication have accelerated in the generation since 1957. The model of society on which the *International Shoe* Court based its opinion is no longer accurate. Business people, no matter how local their businesses, cannot assume that goods remain in the business' locality. Customers and goods can be anywhere else in the country usually in a matter of hours and always in a matter of a very few days.

The conclusion I draw is that constitutional concepts of fairness no longer require the extreme concern for defendants that was once necessary. Rather, as I wrote in dissent from *Shaffer v. Heitner*, *supra*, at 220 (emphasis added), minimum contacts must exist "among the *parties*, the contested transaction, and the forum State." The contacts between any two of these should not be determinative. "[W]hen a suitor seeks to lodge a suit in a State with a substantial interest in seeing its own law applied to the transaction in question, we could wisely act to minimize conflicts, confusion, and uncertainty by adopting a liberal view of jurisdiction, unless considerations of fairness or efficiency strongly point in the opposite direction." 433 U.S. at 225–226. Mr. Justice Black, dissenting in *Hanson v. Denckla*, 357 U.S. at 258–259, expresses similar concerns by suggesting that a State should have jurisdiction over a case growing out of a transaction significantly related to that State "unless litigation there would impose such a heavy and disproportionate burden on a nonresident defendant that it would offend what this Court has referred to as 'traditional notions of fair play and substantial justice.' "Assuming that a State gives a nonresident defendant adequate notice and opportunity to defend, I do not think the Due Process Clause is offended merely because the defendant has to board a plane to get to the site of the trial.

The Court's opinion in No. 78–1078 suggests that the defendant ought to be subject to a State's jurisdiction only if he has contacts with the State "such that he should reasonably anticipate being hailed into court there."...There is nothing unreasonable or unfair, however, about recognizing commercial reality. Given the tremendous mobility of goods and people, and the inability of businessmen to control where goods are taken by customers (or retailers), I do not think that the defendant should be in complete control of the geographical stretch of his amenability to suit. Jurisdiction is no longer premised on the notion that nonresident defendants have somehow impliedly consented to suit. People should understand that they are held responsible for the consequences of their actions and that in our society most actions have consequences affecting many States. When an action in fact causes injury in another State, the actor should be prepared to answer for it there unless defending in that State would be unfair for some reason other than that a state boundary must be crossed.

[...]

I would also...strip the defendant of an unjustified veto power over certain very appropriate fora—a power the defendant justifiably enjoyed long ago when communication and travel over long distances were slow and unpredictable and when notions of state sovereignty were impractical and exaggerated. But I repeat that that is not today's world. If a plaintiff can show that his chosen forum State has a sufficient interest in the litigation (or sufficient contacts with the defendant), then the defendant who cannot show some real injury to a constitutionally protected interest...should have no constitutional excuse not to appear.

The plaintiffs in each of these cases brought suit in a forum with which they had significant contacts and which had significant contacts with the litigation. I am not convinced that the defendants would suffer any "heavy and disproportionate burden" in defending the suits. Accordingly, I would hold that the Constitution should not shield the defendants from appearing and defending in the plaintiff's chosen fora.

MR. JUSTICE MARSHALL, with whom MR. JUSTICE BLACKMUN joins, dissenting.

For over 30 years the standard by which to measure the constitutionally permissible reach of state-court jurisdiction has been well established....The concepts of fairness and substantial justice as applied to an evaluation of "the quality and nature of the [defendant's] activity"...are not readily susceptible of further definition, however, and it is not surprising that the constitutional standard is easier to state than to apply.

This is a difficult case and reasonable minds may differ as to whether respondents have alleged a sufficient "relationship among the defendant[s], the forum and the litigation" ... to satisfy the requirements of *International Shoe*. I am concerned, however, that the majority has reached its result by taking an unnecessarily narrow view of petitioners' forum-related conduct.... [T]he basis for the assertion of jurisdiction is not the happenstance that an individual over whom petitioners had no control made a unilateral decision to take a chattel with him to a distant state. Rather, jurisdiction is premised on the deliberate and purposeful actions of the defendants themselves in choosing to become part of a nationwide, indeed a global, network for marketing and servicing automobiles.

Petitioners are sellers of a product whose utility derives from its mobility. The unique importance of the automobile in today's society, which is discussed in MR. JUSTICE BLACKMUN'S dissenting opinion, *post*,...needs no further elaboration. Petitioners know that their customers buy cars not only to make short trips, but also to travel long distances. In fact, the nationwide service network with which they are affiliated was designed to facilitate and encourage such travel....It is apparent that petitioners have not attempted to minimize the chance that their activities will have effects in other States; on the contrary, they have chosen to do business in a way that increases that change, because it is to their economic advantage to do so.

To be sure, petitioners could not know in advance that this particular automobile would be driven to Oklahoma. They must have anticipated, however, that a substantial portion of the cars they sold would travel out of New York....

It is misleading for the majority to characterize the argument in favor of jurisdiction as one of "foreseeability alone."... As economic entities[,] petitioners reach out from New York knowingly causing effects in other States and receiving economic advantage both from the ability to cause such effects themselves and from the activities of dealers and distributors in other States. While they did not receive revenue from making direct sales in Oklahoma, they intentionally became part of an interstate economic network, which included dealerships in Oklahoma, for pecuniary gain. In light of this purposeful conduct[,] I do not believe it can be said that petitioners "had no reason to expect to be haled before a[n Oklahoma] court."...

The majority apparently acknowledges that if a product is purchased in the forum State by a consumer, that State may assert jurisdiction over everyone in the chain of distribution....With this I agree. But I cannot agree that jurisdiction is necessarily lacking if the product enters the State not through the channels of distribution but in the course of its intended use by the consumer. We have recognized the role played by the automobile in the expansion of our notions of personal jurisdiction....Unlike most other chattels, which may find their way into States far from where they were purchased because their owner takes them there, the intended use of the automobile is precisely as a means of traveling from one place to another. In such a case, it is highly artificial to restrict the concept of the "stream of commerce" to the chain of distribution from the manufacturer to the ultimate consumer.

I sympathize with the majority's concern that persons ought to be able to structure their conduct so as not to be subject to suit in distant forums. But that may not always be possible. Some activities by their very nature may foreclose the option of conducting them in such a way as to avoid subjecting oneself to jurisdiction in multiple forums. This is by no means to say that all sellers of automobiles should be subject to suit everywhere, but a distributor of automobiles to a multistate market and a local automobile dealer who makes himself part of a nationwide network of dealerships can fairly expect that the cars they sell may cause injury in distant States and that they may be called on to defend a resulting lawsuit there.

[. . .]

Of course, the Constitution forbids the exercise of jurisdiction if the defendant had no judicially cognizable contacts with the forum. But as the majority acknowledges, if such contacts are present[,] the jurisdictional inquiry requires a balancing of various interests and policies. . . . I believe such contacts are to be found here and that, considering all of the interests and policies at stake, requiring petitioners to defend this action in Oklahoma is not beyond the bounds of the Constitution. Accordingly, I dissent.

Mr. Justice Blackmun, dissenting.

I confess that I am somewhat puzzled why the plaintiffs in this litigation are so insistent that the regional distributor and the retail dealer, the petitioners here, who handled the ill-fated Audi automobile involved in this litigation, be named defendants. It would appear that the manufacturer and the importer, whose subjectability to Oklahoma jurisdiction is not challenged before this Court, ought not to be judgment-proof. It may, of course, ultimately amount to a contest between insurance companies that, once begun, is not easily brought to a termination. Having made this much of an observation, I pursue it no further.

For me, a critical factor in the disposition of the litigation is the nature of the instrumentality under consideration. It has been said that we are a nation on wheels. What we are concerned with here is the automobile and its peripatetic character. One need only examine our national network of interstate highways, or make an appearance on one of them, or observe the variety of license plates present not only on those highways but in any metropolitan area, to realize that any automobile is likely to wander far from its place of licensure or from its place of distribution and retail sale. Miles per gallon on the highway (as well as in the city) and mileage per tankful are familiar allegations in manufacturers' advertisements today. To expect that any new automobile will remain in the vicinity of its retail sale—like the 1914 electric car driven by the proverbial 'little old lady'—is to blink at reality. The automobile is intended for distance as well as for transportation within a limited area.

It therefore seems to me not unreasonable—and certainly not unconstitutional and beyond the reach of the principles laid down in *International Shoe Co. v. Washington*, 326 U.S. 310 (1945), and its progeny to uphold Oklahoma jurisdiction over this New York distributor and the New York dealer when the accident happened in Oklahoma. Moreover, in assessing "minimum contacts," foreseeable use in another State seems to be little different from foreseeable resale in another State. Yet the Court declares this distinction determinative. . . .

Mr. Justice Brennan points out in his dissent. . .that an automobile dealer derives substantial benefits from States other than its own. The same is true of the regional distributor. Oklahoma does its best to provide safe roads. Its police investigate accidents. It regulates driving within the State. It provides aid to the victim and, thereby it is hoped, lessens damages. All this contributes to and enhances the business of those engaged professionally in the distribution and sale of automobiles. All this also may benefit defendants in the very lawsuits over which the State asserts jurisdiction.

My position need not now take me beyond the automobile and the professional who does business by way of distributing and retailing automobiles. Cases concerning other instrumentalities will be dealt with as they arise and in their own contexts.

I would affirm the judgment of the Supreme Court of Oklahoma. Because the Court reverses that judgment, it will now be about parsing every variant in the myriad of motor vehicle fact situations that present themselves. Some will justify jurisdiction and others will not. All will depend on the "contact" that the Court sees fit to perceive in the individual case.

Notes and Questions

1. At the outset of the second part of the opinion (II), is the Court correct in describing the minimum contacts concept as a device for protecting the defendant from burdensome or unexpected assertions of jurisdiction? The liberalization of the contacts theory in *International Shoe* made the opposite rationale true—that the contacts theory was a means of fostering the plaintiff's right to sue in a favorable forum. Does the Court's historical reference and statement announce a new position? Moreover, does the additional description of the contacts concept as an instrument by which federalism is preserved reinforce the view that *Woodson* will be a landmark opinion? It seems that the Court is saying that new federal constitutional standards for the assertion of jurisdiction are looming and are likely to be intolerant of the jurisdictional exuberance exhibited by state courts in *TACA International* and *Frummer*.

2. How does the Court reconcile its acknowledgement of the national character of commercial transactions and the development of technology

with its view of the due process restrictions on the exercise of state judicial authority? What does the concept of "interstate federalism" mean in the context of the elaboration of the new jurisdictional doctrine?

3. How does the Court's application of the elements of "interstate federalism"—in the form of "reasonableness," "foreseeability," and "purposeful availment"—affect the notion of the formalities of incorporation? What elements must be in place to have courts located in Oklahoma properly assert jurisdiction over the incident? Should the occurrence of the personal injury in Oklahoma be a sufficient element to the assertion of jurisdiction? Can't such a position be fully justified by practicality?

4. The new standard for the proper exercise of jurisdiction by state courts or federal courts that apply state long-arm statutes in the interstate context is "that the defendant's conduct and connection with the forum state are such that he should reasonably anticipate being haled into court there...." How does this standard differ from and modify minimum contacts and what does it mean? Is it also part of fair play?

5. How does Justice Brennan justify his rather mechanical and passive conclusion that "the forum State has an interest in permitting the litigation to go forward, the litigation is connected to the forum, the defendant is linked to the forum, and the burden of defending is not unreasonable.... [I]t is neither unfair nor unreasonable to require these defendants to defend in the forum State." What explains this extraordinarily negative foundation for his desired result? What rule does it propound and how effective is it likely to be?

6. Also, is Justice Brennan right to suggest that the majority misunderstands the impact of the mobile nature of the automobile on the question of jurisdiction? Does that factor dislodge the importance the majority places upon the formalities of incorporation and actual presence in the forum jurisdiction?

7. What benefits attach to Justice Brennan's " 'liberal view of jurisdiction' "? Why is a lack of intellectual discipline and rigor a sensible approach to jurisdiction? If constitutional constraints are meaningless or outmoded, why have them at all?

8. Does a less exuberant view of the assertion of jurisdiction amount to a denial of defendant accountability? Presumably, another court would have jurisdiction. Does the defendant or the Constitution veto the plaintiff's choice of forum?

9. How do you assess Justice Marshall's dissenting contention that "the majority has reached its result by taking an unnecessarily narrow view of petitioners' forum-related conduct"? What are the implications of the defendant's establishment of "a nationwide, indeed a global, network for marketing and servicing automobiles"? How persuasive is the distinction between the commercial "channels of distribution" and "intended use by the consumer" as terms of entry of the product into the forum state? Aren't Marshall's requirements for and characterizations of business conduct profoundly abstract and lacking in any firm reality associated with actual conduct? Under this speculative reasoning, doesn't the sale of a commodity

in Portland, Maine make the merchant liable in all of the courts of the solar system, including Area 51 in the Nevada desert?

10. How might one respond to Justice Blackmun's dissenting puzzlement regarding the lack of suit against the foreign manufacturer and the importer? Does interstate commerce justify suit in any state against any interstate merchant? Why does the nature of the commodity fix jurisdiction rather than conduct or incorporation?

§ 6. THE REFORMULATED STANDARD APPLIED IN INTERNATIONAL LITIGATION

The more conservative rule for the assertion of judicial jurisdiction also responded well to the character of transborder litigation brought before U.S. courts. It closed the gate to complex, difficult, and time-consuming litigation for which the courts lacked the necessary expertise. Unless a specialized federal court were created and given exclusive jurisdiction over such litigation, these cases should probably be resolved through nonjudicial means. Excluding transborder disputes from U.S. court dockets, however, could engender complaints of denial of justice. Ordinary foreign nationals might have been injured by U.S. corporate parties or products. By going abroad, U.S. enterprises, therefore, could escape the accountability generated by U.S. adversarial representation, strict liability statutes, discovery mechanisms, the civil jury, and punitive damages.

Does the U.S. Supreme Court opinion in *Asahi*, the next case, sustain such an evaluation? Is the ruling internationalist or parochial in character? What does it say about extraterritoriality? What factors make jurisdiction over international cases different from jurisdiction in domestic cases? Should foreign nationality be a barrier or an impediment to U.S. court jurisdiction? Does commercial participation—directly or indirectly—in the U.S. market create a sufficient basis for the exercise of U.S. court jurisdiction? Are foreign nationals entitled to constitutional due process protections? Do the burdens of transnational litigation argue for a conservative jurisdictional approach? Is an aggressive posture on the assertion of jurisdiction likely to create diplomatic and foreign policy problems and the prospect of retaliatory foreign conduct? It is also likely to disrupt trade and hamper U.S. company participation in international commerce. Moreover, the clash of national legal standards should argue for the limited application of domestic law to foreign nationals and circumstances. All of these factors appear to make the case for a restrained approach based upon the concept of substantial national and local contacts with the United States and the particular local jurisdiction in which suit is brought.

ASAHI METAL INDUSTRY CO. v. SUPERIOR COURT OF CALIFORNIA

480 U.S. 102, 107 S.Ct. 1026, 94 L.Ed.2d 92 (1987).

[. . .]

This case presents the question whether the mere awareness on the part of a foreign defendant that the components it manufactured, sold, and delivered outside the United States would reach the forum State in the stream of commerce constitutes "minimum contacts" between the defendant and the forum state such that the exercise of jurisdiction "does not offend 'traditional notions of fair play and substantial justice.' " . . .

I.

On September 23, 1978, on Interstate Highway 80 in Solano County, California, Gary Zurcher lost control of his Honda motorcycle and collided with a tractor. Zurcher was severely injured, and his passenger and wife, Ruth Ann Moreno, was killed. In September 1979, Zurcher filed a product liability action in the Superior Court of the State of California in and for the County of Solano. Zurcher alleged that the 1978 accident was caused by a sudden loss of air and an explosion in the rear tire of the motorcycle, and alleged that the motorcycle tire, tube, and sealant were defective. Zurcher's complaint named, *inter alia*, Cheng Shin Rubber Industrial Co., Ltd. (Cheng Shin), the Taiwanese manufacturer of the tube. Cheng Shin in turn filed a cross-complaint seeking indemnification from its co-defendants and from petitioner, Asahi Metal Industry Co., Ltd. (Asahi), the manufacturer of the tube's valve assembly. Zurcher's claims against Cheng Shin and the other defendants were eventually settled and dismissed, leaving only Cheng Shin's indemnity action against Asahi.

California's long-arm statute authorizes the exercise of jurisdiction "on any basis not inconsistent with the Constitution of this state or of the United States." Cal. Code Civ. Proc. Ann. sec. 410.10 (West 1973). Asahi moved to quash Cheng Shin's service of summons arguing the State could not exert jurisdiction over it consistent with the Due Process Clause of the Fourteenth Amendment.

In relation to the motion, the following information was submitted by Asahi and Cheng Shin. Asahi is a Japanese corporation. It manufactures tire valve assemblies in Japan and sells the assemblies to Cheng Shin, and to several other tire manufacturers, for use as components in finished tire tubes. Asahi's sales to Cheng Shin took place in Taiwan. The shipments from Asahi to Cheng Shin were sent from Japan to Taiwan. Cheng Shin bought and incorporated into its tire tubes 150,000 Asahi valve assemblies in 1978; 500,000 in 1979; 500,000 in 1980; 100,000 in 1981; and 100,000 in 1982. Sales to Cheng Shin accounted for 1.24 percent of Asahi's income in 1981 and 0.44 percent in 1982. Cheng Shin alleged that approximately 20 percent of its sales in the United

States are in California. Cheng Shin purchases valve assemblies from other suppliers as well, and sells finished tubes throughout the world.

[. . .]

[T]he Superior Court denied the motion to quash summons, stating that "Asahi obviously does business on an international scale. It is not unreasonable that they defend claims of defect in their product on an international scale." . . .

The Court of Appeal of the State of California issued a peremptory writ of mandate commanding the Superior Court to quash service of summons. The court concluded that "it would be unreasonable to require Asahi to respond in California solely on the basis of ultimately realized foreseeability that the product into which its component was embodied would be sold all over the world including California. . . ."

The Supreme Court of the State of California reversed and discharged the writ issued by the Court of Appeal. . . .The court observed that "Asahi has no offices, property or agents in California. It solicits no business in California and has made no direct sales [in California]." . . .Moreover, "Asahi did not design or control the system of distribution that carried its valve assemblies into California." . . .Nevertheless, the court found the exercise of jurisdiction over Asahi to be consistent with the Due Process Clause. It concluded that Asahi knew that some of the valve assemblies sold to Cheng Shin would be incorporated into tire tubes sold in California, and that Asahi benefited indirectly from the sale in California of products incorporating its components. The court considered Asahi's intentional act of placing its components into the stream of commerce—that is, by delivering the components to Cheng Shin in Taiwan—coupled with Asahi's awareness that some of the components would eventually find their way into California, sufficient to form the basis for state court jurisdiction under the Due Process Clause.

We granted *certiorari* . . . and now reverse.

II.

The Due Process Clause of the Fourteenth Amendment limits the power of a state court to exert personal jurisdiction over a nonresident defendant. "[T]he constitutional touchstone" of the determination whether an exercise of personal jurisdiction comports with due process "remains whether the defendant purposefully established 'minimum contacts' in the forum State." . . . Most recently we have reaffirmed . . . that minimum contacts must have a basis in "some act by which the defendant purposefully avails itself of the privilege of conducting activities within the forum State, thus invoking the benefits and protections of its laws." . . . "Jurisdiction is proper . . . where the contacts proximately result from actions by the defendant himself that create a 'substantial connection' with the forum State." . . .

[. . .]

In *World-Wide Volkswagen* . . . the state court sought to base jurisdiction not on any act of the defendant, but on the foreseeable unilateral actions of the consumer. Since *World-Wide Volkswagen*, lower courts have been confronted with cases in which the defendant acted by placing a product in the stream of commerce, and the stream eventually swept defendant's product into the forum State, but the defendant did nothing else to purposefully avail itself of the market in the forum State. Some courts have understood the Due Process Clause, as interpreted in *World-Wide Volkswagen*, to allow an exercise of personal jurisdiction to be based on no more than the defendant's act of placing the product in the stream of commerce. Other courts have understood the Due Process Clause and . . . *World-Wide Volkswagen* to require the action of the defendant to be more purposefully directed at the forum State than the mere act of placing a product in the stream of commerce.

The reasoning of the Supreme Court of California in the present case illustrates the former interpretation of *World-Wide Volkswagen*. The Supreme Court of California held that, because the stream of commerce eventually brought some valves Asahi sold Cheng Shin into California, Asahi's awareness that its valves would be sold to California was sufficient to permit California to exercise jurisdiction over Asahi consistent with the requirements of the Due Process Clause. The Supreme Court of California's position was consistent with those courts that have held that mere foreseeability or awareness was a constitutionally sufficient basis for personal jurisdiction if the defendant's product made its way into the stream of commerce. . . .

Other courts, however, have understood the Due Process Clause to require something more than that the defendant was aware of its product's entry into the forum State through the stream of commerce in order for the state to exert jurisdiction over the defendant. In the present case, for example, the State Court of Appeal did not read the Due Process Clause, as interpreted by *World-Wide Volkswagen*, to allow "mere foreseeability that the product will enter the forum state [to] be enough by itself to establish jurisdiction over the distributor and retailer." . . .

We now find this latter position to be consonant with the requirements of due process. The "substantial connection" . . . between the defendant and the forum State necessary for a finding of minimum contacts must come about by an action of the defendant purposefully directed toward the forum State. . . . The placement of a product into the stream of commerce, without more, is not an act of the defendant purposefully directed toward the forum State. Additional conduct of the defendant may indicate an intent or purpose to serve the market in the forum State, for example, designing the product for the market in the forum State, advertising in the forum State, establishing channels for providing regular advice to customers in the forum State, or marketing the product through a distributor who has agreed to serve as the sales agent in the forum State. But a defendant's awareness that the stream of commerce may or will sweep the product into the forum State does not convert the mere act of placing the product into the stream into an act purposefully directed toward the forum State.

Assuming, *arguendo*, that respondents have established Asahi's awareness that some of the valves sold to Cheng Shin would be incorporated into tire tubes sold in California, respondents have not demonstrated any action by Asahi to purposefully avail itself of the California market. Asahi does not do business in California. It has no office, agents, employees, or property in California. It does not advertise or otherwise solicit business in California. It did not create, control, or employ the distribution system that brought its valves to California.... There is no evidence that Asahi designed its product in anticipation of sales in California.... On the basis of these facts, the exertion of personal jurisdiction over Asahi by the Superior Court of California exceeds the limits of Due Process.

B.

The strictures of the Due Process Clause forbid a state court from exercising personal jurisdiction over Asahi under circumstances that would offend "traditional notions of fair play and substantial justice."...

We have previously explained that the determination of the reasonableness of the exercise of jurisdiction in each case will depend on an evaluation of several factors. A court must consider the burden on the defendant, the interests of the forum state, and the plaintiff's interest in obtaining relief. It must also weigh in its determination "the interstate judicial system's interest in obtaining the most efficient resolution of controversies; and the shared interest of the several States in furthering fundamental substantive social policies."...

A consideration of these factors in the present case clearly reveals the unreasonableness of the assertion of jurisdiction over Asahi, even apart from the question of the placement of goods in the stream of commerce.

Certainly the burden on the defendant in this case is severe. Asahi has been commanded by the Supreme Court of California not only to traverse the distance between Asahi's headquarters in Japan and the Superior Court of California in and for the Country of Solano, but also to submit its dispute with Cheng Shin to a foreign nation's judicial system. The unique burdens placed upon one who must defend oneself in a foreign legal system should have significant weight in assessing the reasonableness of stretching the long arm of personal jurisdiction over national borders.

When minimum contacts have been established, often the interests of the plaintiff and the forum in the exercise of jurisdiction will justify even the serious burdens placed on the alien defendant. In the present case, however, the interests of the plaintiff and the forum in California's assertion of jurisdiction over Asahi are slight. All that remains is a claim for indemnification asserted by Cheng Shin, a Taiwanese corporation, against Asahi. The transaction on which the indemnification claim is based took place in Taiwan; Asahi's components were shipped from Japan to Taiwan. Cheng Shin has not demonstrated that it is more convenient for it to litigate its indemnification claim against Asahi in California rather than in Taiwan or Japan.

Because the plaintiff is not a California resident, California's legitimate interests in the dispute have considerably diminished. The Supreme Court of California argued that the State had an interest in "protecting its consumers by ensuring that foreign manufacturers comply with the state's safety standards."... The State Supreme Court's definition of California's interest, however, was overly broad. The dispute between Cheng Shin and Asahi is primarily about indemnification rather than safety standards. Moreover, it is not at all clear at this point that California law should govern the question whether a Japanese corporation should indemnify a Taiwanese corporation on the basis of a sale made in Taiwan and a shipment of goods from Japan to Taiwan.... The possibility of being haled into a California court as a result of an accident involving Asahi's components undoubtedly creates an additional deterrent to the manufacture of unsafe components; however, similar pressures will be placed on Asahi by the purchasers of its components as long as those who use Asahi components in their final products, and sell those products in California, are subject to the application of California tort law.

World-Wide Volkswagen also admonished courts to take into consideration the interests of the "several States," in addition to the forum state, in the efficient judicial resolution of the dispute and the advancement of substantive policies. In the present case, this advice calls for a court to consider that the procedural and substantive policies of other *nations* whose interests are affected by the assertion of jurisdiction by the California court. The procedural and substantive interests of other nations in a state court's assertion of jurisdiction over an alien defendant will differ from case to case. In every case, however, those interests, as well as the Federal interest in its foreign relations policies, will be best served by a careful inquiry into the reasonableness of the assertion of jurisdiction in the particular case, and an unwillingness to find the serious burdens on an alien defendant outweighed by minimal interests on the part of the plaintiff or the forum State....

Considering the international context, the heavy burden on the alien defendant, and the slight interests of the plaintiff and the forum State, the exercise of personal jurisdiction by a California court over Asahi in this instance would be unreasonable and unfair.

III.

Because the facts of this case do not establish minimum contacts such that the exercise of personal jurisdiction is consistent with fair play and substantial justice, the judgment of Supreme Court of California is reversed, and the case is remanded for further proceedings not inconsistent with this opinion.

It is so ordered.

JUSTICE BRENNAN, with whom JUSTICE WHITE, JUSTICE MARSHALL, and JUSTICE BLACKMUN join, concurring in part and in the judgment.

I do not agree with the plurality's interpretation of the stream-of-commerce theory, nor with its conclusion that Asahi did not "purposely avail itself of the California market."...I do agree, however, with the Court's conclusion in Part II–B that the exercise of personal jurisdiction over Asahi in this case would not comport with "fair play and substantial justice...." This is one of those rare cases in which "minimum requirements inherent in the concept of 'fair play and substantial justice'...defeat the reasonableness of jurisdiction even [though] the defendant has purposefully engaged in forum activities."... I therefore join Parts I and II–B of the Court's opinion, and write separately to explain my disagreement with Part II–A.

The plurality states that "a defendant's awareness that the stream of commerce may or will sweep the product into the forum State does not convert the mere act of placing the product into the stream into an act purposefully directed toward the forum State."...The plurality would therefore require a plaintiff to show "[a]dditional conduct" directed toward the forum before finding the exercise of jurisdiction over the defendant to be consistent with the Due Process Clause.... I see no need for such a showing, however. The stream of commerce refers not to unpredictable currents or eddies, but to the regular and anticipated flow of products from manufacture to distribution to retail sale. As long as a participant in this process is aware that the final product is being marketed in the forum State, the possibility of a lawsuit there cannot come as a surprise. Nor will the litigation present a burden for which there is no corresponding benefit. A defendant who has placed goods in the stream of commerce benefits economically from the retail sale of the final product in the forum State, and indirectly benefits from the State's laws that regulate and facilitate commercial activity. These benefits accrue regardless of whether that participant directly conducts business in the forum State, or engages in additional conduct directed toward that State. Accordingly, most courts and commentators have found that jurisdiction premised on the placement of a product into the stream of commerce is consistent with the Due Process Clause, and have not required a showing of additional conduct.

[...]

The Court in *World-Wide Volkswagen*...took great care to distinguish "between a case involving goods which reach a distant State through a chain of distribution and a case involving goods which reach the same State because a consumer...took them there."...The California Supreme Court took note of this distinction, and correctly concluded that our holding in *World-Wide Volkswagen* preserved the stream-of-commerce theory....

In this case, the facts found by the California Supreme Court support its finding of minimum contacts. The Court found that "[a]lthough Asahi did not design or control the system of distribution that carried its valve assemblies into California, Asahi was aware of the distribution system's operation, and it knew that it would benefit economically from the sale in California of products incorporating its components."... Accordingly, I cannot join the plurality's determination that Asahi's regular and extensive sales of component parts to a manufacturer it knew was making regular sales of the final product in California is insufficient to establish minimum contacts with California.

JUSTICE STEVENS, with whom JUSTICE WHITE and JUSTICE BLACKMUN join, concurring in part and concurring in the judgment.

The judgment of the Supreme Court of California should be reversed for the reasons stated in Part II–B of the Court's opinion. While I join Parts I and II–B, I do not join Part II–A for two reasons. First, it is not necessary to the Court's decision. An examination of minimum contacts is not always necessary to determine whether a state court's assertion of personal jurisdiction is constitutional.... Part II–B establishes, after considering the factors set forth in *World-Wide Volkswagen Corp. v. Woodson*...that California's exercise of jurisdiction over Asahi in this case would be "unreasonable and unfair."... This finding alone requires reversal; that case fits within the rule that "minimum requirements inherent in the concept of 'fair play and substantial justice' may defeat the reasonableness of jurisdiction even if the defendant has purposefully engaged in forum activities."... Accordingly, I see no reason in this case for the Court to articulate "purposeful direction" or any other test as the nexus between an act of a defendant and the forum State that is necessary to establish minimum contacts.

Second, even assuming that the test ought to be formulated here, Part II–A misapplies it to the facts of this case. The Court seems to assume that an unwavering line can be drawn between "mere awareness" that a component will find its way into the forum State and "purposeful availment" of the forum's market....Over the course of its dealings with Cheng Shin, Asahi has arguably engaged in a higher quantum of conduct than "[t]he placement of a product into the stream of commerce, without more...." Whether or not this conduct rises to the level of purposeful availment requires a constitutional determination that is affected by the volume, the value, and the hazardous character of the components. In most circumstances[,] I would be inclined to conclude that a regular course of dealing that results in deliveries of over 100,000 units annually over a period of several years would constitute "purposeful availment" even though the item delivered to the forum State was a standard product marketed throughout the world.

[. . .]

Notes and Questions

1. Where is the litigation for contribution and indemnification likely to be brought if access to the California courts is foreclosed? The evidence relating to the cause of action is before the California courts and they would have the benefit of the consumer's civil litigation. Can the record be transferred and admitted in a foreign proceeding? If not, there will be duplicative litigation, greater costs, and possibly a denial of remedy. Why does the U.S. Supreme Court command such an impractical result?

2. What role do the concepts of "substantial connection" and "purposeful availment" play in the Court's reasoning on jurisdiction? How and why does it eliminate the "stream of commerce" thinking?

3. Did the court decisions prior to *Woodson* that endorsed the "stream of commerce" thinking, in effect, "punish" mercantile parties for producing products and placing them on the open market? How does the idea of corporate presence replace that thinking and what result does it promote?

4. What "unique burdens" does the submission of disputes to a foreign legal system create for transborder litigation?

5. How would you describe the Court's due process analysis in the opinion? Does foreign nationality or location make for a more rigorous constitutional test for the assertion of jurisdiction?

6. What role do the interests of the forum and of other nations play in the Court's reasoning? What about the concept of reasonableness?

7. Define the expression "international context."

8. Why does this case fracture the Court into so many camps and sub-camps?

Chapter 3

THE IMPACT OF U.S. LAW DOCTRINES ON TRANSBORDER JURISDICTION

Table of Sections

§ 1. THE USE OF CONTRACT TO ESTABLISH JURISDICTION: FORUM–SELECTION CLAUSES

The parties can use the contract to minimize the risk associated with the problems of jurisdiction. Contract remedies are not failsafe, but they can reduce the uncertainty and unpredictability associated with the assertion of jurisdiction by courts. In their agreement, the parties can enter into a forum-selection clause, in which they stipulate that they designate a given court to hear any dispute that might arise under the contract. The stipulation provides some degree of foreseeability in the event of the disruption of the transborder transaction by a commercial conflict between the parties.

The exercise of such contractual authority by private parties once greatly disturbed the courts. The latter would generally invalidate such provisions as an infringement upon their authority and a violation of public policy. Most contract provisions delimiting party liability or dispute resolution modalities were deemed unenforceable. The more modern era has brought overburdened courts and transnational global commercial transactions. The latter two factors *per force* dictated a more accepting judicial attitude and a judicial recognition that self-regulation through contract was both an efficient and effective way to build a rule of law in the international legal vacuum.

The critical concern is that the designated court may not accept the parties' determination and refuse to serve as their forum for litigation. Both public policy reasoning and practicality make such an outcome entirely plausible. Neutrality and expertise, along with convenience, are central to an effective choice.

As noted earlier, few, if any, legal systems have substantive legal rules that address the issues of transnational litigation. Most systems provide only choice-of-law rules to deal with the conflicts that arise between national substantive laws. The U.S. Supreme Court, much like the French Court of Cassation (the highest French court for civil and criminal matters), has filled the law void by elaborating an internationalist doctrine that addresses significant aspects of transborder litigation. The next case is one of the most fundamental and eloquent pronouncements of the U.S. Supreme Court in this area. [Author's Note: The editing of and questions following the case are adapted from my previous publications and are reprinted with permission of Juris Publishing, Inc.]

THE BREMEN v. ZAPATA OFF–SHORE CO.

407 U.S. 1, 92 S.Ct. 1907, 32 L.Ed.2d 513 (1972).

(footnotes omitted)

MR. CHIEF JUSTICE BURGER delivered the opinion of the court.

We granted *certiorari* to review a judgment of the United States Court of Appeals for the Fifth Circuit declining to enforce a forum-selection clause governing disputes arising under an international towage contract between petitioners and respondent. The circuits have differed in their approach to such clauses. For the reasons stated hereafter, we vacate the judgment of the Court of Appeals.

In November 1967, respondent Zapata, a Houston-based American corporation, contracted with petitioner Unterweser, a German corporation, to tow Zapata's ocean-going, self-elevating drilling rig *Chaparral* from Louisiana to a point off Ravenna, Italy, in the Adriatic Sea, where Zapata had agreed to drill certain wells.

Zapata had solicited bids for the towage, and several companies including Unterweser had responded. Unterweser was the low bidder and Zapata requested it to submit a contract, which it did. The contract submitted by Unterweser contained the following provision, which is at issue in this case:

> "Any dispute arising must be treated before the London Court of Justice."

In addition[,] the contract contained two clauses purporting to exculpate Unterweser from liability for damages to the towed barge.

After reviewing the contract and making several changes, but without any alteration in the forum-selection or exculpatory clauses, a Zapata vice-president executed the contract and forwarded it to Unterweser in Germany, where Unterweser accepted the changes, and the contract became effective.

On January 5, 1968, Unterweser's deep sea tug *Bremen* departed Venice, Louisiana, with the *Chaparral* in tow bound for Italy. On January 9, while the flotilla was in international waters in the middle of the Gulf of Mexico, a severe storm arose. The sharp roll of the *Chaparral* in Gulf waters caused its elevator legs, which had been raised for the voyage, to break off and fall into the sea, seriously damaging the *Chaparral*. In this emergency situation[,] Zapata instructed the *Bremen* to tow its damaged rig to Tampa, Florida, the nearest port of refuge.

On January 12, Zapata, ignoring its contract promise to litigate "any dispute arising" in the English courts, commenced a suit in admiralty in the United States District Court at Tampa, seeking $3,500,000 damages against Unterweser *in personam* and the *Bremen in rem*, alleging negligent towage and breach of contract. Unterweser responded by invoking the forum clause of the towage contract, and moved to dismiss for lack of jurisdiction or on *forum non conveniens* grounds, or in the alternative to stay the action pending submission of the dispute to the "London Court of Justice." Shortly thereafter, in February, before the District Court had ruled on its motion to stay or dismiss the United States action, Unterweser commenced an action against Zapata seeking damages for breach of the towage contract in the High Court of Justice in London, as the contract provided. Zapata appeared in that court to contest jurisdiction, but its challenge was rejected, the English courts holding that the contractual forum provision conferred jurisdiction.

In the meantime, Unterweser was faced with a dilemma in the pending action in the United States court at Tampa. The six-month period for filing [an] action to limit its liability to Zapata and other potential claimants was about to expire, but the United States District Court in Tampa had not yet ruled on Unterweser's motion to dismiss or stay Zapata's action. On July 2, 1968, confronted with difficult alternatives, Unterweser filed an action to limit its liability in the District Court in Tampa. That court entered the customary injunction against proceedings outside the limitation court, and Zapata refiled its initial claim in the limitation action.

It was only at this juncture, on July 29, after the six month period for filing the limitation action had run, that the District Court denied Unterweser's January motion to dismiss or stay Zapata's initial action. In denying the motion, that court relied on the prior decision of the Court of Appeals in *Carbon Black Export, Inc. v. The Monrosa*. . . .In that case[,] the Court of Appeals had held a forum-selection clause unenforceable, reiterating the traditional view of many American courts that "agreements in advance of controversy whose object is to oust the jurisdiction of the courts are contrary to public policy and will not be enforced." . . . Apparently concluding that it was bound by the *Carbon Black* case, the District Court gave the forum-selection clause little, if any, weight. Instead, the court treated the motion to dismiss under normal *forum non conveniens* doctrine applicable in the absence of such a clause. . . . Under that doctrine "unless the balance is strongly in favor of the defendant, the plaintiff's choice of forum should rarely be disturbed." . . . The District Court concluded: "The balance of conveniences here is not strongly in favor of [Unterweser] and [Zapata's] choice of forum should not be disturbed."

[. . .]

On appeal, a divided panel of the Court of Appeals affirmed, and on rehearing *en banc* the panel opinion was adopted, with six of the 14 *en banc* judges dissenting. As had the District Court, the majority rested on the *Carbon Black* decision, concluding that "at the very least" that case stood for the proposition that a forum-selection clause "will not be enforced unless the selected state would provide a more convenient forum than the state in which suit is brought." From that premise[,] the Court of Appeals proceeded to conclude that, apart from the forum-selection clause, the District Court did not abuse its discretion in refusing to decline jurisdiction on the basis of *forum non conveniens*. It noted that (1) the flotilla never "escaped the Fifth Circuit's *mare nostrum*, and the casualty occurred in close proximity to the district court"; (2) a considerable number of potential witnesses, including Zapata crewmen, resided in the Gulf Coast area; (3) preparation for the voyage and inspection and repair work had been performed in the Gulf area; (4) the testimony of the *Bremen* crew was available by way of deposition; (5) England had no interest in or contact with the controversy other than the forum-selection clause. The Court of Appeals majority further noted that Zapata was a United States citizen and "[t]he discretion of the district court to remand the case to a foreign forum was consequently limited," especially since it appeared likely that the English courts would enforce the exculpatory clauses. In the Court of Appeals' view, enforcement of such clauses would be contrary to public policy in American courts under *Bisso v. Inland Waterways Corp.* . . . Therefore, "[t]he district court was entitled to consider that remanding Zapata to a foreign forum, with no practical contact with the controversy, could raise a bar to recovery by a United States citizen which its own convenient courts would not countenance."

We hold, with the six dissenting members of the Court of Appeals, that far too little weight and effect were given to the forum clause in resolving this controversy. For at least two decades we have witnessed an expansion of overseas commercial activities by business enterprises based in the United States. The barrier of distance that once tended to confine a business concern to a modest territory no longer does so. Here we see an American company with special expertise contracting with a foreign company to tow a complex machine thousands of miles across seas and oceans. The expansion of American business and industry will hardly be encouraged if, notwithstanding solemn contracts, we insist on a parochial concept that all disputes must be resolved under our laws and in our courts. Absent a contract forum, the considerations relied on by the Court of Appeals would be persuasive reasons for holding an American forum convenient in the traditional sense, but in an era of expanding world trade and commerce, the absolute aspects of the doctrine of the *Carbon Black* case have little place and would be a heavy hand indeed on the future development of international commercial dealings by Americans. We cannot have trade and commerce in world markets and international waters exclusively on our terms, governed by our laws, and resolved in our courts.

Forum-selection clauses have historically not been favored by American courts. Many courts, federal and state, have declined to enforce such clauses on the ground that they were "contrary to public policy," or that their effect was to "oust the jurisdiction" of the court. Although this view apparently still has considerable acceptance, other courts are tending to adopt a more hospitable attitude toward forum-selection clauses. This view, advanced in the well-reasoned dissenting opinion in the instant case, is that such clauses are *prima facie* valid and should be enforced unless enforcement is shown by the resisting party to be "unreasonable" under the circumstances. We believe this is the correct doctrine to be followed by federal district courts sitting in admiralty.... Not surprisingly, foreign businessmen prefer, as do we, to have disputes resolved in their own courts, but if that choice is not available, then in a neutral forum with expertise in the subject matter. Plainly, the courts of England meet the standards of neutrality and long experience in admiralty litigation. The choice of that forum was made in an arm's-length negotiation by experienced and sophisticated businessmen, and absent some compelling and countervailing reason it should be honored by the parties and enforced by the courts.

The argument that such clauses are improper because they tend to "oust" a court of jurisdiction is hardly more than a vestigial legal fiction. It appears to rest at its core on historical judicial resistance to any attempt to reduce the power and business of a particular court and has little place in an era when all courts are overloaded and when businesses once essentially local now operate in world markets. It reflects something of a provincial attitude regarding the fairness of other tribunals....The threshold question is whether that court should have exercised its jurisdiction to do more than give effect to the legitimate expectations of the parties, manifested in their freely negotiated agreement, by specifically enforcing the forum clause.

There are compelling reasons why a freely negotiated private international agreement, unaffected by fraud, undue influence, or overweening bargaining power, such as that involved here, should be given full effect. In this case, for example, we are concerned with a far from routine transaction between companies of two different nations contemplating the tow of an extremely costly piece of equipment from Louisiana across the Gulf of Mexico and the Atlantic Ocean, through the Mediterranean Sea to its final destination in the Adriatic Sea. In the course of its voyage, it was to traverse the waters of many jurisdictions. The *Chaparral* could have been damaged at any point along the route, and there were countless possible ports of refuge. That the accident occurred in the Gulf of Mexico and the barge was towed to Tampa in an emergency were mere fortuities. It cannot be doubted for a moment that the parties sought to provide for a neutral forum for the resolution of any disputes arising during the tow. Much uncertainty and possibly great inconvenience to both parties could arise if a suit could be maintained in any jurisdiction in which an accident might occur or if jurisdiction were left to any place where the *Bremen* or Unterweser might happen to be found. The elimination of all such uncertainties by agreeing in advance on a forum acceptable to both parties is an indispensable element in international trade, commerce, and contracting. There is strong evidence that the forum clause was a vital part of the agreement, and it would be unrealistic to think that the parties did not conduct their negotiations, including fixing the monetary terms, with the consequences of the forum clause figuring prominently in their calculations....

Thus, in the light of present-day commercial realities and expanding international trade we conclude that the forum clause should control absent a strong showing that it should be set aside. Although their opinions are not altogether explicit, it seems reasonably clear that the District Court and the Court of Appeals placed the burden on Unterweser to show that London would be a more convenient forum than Tampa, although the contract expressly resolved that issue. The correct approach would have been to enforce the forum clause specifically unless Zapata could clearly show that enforcement would be unreasonable and unjust, or that the clause was invalid for such reasons as fraud or overreaching. Accordingly, the case must be remanded for reconsideration.

We note, however, that there is nothing in the record presently before us that would support a refusal to enforce the forum clause. The Court of Appeals suggested that enforcement would be contrary to the public policy of the forum under *Bisso*...because of the prospect that the English courts would enforce the clauses of the towage contract purporting to exculpate Unterweser from liability for damages to the *Chaparral*. A contractual choice-of-forum clause should be held unenforceable if enforcement would contravene a strong public policy of the forum in which suit is brought, whether declared by statute or by judicial decision.... It is clear, however, that whatever the proper scope of the policy expressed in *Bisso*, it does not reach this case. *Bisso* rested on considerations with respect to the towage business strictly in American waters, and those considerations are not controlling in an international commercial agreement....

[...]

This case...involves a freely negotiated international commercial transaction between a German and an American corporation for towage of a vessel from the Gulf of Mexico to the Adriatic Sea. As noted, selection of a London forum was clearly a reasonable effort to bring vital certainty to this international transaction and to provide a neutral forum experienced and capable in the resolution of admiralty litigation. Whatever "inconvenience" Zapata would suffer by being forced to litigate in the contractual forum as it agreed to do was clearly foreseeable at the time of contracting. In such circumstances[,] it should be incumbent on the party seeking to escape his contract to show that trial in the contractual forum will be so gravely difficult and inconvenient that he will for all practical purpose be deprived on his day in court. Absent that, there is no basis for concluding that it would be unfair, unjust, or unreasonable to hold that party to his bargain.

[. . .]

The judgment of the Court of Appeals is vacated and the case is remanded for further proceedings consistent with this opinion.

Vacated and remanded.

[. . .]

MR. JUSTICE DOUGLAS, dissenting.

[. . .]

Respondent is a citizen of this country. Moreover, if it were remitted to the English court, its substantive rights would be adversely affected. Exculpatory provisions in the towage [contract] provided (1) that petitioners, the masters and the crews "are not responsible for defaults and/or errors in the navigation of the tow" and (2) that "(d)amages suffered by the towed object are in any case for account of its Owners."

Under our decision in *Dixilyn Drilling Corp.*, . . . "a contract which exempts the tower from liability for its own negligence" is not enforceable, though there is evidence in the present record that it is enforceable in England. That policy was first announced in *Bisso*. . . . Although the casualty occurred on the high seas, the *Bisso* doctrine is nonetheless applicable. . . .

Moreover, the casualty occurred close to the District Court, a number of potential witnesses, including respondent's crewmen, reside in that area, and the inspection and repair work were done there. The testimony of the tower's crewmen, residing in Germany, is already available by way of depositions taken in the proceedings.

All in all, the District Court judge exercised his discretion wisely in enjoining petitioners from pursuing the litigation in England.

[. . .]

Notes and Questions

1. The loss in *The Bremen v. Zapata Off–Shore Co.* was substantial. When *The Bremen* was arrested in Tampa, it was released upon Unterwes-

er's provision of $3,500,000 as security. *See* 407 U.S. at 4 n.3. Moreover, the limitation fund in the Tampa federal district court was $1,390,000 while its counterpart in England contained only $80,000. *See id.* at 8 n.8. In all likelihood, the damage to the *Chaparral* and to Zapata's business represented a multimillion dollar loss. The prospect of recovery was more likely in the United States than England. In addition, although Unterweser's bid included an offer to arrange for insurance coverage, Zapata decided to self-insure. *See id.* at 2 n.2. This was Zapata's general policy regarding all its rigs. *See id.* at 3 n.3. The two exculpatory clauses in "The General Towage Conditions" of the contract transferred all the risk of loss to the owners of the rig and held Unterweser harmless for any acts of negligence by its employees. *See id.* at 2 n.2.

How do or should these factors have influenced the Court's reasoning and determination? Should the quantum of actual damages determine the legality of the contractual allocation of risk? Is this a "bad deal" for Zapata warranting judicial intervention after the fact? Upon what legal basis might the court intervene? Did Zapata enter into the transaction assuming that the special protections of U.S. law would apply, perhaps unbeknownst to its co-contractant? Should the Court take such a circumstance into account?

2. Relief for Zapata is less likely or perhaps unavailable in England. The exculpatory clauses probably would be enforced by English courts, resulting in a dismissal of the action against Unterweser. *See* 407 U.S. at 8 n.8. Moreover, even if Unterweser were held liable, the limitation fund in England, as noted in the foregoing, was modest. Why shouldn't these factors, in addition to the public policy against exculpatory clauses in maritime transactions articulated in *Bisso*, be sufficient to place the litigation within the jurisdiction of U.S. courts and law? Moreover, the incident occurred near a U.S. jurisdiction, involved directly the business assets of a U.S. national, and generally implicated U.S. interests. Why should English courts and law have exclusive jurisdiction over a matter that has no connection or proximity to England or English interests?

3. The Court finds both the policy in *Bisso* and the *Carbon Black* doctrine on forum selection clauses inapplicable to a transborder commercial agreement. The Court, in effect, reverses the rule of *Carbon Black*, holding that forum selection clauses are presumptively enforceable in international contracts. The adverse party can rebut the presumption by establishing that enforcement would result in debilitating inconvenience or a denial of justice. In his dissent, Justice Douglas takes a more insidious view of the interplay between the forum selection clause and the *Bisso* policy against exculpatory clauses. Read the following excerpt from Justice Douglas' dissent and contrast it to the majority's reasoning:

> It is said that because these parties specifically agreed to litigate their disputes before the London Court of Justice, the District Court, absent "unreasonable" circumstances, should have honored that choice by declining to exercise its jurisdiction. The forum-selection clause, however, is part and parcel of the exculpatory provisions in the towing agreement which, as mentioned in the text, is not enforceable in American courts. For only by avoiding litigation in the United States could petitioners hope to evade the *Bisso* doctrine. Judges in this

> country have traditionally been hostile to attempts to circumvent the public policy against exculpatory agreements. For example, clauses specifying that the law of a foreign place (which favors such releases) should control have regularly been ignored. Thus, in *The Kensington*,...the Court held void an exemption from liability despite the fact that the contract provided that it should be construed under Belgian law[,] which was more tolerant....
>
> The instant stratagem of specifying a foreign forum is essentially the same as invoking a foreign law of construction except that the present circumvention also requires the American party to travel across an ocean to seek relief. Unless we are prepared to overrule *Bisso* we should not countenance devices designed solely for the purpose of evading its prohibition. It is argued, however, that one of the rationales of the *Bisso* doctrine, "to protect those in need of goods or services from being overreached by others who have power to drive hard bargains,"... does not apply here because these parties may have been of equal bargaining stature. Yet we have often adopted prophylactic rules rather than attempt to sort the core cases from the marginal ones. In any event, the other objective of the *Bisso* doctrine, to "discourage negligence by making wrongdoers pay damages,"...applies here and in every case regardless of the relative bargaining strengths of the parties.

407 U.S. at 24 n.*

What are the primary and most persuasive arguments in favor of the assertion of U.S. court jurisdiction and the application of existing U.S. law?

4. You should examine the content of the applicable forum selection clause carefully. Are there problems with its construction? For example: (1) to what subject areas does the phrase "any dispute arising" refer; (2) "arising" how and where; (3) what does "treated" mean—adjudication, processing, acknowledgment, or settlement; and (4) what is "the London Court of Justice"? It appears that those sophisticated commercial parties agreed to have "any dispute arising" "treated" before a court in London that does not exist. Don't these problems reveal that the parties failed to consider or to agree upon an appropriate situs for dispute resolution, and that the failures in the clause mean that choice-of-law "localizing"considerations should dictate which court has jurisdiction? Why should the Court remedy the parties' contractual ineptitudes and deficiencies in these circumstances? Isn't the contractual failing a proper foundation for applying the standard doctrines in *Bisso* and *Carbon Black*?

5. The objection in the foregoing notes notwithstanding, it is now clear that the majority opinion in *The Bremen* is good law and acts as the foundation for the Court's progressive articulation of a judicial policy on transborder litigation and international arbitration. *The Bremen* is the first case in which the Court establishes a marked boundary between law for the domestic and international matters, holding that domestic rules may be inapposite in the international sector. It also makes clear that domestic laws need to be either disregarded or adapted for application in the international sector. With *The Bremen*, the Court begins the process of elaborating normative rules of private international law that generally reject the extra-

territorial application of domestic law as a source of law for transborder commercial ventures.

6. Key phrases in the new judicial policy, applicable to forum-selection and arbitral clauses alike, include: "The expansion of American business... will hardly be encouraged if, notwithstanding solemn contracts, we insist on a parochial concept that all disputes must be resolved under our laws and in our courts." "We cannot have trade and commerce in world markets and international waters exclusively on our terms, governed by our laws, and resolved in our courts." "There are compelling reasons why a freely negotiated private international agreement... should be given full effect." "The elimination of... uncertainties by agreeing in advance on a forum acceptable to both parties is an indispensable element in international trade, commerce, and contracting."

Do these statements constitute a rule of law? Do they amount to judicial legislation? How might the Court be in a better position than the Congress to elaborate a framework for regulating international business transactions?

You should isolate the various tenets of the Court's doctrine on matters of transborder litigation and international contracts. They will be echoed, *in haec verba*, in the rulings that deal specifically with international commercial arbitration.

* * * *

The U.S. Supreme Court reaffirmed its doctrine on forum selection clause in a more recent opinion involving a case that was principally domestic in character. The court upheld the validity of the forum selection provision despite its adhesionary character, the respective and unequal status and interests of the parties, and the infringement upon the weaker party's legal right to judicial relief.

CARNIVAL CRUISE LINES, INC. v. SHUTE

499 U.S. 585, 111 S.Ct. 1522, 113 L.Ed.2d 622 (1991).

(citations and footnotes omitted)

JUSTICE BLACKMUN delivered the opinion of the court.

In this admiralty case[,] we primarily consider whether the United States Court of Appeals for the Ninth Circuit correctly refused to enforce a forum-selection clause contained in tickets issued by petitioner Carnival Cruise Lines, Inc., to respondents Eulala and Russel Shute.

I.

The Shutes, through an Arlington, Wash., travel agent, purchased passage for a 7-day cruise on petitioner's ship, the TROPICALE. Respondents paid the fare to the agent who forwarded the payment to petitioner's headquarters in Miami, Fla. Petitioner then prepared the tickets and sent them to respondents in the State of Washington. The face of each ticket, at its left-hand lower corner, contained this admonition:

> "SUBJECT TO CONDITIONS OF CONTRACT ON LAST PAGES **IMPORTANT**! PLEASE READ CONTRACT—ON LAST PAGES 1, 2, 3" App. 15

The following appeared on "contract page 1" of each ticket:

"TERMS AND CONDITIONS OF PASSAGE CONTRACT TICKET

[. . .]

"3. (a) The acceptance of this ticket by the person or persons named hereon as passengers shall be deemed to be an acceptance and agreement by each of them of all of the terms and conditions of this Passage Contract Ticket.

[. . .]

"8. It is agreed by and between the passenger and the Carrier that all disputes and matters whatsoever arising under in connection with or incident to this Contract shall be litigated, if at all, in and before a Court located in the State of Florida, U.S.A., to the exclusion of the Courts of any other state or country." *Id.*, at 16.

The last quoted paragraph is the forum-selection clause at issue.

II.

Respondents boarded the *Tropicale* in Los Angeles, Cal. The ship sailed to Puerto Vallarta, Mexico, and then returned to Los Angeles. While the ship was in international waters off the Mexican coast, respondent Eulala Shute was injured when she slipped on a deck mat during a guided tour of the ship's galley. Respondents filed suit against petitioner in the United States District Court for the Western District of Washington, claiming that Mrs. Shute's injuries had been caused by the negligence of Carnival Cruise Lines and its employees. . . .

Petitioner moved for summary judgment, contending that the forum clause in respondents' tickets required the Shutes to bring their suit against petitioner in a court in the State of Florida. . . . The District Court granted the motion. . . . The Court of Appeals reversed.

[. . .]

III.

We begin by noting the boundaries of our inquiry. First, this is a case in admiralty, and federal law governs the enforceability of the forum-selection clause we scrutinize. . . . Second, we do not address the question whether respondent had sufficient notice of the forum clause before entering the contract for passage. Respondents essentially have conceded that they had notice of the forum-selection provision. . . .

Within this context, respondents urge that the forum clause should not be enforced because, contrary to this Court's teaching in *The Bremen*, the clause was not the product of negotiation, and enforcement effectively would deprive respondents of their day in court. . . .

IV.

A.

Both petitioner and respondents argue vigorously that the Court's opinion in *The Bremen* governs this case, and each side purports to find ample support for its position in that opinion's broad-ranging language. This seeming paradox derives in large part from key factual differences between this case and *The Bremen*, differences that preclude an automatic and simple application of *The Bremen*'s general principles to the facts here.

[. . .]

[I]t would be entirely unreasonable for us to assume that respondents—or any other cruise passenger—would negotiate with petitioner the terms of a forum-selection clause in an ordinary commercial cruise ticket. Common sense dictates that a ticket of this kind will be a form contract the terms of which are not subject to negotiation, and that an individual purchasing the ticket will not have bargaining parity with the cruise line. But by ignoring the crucial differences in the business contexts in which the respective contracts were executed, the Court of Appeals' analysis seems to us to have distorted somewhat this Court's holding in *The Bremen*.

In evaluating the reasonableness of the forum clause at issue in this case, we must refine the analysis of *The Bremen* to account for the realities of form passage contracts. As an initial matter, we do not adopt the Court of Appeals' determination that a nonnegotiated forum-selection clause in a form ticket contract is never enforceable simply because it is not the subject of bargaining. Including a reasonable forum clause in a form contract of this kind well may be permissible for several reasons: First, a cruise line has a special interest in limiting the fora in which it potentially could be subject to suit. Because a cruise ship typically carries passengers from many locales, it is not unlikely that a mishap on a cruise could subject the cruise line to litigation in several different fora. (Citation omitted). Additionally, a clause establishing *ex ante* the forum for dispute resolution has the salutary effect of dispelling any confusion. . . sparing litigants the time and expense of pretrial motions to determine the correct forum, and conserving judicial resources that otherwise would be devoted to deciding those motions. (Citation omitted). Finally, it stands to reason that passengers who purchase tickets containing a forum clause like that at issue in this case benefit in the form of reduced fares reflecting the savings that the cruise line enjoys by limiting the fora in which it may be sued. . . .

[. . .]

It bears emphasis that forum-selection clauses contained in form passage contracts are subject to judicial scrutiny for fundamental fairness. In this case, there is no indication that petitioner set Florida as the forum in which disputes were to be resolved as a means of discouraging cruise passengers from pursuing legitimate claims. Any suggestion of such a bad-faith motive is belied by two facts: petitioner has its principal place of business in Florida, and many of its cruises depart from and return to Florida ports. Similarly, there is no evidence that petitioner obtained respondents' accession to the forum clause by fraud or overreaching. Finally, respondents have conceded that they were given notice of the forum provision and, therefore, presumably retained the option of rejecting the contract with impunity. In the case before us, therefore, we conclude that the Court of Appeals erred in refusing to enforce the forum-selection clause.

[. . .]

V.

The judgment of the Court of Appeals is reversed.

It is so ordered.

JUSTICE STEVENS, with whom JUSTICE MARSHALL joins, dissenting.

[. . .]

Exculpatory clauses in passenger tickets have been around for a long time. These clauses are typically the product of disparate bargaining power between the carrier and the passenger, and they undermine the strong public interest in deterring negligent conduct. . . .

Forum-selection clauses in passenger tickets involve the intersection of two strands of traditional contract law that qualify the general rule that courts will enforce the terms of a contract as written. Pursuant to the first strand, courts traditionally have reviewed with heightened scrutiny the terms of contracts of adhesion, form contracts offered on a take-or-leave basis by a party with stronger bargaining power to a party with weaker power. Some commentators have questioned whether contracts of adhesion can justifiably be enforced at all under traditional contract theory because the adhering party generally enters into them without manifesting knowing and voluntary consent to all their terms. . . .

The common law, recognizing that standardized form contracts account for a significant portion of all commercial agreements, has taken a less extreme position and instead subjects terms in contracts of adhesion to scrutiny for reasonableness. . . .

The second doctrinal principle implicated by forum-selection clauses is the traditional rule that "contractual provisions, which seek to limit the place or court in which an action may . . . be brought, are invalid as contrary to public policy." . . . Although adherence to this general rule has declined in recent years, particularly following our decision in *The Bremen v. Zapata Off–Shore Co.*, 407 U.S. 1, 92 S. Ct. 1907, 32 L.Ed.2d 513 (1972), the prevailing rule is still that forum-selection clauses are not enforceable if they were not freely bargained for, create additional expense for one party, or deny one party a remedy. . . . A forum-selection clause in a standardized passenger ticket would clearly have been unenforceable under the common law before our decision in *The Bremen*, . . . and in my opinion, remains unenforceable under the prevailing rule today.

The Bremen, which the Court effectively treats as controlling this case, had nothing to say about stipulations printed on the back of passenger tickets. That case involved the enforceability of a forum-selection clause in a freely negotiated international agreement between two large corporations providing for the towage of a vessel from the Gulf of Mexico to the Adriatic Sea. The Court recognized that such towage agreements had generally been held unenforceable in American courts, but held that the doctrine of those cases did not extend to commercial arrangements between parties with equal bargaining power.

[. . .]

The stipulation in the ticket that Carnival Cruise sold to respondents certainly lessens or weakens their ability to recover for the slip and fall incident that occurred off the west coast of Mexico during the cruise that originated and terminated in Los Angeles, California. It is safe to assume that the witnesses—whether other passengers or members of the crew—can be assembled with less expense and inconvenience at a west coast forum than in a Florida court several thousand miles from the scene of the accident.

[. . .]

Notes and Questions

1. What rules does the Court establish in regard to adhesionary forum selection clauses? When is such a clause likely to be unenforceable?

2. Does the Court maintain that allowing Carnival Cruise Lines to select unilaterally the forum for prospective litigation is not advantageous? Should the consumer be given a choice or some sort of veto power to achieve "fundamental fairness" in the agreement?

3. What does the reasoning in *Carnival Cruise* add to the doctrine in *The Bremen*? How do you assess the Stevens dissent? Is it forceful and potent? Or, does it complain needlessly about the absence of a bygone doctrine? Could you have been more persuasive?

4. A historical note: For many years, U.S. courts generally refused to give any effect to choice-of-forum clauses. This position was recognized by the first Restatement of the Conflict of Laws. It was not until the landmark decision of *Wm. H. Muller & Co. v. Swedish American Line, Ltd.*, 224 F.2d 806 (2d Cir. 1955), *cert. denied* 350 U.S. 903, 76 S.Ct. 182, 100 L.Ed. 793 (1955), that the courts began to enforce forum selection clauses. In *Muller*, the court emphasized that a forum selection clause could not oust judicial jurisdiction, but "if in the proper exercise of its jurisdiction, by a preliminary ruling the court finds that the agreement is not unreasonable in the setting of the particular case, it may properly decline jurisdiction and relegate a litigation to a forum to which he [the plaintiff] assented." 224 F.2d at 808. The test used by the court was whether the clause was "reasonable" and the burden of proving this was on the plaintiff. This change in position was recognized by the Second Restatement of the Conflict of Laws § 80:

> The parties' agreement as to the place of the action cannot oust a state of judicial jurisdiction, but such an agreement will be given effect unless it is unfair or unreasonable.
>
> Comment:
>
> a. Rationale. Private individuals have no power to alter the rules of judicial jurisdiction. They may not by their contract oust a state of any jurisdiction it would otherwise possess. This does not mean that no weight should be accorded a provision in a contract that any action thereon shall be brought only in a particular state. Such a provision represents an attempt by the parties to insure that the action will be brought in a forum that is convenient for them. A court will naturally be reluctant to entertain an action if it considers itself to be an inappropriate forum. And the fact that the action is brought in a state other than that designated in the contract affords ground for holding that the forum is an inappropriate one and that the court in its discretion should refuse to entertain this action. Such provision, however, will be disregarded if it is the result of overreaching or of unfair use of unequal bargaining power or if the forum chosen by the parties would be a seriously inconvenient one for the trial of the particular action. On the other hand, the provision will be given effect, and the action dismissed, if to do so would be fair and reasonable.

Further recognition of choice-of-forum clauses was incorporated into § 187 of the Second Restatement of the Conflict of Laws:

> (1) The law of the state chosen by the parties to govern their contractual rights and duties will be applied if the particular issue is one which the parties could have resolved by an explicit provision in their agreement directed to that issue.
>
> (2) The law of the state chosen by the parties to govern their contractual rights and duties will be applied, even if the particular issue is one which the parties could not have resolved by an explicit provision in their agreement directed to that issue, unless either
>
> (a) the chosen state has no substantial relationship to the parties or the transaction and there is no other reasonable basis for the parties' choice, or
>
> (b) application of the law of the chosen state would be contrary to a fundamental policy of a state which has a materially greater interest than the chosen state in the determination of the particular issue and which, under the rule of § 188, would be the state of the applicable law in the absence of an effective choice of law by the parties.
>
> (3) In the absence of a contrary indication of intention, the reference is to the local law of the state of the chosen law.

The comments further suggest that the parties to a contract have the contractual capacity to determine the terms of the contract including forum selection unless such terms are against state policy or applicable law.

The Uniform Commercial Code § 1–105 also recognizes the validity of choice-of-forum clauses:

(1) Except as provided hereafter in this section, when a transaction bears a reasonable relation to this state and also to another state or nation the parties may agree that the law either of this state or of such other state or nation shall govern their rights and duties. Failing such agreement this Act applies to transactions bearing an appropriate relationship to this state.

[. . .]

Comment

Purposes:

Subsection (1) states affirmatively the right of the parties to a multi-state transaction or a transaction involving foreign trade to choose their own law. . . .Ordinarily the law chosen must be that of a jurisdiction where a significant enough portion of the making or performance of the contract is to occur or occurs.

In 1968, the National Conference of Commissioners on Uniform State Laws adopted the Model Choice of Forum Act which was modelled after the Convention on the Choice of Court approved by the Hague Conference in 1964. [From: *Documents, Model Choice of Forum Act*, 17 Am. J. Comp. L. 292, 292–93 (1969) (reprinted with permission)]:

Like the Model Act, the convention provides, subject to certain conditions, that a court (a) must entertain an action if it has been designated by the parties in their agreement as a proper forum and (b) must refuse to entertain the action if it is not the court, or one of the courts, designated by the parties as a proper forum. Here the similarity ends. The Model Act is not only drafted in the American style; it also gives the court far more discretion than does the Convention to refuse to entertain the action, although it has been designated by the parties as a proper forum, or to entertain the action, although another court, or courts, have been designated a proper forum in its stead. The Model Act reflects the fact that Americans, in general, are more willing than Continentals to give discretion to their judges.

Section 2 of the Model Act states the circumstances in which the court should entertain an action when it would not have jurisdiction but for the fact that it has been designated a proper forum by the parties in their agreement. . . .This section will, in any event, have a narrow scope of application. This is because it is expressly made inapplicable in the three situations where jurisdiction on the basis of the defendant's consent is exercised most frequently in the United States. These situations involve (1) *cognovit* clauses, in which a party agrees that, upon his failure to comply with his obligations under a contract, judgment may be rendered against him by confession in the courts of one or more states, (2) arbitration clauses and (3) clauses providing for the appointment of an agent for the service of process. These clauses have been excepted from the scope of the Act because they are regulated by statute in many states.

§ 2. JUDICIAL DISCRETION TO DECLINE TO EXERCISE JURISDICTION: THE *FORUM NON CONVENIENS* DOCTRINE

Unlike civil law courts that must rule whenever the law gives them jurisdiction, U.S. and other common law courts have the discretion to refuse to assert the jurisdictional authority that they believe they have. They can exercise their jurisdictional discretion under the doctrine of *forum non conveniens*. The doctrine originated with Scottish courts which wanted to have the ability to dismiss a case if they concluded that trial elsewhere was in the best interest of justice and the litigation. The English courts adopted the practice and it was eventually incorporated into U.S. judicial doctrines, primarily in federal maritime cases.

The U.S. Supreme Court, in the companion cases of *Koster v. (American) Lumbermens Mut. Cas. Co.*, 330 U.S. 518, 67 S.Ct. 828, 91 L.Ed. 1067 (1947), and *Gulf Oil Corp. v. Gilbert*, 330 U.S. 501, 67 S.Ct. 839, 91 L.Ed. 1055 (1947), adopted the doctrine to enhance the ends of justice and the convenience of the parties. The choice of a forum for litigation had to be fair and functional. *Forum non conveniens* was intended to be applied exceptionally—only in circumstances in which the plaintiff's choice of forum imposed an enormous inconvenience on the defendant. Nonetheless, it was meant to provide discipline to the selection of a forum: The plaintiff could not by a choice of forum punish or retaliate against the defendant—" 'vex,' 'harass,' or 'oppress' the defendant by inflicting on him expense or trouble not necessary to his own right to pursue his remedy." The goal was to avoid undue hardship and to prevent forum shopping by either side. Eventually, as the would-be litigation crisis developed, *forum non conveniens* came to serve the goals of efficiency and functionality in the administration of judicial services. For example, in *Piper Aircraft Co. v. Reyno*, 454 U.S. 235, 102 S.Ct. 252, 70 L.Ed.2d 419 (1981), the U.S. Supreme Court concluded that "the American interest in this accident is simply not sufficient to justify the enormous commitment of judicial time and resources that would inevitably be required if the case were to be tried here."

As a consequence, the *forum non conveniens* doctrine came to be regarded as a barrier to judicial access and, thereby, to favor the interests of defendants. While courts were obligated to weigh the public/private interests established in *Gulf Oil* in order to reach a determination, they often concluded that public interest considerations dominated the private interest factors in light of the practicalities of judicial administration. As a result, foreign parties were not allowed to benefit from the greater level of commercial accountability under U.S. law against American corporate interests. The latter, in effect, were insulated from standard U.S. legal accountability.

A court's unwillingness to assert jurisdiction over an international litigation can also be expressed through the doctrine of international *lis pendens*. Like *forum non conveniens*, *lis pendens* is invoked at the court's discretion. It allows a court to decline asserting its authority over a matter when the action is already before a court in another jurisdiction. The actions need not be identical; relatedness is sufficient to trigger the application of the doctrine. It is intended to promote discipline in court dockets and consistent resolutions. The concept is less structured and prominent in federal decisional law on international litigation than *forum non conveniens*. It can result in a stay or dismissal at the court's discretion. The factors or elements to assess are also within the court's discretion.

After reading the court opinion in the next several cases, you should consider whether the U.S. legal system has a public policy obligation to treat U.S. and foreign parties alike for the purpose of access to litigation. Should equal treatment apply only if a U.S. party or interest is involved and only if that involvement is significant? Are there other considerations? Why and why not? Also, should courts use litigation brought against U.S. multinational companies as a means of regulating their global commercial activities? Is that a proper use of judicial power? Finally, would facilitating transborder litigation against U.S. multinationals before U.S. courts create an incentive for them to avoid creating personal injury? How can fairness, balance, and practicality be reconciled in this setting?

PIPER AIRCRAFT CO. v. REYNO

454 U.S. 235, 102 S.Ct. 252, 70 L.Ed.2d 419 (1981).

(footnotes omitted)

Justice MARSHALL delivered the opinion of the Court.

These cases arise out of an air crash that took place in Scotland. Respondent, acting as representative of the estates of several Scottish citizens killed in the accident, brought wrongful-death actions against petitioners that were ultimately transferred to the United States District Court for the Middle District of Pennsylvania. Petitioners moved to dismiss on the ground of *forum non conveniens*. After noting that an alternative forum existed in Scotland, the District Court granted their motions. 479 F. Supp. 727 (1979). The United States Court of Appeals for the Third Circuit reversed. 630 F.2d 149 (1980). The Court of Appeals based its decision, at least in part, on the ground that dismissal is automatically barred where the law of the alternative forum is less favorable to the plaintiff than the law of the forum chosen by the plaintiff. Because we conclude that the possibility of an unfavorable change in law should not, by itself, bar dismissal, and because we conclude that the District Court did not otherwise abuse its discretion, we reverse.

I.

A.

In July 1976, a small commercial aircraft crashed in the Scottish highlands during the course of a charter flight from Blackpool to Perth.

The pilot and five passengers were killed instantly. The decedents were all Scottish subjects and residents, as are their heirs and next of kin. There were no eyewitnesses to the accident. At the time of the crash[,] the plane was subject to Scottish air traffic control.

The aircraft, a twin-engine Piper Aztec, was manufactured in Pennsylvania by petitioner Piper Aircraft Co. (Piper). The propellers were manufactured in Ohio by petitioner Hartzell Propeller, Inc. (Hartzell). At the time of the crash[,] the aircraft was registered in Great Britain and was owned and maintained by Air Navigation and Trading Co., Ltd. (Air Navigation). It was operated by McDonald Aviation, Ltd. (McDonald), a Scottish air taxi service. Both Air Navigation and McDonald were organized in the United Kingdom. The wreckage of the plane is now in a hanger in Farnsborough, England.

The British Department of Trade investigated the accident shortly after it occurred. A preliminary report found that the plane crashed after developing a spin, and suggested that mechanical failure in the plane or the propeller was responsible. At Hartzell's request, this report was reviewed by a three-member Review Board, which held a 9–day adversary hearing attended by all interested parties. The Review Board found no evidence of defective equipment and indicated that pilot error may have contributed to the accident. The pilot, who had obtained his commercial pilot's license only three months earlier, was flying over high ground at an altitude considerably lower than the minimum height required by his company's operations manual.

In July 1977, a California probate court appointed respondent Gaynell Reyno administratrix of the estates of the five passengers. Reyno is not related to and does not know any of the decedents or their survivors; she was a legal secretary to the attorney who filed this lawsuit. Several days after her appointment, Reyno commenced separate wrongful death actions against Piper and Hartzell in the Superior Court of California, claiming negligence and strict liability. Air Navigation, McDonald, and the estate of the pilot are not parties to this litigation. The survivors of the five passengers whose estates are represented by Reyno filed a separate action in the United Kingdom against Air Navigation, McDonald, and the pilot's estate. Reyno candidly admits that the action against Piper and Hartzell was filed in the United States because its laws regarding liability, capacity to sue, and damages are more favorable to her position than are those of Scotland. Scottish law does not recognize strict liability in tort. Moreover, it permits wrongful death actions only when brought by a decedent's relatives. The relatives may sue only for "loss of support and society."

On petitioners' motion, the suit was removed to the United States District Court for the Central District of California. Piper then moved for transfer to the United States District Court for the Middle District of Pennsylvania, pursuant to 28 U.S.C. § 1404(a). Hartzell moved to dismiss for lack of personal jurisdiction, or in the alternative, to transfer. In December 1977, the District Court quashed service on Hartzell and transferred the case to the Middle District of Pennsylvania. Respondent then properly served process on Hartzell.

B.

In May 1978, after the suit had been transferred, both Hartzell and Piper moved to dismiss the action on the ground of *forum non conveniens*. The District Court granted these motions in October 1979. It relied on the balancing test set forth by this Court in *Gulf Oil Corp. v. Gilbert*, 330 U.S. 501, 67 S. Ct. 839, 91 L.Ed. 1055 (1947), and its companion case, *Koster v. Lumbermens Mut. Cas. Co.*, 330 U.S. 518, 67 S. Ct. 828, 91 L.Ed. 1067 (1947). In those decisions, the Court stated that a plaintiff's choice of forum should rarely be disturbed. However, when an alternative forum has jurisdiction to hear the case, and when trial in the chosen forum would "establish...oppressiveness and vexation to a defendant...out of all proportion to plaintiff's convenience," or when the "chosen forum [is] inappropriate because of considerations affecting the court's own administrative and legal problems," the court may, in the exercise of its sound discretion, dismiss the case. *Koster*, *supra*, at 524, 67 S. Ct., at 831–832. To guide trial court discretion, the Court provided a list of "private interest factors" affecting the convenience of the litigants, and a list of "public interest factors" affecting the convenience of the forum. *Gilbert*, *supra*, 330 U.S. at 508–509, 67 S. Ct., at 843.

After describing our decisions in *Gilbert* and *Koster*, the District Court analyzed the facts of these cases. It began by observing that an alternative forum existed in Scotland; Piper and Hartzell had agreed to submit to the jurisdiction of the Scottish courts and to waive any statute of limitations defense that might be available. It then stated that plaintiff's choice of forum was entitled to little weight. The court recognized that a plaintiff's choice ordinarily deserves substantial deference. It noted, however, that Reyno "is a representative of foreign citizens and residents seeking a forum in the United States because of the more liberal rules concerning products liability law," and that "the courts have been less solicitous when the plaintiff is not an American citizen or resident, and particularly when the foreign citizens seek to benefit from the more liberal tort rules provided for the protection of citizens and residents of the United States." 479 F. Supp., at 731.

The District Court next examined several factors relating to the private interests of the litigants, and determined that these factors strongly pointed towards Scotland as the appropriate forum. Although evidence concerning the design, manufacture, and testing of the plane and propeller is located in the United States, the connections with Scotland are otherwise "overwhelming." *Id.* at 732. The real parties in interest are citizens of Scotland, as were all the decedents. Witnesses who could testify regarding the maintenance of the aircraft, the training of the pilot, and the investigation of the accident—all essential to the defense—are in Great Britain. Moreover, all witnesses to damages are located in Scotland. Trial would be aided by familiarity with Scottish topography, and by easy access to the wreckage.

The District Court reasoned that because crucial witnesses and evidence were beyond the reach of compulsory process, and because the defendants would not be able to implead potential Scottish third-party defendants, it would be "unfair to make Piper and Hartzell proceed to trial in this forum." *Id.*, at 733. The survivors had brought separate actions in Scotland against the pilot, McDonald, and Air Navigation. "[I]t would be fairer to all parties and less costly if the entire case was presented to one jury with available testimony from all relevant witnesses." *Ibid.* Although the court recognized that if trial were held in the United States, Piper and Hartzell could file indemnity or contribution actions against the Scottish defendants, it believed that there was a significant risk of inconsistent verdicts.

The District Court concluded that the relevant public interests also pointed strongly towards dismissal. The court determined that Pennsylvania law would apply to Piper and Scottish law to Hartzell if the case were tried in the Middle District of Pennsylvania. As a result, "trial in this forum would be hopelessly complex and confusing for a jury." *Id.*, at 734. In addition, the court noted that it was unfamiliar with Scottish law and thus would have to rely upon experts from that country. The court also found that the trial would be enormously costly and time-consuming, that it would be unfair to burden citizens with jury duty when the Middle District of Pennsylvania has little connection with the controversy; and that Scotland has a substantial interest in the outcome of the litigation.

In opposing the motions to dismiss, respondent contended that dismissal would be unfair because Scottish law was less favorable. The District Court explicitly rejected this claim. It reasoned that the possibility that dismissal might lead to an unfavorable change in the law did not deserve significant weight; any deficiency in the foreign law was a "matter to be dealt with in the foreign forum." *Id.*, at 738.

C.

On appeal, the United States Court of Appeals for the Third Circuit reversed and remanded for trial. The decision to reverse appears to be based on two alternative grounds. First, the Court held that the District Court abused its discretion in conducting the *Gilbert* analysis. Second, the Court held that dismissal is never appropriate where the law of the alternative forum is less favorable to the plaintiff.

[. . .]

We granted *certiorari*. . . to consider the questions. . . concerning the proper application of the doctrine of *forum non conveniens*. 450 U.S. 909, 101 S. Ct. 1346, 67 L.Ed.2d 333 (1981).

The Court of Appeals erred in holding that plaintiffs may defeat a motion to dismiss on the ground of *forum non conveniens* merely by showing that the substantive law that would be applied in the alternative forum is less favorable to the plaintiffs than that of the present forum. The possibility of a change in substantive law should ordinarily not be given conclusive or even substantial weight in the *forum non conveniens* inquiry.

[. . .]

Indeed, by holding that the central focus of the *forum non conveniens* inquiry is convenience, *Gilbert* implicitly recognized that dismissal may not be barred solely because of the possibility of an unfavorable change in law. Under *Gilbert*, dismissal will ordinarily be appropriate where trial in the plaintiff's chosen forum imposes a heavy burden on the defendant or the court, and where the plaintiff is unable to offer any specific reasons of convenience supporting his choice. If substantial weight were given to the possibility of an unfavorable change in law, however, dismissal might be barred even where trial in the chosen forum was plainly inconvenient.

The Court of Appeals' decision is inconsistent with this Court's earlier *forum non conveniens* decisions in another respect. Those decisions have repeatedly emphasized the need to retain flexibility. In *Gilbert*, the Court refused to identify specific circumstances "which will justify or require either grant or denial of remedy." 330 U.S., at 508, 67 S. Ct., at 843. Similarly, in *Koster*, the Court rejected the contention that where a trial would involve inquiry into the internal affairs of a foreign corporation, dismissal was always appropriate. That is one, but only one, factor which may show convenience.... If central emphasis were placed on any one factor, the *forum non conveniens* doctrine would lose much of the very flexibility that makes it so valuable.

In fact, if conclusive or substantial weight were given to the possibility of a change in law, the *forum non conveniens* doctrine would become virtually useless. Jurisdiction and venue requirements are often easily satisfied. As a result, many plaintiffs are able to choose from among several forums. Ordinarily, these plaintiffs will select that forum whose choice-of-law rules are most advantageous. Thus, if the possibility of an unfavorable change in substantive law is given substantial weight in the *forum non conveniens* inquiry, dismissal would rarely be proper.

[. . .]

The Court of Appeals' approach is not only inconsistent with the purpose of the *forum non conveniens* doctrine, but also poses substantial practical problems. If the possibility of a change in law were given substantial weight, deciding motions to dismiss on the ground of *forum non conveniens* would become quite difficult. Choice-of-law analysis would become extremely important, and the courts would frequently be required to interpret the law of foreign jurisdictions. First, the trial court would have to determine what law would apply if the case were tried in the chosen forum, and what law would apply if the case were tried in the alternative forum. It would then have to compare the rights, remedies, and procedures available under the law that would be applied in each forum. Dismissal would be appropriate only if the court concluded that the law applied by the alternative forum is as favorable to the plaintiff as that of the chosen forum. The doctrine of *forum non conveniens*, however, is designed in part to help courts avoid conducting complex exercises in comparative law. As we stated in *Gilbert*, the public interest factors point towards dismissal where the court would be required to "untangle problems in conflict of law, and in law foreign to itself." 330 U.S., at 509, 67 S. Ct., at 843.

Upholding the decision of the Court of Appeals would result in other practical problems. At least where the foreign plaintiff named an American manufacturer as defendant, a court could not dismiss the case on grounds of *forum non conveniens* where dismissal might lead to an unfavorable change in law. The American courts, which are already extremely attractive to foreign plaintiffs, would become even more attractive. The flow of litigation into the United States would increase and further congest already crowded courts.

[. . .]

We do not hold that the possibility of an unfavorable change in law should never be a relevant consideration in a *forum non conveniens* inquiry. Of course, if the remedy provided by the alternative forum is so clearly inadequate or unsatisfactory that it is no remedy at all, the unfavorable change in law may be given substantial weight; the district court may conclude that dismissal would not be in the interests of justice. In these cases, however, the remedies that would be provided by the Scottish courts do not fall within this category. Although the relatives of the decedents may not be able to rely on a strict liability theory, and although their potential damages award may be smaller, there is no danger that they will be deprived of any remedy or treated unfairly.

III.

The Court of Appeals also erred in rejecting the District Court's *Gilbert* analysis. The Court of Appeals stated that more weight should have been given to the plaintiff's choice of forum, and criticized the District Court's analysis of the private and public interests. However, the District Court's decision regarding the deference due plaintiff's choice of forum was appropriate. Furthermore, we do not believe that the District Court abused its discretion in weighing the private and public interests.

A.

The District Court acknowledged that there is ordinarily a strong presumption in favor of the plaintiff's choice of forum, which may be overcome only when the private and public interest factors clearly point towards trial in the alternative forum. It held, however, that the presumption applies with less force when the plaintiff or real parties in interest are foreign.

The District Court's distinction between resident or citizen plaintiffs and foreign plaintiffs is fully justified. In *Koster*, the Court indicated that a plaintiff's choice of forum is entitled to greater deference when the plaintiff has chosen the home forum.... When the home forum has been chosen, it is reasonable to assume that this choice is convenient. When the plaintiff is foreign, however, this assumption is much less reasonable. Because the central purpose of any *forum non conveniens* inquiry is to ensure that the trial is convenient, a foreign plaintiff's choice deserves less deference.

B.

The *forum non conveniens* determination is committed to the sound discretion of the trial court. It may be reversed only when there has been a clear abuse of discretion; where the court has considered all relevant public and private interest factors, and where its balancing of these factors is reasonable, its decision deserves substantial deference.... Here, the Court of Appeals expressly acknowledged that the standard of review was one of abuse of discretion. In examining the District Court's analysis of the public and private interests, however, the Court of Appeals seems to have lost sight of this rule, and substituted its own judgment for that of the District Court.

(1)

In analyzing the private interest factors, the District Court stated that the connections with Scotland are "overwhelming." 479 F. Supp., at 732. This characterization may be somewhat exaggerated. Particularly with respect to the question of relative ease of access to sources of proof, the private interests point in both directions. As respondent emphasizes, records concerning the design, manufacture, and testing of the propeller and plane are located in the United States. She would have greater access to sources of proof relevant to her strict liability and negligence theories if trial were held here. However, the District Court did not act unreasonably in concluding that fewer evidentiary problems would be posed if the trial were held in Scotland. A large proportion of the relevant evidence is located in Great Britain.

[...]

The District Court correctly concluded that the problems posed by the inability to implead potential third-party defendants clearly supported holding the trial in Scotland. Joinder of the pilot's estate, Air Navigation, and McDonald is crucial to the presentation of petitioners' defense....

(2)

The District Court's review of the factors relating to the public interest was also reasonable....

Scotland has a very strong interest in this litigation. The accident occurred in its airspace. All of the decedents were Scottish. Apart from Piper and Hartzell, all potential plaintiffs and defendants are either Scottish or English. As we stated in *Gilbert*, there is "a local interest in having localized controversies decided at home." 330 U.S., at 509, 67 S. Ct., at 843. Respondent argues that American citizens have an interest in ensuring that American manufacturers are deterred from producing defective products, and that additional deterrence might be obtained if Piper and Hartzell were tried in the United States, where they could be sued on the basis of both negligence and strict liability. However, the incremental deterrence that would be gained if this trial were held in an American court is likely to be insignificant. The American interest in this accident is simply not sufficient to justify the enormous commitment of judicial time and resources that would inevitably be required if the case were to be tried here.

[. . .]

Notes and Questions

The circumstances of the case constitute an excellent illustration of a transborder litigation case: There are several relevant nationalities and fora. The central question is not where the litigation can be brought, but rather whether it can remain before a U.S. federal court. What are the public and private interest factors and how does the Court rate them in relation to each other? How much play does trial court discretion have in applying the *forum non conveniens* doctrine? Why is the plaintiff precluded from suit where the most favorable law governs? Is the Court's concept of *forum non conveniens* inspired by the need to manage judicial resources? Primarily? Is State involvement or interest more central?

* * * *

IN RE AIR CRASH DISASTER NEAR BOMBAY, INDIA ON JANUARY 1, 1978

531 F.Supp. 1175 (W.D. Wash. 1982).

(footnotes omitted)

FITZGERALD, District Judge.

On New Year's Day 1978, an Air India Boeing 747 aircraft crashed into the sea shortly after takeoff from Santa Cruz Airport, Bombay, India. All persons aboard, nearly all of whom were Indian Nationals, were killed. After claims against Air India had been settled, the personal representatives of the deceased brought their claims to several United States district courts alleging that the accident was caused by a malfunction in certain components of the aircraft. Plaintiffs contend the United States district courts provide the only proper forum for their claims since the defendants are United States corporations and proof of defendants' liability is to be found among documents and witnesses under defendants' control in the United States. Defendants have taken a contrary position claiming the loss of the aircraft and all persons aboard occurred as a result of faulty operational control of the aircraft and was the responsibility of the pilot and crew. The evidence relied upon to support defendants' position is therefore all in India. Presently before the court are two motions, one to dismiss on the basis of *forum non conveniens* and the other asking for an order settling choice of law issues.... With respect to the *forum non conveniens* motion all defendants have agreed: (1) to submit to the jurisdiction of the courts of India; (2) to make their employees available to testify in India; and (3) to waive any applicable Indian statute of limitations.

A. *Forum Non Conveniens*

The controlling federal decision on *forum non conveniens* is *Gulf Oil Corp. v. Gilbert*, 330 U.S. 501, 67 S. Ct. 839, 91 L.Ed. 1055 (1947). "The principle of *forum non conveniens* is simply that a court may resist imposition upon its jurisdiction even when jurisdiction is authorized by the letter of a general venue statute." *Id.* at 507, 67 S. Ct. at 842. The Court observed that the applicability of the *forum non conveniens* doctrine lies within the sound discretion of the trial court and rests upon consideration of various factors:

> If the combination and weight of factors requisite to given results are difficult to forecast or state, those to be considered are not difficult to name. An interest to be considered, and the one likely to be most pressed, is the private interest of the litigant. Important considerations are the relative ease of access to sources of proof; availability of compulsory process for attendance of unwilling, and the cost of obtaining attendance of willing, witnesses; possibility of view of premises, if view would be appropriate to the action; and all other practical problems that make trial of a case easy, expeditious and inexpensive. There may also be questions as to the enforceability of a judgment if one is obtained. The court will weigh relative advantages and obstacles to fair trial. It is often said that the plaintiff may not, by choice of an inconvenient forum, 'vex,' 'harass,' or 'oppress' the defendant by inflicting upon him expense or trouble not necessary to his own right to pursue his remedy. But unless the balance is strongly in favor of the defendant, the plaintiff's choice of forum should rarely be disturbed.

Id. at 508, 67 S. Ct. at 843. In addition, the Court identified a number of policy considerations which necessarily ought to be taken into account:

> Administrative difficulties follow for courts when litigation is piled up in congested centers instead of being handled at its origin. Jury duty is a burden that ought not to be imposed upon the people of a community which has no relation to the litigation. In cases which touch [the] affairs of many persons, there is reason for holding the trial in their view and reach rather than in remote parts of the country where they can learn of it by report only. There is a local interest in having localized controversies decided at home. There is

> an appropriateness, too, in having the trial of a diversity case in a forum that is at home with the state law that must govern the case, rather than having a court in some other forum untangle problems in conflict of laws, and in law foreign to itself.

Id. at 508–09, 67 S. Ct. at 843.

[. . .]

Because the location of this evidence is in India, defendants doubt their ability to offer an adequate defense at a trial in the United States. They maintain that Air India and responsible agencies of the government of India have consistently thwarted defendants' attempts to obtain documentary and tangible evidence necessary to the defense of these actions. Defendants assert that 1) most of the witnesses in India would be unwilling witnesses whose attendance in a United States court cannot be compelled; and 2) as to those witnesses willing to testify in the United States, the cost of obtaining their attendance would be prohibitive. Consequently, defendants believe they would be forced to present their evidence at trial primarily through the use of depositions. They point out that in *Gulf Oil* the [U.S.] Supreme Court recognized the need for live testimony at trial:

> [T]o fix the place of trial at a point where litigants cannot compel personal attendance and may be forced to try their cases on depositions, is to create a condition not satisfactory to court, jury or most litigants.

330 U.S. at 511, 67 S. Ct. at 844.

[. . .]

Finally, defendants suggest that India has the only true interest in this litigation. India, as the domicile of almost all of the decedents and beneficiaries, has a compelling interest in ensuring fair compensation to the victims of this tragedy. India has a legitimate interest in the safety of India's air transportation and the integrity and operational efficiency of Air India, a governmental entity.

There is merit in defendants' arguments. Evidence relating to operational control and maintenance of the aircraft is located in India. Serious problems have been encountered in efforts to obtain evidence from Indian government agencies regarding the official investigation into the crash and the preparation of the official government report concerning the accident. . . .

Obviously, production of evidence in India or testimony of Indian witnesses cannot be compelled by United States district courts. Faced with similar situations, other courts have not hesitated to dismiss cases on *forum non conveniens* grounds. *See, e.g., Dahl v. United Technologies Corp.*, 472 F. Supp. 696 (D. Del. 1979), *aff'd.*, 632 F.2d 1027 (3d Cir. 1980); *Grodinsky v. Fairchild Industries, Inc.*, 507 F. Supp. 1245 (D. Md. 1981). Given the evidentiary problems inherent in trying this case in the United States, the discovery problems already encountered, and the fact that the accident occurred in India and involves foreign plaintiffs, I believe that this case should be tried in the courts of India if at all possible.

[. . .]

Notes and Questions

Can the court's interpretation and use of the *forum non conveniens* doctrine be separated from their impact upon the merits? Does this decision insulate the manufacturer of the aircraft from liability? What about the accountability of MNEs? Can an operational cause and product cause of the mishap ever be persuasively distinguished? Why does the Indian Government's foot-dragging make U.S. litigation potentially ineffective? Wouldn't a finding of liability in India preclude an additional and duplicative remedy in the United States? Does victim nationality have a critical bearing in the determination? Should it? Is there a presumption against U.S.-based foreign litigation that precedes the application of the balancing test? Is the result here the opposite extreme of *TACA International*? Is holding this litigation in the United States inconceivable? Why?

* * * *

DOW CHEMICAL CO. v. CASTRO ALFARO

786 S.W.2d 674 (Tex. 1990),
cert. denied, 498 U.S. 1024, 111 S.Ct. 671, 112 L.Ed.2d 663 (1991).

RAY, Justice.

At issue in this cause is whether the statutory right to enforce a personal injury or wrongful death claim in the Texas courts precludes a trial court from dismissing the claim on the ground of *forum non conveniens*. The court of appeals held that Texas courts lack the authority to dismiss on the grounds of *forum non conveniens*. 751 S.W.2d 208. Because we conclude that the legislature has statutorily abolished the doctrine of *forum non conveniens* in suits brought under section 71.031 of the Texas Civil Practice and Remedies Code, we affirm the judgment of the court of appeals.

Domingo Castro Alfaro, a Costa Rican resident and employee of the Standard Fruit Company, and eighty-one other Costa Rican employees and their wives brought suit against Dow Chemical Company and Shell Oil Company. The employees claim that they suffered personal injuries as a result of exposure to dibromochloropropane (DBCP), a pesticide manufactured by Dow and Shell, which was allegedly furnished to Standard Fruit. The employees exposed to DBCP allegedly suffered several medical problems, including sterility.

Alfaro sued Dow and Shell in Harris County district court in April 1984. The amended petition alleged that the court had jurisdiction under article 4678 of the Revised Statutes. Following an unsuccessful attempt to remove the suit to federal court, Dow and Shell contested the jurisdiction of the trial court almost three years after the filing of the suit, and contended in the alternative that the case should be dismissed under the doctrine of *forum non conveniens*. Despite a finding of jurisdiction, the trial court dismissed the case on the ground of *forum non conveniens*.

Section 71.031 of the Civil Practice and Remedies Code provides:

> (a) An action for damages for the death or personal injury of a citizen of this state, of the United States, or of a foreign country may be enforced in the courts of this state, although the wrongful act, neglect, or default causing the death or injury takes place in a foreign state or country, if;
>
> (1) a law of the foreign state or country or of this state gives a right to maintain an action for damages for the death or injury;
>
> (2) the action is begun in this state within the time provided by the laws of this state for beginning the action; and
>
> (3) in the case of a citizen of a foreign country, the country has equal treaty rights with the United States on behalf of its citizens.
>
> (b) All matters pertaining to procedure in the prosecution or maintenance of the action in the courts of this state are governed by the law of this state.
>
> (c) The court shall apply the rules of substantive law that are appropriate under the facts of the case.

Tex. Civ. Prac. & Rem. Code Ann. § 71.031 (Vernon 1986). At issue is whether the language "may be enforced in the courts of this state" of Section 71.031(a) permits a trial court to relinquish jurisdiction under the doctrine of *forum non conveniens*.

The statutory predecessors of Section 71.031 have existed since 1913. The original law states "[t]hat whenever the death or personal injury of a citizen of this State or of a country having equal treaty rights with the United States on behalf of its citizens, has been or may be caused by a wrongful act, neglect or default...such right of action may be enforced...in the courts of this State...."...

Dow and Shell argued before this Court that the legislature did not intend to make section 71.031 a guarantee of an absolute right to enforce a suit in Texas brought under that provision. In his dissent, Justice Gonzalez agrees, concluding that the legislature could not have intended to preclude application of *forum non conveniens* to suits brought under the statute because "*[f]orum non conveniens* did not arrive upon the judicial landscape of this state until after the predecessors to section 71.031 were enacted." 786 S.W.2d 691. This conclusion is false. The doctrine of *forum non conveniens* appeared in Texas well before the enactment of article 4678 by the legislature in 1913.

[...]

Texas courts applied the doctrine of *forum non conveniens* in several cases prior to the enactment of article 4678 in 1913. In 1890, this court in *dicta* recognized the power of a court to refuse to exercise jurisdiction on grounds essentially the same as those of *forum non conveniens. See Morris v. Missouri Pac. Ry.*, 78 Tex. 17, 21, 14 S.W. 228, 230 (1890). In *Morris*, we stated:

> We do not think the facts alleged show the action to be transitory. But, if so, it has been held in such actions, where the parties were non-residents and the cause of action originated beyond the limits of the state, these facts would justify the court in refusing to entertain jurisdiction. *Railway Co. v. Miller*, 19 Mich. 305. Jurisdiction is entertained in such cases only upon principles of comity, and not as a matter of right. *Gardner v. Thomas*, 14 Johns. 136; Wells, Juris. § 115.

Id. In *Mexican National Railroad v. Jackson*, 89 Tex. 107, 33 S.W. 857 (1896), this court discussed both the dissimilarity doctrine and the potentiality of docket backlog. With regard to the latter, we stated:

> If our courts assume to adjust the rights of parties against those railroads, growing out of such facts as in this case, we will offer an invitation to all such persons who might prefer to resort to tribunals in which the rules of procedure are more certainly fixed, and the trial by jury secured, to seek the courts of this state to enforce their claims. Thus we would add to the already overburdened condition of our dockets in all the courts, and thereby make the settlement of rights originating outside the state, under the laws of a different government, a charge upon our own people.

Id., 89 Tex. at 112, 33 S.W. at 862. Finally, we made a statement closely resembling a current argument for *forum non conveniens*:

> If the facts showed that this [suit] was necessary in order to secure justice, and the laws were such as we could properly enforce, this consideration [docket backlog] would have but little weight; but we feel that it is entitled to be considered *where the plaintiff chooses this jurisdiction as a matter of convenience, and not of necessity.*

Id. (Emphasis added).

In *Southern Pacific Co. v. Graham*, 12 Tex. Civ. App. 565, 34 S.W. 135 (1896, writ ref'd), the court stated that a district court could, in the exercise of its sound discretion, refuse to entertain jurisdiction in a case involving foreign parties. In *Missouri, Kansas & Texas Railway v. Godair Commission Co.*, 39 Tex. Civ. App. 298, 87 S.W. 871 (1905, writ ref'd), the court stated:

> Appellant's first proposition . . . is . . . that all parties being nonresidents, and the injuries complained of having occurred outside of the state of Texas, the courts of this state are not bound to entertain jurisdiction. The language of this proposition implies that the state courts may entertain jurisdiction of causes in which all parties are nonresidents when the injuries complained of occurred outside of the state, though they are not bound to do so. This being true, the court in this case having entertained jurisdiction, and thus [having]

> determined the question of public policy in favor of entertaining jurisdiction, the appellant has no right to complain.

Id. 39 Tex. Civ. App. at 301; 87 S.W. at 872. Thus, although Justice Gonzalez is correct that the first reported case using the term "*forum non conveniens*" is *Garrett v. Phillips Petroleum Co.*, 218 S.W.2d 238, 239 (Tex. Civ. App.—Amarillo 1949, writ dism'd), the doctrine itself was effectively established in Texas before the enactment of article 4678 by the legislature in 1913.

II.

We therefore must determine whether the legislature in 1913 statutorily abolished the doctrine of *forum non conveniens* in suits brought under article 4678 [now section 71.031].

[. . .]

Asking that this court reverse the decision of the Court of Civil Appeals and affirm the judgment of the trial court dismissing the action, the petitioners in *Allen* quoted from *Atchison, T. & S.F. Ry. Co. v. Weeks*, 254 F. 513 (5th Cir. 1918). *Id.* at 5. In *Weeks*, the United States Court of Appeals for the Fifth Circuit discussed several of the same rationales given today for the application of the doctrine of *forum non conveniens*:

> Manifestly, there are many advantages in trying such a case where the cause of action arises. The law of the cause of action is the law of the place. It may be assumed that the courts of the state can more satisfactorily administer the laws of the state than can the courts of any other state. The expense incident to a trial would usually be materially less at the place of the tort than elsewhere. The imposition upon a state of the expense of maintaining courts to try causes in which the state has no interest would be difficult to justify. The maintenance of the judicial machinery involves no light burden. Many of the states, including Texas, have been unable to provide adequate machinery. No good reason could probably be made to appear why her overworked courts should be compelled to carry any part of the burdens of other states.

[. . .]

We conclude that the legislature has statutorily abolished the doctrine of *forum non conveniens* in suits brought under section 71.031. Accordingly, we affirm the judgment of the court of appeals, remanding the cause to the trial court for further proceedings.

Notes and Questions

In a concurring opinion Justice Doggett stated that: "Both as a matter of law and of public policy, the doctrine of *forum non conveniens* is without justification.... In fact, the doctrine is favored by multinational defendants because a *forum non conveniens* dismissal is often outcome–determinative, effectively defeating the claim and denying the plaintiff recovery." What is your assessment?

Do unstated policy factors dominate the court's reasoning in *Dow Chemical*? Is that policy justified or valid in light of the court's authority? How are equivalent rights by treaty to be determined? Do they function in the opinion? Why doesn't the occurrence of the harm in a foreign venue resolve the jurisdictional issue? Is *forum non conveniens* or some version of it embedded in other doctrines necessary to contain expansionist and exorbitant assertions of judicial jurisdiction?

Assuming that Dow Chemical was unaware of the effect of the product or that the Dow Chemical product was a major causative agent of the plaintiff's injury, why should Costa Rican workers be entitled to U.S. process or U.S.-measured damages? Isn't the law of the place of investment controlling? Shouldn't Dow Chemical be entitled to benefit from the local law or at least have it measure or anticipate the quantum of its potential liability? Wouldn't a rational business plan factor in lower liability exposure and lower insurance costs? Isn't the court's ruling *post facto* and doesn't it constitute unfair surprise? If entry to U.S. courts is allowed, should special procedures apply like placing a ceiling on damages? Does a bias against successful companies and merchants permeate the judiciary? Is that a fair observation? Why is Costa Rica exempt from regulatory responsibility? Shouldn't the Texas state legislature correct the court's eccentric historical revisionism?

§ 3. PARALLEL PROCEEDINGS AND THE ANTI-SUIT INJUNCTION

Judicial jurisdiction can also be affected by the actions of foreign courts. Parties to an international tort or contract dispute can file lawsuits in a number of jurisdictions for various reasons: To retaliate against the other side by increasing the costs and complications of dispute resolution; to obtain a better opportunity for a favorable result; for other litigious advantage; or to hedge against the uncertainty of judgment enforcement. These circumstances demonstrate the critical need for an international agreement on the assertion of judicial jurisdiction. Further, they illustrate the type of conflicts that can be created as result of competing national legal actions. The choice of a single proper forum for litigation would obviate many of the difficulties and increase the efficiency and effectiveness of transborder litigation. A workable and reasonably orderly system should be preferable to a chaotic one. Any international consensus on this matter, however, remains elusive—even between like-minded States. The unwillingness to surrender national prerogatives is especially strong with respect to adjudicatory authority.

The anti-suit injunction is a device by which courts can attempt to force the selection of a single venue for suit and by which they can safeguard their authority. Once a court asserts jurisdiction properly under its law and receives notice of a parallel action in another country, it can issue an anti-suit injunction, prohibiting a litigating party from proceeding in the foreign court. The foreign court can respond by issuing its own anti-suit injunction against the other party. With an irreconcilable clash of authority, the resolution of the dispute becomes more uncertain, more difficult, and more expensive.

From a more measured perspective, the anti-suit injunction is perceived by many courts to be a form of extraordinary relief. It is intended to apply in circumstances of bad faith litigation practices that impede justified recovery by creating unnecessary delay, costs, and inconvenience. Anti-suit injunctions run coarsely against the grain of deference and mutual respect. They represent aggression, intolerance, and intrusion. Given judicial temperaments and the stake placed in national autonomy and independence, anti-suit injunctions are unlikely to succeed. They may, in fact, generate even greater conflict by creating foreign policy and diplomatic problems.

In any event, the federal courts are split on the utility and desirability of anti-suit injunctions. The Fifth, Seventh, and Ninth Circuits are more likely to issue them in order to avoid nonsensical litigation or duplication, whereas the Second, Sixth, and D.C. Circuits rarely grant requests for anti-suit injunctions. They deem them to violate comity and frustrate international judicial assistance.

Generally, requests for anti-suit injunctions are unlikely to be granted against foreign litigation that has progressed substantially. The policy favoring the efficient use of judicial resources will prevail in all but truly exceptional circumstances. If a U.S. court accedes to the order of the foreign tribunal in these circumstances, the result will usually be a conditional stay or dismissal. In *China Trade & Development Corp. v. M/V Choong Yong*, 837 F.2d 33, 36 (2d Cir. 1987), the Second Circuit established a number of basic requirements for issuing an anti-suit injunction. The action would be warranted if a policy of the issuing forum were being frustrated or evaded; if the lawsuit abroad were vexatious in character; if the foreign action undermined the issuing court's authority and jurisdiction. In addition, the anti-suit injunction could be used to stem a race to judgment or to avoid delay, costs, and inconvenience. It can also be a device by which a U.S. court declares that it is the best venue for conducting the litigation—in effect, a *forum non conveniens* ruling in reverse. Further, it can be used to express the view that, if all other factors are equal, the tribunal in which the suit was initially filed should have exclusive jurisdiction.

GAU SHAN CO., LTD. v. BANKERS TRUST CO.

956 F.2d 1349 (6th Cir. 1992).

[International comity precludes an anti-suit injunction].

RYAN, Circuit Judge.

This is an appeal from a preliminary injunction enjoining defendant Bankers Trust Company, an American corporation, from filing a lawsuit in Hong Kong against plaintiff Gau Shan Company, a Hong Kong corporation. The issue for decision is whether the district court offended principles of international comity in issuing its preliminary injunction.

We conclude that the lower court misinterpreted the relevant principles of international comity and, as a result, abused its discretion in restraining Bankers Trust from prosecuting the foreign action. Therefore, we reverse.

I.

Gau Shan Company is a cotton merchant engaged in marketing cotton to the People's Republic of China. One of Gau Shan's sources for American cotton was the Julien Company, a Tennessee corporation. Bankers Trust was the primary source of Julien's financing for its cotton sales. Gau Shan became aware of Bankers Trust through its dealings with Julien.

[. . .]

A. International Comity

It is well settled that American courts have the "power to control the conduct of persons subject to their jurisdiction to the extent of forbidding them from suing in foreign jurisdictions." *Laker Airways Ltd. v. Sabena, Belgian World Airlines*, 731 F.2d 909, 926 (D.C. Cir. 1984) (footnote omitted). However, "parallel proceedings on the same *in personam* claim should ordinarily be allowed to proceed simultaneously, at least until a judgment is reached in one [jurisdiction] which can be pled as *res judicata* in the other." *Id.* at 926–27 (footnote omitted). For this reason, injunctions "restraining litigants from proceeding in courts of independent countries are rarely issued." *Id.* at 927. (Footnote omitted).

The circuits are split concerning the proper standards to be applied, in the context of considerations of international comity, in determining whether a foreign antisuit injunction should be issued. The Ninth and Fifth Circuits hold that a duplication of the parties and issues, alone, is generally sufficient to justify the issuance of such an injunction. *See, e.g., Seattle Totems Hockey Club, Inc. v. National Hockey League*, 652 F.2d 852, 856 (9th Cir. 1981), *cert. denied*, 457 U.S. 1105, 102 S. Ct. 2902, 73 L.Ed.2d 1313 (1982); *In re Unterweser Reederei, GmbH*, 428 F.2d 888, 896 (5th Cir. 1970), *rev'd on other grounds*, 407 U.S. 1, 92 S. Ct. 1907, 32 L.Ed.2d 513 (1972). These courts rely primarily upon considerations of vexatiousness or oppressiveness in a race to judgment in the foreign forum as sufficient grounds for an injunction. But, the Second and D.C. Circuits have held that the standard for granting a foreign antisuit injunction is whether the injunction is necessary to protect the forum court's jurisdiction or to prevent evasion of the forum court's important public policies. *See, e.g., Sea Containers Ltd. v. Stena AB*, 890 F.2d 1205, 1214 (D.C. Cir. 1989); *China Trade & Dev. Corp. v. M/V. Choong Yong*, 837 F.2d 33, 36 (2d Cir. 1987); *Laker Airways*, 731 F.2d at 927, 937. This circuit has not addressed the question.

1. Fifth and Ninth Circuits' View

In *Seattle Totems*, the Ninth Circuit affirmed the issuance of an antisuit injunction against the defendants in an antitrust suit brought against the National Hockey League (NHL) which had sought to file a suit involving the same breach of contract claim in Canadian courts. 652 F.2d at 856. The NHL, plaintiffs in the Canadian action, admitted that under Fed. R. Civ. P. 13(a) their contract claim would constitute a compulsory counterclaim in the antitrust lawsuit pending in the United States court. *Id.* at 853. However, Canadian law did not require that the defendant raise its compulsory counterclaim. *Id.* at 854. The Ninth Circuit found that the district court properly invoked Rule 13(a) to govern the pending litigation rather than Canadian law and held that the injunction against the Canadian suit was proper. *Id.* at 853–54.

The court in *Seattle Totems* stated that "foreign litigation may be enjoined when it would (1) frustrate a policy of the forum issuing the injunction; (2) be vexatious or oppressive; (3) threaten the issuing courts [sic] [court's] in rem or quasi in rem jurisdiction, or (4) where the proceedings prejudice other equitable considerations." *Id.* at 855. The court held that the lower court did not abuse its discretion by enjoining the prosecution of the contract claim in Canada in view of relevant factors, including "the convenience to the parties and witnesses, the interests of the court in promoting the efficient administration of justice and the potential prejudice to one party or another." *Id.* at 856.

The court in *Seattle Totems* cited as authority the Fifth Circuit case in *In re Unterweser Reederei*, 428 F.2d 888, 896 (5th Cir. 1970), wherein the Fifth Circuit affirmed the lower court's decision enjoining one of the parties from prosecuting in English courts a claim which had been pled as a counterclaim in the pending district court action. The Fifth Circuit stated that, "allowing simultaneous prosecution of the same action in a foreign forum thousands of miles away would result in 'inequitable hardship' and 'tend to frustrate and delay the speedy and efficient determination of the cause.' "*Id.* at 896 (footnote omitted).

Thus, the Fifth and Ninth Circuits hold that a duplication of the parties and issues, alone, is sufficient to justify a foreign antisuit injunction.

2. *Second and D.C. Circuits' View*

In *Laker Airways*, American and other non-British defendants were enjoined from seeking relief in English courts as an attempt to escape United States antitrust laws for their conduct in the United States. 731 F.2d at 956. The D.C. Circuit upheld the trial court's injunction, finding that the antitrust laws were clearly applicable to the conduct which was the subject of the claims. The court held that "a preliminary injunction [was] imperative to preserve the court's jurisdiction." *Id.*

Similarly, the Second Circuit adopted the *Laker Airways* analysis in deciding to reverse the lower court's decision to issue an injunction. *China Trade*, 837 F.2d at 35. The Second Circuit held that a foreign antisuit injunction was not justified because the Korean litigation did not threaten the district court's jurisdiction or threaten any important public policies. *Id.* at 37.

Thus, the Second and D.C. Circuits hold that the only proper grounds to grant a foreign antisuit injunctions are: 1) to protect the forum's jurisdiction, or 2) to prevent evasion of the forum's important public policies. These circuits hold that a duplication of the parties and issues, alone, is not sufficient to justify a foreign antisuit injunction. *China Trade*, 837 F.2d at 36; *Laker Airways*, 731 F.2d at 928.

The district court in this case, in concluding that the dictates of international comity did not preclude the issuance of an injunction here, did not adopt the approaches of either the Fifth and Ninth Circuits or the Second and D.C. Circuits. Instead, the court used elements from each and found that because parallel proceedings duplicate the parties and issues, the federal courts' important public policy of a just, speedy and inexpensive determination of every action under Fed. R. Civ. P. 1 and 13 would be evaded should Bankers Trust be permitted to sue Gau Shan in Hong Kong. Gau Shan agrees and argues that these and other factors favor litigation of Bankers Trust's collection claim in Tennessee.

Bankers Trust responds that this court should adopt the analysis of the Second and D.C. Circuits that a foreign antisuit injunction should issue only when the foreign proceeding 1) threatens the jurisdiction of the United States court, or 2) evades strong public policies of the United States. Bankers Trust contends there is no threat to this court's jurisdiction because the Hong Kong suit would not affect this suit. It also contends that a suit in Hong Kong would not evade any important public policies of the United States. We agree.

III.

Comity dictates that foreign antisuit injunctions be issued sparingly and only in the rarest of cases. *Laker Airways*, 731 F.2d at 927. The days of American hegemony over international economic affairs have long since passed. The United States cannot today impose its economic will on the rest of the world and expect meek compliance, if indeed it ever could. The modern era is one of world economic interdependence, and economic interdependence requires cooperation and comity between nations. In an increasingly international market, commercial transactions involving players from multiple nations have become commonplace. Every one of these transactions presents the possibility of concurrent jurisdiction in the courts of the nations of the parties involved concerning any dispute arising in the transaction. This case is an example. Here, we have the possibility of concurrent jurisdiction in Hong Kong and the United States. Gau Shan asks this court to disregard the principles of international comity and affirm the issuance of an antisuit injunction which effectively denies the Hong Kong court jurisdiction over a matter otherwise properly before it, and reserves to a United States court exclusive jurisdiction over a dispute involving parties from different nations. Before taking such a drastic step, this court must consider carefully the implications of such action under principles of international comity.

Although an antisuit injunction does not directly interfere in a foreign court's jurisdiction, it "effectively restrict[s] the foreign court's ability to exercise its jurisdiction." *Laker Airways*, 731 F.2d at 927. In this case, for example, the injunction restricts the Hong Kong court's ability to exercise its jurisdiction by enjoining Bankers Trust from bringing suit in Hong Kong. In a case in which parties to an international transaction file separate suits in different forums, the availability of antisuit injunctions presents the possibility that no relief will be granted. If both the foreign court and the United States court issue injunctions preventing their respective nationals from prosecuting a suit in the foreign forum, both actions will be paralyzed and neither party will be able to obtain any relief. The more readily courts resort to this extraordinary device, the more frequently this sort of undesirable stalemate will occur.

The inappropriate use of antisuit injunctions can have unintended, widespread effects. International commerce depends in no small part on the ability of merchants to predict the likely consequences of their conduct in overseas markets. Predictability depends in turn on an atmosphere of cooperation and reciprocity between nations. The issuance of antisuit injunctions threatens predictability by making cooperation and reciprocity between courts of different nations less likely.

In this regard, antisuit injunctions are even more destructive of international comity than, for example, refusals to enforce foreign judgments. At least in the latter context foreign courts are given the opportunity to exercise their jurisdiction. Antisuit injunctions, on the other hand, deny foreign courts the right to exercise their proper jurisdiction. Such action conveys the message, intended or not, that the issuing court has so little confidence in the foreign court's ability to adjudicate a given dispute fairly and efficiently that it is unwilling even to allow the possibility. Foreign courts can be expected to reciprocate such disrespect. Reciprocity and cooperation can only suffer as a result. Accordingly, foreign antisuit injunctions should be issued only in the most extreme cases.

[. . .]

Factors such as "vexatiousness" or "oppressiveness" and a "race to judgment" are "likely to be present whenever parallel actions are proceeding concurrently." *China Trade*, 837 F.2d at 36. An antisuit injunction based upon these factors would tend to debilitate the policy that permits parallel actions to continue and that disfavors antisuit injunctions. *Id.* We think the reasoning of the Second and D.C. Circuits, identifying the proper criteria for issuance of antisuit injunctions, more satisfactorily accommodates the important principles of international comity a federal court should take into account. . . .

[. . .]

Notes and Questions

Judicial comity discourages unilateralism and inhospitable assertions of jurisdiction. This practice leads to relative harmony among national and foreign courts because there are no attempts to exorbitantly and unlawfully police each other's judicial authority. In extraordinary and rare circumstances, situations can arise in which there is manifestly a single tribunal that should exercise jurisdiction. The means for expressing such a conclusion, however, probably should not be an order directed at one of the litigating parties, but a type of letter of request addressed to the foreign court before which the parallel action has been filed. In the document, the issuing court would make its case to the other tribunal, for example, on the basis of the impact of the litigation upon national or local interests, nationality factors, public policy, or upon some other suitable basis. The foreign tribunal could choose to acquiesce to or reject the request. Is this a better approach or system? How likely is it to work? What are the potential problems?

Of the two rationales advanced for anti-suit injunctions—policing the conduct of wayward litigants or protecting fundamental national interests, which do you find more persuasive and for what reason(s)? Should there be a legislative rule, a U.S. Supreme Court opinion, or a treaty provision? What is the *Laker Airways* analysis? Is economic interdependence or the internationalization of the marketplace a good basis for adopting a policy of meekness? Why should stammering at a problem provide resolution? Is the management of judicial resources part of U.S. public policy interests? Who says? How can a court justify limiting a litigant's freedom of action and choice in relation to other tribunals? Is the issuing court really trying to control or define a foreign court's jurisdiction?

* * * *

KAEPA, INC. v. ACHILLES CORP.

76 F.3d 624 (5th Cir. 1996)

[Upholding issuance of anti-suit injunction].

(footnotes omitted)

WIENER, Circuit Judge:

The primary issue presented by this appeal is whether the district court erred by enjoining Defendant–Appellant Achilles Corporation from prosecuting an action that it filed in Japan as plaintiff, which essentially mirrored a lawsuit previously filed by Plaintiff–Appellee Kaepa, Inc. in state court and then being prosecuted in federal district court by Kaepa. Given the private nature of the dispute, the clear indications by both parties that claims arising from their contract should be adjudicated in this country, and the duplicative and vexatious nature of the Japanese action, we conclude that the district court did not abuse its discretion by barring the prosecution of the foreign litigation. Accordingly, we affirm the grant of the antisuit injunction.

I. Facts and Proceedings

This case arises out of a contractual dispute between two sophisticated, private corporations: Kaepa, an American company which manufactures athletic shoes; and Achilles, a Japanese business enterprise with annual sales that approximate one billion dollars. In April 1993, the two companies entered into a distributorship agreement whereby Achilles obtained exclusive rights to market Kaepa's footwear in Japan. The distributorship agreement expressly provided that Texas law and the English language would govern its interpretation, that it would be enforceable in San Antonio, Texas, and that Achilles consented to the jurisdiction of the Texas courts.

Kaepa grew increasingly dissatisfied with Achilles's performance under the contract. Accordingly, in July of 1994, Kaepa filed suit in Texas state court, alleging (1) fraud and negligent misrepresentation by Achilles to induce Kaepa to enter into the distributorship agreement, and (2) breach of contract by Achilles. Thereafter, Achilles removed the action to federal district court, and the parties began a laborious discovery process which to date has resulted in the production of tens of thousands of documents. In February 1995, after appearing in the Texas action, removing the case to federal court, and engaging in comprehensive discovery, Achilles brought its own action in Japan, alleging mirror-image claims: (1) fraud by Kaepa to induce Achilles to enter into the distributorship agreement, and (2) breach of contract by Kaepa.

Back in Texas, Kaepa promptly filed a motion asking the district court to enjoin Achilles from prosecuting its suit in Japan (motion for an antisuit injunction). Achilles in turned moved to dismiss the federal court action on the ground of *forum non conveniens*. The district court denied Achilles's motion to dismiss and granted Kaepa's motion to enjoin, ordering Achilles to refrain from litigating the Japanese action and to file all of its counterclaims with the district court. Achilles timely appealed the grant of the antisuit injunction.

II. Analysis

A. *Propriety of the Antisuit Injunction*

[. . .]

It is well settled among the circuit courts—including this one—which have reviewed the grant of an antisuit injunction that the federal courts have the power to enjoin persons subject to their jurisdiction from prosecuting foreign suits. The circuits differ, however, on the proper legal standard to employ when determining whether that injunctive power should be exercised. We have addressed the propriety of an antisuit injunction on two prior occasions, in *In re Unterweser Reederei Gmbh* and *Bethell v. Peace*. Emphasizing in both cases the need to prevent vexatious or oppressive litigation, we concluded that a district court does not abuse its discretion by issuing an antisuit injunction when it has determined "that allowing simultaneous prosecution of the same action in a foreign forum thousands of miles away would result in 'inequitable hardship' and 'tend to frustrate and delay the speedy and efficient determination of the cause.'" The Seventh and the Ninth Circuits have either adopted or "incline[d] toward" this approach, but other circuits have employed a standard that elevates principles of international comity to the virtual exclusion of essentially all other considerations.

...We decline...to require a district court to genuflect before a vague and omnipotent notion of comity every time that it must decide whether to enjoin a foreign action.

[...]

For the foregoing reasons, the district court's grant of Kaepa's motion to enjoin the litigation of Achilles's action in Japan is

AFFIRMED.

EMILIO M. GARZA, Circuit Judge, dissenting:

International comity represents a principle of paramount importance in our world of ever increasing economic interdependence. Admitting that "comity" may be a somewhat elusive concept does not mean that we can blithely ignore its cautionary dictate. Unless we proceed in each instance with respect for the independent jurisdiction of a sovereign nation's courts, we risk provoking retaliation in turn, with detrimental consequences that may reverberate far beyond the particular dispute and its private litigants. Amicable relations among sovereign nations and their judicial systems depend on our recognition, as federal courts, that we share the international arena with co-equal judicial bodies, and that we therefore act to deprive a foreign court of jurisdiction only in the most extreme circumstances. Because I feel that the majority's opinion does not grant the principle of international comity the weight it deserves, I must respectfully dissent.

[...]

Notes and Questions

The majority's refusal "to genuflect before a vague and omnipotent notion" forcefully states its position. The federal court views with contempt any attempt to limit its authority to do what it believes it must do to fulfill its public obligations. How would you describe the dissenting position? Does it argue for a cowering form of passivity? What does international comity require in such matters? If you could legislate an approach, what rules would you devise? Why?

* * * *

GENERAL ELECTRIC CO. v. DEUTZ AG

270 F.3d 144 (3d Cir. 2001).

[International comity precludes an anti-suit injunction].

(footnotes omitted)

OPINION OF THE COURT

WEIS, Circuit Judge.

In this breach of contract suit, the District Court found that the defendant, a German guarantor, had sufficient contacts with Pennsylvania to be subject to personal jurisdiction. After a jury determination, the Court also found that the defendant was not entitled to invoke the arbitration clause in the underlying contract signed by its subsidiary. We will affirm these rulings. The Court also enjoined the defendant from applying to the English courts to enforce the alleged right to arbitration. We will reverse the grant of that injunction principally on the grounds of comity.

In June 1993, plaintiff General Electric, a New York corporation with manufacturing facilities in western Pennsylvania, entered into a contract with Motoren–Werke Mannheim AG, a German corporation with headquarters in Mannheim, Germany. Essentially, the agreement provided that Motoren–Werke would design, and General Electric would manufacture, high horsepower diesel engines for locomotives. The contract also included a section in which Deutz AG, the parent company of Motoren–Werke, guaranteed the obligations of its subsidiary.

By late 1997, the joint venture was encountering difficulties, and General Electric eventually called upon Deutz to provide the additional funding necessary for the work to continue. The parties held extended discussions, but were unable to resolve their differences. In December 1998, General Electric filed suit in the United States District Court for the Western District of Pennsylvania, asserting breach of contract claims against Deutz. The complaint sought damages as a result of lost sales and diversion of resources toward tasks that were the contractual responsibility of Motoren–Werke.

Deutz moved to dismiss for lack of personal jurisdiction or, alternatively, to compel international arbitration as it alleged the contract required. In July 1999, while these matters were proceeding in the District Court, Deutz sought arbitration before a panel of the International Arbitration Association in London.

The District Court issued an Opinion and Order on December 29, 1999, holding that Deutz's contacts with the forum state, made in the course of pre-contract negotiations and post-contract visits by Deutz executives in an effort to resolve the parties' dispute, provided sufficient evidence to support a finding of specific jurisdiction. The Court also ruled that the language of the contract did not unambiguously include Deutz within the scope of its arbitration provisions. The issue was submitted to a jury, which found that Deutz was not entitled to arbitration.

In April 2000, before the arbitration panel issued a decision, Deutz petitioned the High Court in London to enjoin General Electric from further proceedings in the Western District of Pennsylvania. The High Court declined to issue an injunction.

On July 31, 2000, the District Court enjoined Deutz form resorting to the High Court in the future. It was not until November 14, 2000, that the arbitration panel held that General Electric and Deutz had not agreed to arbitrate their contractual disputes. Deutz has appealed all of the orders of the District Court.

[. . .]

IV. The Injunction

As noted earlier, while the parties were litigating in Pennsylvania, Deutz initiated an arbitration proceeding before the International Chamber of Commerce Court of Arbitration in July 1999. Despite General Electric's objections, the ICC assembled a panel of arbitrators to consider the jurisdictional issue.

After the ICC Panel set a schedule for its proceedings, Deutz applied to the Queen's Bench Division of the High Court in London for an order restraining General Electric from seeking an injunction in the District Court in Pennsylvania against Deutz proceeding before the ICC.

Justice Thomas of the High Court, in a judgment dated April 14, 2000, dismissed the request. He emphasized that in the posture of the matter before the Court that he was "not in any way finally deciding the point." Nonetheless, it appeared that "the words by which Deutz became a party to the agreement [did] not establish a serious issue to be tried on the question of whether [it] became a party to the arbitration clause."

The High Court also recognized that each party had been given a full opportunity to produce evidence in the District Court, which had applied principles similar to those adhered to by the Queen's Bench. Finally, Justice Thomas remarked that Deutz would be able to assert its contentions in the forthcoming District Court proceedings, particularly the argument that comity should inform the deference to be accorded the jurisdiction of the ICC Panel. In the meantime, the ICC Panel continued to receive memorials and expert opinions from the parties bearing on the jurisdictional question.

After argument and further briefing, the District Court, citing its authority to enjoin parties from pursuing parallel litigation in foreign as well as domestic courts, issued an order on July 31, 2000, "permanently enjoin[ing] Deutz from appealing the forthcoming jurisdictional order of the Arbitral Tribunal to the English courts or from taking any other action in furtherance of its prosecution of the ICC arbitration." Because the parties had purportedly completed their submissions to the arbitration panel, and nothing remained but the issuance of a decision, the

Court limited its order, enjoining Deutz from appealing the ICC ruling to the English courts or taking further steps in arbitration thereafter.

The District Court acknowledged that its injunctive power must be exercised sparingly; parallel proceedings are ordinarily permitted to proceed simultaneously, at least until one has reached the stage where its ruling becomes *res judicata*. Recognizing that an intercircuit split has developed over the degree of deference owed foreign courts, the District Court concluded that the better approach emphasizes international comity. Using this standard, it would issue an injunction only if *res judicata* applied, or if the foreign proceeding threatened the Court's jurisdiction over the matter at hand or a strong public policy of the United States.

[. . .]

We are persuaded that none of the bases relied upon by the District Court supports the issuance of an injunction in this case. . . .

[. . .]

The circumstances here were not so aggravated as to justify interference with the jurisdiction of the courts of another sovereign state, and there is no indication that the English courts would have prevented General Electric from arguing the *res judicata* effect of the February 28, 2000 order.

General Electric argues that if Deutz had not been so restrained, it might have destroyed the District Court's jurisdiction by securing an order from the High Court compelling arbitration. The record, however, reveals little basis for such qualms. Deutz petitioned the High Court two months after the District Court had dismissed the arbitration request, and the High Court declined to issue an injunction restraining General Electric from proceeding in the federal court, voicing serious doubts about the strength of Deutz's position. Thus, the District Court knew before it enjoined Deutz that the High Court had shown no inclination to disagree with the non-arbitrability ruling.

Similarly ill-founded is General Electric's assertion that the sanctity of the jury verdict would be jeopardized by permitting Deutz to repair once again to the High Court in London. Although the jury unquestionably has a more important role in the American jurisprudential system than in that of any other nation, its verdict is neither infallible nor immune from judicial scrutiny.

We have been cited to no authority that endorses enjoining proceedings in a foreign court on the grounds that an American jury verdict might be called into question. Indeed, in denying Deutz's application, the High Court took pains to mention that the findings of fact had been made by a jury. There is little reason to believe that the High Court could give any less deference to the jury's role as fact-finder if the issue were presented a second time.

V. Comity

In parallel litigation, the issue of comity is an important and omnipresent factor. Although it is a consideration in federal and state litigation, it assumes even more significance in international proceedings. . . .

The Court of Appeals for the D.C. Circuit has described comity as a "complex and elusive concept," the deference a domestic court should pay to the actions of a foreign government, not otherwise binding on the forum. *Laker Airways Ltd. v. Sabena, Belgian World Airlines*, 731 F.2d 909, 937 (D.C. Cir. 1984). The primary reason for giving effect to the rulings of foreign tribunals is that such recognition fosters international cooperation and encourages reciprocity. Thus, comity promotes predictability and stability in legal expectations, two critical components of successful international commercial enterprises. It also encourages the rule of law, which is especially important because as trade expands across international borders, the necessity for cooperation among nations increases as well. *Id.*

[. . .]

The federal Courts of Appeals have not established a uniform rule for determining when injunctions on foreign litigation are justified. Two standards, it appears, have developed. Courts following the "liberal" or "lax" standard will issue an injunction where policy in the enjoining forum is frustrated, the foreign proceeding would be vexatious or would threaten a domestic court's *in rem* or *quasi in rem* jurisdiction or other equitable considerations, and finally, where allowing the foreign proceedings to continue would result in delay. The Courts of Appeals for the Fifth, Seventh, and Ninth Circuits generally apply this standard.

By contrast, the Second, Sixth and District of Columbia Circuits use a more restrictive approach, rarely permitting injunctions against foreign proceedings. These courts approve enjoining foreign parallel proceedings only to protect jurisdiction or an important public policy. Vexatiousness and inconvenience to the parties carry far less weight.

Our Court is among those that resort to the more restrictive standard. . . .

Our jurisprudence . . . reflects a serious concern for comity. This Court may properly be aligned with those that have adopted a strict approach when injunctive relief against foreign judicial proceedings is sought. Although it recognized our adherence to that restrictive standard, the District Court in this case invoked the threat to jurisdiction and violation of public policy factors to justify the injunction. As we noted earlier, the evidence supporting application of these factors was extremely weak, and any doubts to the contrary should have been put to rest by the High Court's judgment, issued before the injunction was granted.

[. . .]

Notes and Questions

1. When the court refers to the ICC Court of Arbitration in London, it must mean either an ICC arbitration that took place in London or an arbitral proceeding conducted in London pursuant to the rules of the LCIA (the London Court of International Arbitration). There is no ICC Court of Arbitration in London; there is an ICC Court of International Arbitration in Paris, France at the ICC headquarters there. It, however, does not conduct arbitral proceedings, but rather performs general administrative duties and provides a type of quality control review of ICC arbitral awards. Moreover, whether the parties are bound by a valid contract of arbitration, under the arbitration law of most States, is decided by the arbitrators rather than a court. The *kompetenz-kompetenz* doctrine provides that jurisdictional challenges are first addressed to the sitting arbitral tribunal and thereafter the arbitrators' ruling can be subject to judicial supervision. The action of the U.S. district court, however, is perfectly in line with Federal Arbitration Act (FAA) § 3 and even the modifying holding in the *Kaplan* case. Under U.S. law, courts decide whether a contractual foundation exists for arbitration and under FAA § 4 the question of the existence or scope of a contract of arbitration can be decided by a jury.

2. The High Court's refusal to issue an anti-suit injunction is peculiar in some respects. It must reflect the court's view that the interests of justice did not warrant judicial intervention. Indirectly, it represents a refusal to provide judicial assistance to arbitration. The latter posture is unusual for English and other Western courts. These points of refinement on arbitration law, however, are moot in light of the arbitral tribunal's eventual ruling that the parties were not bound by an arbitration agreement. You should map out the procedural consequences of a hypothetical ruling by the arbitral tribunal that it had jurisdiction to rule because the parties were bound by an enforceable arbitration agreement. Wouldn't such a determination set the litigation in procedural upheaval or would the issue be resolved quickly and neatly in favor of arbitration and the arbitral tribunal's assertion of jurisdiction?

3. Further, you should assess the court's description of the decisional tests and positions for ordering anti-suit relief. Does the discussion clarify the issues and the interests involved? What evaluation do you have of the court's adherence to the comity analysis?

4. Finally, compare and contrast the following statements from English court opinions for their impact upon the law of anti-suit injunctions:

THE ATLANTIC STAR

[1972] 3 All E.R. 705, 709 (Ct. App. 1972).

"The right to come here is not confined to Englishmen. It extends to any friendly foreigner. He can seek the aid of our court if he desires to do so. You may call this 'forum shopping' if you please, but if the forum is England, it is a good place to shop in, both for the quality of the goods and the speed of service."

SMITH KLINE & FRENCH LABORATORIES LTD. v. BLOCH

[1983] 2 All E.R. 72 (Ct. App. 1983).

"As a moth is drawn to the light, so is a litigant drawn to the United States. If he can only get his case into their courts, he stands to win a fortune. At no cost to himself, and at no risk of having to pay anything to the other side. The lawyers there will conduct the case 'on spec' as we say, or on a 'contingency fee' as they say. The lawyers will charge the litigant nothing for their services but instead they will take 40% of the damages, if they win the case in court, or out of court on a settlement. If they lose, the litigant will have nothing to pay to the other side. The courts in the United States have no such costs deterrent as we have. There is also in the United States a right to trial by jury. These are prone to award fabulous damages. They are notoriously sympathetic and know that the lawyers will take their 40% before the plaintiff gets anything. All this means that the defendant can be readily forced into a settlement. The plaintiff holds all the cards...."

CASTANHO v. BROWN & ROOT (UK) LTD.

[1980] 3 All E.R. 72, 76 (Ct. App. 1980).

"A Texas-style claim is big business."

§ 4. STATE STATUS AS A BARRIER TO COURT JURISDICTION

Sovereign immunity is a doctrine under which foreign States, their instrumentalities, and their property enjoy immunity from the exercise of jurisdiction and the enforcement of judgments by courts of other States. The rationale for the doctrine is that no State is superior to another. If all States are equally independent, the courts of one State cannot sit in judgment of the legality of another State's acts.

Historically, sovereign immunity can be traced to a time when most States were ruled by individual sovereigns who, in a very real sense, personified the State. "When states were identified with their sovereigns, and the relations of states were in great measure personal relations of individuals, considerations of courtesy were naturally prominent....Supposing reasons of courtesy to be disregarded, immunities would still be required upon the ground of practical necessity. If a sovereign, while in a foreign state, were subjected to its jurisdiction, the interests of his own state might readily be jeopardized by the consequences of his position." W. Hall, International Law 178 (Higgins, ed. 7th ed. 1917). The doctrine of sovereign immunity eventually acquired two different characterizations: The absolute theory and the restrictive theory.

The U.S. Supreme Court originally adopted a theory of absolute immunity in *Schooner Exchange v. McFaddon*, 11 U.S. (7 Cranch) 116, 3

L.Ed. 287 (1812). "This full and absolute territorial jurisdiction being alike the attribute of every sovereign, and being incapable of conferring extra-territorial power, would not seem to contemplate foreign sovereigns nor their sovereign rights as its objects. One sovereign being in no respect amenable to another; and being bound by obligations of the highest character not to degrade the dignity of his nation, by placing himself or its sovereign rights within the jurisdiction of another, can be supposed to enter a foreign territory only under an express license, or in the confidence that the immunities belonging to his independent sovereign station, though not expressly stipulated, are reserved by implication, and will be extended to him." *Id.*

Gradually, during the industrial revolution, foreign States began to emphasize the exceptions to sovereign immunity and to differentiate between acts of a state *jure gestionis* and acts *jure imperii*, the former being exempt from sovereign immunity. This differentiation eventually led to the adoption by the United States of the "restrictive theory" of sovereign immunity that protected actions by a foreign State performed in its capacity as a sovereign, but excepted those actions performed by a foreign State in its capacity as a private entity. The acceptance of the restrictive theory was first articulated in the "Tate Letter," 26 Dep't State Bull. 984 (1952):

> It is thus evident that with the possible exception of the United Kingdom little support has been found except on the part of the Soviet Union and its satellites for continued full acceptance of the absolute theory of sovereign immunity. There are evidences that British authorities are aware of its deficiencies and ready for a change. The reasons which obviously motivate state trading countries in adhering to the theory with perhaps increasing rigidity are most persuasive that the United States should change its policy. Furthermore, the granting of sovereign immunity to foreign governments in the courts of the United States is most inconsistent with the action of the Government of the United States in subjecting itself to suit in these same courts in both contract and tort and with its long established policy of not claiming immunity in foreign jurisdictions for its merchant vessels. Finally, the Department feels that the widespread and increasing practice on the part of governments of engaging in commercial activities makes necessary a practice which will enable persons doing business with them to have their rights determined in the courts. For these reasons it will hereafter be the Department's policy to follow the restrictive theory of sovereign immunity in the consideration of requests of foreign governments for a grant of sovereign immunity.

The trend toward a restrictive application of sovereign immunity culminated in 1976 with the Foreign Sovereign Immunities Act, 28 U.S.C.A. §§ 1602–1611 (1977).

United States Foreign Sovereign Immunities Act of 1976

[FSIA]

[. . .]

An Act

To define the jurisdiction of the United States courts in suits against foreign states, the circumstances in which foreign states are immune from suit and in which execution may not be levied on their property, and for other purposes.

[. . .]

§ 1330. Actions against foreign states.

(a) The district courts shall have original jurisdiction without regard to amount in controversy of any nonjury civil action against a foreign state as defined in section 1603(a) of this title as to any claim for relief in personam with respect to which the foreign state is not entitled to immunity either under sections 1605–1607 of this title or under any applicable international agreement.

(b) Personal jurisdiction over a foreign state shall exist as to every claim for relief over which the district courts have jurisdiction under subsection (a) where service has been made under section 1608 of this title.

(c) For purposes of subsection (b), an appearance by a foreign state does not confer personal jurisdiction with respect to any claim for relief not arising out of any transaction or occurrence enumerated in sections 1605–1607 of this title.

[. . .]

§ 1602. Findings and declaration of purpose.

The Congress finds that the determination by United States courts of the claims of foreign states to immunity from the jurisdiction of such courts would serve the interests of justice and would protect the rights of both foreign states and litigants in United States courts. Under international law, states are not immune from the jurisdiction of foreign courts insofar as their commercial activities are concerned, and their commercial property may be levied upon for the satisfaction of judgments rendered against them in connection with their commercial activities. Claims of foreign states to immunity should henceforth be decided by courts of the United States and of the States in conformity with the principles set forth in this chapter.

§ 1603. Definitions.

For purposes of this chapter—

(a) A 'foreign state', except as used in section 1608 of this title, includes a political subdivision of a foreign state or an agency or instrumentality of a foreign state as defined in subsection (b).

(b) An 'agency or instrumentality of a foreign state' means any entity—

(1) which is a separate legal person, corporate or otherwise, and

(2) which is an organ of a foreign state or political subdivision thereof, or a majority of whose shares or other ownership interest is owned by a foreign state or political subdivision thereof, and

(3) which is neither a citizen of a State of the United States as defined in section 1332 (c) and (d) of this title, nor created under the laws of any third country.

(c) The 'United States' includes all territory and water, continental or insular, subject to the jurisdiction of the United States.

(d) A 'commercial activity' means either a regular course of commercial conduct or a particular commercial transaction or act. The commercial character of an activity shall be determined by reference to the nature of the course of conduct or particular transaction or act, rather than by reference to its purpose.

(e) A 'commercial activity carried on in the United States by a foreign state' means commercial activity carried on by such state and having substantial contact with the United States.

§ 1604. Immunity of a foreign state from jurisdiction.

Subject to existing international agreements to which the United States is a party at the time of enactment of this Act[,] a foreign state shall be immune from the jurisdiction of the courts of the United States and of the States except as provided in section 1605 to 1607 of this chapter.

§ 1605. General exceptions to the jurisdictional immunity of a foreign state.

(a) A foreign state shall not be immune from the jurisdiction of courts of the United States or of the States in any case—

(1) in which the foreign state has waived its immunity either explicitly or by implication, notwithstanding any withdrawal of the waiver which the foreign state may purport to effect except in accordance with the terms of the waiver;

(2) in which the action is based upon a commercial activity carried on in the United States by the foreign state; or upon an act performed in the United States in connection with a commercial activity of the foreign state elsewhere; or upon an act outside the territory of the United States in connection with a commercial activity of the foreign state elsewhere and that act causes a direct effect in the United States;

(3) in which rights in property taken in violation of international law are in issue and that property or any property exchanged for such property is present in the United States in connection with a commercial activity carried on in the United States by the foreign

state; or that property or any property exchanged for such property is owned or operated by an agency or instrumentality of the foreign state and that agency or instrumentality is engaged in a commercial activity in the United States;

(4) in which rights in property in the United States acquired by succession or gift or rights in immovable property situated in the United States are in issue; or

(5) not otherwise encompassed in paragraph (2) above, in which money damages are sought against a foreign state for personal injury or death, or damage to or loss of property, occurring in the United States and caused by the tortious act or omission of that foreign state or of any official or employee of that foreign state while acting within the scope of his office or employment; except this paragraph shall not apply to—

(A) any claim based upon the exercise or performance or the failure to exercise or perform a discretionary function regardless of whether the discretion be abused, or

(B) any claim arising out of malicious prosecution, abuse of process, libel, slander, misrepresentation, deceit, or interference with contract rights.

(6) in which the action is brought, either to enforce an agreement made by the foreign state with or for the benefit of a private party to submit to arbitration all or any differences which have arisen or which may arise between the parties with respect to a defined legal relationship, whether contractual or not, concerning a subject matter capable of settlement by arbitration under the laws of the United States, or to confirm an award made pursuant to such an agreement to arbitrate, if (A) the arbitration takes place or is intended to take place in the United States, (B) the agreement or award is or may be governed by a treaty or other international agreement in force for the United States calling for the recognition and enforcement of arbitral awards, (C) the underlying claim, save for the agreement to arbitrate, could have been brought in a United States court under this section or section 1607, or (D) paragraph (1) of this subsection is otherwise applicable.

(b) A foreign state shall not be immune from the jurisdiction of the courts of the United States in any case in which a suit in admiralty is brought to enforce a maritime lien against a vessel or cargo of the foreign state, which maritime lien is based upon a commercial activity of the foreign state: *provided*, That—

(1) notice of the suit is given by delivery of a copy of the summons and of the complaint to the person, or his agent, having possession of the vessel or cargo against which the maritime lien is asserted; but such notice shall not be deemed to have been delivered, nor may it thereafter be delivered, if the vessel or cargo is arrested pursuant to process obtained on behalf of the party bringing the

suit—unless the party was unaware that the vessel or cargo of a foreign state was involved, in which event the service of process of arrest shall be deemed to constitute valid delivery of such notice; and

(2) notice to the foreign state of the commencement of suit as provided in section 1608 of this title is initiated within ten days either of the delivery of notice as provided in subsection (b) (1) of this section or, in the case of a party who was unaware that the vessel or cargo of a foreign state was involved, of the date such party determined the existence of the foreign state's interest.

(c) Whenever notice is delivered under subsection (b)(1), the suit to enforce a maritime lien shall thereafter proceed and shall be heard and determined according to the principles of law and rules of practice of suits *in rem* whenever it appears that, had the vessel been privately owned and possessed, a suit *in rem* might have been maintained. A decree against the foreign state may include costs of the suit and, if the decree is for a money judgment, interest as ordered by the court, except that the court may not award judgment against the foreign state in an amount greater than the value of the vessel or cargo upon which the maritime lien arose. Such value shall be determined as of the time notice is served under subsection (b)(1). Decrees shall be subject to appeal and revision as provided in other cases of admiralty and maritime jurisdiction. Nothing shall preclude the plaintiff in any proper case from seeking relief *in personam* in the same action brought to enforce a maritime lien as provided in this section.

(d) A foreign state shall not be immune from the jurisdiction of the courts of the United States in any action brought to foreclose a preferred mortgage, as defined in the Ship Mortgage Act, 1920 (46 U.S.C. 911 and following). Such action shall be brought, heard, and determined in accordance with the provisions of that Act and in accordance with the principles of law and rules of practice of suits *in rem*, whenever it appears that had the vessel been privately owned and possessed a suit *in rem* might have been maintained.

§ 1606. Extent of Liability.

As to any claim for relief with respect to which a foreign state is not entitled to immunity under section 1605 or 1607 of this chapter, the foreign state shall be liable in the same manner and to the same extent as a private individual under like circumstances; but a foreign state except for an agency or instrumentality thereof shall not be liable for punitive damages; if, however, in any case wherein death was caused, the law of the place where the action or omission occurred provides, or has been construed to provide, for damages only punitive in nature, the foreign state shall be liable for actual or compensatory damages measured by the pecuniary injuries resulting from such death which were incurred by the persons for whose benefit the action was brought.

§ 1607. Counterclaims.

In any action brought by a foreign state, or in which a foreign state intervenes, in a court of the United States or of a State, the foreign state shall not be accorded immunity with respect to any counterclaim—

(a) for which a foreign state would not be entitled to immunity under section 1605 of this chapter had such claim been brought in a separate action against the foreign state; or

(b) arising out of the transaction or occurrence that is the subject matter of the claim of the foreign state; or

(c) to the extent that the counterclaim does not seek relief exceeding in amount or differing in kind from that sought by the foreign state.

§ 1608. Service; time to answer; default.

(a) Service in the courts of the United States and of the States shall be made upon a foreign state or political subdivision of a foreign state:

(1) by delivery of a copy of the summons and complaint in accordance with any special arrangement for service between the plaintiff and the foreign state or political subdivision; or

(2) if no special arrangement exists, by delivery of a copy of the summons and complaint in accordance with an applicable international convention on service of judicial documents; or

(3) if service cannot be made under paragraphs (1) or (2), by sending a copy of the summons and complaint and a notice of suit, together with a translation of each into the official language of the foreign state, by any form of mail requiring a signed receipt, to be addressed and dispatched by the clerk of the court to the head of the ministry of foreign affairs of the foreign state concerned, or

(4) if service cannot be made within 30 days under paragraph (3), by sending two copies of the summons and complaint and a notice of suit, together with a translation of each into the official language of the foreign state, by any form of mail requiring a signed receipt, to be addressed and dispatched by the clerk of the court to the Secretary of State in Washington, District of Columbia, to the attention of the Director of Special Consular Services—and the Secretary shall transmit one copy of the papers through diplomatic channels to the foreign state and shall send to the clerk of the court a certified copy of the diplomatic note indicating when the papers were transmitted.

[. . .]

§ 1609. Immunity from attachment and execution of property of a foreign state.

Subject to existing international agreements to which the United States is a party at the time of enactment of this Act[,] the property in the United States of a foreign state shall be immune from attachment arrest and execution except as provided in sections 1610 and 1611 of this chapter.

§ 1610. Exception to the immunity from attachment or execution.

(a) The property in the United States of a foreign state, as defined in section 1603(a) of this chapter, used for a commercial activity in the United States, shall not be immune from attachment in aid of execution, or from execution, upon a judgment entered by a court of the United States or of a State after the effective date of this Act, if—

(1) the foreign state has waived its immunity from attachment in aid of execution or from execution either explicitly or by implication, notwithstanding any withdrawal of the waiver the foreign state may purport to effect except in accordance with the terms of the waiver, or

(2) the property is or was used for the commercial activity upon which the claim is based, or

(3) the execution relates to a judgment establishing rights in property which has been taken in violation of international law or which has been exchanged for property taken in violation of international law, or

(4) the execution relates to a judgment establishing rights in property—

(A) which is acquired by succession or gift, or

(B) which is immovable and situated in the United States: *Provided*, That such property is not used for purpose of maintaining a diplomatic or consular mission or the residence of the Chief of such mission, or

(5) the property consists of any contractual obligation or any proceeds from such a contractual obligation to indemnify or hold harmless the foreign state or its employees under a policy of automobile or other liability or casualty insurance covering the claim which merged into the judgment.

(b) In addition to subsection (a), any property in the United States of an agency or instrumentality of a foreign state engaged in commercial activity in the United States shall not be immune from attachment in aid of execution, or from execution, upon a judgment entered by a court of the United States or of a State after the effective date of this Act, if—

(1) the agency or instrumentality has waived its immunity from attachment in aid of execution or from execution either explicitly or implicitly, notwithstanding any withdrawal of the waiver the agency or instrumentality may purport to effect except in accordance with the terms of the waiver, or

(2) the judgment relates to a claim for which the agency or instrumentality is not immune by virtue of section 1605(a) (2), (3),

or (5) or 1605(b) of this chapter, regardless of whether the property is or was used for the activity upon which the claim is based.

(c) No attachment or execution referred to in subsections (a) and (b) of this section shall be permitted until the court has ordered such attachment and execution after having determined that a reasonable period of time has elapsed following the entry of judgment and the giving of any notice required under section 1608(e) of this chapter.

(d) The property of a foreign state, as defined in section 1603(a) of this chapter, used for a commercial activity in the United States, shall not be immune from attachment prior to the entry of judgment in any action brought in a court of the United States or of a State, or prior to the elapse of the period of time provided in subsection (c) of this section, if—

(1) the foreign state has explicitly waived its immunity from attachment prior to judgment, notwithstanding any withdrawal of the waiver the foreign state may purport to effect except in accordance with the terms of the waiver, and

(2) the purpose of the attachment is to secure satisfaction of a judgment that has been or may ultimately be entered against the foreign state, and not to obtain jurisdiction.

(e) The vessels of a foreign state shall not be immune from arrest *in rem*, interlocutory sale, and execution in actions brought to foreclose a preferred mortgage as provided in section 1605(d).

§ 1611. Certain types of property immune from execution.

(a) Notwithstanding the provisions of section 1610 of this chapter, the property of those organizations designated by the President as being entitled to enjoy the privileges, exemptions, and immunities provided by the International Organizations Immunities Act shall not be subject to attachment or any other judicial process impeding the disbursement of funds to, or on the order of, a foreign state as the result of an action brought in the courts of the United States or of the States.

(b) Notwithstanding the provisions of section 1610 of this chapter, the property of a foreign state shall be immune from attachment and from execution, if–

(1) the property is that of a foreign central bank or monetary authority held for its own account, unless such bank or authority, or its parent foreign government, has explicitly waived its immunity from attachment in aid of execution, or from execution, notwithstanding any withdrawal of the waiver which the bank, authority or government may purport to effect except in accordance with the terms of the waiver; or

(2) the property is, or is intended to be, used in connection with a military activity and

(A) is of a military character, or

(B) is under the control of a military authority or defense agency.

[. . .]

Commentary

"The basic premise of. . .[the] doctrine [of restrictive immunity as codified in the FSIA] is that in commercial matters. . .a foreign sovereign should not have available the defense of sovereign immunity. In essence, that doctrine restricts the immunity of a foreign state to suits involving a foreign state's public acts (*acta jure imperii*) and does not extend immunity to suits based on its commercial or private acts (*acta jure gestionis*)." Von Mehren, *The Foreign Sovereign Immunities Act of 1976*, 17 Colum. J. Trans. L. 33, 33–34 (1978).

By 1976, all of the important trading and industrial countries in the Western world with the exception of the United Kingdom had adopted the restrictive theory of sovereign immunity. Then, in 1981, the English court, in *Playa Larga and Marble Island v. I Congreso del Partido*, (1981) 3 W.L.F. 328, 336 (H.L.), recognized and described the doctrine:

> The relevant exception, or limitation, which has been engrafted upon the principle of immunity of states, under the so-called 'restrictive theory,' arises from the willingness of states to enter into commercial or other private law transactions with individuals. It appears to have two main foundations: (a) It is necessary in the interest of justice to individuals having such transactions with states to allow them to bring such transactions before the courts. (b) To require a state to answer a claim based upon such transactions does not involve a challenge to or inquiry into any act of sovereignty or governmental act of that state. It is, in accepted phrases, neither a threat to the dignity of that state, nor any interference with its sovereign functions.
>
> When therefore a claim is brought against a state. . .and state immunity is claimed, it is necessary to consider what is the relevant act which forms the basis of the claim: is this, under the old terminology, an act '*jure gestonis*' or is it an act '*jure imperii*': is it (to adopt the translation of these catchwords used in the 'Tate Letter') a 'private act' or is it a 'sovereign or public act,' a private act meaning in this context an act of a private law character such as a private citizen might have entered into. It is upon this point that the arguments in these appeals is focused.

On appeal, the court reiterated its acceptance of the restrictive theory: "In view of these developments [the American adoption of the FSIA in 1976 and the United Kingdom adoption of the State Immunity Act in 1978] I think it plain that the absolute doctrine is no longer part of international law, and by reason of the doctrine of incorporation it should be applied by the English courts, not only in actions *in rem* but also in actions *in personam*." (1981) 1 All E.R. 1092, 1100.

The FSIA thus became internationally significant as a statement of policy and as the vehicle of a trend. "Viewed broadly, the Immunities Act adopts four basic strategies. First, it adopts the restrictive theory of foreign sovereign immunity both with respect to jurisdiction and execution. Second, it places in the judiciary the duty to decide whether a foreign sovereign is entitled to immunity. Third, it restricts jurisdiction over foreign sovereigns to *in personam* jurisdiction and, in so doing, in effect eliminates *in rem* and *quasi in rem* jurisdiction against foreign sovereigns. Fourth, in a number of respects, it places the foreign sovereign in a position similar to the domestic sovereign." Von Mehren, *supra*, 17 COLUM. J. TRANS. L. at 44–45.

"Congress chose to pursue *in personam* jurisdiction to the exclusion of *in rem* jurisdiction because of a conviction that the 'fortuitous' location of property in this country should not necessitate trial in our courts under foreign law and that attachment of such property serves to unduly strain foreign relations." *Id.* at 46–47.

One difficulty the courts have encountered with respect to the restrictive theory has been classifying a certain act as a commercial activity and thus exempt from sovereign immunity. In *Victory Transport v. Comisaria General de Abastecimientos*, 336 F.2d 354 (2d Cir. 1964), *cert. denied*, 381 U.S. 934 (1965), the court established five areas in which it would allow the claim of sovereign immunity: (1) internal administrative acts, such as expulsion of an alien; (2) legislative acts, such as nationalization; (3) acts concerning the armed forces; (4) acts concerning diplomatic activity; and (5) public loans. This approach was a forerunner of the FSIA and differs in two significant respects. "First, *Victory Transport* establishes a classification of political and public acts and says that, if such acts are in issue, the sovereign is entitled to immunity. The Immunities Act does the opposite; it establishes a classification of 'commercial acts' and says that, if such acts are in issue, the foreign sovereign is not entitled to immunity. Second, the *Victory Transport* classification is based upon a consideration both of the nature and the purpose of the act." Von Mehren, *supra*, 17 COLUM. J. TRANS. L. at 43. Thus, *Victory Transport*, although useful in tracing the development of the restrictive theory of sovereign immunity in American law, is no longer controlling in either its approach or its conclusions. More recent decisions have modified the commercial activity exception in light of the FSIA.

Notes and Questions

1. It should be noted that State immunity is the rule and amenability to suit the exception. The FSIA codifies both aspects of that rule. In practical terms, if an exception to immunity is unlikely to be available, the State cannot be sued and made accountable for its conduct. Losses will fall on the private party, unless there is political risk or another form of insurance. Another remedy may be the governmental espousal of the private claim for possible litigation before the International Court of Justice or for diplomatic

intervention and negotiation. The latter is extremely rare and is effective for a private party only when its interests truly coincide with those of the government. Clients should be informed by counsel that dealing with foreign governments or their entities can be a highly perilous activity and that the FSIA is hardly a failsafe solution and may promise much more than it actually delivers.

2. You should evaluate § 1330 and determine the elements of the jurisdictional test for litigation involving foreign States. Identify and explain the rationale that underlies each paragraph of § 1330.

3. One of the most significant provisions of the FSIA is § 1603(d) which defines the notion of a "commercial activity." After reading the provision, identify when a State or its entities engage in commercial activities. Is the definition supplied in the Act too taxonomic? What reasoning underlies the distinction between "nature" and "purpose"? You should read § 1603(e) with equal care. Doesn't it supply an overly abstract definition of State commercial activity in the United States? What effect does such an approach have?

4. Section 1605 supplies the list of exceptions to the rule of State immunity. Assuming that implied and express waivers can be effectively distinguished, what circumstances are necessary to constitute either waiver? Are express waivers ever likely to be achieved? If so, would you trust such a statement by a foreign State or its entities? Can't the State simply revoke its promise later in light of changed circumstances?

What purpose underlies the tripartite structure of § 1605(a)(2)? Doesn't the provision give the legislation extraterritorial reach? Is its effectiveness, therefore, in jeopardy? How might such a provision be given real impact?

5. It should be noted that, prior to the FSIA, the question of the immunity of foreign States from suit was often referred by courts to the U.S. Department of State. The referral was made for reasons of separation of powers and justiciability. The Executive Branch has the constitutional authority to conduct the foreign policy of the United States and relations with foreign States generally is the centerpiece of that foreign policy. The proponents of the FSIA believed that this process was overly political and that courts should make their own would-be objective juridical determinations on the amenability of foreign States to suit. Section 1605(3), addressing expropriated property as a basis for jurisdiction against foreign States, incorporates a political element into the statute. You should explain the purpose and rationale of the section. The statute otherwise maintains the supposedly objective character of immunity determinations. Are determinations reached under the FSIA devoid of political content or undertones? Should or can they be? The case law provides some dramatic and interesting answers to these questions, challenging the Congress's ability to neutralize immunity determinations.

You should also examine § 1605(5) in some detail. It provides the domestic purpose for the FSIA and illustrates its domestic application. Identify the basic test and its elements. Describe the circumstances of its intended and actual application. How would the provision apply to circumstances in which a diplomat/spy from a former Soviet Republic (say, Georgia) drives drunk in the late evening in a residential area of the District of

Columbia and careens onto the sidewalk in his drunken stupor, killing a pedestrian—a college student who was lawfully on the street?

6. Section 1605(a)(6) is a recent addition to the statute. It was added in 1988 under Public Law 100–669, 102 Stat. 3969 (1988). It is known as "the arbitration exception." It provides that States are not immune in legal proceedings in which a party seeks to enforce an arbitration agreement or award. Does the provision achieve its objective? What impact should the content of this provision have upon the counseling of clients who intend to pursue foreign investment or other transactions involving foreign States?

7. What FSIA rules apply to maritime transactions? Are they workable and likely to be effective?

8. Section 1606 establishes the scope of State liability under the Act. Are there any significant restrictions or limitations?

9. Compare and contrast the foregoing provisions with the "back-end" provisions—§§ 1609–1611. Is there a significant departure from the law articulated at the "front-end" of the statute? Are foreign States liable for their commercial conduct in terms of collectible judgments? Under what circumstances?

10. The critical concern for purposes of transborder litigation is to understand when a federal court is likely to rule that the State was not engaged in a commercial activity and, therefore, is not subject to suit—even though the court may have a fully proper and constituted basis for asserting its jurisdiction. The law, not judicial discretion, divests the court in such circumstances of otherwise applicable jurisdiction for reasons of politics and foreign relations. Another issue of significance is the effectiveness of the statutory language of the FSIA—is a State commercial activity readily found and are State waivers of immunity given effect? It should also be emphasized that there are two prongs to sovereign immunity: (1) from suit, and (2) from execution. A failure to find both prongs can result in the *de facto* absolute immunity of the State. The following cases should be read with these considerations in mind.

The Cases

The first case constitutes a useful illustration of when a foreign State acts in a classically political capacity. The functions that can be uniquely performed by a State include: imposing taxation, providing for police services and imprisonment, the conduct of foreign policy and diplomacy, declaring war, and pursuing covert activities. The regulations that apply to customs and immigration—the importing and exporting of goods and the admission of people to the country and granting citizenship—across national boundaries are part of the State's quintessential political responsibilities.

FROLOVA v. U.S.S.R.

761 F.2d 370 (7th Cir. 1985).

Before Bauer, Wood and Coffey, Circuit Judges.

Per Curiam.

Lois Becker, an American citizen and a graduate student at Stanford University, traveled to the Soviet Union in 1981 to do research for her dissertation on nineteenth century Russian political literature. While there, she met and fell in love with Andrei Frolov, a Soviet citizen, and the two of them were married in Moscow on May 19, 1981. The plaintiff, now as Lois Frolova, returned to the United States when her visa expired in June 1981. Her husband was forced to stay behind because he did not yet have the documentation or official permission needed to leave the Soviet Union. In September 1981[,] Mr. Frolov's request to leave the U.S.S.R. was denied because of "bad relations with the United States."

Mr. Frolov renewed his request in March 1982 (apparently there is a six-month waiting period before a person can reapply for permission to leave the U.S.S.R.), shortly after his wife arrived in Moscow on a twenty-day tourist visa. This request was turned down in April 1982; the reason given this time was that Frolov's departure was "not in the interest of the Soviet State." The next month[,] Mr. Frolov began a hunger strike, along with six other Muscovites who also had spouses living abroad.

On May 20, 1982, Lois Frolova filed the instant action, seeking an injunction and damages against the Soviet Union. She alleged that, as a result of the U.S.S.R.'s refusal to permit her husband to emigrate, she had suffered mental anguish, physical distress and loss of her rights of consortium. Ten days later, Mr. Frolov was informed by the Soviet secret police, the KGB, that he should apply for an exit visa. He did so and left the Soviet Union on June 20, 1982.

After her husband arrived in the United States, plaintiff abandoned her request for injunctive relief but not her claim for damages. The district court, acting *sua sponte*, dismissed the action.... The court discussed, but did not decide, whether the Soviet Union was immune from suit under the Foreign Sovereign Immunities Act of 1976.... Instead, the court ruled that dismissal was required by the act of state doctrine because the denial of Mr. Frolov's emigration request was an act of state that was not the proper subject of litigation in American courts....

We need not discuss the applicability of the act of state doctrine because we conclude that under the FSIA the Soviet Union was entitled to sovereign immunity and that the district court, as a result, lacked jurisdiction. Accordingly, we affirm the district court's dismissal of this action.

I.

For most of this nation's history[,] foreign countries have traditionally been granted complete immunity from suit in American courts....In 1952[,] the State Department adopted the "restrictive" theory of foreign sovereign immunity in the so-called Tate Letter...by which the United States would recognize another sovereign's immunity with regard to sovereign or public acts, but not for private acts. The application of the new doctrine was left principally to the discretion of the State Department until Congress passed the FSIA in 1976....

The FSIA—which, in general, codifies the restrictive theory of sovereign immunity—was designed to move resolution of foreign sovereign immunity issues from the Executive Branch to the judiciary. . . . In addition, Congress intended the provisions of the FSIA to be the "sole and exclusive standards to be used in resolving questions of sovereign immunity raised by foreign states before Federal and State courts in the United States." . . .

The FSIA begins with the presumption that foreign states are immune from suit, subject to specified exceptions. . . . Because the absence of sovereign immunity is a prerequisite to subject matter jurisdiction, the question of immunity must be considered by a district court even though the foreign country whose immunity is at issue has not entered an appearance. . . .

Frolova asserts on appeal that the Soviet Union's immunity is waived by two international agreements and three statutory provisions. We shall consider each in turn.

II.

Frolova's first argument is that the U.S.S.R. is not entitled to sovereign immunity because of the international agreement exception found in 28 U.S.C. § 1604 ("Subject to existing international agreements . . ."). She contends that the provisions of the United Nations Charter, 59 Stat. 1033 (1945), and the Helsinki Accords (Officially entitled Conference on Security and Cooperation in Europe: Final Act), 73 Dept. of State Bull. 323 (1975), may be enforced by private litigants.

Treaties made by the United States are the law of the land, U.S. Const. art. VI, but if not implemented by appropriate legislation they do not provide the basis for a private lawsuit unless they are intended to be self-executing. . . . Whether a treaty is self-executing is an issue for judicial interpretation, Restatement (Second) of Foreign Relations Law of the United States, § 154(1) (1965).

The provisions of the United Nations Charter on which plaintiff relies are Articles 55 and 56. We have found no case holding the U.N. Charter is self-executing nor has plaintiff provided us with one. There are, however, quite a few decisions stating that the Charter is not self-executing. Indeed, a significant number of decisions have [sic] [has] rejected the precise argument made here with respect to Articles 55 and 56. We agree with those rulings: Article 55 and 56 do not create rights enforceable by private litigants in American courts.

To begin with, the articles are phrased in broad generalities, suggesting that they are declarations of principles, not a code of legal rights. . . . Articles 55 and 56 create obligations on the member nations (and the United Nations itself); they do not confer rights on individual citizens. . . .

Moreover, judicial resolution of cases bearing significantly on sensitive foreign policy matters, like the case before us, might have serious foreign policy implications which courts are ill-equipped to anticipate or handle.... Soviet emigration policies have been the subject of a long-running battle between American policymakers and the Kremlin, often generating conflict between the White House and Congress. Judicial intervention into such a delicate political issue would be ill-advised and could have unforeseen consequences for American–Soviet relations.

There is no basis for concluding that Article 55 and 56 are privately enforceable. Unless the United Nations alters its fundamental nature and amends its Charter, individuals having grievances based on Articles 55 and 56 will have to be satisfied with diplomatic channels and the court of world opinion to resolve their disputes; they may not bring suit in American courts.

A treaty is primarily a compact between independent nations. It depends for the enforcement of its provisions on the interest and the honor of the governments which are parties to it. If these fail, its infraction becomes the subject of international negotiations and reclamations, so far as the injured party chooses to seek redress, which may in the end be enforced by actual war. It is obvious that with all this the judicial courts have nothing to do and can give no redress....

Similarly, we hold that the Helsinki Accords are not self-executing. Frolova contends that certain sections of that agreement create judicially-enforceable rights, including provisions concerning (1) contacts and regular meetings on the basis of family ties; (2) reunification of families; and (3) marriage between citizens of different states.

To begin with, the caution against judicial involvement in this nation's foreign relations is as applicable to the Helsinki agreement as it is to the U.N. Charter. In addition, the sections of the Helsinki Accords with which we are concerned are, like the U.N. Charter (although to a lesser degree), phrased in generalities, and there is no indication that the nations signing the agreement anticipated that it would be enforced by private litigants. Indeed, the Accords reaffirm respect for the sovereignty of its signers...and pledge noninterference in the internal affairs of those nations.... Rather, the Accords create obligations on the signatory countries and establish goals which the nations will try to reach on their own.

[...]

III.

Plaintiff next raises an argument closely related to that discussed in Part II: the Soviet Union has waived its defense of sovereign immunity. The FSIA provides that foreign countries are not immune in cases "in which the foreign state has waived its immunity either explicitly or by implication, notwithstanding any withdrawal of the waiver which the foreign state may purport to effect except in accordance with the terms of the waiver."... Frolova contends that the U.S.S.R. implicitly waived its sovereign immunity when it signed the United Nations Charter and the Helsinki Accords; in addition, she argues that waiver can be implied from the Soviet Union's failure to enter an appearance in this action.

The legislative history of the FSIA gives three examples of cases in which courts have found implied waivers: (1) a foreign state has agreed to arbitration in another country; (2) a foreign state has agreed that a contract is governed by the law of a particular country; and (3) a foreign state has filed a responsive pleading in a case without raising the defense of sovereign immunity.... Since the FSIA became law, courts have been reluctant to stray beyond these examples when considering claims that a nation has implicitly waived its defense of sovereign immunity.

Cases involving arbitration clauses illustrate that provisions allegedly waiving sovereign immunity are narrowly construed. Courts have found an implicit waiver under § 1605(a)(1) in cases involving contracts in which a foreign state has agreed to arbitrate disputes without specifying jurisdiction in a particular country or forum...or where another nation has stipulated that American law should govern any contractual disputes.... But most courts have refused to find an implicit waiver of immunity to suit in American courts from a contract clause providing for arbitration in a country other than the United States.

[...]

The discussions of § 1605(a)(1) in the committee reports refer to waiver by treaty, but only in the context of *explicit* waivers of sovereign immunity; waiver by treaty is not included in the list of examples of implicit waivers.... Courts have generally required convincing evidence that a treaty was intended to waive sovereign immunity before holding that a foreign state may be sued in this country....

Here there is absolutely no evidence from the language, structure[,] or history of the agreements at issue that implies a waiver of the U.S.S.R.'s sovereign immunity. There is no basis for finding a waiver from the vague, general language of the agreements nor is there any reason to conclude that the nations that are parties to these agreements anticipated when signing them that American courts would be the means by which the documents' provisions would be enforced.... Neither document implicitly waives the Soviet Union's defense of sovereign immunity.

Frolova's argument that the Soviet Union implicitly waived its immunity by not defending this action is also without merit. As the Supreme Court indicated in *Verlinden*, even in cases in which the defendant has not entered an appearance[,] the district court has an obligation to satisfy itself that the defense of sovereign immunity is not available before it has subject-matter jurisdiction.... Moreover, the example given in the legislative history—filing a responsive pleading without raising an immunity defense—demonstrates that Congress anticipated, at a minimum, that waiver would not be found absent a conscious decision to take part in the litigation and a failure to raise sovereign immunity despite the opportunity to do so. The case law evidences a reticence to find a waiver from the nature of a foreign state's participation in litigation....

The last statutory section on which plaintiff attempts to hang her jurisdictional hat is 28 U.S.C. § 1605(a)(5), which provides in pertinent part that immunity is waived in cases

> in which money damages are sought against a foreign state for personal injury or death, or damage to or loss of property, occurring in the United States and caused by the tortious act or omission of that foreign state or of any official or employee of that foreign state while acting within the scope of his office or employment....

At first blush, it appears that there is jurisdiction if the injury, as here, occurs in this country, regardless of whether the tortious act causing the injury occurred within this nation's borders. At least one district court has read § 1605(a)(5) this broadly...but this interpretation has been rejected by the Court of Appeals for that circuit....

The reason that the decisions...reject the broad construction of § 1605(a)(5) posited by plaintiff, and the reason we join them today, is that there is explicit legislative history indicating that Congress intended that the tortious act or omission, as well as the injury, occur in the United States.

Notes and Questions

1. The plaintiff's dispute with the U.S.S.R. involved intense and highly personal emotions. Her strategy was to file a provocative lawsuit to generate public attention to and interest in her marital and immigration plight. Are any of the legal arguments she makes—from injunctive relief to self-executing treaty law to her reading of the FSIA—even conceivable, let alone sound? Does the court take these arguments too seriously? Is the case simply another small episode in cold war theatrics and rhetoric? Is there any diminution of separation of powers as a result?

2. There must have been some powerful political and private forces at work to achieve the outcome. The most effective way to deal with a political entity like a State is by marshalling political pressures. There is, of course, no way to verify this speculation because there is no public record of the possible maneuvering. This aspect of the matter illustrates the respective functions of the executive and the judiciary and how differently they perform their tasks. The larger lesson of the case may be that the State can be held accountable only on its own terms and that the reach of the judiciary in its regard is extremely limited in all, even statutorily permissible, circumstances.

3. You should pay particular attention to the part of the opinion that describes the old function of FSIA § 1605(a)(1) on implied and express waivers. The prior law provided in some cases that the State's agreement to arbitrate disputes amounted to an implied waiver of sovereign immunity. Under the arbitration agreement, the State had agreed to the exercise of jurisdiction by the arbitral tribunal and impliedly agreed to the exercise of state judicial jurisdiction in connection with the arbitration: To enforce the agreement and supervise the award. FSIA § 1605(a)(6), the "arbitration exception," make that prior position unnecessary.

TEXAS TRADING & MILLING CORP. v. FEDERAL REPUBLIC OF NIGERIA

500 F.Supp. 320 (S.D.N.Y.1980), *reversed*, 647 F.2d 300 (2d Cir.1981), *cert. denied*, 454 U.S. 1148, 102 S.Ct. 1012, 71 L.Ed.2d 301 (1982).

IRVING R. KAUFMAN, Circuit Judge:

These four appeals grow out of one of the most enormous commercial disputes in history, and present questions which strike to [sic] [at] the very heart of the modern international economic order. An African nation, developing at breakneck speed by virtue of huge exports of high-grade oil, contracted to buy huge quantities of Portland cement, a commodity crucial to the construction of its infrastructure. It overbought, and the country's docks and harbors became clogged with ships waiting to unload. Imports of other goods ground to a halt. More vessels carrying cement arrived daily; still others were steaming towards the port. Unable to accept delivery of the cement it had bought, the nation repudiated its contracts. In response to suits brought by disgruntled suppliers, it now seeks to invoke an ancient maxim of sovereign immunity—*par in parem imperium non habet*—to insulate itself from liability. But Latin phrases speak with a hoary simplicity inappropriate to the modern financial world. For the ruling principles here, we must look instead to a new and vaguely-worded statute, the Foreign Sovereign Immunities Act of 1976 ("FSIA" or "Act")—a law described by its draftsmen as providing only "very modest guidance" on issues of preeminent importance. For answers to those most difficult questions, the authors of the law "decided to put [their] faith in the U.S. courts." Guided by reason, precedent, and equity, we have attempted to give form and substance to the legislative intent. Accordingly, we find that the defense of sovereign immunity is not available in any of these four cases.

I.

The facts of the four appeals are remarkably parallel, and can be stated in somewhat consolidated form. Early in 1975, the Federal Military Government of the Federal Republic of Nigeria ("Nigeria") embarked on an ambitious program to purchase immense amounts of cement.... Nigeria executed 109 contracts, with 68 suppliers. It purchased, in all, over 16 million metric tons of cement. The price was close to one billion dollars.

A.

Four of the 109 contracts were made with American companies.... The four plaintiffs are not industrial corporations; they are, instead, "trading companies," which buy from one person and sell to another in hope[] of making a profit on the differential. Each of the plaintiffs is a New York corporation.

The contracts at issue were signed early in 1975. Each is substantially similar; indeed, Nigeria seems to have mimeographed them in blank, and filled in details with individual suppliers. Overall, each contract called for the sale by the supplier to Nigeria of 240,000 metric tons of Portland cement. Specifically, the contracts required Nigeria, within a time certain after execution, to establish in the seller's favor "an Irrevocable, Transferable abroad, Divisible and Confirmed letter of credit" for the total amount due under the particular contract, slightly over $14 million in each case. The contract also named the bank through which the letter of credit was to be made payable.... Drafts under the letters of credit were to be "payable at sight, on presentation" of certain documents to the specified bank.

Within a certain time after establishment and receipt of the letter of credit, each seller was to start shipping cement to Nigeria. The cement was to be bagged, and was to meet certain chemical specifications. Shipments were to be from ports named in the contracts, mostly Spanish, and were to proceed at approximately 20,000 tons per month. Delivery was to the port of Lagos/Apapa, Nigeria, and the seller was obligated to insure the freight to the Nigerian quay. Each contract also provided for demurrage....

In short, performance under the contracts was to proceed as follows. Nigeria was to establish letters of credit. The suppliers were to ship cement. Each time a supplier had loaded a ship and insured its cargo to Lagos/Apapa, the supplier could take documents so proving to the bank named in the contract and, "at sight," be paid for the amount of cement it shipped. The ship might sink on the way to Nigeria, or it might never leave the Spanish port at all, but—on presentation of proper documents showing a loaded ship and an insured cargo—the supplier had a right to be paid. Demurrage was to operate in the same manner: if a ship was detained in Nigerian waters, the supplier would receive certain documents. It could present the documents to the bank, and receive payment.

The actual financial arrangements differed from those set forth in the cement contracts. Instead of establishing "confirmed" letters of credit with the banks named, Nigeria established what it called "irrevocable" letters of credit with the Central Bank of Nigeria ("Central Bank"), an instrumentality of the Nigerian government, and advised those letters of credit through the Morgan Guaranty Trust Company ("Morgan") of New York. That is, under the letters of credit as established, each seller was to present appropriate documents not to the named bank, but to Morgan. And, since the letters were not "confirmed," Morgan did not promise to pay "on sight"; it assumed no independent liability. Each of the letters of credit provided it was to be governed by the Uniform Customs and Practice for Documentary Credits ("UCP") (1962 Revision), as set forth in Brochure No. 222 of the International Chamber of Commerce.

Nigeria's choice of Morgan as a bank to which suppliers presented documents and from which suppliers secured payments came in the course of a longstanding relationship between Nigeria and Morgan. Central Bank used Morgan as its correspondent bank in the United

States, and Morgan conducted myriad transactions on Nigeria's behalf. Employees of Central Bank regularly came to Morgan for training seminars. On Nigeria's request, Morgan made payments to Nigerian students in the United States, to American corporations to which Nigeria owed money, and to the Nigerian embassy and consulates in the United States. Indeed, Nigeria used Morgan to make payments (for salaries, operating expenses, and the like) to Nigerian embassies in other countries as well. Until 1974, Morgan had the right to draw up to $1 million per day from Nigeria's account at the Federal Reserve Bank of New York to satisfy Nigeria's obligations. Nigeria raised the limit to $3 million per day in 1974, and Morgan enjoyed unlimited drawing rights on Nigeria's funds beginning in November 1975. Central Bank kept over $200 million of securities in a custody account at Morgan. Morgan advised as much as $200 million in letters of credit established by Nigeria, and confirmed, in addition, letters of credit totaling at least $70 million more.

After receiving notice that the letters of credit ha[d] been established, the suppliers set out to secure subcontracts to procure the cement, and shipping contracts to transport it. They, through their subcontractors, began to bag the cement and load it on ships, as suppliers across the globe were doing the same. Hundreds of ships arrived in Lagos/Apapa in the summer of 1975, and most were carrying cement. Nigeria's port facilities could accept only one to five million tons of cement per year; at any rate, they could not begin to unload the over sixteen million tons Nigeria had slated for delivery in eighteen short months. Based on prior experience, Nigeria had made the contracts expecting only twenty percent of the suppliers to be able to perform. By July, when the harbor held over 400 ships waiting to unload—260 of them carrying cement—Nigeria realized it had misjudged the market considerably.

C.

With demurrage piling up at astronomical rates, and suppliers, hiring, loading, and dispatching more ships daily, Nigeria decided to act. On August 9, 1975, Nigeria caused its Ports Authority to issue Government Notice No. 1434, a regulation which stated that, effective August 18, all ships destined for Lagos/Apapa would be required to convey to the Ports Authority, two months before sailing, certain information concerning their time of arrival in the port. The regulation also stated vaguely that the Ports Authority would "co-ordinate all sailing," and that it would "refus[e] service" to vessels which did not comply with the regulation. Then, on August 18, Nigeria cabled its suppliers and asked them to stop sending cement, and to cease loading or even chartering ships. In late September, Nigeria took the crucial step: Central Bank instructed Morgan not to pay under the letters of credit unless the supplier submitted—in addition to the documents required by the letter of credit as written—a statement from Central Bank that payment ought to be made. Morgan notified each supplier of Nigeria's instructions, and

Morgan commenced refusing to make payment under the letters of credit as written. Almost three months later, on December 19, 1975, Nigeria promulgated Decree No. 40, a law prohibiting entry into a Nigerian port to any ship which had not secured two months' prior approval, and imposing criminal penalties for unauthorized entry.

Nigeria's unilateral alteration of the letters of credit took place on a scale previously unknown to international commerce. Officers of Morgan explained the potential consequences of Nigeria's action to representatives of Central Bank; Central Bank was adamant that Morgan not pay. After a meeting with Central Bank personnel, one Morgan officer stated that Central Bank's Deputy Governor "responded that the [Nigerian] Government was willing to go to court if we did pay." Within weeks of Nigeria's instructions to Morgan not to pay without the additional documentation, Morgan warned Central Bank in a telex: "We believe that there is an increasing possibility that litigation against you may be instituted in New York."

Nigeria's next step was to invite its suppliers to cancel the contracts. As part of the program, Nigeria convened a meeting at Morgan's offices in New York, to discuss Nigeria's position with members of the American financial community. Over forty suppliers eventually did settle....

Cement suppliers who did not settle sued in courts all over the world. The four suppliers at issue here—Texas Trading, Nikkei, East Europe, and Chenax—sued in the Southern District of New York. Named as defendants were both Nigeria and Central Bank. The complaints alleged that Central Bank's September instructions to Morgan, changing the terms of payment under the letters of credit, constituted anticipatory breaches of both the cement contracts (requiring Nigeria to establish "Irrevocable" letters of credit with certain terms of payment) and the letters of credit (requiring Central Bank to authorize payment when certain documents were presented to Morgan). Defendants do not seriously dispute that their actions constitute such anticipatory breaches; their defenses go more to the propriety of jurisdiction under the FSIA....

II.

The law before us is complex and largely unconstrued, and has introduced sweeping changes in some areas of prior law.... In structure, the FSIA is a marvel of compression. Within the bounds of a few tersely-worded sections, it purports to provide answers to three crucial questions in a suit against a foreign state: the availability of sovereign immunity as a defense, the presence of subject matter jurisdiction over the claim, and the propriety of personal jurisdiction over the defendant.... Through a series of intricately coordinated provisions, the FSIA seems at first glance to make the answer to one of the questions, subject matter jurisdiction, dispositive of all three.... This economy of decision has come, however, at the price of considerable confusion in the district courts. In fact, Congress intended the sovereign immunity and subject matter jurisdiction decisions to remain slightly distinct, and it drafted the Act accordingly. Moreover, Congress has only an incomplete power to tie personal jurisdiction to subject matter jurisdiction; its prerogatives are constrained by the due process clause. These cases present an opportunity to untie the FSIA's Gordian knot, and to vindicate the Congressional purposes behind the Act.

A.

Turning to the specific provisions of the law, a description of the FSIA's analytic structure is helpful. The jurisdiction-conferring provision of the Act . . . creates [original jurisdiction] in the district courts. . . . Crucial to . . . [jurisdiction] is the phrase "commercial activity." In it is lodged centuries of Anglo–American and civil law precedent constructing [sic] [construing] the term "sovereign immunity." If the activity is not "commercial," but rather, is "governmental," then the foreign state is entitled to immunity under section 1605, and "original jurisdiction" is not present under § 1330(a).

. . . If commercial activity under § 1603(d) is present, and if it bears the relation to the United States required by § 1605(a)(2), then the foreign state is "not entitled to immunity," and the district court has statutory subject matter jurisdiction over the claim through § 1330(a). And, if the exercise of that jurisdiction falls within the judicial power set forth by Article III of the Constitution, subject matter jurisdiction over the claim exists.

Our analysis next proceeds to the question of personal jurisdiction. . . . The Act . . . makes the statutory aspect of personal jurisdiction simple: subject matter jurisdiction plus service of process equals personal jurisdiction. . . . But, the Act cannot create personal jurisdiction where the constitution forbids it. Accordingly, each finding of personal jurisdiction under the FSIA requires, in addition, a due process scrutiny of the court's power to exercise its authority over a particular defendant.

In short, a "§ 1605(a)(2) case" calls for the resolution of a series of five questions:

1) Does the conduct the action is based upon or related to qualify as "commercial activity"?

2) Does that commercial activity bear the relation to the cause of action and to the United States described by one of the three phrases of § 1605(a)(2), warranting the Court's exercise of subject matter jurisdiction under § 1330(a)?

3) Does the exercise of this congressional subject matter jurisdiction lie within the permissible limits of the "judicial power" set forth in Article III?

4) Do subject matter jurisdiction under § 1330(a) and service under § 1608 exist, thereby making personal jurisdiction proper under § 1330(b)?

5) Does the exercise of personal jurisdiction under § 1330(b) comply with the due process clause, thus making personal jurisdiction proper?

[. . .]

B.

Before undertaking the threshold "commercial activity" analysis, our first task is to identify what particular conduct in this case is relevant. Subsection 1603(d) states that "commercial activity" might consist of either "a regular course of commercial conduct" or "a particular commercial transaction or act." The words "regular course of. . .conduct" seem to authorize courts to cast the net wide, and to identify a broad series of acts as the relevant set of activities. . . . Here the relevant "course of. . .conduct" is undoubtedly Nigeria's massive cement purchase program. Alternatively, each of its contracts or letters of credit with these four plaintiffs would qualify as "a particular. . .transaction."

The determination of whether particular behavior is "commercial" is perhaps the most important decision a court faces in an FSIA suit. This problem is significant because the primary purpose of the Act is to "restrict" the immunity of a foreign state to suits involving a foreign state's public acts. . . . If the activity is not "commercial," it satisfies none of the three clauses of § 1605(a)(2), and the foreign state is (at least under that subsection) immune from suit. Unfortunately, the definition of "commercial" is the one issue on which the Act provides almost no guidance at all. Subsection 1603(d) advances the inquiry somewhat, for it provides: "The commercial character of an activity shall be determined by reference to the nature of the course of conduct or particular transaction or act, rather than by reference to its purpose." No provision of the Act, however, defines "commercial." Congress deliberately left the meaning open and, as noted above, "put [its] faith in the U.S. courts to work out progressively, on a case-by-case basis. . .the distinction between commercial and governmental.". . . We are referred to no less than three separate sources of authority to resolve this fundamental definitional question.

The first source is statements contained in the legislative history itself. Perhaps the clearest of them was made by Bruno Ristau, then Chief of the Foreign Litigation Section of the Civil Division, Department of Justice. Ristau stated: "[I]f a government enters into a contract to purchase goods and services, that is considered a commercial activity. It avails itself of the ordinary contract machinery. It bargains and negotiates. It accepts an offer. It enters into a written contract and the contract is to be performed." . . . The House Report seems to conclude that a contract or series of contracts for the purchase of goods would be *per se* a "commercial activity,". . .and the illustrations cited by experts who testified on the bill—contracts, for example, for the sale of army boots or grain—support such a rule. Or, put another way, if the activity is one in which a private person could engage, it is not entitled to immunity. . . .

The second source for interpreting the phrase "commercial activity" is the "very large body of case law which exist[ed]" in American law upon passage of the Act in 1976.... Testifying on an earlier version of the bill, Charles N. Brower, then Legal Adviser of the Department of State, stated:

> [T]he restrictive theory of sovereign immunity from jurisdiction, which has been followed by the Department of State and the courts since it was articulated in the familiar letter of Acting Legal Adviser Jack B. Tate of May 29, 1952, would be incorporated into statutory law. This theory limits immunity to public acts, leaving so-called private acts subject to suit. The proposed legislation would make it clear that immunity cannot be claimed with respect to acts or transactions that are commercial in nature, regardless of their underlying purpose.

[...]

Finally, current standards of international law concerning sovereign immunity add content to the "commercial activity" phrase of the FSIA....

Under each of these three standards, Nigeria's cement contracts and letters of credit qualify as "commercial activity." Lord Denning, writing in *Trendtex Trading Corp. v. Central Bank of Nigeria*, [1977] 2 W.L.R. 356, 369, 1 All E.R. 881...stated: "If a government department goes into the market places of the world and buys boots or cement—as a commercial transaction—that government department should be subject to all the rules of the marketplace." Nigeria's activity here is in the nature of a private contract for the purchase of goods. Its purpose—to build roads, army barracks, whatever—is irrelevant. Accordingly, courts in other nations have uniformly held Nigeria's 1975 cement purchase program and appurtenant letters of credit to be "commercial activity," and have denied the defense of sovereign immunity. We find defendants' activity here to constitute "commercial activity," and we move on to the next step of analysis.

C.

1.

We need look no further than the third clause of § 1605(a)(2) to find statutory subject matter jurisdiction here. That clause provides: "A foreign state shall not be immune...in any case...in which the action is based...upon an act outside the territory of the United States in connection with a commercial activity of the foreign state elsewhere and that act causes a direct effect in the United States."

The focus of our analysis is to determine whether "the act cause[d] a direct effect in the United States" within the meaning of the FSIA. The "direct effect" clause has been the subject of considerable commentary, but remains somewhat abstruse....Here, under either theory of recovery, breach of the cement contracts or breach of the letters of credit, the effect on the suppliers was "direct." They were beneficiaries of the contracts that were breached....

Finally, the most difficult aspect of the direct effect clause concerns its phrase, "in the United States." State law abounds with decisions locating "effects" for personal jurisdiction purposes. But those cases are not precisely on point, for they are concerned more with federalism, and less with international relations, than was Congress in passing the FSIA. Reliance on state cases is not necessary here because the financial loss in these cases occurred "in the United States" for two much simpler reasons. First, the cement suppliers were to present documents and collect money in the United States, and the breaches precluded their doing so. Second, each of the plaintiffs is an American corporation. Whether a failure to pay a foreign corporation in the United States or to pay an American corporation overseas creates an effect "in the United States" under § 1605(a)(2) is not before us. Both factors are present here, and the subsection is clearly satisfied....

The foregoing analysis demonstrates that neither "direct" nor "in the United States" is a term susceptible of easy definition. A corporation is no more than a series of conduits, filtering profit—or loss—through each stage from the company's customers to its shareholders, who may themselves be fictional entities as well. Harm to any component is somewhat "indirect," and locating the site of the injury, especially when the harm consists in an omission, is an enterprise fraught with artifice. Courts construing either term should be mindful more of Congress's concern with providing "access to the courts" to those aggrieved by the commercial acts of a foreign sovereign... than with cases defining "direct" or locating effects under state statutes passed for dissimilar purposes. Before the FSIA, plaintiffs enjoyed a broad right to bring suits against foreign states, subject only to State Department intervention and the presence of attachable assets. Congress in the FSIA certainly did not intend significantly to constrict jurisdiction; it intended to regularize it....The question is, was the effect sufficiently "direct" and sufficiently "in the United States" that Congress would have wanted an American court to hear the case? No rigid parsing of § 1605(a)(2) should lose sight of that purpose. We have no doubt that Congress intended to bring suits like these into American courts...and we hold that statutory subject matter jurisdiction here exists.

2.

The final step in establishing the court's right to hear the claim is to find a constitutional basis for the statutory exercise of subject matter jurisdiction.... Each of these four suits is "between a State, or the Citizens thereof, and foreign States," U.S. Const., art. III, § 2, cl. 1, and therefore comes within the judicial power by way of the diversity grant. Indeed, it is to that clause that the drafters of the FSIA looked in securing a constitutional basis for FSIA suits generally.... The district court, we conclude, had the power to hear these claims.

D.

1.

Subsequent to the determination of subject matter jurisdiction is the issue of personal jurisdiction. The statutory aspects of the analysis are quite simple. Subsection 1330(b) provides for personal jurisdiction over the foreign state as to any claim the district court has power to hear under § 1608. Service here has been made, or at least not objected to.... Subject matter jurisdiction exists, so statutory personal jurisdiction exists as well.

Turning to the constitutional constraints on personal jurisdiction, our first inquiry must be whether the safeguards of due process, which otherwise regulate every exercise of personal jurisdiction, apply to FSIA cases at all. Specifically, is a foreign state a "person" within the meaning of the due process clause?...[In prior cases,] we applied constitutional due process analysis to a suit against a foreign state. We affirm that holding today....

Since the constitutional constraints apply here, our next concern must be to delineate the contacts that are relevant. The inquiry has two aspects: whose contacts, and with what? To bring any defendant before the court, of course, the due process analysis must be satisfied as to him. Nonetheless, it is not only defendant's activities in the forum, but also actions relevant to the transaction by an agent on defendant's behalf, which support personal jurisdiction.... Central Bank's activities with respect to the "commercial activity" are chargeable to Nigeria, and Morgan's activities are chargeable to both. If Morgan had not performed for Central Bank, and Central Bank for Nigeria, the entire payment mechanism supporting cement contracts, Nigeria would have been required to make the payments directly.... Since service was made under § 1608, the relevant area in delineating contacts is the entire United States, not merely New York....

The facts of these cases establish that Central Bank, and through Central Bank Nigeria, repeatedly and "purposefully avail[ed themselves]" of the privilege of conducting activities in the United States.... Central Bank alone sent its employees to New York for training, kept large cash balances here, and maintained a custody account as well. If Morgan had converted Central Bank's funds from either account, New York law would have protected Central Bank, and allowed it to sue. Central Bank made it a regular practice to advise letters of credit through Morgan, and to use Morgan as its means of paying bills throughout the world. New York law protected Central Bank in each of its instructions, transfers, and withdrawals. Central Bank's activities with respect to the cement contracts and the letters of credit, [activities] directly chargeable to Nigeria...show the same pattern. In Nigeria's behalf and on Nigeria's instructions, Central Bank advised each of the letters of credit through Morgan, in the United States, regardless of the individual supplier's wishes. Having chosen American law and process as their protectors, Nigeria and Central Bank were not hesitant to invoke them; at the mere hint Morgan was reluctant to honor defendants' amendments to the letters of credit, an officer of Central Bank threatened to "go to court" to enforce them.

[. . .]

. . . In light of defendants' intentional activities in the United States, litigation was clearly foreseeable here.

Although the United States is certainly distant from Nigeria, litigation here is not unduly inconvenient for defendants. Every modern transnational commercial contract presents problems of adjudicatory cost; in the cement purchase program, where Nigeria bargained with corporations from the plethora of nations, required in the contracts that the goods came mostly from Europe, and provided in some letters of credit that payment was to be made in the United States, the inconvenience was at least expected. Moreover, Nigeria in the cement contracts agreed to submit to arbitration by the International Chamber of Commerce ("ICC"). The ICC's headquarters are in Paris, but its arbitrations can take place anywhere in the world. . . .

Here, we should not be unmindful that Congress has passed the FSIA specifically to provide "access to the court." . . . Similarly, the plaintiff has an "interest in obtaining convenient and effective relief." . . . Accordingly, we hold that defendants' relation to the forum here satisfied the "minimum contacts" requirement. . . .

III.

Our rulings today vindicate more than Congressional intent. They affirm the right of all participants in the marketplace of the world to be treated as equals, and to ascribe to principles of trade which found their birth in the law merchant, centuries ago. Corporations can enter contracts without fear that the defense of sovereign immunity will be inequitably interposed, and foreign states can bargain without paying a premium required by a trader in anticipation of a judgment-proof client. Commerce is fostered, and all interests are advanced.

. . . [T]he district court held jurisdiction to be present, and proceeded to the trial of plaintiffs' claims. We find no error in its rulings on the merits, and affirm those three judgments in full. In *Texas Trading*, the district court ordered the complaint dismissed for lack of jurisdiction. That order is reversed, and the case is remanded for proceedings consistent with this opinion.

Notes and Questions

1. *Texas Trading* is a justly famous case. It represents a sound and predictable application and construction of the text of the FSIA and its "commercial activity" exception. The ruling eliminates the State's shield to jurisdictional and other forms of accountability whenever the governmental entity engages in private commercial conduct. It also represents a substantial embarrassment to the Government of Nigeria because the ministerial

appraisal of market conditions was so erroneous and ultimately costly. As the court reports: "Nigeria executed 109 contracts, with 68 suppliers. It purchased, in all, over 16 million metric tons of cement. The price was close to one billion dollars." This was $1 billion in the late 1970s. Should the court have made some effort to adjust matters in light of Nigeria's status as a developing African country? Does the FSIA permit such adjustments? Are such solutions within judicial discretion and authority? Was the dispute justiciable? Why and why not? What would have been the result if the U.S. State Department submitted an *amicus curia* brief, stating that the lawsuit would cause significant damage to the U.S. foreign policy interest in Nigeria and the African region?

2. Explain what the court means when it describes the FSIA as a "marvel of compression," which in its "vaguely-worded" provisions provides "very modest guidance" on critical issues. Do you agree with the court's assessment?

3. How does the court address the issues of subject matter jurisdiction, personal jurisdiction, and the availability of the sovereign immunity defense? Are the three factors separable under the FSIA and the circumstances of the case? How do you assess the court's five-part test?

4. How do the comments of Ristau and Brower clarify the meaning of "commercial activity" under the FSIA?

5. What contact exists between the United States and the transaction for purposes of jurisdiction?

6. Do you agree with the court's evaluation of its opinion that appears after "III"?

7. Assess the court's reference to the arbitral clauses in the purchase contracts? Do they or should they have eliminated U.S. court jurisdiction? Why aren't these cases in arbitration?

8. When does the State engage in a commercial activity?

* * * *

A subsequent opinion addressing the same Nigerian purchase of cement transaction concluded that the FSIA allowed foreign plaintiffs to sue the Nigerian State in U.S. court. The legislation thereby acquired an extraterritorial reach and U.S. substantive standards came to regulate the commercial liability of foreign States in regard to private foreign parties. Not only could such a position enhance the volume of U.S. litigation, but it could also have a highly disruptive impact upon U.S. foreign policy.

VERLINDEN v. CENTRAL BANK OF NIGERIA

461 U.S. 480, 103 S.Ct. 1962, 76 L.Ed. 2d 81 (1983).

Chief Justice Burger delivered the opinion of the Court.

[. . .]

We granted *certiorari* to consider whether the Foreign Sovereign Immunities Act of 1976, by authorizing a foreign plaintiff to sue a foreign state in the United States district court on a nonfederal cause of action, violates Article III of the Constitution.

I.

On April 21, 1975, the Federal Republic of Nigeria and petitioner Verlinden B.V., a Dutch corporation with its principal offices in Amsterdam, the Netherlands, entered into a contract providing for the purchase of 240,000 metric tons of cement by Nigeria. The parties agreed that the contract would be governed by the laws of the Netherlands and that disputes would be resolved by arbitration before the International Chamber of Commerce, Paris, France.

The contract provided that the Nigerian Government was to establish an irrevocable, confirmed letter of credit.... According to petitioner's amended complaint, however, respondent Central Bank of Nigeria, an instrumentality of Nigeria, improperly established an unconfirmed letter of credit payable through Morgan Guaranty Trust Co. in New York.

II.

In August 1975, Verlinden subcontracted with a Liechtenstein corporation, Interbuco, to purchase the cement needed to fulfill the contract. Meanwhile, the ports of Nigeria had become clogged with hundreds of ships carrying cement, sent by numerous other cement suppliers with whom Nigeria also had entered into contracts. In mid-September, Central Bank unilaterally directed its correspondent banks, including Morgan Guaranty, to adopt a series of amendments to all letters of credit issued in connection with the cement contracts. Central Bank also directly notified the suppliers that payment would be made only for those shipments approved by Central Bank two months before their arrival in Nigerian waters.

Verlinden then sued Central Bank in the United States District Court for the Southern District of New York, alleging that Central Bank's actions constituted an anticipatory breach of the letter of credit. Verlinden alleged jurisdiction under the Foreign Sovereign Immunities Act, 28 USC § 1330 [28 USCS § 1330]. Respondent moved to dismiss for, among other reasons, lack of subject matter and personal jurisdiction.

[. . .]

III.

[. . .] The District Court and the Court of Appeals both held that the Foreign Sovereign Immunities Act purports to allow a foreign plaintiff to sue a foreign sovereign in the courts of the Untied States, provided the substantive requirements of the Act are satisfied. We agree.

On its face, the language of the statute is unambiguous. The statute grants jurisdiction over "any nonjury civil action against a foreign state. . . with respect to which the foreign state is not entitled to immunity." 28 USC § 1330(a) [28 USCS § 1330(a)]. The Act contains no indication of any limitation based on the citizenship of the plaintiff.

The legislative history is less clear in this regard. The House Report recites that the Act would provide jurisdiction for "*any* claim with respect to which the foreign state is not entitled to immunity under sections 1605–1607." HR Rep. No. 94–1487, *supra*, at 13 (emphasis added), and also states that its purpose was "to provide when and how *parties* can maintain a lawsuit against a foreign state or its entities," *id.*, at 6 (emphasis added). At another point, however, the Report refers to the growing number of disputes between "American citizens" and foreign states, *id.*, at 6–7, and expresses the desire to ensure "*our citizens*. . . access to the courts," *id.*, at 6 (emphasis added).

Notwithstanding this reference to "our citizens," we conclude that when considered as a whole, the legislative history reveals an intent not to limit jurisdiction under the Act to actions brought by American citizens. Congress was aware of concern that "our courts [might be] turned into small 'international courts of claims[,]'. . .open. . .to all comers to litigate any dispute which any private party may have with a foreign state anywhere in the world." Testimony of Bruno A. Ristau, Hearings on HR 11315, at 31. As the language of the statute reveals, Congress protected against this danger not by restricting the class of potential plaintiffs, but rather by enacting substantive provisions requiring some form of substantial contact with the United States. *See* 28 USC § 1605 [28 USCS § 1605]. If an action satisfies the substantive standards of the Act, it may be brought in federal court regardless of the citizenship of the plaintiff.

IV.

[. . .] We now turn to the core question presented by this case: whether Congress exceeded the scope of Art. III of the Constitution by granting federal courts subject matter jurisdiction over certain civil actions by foreign plaintiffs against foreign sovereigns where the rule of decision may be provided by state law.

This Court's cases firmly establish that Congress may not expand the jurisdiction of the federal court beyond the bounds established by the Constitution. *See, e.g., Hodgson v. Bowerbank*, 5 Cranch 303, 3 L. Ed. 108 (1809); *Kline v. Burke Construction Co.*, 260 U.S. 226, 234, 67 L.Ed. 226, 43 S. Ct. 79 (1922). Within Art. III of the Constitution, we find two sources authorizing the grant of jurisdiction in the Foreign Sovereign Immunities Act: The Diversity Clause and the "Arising Under" Clause. The Diversity Clause, which provides that the judicial power extends to controversies between "a State, or the Citizens thereof, and foreign States," covers actions by citizens of states. Yet diversity jurisdiction is not sufficiently broad to support a grant of jurisdiction over actions by foreign plaintiffs, since a foreign plaintiff is not "a State or [a] Citize[n] thereof." *See Moseman v. Higginson*, 4 Dall 12, 1 L.Ed. 720 (1800). We conclude however, that the "Arising Under" Clause of Art. III provides an appropriate basis for the statutory grant of subject matter jurisdiction to actions by foreign plaintiffs under the Act.

The controlling decision on the scope of Art. III "arising under" jurisdiction is Chief Justice Marshall's opinion for the Court in *Osborn v. Bank of United States*, 9 Wheat 738, 6 L. Ed. 204 (1824). In *Osborn*, the Court upheld the constitutionality of a statute that granted the Bank of the United States the right to sue in federal court on causes of action based upon state law. There, the Court concluded that the "judicial department may receive...the power of construing every...law" that "the Legislature may constitutionally make."... The rule was laid down that "it [is] a sufficient foundation for jurisdiction that the title or right set up by the party may be defeated by one construction of the constitution or law[s] of the United States and sustained by the opposite construction."...[T]he present case does not involve a mere speculative possibility that a federal question may arise at some point in the proceeding. Rather, a suit against a foreign state under this Act necessarily raises questions of substantive federal law at the very outset, and hence clearly "arises under" federal law, as that term is used in Art. III.

[...] By reason of its authority over foreign commerce and foreign relations, Congress has the undisputed power to decide, as a matter of federal law, whether and under what circumstances foreign nations should be amenable to suit in the United States. Actions against foreign sovereigns in our courts raise sensitive issues concerning the foreign relations of the United States, and the primacy of federal concerns is evident....Congress exercised its Art. I powers by enacting a statute comprehensively regulating the amenability of foreign nations to suit in the United States. The statute must be applied by the district courts in every action against a foreign sovereign, since subject matter jurisdiction in any such action depends on the existence of one of the specified exceptions to foreign sovereign immunity, 28 USC § 1330(a) [28 USCS § 1330(a)]. At the threshold of every action in a district court against a foreign state, therefore, the court must satisfy itself that one of the exceptions applies—and in doing so it must apply the detailed federal law standards set forth in the Act. Accordingly, an action against a foreign sovereign arises under federal law, for purposes of Art. III jurisdiction.

[...]

[I]n enacting the Foreign Sovereign Immunities Act, Congress expressly exercised its power to regulate foreign commerce along with other specified Art. I powers....As the House Report clearly indicates, the primary purpose of the Act was to "se[t] forth comprehensive rules governing sovereign immunity," HR Rep. No. 94–1487, p. 12 (1976); the jurisdictional provisions of the Act are simply one part of this comprehensive scheme. The Act thus does not merely concern access to the federal courts. Rather, it governs the types of actions for which foreign sovereigns may be held liable in a court in the United States, federal or state. The Act codifies the standards governing foreign sovereign immunity as an aspect of substantive federal law,...and applying those standards will generally require interpretation of numerous points of federal law. Finally, if a court determines that none of the exceptions to sovereign immunity applies, the plaintiff will be barred from raising his claim in any court in the United States—manifestly, "the title or right set up by the party, may be defeated by one construction of the. . . laws of the United States, and sustained by the opposite construction." *Osborn v. Bank of United States*, 9 Wheat, at 822, 6 L. Ed. 204. That the inquiry into foreign sovereign immunity is labeled under the Act as a matter of jurisdiction does not affect the constitutionality of Congress' action in granting federal courts jurisdiction over cases calling for application of this comprehensive regulatory statute.

[. . .] Congress, pursuant to its unquestioned Art. I powers, has enacted a broad statutory framework governing assertions of foreign sovereign immunity. In so doing, Congress deliberately sought to channel cases against foreign sovereigns away from the state courts and into federal courts, thereby reducing the potential for a multiplicity of conflicting results among the courts of the 50 States. The resulting jurisdictional grant is within the bounds of Art. III, since every action against a foreign sovereign necessarily involves application of a body of substantive federal law, and accordingly "arises under" federal law, within the meaning of Art. III.

V.

[. . .] A conclusion that the grant of jurisdiction in the Foreign Sovereign Immunities Act is consistent with the Constitution does not end the case. An action must not only satisfy Art. III but must also be supported by a statutory grant of subject matter jurisdiction. As we have made clear, deciding whether statutory subject matter jurisdiction exists under the Foreign Sovereign Immunities Act entails an application of the substantive terms of the Act to determine whether one of the specified exceptions to immunity applies.

In the present case, the District Court, after satisfying itself as to the constitutionality of the Act, held that the present action does not fall within any specified exception. The Court of Appeals, reaching a contrary conclusion as to jurisdiction under the Constitution, did not find it necessary to address this statutory question. Accordingly, on remand the Court of Appeals must consider whether jurisdiction exists under the act itself. If the Court of Appeals agrees with the District Court on that issue, the case will be at an end. If, on the other hand, the Court of Appeals concludes that jurisdiction does exist under the statute, the action may then be remanded to the District Court for further proceedings.

It is so ordered.

* * * *

In 1992, the U.S. Supreme Court affirmed the approach that had been adopted in *Texas Trading*. The issuing of bonds by a foreign government was a commercial act under the FSIA no matter what purpose or motivation underlay the State conduct. The bonds were "garden-variety debt instruments." Here, the foreign government was not a regulator of the financial market, but rather assumed the role of a player. Therefore, the foreign government could not unilaterally reschedule the repayment of its debt. Moreover, the transaction between the foreign State and foreign parties had enough of a "direct effect" in the United States to attribute jurisdiction to U.S. courts. The linkage in these circumstances was to a U.S. bank in New York City.

REPUBLIC OF ARGENTINA v. WELTOVER, INC.

504 U.S. 607, 112 S.Ct. 2160, 119 L.Ed.2d 394 (1992).

(footnotes omitted)

JUSTICE SCALIA delivered the opinion of the Court.

This case requires us to decide whether the Republic of Argentina's default on certain bonds issued as part of a plan to stabilize its currency was an act taken "in connection with a commercial activity" that had a "direct effect in the United States" so as to subject Argentina to suit in an American court under the Foreign Sovereign Immunities Act of 1976, 28 U.S.C. § 1602 *et seq.*

I.

Since Argentina's currency is not one of the mediums of exchange accepted on the international market, Argentine businesses engaging in foreign transactions must pay in United States dollars or some other internationally accepted currency. In the recent past, it was difficult for Argentine borrowers to obtain such funds, principally because of the instability of the Argentine currency. To address these problems, petitioners, the Republic of Argentina and its central bank, Banco Central (collectively Argentina), in 1981 instituted a foreign exchange insurance contract program (FEIC), under which Argentina effectively agreed to assume the risk of currency depreciation in cross-border transactions involving Argentine borrowers. This was accomplished by Argentina's agreeing to sell to domestic borrowers, in exchange for a contractually predetermined amount of local currency, the necessary United States dollars to repay their foreign debts when they matured, irrespective of intervening devaluations.

Unfortunately, Argentina did not possess sufficient reserves of United States dollars to cover the FEIC contracts as they became due in 1982. The Argentine Government thereupon adopted certain emergency measures, including refinancing of the FEIC-backed debts by issuing to the creditors government bonds. These bonds, called "Bonods," provide for payment of interest and principal in United States dollars; payment may be made through transfer on the London, Frankfurt, Zurich, or New York market, at the election of the creditor. Under this refinancing program, the foreign creditor had the option of either accepting the Bonods in satisfaction of the initial debt, thereby substituting the Argentine Government for the private debtor, or maintaining the debtor/creditor relationship with the private borrower and accepting the Argentine Government as guarantor.

When the Bonods began to mature in May 1986, Argentina concluded that it lacked sufficient foreign exchange to retire them. Pursuant to a Presidential Decree, Argentina unilaterally extended the time for payment and offered bondholders substitute instruments as a means of rescheduling the debts. Respondents, two Panamanian corporations and a Swiss bank who hold, collectively, $1.3 million of Bonods, refused to accept the rescheduling and insisted on full payment, specifying New York as the place where payment should be made. Argentina did not pay, and respondents then brought this breach-of-contract action in the United States District Court for the Southern District of New York, relying on the Foreign Sovereign Immunities Act of 1976 as the basis for jurisdiction. Petitioners moved to dismiss for lack of subject-matter jurisdiction, lack of personal jurisdiction, and *forum non conveniens*. The District Court denied these motions, 753 F. Supp. 1201 (1991), and the Court of Appeals affirmed, 941 F. 2d 145 (2d Cir. 1991). We granted Argentina's petition for *certiorari*, which challenged the Court of Appeals' determination that, under the Act, Argentina was not immune from the jurisdiction of the federal courts in this case. 502 U.S. 1024 (1992).

II.

The Foreign Sovereign Immunities Act of 1976 (FSIA), 28 U.S.C. § 1602 *et seq.*, establishes a comprehensive framework for determining whether a court in this country, state or federal, may exercise jurisdiction over a foreign state. Under the Act, a "foreign state *shall* be immune from the jurisdiction of the courts of the United States and of the States" unless one of several statutorily defined exceptions applies. § 1604 (emphasis added). The FSIA thus provides the "sole basis" for obtaining jurisdiction over a foreign sovereign in the United States. *See Argentine Republic v. Amerada Hess Shipping Corp.*, 488 U.S. 428, 434–439 (1989). The most significant of the FSIA's exceptions—and the one at issue in this case—is the "commercial" exception of § 1605(a)(2), which provides that a foreign state is not immune from suit in any case

> "in which the action is based upon a commercial activity carried on in the United States by the foreign state; or upon an act performed in the United States in connection with a commercial activity of the foreign state elsewhere; or upon an act outside the territory of the United States in connection with a commercial activity of the foreign state elsewhere and that act causes a direct effect in the United States." § 1605(a)(2).

In the proceedings below, respondents relied only on the third clause of § 1605(a)(2) to establish jurisdiction, 941 F.2d, at 149, and our analysis is therefore limited to considering whether this lawsuit is (1) "based...upon an act outside the territory of the United States"; (2) that was taken "in connection with a commercial activity" of Argentina outside this country; and (3) that "cause[d] a direct effect in the United

States." The complaint in this case alleges only one cause of action on behalf of each of the respondents, viz., a breach-of-contract claim based on Argentina's attempt to refinance the Bonods rather than to pay them according to their terms. The fact that the cause of action is in compliance with the first of the three requirements—that it is "based upon an act outside the territory of the United States" (presumably Argentina's unilateral extension)—is uncontested. The dispute pertains to whether the unilateral refinancing of the Bonods was taken "in connection with a commercial activity" of Argentina, and whether it had a "direct effect in the United States." We address these issues in turn.

A.

Respondents and their *amicus*, the United States, contend that Argentina's issuance of, and continued liability under, the Bonods constitute a "commercial activity" and that the extension of the payment schedules was taken "in connection with" that activity. The latter point is obvious enough, and Argentina does not contest it; the key question is whether the activity is "commercial" under the FSIA.

The FSIA defines "commercial activity" to mean:

> "[E]ither a regular course of commercial conduct or a particular commercial transaction or act. The commercial character of an activity shall be determined by reference to the nature of the course of conduct or particular transaction or act, rather than by reference to its purpose." 28 U.S.C. § 1603(d).

This definition, however, leaves the critical term "commercial" largely undefined: The first sentence simply establishes that the commercial nature of an activity does *not* depend upon whether it is a single act or a regular course of conduct; and the second sentence merely specifies what element of the conduct determines commerciality (*i.e.*, nature rather than purpose), but still without saying what "commercial" means....

...[W]e conclude that when a foreign government acts, not as regulator of a market, but in the manner of a private player within it, the foreign sovereign's actions are "commercial" within the meaning of the FSIA. Moreover, because the Act provides that the commercial character of an act is to be determined by reference to its "nature" rather than its "purpose," 28 U.S.C. § 1603(d), the question is not whether the foreign government is acting with a profit motive or instead with the aim of fulfilling uniquely sovereign objectives. Rather, the issue is whether the particular actions that the foreign state performs (whatever the motive behind them) are the *type* of actions by which a private party engages in "trade and traffic or commerce."... Thus, a foreign government's issuance of regulations limiting foreign currency exchange is a sovereign activity, because such authoritative control of commerce cannot be exercised by a private party; whereas a contract to buy army boots or even bullets is a "commercial" activity, because private companies can similarly use sales contracts to acquire goods....

The commercial character of the Bonods is confirmed by the fact that they are in almost all respects garden-variety debt instruments: They may be held by private parties; they are negotiable and may be traded on the international market (except in Argentina); and they promise a future stream of cash income....

We agree with the Court of Appeals, see 941 F.2d, at 151, that it is irrelevant *why* Argentina participated in the bond market in the manner of a private actor; it matters only that it did so. We conclude that Argentina's issuance of the Bonods was a "commercial activity" under the FSIA.

B.

The remaining question is whether Argentina's unilateral rescheduling of the Bonods had a "direct effect" in the United States, 28 U.S.C. § 1605(a)(2)....

We...have little difficulty concluding that Argentina's unilateral rescheduling of the maturity dates on the Bonods had a "direct effect" in the United States. Respondents had designated their accounts in New York as the place of payment, and Argentina made some interest payments into those accounts before announcing that it was rescheduling the payments. Because New York was thus the place of performance for Argentina's ultimate contractual obligations, the rescheduling of those obligations necessarily had a "direct effect" in the United States: Money that was supposed to have been delivered to a New York bank for deposit was not forthcoming. We reject Argentina's suggestion that the "direct effect" requirement cannot be satisfied where the plaintiffs are all foreign corporations with no other connections to the United States. We expressly stated in *Verlinden* that the FSIA permits "a foreign plaintiff to sue a foreign sovereign in the courts of the United States, provided the substantive requirements of the Act are satisfied," 461 U.S. at 489.

[...]

We conclude that Argentina's issuance of the Bonods was a "commercial activity" under the FSIA; that its rescheduling of the maturity dates on those instruments was taken in connection with that commercial activity and had a "direct effect" in the United States; and that the District Court therefore properly asserted jurisdiction, under the FSIA, over the breach-of-contract claim based on that rescheduling. Accordingly, the judgment of the Court of Appeals is

Affirmed.

* * * *

Two other cases appear to establish that judicial determinations of state immunity are less than objective and devoid of political considerations. In *SEDCO* and *Nelson*, state conduct is held to be non-commercial in character, although it would seem that a proper application of *Texas Trading* and *Weltover* would dictate the opposite conclusion. In each case, the participating State was significant to U.S. foreign policy interests and a disruption of the existing relationship could have proven costly. The reasoning in both *SEDCO* and *Nelson* appears to be transparently calculated to shield an ally from judicial accountability for acts done clearly in connection with a commercial activity. To some degree, the net effect of the 1976 FSIA was to transfer the function of making political assessments in connection with assertions of State immunity from the U.S. Department of State to the federal judiciary. This systemic reordering was not an express objective of the statute and it could, therefore, create separation of powers problems. In any event, the case law has rendered the FSIA unstable and unpredictable in terms of the rules it established for the amenability of States to suits and enforcement.

When reading the next two cases, you should concentrate on the issue of how the ruling court avoids FSIA § 1603(d). Can there be any doubt that the State's liability in each case proceeds from its engagement in "garden-variety" commercial conduct? Is there any rhetorical trick that can justify describing oil drilling activities and the administration of a hospital as anything other than private commercial conduct? Do you agree with the foregoing contentions? You should identify how the courts reach an opposite conclusion. Can you be more persuasive than the courts on this point? Are the distinctions drawn between other cases convincing? What advice do you give to clients in light of these opinions?

IN MATTER OF SEDCO

543 F.Supp. 561 (S.D. Tex. 1982).

O'CONNOR, District Judge.

INTRODUCTION

The 1979 IXTOC I well disaster in the Bay of Campeche has produced a tangle of litigation. Before the Court, at this time, is a series of jurisdictional issues which must be untangled before discovery on the merits can begin. . . .

PEMEX

Petroleos Mexicanos (Pemex), which is both a direct defendant to certain private and public plaintiffs and a third party defendant to claims asserted by SEDCO, has moved to be dismissed from all claims on the basis of the grant of sovereign immunity provided by the Foreign Sovereign Immunity Act, 28 U.S.C. § 1602 et seq. (FSIA). By asserting this motion, Pemex alleges that this Court lacks jurisdiction to hear claims based upon acts purportedly done in this capacity as a foreign sovereign. . . .

Federal courts generally have jurisdiction over actions against foreign states pursuant to 28 U.S.C. § 1330(a). This section provides that original subject matter jurisdiction lies in federal district courts "as to any claim for relief in personam with respect to which the foreign state is not entitled immunity under the [FSIA] or under any applicable international agreement." Personal jurisdiction over the foreign state is achieved through service of process under 28 U.S.C. § 1608 which provides for special service through international channels. 28 U.S.C. § 1330(b)....

Generally, the statute [FSIA] grants immunity to foreign states and their agencies or instrumentalities, 28 U.S.C. 1604. It thereafter creates five exceptions to this grant of immunity of which two have been asserted by Plaintiffs in the present case: the "commercial activity" exception 1605(a)(2); and the "noncommercial tort" exception 1605(a)(5). Once a basis for jurisdiction is alleged, the burden of proof rests on that foreign state to demonstrate that immunity should be granted....

Section 1605(a)(2)—Commercial Activity Exception

[...]

Petroleos Mexicanos was created in 1938 as a decentralized governmental agency charged with the exploration and development of Mexico's hydrocarbon resources. Unlike in the United States, the government of Mexico owns its country's natural resources, in particular, its hydrocarbon deposits. Mex. Political Const. art. 27. The Regulatory Law passed pursuant to the Mexican Constitution specifically creates a national oil company, Pemex, to implement the National Development Plan for hydrocarbon resources. Pemex is not privately owned and is governed by a council (*Consejo de Administration*) composed of Presidential appointees. Decisions made by the governing council are made in furtherance of Mexican National policy concerning its Petroleum resources. Beyond a doubt, Pemex is a "foreign state" as contemplated by § 1603(a) of the FSIA....

Whether Pemex was engaged in commercial activity when it performed the acts complained of by Plaintiffs in this lawsuit is a difficult issue. The statute generally defines "commercial activity" as:

> a regular course of commercial conduct or a particular commercial transaction or act. The commercial character of an activity shall be determined by reference to the nature of the course of conduct or particular transaction or act, rather than by reference to its purpose.

28 U.S.C. § 1603(d). Undeniably, Pemex, as a national oil company, engages in a substantial amount of commercial activity.... However, this Court must focus on the specific acts made the basis of the present lawsuit in applying the FSIA. It is whether these particular acts constituted or were in connection with commercial activity, regardless of the defendant's general commercial or governmental nature that is in issue....

There is little doubt that where a foreign nation enters into the world marketplace to purchase or sell goods, it has engaged in commercial activity for purposes of the FSIA.... This is not to say that every act done by a foreign state which could be done by a private citizen in the

United States is "commercial activity" under § 1605(a)(2). Such a world view unrealistically denies the existence of other types of governments and economic systems. . . .

While the existence of a contractual relationship is not essential to a finding of commercial activity by a foreign state, it is often indicative of such conduct. The term "commercial activity" could embrace world-wide shipping activities by a state-owned shipping company. . .or the operation of a state-owned hotel. . . . Torts committed by the foreign state in the absence of a commercial contract but in connection with this type of activity could be found to be commercial under the provisions of the FSIA and subject the foreign state to jurisdiction in United States federal courts.

Here, Pemex was engaged in drilling an exploratory oil well in its patrimonial waters, the Bay of Campeche. The data derived from this exploration was integral to the Mexican government's long range planning and policy making process concerning the production and utilization of state-owned minerals. Such policy is not made by Pemex, but is formed by higher levels of government. Mexican law, however, mandates that Pemex gather information concerning these resources and create programs to implement the six-year national development plan devised by the various government ministries and adopted by the President of Mexico. Pemex had not entered into a contract with anyone for the oil and gas produced from the IXTOC I well, nor has it contracted with a United States business to drill the well. In fact, Pemex was attempting to determine if deposits of oil and gas were located offshore under Campeche Bay. Acting by authority of Mexican law within its national territory and in intragovernmental cooperation with other branches of the Mexican government, Pemex was not engaged in commercial activity as contemplated by Congress in the FSIA when the IXTOC I well was drilled.

The FSIA requires the Court to focus on the specific act by a foreign state made the basis of the lawsuit. The Court must regard carefully a sovereign's conduct with respect to its natural wealth. A very basic attribute of sovereignty is the control over its mineral resources and short of actually selling these resources on the world market, decisions and conduct concerning them are uniquely governmental in nature. . . .Because the nature of Pemex' act in determining the extent of Mexico's natural resources was uniquely sovereign, this Court finds that the commercial activity exception to the FSIA, § 1605(a)(2), is inapplicable to the facts presented by this case.

Section 1605(a)(5)—Noncommercial Tort Exception

Alternatively, it is urged that this Court exercise jurisdiction over Pemex under the "noncommercial tort" exception to the FSIA, § 1605(a)(5). Section 1605(a)(5) provides that a suit for damages based on alleged noncommercial tort committed by a foreign state in the United States is actionable in federal court. For jurisdiction to exist, the following must be shown: (1) a noncommercial act by the foreign state;

(2) causing personal injury or damages to, or loss of property; and (3) that the claim is not based upon the exercise of a discretionary function, or upon libel, slander, misrepresentation, or interference with contract rights.

Section 1605(a)(5) is silent with respect to where the noncommercial tort must occur for jurisdiction to exist. Plaintiffs argue the tort may occur, in whole or in part, in the United States, and that the tort occurs in the United States if the acts or omissions directly affect this country. This argument may be correct in other circumstances. . . however, legislative history appears to reject this theory with respect to the FSIA. In describing the purpose of § 1605(a)(5), the House Committee Report accompanying the House Bill, which ultimately became the FSIA, states:

> It denies immunity as to claims for personal injury or death, or for damage to or loss of property caused by the tortious act or omission of a foreign state or its officials or employees, acting within the scope of their authority, the tortious act or omission must occur within the jurisdiction of the United States. . . .

House Report. . . at 6619. The primary purpose of this exception is to cover the problem of traffic accidents by embassy and governmental officials in this country. *Id.* While the exception does extend generally to all noncommercial torts committed in this country. . . this Court finds that the tort, in whole, must occur in the United States. The alleged acts or omissions made the basis of this lawsuit all took place in Mexico or its territorial waters in the Bay of Campeche, and § 1605(a)(5) is, therefore, inapplicable. . . .

Notwithstanding the fact that the tort did not occur wholly within the United States, the acts complained of were discretionary in nature, done in furtherance of Pemex' legal mandate to explore for Mexico's hydrocarbon deposits. Discretionary acts by a sovereign are specifically immunized from suit under the FSIA. 28 U.S.C. § 1605(a)(5)(A). The language of this exemption and its legislative history demonstrate that it parallels the discretionary act exception of the Federal Tort Claims Act, 28 U.S.C. § 2680(a). . . . The scope of this discretionary act exception has troubled courts for years. . . . However, the facts of this case closely resemble those of *Dalehite v. United States*, 346 U.S. 15, 73 S. Ct. 956, 97 L. Ed. 1427 (1953), still the leading case on the issue. In *Dalehite*, the Supreme Court found the government's actions in formulating and then directing the execution of a formal plan for a fertilizer export program could not form the basis of a suit under the Federal Tort Claims Act. Such actions were found to be discretionary under § 2860(a), even though an alleged abuse of that discretion resulted in the 1947 Texas City disaster.

Pemex, in this case, was executing a national plan formulated at the highest levels of the Mexican government by exploring for Mexico's natural resources. Any act performed by a subordinate of Pemex in furtherance of this exploration plan was still discretionary in nature and immune from suit under the FSIA. To deny immunity to a foreign state for the implementation of its domestic economic policies would be to completely abrogate the doctrine of foreign sovereign immunity by allowing an exception to swallow the grant of immunity preserved by § 1604. Therefore, Pemex Motion to Dismiss all claims against it on the basis of foreign sovereign immunity must be granted.

[. . .]

SAUDI ARABIA v. NELSON

507 U.S. 349, 113 S.Ct. 1471, 123 L.Ed.2d 47 (1993).

(footnotes omitted)

JUSTICE SOUTER delivered the opinion of the Court.

The Foreign Sovereign Immunities Act of 1976 entitles foreign states to immunity from the jurisdiction of courts in the United States, 28 U.S.C. § 1604, subject to certain enumerated exceptions. § 1605. One is that a foreign state shall not be immune in any case "in which the action is based upon a commercial activity carried on in the United States by the foreign state." § 1605(a)(2). We hold that respondents' action alleging personal injury resulting from unlawful detention and torture by the Saudi Government is not "based upon a commercial activity" within the meaning of the Act, which consequently confers no jurisdiction over respondents' suit.

I.

[. . .]

Petitioner Kingdom of Saudi Arabia owns and operates petitioner King Faisal Specialist Hospital in Riyadh, as well as petitioner Royspec Purchasing Services, the hospital's corporate purchasing agent in the United States. . . . The Hospital Corporation of America, Ltd. (HCA), an independent corporation existing under the laws of the Cayman Islands, recruits Americans for employment at the hospital under an agreement signed with Saudi Arabia in 1973. . . .

In its recruitment effort, HCA placed an advertisement in a trade periodical seeking applications for a position as a monitoring systems engineer at the hospital. The advertisement drew the attention of respondent Scott Nelson in September 1983, while Nelson was in the United States. After interviewing for the position in Saudi Arabia, Nelson returned to the United States, where he signed an employment contract with the hospital, . . . satisfied personnel processing requirements, and attended an orientation session that HCA conducted for hospital employees. In the course of that program, HCA identified Royspec as the point of contact in the United States for family members who might wish to reach Nelson in an emergency. . . .

In December 1983, Nelson went to Saudi Arabia and began work at the hospital, monitoring all "facilities, equipment, utilities and maintenance systems to insure the safety of patients, hospital staff, and others."...He did his job without significant incident until March 1984, when he discovered safety defects in the hospital's oxygen and nitrous oxide lines that posed fire hazards and otherwise endangered patients' lives....Over a period of several months, Nelson repeatedly advised hospital officials of the safety defects and reported the defects to a Saudi Government commission as well....Hospital officials instructed Nelson to ignore the problems....

The hospital's response to Nelson's reports changed, however, on September 27, 1984, when certain hospital employees summoned him to the hospital's security office where agents of the Saudi Government arrested him. The agents transported Nelson to a jail cell, in which they "shackled, tortured and bea[t]" him...and kept him four days without food.... Although Nelson did not understand Arabic, government agents forced him to sign a statement written in that language, the content of which he did not know; a hospital employee who was supposed to act as Nelson's interpreter advised him to sign "anything" the agents gave him to avoid further beatings.... Two days later, government agents transferred Nelson to the Al Sijan Prison "to await trial on unknown charges."...

At the prison, Nelson was confined in an overcrowded cell area infested with rats, where he had to fight other prisoners for food and from which he was taken only once a week for fresh air and exercise....Although police interrogators repeatedly questioned him in Arabic, Nelson did not learn the nature of the charges, if any, against him.... For several days, the Saudi Government failed to advise Nelson's family of his whereabouts, though a Saudi official eventually told Nelson's wife, respondent Vivian Nelson, that he could arrange for her husband's release if she provided sexual favors....

Although officials from the United States Embassy visited Nelson twice during his detention, they concluded that his allegations of Saudi mistreatment were "not credible" and made no protest to Saudi authorities.... It was only at the personal request of a United States Senator that the Saudi Government released Nelson, 39 days after his arrest, on November 5, 1984.... Seven days later, after failing to convince him to return to work at the hospital, the Saudi Government allowed Nelson to leave the country....

In 1988, Nelson and his wife filed this action against petitioners in the United States District Court for the Southern District of Florida seeking damages for personal injury. The Nelsons' complaint sets out 16 causes of action, which fall into three categories. Counts II through VII and counts X, XI, XIV, and XV allege that petitioners committed various intentional torts, including battery, unlawful detainment, wrongful arrest and imprisonment, false imprisonment, inhuman torture, disruption of normal family life, and infliction of mental anguish.... Counts I, IX and XIII charge petitioners with negligently failing to warn Nelson of otherwise undisclosed dangers of his employment, namely, that if he attempted to report safety hazards the hospital would likely retaliate against him and the Saudi Government might detain and physically abuse him without legal cause.... Finally, counts VIII, XII, and XVI allege that Vivian Nelson sustained derivative injury resulting from petitioners' actions.... Presumably because the employment contract provided that Saudi courts would have exclusive jurisdiction over claims for breach of contract,... the Nelsons raised no such matters.

The District Court dismissed for lack of subject-matter jurisdiction under the Foreign Sovereign Immunities Act of 1976, 28 U.S.C. §§ 1330, 1602 *et seq.* It rejected the Nelsons' argument that jurisdiction existed, under the first clause of § 1605(a)(2), because the action was one "based upon a commercial activity" that petitioners had "carried on in the United States." Although HCA's recruitment of Nelson in the United States might properly be attributed to Saudi Arabia and the hospital, the District Court reasoned, it did not amount to commercial activity "carried on in the United States" for purposes of the Act.... The court explained that there was no sufficient "nexus" between Nelson's recruitment and the injuries alleged. "Although [the Nelsons] argu[e] that but for [Scott Nelson's] recruitment in the United States, he would not have taken the job, been arrested, and suffered the personal injuries," the court said, "this 'connection' [is] far too tenuous to support jurisdiction" under the Act.... Likewise, the court concluded that Royspec's commercial activity in the United States, purchasing supplies and equipment for the hospital... had no nexus with the personal injuries alleged in the complaint; Royspec had simply provided a way for Nelson's family to reach him in an emergency....

The Court of Appeals reversed. 923 F.2d 1528 (CA11 1991). It concluded that Nelson's recruitment and hiring were commercial activities of Saudi Arabia and the hospital, carried on in the United States for purposes of the Act... and that the Nelsons' action was "based upon" these activities within the meaning of the statute.... There was, the court reasoned, a sufficient nexus between those commercial activities and the wrongful acts that had allegedly injured the Nelsons: "the detention and torture of Nelson are so intertwined with his employment at the Hospital," the court explained, "that they are 'based upon' his recruitment and hiring" in the United States.... The courts also found jurisdiction to hear the claims against Royspec.... After the Court of Appeals denied petitioners' suggestion for rehearing *en banc*,... we granted *certiorari*, 504 U.S. 972 (1992). We now reverse.

II.

The Foreign Sovereign Immunities Act "provides the sole basis for obtaining jurisdiction over a foreign state in the courts of this country."... Under the Act, a foreign state is presumptively immune from the jurisdiction of United States courts; unless a specified exception applies, a federal court lacks subject-matter jurisdiction over a claim against a foreign state....

Only one such exception is said to apply here. The first clause of § 1605(a)(2) of the Act provides that a foreign state shall not be immune from the jurisdiction of United States courts in any case "in which the action is based upon a commercial activity carried on in the United States by the foreign state." The Act defines such activity as "commercial activity carried on by such state and having substantial contact with the United States," § 1603(e), and provides that a commercial activity may be "either a regular course of commercial conduct or a particular commercial transaction or act," the "commercial character of [which] shall be determined by reference to" its "nature," rather than its "purpose," § 1603(d).

There is no dispute here that Saudi Arabia, the hospital, and Royspec all qualify as "foreign state[s]" within the meaning of the Act....

[...]

Under the restrictive, as opposed to the "absolute," theory of foreign sovereign immunity, a state is immune from the jurisdiction of foreign courts as to its sovereign or public acts (*jure imperii*), but not as to those that are private or commercial in character (*jure gestionis*).... We explained in *Weltover*,...that a state engages in commercial activity under the restrictive theory where it exercises " 'only those powers that can also be exercised by private citizens,' "as distinct from those " 'powers peculiar to sovereigns.' " Put differently, a foreign state engages in commercial activity for purposes of the restrictive theory only where it acts "in the manner of a private player within" the market....

We emphasized in *Weltover* that whether a state acts "in the manner of" a private party is a question of behavior, not motivation....We did not ignore the difficulty of distinguishing " 'purpose' (*i.e.*, the *reason* why the foreign state engages in the activity) from 'nature' (*i.e.*, the outward form of the conduct that the foreign state performs or agrees to perform)," but recognized that the Act "unmistakably commands" us to observe the distinction....Because Argentina had merely dealt in the bond market in the manner of a private player, we held, its refinancing of the bonds qualified as a commercial activity for purposes of the Act despite the apparent governmental motivation....

Unlike Argentina's activities that we considered in *Weltover*, the intentional conduct alleged here (the Saudi Government's wrongful arrest, imprisonment, and torture of Nelson) could not qualify as commercial under the restrictive theory. The conduct boils down to abuse of the power of its police by the Saudi Government, and however monstrous such abuse undoubtedly may be, a foreign state's exercise of the power of its police has long been understood for purposes of the restrictive theory as peculiarly sovereign in nature....Exercise of the powers of police and penal officers is not the sort of action by which private parties can engage in commerce. "[S]uch acts as legislation, or the expulsion of an alien, or a denial of justice, cannot be performed by an individual acting in his own name. They can be performed only by the state acting as such." Lauterpacht, *The Problem of Jurisdictional Immunities of Foreign States*, 28 BRIT. Y.B. INT'L. L. 220, 225 (1952)....

III.

The Nelsons' action is not "based upon a commercial activity" within the meaning of the first clause of § 1605(a)(2) of the Act, and the judgment of the Court of Appeals is accordingly reversed. *It is so ordered.*

JUSTICE WHITE, with whom JUSTICE BLACKMUN joins, concurring in the judgment.

[. . .]

The majority concludes that petitioners enjoy sovereign immunity because respondents' action is not "based upon a commercial activity." I disagree. I nonetheless concur in the judgment because in my view the commercial conduct upon which respondents base their complaint was not "carried on in the United States."

I.

[. . .]

B.

To run and operate a hospital, even a public hospital, is to engage in a commercial enterprise. The majority never concedes this point, but it does not deny it either, and to my mind the matter is self-evident. By the same token, warning an employee when he blows the whistle and taking retaliatory action, such as harassment, involuntary transfer, discharge, or other tortious behavior, although not prototypical commercial acts, are certainly well within the bounds of commercial activity. The House and Senate Reports accompanying the legislation virtually compel this conclusion, explaining as they do that "a foreign government's. . .employment or engagement of laborers, clerical staff or marketing agents. . .would be among those included within" the definition of commercial activity. H.R. Rep. No. 94–1487, p. 16 (1976) (House Report); S. Rep. No. 94–1310, p. 16 (1976) (Senate Report). Nelson alleges that petitioners harmed him in the course of engaging in their commercial enterprise, as a direct result of their commercial acts. His claims, in other words, is "based upon commercial activity."

Indeed, I am somewhat at a loss as to what exactly the majority believes petitioners have done that a private employer could not. As countless cases attest, retaliation for whistle-blowing is not a practice foreign to the marketplace. Congress passed a statute in response to such behavior, see Whistleblower Protection Act of 1989, 5 U.S.C. § 1213 *et seq.* (1988 ed., Supp. III), as have numerous States. On occasion, private employers also have been known to retaliate by enlisting the help of police officers to falsely arrest employees. . . .More generally, private parties have been held liable for conspiring with public authorities to effectuate an arrest. . .and for using private security personnel for the same purposes. . . .

Therefore, had the hospital retaliated against Nelson by hiring thugs to do the job, I assume the majority—no longer able to describe this conduct as "a foreign state's exercise of the power of its police," *ante*,...—would consent to calling it "commercial." For, in such circumstances, the state-run hospital would be operating as any private participant in the marketplace and respondents' action would be based on the operation by Saudi Arabia's agents of a commercial business.

At the heart of the majority's conclusion, in other words, is the fact that the hospital in this case chose to call in government security forces. *See ante*, at 362. I find this fixation on the intervention of police officers, and the ensuing characterization of the conduct as "peculiarly sovereign in nature," *ante*, at 361, to be misguided....

II.

Nevertheless, I reach the same conclusion as the majority because petitioners' commercial activity was not "carried on in the United States."...Neither the hospital's employment practices, nor its disciplinary procedures, has any apparent connection to this country. On that basis, I agree that the Act does not grant the Nelsons access to our courts.

[...]

* * * *

The Act of State Doctrine and Transborder Judicial Jurisdiction

The Act of State Doctrine emerged from the U.S. constitutional doctrine of separation of powers. Like sovereign immunity, it can eliminate a U.S. court's power to rule in a litigation involving a foreign State. Therefore, it has the same effect as sovereign immunity and it, too, is raised at the outset of the proceeding. It centers upon the foreign State's conduct, however, not its political status. The next case defines Act of State and distinguishes it from sovereign immunity.

INTERNATIONAL ASS'N. OF MACHINISTS AND AEROSPACE WORKERS v. ORGANIZATION OF PETROLEUM EXPORTING COUNTRIES (OPEC)

649 F.2d 1354 (9th Cir. 1981).

[...]

SOVEREIGN IMMUNITY

[...]

In 1976, Congress enacted the FSIA and declared that the federal courts will apply an objective nature-of-the-act test in determining whether activity is commercial and thus not immune: "The commercial character of an activity shall be determined by reference to the nature of the course of conduct or particular transaction or act, rather than by reference to its purpose." 28 U.S.C. § 1603(d).

A critical step in characterizing the nature of a given activity is defining exactly what that activity is. The immunity question may be determined by how broadly or narrowly that activity is defined. In this case, IAM [International Association of Machinists and Aerospace Workers] insists on a very narrow focus on the specific activity of "price fixing." IAM argues that the FSIA does not give immunity to this activity. Under the FSIA a commercial activity is one which an individual might "customarily carr[y] on for profit." H.R.Rep. No. 94–1487, 94th Cong., 2d Sess. 16, *reprinted in* [1976] U.S. Code Cong. & Ad. News 6604, 6615. OPEC's activity, characterized by IAM as making agreements to fix prices, is one which is presumably done for profit; it is thus commercial and immunity does not apply.

The court below defined OPEC's activity in a different way: "[I]t is clear that the nature of the activity engaged in by each of these OPEC member countries is the establishment by a sovereign state of the terms and conditions for the removal of a prime natural resource—to wit, crude oil—from its territory." 477 F.Supp. at 567. The trial judge reasoned that, according to international law, the development and control of natural resources is a prime governmental function. *Id.* at 567–78. The opinion cites several resolutions of the United Nations' General Assembly, which the United States supported, and the United States Constitution, Art. 4, § 3, cl. 2, which treat the control of natural resources as governmental acts.

IAM argues that the district court's analysis strays from the path set forth in the FSIA. The control of natural resources is the purpose behind OPEC's actions, but the act complained of here is a conspiracy to fix prices. The FSIA instructs us to look upon the act itself rather than underlying sovereign motivations.

The district court was understandably troubled by the broader implications of an anti-trust action against the OPEC nations. The importance of the alleged price-fixing activity to the OPEC nations cannot be ignored. Oil revenues represent their only significant source of income. Consideration of their sovereignty cannot be separated from their near total dependence upon oil. We find that these concerns are appropriately addressed by application of the act of state doctrine. While we do not apply the doctrine of sovereign immunity, its elements remain relevant to our discussion of the act of state doctrine.

B. The Act of State Doctrine

The act of state doctrine declares that a United States court will not adjudicate a politically sensitive dispute which would require the court to judge the legality of the sovereign act of a foreign state. This doctrine was expressed by the Supreme Court in *Underhill v. Hernandez*, 168 U.S. 250, 252, 18 S. Ct. 83, 84 42 L. Ed. 456 (1897):

> Every sovereign State is bound to respect the independence of every other sovereign State, and the courts of one country will not sit in

judgment on the acts of the government of another done within its own territory.

The doctrine recognizes the institutional limitations of the courts and the peculiar requirements of successful foreign relations. To participate adeptly in the global community, the United States must speak with one voice and pursue a careful and deliberate foreign policy. The political branches of our government are able to consider the competing economic and political considerations and respond to the public will in order to carry on foreign relations in accordance with the best interests of the country as a whole. The courts, in contrast, focus on single disputes and make decisions on the basis of legal principles. The timing of our decisions is largely a result of our caseload and of the random tactical considerations which motivate parties to bring lawsuits and to seek delay or expedition. When the courts engage in piecemeal adjudication of the legality of the sovereign acts of states, they risk disruption of our country's international diplomacy. The executive may utilize protocol, economic sanction, compromise, delay, and persuasion to achieve international objectives. Ill-timed judicial decisions challenging the acts of foreign states could nullify these tools and embarrass the United States in the eyes of the world.

The act of state doctrine is similar to the political question doctrine in domestic law. It requires that the courts defer to the legislative and executive branches when those branches are better equipped to resolve a politically sensitive question. Like the political question doctrine, its applicability is not subject to clear definition. The courts balance various factors to determine whether the doctrine should apply.

While the act of state doctrine has no explicit source in our Constitution or statutes, it does have "constitutional underpinnings." *Banco Nacional de Cuba v. Sabbatino*, 376 U.S. 398, 423, 84 S. Ct. 923, 937 11 L.Ed. 2d 804 (1964). The Supreme Court has stated that the act of state doctrine:

> arises out of the basic relationships between branches of government in a system of separation of powers.... The doctrine as formulated in past decisions expressed the strong sense of the Judicial Branch that its engagement in the task of passing on the validity of foreign acts of state may hinder rather than further this country's pursuit of goals both for itself and for the community of nations as a whole in the international sphere. *Id.*

The principle of separation of powers is central to our form of democratic government. Just as the courts have carefully guarded their primary role as interpreters of the Constitution and the laws of the United States, so have they recognized the primary role of the President and Congress in resolution of political conflict and the adoption of foreign policy....

The doctrine of sovereign immunity is similar to the act of state doctrine in that it also represents the need to respect the sovereignty of foreign states. The two doctrines differ, however, in significant respects. The law of sovereign immunity goes to the jurisdiction of the court. The act of state doctrine is not jurisdictional. *Ricaud v. American Metal Co.*, 246 U.S. 304, 309, 38 S. Ct. 312, 313, 62 L.Ed. 733 (1918). Rather, it is a prudential doctrine designed to avoid judicial action in sensitive areas. Sovereign immunity is a principle of international law, recognized in the United States by statute. It is the states themselves, as defendants, who may claim sovereign immunity. The act of state doctrine is a domestic legal principle, arising from the peculiar role of American courts. It recognizes not only the sovereignty of foreign states, but also the spheres of power of the co-equal branches of our government. Thus a private litigant may raise the act of state doctrine, even when no sovereign state is a party to the action. *See, e.g., Timberlane Lumber Co. v. Bank of America*, 549 F.2d 597, 606 (9th Cir. 1976). The act of state doctrine is apposite whenever the federal courts must question the legality of the sovereign acts of foreign states.

It has been suggested that the FSIA supersedes the act of state doctrine, or that the amorphous doctrine is limited by modern jurisprudence. We disagree.

[. . .]

The act of state doctrine is not diluted by the commercial activity exception which limits the doctrine of sovereign immunity. While purely commercial activity may not rise to the level of an act of state, certain seemingly commercial activity will trigger act of state considerations. As the district court noted, OPEC's "price-fixing" activity has a significant sovereign component. While the FSIA ignores the underlying purpose of a state's action, the act of state doctrine does not. This court has stated that the motivations of the sovereign must be examined for a public interest basis. *Timberlane*, 549 F.2d at 607. . . . When the state qua state acts in the public interest, its sovereignty is asserted. The courts must proceed cautiously to avoid an affront to that sovereignty.

Because the act of state doctrine and the doctrine of sovereign immunity address different concerns and apply in different circumstances, we find that the act of state doctrine remains available when such caution is appropriate, regardless of any commercial component of the activity involved.

In addition to the public interest factor, a federal court must heed other indications which call for act of state deference. The doctrine does not suggest a rigid rule of application. In the *Sabbatino* case, the Supreme Court suggested a balancing approach:

> Some aspects of international law touch more sharply on national nerves than do others; the less important the implications of an issue are for our foreign relations, the weaker the justification for exclusivity in the political branches. 376 U.S. at 428, 84 S. Ct. at 940.

The decision to deny access to judicial relief is not one we make lightly. In *Timberlane Lumber Co. v. Bank of America*, 549 F.2d 597, 606 (9th Cir. 1976), this court noted that "not every case is identical in its potential impact on our relations with other nations." The "touchstone" or "crucial element" is the potential for interference with our foreign relations. *Timberlane*, 549 F.2d at 607. . . .

There is no question that the availability of oil has become a significant factor in international relations. The growing world energy crisis has been judicially recognized in other cases. . . . The record in this case contains extensive documentation of the involvement of our executive and legislative branches with the oil question. IAM does not dispute that the United States has a grave interest in the petro-politics of the Middle East, or that the foreign policy arms of the executive and legislative branches are intimately involved in this sensitive area. It is clear that OPEC and its activities are carefully considered in the formulation of American foreign policy.

The remedy IAM seeks is an injunction against the OPEC nations. The possibility of insult to the OPEC states and of interference with the efforts of the political branches to seek favorable relations with them is apparent from the very nature of this action and the remedy sought. While the case is formulated as an anti-trust action, the granting of any relief would in effect amount to an order from a domestic court instructing a foreign sovereign to alter its chosen means of allocating and profiting from its own valuable natural resources. On the other hand, should the court hold [that] the OPEC's actions are legal, this "would greatly strengthen the bargaining hand" of the OPEC nations in the event that Congress or the executive chooses to condemn OPEC's actions. *Sabbatino*, 376 U.S. at 432, 84 S. Ct. at 942.

[. . .]

IV. Conclusion

The act of state doctrine is applicable in this case. The courts should not enter at the will of litigants into a delicate area of foreign policy which the executive and legislative branches have chosen to approach with restraint. The issue of whether the FSIA allows jurisdiction in this case need not be decided, since a judicial remedy is inappropriate regardless of whether jurisdiction exists. Similarly, we need not reach the issues regarding the indirect-purchaser rule, the extraterritorial application of the Sherman Act, the definition of "person" under the Sherman Act, and the propriety of injunctive relief.

The decision of the district court dismissing this action is AFFIRMED.

* * * *

In *Republic of Austria v. Altmann*, 124 S. Ct. 2240, 159 L.Ed.2d 1 (2004), the U.S. Supreme Court held that the FSIA could be applied retroactively to claims that were based on conduct that occurred prior to the statute's enactment or even prior to the U.S. adoption of the restrictive theory of sovereign immunity. The case involved an action against Austria and a government-owned art gallery for the misappropriation of art works from 1941 to 1948.

* * * *

Note on the Alien Tort Statute (ATS)

The ATS supplies the jurisdictional basis for lawsuits brought by foreign nationals against former foreign government officials in federal district courts. The plaintiffs allege that they were injured by the tortious conduct of a foreign official who acted under color of governmental authority. The conduct complained of amounts to a violation of customary international law or a treaty to which the United States is a party. The action does not constitute a lawsuit against a foreign government or its instrumentality; if it did, it would be governed by the FSIA. *See Abdi Jama v. INS*, 22 F. Supp. 2d (D.N.J. 1998); *Argentine Republic v. Amerada Hess Shipping Corp.*, 488 U.S. 428, 109 S. Ct. 683, 102 L.Ed.2d 818 (1989). The action is directed against an individual who allegedly used his/her governmental authority and position to harm the plaintiff and the harm amounts to a violation of international human rights norms.

The ATS arises from the 1789 Judiciary Act which gives U.S. district courts non-exclusive jurisdiction over tort litigation brought by aliens for conduct that violates international law or the provisions of treaties to which the United States is a party. As incorporated in 28 U.S.C.A. § 1350, the ATS allows "civil action[s] by an alien for a tort only, committed in violation of the law of nations or a treaty of the United States." The provision, in effect, allows federal district courts to act as a transborder venue for assessing the civil liability of international human rights violations. It thereby gives extraterritorial effect to U.S. legal procedure and interpretations of transnational public law.

The ATS' significance as a cause of action became apparent only in the 1980s when the U.S. Court of Appeals for the Second Circuit decided *Filartiga v. Pena–Irala*, 630 F.2d 876 (2d Cir. 1980). The case illustrated the basic circumstances of a likely suit: The claimants sued a former Paraguayan police official in tort for the alleged torture and wrongful death of a relative. The substantive basis for the suit was that torture by a state actor in the exercise of his official capacity constituted a violation of customary international law for which civil liability would lie against the individual. In its opinion, the court attempted to limit the reach of the ATS to violations of "universally recognized norms of international law" that were expressly recognized in specific transborder instruments. Part of the ensuing judicial debate involved precisely the question of what conduct amounted to a violation of international law. Invoking the history relating to the 1789 Judiciary Act, the Second Circuit provided a conservative and disciplined answer. Historically, the contemplated public law torts had been limited to "violations of safe conduct, infringement of the rights of ambassadors, and piracy." 124 S.Ct. at 2761. In the modern context, informed by international human rights conventions, most federal courts limited the public law torts under the ATS to slave trading, forced labor, torture, murder, genocide, and war crimes. *See Tachiona v. Mugabe*, 234 F. Supp. 2d 401 (S.D.N.Y. 2002); *Abdullahi v. Pfizer, Inc.*, No. 01 CIV. 8118, 2002 WL 31082956 (S.D.N.Y. Sept. 17, 2002); *John Doe I v. Unocal*, Nos. 00–56603, 00–57197, 00–56628, 00–57195, 2002 WL 31063976 (9th Cir. Sept. 18, 2002). Most courts exclude the seizure of private property and the causation of environmental harm from the category of justiciable torts under the ATS. *See Flores v. S. Peru Copper Corp.*, 253 F. Supp. 2d 510 (S.D.N.Y. 2002); *Beanal v. Freeport McMoran Copper & Gold, Inc.*, 969 F. Supp. 362 (E.D. La. 1997), *aff'd other grounds*, 197 F.3d 161 (5th Cir. 1999).

ATS suits can be brought against private companies as well as former government officials. State action is not necessary but is usually present. *See Kadic v. Karadzic*, 70 F.3d 232 (2d Cir. 1995), *cert. denied*, 518 U.S. 1005 (1996); *In re Estate of Ferdinand E. Marcos HR Litig.*, 978 F.2d 493 (9th Cir. 1992), *cert. denied*, 508 U.S. 972 (1993); *Tel-Oren v. Libyan Arab Republic*, 726 F.2d 774 (D.C. Cir. 1984), *cert. denied*, 470 U.S. 1003 (1985); *Klinghoffer v. S.N.C. Achille Lauro*, 937 F.2d 44 (2d Cir. 1991). The actions are subject to the usual defenses: *forum non conveniens*; nonjusticiability based upon a political question; and international comity. The successful pleading of a defense can lead to a dismissal of the action. Both compensatory and punitive damages are available. The contemporary usage of the ATS was reinforced in 1991 by the passage of the Torture Victims Protection Act—a narrower statute establishing federal jurisdiction over torture and extrajudicial killings. *See* 106 Stat. 73.

In 2004, the U.S. Supreme Court decided *Sosa v. Alvarez–Machain*, 124 S. Ct. 2739, 159 L.Ed.2d 718 (2004), and *United States v. Alvarez–Machain*, 124 S. Ct. 821, 157 L.Ed.2d 692 (2003). There, the Court held that a Mexican national was not entitled to relief, *inter alia*, under the ATS even though he had been abducted by the DEA from Mexico. The court made a number of observations about the role and purpose of the ATS, clarifying its underlying gravamen. Several of these observations are reproduced below. You should assess their impact upon the ATS and your understanding of international human rights and activist litigation in the contemporary age:

1. "As enacted in 1789, the ATS gave district courts 'cognizance' of certain causes of action, and the term bespoke a grant of jurisdiction, not power to mold substantive law." 124 S. Ct. at 2754.
2. "In sum, we think the statute was intended as jurisdictional in the sense of addressing the power of the courts to entertain cases concerned with a certain subject." 124 S. Ct. at 2755.
3. "It was this narrow set of violations of the law of nations ['violations of safe conduct, infringement of the rights of ambassadors, and piracy'], admitting of a judicial remedy and at the same time threatening serious consequences in international

affairs, that was probably on [the] minds of the men who drafted the ATS with its reference to tort." 124 S. Ct. 2756.

4. "Congress intended the ATS to furnish jurisdiction for a relatively modest set of actions alleging violations of the law of nations." 124 S. Ct. at 2759.

5. "Accordingly, we think courts should require any claim based on the present-day law of nations to rest on a norm of international character accepted by the civilized world and defined with a specificity comparable to the features of the 18th-century paradigms we have recognized." 124 S. Ct. at 2763.

6. "Since many attempts by federal courts to craft remedies for the violation of new norms of international law would raise risks of adverse foreign policy consequences, they should be undertaken, if at all, with great caution." 124 S. Ct. at 2763.

7. "[W]e are persuaded that federal courts should not recognize private claims under federal common law for violations of any international law norm with less definite content and acceptance among civilized nations than the historical paradigms familiar when § 1350 was enacted." 124 S. Ct. at 2765.

8. "[W]e now tend to understand common law not as a discoverable reflection of universal reason but, in a positivistic way, as a product of human choice. And we now adhere to a conception of limited judicial power first expressed in reorienting federal diversity jurisdiction, see *Erie R. Co. v. Tompkins* . . . , that federal courts have no authority to derive 'general' common law." 124 S. Ct. at 2764.

The last statement is of monumental, even revolutionary, significance. It embodies a complete reassessment of the historical and systemic function of the common law enterprise. It advances a new conception of law-making. It also redefines the role of courts in achieving societal regulation. The statement represents an exercise in truth-speaking that is rare among institutions that bear public responsibility and authority. What do you think?

§ 5. JURISDICTION TO ADJUDICATE: THE LAW OF OTHER COUNTRIES

French law requires that plaintiffs sue at the place of defendant's domicile. "Thus domicile of a defendant in France always affords a jurisdictional basis, even if plaintiff and defendant are aliens. Residence also may be sufficient, but bare presence ("transient jurisdiction" in the United States or England) will not suffice. For corporations, the principal office (*siège social*) serves as the equivalent of domicile. It appears that corporations with offices (but not principal offices) in France can be sued there on causes of action related to their French activities." *See* H. Steiner & D. Vagts, Transnational Legal Problems 753 (2d ed. 1976).

Under **English law**, *in personam* jurisdiction is also tied to the concept of "presence" which is identified with the idea of local "transaction of business." Common law requires that the defendant be personally served within the jurisdiction and service of a writ abroad is possible only to the extent permitted by statute. Order 11 of the Rules of the Supreme Court of Judicature, [1962] 3 Stat. Instr. 2529, 2552 (No. 2145),

> [u]nlike the United States long-arm statutes[,] requires plaintiffs to obtain authorization from a court before they can use these special rules. Excerpts from Order 11, as amended in minor respects in 1962, appear below:
>
> Principal cases in which service of writ out of jurisdiction is permissible
>
> 1.—(1) Subject to [certain other provisions], service of a writ, or notice of a writ, out of the jurisdiction is permissible with the leave of the Court in the following cases, that is to say—
>
> [. . .]
>
> (c) if in the action begun by the writ relief is sought against a person domiciled or ordinarily resident within the jurisdiction;
>
> [. . .]
>
> (f) if the action begun by the writ is brought against a defendant not domiciled or ordinarily resident in Scotland to enforce, rescind, dissolve, annul or otherwise affect a contract, or to recover damages or obtain other relief in respect of the breach of a contract, being (in either case) a contract which—
>
> [. . .]
>
> (i) was made within the jurisdiction, or
>
> (ii) was made by or through an agent trading or residing within the jurisdiction on behalf of a principal trading or residing out of the jurisdiction, or
>
> (iii) is by its terms, or by implication, governed by English law;
>
> (h) if the action begun by the writ is founded on a tort committed within the jurisdiction. . . .

See H. STEINER & D. VAGTS, *supra*, at 750–51.

In **Germany**, corporations may be sued where they have their seat, where the obligation in question is to be fulfilled (Section 29 Zivilprozessordnung), where the wrongful conduct took place (in the case of tort action), or where there is a local branch of the corporation.

In practice, Section 23 has been most used to confer jurisdiction on German courts over foreigners. It has also been subject to the sharpest criticism as being exceptional or 'exorbitant.' It reads:

> For complaints asserting pecuniary claims against a person who has no domicile within the country, the court of the district within which this person has property, or within which is found the object claimed by the complaint, has jurisdiction...

"As interpreted, the section permits a plaintiff to recover judgment for any amount, regardless of the value of the defendant's property within Germany. It has not been interpreted as equivalent to '*quasi in rem*' jurisdiction, as generally understood in the United States, under which a court's judgment is limited to the value of the property which was attached or garnished. German courts have applied Section 23 to situations where property of trivial value (such as a commercial account book of defendant) was within the jurisdiction."

See id. at 753–54.

Because the **Japanese legal system** is patterned on the civil law model, the Japanese rules on court jurisdiction resemble the common law rules on venue. The courts' ability to entertain an action is stated basically in territorial terms. Jurisdiction in private law cases is *in personam*, the notions of *in rem* or *quasi in rem* jurisdiction do not exist. Also, jurisdiction assertion is not the expression of the court's coercive power. According to Japanese notions, jurisdiction merely defines the "competence" of the court to adjudicate (to build a record, identify and apply the law, and render a judgment). Also, the defendant need not be physically present in the territory of the court; service of process is not required; and *forum non conveniens* does not exist.

The court's ability to entertain an action is based primarily on the defendant's domicile or residence. Courts in the district of the defendant's general forum can entertain lawsuits against the defendant. Unless a special forum rule applies, Japanese courts have no ability to hear suits against individuals who do not have either a domicile or residence in Japan. The special forum rules provide that actions involving monetary obligations can be brought at the place of performance and that tort claims can be adjudicated at the place of the tort or of the personal injury. Japan has the equivalent of Section 23 of the German Code of Civil Procedure. It allows suit against individuals without a general forum in Japan where the subject matter of the claim or other attachable property is located. There is also a form of joint liability jurisdiction under which a person without general forum can be sued in the district in which a co-adventurer satisfies the general forum requirements.

Japanese law has no rules on international jurisdiction. The jurisdictional provisions in the Code are seen as exclusively as domestic rules. No enacted statute on the issue exists. Japan is not a party to any international instrument on court jurisdiction in international litigation cases. In the absence of any legislation guidance, the Japanese courts—relying on *jori* or "common sense" or "natural reason"—have elaborated three doctrines to deal with the issues of international jurisdiction. *Jori* requires in matters of procedure that the parties be treated fairly and given access to a suitable and expeditious trial. The location of the action must be fair and reasonable.

1. The *retrospective surmise doctrine* (*gyaku-suichi-setsu*) provides that jurisdiction in an international case can be asserted by a Japanese court if the provisions of the Code of Civil Procedure allow for the assertion of jurisdiction in a domestic setting. In other words, the basis for domestic jurisdiction acts as the foundation for international jurisdiction by ricochet. Therefore, international jurisdiction is deduced retrospectively from the domestic provisions on venue and jurisdiction.

2. The *distributive jurisdiction doctrine* (*kankatsu-haibun-setsu*) provides that judicial jurisdiction in international matters is premised upon the ability of the tribunal to dispense justice on an international scale. Given the international character of the litigation, the municipal court that is designated to have jurisdiction should be best able to respond to the particularities of the litigation and provide the best means for achieving justice and providing for stable international relations. Hence, conflicts rules would "distribute" jurisdiction to the tribunal that is best suited to handle the litigation.

3. The *balancing doctrine* (*hikaku-koryo-setsu*) provides that whether a court has jurisdiction over an international litigation should be decided in an *ad hoc* fashion—by "balancing" in every case a variety of factors that attend the litigation (*e.g.*, the interests and convenience of the parties [especially those of the defendant], the subject matter of the litigation, and the "contacts" between the litigation and the country in which suit is brought).

The current approach of the Japanese courts to the assertion of jurisdiction in international litigation appears to merge the "retrospective surmise doctrine" with some of the general elements of the "balancing doctrine." Provisions of domestic law provide the juridical foundation for the exercise of jurisdiction, if the assertion of the court's authority satisfies the interests of justice given the international character of the suit. The acceptance of this approach arose from the decision of the Japanese Supreme Court in the landmark *Malaysia Airline Systems* case. *See* Judgment of Oct. 16, 1981 (Sup. Ct.), 35–7 Sup. Ct. Civ. Case Rep. 1224.

There, the survivors of the plaintiff, a Japanese national who had died in an airplane crash in Malaysia while on board a Malaysian airline flight, brought suit before a Japanese court. The Nagoya District Court dismissed the suit, holding that it lacked jurisdiction. The court reasoned that the question of whether international jurisdiction existed was to be decided by reference to "*naturalis ratio*" because Japanese law contained no provisions on this question. Because the transaction and the accident were all localized in Malaysia and despite the fact that the plaintiff's domicile was in Japan and the defendant had a place of business in Japan, the court deemed that the courts of Malaysia had jurisdiction. On appeal, the Nagoya High Court remanded the case to the district court, holding—pursuant to the domestic provision in the Code of Civil Procedure—that the defendant's appointment of a representative in Japan and establishment of a business office subjected the defendant to suit in Japan under Japanese law. Moreover, the place of performance of the contract had been Japan and this factor made Japan a suitable forum for the suit under the "*naturalis ratio*."

On appeal to the Supreme Court, that Court upheld the appellate court reasoning and determination:

> ...[I]t is a principle that Japanese jurisdiction cannot be extended to a defendant who is a foreign juridical person whose principal office is located in a foreign country, unless the juridical person is willing to submit to [Japanese court] jurisdiction. Exceptionally, however,...it may be appropriate in some cases to have the defendant submit to our jurisdiction regardless of the defendant's nationality of residence. Regarding the extent of this exceptional treatment, there is no statute that directly provides for international jurisdiction, nor any relevant treaty or any clear principle generally recognized under international law. In such a situation, it is proper to decide according to "*naturalis ratio*"—from the point of view of fairness to the parties, justice, and the efficiency of litigation. If Japanese law provides for a forum of litigation in its provision on domestic venue in the Code of Civil Procedure, such as the defendant's residence (art. 2), a juridical person's...place of business (art. 4), the place of performance (art. 5), the location of the defendant's property (art. 8), or the place of the tort (art. 15),...it satisfies the *naturalis ratio* to have the defendant submit to our jurisdiction in such a case.

On the basis of this reasoning, the court decided that the defendant could be sued in Japan because it had appointed a representative in Japan and maintained a place of business in Tokyo.

Since the Supreme Court's decision in *Malaysia Airline Systems*, Japanese courts generally have premised their international jurisdiction on the venue provisions of the Code of Civil Procedure and made exceptions when a special circumstance was found to exist.

See generally S. KIDANA, H. MATSUOKA, & S. WATANABE, OUTLINE OF PRIVATE INTERNATIONAL LAW 227, 228 (1985).

Chapter 4

DIVERSE TRIAL CONCEPTS

Table of Sections

---

§ 1. NATIONAL LEGAL TRADITIONS

(i)

The Civilian Trial Process

Procedure is not pure form...It is the "Cape Wrath" where Rapidity and Efficiency have to be combined with Justice; it is also the "Cape of Good Hope" where Individual Liberty has to be combined with Equality of Opportunities. Procedure is, in fact, the faithful mirror of all of the major exigencies, problems, and trials of our epoch—of the immense challenge of our time.[1]

I. General Observations

The continental civil law view of procedural justice contrasts sharply with U.S. common law notions of due process of law. In civil law systems, like France, judges are civil servants—magistrates whose responsibility is to administer justice in the name of the State. In this bureaucratized system of justice, there are no civil juries or complex rules of evidence. Judges are entrusted with the task of finding and evaluating evidence. They conduct and control trials, and have primary allegiance to the integrity of the substantive law.

As a consequence, party-driven trials, cross-examination, lawyer-conducted depositions, and contingency fee arrangements are unknown in civil law systems. The single-event trial is replaced by a series of hearings, in which evidence is gathered and relevant legal questions are examined. Witnesses are not heard under oath and are examined primarily by the judge; they often relate free-flowing narrative accounts of their observations. Judges determine both liability and damages. The court rules as a unitary public body, without expressing dissenting views. A *de novo* reconsideration of the entire matter is available on appeal.

Despite the inquisitorial character of the judges' procedural powers, the parties establish the subject matter of the litigation in the civil law trial.[2] Judges cannot commence an action or render a decision beyond the case presented by the parties. An infringement of these principles constitutes a denial of justice and subjects the judge to civil or criminal sanctions.[3]

Moreover, civil law judges are not lawyers. They enter their profession immediately upon completing their legal training, and never loose sight of the theoretical and substantive (versus "exigent" and "practical") academic approach to the law.[4] The French judge approaches the analysis of legal questions "in terms of general principles, with the use of generalizations and conceptual abstractions. In other words, the judicial operation is perfectly suited to a civil law system with its

1. Mauro Cappelletti, *Social and Political Aspects of Civil Procedure—Reforms and Trends in Western and Eastern Europe*, 69 MICH. L. REV. 847–886 (1971).

2. In light of the essentially private rights involved in civil proceedings, the proceedings must be initiated by parties themselves, who alone may defend their personal rights. NCPC art. 1 (Fr.).

3. *See* J.A. Jolowicz. *The Active Role of the Court in Civil Litigation*, *in* PUBLIC INTEREST PARTIES AND THE ACTIVE ROLE OF THE JUDGE IN CIVIL LITIGATION 155–277, 169–171 (Mauro Cappelletti, ed. 1975). *See also* JACQUES NORMAND, LE JUGE ET LE LITIGE 43–51 (1965).

4. See Joseph Dainow, *The Constitutional and Judicial Organization of France and Germany and Some Comparisons of the Civil Law and Common Law Systems*, 37 INDIANA L. REV. 1, 43 (1961): "In common law countries, there is no particular training for judges because the judges are drawn from the successful practitioners who have made a good name for themselves. All their experience has been of a practical nature, and their approach as judges continues to be the same. With a legal system based essentially on decided cases, the judges must necessarily be practical, and the elevation of a member of the bar to a seat on the bench is the perfectly natural procedure."

codification of integrated and coordinated principles of a systematic plan."[5]

The French judiciary's response to the silence or insufficiency of the written law is also characteristically civilian. In common law jurisdictions, written law is the exception. In most subject areas, it is inevitably supplanted by the evolving common law. In the Romanist tradition, by contrast, the written law is primary. As a result, civil law courts encounter problems when the written law is incomplete or nonexistent. For instance, article 4 of the French Civil Code compels the court to render a judgment. Refusing to decide a case because the written law is somehow deficient constitutes a punishable offense. The court can employ a variety of gap-filling measures to reach a determination.[6]

Moreover, the common law doctrines of precedent and *stare decisis* generally are unknown in civil law systems. Decisions are consistent, but this is nothing like claiming that the courts are *bound* to follow prior decisions. The French courts must state the reasons for their judgment,[7] and merely citing prior case law is deemed an inadequate justification for a holding.[8] The French courts, however, recognized the doctrine of *jurisprudence constante* or *établie*: Once a legal question has been decided the same way numerous times by the Court of Cassation, the opinions establish an official interpretation of the written law. In effect, a series of consistent judicial decisions has the status of an interpretation of the written law provided by custom.[9]

II. The Proceedings

The plaintiff's lawyer commences a lawsuit by the service of a summons, called an *assignation*.[10] As in the U.S. complaint, the parties must set out the matters of fact and the relevant law on the pertinent legal questions.[11] Unlike the U.S. complaint, however, the parties must also propose an appropriate means of proving their main factual contentions, thereby revealing the major written materials in their possession.[12]

5. *Id.* at 11.

6. Because the written law is designed to provide a certain and comprehensive statement of the law, court judgments do not need to fulfill this function. Instead, they add an element of flexibility to legal processes. *See* D.L. Lipstein, *The Doctrine of Precedent in Continental Law with Special Reference to French and German Law*, 28 J. COMP. LEG. & INT'L L. 34 (Soc'y of Comparative Legislation 3d Series 1946).

7. NCPC art. 455.

8. *See* Loussouarn, *The Relative Importance of Legislation, Custom, Doctrine and Precedence in French Law*, 18 LA. L. REV. 235 (1958).

9. In both France and Louisiana, custom is "generally accepted as having acquired the force of law. However, it may not abrogate legislation." La. Civ. Code art. 3 (West 1993). *See also* Loussouarn, *supra* note 8, at 250–54; J.P. DAWSON. THE ORACLES OF THE LAW 416–31 (1968). Jurisprudence, on the other hand, constitutes no more than a persuasive legal source. A.N. YIANNOPOULOS, LOUISIANA CIVIL LAW SYSTEM sec. 31–32 (1977); La. Civ. Code art. 1 cmt. (b) (West 1993).

10. NCPC art. 54.

11. *See* NCPC art. 56, pars. 2–4: "It is also in the *conclusions* that the parties make their request for whatever investigative measure (*mesure d'instruction, e.g. expertise, enquête, visite des lieux, comparution des parties*) they would like the judge to order."

12. In the absence of sufficient detail, the other party may raise the objection known as *obscure Lbelli*. XVI–6 INTERNATION-

The parties may add related claims at any time during the proceedings.[13] Counterclaims (*demandes reconventionnelles*), included in the *conclusions en defense*, are decided with the main action.[14]

Civil law systems traditionally have relatively unsophisticated discovery procedures. Revising the New Code of Civil Procedure to strengthen France's historically weak discovery rules has not had much effect:

> In spite of the high-sounding programmatic announcement in Art. 10 of the Civil Code. . .that 'Everyone must cooperate with the judiciary (*la justice*) in order that truth may prevail,' the recent version of French civil procedure does not seem to have brought about a radical change in this respect. Some discovery devices, it is true, have been introduced ... and are now embodied in the new Code of Civil Procedure. Articles 138 to 142 of that Code provide for some discovery of documents in the possession of an adverse party or a third person; a judicial order for such discovery is enforceable by a fine (*astreinte*). Pursuant to Arts. 184–198, a party can be ordered to appear personally before the court, in order to answer questions. But the interrogation will be conducted by the court rather than by counsel, and will not be under oath. All of these measures of discovery, moreover, take place only if ordered by the court, which has much discretion in the matter. In this connection, it must be remembered that effective discovery in civil litigation runs counter to a French tradition of long standing.[15]

Upon receiving the *assignation*, the president of the court submits the case to a particular chamber of the court. That section then determines whether the case can be heard without preparation or requires development by an examining judge (*juge de la mise en état*).[16] When a case requires development, the president of the section appoints an examining judge to conduct the interlocutory stage of the proceedings.[17] Otherwise, the case proceeds directly to trial.[18]

In the interlocutory stage of proceedings (*instruction*), the examining judge directs the development of the factual and legal issues and fixes the time limits for preparing the case.[19] Article 179 requires the judge to give parties notice of any proceeding, thereby allowing them to

AL ENCYCLOPEDIA OF COMPARATIVE LAW 71 (Mauro Cappelletti, ed. 1984) [hereinafter Encyclopedia] (citing Fettweis, *Éléments de la competence et de la procedure civile II* [Liège 1962] 4–4–05).

13. NCPC art. 68.

14. *Id.*

15. R. SCHLESINGER, et al., COMPARATIVE LAW 426, n. 32 (5th ed. 1988) (citing James Beardsley, *Proof of Fact in French Civil Procedure*, 34 AM. J. COMP. LAW 459 [1986]) (citations omitted); *see also* Robert W. Miller, *The Mechanisms of Fact–Discovery: A Study in Comparative Civil Procedure* (pts. 1–2). 32 ILL. L. REV. 261, 424 (1937); *Pain* v. *United Technologies Corp.*, 637 F.2d 775, 789 (D.C. Cir. 1980), *cert. denied*, 454 U.S. 1128 (1981); *cf. Mobil Tankers Co., S.A.* v. *Mene Grande Oil Co.*, 363 F.2d 611, 614–15 (3d Cir. 1966).

16. NCPC arts. 760–63. Some investigations may be conducted by preliminary orders issued in an accelerated proceeding (*référé*). This proceeding takes place even before the investigating judge is appointed. *See* NCPC arts. 808–11.

17. NCPC art. 762.

18. NCPC art. 760.

19. NCPC art. 762.

be present and to respond. The judge may inquire into the facts by issuing procedural orders (*mesures d'instruction*).[20] In addition, the judge may: take advice from persons possessing technical or specialized knowledge[21] or appoint an expert,[22] call the parties to give their version of the facts,[23] order the taking of oral testimony from witnesses,[24] or rule on procedural defenses.[25]

French civil procedure functions without the sequence rules so familiar in U.S. litigation.[26] Because the court presides over the entire case, the concepts of "plaintiff's case," and "defendant's case"—that determine the sequence of presentation and consideration of issues before a U.S. court—are unnecessary. As a result, the court may freely investigate any part of the dispute, and usually begins its inquiry by considering the most important issues. For example, the court might first examine an affirmative defense, which could not be considered under U.S. procedure until the plaintiff had rested its case.

Once the investigating judge is satisfied that the case is adequately prepared for trial, the preparatory phase is closed (*clôture des débats*). The parties may no longer exchange written pleadings or refer to additional documents. The president of the chamber then fixes the date for the final hearing (*audience de plaidoirie*), at which the parties make their oral arguments. At the conclusion of the arguments, the parties submit *dossiers* to the court that contain their pleadings and documentary evidence.[27]

French civil procedure is marked by a strong distrust of oral evidence.[28] In fact, the bulk of the evidence consists of written statements from witnesses. Strict rules limit the admissibility of oral evidence. When oral evidence is taken,[29] one of the parties has usually requested it and identified the questions it believes require such proof.[30] If convinced of its need, the investigating judge will issue an order for the testimony, specifying the issues upon which the witness will be allowed to testify.[31] The examination of the witness (called an *enquête*) usually takes place in the judge's chambers in the presence of the respective *avocats*.[32]

20. For example, the investigating judge, upon the application of one of the parties, may order the production of relevant evidence from an opposing party or a third party. NCPC art. 770.

21. NCPC arts. 249–55.

22. NCPC arts. 263–284.

23. NCPC arts. 184–98.

24. NCPC arts. 204–31, 771.

25. NCPC art. 771, par. 1.

26. John H. Langbein, *The German Advantage in Civil Procedure*, 52 U. Chi. L. Rev. 823, 830 (1985).

27. *See id.* at 831.

28. James Beardsley identified Loysel's maxim, "*Qui mieux abreuve, mieux prevue*" ("a witness who is well wined and dined will testify well") as illustrative of the "distrust which has marked French civil procedure for centuries." Beardsley, *supra* note 15, at 478; *cf.* C. Civ. arts. 1317–69 [hereinafter CC].

29. *See* NCPC arts. 232–84. Apparently, resort to oral testimony is generally limited to family law matters. *Id.*

30. NCPC arts. 222–24. The investigating judge, however, has the power to order such testimony on his/her own motion. NCPC art. 218.

31. NCPC art. 205.

32. *See* NCPC arts. 208–09.

The judge begins the *enquête* by informing the witness of the subject of the inquiry and instructing the witness to give a narrative account of his/her knowledge of the matters in question.[33] The judge also serves as the examiner-in-chief, interrupting the witness on occasion to ask specific questions. The *avocats* may not address the witness directly, but they can suggest questions to the judge.[34] Rather than having the testimony transcribed, the judge dictates a summary of it to the court clerk. The witness may examine the summary and make alterations or additions.[35] The court relies exclusively on the written record of the examination when making findings of fact.[36]

Partisan preparation, examination, and cross-examination of witnesses are unknown in the French trial process. Not only would preparation of a witness constitute a serious breach of ethics, but any substantial contact between a lawyer and a witness impeaches the credibility of the witness.[37] The combat of the parties is not given the primary role—no matter how vast the available body of information. The goal of resolution is achieved through the written law and the court's primary task of normative decision-making.[38]

In France, experts are almost always appointed by the court, often from a permanent official list. In civil matters, however, judges may appoint whomever they choose unless restricted by legislation or regulations.[39] This continental tradition of expert selection by the court avoids partisanship and its distortions.

> European legal systems are... expert-prone. Expertise is frequently sought. The literature emphasizes the value attached to having expert assistance available to the courts in an age in which litigation involves facts of ever-greater technical difficulty. The essential insight of Continental civil procedure is that credible

33. *See* NCPC arts. 210–14.

34. NCPC arts. 213–14.

35. NCPC arts. 219–20.

36. Obviously, such a process runs the risk of distortion or inaccuracy via the judge's interpretation of the witness' testimony. Placing faith in a professional adjudicator for efficiency and expediency in the fact-finding process, however, goes a long way toward justifying the risk.

37. *See* NCPC art. 214. A related issue revolves around the lack of anything comparable to U.S. exclusionary rules of evidence in the civilian codes. *See generally*, Hans W. Baade, *Illegally Obtained Evidence in Criminal and Civil Cases: A Comparative Study of a Classic Mismatch*, 51 TEX. L. REV. 1325 (1973); Hans W. Baade, *Illegally Obtained Evidence in Criminal and Civil Cases: A Comparative Study of a Classic Mismatch II*, 52 TEX. L. REV. 621, 621–24 (1974). Rules excluding probative evidence due to concerns of prejudice and the like are simply nonexistent. *See* Baade, *supra*, 52 TEX. L. REV. at 624. For example, hearsay evidence is not excluded and therefore allows the court to freely pursue the most probative—versus the least prejudicial—evidence. Thus, all manner of second-hand methods of oral proof, including police reports and other official accounts of interrogations, are admissible (and welcomed) into evidence.

38. NCPC art. 199.

39. NCPC art. 198. "The civilians still hold to the idea that a party cannot be a 'witness'; but their codes...do so provide for judicial examination of the parties so that they may clarify their contentions and assist the court in finding the truth." R. SCHLESINGER, et al., *supra* note 15, at 428. *See also* Langbein, *supra* note 26, at 836. NCPC art. 232. For example, artificial persons may be appointed by the court as experts. *Id. Cf.* Loi No. 71–498 relative aux experts judiciaries (1) of 29 June 1971 (JO 30 June, p. 6300) art. 2.

expertise must be neutral expertise. Thus, the responsibility for selecting and informing experts is placed upon the courts, although with important protections for party interests.[40]

The French code of civil procedure gives the expert a status akin to an auxiliary judicial officer.[41] The role of the expert in French procedure is reminiscent of that of a judge in many respects:

> When carried out by an expert who examines the evidence broadly, interrogates third persons, allows the parties to participate fully, the expertise [or investigatory proceeding conducted by the expert], though lacking in judicial formality and conducted by a layman, takes on some of the characteristics of the "trial" which is otherwise not to be found the French system of civil procedure. This is so, not only because of the approach taken by the expert but also because, notwithstanding the overriding responsibility of the court for determinations of fact, the expert's report is usually decisive.[42]

The order appointing the expert identifies the specific issues to be investigated and the time within which the expert must submit findings to the court.[43] The expert is bound to conduct the investigation "contradictorily," that is, where necessary, the parties must be given the opportunity to be present and to participate in the investigatory proceedings. In the course of the investigations, the expert may hear or hire individuals whose skills or knowledge are necessary, may conduct discovery, and may even examine witnesses. The expert does not testify before the court, but rather submits a written report[44] outlining the findings and the opinion.[45] The expert, however, may be examined in open court regarding specific points or conclusions contained in the report. The Code provides that an expert "must never express opinions on points of law."[46]

After developing the facts and hearing the oral arguments of the parties, the court must decide the case.[47] The court cannot render a general ruling: its decision must clearly apply the relevant codal provisions to the particular facts and parties involved. During the court's deliberations, the investigating judge presents an opinion to the court.[48] After deliberations, the court normally announces its judgment in open court. Occasionally, if the case is relatively simple, the judges will consult briefly and the presiding judge will deliver judgment at the hearing

40. Langbein, *supra* note 26, at 836–37 (footnotes omitted).

41. *See, e.g.*, NCPC arts. 242, 243, 266, 275, 278, 279. *See also* E.J. Cohn, *The Rules of Arbitration of the United Nations Economic Commission for Europe*, 16 Int'l & Comp. L.Q. 946, 968 (1967) (discussing such procedures in general for civil law jurisdictions and providing further references).

42. Beardsley, *supra* note 15, at 481. It is interesting to note that this process to some extent injects some of the substantial benefits of arbitration into the judicial process without completely abandoning the integrity of the substantive law to private dispute resolution.

43. NCPC art. 265.

44. NCPC art. 282.

45. NCPC arts. 276–79, 282–83.

46. NCPC art. 238.

47. CC art. 4.

48. NCPC art. 786, 450–51, 452, 456, 455, 458.

without having the court retire to deliberate. The clerk of court establishes the text of the judgment as it is read in court, and then delivers it to the judges for signature. The judgment must include a summary of the evidence and respective arguments of the parties, the reasons upon which the court based its decision (*les motifs*), and a statement of the decision itself (*le dispositif*).

III. Conclusion

The primacy of the written law even dominates procedure in civil law systems. Civilian systems reflect the conviction that the resolution of disputes emerges from the application of substantive legal principles rather than the discovery of facts. The first question of any litigation is whether the dispute falls within the ambit of one or more code articles. If not, the next step requires reasoning by analogy. Either way, the starting point is a provision, or a number of provisions, of the Code. The judge is bound to look to the general principles of the Code to identify a basis for the decision.

Active, professional judges control the trial process, guaranteeing that procedural considerations never overwhelm the status or significance of the written law. Litigation is conceived of as a process through which the judiciary gathers the relevant information to which it applies the fixed meaning of the Code provisions. Fairness is achieved by the rectitude of conformity to established principles of the Civil Code.

[Prepared, researched, and written by Tulane law students who worked on a comparative law dictionary under my supervision at the end of 1980s.]

Notes and Questions

1. The reading presents in great detail the operation of the French trial process and the contrast to its American counterpart. There are many formal and substantive points of departure. The objective of the description is not to train the reader in French procedure (most readers will never enter into a French courtroom), but rather to convey a sense of the enormous differences that can separate like-minded, allied systems. From a structural and operational perspective, the differences in process are staggering. The French trial process comes across as more academic, impractical, and repressive than the American. Do you share this assessment? What impact would those factors have on your relationship to a client with business interests in France or to a French lawyer who is an ally or an adversary? Could you trust the French courts to reach a fair determination? What aspect of the process might lead you to distrust or to trust it?

2. Judges especially in the French system, along with French university law professors, act as the high priests of law. Law—in the form of codified texts—proclaims what is right, good, and desirable in human society. It is a veritable religion. Would it be accurate to say that law in continental European systems, like the French, looms as a cultural, historical, and intellectual force, whereas it is the power and force of law that is at the core of the American legal system? Why might you find this question disturbing?

3. There are numerous procedural differences between the trial systems that are noteworthy. For example, there is no verbatim transcript of the proceeding in the French system. The presiding judge simply dictates his or her recollection of the various meetings to the clerk of court. Appeal is not, therefore, based on the minutes of the meetings. Appeal represents a *de novo* reconsideration of the entire matter, including a new trial. In the French system, this feature is known as *le deuxième degré de juridiction* and is a substantial part of the system's due process guarantees. Further appeal, to the highest court with subject matter jurisdiction, is available only on the basis of a question of law. Moreover, it is difficult to challenge evidentiary determinations because there are so few rules and wide judicial discretion. In this judicial framework, a verbatim transcript would be of little utility. Do you agree? Do you find it, as Baudelaire said of Poe's poetry in an admiring way, "shocking"?

4. *L'expertise judiciaire* is another important contrast that highlights the differences between the two procedural systems. Legal experts in the French system are appointed by the court and serve as a quasi-judicial officers. The report they submit is like the opinion of a magistrate in the federal system; it is very likely to be adopted fully or nearly so by the court. The use of experts, therefore, is radically different in the two processes. How would you explain this distinction to your client and how would you evaluate it?

La partie civile is another telling illustration. Tort law is practiced very differently in the French legal system. There are no juries; damages and liability are established by the court. When the commission of a tort gives rise to the criminal prosecution of the tortfeasor, the victim of the tort can join the criminal proceeding as the "civil" party (*la partie civile*). This procedure allows the civil claimant to benefit from the district attorney's conduct of the trial, including discovery and expert reports. The conviction of the tortfeasor for a crime will result in the assessment of civil damages for the plaintiff. Under French law, criminal determinations and findings are binding on the civil proceedings. The joinder of actions facilitates the plaintiff's case and promotes efficiency and economy in personal injury litigation. It is safe to say that such a procedure would be unthinkable in the U.S. system. Why would it be so repugnant to U.S. concepts of tort litigation?

5. As a final point, it should be emphasized that characteristic U.S. trial techniques, *e.g.*, preparing witnesses, is deemed unethical and probably illegal in the French system. Explain why such techniques are reprehensible in the French system?

6. For a more detailed discussion of these comparative law considerations, see H. PATRICK GLENN, LEGAL TRADITIONS OF THE WORLD (2d ed. 2004).

(ii)

Summary of
David J. Przeracki, *"Working It Out": A Japanese Alternative To Fighting It Out,*

37 Clev. St. L. Rev. 149 (1989)
(reprinted with permission).

[. . .]

B. Socio-legal History

1. The Confucian Influence

In stark contrast to America's legal and cultural heritage, and essential to an understanding of contemporary Japan, is the recognition of the pervasive influence of Confucian philosophy on Japanese society from the earliest times. Best known for its moral philosophy, Confucianism "gives primary emphasis to the ethical meaning of *human relationships*, finding and grounding the moral in the divine transcendence." The relationships one has with others, if harmonious, lead to achievement of the basic Confucian virtue of *jen* (translated as compassion, human-heartedness or "man-to-manness"). For the Japanese,

> [t]he spirit of harmony and concord [is] expressed in the virtue of *wa*. If people abided by *wa*, disputes would not arise. It is the one's duty to avoid discord. *En* is the principle of social tie. The net effect of these two principles [constitutes the foundation of] . . . the Japanese [perspective]. Maintaining the relationship bound together by these two forces is the paramount concern.
>
> [Watts, *Briefing the American Negotiator in Japan*, 16 Int'l Law. 597, 600 (1982).]

Wa is the principle of harmony which the Japanese feel is a condition of one's being in any relationship, including contractual. Accordingly, *wa* may prevent discord in all activities.

Owing to simple Confucian principles, the Japanese are socialized to avoid interpersonal disputes in every realm, including social and business. The principles of *wa* and *en* are still practiced in contemporary Japan, as evidenced in Japanese contract methodology and Japanese dispute resolution techniques which are characterized by conciliation, less litigation, and very few lawyers.

[. . .]

2. Contemporary Japanese Legal System

Because of the myriad of influences on the development of law in Japan, the Japanese legal system of the twentieth century has been described as a *mélange* of (1) civil law, (2) American law, and (3) Japanese Legal Consciousness. The first element, civil law, refers to the Japanese Civil Code based on the German Civil Code. While the Code remains in effect [today], these legal rules function merely as guiding principles (*tatemae*) in the development of the more important social-political consensus. According to Judge Sho Watanabe, a veteran judge of the Tokyo District Court, this societal consensus, coupled with the judge's innate or "gut" feeling, constitute "*honei*," the ultimate basis for judicial decisions.

The second element of Professor Taniguci's description of the modern-day Japanese legal system is American law. The American-style constitution, imposed upon Japan during the Occupation after World War II, was accompanied by Code revisions concerning both family law and corporate law. Furthermore, a new Securities Exchange Law, Anti–Monopoly Law, and Income Tax Code—all patterned after American law—were enacted.

"Japanese Legal Consciousness," the third element, can be described as a natural, collective abhorrence to confrontation at any level. It is:

> [A] combination of native attitudes, traditions, and social norms that make the Japanese process different from any other, despite the highly imitative nature of Japanese statutory law. [G]enerally, this special legal consciousness results from the fact that in Japan relationships, including economic relationships, are considered basically to be social rather than legal.
>
> [Stevens, *Modern Japanese Law as an Instrument of Comparison*, 19 Am. J. Comp. L. 665, 667–68 (1971).]

[. . .]

Finally, while there exists in contemporary Japan a concept of duty to another, or duty to the group (both are *giri*), unlike in America, *there does not exist any notion of individual right*. For instance, the Japanese word for law, *ho*, bears no notion of substantive rights as incorporated in Western law. The law for most persons means government restraints on individuals for governmental purposes. Fundamentally, to insist on an individual right would be to violate one's own *giri*. "The Japanese aversion to the law is really an aversion to the use of law in the legal process, to the shame of the courtroom, to the judgment that blames." "Shame here implies the immense social pressure brought to bear on the individuals to resolve their conflicts without disturbing the social order." Hence, in contract negotiation, positions are not asserted adversarially. Rather, contracts are made by the parties without substantial disagreement.

C. Japanese Contracts

1. *Formation*

According to one definition, a Japanese contract (*kuwaiti*) is "[a]n agreement of two or more parties which is intended to produce fixed effects under private law among such persons." Practically speaking, however, a Japanese contract is really something quite different. Consistent with Confucian ideology, the Japanese businessman believes that the *relationship* he has with the other contracting party is of most importance:

> For the Japanese, a contract is the end result of having established a relationship of trust and friendship. This relationship of mutual trust is more important than the obligations embodied in the contract, for it indicates that both parties possess an understanding that can be employed if and when future problems arise.
>
> [Lansing & Wechselblatt, *Doing Business in Japan: The Importance of the Unwritten Law*, 17 INT'L LAW. 647, 654 (1983) (emphasis added).]

Furthermore, "[i]f a contract is concluded between two parties, for instance, its precise content will depend more upon what the parties feel their relationship is or is expected to be than upon the objective words used to frame the contract."

It is clear, therefore, that business relationships are *giri* relationships, replete with emotive qualities. Contracting parties strive to achieve the spirit of harmony (*wa*) and trust, and are dedicated to the long-term relationship. The Japanese Ministry of International Trade and Industry observed that many Japanese business relationships stretch back over three generations.

During the course of contract formation, the Japanese are not really negotiat[ing] contracts, but rather relationships. Elements of mutual dignity and reciprocal respect, both aimed at harmony maintenance, are critical to successful contract negotiations with the Japanese. Japanese Legal Consciousness, which directs all aspects of Japanese legal relations, implies a notion of good faith requirement in American contract law.

Because of the Japanese emphasis on relationships, it should not be surprising that lawyers are typically not involved in contract negotiations. "In the past, the Japanese believed that lawyers destroyed *wa* by stressing their client's position and by ignoring compromises that benefit society as a whole."

It should also not be surprising that because the Japanese negotiate relationships rather than contract terms, *the concept of consideration does not exist in Japan*. There is no bargained-for-exchange in Japanese contract negotiations. In Japan, the long-term relationship is more important than the short-term profit.

Consequently, the written document is not particularly important to the Japanese businessman. When a contract is reduced to a writing, it is typically very short, often not longer than one page. The writing does not attempt to account for every contingency, but rather leaves areas intentionally grey to allow for future modification. The terms are vague and sketch only a general outline of the course of exchanges to take place. Again, mutual trust and commitment to the business relationship will define the terms ultimately performed. Consequently, after the signing it is unlikely that a Japanese businessman will ever again look at the written document.

2. *Performance*

As seen earlier, Japanese contract terms are generally amorphous and vague. Consequently, performance is not restrictively defined. Rather, the general terms are guided by Japanese Legal Consciousness. This principle, as it applies to contract performance, is enshrined in the doctrine of good faith and is codified in Article 1(2) of the Japanese Civil Code. In relevant part, this section reads, "the ... performance of duties shall be done in faith and in accordance with the principles of trust."

3. *Dispute Resolution*

It is worthy of reiteration that there exists no concept of right in Japanese society. Historically, the emphasis has been on duty, specifically, a duty to maintain harmonious relationships. As a consequence, the Japanese approach to dispute resolution reverses the order of practice in America; the Japanese strongly prefer extra-judicial, informal means as opposed to litigation. "When a dispute arises, the *relationship* functions as the dispute settling mechanism." Dispute resolution is usually initiated by the introduction of "*naniwabushi*," a tear-jerking statement. "Since the Japanese are more aesthetic and sentimental than logical and rational they are susceptible to sad stories.... Compromise is not difficult to achieve."

The procedure by which interpersonal settlements are made has been called "reconcilement." Reconcilement is described as "the process by which parties in the dispute confer with each other and reach a point at which they can come to terms and restore or create harmonious relationships." Japanese confidence in reconcilement is perhaps best exemplified in the "We Can Work It Out" clause which invariably appears at the end of Japanese contracts. The clause will typically take one of two forms:

> If in the future a dispute arises between the parties with regard to the ... [provisions] ... stipulated in this contract, the parties will confer in good faith [*Sei-i o motte Kyogi Suru*].
>
> or
>
> ... will settle [the dispute] harmoniously by consultation [*Kyogi Ni Yori emman Ni Kaiketsu Suru*].
>
> [D. Henderson, Conciliation and Japanese Law 194 (1965)]

The notion of reconcilement recalls the traditional idea that both parties are to blame when a conflict arises (*kenka ryoseibei*) because they both failed to maintain harmonious relations. It is, therefore, in the best interest of each party to settle the dispute privately.

A second level of dispute resolution in Japan is conciliation (*chotei*). Also rooted in Confucian philosophy, and first codified during the Tokugawa Shogunate, conciliation is now provided for in the Civil Conciliation Law of 1951. According to Article 1, "[t]he purpose of this law is to devise, by mutual concessions of the parties, solutions for disputes concerning civil matters, which are consistent with reason and befitting actual circumstances." The negotiations are conducted through a third party (a conciliator or a judge) or a committee. When a compromise is reached, the settlement is enforceable as if determined by a court.

Conciliation is very popular in Japan. Surveys conducted over a three-year period indicate that 80% of Japanese would seek settlement through conciliation. Only 20% would prefer settlement in court (after first attempting reconcilement). The Western practice of arbitration, however, is not very popular in Japan. The Japanese dislike arbitration because it "*imposes* a decision on the parties rather than allowing [them] to mold the outcome under the [influence] of a social superior."

Litigation, consequently, is considered exclusively a last resort. "To bring a case to court emphasizes a failure of society and individuals to resolve suits through traditional means. Any hope of restoring harmony is thus destroyed."

The non-litigious nature of the Japanese is generally attributed to their desire to maintain social harmony. However, several other reasons have been proffered to explain their non-litigious propensities. The first of these is the dearth of effective legal sanctions. In Japanese civil cases, the ultimate sanction is to attach property. While other sanctions include civil fines, the ability to collect them is heavily reliant upon the party's willingness to pay. Another reason is the relative expense to bring suit in Japan. Filing fees, for example, are pro-rated to the amount in controversy, and can be very costly. A final reason to explain the scarcity of litigation is the modest supply of lawyers in Japan.

[. . .]

Notes and Questions

1. Japanese law and society's difference with and distance from the U.S. legal system and culture are very substantial. The diversity no longer represents merely a variation on a Western theme, but rather symbolizes the clash of fixed, unyielding worlds. The manners, approach, and assumptions are opposed and probably incompatible. It is not possible to engage in exchanges, unless one side cedes to the practices of the other. Necessity may motivate the concession, while the superiority of economic strength defines it. When Japanese merchants enter into Western-styled contracts, for example, they do so because they find the business prospects too lucrative to forgo. They also enter into such contracts with a vengeance; in other words, they behave just as adversarially as their American partners in terms of the content and performance of the agreement. The English language and U.S. lawyering practices continue to dominate global business transactions. The necessity of adaptation, however, does not eliminate ultimate cultural allegiance.

2. One could speculate about what would transpire if the tables were turned. Would Japanese business practices and legal concepts prevail over

their American counterparts? Would they be suitable for conducting global business? As with U.S. foreign policy, is there a messianic quality to American law? Are U.S. business law and trial techniques among the most viable and successful of all American exports? Or, are the strings of the international marketplace always pulled by the country with the strongest and longest arms?

3. The statistics given earlier on the Japanese bar (*see* chapter one *supra*) reveal a society that both differs from and resembles U.S. society. There are few attorneys in Japan, but many professionals have a basic law degree and legal education. Many of them obtain a U.S. LL.M. degree. Government bureaucracy and cultural hierarchies have an all-powerful position in Japan, but it is equally true that Japanese business seeks to be competitive on a worldwide basis. How truly different are Japanese law, society, and business? Are these differences meaningful or simply historical and confined to domestic life? How much play should be given to the lack of individual rights and the duty owed to the group?

4. To illustrate dichotomies further: Japan had no law on product liability until the mid–1990s, a situation which by Western standards was incredible for a major world economic power. The lack of law also was a means of thwarting lawsuits for product liability at least within Japan. Japanese companies, of course, remained vulnerable to suits in other countries. Their liability, therefore, became a factor of the enforceability of foreign judgments in Japan or of enforcement at the place of rendition. The new law modernizes the applicable legal regime and communicates the view that the legal system is not engaging in protectionist obsolescence and is responsive to corporate accountability and consumer protection.

A new arbitration law took effect in March 2004. *See* 15 World Arb. & Mediation Rep. 134 (May 2004). It was enacted in part to dispell the impression that Japan was less than enthusiastic about arbitration and to herald a new day for arbitration in Japan. The law took more than ten years to make its way to the Japanese Diet and was the product of an expert drafting group. It is a complex legislative scheme that borrows from a wide variety of sources. It is, therefore, unlikely to change the status of arbitration in Japan overnight. It is a long-awaited, but hesitant step in the transborder direction.

(iii)

Chris X. Lin, *A Quiet Revolution: An Overview of China's Judicial Reform*,

4 Asian-Pac. L. & Pol'y J. 9 (2003)
(reprinted with permission)
(footnotes omitted).

[. . .]

I. Introduction: Changing with the Times, A New Mindset

China's accession to the World Trade Organization (WTO) has been hailed as the harbinger of a new age. Contrary to their past reservations based on ideological reasons, policy makers and opinion molders in China now openly embrace the notion that, in order for China to be a respectable member of the international community, it must follow certain universally accepted norms, whether they be the United Nations Human Rights Convention, or rules proscribed by the WTO. Indeed, this recognition has become so much of the national consciousness that a new term has been coined and widely circulated. It is comprised of five Chinese characters: "*yu guo ji jie gui*," and literally means "making (the railroad) tracks consistent with the international gauge."

China's entry into the WTO has provided a much-needed outside impetus for it to adopt certain universally accepted principles such as transparency and judicial review. But China's resolve to enter the WTO, even if it meant that fundamental changes are necessary, reflects a much deeper current in thinking. The conversion of Chinese society from a planned economy to a market economy has fundamentally changed the relationship between the individual and the government, or at least it requires such a change. As Nobel Prize winning economist Milton Friedman recently put it, the key to the success of such a transition is not privatization, as he thought ten years ago, but rule of law.

When a government agency issues a directive depriving businesses of their right to free competition, can an individual ask the Court to declare it unlawful on the grounds that it violates the Administrative Procedure Law? When the legislature passes a law depriving an individual citizen of a fundamental right, can that individual ask the Court to strike down the statute on the grounds that it unconstitutional? Such are the fundamental issues facing China in its drive towards a modern economy and towards a modern society based on rule of law. It is in this arena that the judiciary shall play a key role.

Starting in the late 1980s and up until recent years, Chinese legal reform has largely centered on efforts to enact new legislation (including administrative regulations) in various areas of substantive law. Within the judiciary, reform has taken the form of developing a modern adversarial trial system, including the introduction of some elementary rules of evidence. Such reforms were deemed necessary to resolve the civil and commercial disputes arising from China's transformation from a planned to a market economy.

An overhaul of China's trial system alone, however, has not been enough to enable the Chinese courts to fulfill their functions in achieving justice. Indeed, some experts believe that such efforts have failed woefully. There is a new awareness among many within the Chinese legal community that all the reform measures will mean nothing without the establishment of judicial independence. In other words, an "institutional reform" is needed to reset the status of the courts and their relationship with other branches of the government.

Now we seem to be witnessing a second phase of China's legal reform, one that focuses on the need to bring the judiciary to the center stage as an arbiter between private citizens and the government and a guardian of the citizens' rights against government encroachment. As this new chapter of judicial reform unfolds, many of China's lower courts have taken initiative to introduce various innovative measures. But more important, in this course of experimenting, traditional thinking has been challenged, ideological taboos have been broken, the relationship between the individual and the government has been perceived in a new light, and the roles of the courts are under constant reassessment.

Several interwoven "mega-trends," which also constitute the most urgent tasks on the agenda of China's judicial reform today, have emerged from the current innovations. Among other things, they are: a recognition that rule of law is the benchmark of modern civilization; an emphasis on the vital role to be played by an independent judiciary in achieving rule of law; an acknowledgement of the relationship between constitutional protection of individual rights and rule of law; the requirement for judicial independence by China's commitment made in joining the WTO; the need to create a system of binding precedents and case law to achieve greater consistency among courts in their applications of the law and to reduce abuse of discretion on the part of judges; and finally, the need for transparency of the judicial process.

Such themes in China's current judicial reform may sound quite familiar to an American lawyer since many of their underlying concepts originated from the American experience with rule of law, including the development of an independent judiciary as the ultimate guardian of citizens' constitutional rights. Indeed, detailed references to American law permeate Chinese legal scholars' discussions and provide inspiration to Chinese courts for their innovative measures. Such American influence should not come as a surprise, since numerous Chinese law school professors have received degrees or training in the United States and numerous judges, lawyers, and law enforcement officials have visited this country and received short-term training. Now, the seeds sown are bearing fruit. To borrow a phrase from Michael Rosenfeld, an impressive amount of transplanting has taken place.

[. . .]

II. Recognition of Rule of Law as a Universal Value & Benchmark for Modern Civilization

Discussions among Chinese legal scholars about the need for rule of law as a major component in China's modernization drive started in the mid–1990s. The importance of the rule of law, however, has never been as relevant or important as it is today. There are at least two explanations for this. First, the progress of China's economic reforms has created many complex problems, such as increasing commercial and international disputes and rampant corruption and economic crime, which can only be effectively addressed by a fair and efficient judiciary. Second, the conversion to a "socialist market economy" has loosened the ideological control that the Chinese Communist Party (CCP) exercises over China's political reforms, which is the larger context within which China's judicial reform has progressed.

[...]

[T]he CCP leadership is moving towards a new understanding of the term "justice." It now understands that justice includes both substantive and procedural justice, that procedural laws play an important role in achieving just outcomes, and that a country with rule of law must first be a country with rule of procedural law. This constitutes a correction of the country's long overemphasis on substantive law at the expense of procedural law. It is important to stress ... that litigation procedure serves a dual function: it is both an instrument to implement substantive laws, and something of inherent value with an independent function.

What the Chinese call "procedural justice" is certainly not unfamiliar to American lawyers. It is essentially the same concept as the American Constitution calls "due process of law." Indeed, as a leading jurist in China puts it, procedure is "the life of law." This includes the procedure to pass a law or to promulgate a regulation, the procedure to conduct public hearings for public comment, the procedure for court enforcement of laws and regulations, the procedure for the police to obtain a warrant for search and seizure, or a warrant of arrest....

The profoundness of this conceptual revolution can be gleaned from the shift of the focus from "rule by law" to "rule of law," two terms in Chinese reflecting somewhat different understandings of the goals of China's legal reform. The first term comprises the Chinese characters "*yi fa zhi guo*," which can be literally translated into governing the country according to law or government by law. While this formulation is a departure from the old ideology that the state could act arbitrarily, it carries an inherent ambiguity. Does it mean that the government must rule through laws (such as statutes and regulations) or that the state must act within the limit of laws (especially those laws that are aimed at protecting individual rights) while ruling the country? It is no coincidence that government leaders have a preference for the former construction of the term. To many of China's leaders, the function of the law is to provide a code of conduct for citizens so that they will have rules to follow and laws to abide. The second term, now most often used by advocates of legal reforms, but becoming increasingly accepted in China, is "*fa zhi*," which can be translated into English as rule of law and seems to have been a Chinese translation of that English term. Because it does not contain the noun country as the object of the verb rule, this formulation seems to carry a greater emphasis on the limitations on government power. Or at least it means that the ruler, as well as the ruled, must act within the bounds of laws.

[...]

To sum up, a major shift in perspective took place among Chinese jurists in the past decade. Previously law was perceived as an instrument to impose the will of the state on the people, albeit a less arbitrary and more rational instrument compared to the ruthless and capricious rule of man in the past. Now emphasis is on the need to use law to limit the powers of the government so that the rights of individual citizens will be respected. With the acceleration of economic reforms, the dominant trend in Chinese legal thinking has been to recognize that the protection of citizens' rights is the *raison d'être* of a constitutional system.

III. Constitutionalism and the Roles of the Judiciary in Constitutional Reform

A. *The Awakening of Constitutionalism in China*

No student of China's legal reform during the past two decades will fail to notice the trajectory that reforms have taken—from commercial law, to civil law, then through administrative law and criminal law, and eventually culminating in the gradual reform of constitutional law. Constitutional law, being the closest to the distribution of political power, and hence the most sensitive to the Communist leadership, has had to wait until just recently to become the focus of reform. Of course, for quite some time Chinese scholars of constitutional law have pointed out that supremacy of the constitution over both the government and Chinese Communist Party is a predicate for rule of law, and without constitutional limitations on government powers, there can only be rule of man, not rule of law. While the taboos against discussion of constitutional reform have gradually disappeared since the late 1980s, only recently have meaningful changes become a realistic prospect.

[. . .]

[M]any of the problems facing the Chinese judiciary today cannot be effectively solved unless China restructures its constitutional framework. Many prominent Chinese legal scholars have pointed out that meaningful constitutional reform first requires the recognition of individual freedoms, or citizens' rights, as they are more commonly called in China. . . .

The current recognition of the importance of individuals' rights and the need to limit the government through the constitution marks a dramatic departure from the Chinese Communist Party orthodox that long belittled the importance of constitutional rights in favor of the totalitarian rule of the Party. It is, no doubt, an important step. How to make the constitution function as a guarantee of the citizens' rights remains an enormous challenge to reformers in China, because in the past courts have been prohibited from applying and interpreting the constitution in individual cases.

[. . .]

IV. The Changing Perception of Judicial Independence and its Prospect in China Post WTO Entry

While China's entry into the WTO provided a significant movement towards judicial independence, WTO accession is certainly not the only driving force. In recent years, advocates for judicial independence have become increasingly vocal. To understand the significance of this recent development, some historical perspective will be helpful.

A. From Rejection to Acceptance: A Radical Departure from the Past

Barely a decade ago, an authoritative book published in China on the Chinese judicial system, entitled Judicial System in China, declared, "the nature of judicial system is to prosecute, on behalf of the state, activities that are against the ruling order and to implement the will of the state with coercive force." With undertones of the Marxist "class struggle" the author continued:

> "Separation of powers" as conceived by Montesquieu can never become a reality. No matter how "separated," the purpose of the bourgeois state is to suppress the rebellions of the working class and maintain the bourgeois state. The concept of "judicial independence," derived from the concept of separation of powers, has been used to portray the courts as an institution above the classes and administering justice. But this is just to pacify the working class to prevent their rebellions. Although the constitution and laws provide for "judicial independence" as a principle, in reality the courts are both "independent" and "nonindependent" at the same time, and their function is to disguise the reactionary nature of the bourgeois judiciary.

How much has changed in the short decade since Professor Wu made his negative comment on the theory of Western style separation of powers and judicial independence. A book published in 2000, also entitled Judicial System in China and edited by the Chief Judge of the High Court of Tianjin, recognizes that judicial reform is a universal and irreversible trend: "While the legal systems in the world are divided into two, *i.e.*, the socialist system and the capitalist system, which overlapped with the traditional division between the common law system and the continental system, a commonality between all of them is [that] they all have been undergoing constant reforms." While the book mentions the socialist nature of the Chinese legal system in passing, as most official writings in China still do, it is devoid of the ideological rhetoric of its predecessor and focuses primarily on the roles of the judiciary in an increasingly complex market economy. But even such a view appears outdated since both judicial reform and the modernization drive have accelerated rapidly in the two years between 2000 and 2002. Today, both separation of powers and checks and balances have both been accepted in China as valuable political theories, if not wholly adaptable within the current legal system. Moreover, the Communist leadership has openly embraced judicial independence, as a principle, despite the fact that there are still different interpretations as to what "judicial independence" actually means.

B. Rampant Judicial Corruption: An Internal Impetus for Reform

Judicial corruption is another important impetus for adopting reform measures to increase judicial independence. Perhaps there is no better example to illustrate this point than the legal community's reactions to *Cangnan County v. Long Gang Rubber Molding, Inc*. In this much-publicized case, a court at the county level totally disregarded both the facts and law in entering judgment in favor of the county department of treasury and a perpetrator of fraud who controlled the agency, for the sole reason that the court's funding came from that department.

Outraged by the result in *Cangnan County v. Long Gang Rubber Molding, Inc.*, two prominent legal scholars, Professor Su Huiyu, Vice President of China Society of Criminal Law Studies, and Professor Zheng Wei of Eastern China University of Legal and Political Studies, lamented in 1999 that such phenomena are the inevitable result of the absurd situation in China where "those who manage the money bags manage those who manage the law," and called for immediate restructuring of the Chinese judiciary. As they pointed out, the Chinese court system suffers from the following problems: (1) abuse of discretion by the judges, which makes the outcome of litigation unpredictable; (2) local protectionism, (3) corruption among judicial officials, and (4) lack of authority and efficiency of the judiciary. Unless this system is reformed, they warned, the people will completely lose their confidence in the government, jeopardizing the survival of the Communist regime.

[. . .]

. . . Not separated from the more active executive and legislative branches, the judiciary is heavily influenced by local party and government officials who often abuse their power by interfering with the courts' business. The only solution lies in the adoption of the separation of powers principle and gradually increasing judicial independence through the various measures proposed by the Chinese jurists.

C. *China's Accession to the WTO: An Impetus from the Outside*

Increasing judicial independence is not only necessary to check the judicial corruption rampant in China, it is also a reform necessitated by China's Accession to the WTO. As Professor Mi Jian, Deputy Chief Justice of the Qinghai Provincial High Court, pointed out, judicial independence is an essential prerequisite for all WTO members, as it is a foundation for all the rules and mechanisms under WTO. Without judicial independence, China will not be able to meet WTO's requirements for uniform enforcement of law, impartial judicial review, including annual review of trade policies, transparency of the adjudication process, etc. As a consequence of such failure, warned Professor Mi, China will lose its credibility with other members of the WTO and eventually be precluded from the international mechanisms of settling trade disputes.

[. . .]

V. The Function of Case-Law Precedents Within the Code-Law Framework

In recent years, there have been vigorous discussions in China among jurists and judges about whether the Chinese court system should adopt the practice of following case law precedents. While such debates are not new among Chinese legal scholars, recently the focal point has shifted. Whereas in the past the issue was whether the doctrine of *stare decisis* should even be considered in China's judicial reform, now the differences between the participants in the debate mostly center on how much of that doctrine should be adopted. The latest round of debate within the Chinese legal community indicates that there is now a general consensus that at least some court decisions should be treated as binding precedents for lower courts....

[...]

VI. Innovative Measures Taken to Increase Transparency and Accountability of the Judiciary

Adoption of a precedent system is only one of the innovations in China's process of judicial reform that will have a tremendous impact in shaping the Chinese judiciary in the years to come. There are other developments, each of which is a "first" in China's history. Most of these measures aim at making the judiciary more accountable and the judicial process more transparent.

A. *Publication of Court Opinions, Including the Dissent*

One of these measures is for the courts to include dissenting opinions in their decisions....

To understand the significance of this development, one must bear in mind that the China has followed a continental legal system model in which court decisions did not have binding precedential value. "In many cases, a court will decide a case by issuing an order that is no more than one or two sentences in length with no legal reasoning or analysis." Therefore, for the court to issue opinions with detailed reasoning is already a departure from the Chinese judiciary's past practice.

There are two stated rationales behind the Shanghai court's decision to start including dissenting opinions in its decisions. First, allowing the public to see how a court reaches its decision ultimately results in greater fairness of the judicial process and increases the public's trust in the system. Indeed, as one commentator said, "sunlight is the best disinfectant." Second, making judges document their opinions in a distinctive manner also helps raise the professional and ethical standards of judges because they will be more careful in their reasoning if their decisions are subject to public scrutiny.

To appreciate the importance of this development, American readers should be reminded of an important difference between the Chinese and American legal systems. With few exceptions, trials in the United States are presided over by a single judge, and "panels" exist only at the appellate level. In contrast, trials in China are mostly presided over by a "trial panel." The Organic Law of the People's Courts (OLPC) provides that only simple civil cases, non-serious criminal cases and those specifically allowed by law may be heard by individual judges; for all other cases, trials and appeals must be heard by panels of judges and "people's" jurors. "Decisions of greater importance" have to be made by "trial committees," which consist of the chief judge (president), the deputy chief judge, and senior judges. This means that difficult or controversial cases heard by a collegiate panel in a certain court will be reviewed and decided by its trial committee; a judge from the panel will normally make a short report to the trial committee to brief it on the facts and issues. After reviewing the report, the committee will normally instruct the panel on how to decide the case.

This "panel" system has played a positive role in preventing abuse of judicial discretion and miscarriage of justice. Too often, local governments and party officials pressure judges to make decisions that will advance their particular interests. Typically, a government official approaches the chief judge, who in turn exerts pressure on the judges working under his supervision. Indeed, the chief judge in China is not just a presiding judge as in the United States—he also serves as the "president" of the court. He even has the power to discharge judges working in his court. Under such a structure, the collective decision-making process of the trial-panel-trial committee system may serve as a check, albeit a very weak one, against abuses of power by individual judges, including the chief judges.

This two-level structure, however, also comes with reduced accountability, because the judges that determine cases are not those before whom the parties submit their testimonies and evidence. The same problem exists in the Chinese practice that upper courts may "guide" lower courts to help them "solve" difficult cases. A former vice chief judge (vice-president) of the Chinese Supreme Court explained that this practice arose from the need to avoid erroneous decisions. Given that what constitutes "difficult" can be purely subjective, this practice has undermined the notion of due process throughout the entire Chinese justice system.

Since "panels" exist at both the trial and appellate level, publishing all dissenting opinions is more difficult and costly in China. However, the current statutory framework does provide a certain degree of accommodation for registering the minority voice. While the Criminal Procedure Law of 1979 provides that trial panels shall adopt the majority opinions in reaching their decisions, a 1996 amendment provides that minority opinions should be kept in the record. Should the Chinese judiciary continue its strict adherence to the Continental tradition of not publishing dissenting opinions or should it adopt the Anglo–American practice of doing so? While my survey has not discovered any published articles opposing adoption of the Anglo–American practice, it has uncovered several supporting it. In one of them, the author argued that it promotes judicial transparency and democratic principles. However, the author also recommends limiting publication to appellate opinions and, as a first step, publishing such opinions in civil cases only.

B. *Adopting the Single Judge Trial System*

In view of China's limited judicial resources, its practice of requiring most trials to be conducted by a panel of judges rather than individual judges may strike an outside observer as contrary to common sense. But one must realize that, historically, the courts played a very limited function in the Chinese society, especially in non-criminal matters. Only recently have laws become a significant part of the daily life in China. But now the explosion of cases has made the old panel system too expensive to maintain. In 1999, the Intermediate Court of Qingdao in Shandong Province initiated a new system in which all trials except the most important ones are conducted by a single judge.

This is not just a matter of efficiency. When cases are tried by trial committees, the relationship between junior judges and senior judges, just as between lower courts and higher courts, is one of administrative supervision and obedience. Judges have no sense of independence and are often influenced by their superiors in reaching decisions. Some people argue that given the low quality of Chinese judges, trial committees are a necessity—individual judges simply do not have the capability to decide cases. But according to Professor He Weifang, the mechanism of trial committees is not the solution, but the very cause of the problem. As a whole, Chinese judges are poorly educated even though the Judges Law of 1995 provides they must have a college education. Therefore, there is nothing to guarantee that judges in the trial committees are sufficiently equipped to make well-reasoned decisions. On the contrary, the current system increases the possibility that judicial decisions are the result of interventions from superiors, including local governments.

To understand this better, one must realize that in China's legal culture, a judge means something entirely different from what that term brings to mind in America. In China, courts operate more like a bureaucracy where cases are heard by panels and determined by committees, and the presiding judge (the president) typically has the strongest voice. Lower judges rarely have the power to make independent decisions determining the outcome of cases. In fact, many lower judges do not adjudicate at all. Some even function as administrative staff. Others play a role similar to judicial clerks in the United States, researching cases and drafting memoranda. The Chinese Supreme Court, for instance, has one president (chief justice), eight vice presidents (vice-chief justices), eighty judges, and 120 assistant judges.

While the trial committee system is not likely to disappear given the low quality of junior judges in China, it is highly possible that its influence will gradually diminish while individual judges are given more power to decide cases independently. Already, there seems to be a trend among courts to delegate to individual judges the power and responsibility to decide certain categories of cases.

VII. Conclusion

. . . The general perception [previously] among government officials and intellectuals was that, since China was a "socialist" country with a non-Western cultural tradition, Western concepts in legal and political thinking should be viewed with reservation and adopted with even greater caution. Now the Chinese regard many, if not most, of these rules as international norms, and are willing to accept them as such. It appears that more and more judges, legal scholars, other academics, and government officials have openly embraced the underlying values of many Western-originated practices as universally applicable. This change in thinking is certainly more profound than the structural reforms introduced thus far and will determine the direction, as well as the extent, of future reforms.

What has caused such profound shift in China's legal thinking? I believe there are at least three possible explanations. First, since the market economy has taken root in China, the relationship between individual citizens and the government has undergone tremendous change. The government's role in society has steadily eroded and China is evolving into a much more rights-oriented society than it was ten or twenty years ago. As one scholar points out, currently the market economy in China has entered a stage of development in which further progress requires a new type of government with the following features: its functions must be limited; its conduct must be in compliance with the laws; its powers must be fragmented, based on self-rule; its operation must be institutionalized and open to the public; and its legitimacy must be based on popular elections or laws. Most important, with ongoing economic reform comes the recognition of private property and the need to protect it. This makes limitation of government power necessary, since unless the power structure of the state is also changed, holding power would mean holding property. The prospect of absolute power combined with property, is quite disturbing. Therefore, if the sanctity of private property is to be protected by the Constitution, then the role of the government has to be redefined and its power has to be limited. Professor Ji Weidong calls this an opportunity for a "historical compromise."

The second possible explanation, which is closely related to the first, is that as the Chinese economic system has become more like the dominant Western model, and as China has gradually accumulated greater economic power, Western legal and political ideas have become less menacing and more appealing to the Chinese.... To the Chinese, the so-called international norms [previously] reflected mostly the values of the predatory imperialist West (including Japan) and served mostly its interests. China could not adopt the rules of the game because it was not China's game. The increasingly important role China plays in the international community and the success of its economic reforms has radically changed the Chinese perception of the world. Not only do international norms developed in the West now benefit China much as they benefit Western countries, but China now has a voice in making such rules....

The third possible explanation, which is also closely related to the first two, is the rejuvenation of the Chinese leadership....

[. . .]

(iv)

Mo Zhang & Paul Zwier, *Burden of Proof: Developments in Modern Chinese Evidence Rules,*

10 TULSA J. COMP. & INT'L L. 419 (2003)
(reprinted with permission)
(footnotes omitted).

One of the most interesting developments in China since its entrance into the World Trade Organization (WTO) has been the Chinese government's apparent commitment to the "rule of law." As a matter of fact, since 1999 when the Chinese Constitution was amended by the nation's legislative body, the National People's Congress, promoting the rule of law has become the constitutional mandate in the nation. Although there exists significant conceptual differences between Chinese and Western scholars in what would constitute the rule of law, the rule of law has been commonly understood in China to mean construction/development of the legal system to ensure that the nation is governed by law.

As part of its effort to put substance behind this commitment, the Chinese government is engaged on a number of levels in judicial reform, aiming at improving the judiciary. In 2001, the Supreme People's Court of China made it the "century theme" to achieve "Impartiality and Efficiency" in the people's courts. In his working report to the Annual Conference of the National People's Congress of China in March 2002, the President of the Supreme People's Court stated that the people's courts would continue the ongoing judicial reform, with impartiality and efficiency as the main theme. A major part of the judicial reform rests with efforts to develop sound evidence rules as applied to both civil and criminal proceedings.

China has no unified evidence code, *per se*, and the current evidence law exists in evidence rules that are scattered in the Criminal Procedure Law, Civil Procedure Law (CPL), and Administrative Procedure Law. Adopted on July 1, 1979, the Criminal Procedure Law contains some eight articles that deal with evidence. On March 17, 1996, the Criminal Procedure Law was amended with the significant addition of the principle of "presumption of innocence" in a criminal proceeding. The presumption of innocence shifted the burden of proving the guilt of the accused on to the shoulder of the government. The Administrative Procedure Law adopted on April 4, 1989 contains six articles for evidence. On April 9, 1991, the Civil Procedure Law was promulgated. Of 320 articles in the Civil Procedure Law, only twelve articles are provisions of evidence.

For many years, there has been strong criticism in China that courts are given little guidance in setting standards of proof and there is a clear lack of detailed and readily "operable" evidence rules. The concerns are that the insufficiency of evidence rules has become a great obstacle to achieving justice and fairness of the judiciary, and consequently there are increasing calls for the adoption of a separate evidence law among scholars and legislators. As noted, China's entry into the WTO is posing great challenges to the Chinese judicial system in that more profound reforms are needed. In this context, the Chinese government's motives to promote the rule of law in China may not be the purest, but an understanding of due process through the requirements of proof and the presentation of evidence seem[] to be rising in the nation. This trend will help bring about not only economic prosperity in China, but also entrance of the country into the international mainstream of human rights protection.

Recognizing the need for more clearly defined evidence rules, the Supreme People's Court has been taking efforts to perfect the existing evidence provisions in the procedure laws through the power of judicial interpretation and administration. In the meantime, the Supreme People's Court is enacting new evidence law in the area of procedure. For example, in its Several Opinions on Application of the Procedure Law of the People's Republic of China which was issued on July 14, 1992, the Supreme People's Court construed who has the burden of proof in different types of tort cases. The Court also listed situations in which the people's court shall be responsible for collecting evidence. On September 2, 1998, in order to implement the amended Criminal Procedure Law (1996), the Supreme People's Court issued the Interpretations on Questions Concerning Implementation of the Criminal Procedure Law of China (Interpretations). The Interpretations specified in particular what must be proved by evidence in criminal proceedings.

The most important attempt of the Supreme People's Court to help further improve judicial justice in China is the adoption of the Several Rules of Evidence Concerning Civil Litigation (Civil Evidence Rules). The Civil Evidence Rules are essentially the judicial interpretations made by the Supreme People's Court under Chinese laws. Effective April 1, 2002, the Civil Evidence Rules are acclaimed as the major development of evidence law in China. Although theoretically, the judicial interpretations are not the "laws" in China, they have played a significant role in shaping the legal regime and provided the courts with "urgently needed gap-fillers." More importantly, in the adoption of the Civil Evidence Rules, the Supreme Court made it clear that matters of evidence are the core of civil procedure, which obviously demonstrates the Court's serious view on the importance of evidence. It is expected that the Civil Evidence Rules and application of them will provide experimental experiences in helping China to ultimately adopt civil evidence law in China.

[. . .]

I. Evolution of Civil Evidence Rules in China—On Paper and in Practice

Evidence rules in China were not well-developed and there was barely any evidence provision until 1979 when the Criminal Procedure

Law of China was adopted. The lack of evidence rules was rooted in the misconception of the role of procedure law.

First, before the adoption of the Criminal Procedure Law, "State Policy" was regarded as the primary source of rules governing judicial proceedings. As a result, policy took the place of law. Due to the government interest oriented nature of the State policy, the application of the policy would almost always sacrifice the interest of the individual in order to maintain the supremacy of the State interest. Therefore, the procedural law and evidence rules were almost ignored.

Secondly, it had been a very common phenomenon in China to give substantive law more weight than procedural law. The notion was that the substantive law would best serve the need of the State in protecting its interests against individuals while the procedures tended to protect individual interests and rights. This notion was particularly in effect whenever the government chose to interfere with judicial proceedings. Procedures were viewed as an attachment to the substance and played a secondary role in the judicial proceedings.

Thirdly, judges had long been regarded as the "State workers" or the "public servants," and their function was to implement the State policy and protect the State interest. Partly affected by that, the doctrine of *ex officio* (by virtue of the office) of justice had excessively dominated the judicial proceedings, both criminal and civil, and actually became an "*ultra ex officio*." The *ex officio* customized the procedure to the needs of the state at the time. Under this scenario, judges were responsible for all matters in the proceeding, and parties to the litigation would not have much to do as long as the case was brought to the court. Consequently, the procedures had never been the center of attention in the court trials before 1979.

In 1979, stimulated by the move to open up to the outside world, China began to restore a legal system that was destroyed during the ten-year chaos of Cultural Revolution (1966–1976). The most concrete step in this regard was the adoption of the Criminal Law and Criminal Procedure Law. It was at this time that the Civil Evidence Rules were first provided in the procedure law. In the same year, attempting to improve the quality of trials in civil cases, the Supreme People's Court issued the Civil Evidence Rules Concerning Procedural System in the Trials of Civil Cases in the People's Courts (Provisional). However, these procedural rules did not contain any evidence provisions.

The absence of evidence rules in the trials of civil cases ended in 1982 when the Civil Procedural Law of China (Provisional) was adopted. Effective on October 1, 1982, the Civil Procedural Law (Provisional) had a special chapter dealing with evidence, which consisted of eleven articles. The Civil Procedural Law (Provisional) was later replaced by Civil Procedural Law stipulated by the National People's Congress on April 9, 1991. In 1992, the Supreme People's Court issued the Opinions on Application of the Civil Procedural Law of the People's Republic of China (Opinions on the CPL). The Opinions on the CPL explicitly state, among other things, the burden of proof of presenting evidence in specific cases.

[. . .]

C. Attempts at Trial Reform in the "Rules on Trial Methods"

In response to the problems facing the CPL concerning evidence, the Supreme People's Court implemented a number of efforts to clear up the clouds over the evidence provisions. In addition to the Opinions on the CPL, the Supreme Court in 1998 issued Several Rules on the Matters Concerning Reform of Civil and Economic Trial Methods (Rules on Trial Methods), which is regarded as the overture to the judicial reform initiative of the people's courts.

The Rules on Trial Methods, with an effort to promote procedural justice, address, *inter alia*, such specific questions as (a) burden of proof of the parties and investigation and collection of evidence by the court; (b) pretrial preparation and requirements for a fair trial; (c) improvement of court trials; and (d) examination and determination of evidence. In the same year, the Supreme People's Court published "A Guideline of 5–Year Reform of the People's Courts," which made it a top priority of the reform to improve evidence rules in the civil litigation. As part of the reform, on December 6, 2001, the Supreme People's Court adopted the Civil Evidence Rules.

It should be noted that unlike Western courts, during the course of adjudication in Chinese people's courts, there is no distinction between law and fact in terms of roles to be played between judge and jury for the finding of fact. The Chinese judicial system does not recognize a jury, though there are "judicial assessors" in many of the trials. Therefore, a judge in a Chinese people's court actually has two duties: to ascertain fact and to apply law.

II. The Civil Evidence Rules and Their Implications

Standing at the threshold of the ambitious judicial reform engaged in by the Supreme People's Court of China, the Civil Evidence Rules reflect the general recognition of the importance of procedural justice by the Chinese judiciary. Adoption of the Civil Evidence Rules also, at least in part, represents the judicial adjustment in China to the mandate of the WTO system. As noted however, since the Supreme People's Court has no law-making power, the Civil Evidence Rules are defined as judicial interpretation, which is used to help implement law.

The Civil Evidence Rules contain 83 articles, which are divided into six parts. The issues addressed in each part are: (a) production of evidence by the parties; (b) investigation and collection of evidence by the people's courts; (c) time limits for production of evidence and exchange of evidence; (d) cross-examination of evidence; (e) examination and determination of evidence; and (f) others.

What seems significant is that the Civil Evidence Rules are intended to minimize the role of people's courts in evidence production. To that end, the Civil Evidence Rules not only clarify the burden of proof on the parties with detailed provisions, but also define the scope and requirements for the investigation of evidence by the people's courts. Another important change is the imposition of time limits on the production of evidence, particularly new evidence.

With regard to the requirements and standard of proof, the Civil Evidence Rules depart from the doctrine of actuality by promoting an approach of "legal trueness" instead of "objective trueness." In the meantime, the Civil Evidence Rules open the door to the acceptance of discretionary evaluation of evidence by judges. Additionally, the Civil Evidence Rules readdress the exclusion rule as applied to illegal evidence.

A. *Burden of Proof and Distribution of the Burden*

The Civil Evidence Rules place significant reliance on the production of evidence by the parties. Under Article 1 of the Civil Evidence Rules, when a plaintiff commences a lawsuit in the people's court or a defendant raises a counterclaim, the relevant evidence materials that meet the requirements for bringing the lawsuit shall be attached. This would mean that the parties to an action are required to present evidence materials to commence the action (also called "commencement evidence") when making the claim(s). What is also implied in Article 1 is that the people's court may dismiss the action or claim if there are no evidence materials. As far as the burden of proof is concerned, the Civil Evidence Rules focus further on the parties through the specific provisions that are aimed at allocating the burden of proof.

1. General Rule: Whoever Makes Allegations Bears the Burden of Proof

Article 2 of the Civil Evidence Rules provides that the party to a civil action is responsible for providing evidence to prove the facts on which his claims or rebuttal against the claims of the other party stand. This provision is generally regarded as the restatement of Article 64 of the CPL that requires parties to a civil action to produce evidence in support of their allegations.

However, what is important is that the Civil Evidence Rules specifically state the consequence the party would have to face for a failure to provide evidence. According to Article 2 of the Civil Evidence Rules, if there is no evidence or the evidence is not sufficient to prove the facts of the claim, the party who has the burden of proof shall bear the adverse consequences. Thus, under the Civil Evidence Rules, the claiming party to an action not only is responsible for providing evidence, but also shall take the risk of any failure in this regard. This would mean that a failure in producing evidence could result in a dismissal of the case or a court decision in the other party's favor.

2. Role of the People's Court

While the Civil Evidence Rules impose burdens of proof on the parties to an action, the role of the people's court is not diminished in the production of evidence. Article 3 of the Civil Evidence Rules clearly requires the people's court to inform the parties of their duty to produce evidence and any possible legal consequences that would arise from their failure to do so. The purpose is to help the parties actively, completely, correctly, and honestly fulfill their evidence obligation. In addition, under Article 3, a party may ask the people's court to investigate and collect evidence if for objective reasons the party could not collect the evidence himself. This provision is said to serve twofold functions: to impose a duty to inform the people's court about their case and to grant rights of request to the parties.

Another provision worthy of attention is Article 7. It provides that if there is no specific provision in the law or if the burden of proof could not be ascertained under the Civil Evidence Rules, or other judicial interpretation, the people's court may make a determination on the matter of the burden of proof. But it is required that the determination as such be made on the basis of principles of fairness and good faith with a consideration of the party's ability to produce the evidence.

3. Reversed and Specific Burden of Proof

An exception to the general principle of the burden of proof on a claiming party is the situation where the burden of proof is reversed. The issue of reversed burden of proof is stated in the Opinions on the CPL, though the CPL itself is silent on the issue. The Civil Evidence Rules further specify the cases to which the reversed burden of proof applies as stated in the Opinions on the CPL, and also extends its application to defective products and joint acts of tort and medical injury cases.

[. . .]

In addition to the provisions of reversed burden of proof, the Civil Evidence Rules also specifically impose the burden of proof on the shoulder of a particular party in certain contract cases and labor dispute cases. The imposition once again reflects the tendency of the Supreme People's Court to advance allocation of the burden in civil actions.

[. . .]

D. Cross–Examination of Evidence

The Civil Evidence Rules make it crucial that the evidence is cross-examined by the parties in court. Article 47 explicitly requires that all evidence be presented in the court and cross-examined by the parties. Additionally, no evidence may be used to determine the facts of the case without being cross-examined. However, the evidence that is admitted by the party, recorded during the process of evidence exchange, and explained accordingly by the judge during the court hearing may be considered without cross-examination. Also, as set forth in Article 48, an exception to cross-examination may also apply if the evidence involves state secrets, business secrets, individual privacy, or other evidence that shall be kept secret under the law.

For purposes of cross-examination, the Civil Evidence Rules contain the provisions that reflect both the interpretations previously made and the practices readily accepted by the Supreme People's Court. Of particular significance are the provisions concerning original evidence, scope and sequence of the cross-examination, and testimonial evidence. The Civil Evidence Rules attempt to premise the cross-examination on two principles: direct trial and verbal trial.

When the cross-examination deals with documentary evidence, real evidence, or audiovisual materials, Article 49 provides that the party has the right to request the presentation of the original document or materials of the evidence. Such request will not be granted if a copy or duplicate of the evidence is permitted by the people's court to be presented due to real difficulty in obtaining the original, or if the original evidence no longer exists, as long as the copy or duplicate is proven to be authentic to the original.

The extent to which the parties may cross-examine evidence is subject to certain limits. Under Article 50, during cross-examination, the parties to an action shall explain and argue the provability of the evidence or weight of proof with a focus on reality, relevance, and legality of the evidence in question. In addition, cross-examination must be made in a certain order. In accordance with Article 51, cross-examination shall begin with the plaintiff's evidence, cross-examined by the defendant and a third party. The defendant's evidence is presented next, cross-examined by the plaintiff and any third party.

If the evidence is collected by the people's court upon the request of a party, the evidence shall be deemed as presented by the requesting party. If the evidence is obtained by the people's court on its own initiative, the people's court shall make explanation to the parties while showing the evidence for their opinion during the hearing.

A major part of the cross-examination is the testimonial evidence. An increasingly important consideration concerning the testimonial evidence is court witnesses. In this regard, a number of issues are specially addressed in the Civil Evidence Rules, which provide useful guidance in the use of witnesses during the court hearing.

[. . .]

E. Evaluation and Determination of Evidence

The question as to how the evidence would be examined and determined by the people's court seems to be a major concern of the Supreme People's Court. The Civil Evidence Rules clearly reflect the Court's desire to make experimental progress in carefully defining the role of court with regard to the admission of evidence. To that end, several rules governing determination of evidence are developed in the Civil Evidence Rules, which significantly change the basic notions of evidence found in the CPL.

1. "Facts of the Case" Rule

Under Article 63 of the Civil Evidence Rules, the people's court shall base its decision on the facts of the case that the evidence would prove. The provision in essence repeals the doctrine of "factuality" that requires "objective trueness." In the light of Article 63, the people's court would not have to exhaust all possible resources trying to find the "objective trueness" of the case. All the court would need to do is to see if the facts in the case could be proved by credible evidence in order to achieve "legal trueness."

2. Discretionary Determination of Evidence Rule

Article 64 of Civil Evidence Rules gives the judge discretion to make an independent determination on provability of the evidence after a full and objective examination of the evidence under prescribed procedures. Importantly, when making the determination, the judge is enabled to use logical reasoning and daily living experiences in addition to adherence to law and judicial ethics (conscience of the judge). Another requirement is that the judge examine and evaluate all evidence of the case from such aspects as the degree of relevance between each element of evidence and the facts of the case, as well as the relationship among various elements of evidence.

[. . .]

3. Exclusion Rule

Under the Civil Evidence Rules, a judge may exclude relevant evidence for statutory reasons. In accordance with Article 67, an admission of facts of a case made by a party during the litigation as comprised for purposes of a mediation agreement or settlement shall not be used as evidence against the party. In addition, pursuant to Article 68, evidence shall not be used as the basis of determining the facts of a case if the evidence is obtained through means that harm the legitimate interests of others or violate prohibitive provisions of law.

Moreover, under Article 69, certain evidence, standing alone, shall not be taken as the ground for fact determination. Evidence in this category includes: (a) testimony made by a minor that is incompatible with the minor's age and intellectual condition; (b) testimony given by a witness who has a biased relationship with a party or the party's agent *ad litem*; (c) audiovisual materials that contain doubtfulness; (d) a copy or duplicate that could not be verified with the original; or (e) testimony of a witness who fails to appear in court for cross-examination without justified reasons.

[. . .]

III. Application of the Civil Evidence Rules in the People's Court and its Impacts

[. . .]

It would be a mistake to infer that the judges in the people's courts would become less active because the Civil Evidence Rules have seemingly departed from the tradition of *ex officio* of justice that once dominated the Chinese judicial system. To be more specific, the increasing emphasis on the role of the parties is not intended to change the inquisitorial nature of the Chinese judicial system. On the contrary, the role of judge in civil proceedings becomes more critical than ever before because the evidence is now viewed as central to the trial and the court is required to make a fair and open determination of it.

It might be too early to tell how much impact the Civil Evidence Rules have already had on people's courts in civil proceedings, but the Supreme People's Court is confident in seeing an "important and far-reaching impact on the reform of civil trials and improvement of civil litigation system in China." As noted, it was not until recent years that evidence has become the focus in litigation.

[. . .]

V. Conclusion

China's evidence law has come a long way in a short period of time. What is the next step for China in the development of its evidence law and the rule of law? It would be unrealistic to insist on China's adopting wholesale common law or Western codes of evidence law, since China is basically a civil law system. To the extent that Hong Kong (formerly a British colony) law applies, China has mixed common law and civil law systems, but the civil law tradition dominates. Still more can be done to improve the rule of law.

A first step would be to ensure that the Civil Evidence Rules would be applied uniformly in the nation, and that the basic evidence principles, such as hearsay rules and exclusion rules, would be made uniform in criminal and civil proceedings. As a part of this development, the Civil Evidence Rules seem to have also made clearer the role of the court as both a fact finder and judgment-maker. In this regard, they recognize that evidence needs to be presented and tested before it can be determined true or false and admitted or discarded accordingly.

Second, China needs to truly make the Chinese system a constitutional system by providing the means to institute the constitutional processes that will ensure the rule of law. As mentioned, these include the requirement of a public hearing, the presentation and testing of evidence, and the important confrontation of witnesses against a party. In addition, the court needs to continue in its efforts to provide for transparency, recordation of evidence and rules, and clear time limits on the gathering, exchange, and consideration of evidence in order to achieve fairness in the hearing.

Two other developments in the Chinese legal system need to be encouraged. The first is to provide for Chinese lawyers a role in the gathering and exchange of evidence and in the presentation of law and evidence in the hearing. What has started to develop with regard to the presentation of expert evidence needs to be encouraged with regard to the presentation of all facts and evidence. Lawyers can provide the incentive for the most efficient gathering of facts and the exchange of those facts. This will greatly alleviate the workload and obligations of the court and allow it to focus on what is most important.

In addition, until judges are truly educated on the developments in Chinese law, lawyers can be the most efficient disseminators of information about the law to these judges. If a party wants an advantage, they hire someone who knows the law so they can decide whether they want to bother the court with the dispute or resolve it outside the courtroom. Over time, providing a role for lawyers will greatly reduce the number of cases the courts will have to hear.

Finally, even as law schools spring up all over China and new lawyers and judges are being trained, China must find ways to provide for the education of existing lawyers, and judges in particular, in the development of laws and rules. What seems essential is to provide innovative ways to educate legal professionals in a way that will make the system work.

[. . .]

Notes and Questions

1. According to Bin Xue Sang, it has been a constant in Chinese legal history to emphasize criminal law and substantive law. As a consequence, civil law and procedural justice have been underdeveloped areas in the Chinese legal system. The enactment of the Civil Procedure Law of the People's Republic of China (the CPL) on April 9, 1991 was a groundbreaking development for China. The first fully effective law of civil procedure in China had been the 1982 Provisional Civil Procedure Law. The new revised law was apparently the product of China's "modernization drive" and "open door policy." Bin Xue Sang, *China's Civil Procedure Law: A New Guide for Dispute Resolution in China*, 26 INT'L LAWYER 413 (1992). How do you assess the historical distinction between criminal law and civil procedure in Chinese legal history? Does it tell you anything about the make-up and character of Chinese society? How valuable is order? How prized is freedom?

2. As a matter of general speculation, what description would you give of the rule of law and of the role of lawyers in Chinese society? For example, does giving all Chinese lawyers the status of state employees differ from having judges in continental European civil law systems be civil servants? Assess generally the significance of state employment for juridical actors.

3. In China, there is a ban on having foreign lawyers appear in Chinese court. It is argued that that policy represents an effort to maintain the integrity and autonomy of the legal professional—to make it free of foreign intrusion and trespass. Foreign lawyers must use Chinese lawyers. *See* Bin Xue Sang, *China's Civil Procedure Law: A New Guide for Dispute Resolution in China*, 26 INT'L LAWYER 413 (1992). Are there less ideologically-motivated and more practical reasons for the policy?

4. There is also a general practice of *pro se* representation. According to Bin Xue Sang, *supra*, there is no legal requirement to hire lawyers. *Id.* What does that say about the Chinese trial system?

5. What role do you think ADR, mediation, and arbitration play in the Chinese legal system? What values are implicated? How do these values determine the hierarchy of remedies?

6. Evaluate the significance of China's accession to the WTO to the current process of legal reforms. Why have human rights, transparency, and procedure become goals of the reformation? What role, if any, does private property play in all of this? Is there less insularity in Chinese policy?

7. Ponder, in some detail, the distinction between "rule by law" and "rule of law." What relationship do the phrases imply between socio-political organization and the legal system? How does the notion of "rights" fit into the difference in phrasing?

8. What values appear to prevail in Chinese legal reform? What values are being supplanted?

9. How might *stare decisis* and dissenting judicial opinions affect the Chinese experience?

10. Compare and contrast the Chinese and American systems of trial. How close are they? Are they at all comparable? Are Western implants or transplants likely to work in China? What does history say?

11. Describe the role of courts in Chinese society and in China's political system.

12. Do burden of proof and cross-examination make a meaningful difference in the Chinese trial process? Why and why not?

13. Compare and contrast U.S. and Chinese due process.

14. What advice would you give to a client who has a specialized heavy equipment manufacturing operation in Illinois and receives an email from the Chinese Natural Resources and Foreign Trade Ministry, requesting an order for an enormous supply of heavy equipment. The anticipated production will occupy the entire plant for 18 to 24 months; the business is a small, family-operated concern with 45 employees that does gross revenues of $1.5 million a year. The email includes a production and delivery schedule, proposes a price, and states that time is of the essence. Transport and delivery are the responsibility of the manufacturer. The English is abbreviated and somewhat unclear. The email says nothing else of substance.

§ 2. DISCOVERY AND EVIDENCE–GATHERING

At the beginning of the 20th century, international judicial assistance was hardly a priority of the first order for U.S. courts. They conceived of jurisdiction in territorial terms and their function as the protection of nationals. Distances were real or at least much less surmountable than they are today. Foreign cultures were not simply tourist destinations, but rather represented alien worlds. Despite the Wilson presidency and the ill-fated League of Nations, the U.S. and its legal institutions remained insular and self-contained.

The next case is a good illustration of the earlier parochial attitude. Of course, this approach was not endorsed solely by U.S. courts; one suspects that most national courts shared the same disposition on these matters. The arm of the law did not reach beyond domestic boundaries.

Can you determine why the federal district judge refuses to render the assistance that is requested? What does the Mexican court want from its U.S. counterpart? Why does the request of the foreign court raise such a difficult problem? How does the U.S. court perceive the issue presented and its judicial capacity? What is so "novel" about the possible exercise of jurisdiction for this purpose? Why can service not be effectuated here? Should the defendant's legal accountability be available only when he owns real property in the foreign jurisdiction and not when he transacts business through contract? In your view, what position might represent a better approach? Is a neutral transnationalism always preferable to the protection of nationals and local interests? What role does public policy play in all of this? Which version of public policy is applicable?

IN RE LETTERS ROGATORY OUT OF FIRST CIVIL COURT OF CITY OF MEXICO

261 Fed. 652 (S.D.N.Y. 1919).

AUGUSTUS N. HAND, District Judge. This is a motion to vacate an order directing the service of a summons within the district upon a resident to answer to a suit brought against him in the Republic of Mexico for the payment of rent and redelivery of certain property which is claimed by virtue of a contract of lease made in the city of Mexico for the term of one year, from June, 1914, to June, 1915. The process was accompanied by a request from the judge of the court having jurisdiction in the city of Mexico that process of that court be served upon defendant in New York. This judicial request is said to come within the definition of letters rogatory in the civil law, is addressed to any one who may be a judge having jurisdiction over a civil case in the city of New York....

[I]t is apparently possible through the aid of this court to render the person sought to be served subject to a personal judgment in Mexico, because the contract sued upon was to be performed there. Such a result is contrary to our own system of jurisprudence, which treats the legal jurisdiction of a court as limited to persons and property within its territorial jurisdiction.... It is undesirable, in my opinion, to aid a process which may require residents of this district to submit to the burden of defending foreign suits brought in distant countries, where they have no property, or as an alternative to suffer a personal judgment by default, which will be enforceable against them personally whenever they may enter the foreign territory. As a matter of policy, the matter would be quite different, if the effect of the service would only be a judgment enforceable against property of the defendant in Mexico.

While this court has power to execute letters rogatory in the sense in which the term is used in the American and English law, neither it nor, so far as I can discover from the reported decisions, any other American or English court, has by an order directing the service of process aided a foreign tribunal to acquire jurisdiction over a party within the United States. Letters rogatory have been so long familiar to our courts, and so exclusively limited by understanding and in practice to proceedings in the nature of commissions to take depositions of witnesses at the request of a foreign court, that I should hardly feel inclined to assume such a novel jurisdiction as is proposed without statutory authority, even if I regarded the case as one where, as a matter of sound policy, aid should be given to the foreign tribunal.

[...]

The motion to vacate the order is granted, both on the ground that the judicial aid invoked is without precedent, and also because it is contrary to the ideas of American courts as to the limits of judicial jurisdiction.

* * * *

In re Romero reinforces the position that the court assumed in the foregoing case and does so without the anguish of self-doubt. The circumstances again involve a proceeding before a Mexican court, brought presumably by a Mexican national to collect an alleged debt owed by an absentee U.S. party. What rule of transborder jurisdiction does the New York state court propound? When is a multinational corporate enterprise, headquartered in the United States, subject to suit abroad? What are the most critical elements of judicial jurisdiction? Is this the right approach?

IN RE ROMERO

56 Misc. 319, 107 N.Y.S. 621 (1907).

O'Gorman, J. This is a motion by the Manhattan Trust Company of the city of New York to vacate an order entered herein on October 30, 1907, directing the service upon the trust company of certain so-called letters rogatory issuing out of the Second civil court of the city of Mexico. The papers issued by the Mexican court are not in the nature of letters rogatory, but appear to be a summons and complaint in an action instituted in that court by a resident of Mexico for legal services alleged to have been rendered in that country to the Manhattan Trust Company. In substance the Mexican court requests the courts of this state to order the service of a summons and complaint issuing out of a foreign court upon a resident of this state. It is clear that the courts of this state possess no power to perform such a function. By statute our courts will assist in the execution of foreign letters rogatory for the examination of witnesses within our jurisdiction; but even as to such process there is no inherent or implied power in the court. The authority must be found in the statute....

If, however, the court possessed the power, it should not be exercised in this case. The Manhattan Trust Company has no office in Mexico. It has no business and has no property in that republic. It is a

New York corporation, with its offices in New York City. The Mexican court, therefore, has not and cannot obtain jurisdiction over the defendant. The principle is well recognized that no court can acquire jurisdiction over a person not located within the jurisdiction and having no property therein. The authority of every tribunal is confined to person and property within the territorial limits of the state or country in which it is established.... It is conceded that our own courts could not by the service of a summons in the republic of Mexico acquire jurisdiction of a citizen of Mexico having no property in this state. The doctrine is well established that the laws of a foreign country will not be enforced, if such enforcement will contravene the settled policy of the forum or be prejudicial to the interests of its own citizens....Motion to vacate order granted....

* * * *

The federal law is now supportive of international judicial assistance—perhaps even to a fault. U.S. courts can be asked to effectuate service or assist a foreign tribunal in gathering information for a litigation being conducted abroad. Is such assistance likely to be mutual and reciprocal? Are the latter two characteristics necessary? Why? What issues might arise when foreign courts are asked to assist their U.S. counterparts? What formal requirements, if any, exist under federal law for making a request? What is the basis for the U.S. court's jurisdiction? Do these provisions give extraterritorial effect to foreign court jurisdiction in the United States? Are there any limits to these accommodations?

28 U.S.C. § 1696. Service in foreign and international litigation

(a) The district court of the district in which a person resides or is found may order service upon him of any document issued in connection with a proceeding in a foreign or international tribunal. The order may be made pursuant to a letter rogatory issued, or request made, by a foreign or international tribunal or upon application of any interested person and shall direct the manner of service. Service pursuant to this subsection does not, of itself, require the recognition or enforcement in the United States of a judgment, decree, or order rendered by a foreign or international tribunal.

(b) This section does not preclude service of such a document without an order of court.

28 U.S.C. § 1781. Transmittal of letter rogatory or request

(a) The Department of State has power, directly, or through suitable channels—

(1) to receive a letter rogatory issued, or request made, by a foreign or international tribunal, to transmit it to the tribunal, officer, or agency in the united States to whom it is addressed, and to receive and return it after execution; and

(2) to receive a letter rogatory issued, or request made, by a tribunal in the United States, to transmit it to the foreign or international tribunal, officer, or agency to whom it is addressed, and to receive and return it after execution.

(b) This section does not preclude—

(1) the transmittal of a letter rogatory or request directly from a foreign or international tribunal to the tribunal, officer, or agency in the United States to whom it is addressed, and its return in the same manner; or

(2) the transmittal of a letter rogatory or request directly from a tribunal in the United States to the foreign or international tribunal, officer, or agency to whom it is addressed, and its return in the same manner. . . .

28 U.S.C. § 1782. Assistance to foreign and international tribunals and to litigants before such tribunals

(a) The district court of the district in which a person resides or is found may order him to give his testimony or statement or to produce a document or other thing for use in a proceeding in a foreign or international tribunal. The order may be pursuant to a letter rogatory issued, or request made, by a foreign or international tribunal or upon the application of any interested person and may direct that the testimony or statement be given, or the document or other thing be produced, before a person appointed by the court. By virtue of his appointment, the person appointed has power to administer any necessary oath and take the testimony or statement. The order may prescribe the practice and procedure, which may be in whole or part the practice and procedure of the foreign country or the international tribunal, for taking the testimony or statement or producing the document or other thing. To the extent that the order does not prescribe otherwise, the testimony or statement shall be taken, and the document or other thing produced, in accordance with the Federal Rules of Civil Procedure.

A person may not be compelled to give his testimony or statement or to produce a document or other thing in violation of any legally applicable privilege.

(b) This chapter does not preclude a person within the United States from voluntarily giving his testimony or statement, or producing a document or other thing, for use in a proceeding in a foreign or international tribunal before any person and in any manner acceptable to him. . . .

28 U.S.C. § 1783. Subpoena of person in foreign country

(a) A court of the United States may order the issuance of a subpoena requiring the appearance as a witness before it, or before a person or body designated by it, of a national or resident of the United

States who is in a foreign country, or requiring the production of a specified document or other thing by him, if the court finds that particular testimony or the production of the document or other thing by him is necessary in the interest of justice, and, in other than a criminal action or proceeding, if the court finds, in addition, that it is not possible to obtain his testimony in admissible form without his personal appearance or to obtain the production of the document or other thing in any other manner.

(b) The subpoena shall designate the time and place for the appearance or for the production of the document or other thing. Service of the subpoena and any order to show cause, rule, judgment, or decree authorized by this section or by section 1784 of this title shall be effected in accordance with the provisions of the Federal Rules of Civil Procedure relating to service of process on a person in a foreign country. The person serving the subpoena shall tender to the person to whom the subpoena is addressed his estimated necessary travel and attendance expenses, the amount of which shall be determined by the court and stated in the order directing the issuance of subpoena.

Notes and Questions

1. In § 1696(a), what is the distinction between a "foreign" and an "international" tribunal? Do both terms refer solely or principally to courts? What leads you to your conclusion? Other than the International Court of Justice (ICJ), is there any international court?

2. Under § 1696(a), who has standing to make the contemplated request to effectuate service? Isn't the permissible scope too wide? What purpose does the enormous latitude serve?

3. Under § 1696(a), what significance do you ascribe to the last sentence of the section? Does it constitute "giving with one hand and taking with the other"?

4. What does § 1696(b) mean? When could nonjudicial service take place and how should it be effectuated? This provision may be significant for the purposes of the Hague Service Convention.

5. What impact does § 1781 have upon the transborder service of process? What role does the U.S. State Department have in this process? Why does the entire process appear optional? Isn't it important enough to have real rules? This provision may also partly implement the Hague Service Convention.

6. Sections 1782 and 1783 address the role and participation of U.S. federal courts in transborder discovery and evidence-gathering. Section 1783 authorizes a federal court to issue a subpoena to an absentee resident or national to secure testimony or documents. The federal court, therefore, has the power under U.S. law to issue extraterritorial commands to absentee residents and nationals. Whether they will be respected in the implicated foreign country depends upon the foreign law. The order contemplated under § 1783 is directed to U.S. nationals or residents abroad. In that sense,

the subpoenas are more likely to be effective for foreign enforcement because they may not be seen as violating sovereign autonomy.

The Act of March 2, 1855, 10 Stat. 630, was the first U.S. statute to authorize courts to act on letters rogatory. The legislation gave the federal circuit courts the authority to appoint a commissioner to question the witnesses who were designated in the letter. In 1863, the law was modified; its application was restricted to pending actions involving money or property in which the requesting State had no interest. (12 Stat. 769–770.) In 1948, the statute became § 1782 and was expanded to cover all pending civil and criminal actions. (63 Stat. 103.) Finally, in 1964, Congress amended § 1782 to make it easier for foreign parties to obtain discovery within the United States and to encourage other countries to liberalize international judicial assistance. *See* 28 U.S.C.A. § 1782 (1997).

In particular, § 1782 now permitted U.S. district courts to assist foreign parties in securing documents and other tangible evidence—in addition to depositions and testimony, which previously had been all that was allowed. Foreign parties, therefore, could engage in the full range of litigious evidence-gathering. The term "foreign tribunal" was adopted, giving quasi-judicial and administrative agencies standing to invoke the measure. The other new term, "interested person," was also more inclusive, allowing foreign magistrates to request judicially-assisted U.S. discovery. Finally, judicial assistance was available even if there was no litigation pending abroad.

Idealism and a strong sense of internationalism undergirded the provision. It was intended to foster and facilitate litigation with international aspects, to encourage international judicial assistance and cooperation, to allow U.S. nationals to participate effectively in foreign proceedings, and to generate respect for the sovereign integrity of nations. It was not premised on the *quid pro quo* of reciprocity. *See In re Application of Malev Hungarian Airlines*, 964 F.2d 97 (2d Cir. 1992); *In re Application for Order for Judicial Assistance in Foreign Proceeding*, 147 F.R.D. 223 (C.D.Cal. 1993); *Lancaster Factoring Co. v. Mangone*, 90 F.3d 38 (2d Cir. 1996).

The party being deposed or supplying documents did not need to be a party to the litigation. The term "person" in § 1782 could cover partnerships, companies, or other business associations, but not sovereign governments. *See Al Fayed v. CIA*, 229 F.3d 272 (D.C. Cir. 2000). Generally, it required that evidence should be within the territorial limits of the United States. *See Four Pillars Enterprises Co. v. Avery Dennison Corp.*, 308 F.3d 1075 (9th Cir. 2002). The foreign proceeding for which the information is sought must be adjudicative and neutral in character—not investigatory or an action for enforcement. *See In re Gianoli Aldunate*, 3 F.3d 54 (2d Cir. 1993).

Problems with Section 1782 arose on two points. First, the Second and Fifth U.S. Circuits held that the phrase "foreign or international tribunal" did not include international arbitral tribunals. *See Kazakhstan v. Biedermann International*, 168 F.3d 880 (5th Cir. 1999); *NBC v. Bear Stearns & Co. Inc.*, 165 F.3d 184 (2d Cir. 1999). The rulings must have been based upon an institutional status consideration—*i.e.*, that a public law court could only transact with and be solicited by another public law entity. Arbitral tribunals are creatures of contract and private authority. As a result, public jurisdiction could not be used to facilitate arbitral proceedings. The courts also stated that judicial discovery could only be used in arbitral proceedings if the agreement to arbitrate so provided. The case law was unfortunate because it made federal international litigation assistance much less likely for purely formalistic reasons. The vast majority of international commercial litigation takes place through transborder arbitration. Most requests for discovery are made by arbitral tribunals. By ruling them ineligible for assistance, the courts made first-rate professional evidence less accessible and the arbitrators' adjudicatory tasks more difficult.

Second, practitioners expressed concern about the apparent lack of reciprocity under § 1782. Under the provision, foreign courts and lawyers are provided with evidence or testimony gathered under U.S. procedures and rules. Their rigor guarantees that the evidence will be fully "usable" in the proceeding abroad—witnesses will be heard under oath, all parties will be represented, each party can ask questions, and a verbatim transcript will be made. Section 1782 does not, however, apply in the other direction. It does not create a right for U.S. counsel to obtain professional evidence abroad that is "serviceable" in U.S. legal proceedings. Evidence gathered abroad is subject to the rules and procedures of the local foreign jurisdiction. The foreign framework probably does not include any of the federal procedures. It is, therefore, unlikely to be of any value in the U.S. litigation. Section 1782 does not cure, but rather reinforces the disparity and imbalance.

This concern is expressed in somewhat less straightforward fashion as an issue of "discoverability." In other words, should U.S. courts ruling pursuant to § 1782 ascertain whether the requested evidence is discoverable under the laws of the foreign jurisdiction in which the litigation is taking place? The majority rule among federal circuits is that U.S. courts have no obligation to determine the foreign "discoverability" of the requested evidence. *See In re Letter Rogatory From the First Court of First Instance in Civil Matters*, 42 F.3d 308 (5th Cir. 1995). Some courts, however, have required foreign discoverability especially when the request is made by a private party rather than a court. *See United States v. Morris*, 82 F.3d 590 (4th Cir. 1996); *In re Asta Medica*, 981 F.2d 1 (1st Cir. 1992). The assumption is that a foreign court knows how to apply its own law on evidence-gathering.

There was no U.S. Supreme Court ruling on § 1782 until recently. The U.S. Supreme Court ruled on Section 1782 and its requirements, in *Intel Corporation v. Advanced Micro Devices, Inc.*, 124 S.Ct. 2466, 159 L.Ed.2d 355 (2004). It held that the so-called discoverability requirement was not part of the statute. Prior to the holding, the First and Eleventh Circuits had held that documents sought by a party to a foreign litigation needed to be "discoverable" in that jurisdiction in order to be subject to discovery under § 1782. The Court agreed with the position of the Second, Third, and Ninth Circuits and rejected the equivalence of discovery requirement. Nothing in the statutory provision's legislative history or text referred to or justified such a requirement. The comity rationale of offense to a foreign government by allowing greater discovery under U.S. law was not persuasive. Moreover, giving foreign litigants more discovery than U.S. litigants could obtain from a foreign court did not place the latter in a disadvantageous position. Any inequality could be remedied by the district court by requiring reciprocal discovery in the production order.

The strict construction of the text of the statute is accurate, but fails to account effectively, it seems, for the displeasure of practitioners with uneven access to information in different jurisdictions. Moreover, is the reference to the district court's discretion any solace? Can courts really customize production orders in this matter, especially those that are to be applied abroad (in effect) in systems that find U.S. notions of record-building alien? Is the Court's opinion a solution or the expression of something else?

7. In *Fonseca v. Blumenthal*, 620 F.2d 322 (2d Cir. 1980), the court provided some elucidation on the phrase "foreign or international tribunal." Does the court's discussion add to your understanding of the judicial power to undertake international judicial assistance? Is that what Congress intended?

[. . .]

In 1964, § 1782 was amended to provide for obtaining testimony or documents for use "in a proceeding in a foreign or international tribunal." The word "tribunal" was used deliberately "to make it clear that assistance is not confined to proceedings before conventional courts . . . [but extends to] proceedings before a foreign administrative tribunal or quasi-judicial agency as in proceedings before a conventional foreign court." . . .

As we pointed out in *India* [385 F.2d 1017, 1020 (2d Cir. 1967)], "[w]hile Congress materially expanded the scope of 28 U.S.C. § 1782 in 1964, it did not go to the full extent of authorizing a district court to execute letters rogatory whenever requested by a foreign country or a party there. . . ." It is evident that Congress intended "tribunal" to have an adjudicatory connotation.

We also observed in *India* that one concern of Congress in amending § 1782 in 1964 was to insure judicial assistance for French *juges d'instruction*. The *juge* is roughly equivalent to our grand jury. It is he who determines whether evidence against an individual charged with a major crime is sufficient to require him to stand trial. *Id.*

Although the *juge* directs the investigation, he represents "neither the interest of the police nor that of the state prosecutors." . . . In determining whether to proceed to trial, the government and the accused each are represented to an equal degree before the *juge*. "[H]is aim is simply to ensure that justice is done." . . . This is the hallmark of a tribunal—impartial adjudication.

Unlike the *juges d'instruction*, the Superintendent of Exchange Control is charged to act in the government's interest to enforce the law. He is required to protect the balance of payments by restraining the outward flow of capital from Colombia. He has extraordinary powers to order and conduct far-reaching investigations; he is empowered to determine whether violation of the law has occurred. Although the subject of an investigation may be represented by counsel, the government's sole representative is the Superintendent himself.

The essence of the Superintendent's responsibility is the direction of a law enforcement agency. Unlike the *juge*, he has what Judge Friendly referred to in *India* as "an institutional interest in a particular result." ... This interest is inconsistent with the concept of impartial adjudication intended by the term "tribunal."

We therefore hold that the district court erred in concluding that the Superintendent of Exchange Control is "tribunal" within the meaning of § 1782. In so holding, we do not express or imply any adverse reflection on the Superintendent or his legitimate function under Colombian law. Rather, our holding is compelled by the terms of § 1782 as enacted by Congress.

[...]

8. In *Shin v. United States*, 555 F.2d 720 (9th Cir. 1977), the court established a useful distinction between due process requirements and the need to establish whether the "foreign or international tribunal" has proper jurisdiction:

[...]

Under the statute the only restrictions explicitly stated are that the request be made by a foreign or international tribunal, and that the testimony or material requested be for use in a proceeding in such a tribunal. This court has also held that the investigation in connection with which the request is made must relate to a judicial or quasi-judicial controversy....

There is no question but that such conditions are met here. The question raised by appellant is whether a tribunal that has already entertained trial of the controversy and thus is aware of the issues presented and of what evidence would be relevant to those issues, can, under Korean law, request assistance on behalf of the tribunal where review is now pending. In our judgment[,] our federal courts, in responding to requests, should not feel obliged to involve themselves in technical questions of foreign law relating to subject-matter jurisdiction of foreign or international tribunals, or the admissibility before such tribunals of the testimony or material sought.

This is not to say that jurisdiction of the requesting court is never an appropriate inquiry. If departures from our concepts of fundamental due process and fairness are involved, a different question is presented—one that is not presented here and which we do not reach. A request for judicial assistance is an appeal to the discretion of the district court.... Here it is not disputed that the Korean courts have a legitimate basis for the exercise of judicial authority over appellant and that a controversy is there entertained in which the records would be of use. We find no abuse of discretion in honoring the request under these circumstances.

[...]

* * * *

The Federal Rules of Civil Procedure contain a number of provisions that address the role of the federal courts in conducting transborder litigation. The rules are forged on the basis of domestic law and generally ignore the rules that prevail in the requested foreign jurisdiction. They lack any comparative or foreign law content. They reflect an almost naïve liberalism about how to achieve and conduct international judicial assistance. The rules are founded upon a form of unquestioning idealism that minimizes the very substantial difficulties of transborder judicial cooperation. The rules seem to be based upon the assumption that a would-be enlightened domestic concept will melt away all the problems and the resistance of foreign legal processes. After evaluating the rules and assessing their content, can you propose a rule that could achieve enforcement in a predictable and consistent manner?

Federal Rule of Civil Procedure 4(e)

(e) Summons: Service Upon a Party Not Inhabitant of or Found Within State. Whenever a statute of the United States or an order of court thereunder provides for service of a summons, or of a notice, or of an order in lieu of summons upon a party not an inhabitant of or found within the state in which the district court is held, service may be made under the circumstances and in the manner prescribed by the statute or order, or, if there is no provision therein prescribing the manner of service, in a manner stated in this rule. Whenever a statute or rule of court of the state in which the district court is held provides (1) for service of a summons, or of a notice, or of an order in lieu of summons upon a party not an inhabitant of or found within the state, (2) for service upon or notice to him to appear and respond or defend in an action by reason of the attachment or garnishment or similar seizure of his property located within the state, service may in either case be made under the circumstances and in the manner prescribed in the statute or rule.

Notes and Questions

To what extent, however, should consideration be given to the domestic law of the country in which service is to be performed? Suppose the service, though valid and effective under American law, would be ineffective under foreign law? Does that circumstance have any bearing? Suppose the act of service, as contemplated, is deemed to violate foreign law? Consider whether Rule 4(1), which follows, is more responsive to these concerns.

Federal Rule of Civil Procedure 4(1)

(i) Alternative Provisions for Service in a Foreign Country

(1) Manner. When the federal or state law referred to in subdivision (e) of this rule authorizes service upon a party not an inhabitant of or found within the state in which the district court is held, and service is to be effected upon the party in a foreign country, it is also sufficient if service of the summons and complaint is made: (A) in the manner prescribed by the law of the foreign country for service in that country in an action in any of its courts of general jurisdiction; or (B) as directed by the foreign authority in response to a letter rogatory, when service in

either case is reasonably calculated to give actual notice; or (C) upon an individual, by delivery to him personally, and upon a corporation or partnership or association, by delivery to an officer, a managing or general agent; or (D) by any form of mail, requiring a signed receipt, to be addressed and dispatched by the clerk of the court to the party to be served; or (E) as directed by order of the court. Service under (C) or (E) above may be made by any person who is not a party and is not less than 18 years of age or who is designated by order of the district court or by the foreign court. On request, the clerk shall deliver the summons to the plaintiff for transmission to the person or the foreign court or officer who will make the service.

(2) Return. Proof of service may be made as prescribed by subdivision (g) of this rule, or by the law of the foreign country, or by order of the court. When service is made pursuant to subparagraph (1)(D) of this subdivision, proof of service shall include a receipt signed by the addressee or other evidence of delivery to the addressee satisfactory to the court.

Notes and Questions

Rules 28 and 29 continue to apply an approach of facile accommodation, under which self-evident conflicts are ignored and opposing positions are simply left to coexist. The ultimate statement of that approach is achieved when Rule 28 provides, in effect, that evidence gathered pursuant to foreign rules need not be excluded if it does not comply with basic U.S. evidentiary standards. What is the precise duty of the court in regard to such evidence? Of what use is the evidence likely to be? What if it prejudices the rights of one of the parties? Is it worth the cost of time and money to collect? What can a practitioner do in light of these provisions? How would you state a more workable rule?

Federal Rules of Civil Procedure 28(b), 29

Rule 28. Persons Before Whom Depositions May Be Taken

[. . .]

(b) In Foreign Countries. In a foreign country, depositions may be taken (1) on notice before a person authorized to administer oaths in the place in which the examination is held, either by the law thereof or by the law of the United States, or (2) before a person commissioned by the court, and a person so commissioned shall have the power by virtue of this commission to administer any necessary oath and take testimony, or (3) pursuant to a letter rogatory. A commission or a letter rogatory shall be issued on application and notice and on terms that are just and appropriate. It is not requisite to the issuance of a commission or a letter rogatory that the taking of the deposition in any other manner is impracticable or inconvenient; and both a commission and a letter rogatory may be issued in proper cases. A notice or commission may designate the person before whom the deposition is to be taken either by name or descriptive title. A letter rogatory may be addressed "To the

Appropriate Authority in [here name the country]." Evidence obtained in response to a letter rogatory need not be excluded merely for the reason that it is not a verbatim transcript or that the testimony was not taken under oath or for any similar departure from the requirements for depositions taken within the United States under these rules.

Rule 29. Stipulations Regarding Discovery Procedure

Unless the court orders otherwise, the parties may by written stipulation (1) provide that depositions may be taken before any person, at any time or place, upon any notice, and in any manner and when so taken may be used like other depositions, and (2) modify the procedures provided by these rules for other methods of discovery, except that stipulations extending the time provided in Rules 33, 34, and 36 for responses to discovery may be made only with the approval of the court.

* * * *

The Hague Convention framework was instituted to establish a transborder regime for service of process and evidence-gathering. One of its primary goals was to reconcile the U.S. common law techniques in the area with the continental civil law approach to the making of a record. It sought to reduce the conflicts that attended the commencement and pursuit of transborder litigation. Its provisions protect the sovereignty and territorial autonomy of signatory States yet provide the means of securing foreign evidence that might be useful in U.S. proceedings. As such, the Hague framework reflects a moment of reconciliation in the long-standing European–American battle for legal, political, and business supremacy.

Because it was negotiated and drafted by political agents, it achieves only approximative solutions to the problem of disparate trial processes. In fact, it has not remedied the previously existing problems at all—there is now greater delay, costs, and conflict. The politicians may have found suitably general language upon which to agree, but they consequently ignored the practical difficulties they were commissioned to solve.

In reading the texts of the conventions, you should first determine whether the foregoing negative assessment is warranted. What provisions of the conventions demonstrate its failure to serve as a practical protocol for transborder practitioners? How might the treaty framework create even more delay and make litigation even more expensive? Where are the textual references to the civil law and common law processes? Isn't it curious that an instrument that purports to reconcile the different legal processes gives them so little presence in its provisions? Can you identify the political compromise, if any, that is embedded in the convention texts? What is a "central authority," where is it located, and what does it do? Are there real limits on the State's authority to refuse or to modify requests for litigation assistance? What crucial provisions exist on that score? How would you use the conventions if you were an international practitioner? Can you propose a better protocol?

CONVENTION ON THE SERVICE ABROAD OF JUDICIAL AND EXTRAJUDICIAL DOCUMENTS IN CIVIL OR COMMERCIAL MATTERS

20 U.S.T. 361, T.I.A.S. No.6638 (1965) (done on Nov. 15, 1965, ratified by the U.S. on April 24, 1967, entered into force February 10, 1969).

The States signatory to the present Convention,

Desiring to create an appropriate means to ensure that judicial and extrajudicial documents to be served abroad shall be brought to the notice of the addressee in sufficient time,

Desiring to improve the organization of mutual judicial assistance for that purpose by simplifying and expediting the procedure,

Have resolved to conclude a Convention to this effect and have agreed upon the following provisions:

Article 1

The present Convention shall apply in all cases, in civil or commercial matters, where there is occasion to transmit a judicial or extrajudicial document for service abroad.

This Convention shall not apply where the address of the person to be served with the document is not known.

Chapter I—Judicial Documents

Article 2

Each contracting state shall designate a Central Authority which will undertake to receive requests for service coming from other contracting states and to proceed in conformity with the provisions of articles 3 to 6.

Each state shall organize the Central Authority in conformity with its own law.

Article 3

The authority or judicial officer competent under the law of the State in which the documents originate shall forward to the Central Authority of the State addressed a request conforming to the model annexed to the present Convention, without any requirement of legalisation or equivalent formality.

The document to be served or a copy thereof shall be annexed to the request. The request and the document shall both be furnished in duplicate.

Article 4

If the Central Authority considers that the request does not comply with the provisions of the present Convention it shall promptly inform the applicant and specify its objections to the request.

Article 5

The Central Authority of the State addressed shall itself serve the document or shall arrange to have it served by an appropriate agency, either-

(a) by a method prescribed by its internal law for the service of documents in domestic actions upon persons who are within its territory, or

(b) by a particular method requested by the applicant, unless such a method is incompatible with the law of the State addressed.

Subject to sub-paragraph (b) of the first paragraph of this article, the document may always be served by delivery to an addressee who accepts it voluntarily.

If the document is to be served under the first paragraph above, the Central Authority may require the document to be written in, or translated into, the official language or one of the official languages of the State addressed.

The part of the request, in the form attached to the present Convention, which contains a summary of the document to be served, shall be served with the document.

Article 6

The Central Authority of the State addressed, or any authority which it may have designated for that purpose, shall complete a certificate in the form of the model annexed to the present Convention.

The certificate shall state that the document has been served, and shall include the method, the place, and the date of service and the person to whom the document was delivered.

If the document has not been served, the certificate shall set out the reasons which have prevented service.

The applicant may require that a certificate not completed by a Central Authority or by a judicial authority shall be countersigned by one of these authorities.

The certificate shall be forwarded directly to the applicant.

Article 7

The standard terms in the model annexed to the present Convention shall in all cases be written either in French or in English. They may also be written in the official language, or in one of the official languages, of the state in which the documents originate.

The corresponding blanks shall be completed either in the language of the State addressed or in French or in English.

Article 8

Each contracting State shall be free to effect service of judicial documents upon persons abroad, without application of any compulsion, directly through its diplomatic or consular agents.

Any State may declare that it is opposed to such service within its territory, unless the document is to be served upon a national of the State in which the documents originate.

Article 9

Each contracting State shall be free, in addition, to use consular channels to forward documents, for the purpose of service, to those authorities of another contracting State which are designated by the latter for this purpose.

Each contracting State may, if exceptional circumstances so require, use diplomatic channels for the same purpose.

Article 10

Provided the State of destination does not object, the present Convention shall not interfere with:

(a) the freedom to send judicial documents, by postal channels, directly to persons abroad,

(b) the freedom of judicial officers, officials or other competent persons of the State of origin to effect service of judicial documents directly through the judicial officers, officials or other competent persons of the State of destination,

(c) the freedom of any person interested in a judicial proceeding to effect service of judicial documents directly through the judicial officers, officials or other competent persons of the State of destination.

Article 11

The present Convention shall not prevent two or more contracting States from agreeing to permit, for the purpose of service of judicial documents, channels of transmission other than those provided for in the preceding articles and, in particular, direct communication between their respective authorities.

Article 12

The service of judicial documents coming from a contracting State shall not give rise to any payment or reimbursement of taxes or costs for the services rendered by the State addressed. The applicant shall pay or reimburse the costs occasioned by—

(a) the employment of a judicial officer or of a person competent under the law of the State of destination,

(b) the use of a particular method of service.

Article 13

Where the request for service complied with the terms of the Convention, the State addressed may refuse to comply therewith only if it deems that compliance would infringe its sovereignty or security.

It may not refuse to comply solely on the ground that, under its internal law, it claims exclusive jurisdiction over the subject-matter of the action or that its internal law would not permit the action upon which the application is based.

The Central Authority shall, in case of refusal, promptly inform the applicant and state the reasons for the refusal.

Article 14

Difficulties which may arise in connection with the transmission of judicial documents for service shall be settled through diplomatic channels.

Article 15

Where a writ of summons or an equivalent document had to be transmitted abroad for the purpose of service, under the provisions of the present Convention, and the defendant has not appeared, judgment shall not be given until it is established that-

(a) the document was served by a method prescribed by the internal law of the State addressed for the service of documents in domestic actions upon persons who are within its territory, or

(b) the document was actually delivered to the defendant or to his residence by another method provided for by this Convention,

and that in either of these cases the service or the delivery was effected in sufficient time to enable the defendant to defend.

Each contracting state shall be free to declare that the judge, notwithstanding the provisions of the first paragraph of this article, may give judgment even if no certificate of service or delivery has been received, if all the following conditions are fulfilled:

(a) the document was transmitted by one of the methods provided for in this Convention,

(b) a period of time of not less than six months, considered adequate by the judge in the particular case, has elapsed since the date of the transmission of the document,

(c) no certificate of any kind has been received, even though every reasonable effort has been made to obtain it through the competent authorities of the State addressed.

Notwithstanding the provisions of the preceding paragraphs the judge may order, in case of urgency, any provisional or protective measures.

Article 16

When a writ of summons or an equivalent document had to be transmitted abroad for the purpose of service, under the provisions of the present convention, and a judgment has been entered against a defendant who has not appeared, the judge shall have the power to relieve the defendant from the effects of the expiration of the time for appeal from the judgment if the following conditions are fulfilled—

(a) the defendant, without any fault on his part, did not have knowledge of the document in sufficient time to defend, or knowledge of the judgment in sufficient time to appeal, and

(b) the defendant has disclosed a *prima facie* defense to the action on the merits.

An application for relief may be filed only within a reasonable time after the defendant has knowledge of the judgment.

Each contracting State may declare that the application will not be entertained if it is filed after the expiration of a time to be stated in the declaration, but which shall in no case be less than one year following the date of the judgment.

This article shall not apply to judgments concerning status or capacity of persons.

Chapter II—Extrajudicial Documents

Article 17

Extrajudicial documents emanating from authorities and judicial officers of a contracting State may be transmitted for the purpose of service in another contracting State by methods and under the provisions of the present Convention.

Chapter III—General Clauses

Article 18

Each contracting State may designate other authorities in addition to the Central Authority and shall determine the extent of their competence.

The applicant shall, however, in all cases, have the right to address a request directly to the Central Authority.

Federal States shall be free to designate more than one Central Authority.

Article 19

To the extent that the internal law of a contracting State permits methods of transmission, other than those provided for in the preceding articles, of documents coming from abroad, for service within its territory, the present Convention shall not effect such provisions.

Article 20

The present Convention shall not prevent an agreement between any two or more contracting States to dispense with—

(a) the necessity for duplicate copies of transmitted documents as required by the second paragraph of article 3,

(b) the language requirements of the third paragraph of article 5 and article 7,

(c) the provisions of the fourth paragraph of article 5,

(d) the provisions of the second paragraph of article 12.

[. . .]

CONVENTION ON THE TAKING OF EVIDENCE ABROAD IN CIVIL OR COMMERCIAL MATTERS,

25 U.S.T. 2555, T.I.A.S. No. 744,
reprinted in 12 I.L.M. 3274 (1973).

The States signatory to the present Convention,

Desiring to facilitate the transmission and execution of Letters of Request and to further the accommodation of the different methods which they use for this purpose,

Desiring to improve mutual judicial co-operation in civil or commercial matters,

Have resolved to conclude a Convention to this effect and have agreed upon the following provisions:

Chapter I—Letters of Request

Article 1

In civil or commercial matters a judicial authority of a Contracting State may, in accordance with the provisions of the law of that State, request the competent authority of another Contracting State, by means of a Letter of Request, to obtain evidence, or to perform some other judicial act.

A Letter shall not be used to obtain evidence which is not intended for use in judicial proceedings, commenced or contemplated.

The expression "other judicial act" does not cover the service of judicial documents or the issuance of any process by which judgments or orders are executed or enforced, or orders for provisional or protective measures.

Article 2

A Contracting State shall designate a Central Authority which will undertake to receive Letters of Request coming from a judicial authority of another Contracting State and to transmit them to the authority competent to execute them. Each State shall organize the Central Authority in accordance with its own law.

Letters shall be sent to the Central Authority of the State of execution without being transmitted through any other authority of that State.

Article 3

A Letter of Request shall specify:

(a) the authority requesting its execution and the authority requested to execute it, if known to the requesting authority;

(b) the names and addresses of the parties to the proceedings and their representatives, if any;

(c) the nature of the proceedings for which the evidence is required, giving all necessary information in regard thereto;

(d) the evidence to be obtained or other judicial act to be performed;

(e) the names and addresses of the persons to be examined;

(f) the questions to be put to the persons to be examined or a statement of the subject-matter about which they are to be examined;

(g) the documents or other property, real or personal, to be inspected;

(h) any requirement that the evidence is to be given on oath or affirmation, and any special form to be used;

(i) any special method or procedure to be followed under Article 9.

A Letter may also mention any information necessary for the application of Article 11.

No legalization or other like formality may be required.

Article 4

A Letter of Request shall be in the language of the authority requested to execute it or be accompanied by a translation into that language.

Nevertheless, a Contracting State shall accept a Letter in either English or French, or a translation into one of these languages, unless it has made the reservation authorized by Article 33.

A Contracting State which has more than one official language and cannot, for reasons of internal law, accept Letters in one of these languages for the whole of its territory, shall by declaration, specify the language in which the Letter or translation thereof shall be expressed for execution in the specified parts of its territory. In case of failure to comply with this declaration, without justifiable excuse, the costs of translation into the required language shall be borne by the State of origin.

A Contracting State may, by declaration, specify the language or languages other than those referred to in the preceding paragraphs, in which a Letter may be sent to its Central Authority.

Any translation accompanying a Letter shall be certified as correct, either by a diplomatic officer or consular agent or by a sworn translator or by any other person so authorized in either State.

Article 5

If the Central Authority considers that the request does not comply with the provisions of the present Convention, it shall promptly inform the authority of the State of origin which transmitted the Letter of Request, specifying the objections to the Letter.

Article 6

If the authority to whom a Letter of Request has been transmitted is not competent to execute it, the Letter shall be sent forthwith to the authority in the same State which is competent to execute it in accordance with the provisions of its own law.

Article 7

The requesting authority shall, if it so desires, be informed of the time when, and the place where, the proceedings will take place, in order that the parties concerned, and their representatives, if any, may be present. This information shall be sent directly to the parties or their representatives when the authority of the State of origin so requests.

Article 8

A Contracting State may declare that members of the judicial personnel of the requesting authority of another Contracting State may be present at the execution of a Letter of Request. Prior authorization by the competent authority designated by the declaring State may be required.

Article 9

The judicial authority which executed a Letter of Request shall apply its own law as to the methods and procedures to be followed.

However, it will follow a request of the requesting authority that a special method or procedure be followed, unless this is incompatible with the internal law of the State of execution or is impossible of performance by reason of its internal practice and procedure or by reason of practical difficulties.

A Letter of Request shall be executed expeditiously.

Article 10

In executing a Letter of Request, the requested authority shall apply the appropriate measures of compulsion in the instances and to the same extent as are provided by its internal law for the execution of orders issued by the authorities of its own country or of requests made by parties in internal proceedings.

Article 11

In the execution of a Letter of Request, the person concerned may refuse to give evidence in so far as he has a privilege or duty to refuse to give the evidence—

(a) under the law of the State of execution; or

(b) under the law of the State of origin, and the privilege or duty has been specified in the Letter, or, at the instance of the requested authority, has been otherwise confirmed to that authority by the requesting authority.

A Contracting State may declare that, in addition, it will respect privileges and duties existing under the law of States other than the State of origin and the State of execution to the extent specified in that declaration.

Article 12

The execution of a Letter of Request may be refused only to the extent that—

(a) in the State of execution the execution of the Letter does not fall within the functions of the judiciary; or

(b) the State addressed considers that its sovereignty or security would be prejudiced thereby.

Execution may be refused solely on the ground that under its internal law the State of execution claims exclusive jurisdiction over the subject matter of the action or that its internal law would not admit a right of action on it.

Article 13

The documents establishing the execution of the Letter of Request shall be sent by the requested authority by the same channel which was used by the latter.

In every instance where the Letter is not executed in whole or in part, the requesting authority shall be informed immediately through the same channel and advised of the reasons.

Article 14

The execution of the Letter of Request shall not give rise to any reimbursement of taxes or costs of any nature.

Nevertheless, the State of execution has the right to require the State of origin to reimburse the fees paid to experts and interpreters and the costs occasioned by the use of a special procedure requested by the State of origin under Article 9, paragraph 2.

The requested authority whose law obliges the parties themselves to secure evidence, and which is not able itself to execute the Letter, may, after having obtained the consent of the requesting authority, appoint a suitable person to do so. When seeking this consent the requested authority shall indicate the approximate costs which would result from this procedure. If the requesting authority gives its consent it shall reimburse any costs incurred; without such consent the requesting authority shall not be liable for the costs.

CHAPTER II—TAKING OF EVIDENCE BY DIPLOMATIC OFFICERS, CONSULAR AGENTS AND COMMISSIONERS

Article 15

In a civil or commercial matter, a diplomatic officer or consular agent of a Contracting State may, in the territory of another Contracting

State and within the area where he exercised his functions, take the evidence without compulsion of nationals of a State which he represents in aid of proceedings commenced in the courts of a State which he represents.

A Contracting State may declare that evidence may be taken by a diplomatic officer or consular agent only if permission to that effect is given upon application made by him or on his behalf to the appropriate authority designated by the declaring State.

Article 16

A diplomatic officer or consular agent of a Contracting State may, in the territory of another Contracting State and within the area where he exercises his functions, also take the evidence, without compulsion, of nationals of the State in which he exercises his functions or of a third State, in aid of proceedings commenced in the courts of a State which he represents, if—

(a) a competent authority designated by the State in which he exercises his functions has given its permission either generally or in the particular case, and

(b) he complies with the conditions which the competent authority has specified in the permission.

A Contracting State may declare that evidence may be taken under this Article without its prior permission.

Article 17

In a civil or commercial matter, a person duly appointed as a commissioner for the purpose may, without compulsion, take evidence in the territory of a Contracting State in aid of proceedings commenced in the courts of another Contracting State if—

(a) a competent authority designated by the State where the evidence is to be taken has given its permission either generally or in the particular case; and

(b) he complies with the conditions which the competent authority has specified in the permission.

A Contracting State may declare that evidence may be taken under this Article without its prior permission.

Article 18

A Contracting State may declare that a diplomatic officer, consular agent or commissioner authorized to take evidence under Articles 15, 16 or 17, may apply to the competent authority designated by the declaring State for appropriate assistance to obtain the evidence by compulsion. The declaration may contain such conditions as the declaring State may see fit to impose.

If the authority grants the application it shall apply any measures of compulsion which are appropriate and are prescribed by its law for use in internal proceedings.

Article 19

The competent authority, in giving the permission referred to in Articles 15, 16, or 17, or in granting the application referred to in Article 18, may lay down such conditions as it deems fit, *inter alia*, as to the time and place of the taking of the evidence. Similarly it may require that it be given reasonable advance notice of the time, date and place of the taking of the evidence; in such a case a representative of the authority shall be entitled to be present at the taking of the evidence.

Article 20

In the taking of evidence under any Article of this Chapter persons concerned may be legally represented.

Article 21

Where a diplomatic officer, consular agent or commissioner is authorized under Articles 15, 16, or 17 to take evidence—

(a) he may take all kinds of evidence which are not incompatible with the law of the State where the evidence is taken or contrary to any permission granted pursuant to the above Articles, and shall have power within such limits to administer an oath or take an affirmation;

(b) a request to a person to appear or to give evidences shall, unless the recipient is a national of the State where the action is pending, be drawn up in the language of the place where the evidence is taken or be accompanied by a translation into such language;

(c) the request shall inform the person that he may be legally represented and, in any State that has not filed a declaration under Article 18, shall also inform him that he is not compelled to appear or to give evidence;

(d) the evidence may be taken in the manner provided by the law applicable to the court in which the action is pending provided that such manner is not forbidden by the law of the State where the evidence is taken;

(e) a person requested to give evidence may invoke the privileges and duties to refuse to give the evidence contained in Article 11.

Article 22

The fact that an attempt to take evidence under the procedure laid down in this Chapter has failed, owing to the refusal of a person to give evidence, shall not prevent an application being subsequently made to take the evidence in accordance with Chapter 1.

CHAPTER III—GENERAL CLAUSES

Article 23

A Contracting State may, at the time of signature, ratification or accession, declare that it will not execute Letters of Request issued for the purpose of obtaining pretrial discovery of documents as known in Common Law countries.

Article 24

A Contracting State may designate other authorities in addition to the Central Authority and shall determine the extent of their competence. However, Letters of Request may in all cases be sent to the Central Authority.

Federal States shall be free to designate more than one Central Authority.

Article 25

A Contracting State which has more than one legal system may designate the authorities of one of such systems, which shall have exclusive competence to execute Letters of Request pursuant to this Convention.

Article 26

A Contracting State, if required to do so because of constitutional limitations, may request the reimbursement by the State of origin of fees and costs, in connection with the execution of Letters of Request, for the service of process necessary to compel the appearance of a person to give evidence, the costs of attendance of such persons, and the cost of any transcript of the evidence.

Where a State has made a request pursuant to the above paragraph, any other Contracting State may request from that State the reimbursement of similar fees and costs.

Article 27

The provisions of the present Convention shall not prevent a Contracting State from—

(a) declaring that Letters of Request may be transmitted to its judicial authorities through channels other than those provided for in Article 2;

(b) permitting, by internal law or practice, any act provided for in this Convention to be performed upon less restrictive conditions;

(c) permitting, by internal law or practice, methods of taking evidence other than those provided for in this Convention.

Article 28

The present Convention shall not prevent an agreement between any two or more Contracting States to derogate from—

(a) the provisions of Article 2 with respect to methods of transmitting Letters of Request;

(b) the provisions of Article 4 with respect to the language which may be used;

(c) the provisions of Article 8 with respect to the presence of judicial personnel at the execution of Letters;

(d) the provisions of Article 11 with respect to the privileges and duties of witnesses to refuse to give evidence;

(e) the provisions of Article 13 with respect to the methods of returning executed Letters to the requesting authority;

(f) the provisions of Article 14 with respect to fees and costs;

(g) the provisions of Chapter 11.

[. . .]

* * * *

The central U.S. case on the Hague Evidence Convention follows. In many respects, *Aérospatiale* is an unusual ruling for the U.S. Supreme Court. All of the Court's other decisions on matters of private international litigation have supported the development of an "anational" legal order and process designed for global commerce. *Aérospatiale* departs from that tradition. The Court is less than supportive of the Hague Evidence Convention; in fact, it chooses to privilege the legal regime that is most detrimental to the Convention and its continued viability. It, in effect, squarely places matters of transborder discovery into a domestic legal framework. That decision has the effect of leaving many evidentiary requests unfulfilled because, without compliance with the Convention, blocking statutes will prevent the gathering of evidence, discovery, and the taking of testimony. What objective is the Court pursuing? What point it is trying to make? Is its determination right? What does it say about the Hague Evidence Convention? What should practitioners now do to represent their international clients? You should note from statements made early in the opinion that the Hague Evidence Convention is hardly a universal instrument. How do you assess the modest number of accessions?

SOCIÉTÉ NATIONALE INDUSTRIELLE AÉROSPATIALE v. U.S. DISTRICT COURT

482 U.S. 522, 107 S.Ct. 2542, 96 L.Ed.2d 461 (1987).

Justice STEVENS delivered the opinion of the Court.

The United States, the Republic of France, and 15 other Nations have acceded to the Hague Convention on the Taking of Evidence Abroad in Civil or Commercial Matters . . . . This Convention—sometimes referred to as the "Hague Convention" or the "Evidence Convention"—prescribes certain procedures by which a judicial authority in one contracting State may request evidence located in another contracting State. The question presented in this case concerns the extent to which a Federal District Court must employ the procedures set forth in the Convention when litigants seek answers to interrogatories, the production of documents, and admissions from a French adversary over whom the court has personal jurisdiction.

I.

The two petitioners are corporations owned by the Republic of France. They are engaged in the business of designing, manufacturing, and marketing aircraft. One of their planes, the "Rallye," was allegedly advertised in American aviation publications as "the World's safest and most economical STOL plane." On August 19, 1980, a Rallye crashed in Iowa, injuring the pilot and a passenger. Dennis Jones, John George, and Rosa George brought separate suits based upon this accident in the United States District Court for the Southern District of Iowa, alleging that petitioners had manufactured and sold a defective plane and that they were guilty of negligence and breach of warranty. Petitioners answered the complaints, apparently without questioning the jurisdiction of the District Court. With the parties' consent, the cases were consolidated and referred to a magistrate....

Initial discovery was conducted by both sides pursuant to the Federal Rules of Civil Procedure without objection. When plaintiffs served a second request for the production of documents pursuant to Rule 34, a set of interrogatories pursuant to Rule 33, and requests for admission pursuant to Rule 36, however, petitioners filed a motion for a protective order.... The motion alleged that because petitioners are "French corporations, and the discovery sought can only be found in a foreign state, namely France," the Hague Convention dictated the exclusive procedures that must be followed for pretrial discovery....In addition, the motion stated that under French penal law, the petitioners could not respond to discovery requests that did not comply with the Convention....

The Magistrate denied the motion insofar as it related to answering interrogatories, producing documents, and making admissions. After reviewing the relevant cases, the Magistrate explained:

> "To permit the Hague Evidence Convention to override the Federal Rules of Civil Procedure would frustrate the courts' interests, which particularly arise in products liability cases, in protecting United States citizens from harmful products and in compensating them for injuries arising from use of such products."

[...]

II.

In the District Court and the Court of Appeals, petitioners contended that the Hague Evidence Convention "provides the exclusive and mandatory procedures for obtaining documents and information located within the territory of a foreign signatory." 782 F.2d at 124. We are satisfied that the Court of Appeals correctly rejected this extreme position. We believe it is foreclosed by the plain language of the Convention. Before discussing the test of the Convention, however, we briefly review its history.

[...]

... The Convention's purpose was to establish a system for obtaining evidence located abroad that would be "tolerable" to the state executing the request and would produce evidence "utilizable" in the requesting state ....

... The Convention was fairly summarized in the Secretary of State's letter of submittal to the President. "The willingness of the Conference to proceed promptly with work on the evidence convention is perhaps attributable in large measure to the difficulties encountered by courts and lawyers in obtaining evidence abroad from countries with markedly different legal systems. Some countries have insisted on the exclusive use of the complicated, dilatory and expensive system of letters rogatory or letters of request. Other countries have refused adequate judicial assistance because of the absence of a treaty or convention regulating the matter. The substantial increase in litigation with foreign aspects arising, in part, from the unparalleled expansion of international trade and travel in recent decades has intensified the need for an effective international agreement to set up a model system to bridge differences between the common law and civil law approaches to the taking of evidence abroad.

"Civil law countries tend to concentrate on commissions rogatories, while common law countries take testimony on notice, by stipulation and through commissions to consuls or commissioners. Letters of request for judicial assistance from courts abroad in securing needed evidence have been the exception, rather than the rule. The civil law technique results normally in a resume of the evidence, prepared by the executing judge and signed by the witness, while the common law technique results normally in a verbatim transcript of the witness's testimony certified by the reporter.

"Failure by either the requesting state or the state of execution fully to take into account the differences of approach to the taking of evidence abroad under the two systems and the absence of agreed standards applicable to letters of request have frequently caused difficulties for courts and litigants. To minimize such difficulties in the future, the enclosed convention, which consists of a preamble and forty-two articles, is designed to:

"1. Make the employment of letters of request a principal means of obtaining evidence abroad;

"2. Improve the means of securing evidence abroad by increasing the powers of consuls and by introducing in the civil law world, on a limited basis, the concept of the commissioner;

"3. Provide means for securing evidence in the form needed by the court where the action is pending; and

"4. Preserve all more favorable and less restrictive practices arising from internal law, internal rules of procedure and bilateral or multilateral conventions.

"What the convention does is to provide a set of minimum standards with which contracting states agree to comply. Further, through articles 27, 28 and 32, it provides a flexible framework within which any future liberalizing changes in policy and tradition in any country with respect to international judicial cooperation may be translated into effective change in international procedures. At the same time it recognizes and preserves procedures of every country which now or hereafter may provide international cooperation in the taking of evidence on more liberal and less restrictive bases, whether this is effected by supplementary agreements or by municipal law and practice." ...

III.

In arguing their entitlement to a protective order, petitioners correctly assert that both the discovery rules set forth in the Federal Rules of Civil Procedure and the Hague Convention are the law of the United States.... This observation, however, does not dispose of the question before us; we must analyze the interaction between these two bodies of federal law. Initially, we note that at least four different interpretations of the relationship between the federal discovery rules and the Hague Convention are possible. Two of these interpretations assume that the Hague Convention by its terms dictates the extent to which it supplants normal discovery rules. First, the Hague Convention might be read as requiring its use to the exclusion of any other discovery procedures whenever evidence located abroad is sought for use in an American court. Second, the Hague Convention might be interpreted to require first, but not exclusive, use of its procedures. Two other interpretations assume that international comity, rather than the obligations created by the treaty, should guide judicial resort to the Hague Convention. Third, then, the Convention might be viewed as establishing a supplemental set of discovery procedures, strictly optional under treaty law, to which concerns of comity nevertheless require first resort by American courts in all cases. Fourth, the treaty may be viewed as an undertaking among sovereigns to facilitate discovery to which an American court should resort when it deems that course of action appropriate, after considering the situations of the parties before it as well as the interests of the concerned foreign state.

[...]

We reject the first two of the possible interpretations as inconsistent with the language and negotiating history of the Hague Convention. The Preamble of the Convention specifies its purpose "to facilitate the transmission and execution of Letters of Request" and to "improve mutual judicial co-operation in civil or commercial matters." ... The

Preamble does not speak in mandatory terms which would purport to describe the procedures for all permissible transnational discovery and exclude all other existing practices. The text of the Evidence Convention itself does not modify the law of any contracting State, require any contracting State to use the Convention procedures, either in requesting evidence or in responding to such requests, or compel any contracting State to change its own evidence-gathering procedures.

The Convention contains three chapters. [Both] Chapter I ... and Chapter III ... use permissive rather than mandatory language. Thus, Article 1 provides that a judicial authority in one contracting State "may" forward a letter of request to the competent authority in another contracting State for the purpose of obtaining evidence. Similarly, Articles 15, 16 and 17 provide that diplomatic officers, consular agents, and commissioners "may ... without compulsion," take evidence under certain conditions. The absence of any command that a contracting State must use Convention procedures when they are not needed is conspicuous.

Two of the articles in Chapter III, entitled, "General Clauses," buttress our conclusion that the Convention was intended as a permissive supplement, not a preemptive replacement, for other means of obtaining evidence located abroad. Article 23 expressly authorizes a contracting State to declare that it will not execute any letter of request in aid of pretrial discovery in a common law country. Surely, if the Convention had been intended to replace completely the broad discovery powers that the common law courts in the United States previously exercised over foreign litigants subject to their jurisdiction, it would have been most anomalous for the common law contracting Parties to agree to Article 23, which enables a contracting Party to revoke its consent to the treaty's procedures for pretrial discovery. In the absence of explicit textual support, we are unable to accept the hypothesis that the common law contracting States abjured recourse to all pre-existing discovery procedures at the same time that they accepted the possibility that a contracting Party could unilaterally abrogate even the Convention's procedures. Moreover, Article 27 plainly states that the Convention does not prevent a contracting State from using more liberal methods of rendering evidence than those authorized by the Convention. Thus, the text to the Evidence Convention, as well as the history of its proposal and ratification by the United States, unambiguously supports the conclusion that it was intended to establish optional procedures that would facilitate the taking of evidence abroad....

An interpretation of the Hague Convention as the exclusive means for obtaining evidence located abroad would effectively subject every American court hearing a case involving a national of a contracting State to the internal laws of that State. Interrogatories and document requests are staples of international commercial litigation, no less than of other suits, yet a rule of exclusivity would subordinate the court's supervision of even the most routine of these pretrial proceedings to the actions, or equally, to the inactions of foreign judicial authorities....

[. . .]

The Hague Convention . . . contains no . . . plain statement of a pre-emptive intent. We conclude accordingly that the Hague Convention did not deprive the District Court of the jurisdiction it otherwise possessed to order a foreign national party before it to produce evidence physically located within a signatory nation.

While the Hague Convention does not divest the District Court of jurisdiction to order discovery under the Federal Rules of Civil Procedure, the optional character of the Convention's procedures sheds light on one aspect of the Court of Appeals' opinion that we consider erroneous. That court concluded that the Convention simply "does not apply" to discovery sought from a foreign litigant that is subject to the jurisdiction of an American court. 782 F.2d, at 124. . . .

[I]t appears clear to us that the optional Convention procedures are available whenever they will facilitate the gathering of evidence by the means authorized in the Convention. Although these procedures are not mandatory, the Hague Convention does "apply" to the production of evidence in a litigant's possession in the sense that it is one method of seeking evidence that a court may elect to employ. . . .

V.

Petitioners contend that even if the Hague Convention's procedures are not mandatory, this Court should adopt a rule requiring that American litigants first resort to those procedures before initiating any discovery pursuant to the normal methods of the Federal Rules of Civil Procedure. . . . The Court of Appeals rejected this argument because it was convinced that an American court's order ultimately requiring discovery that a foreign court had refused under Convention procedures would constitute "the greatest insult" to the sovereignty of that tribunal. 782 F.2d, at 125–126. We disagree with the Court of Appeals' view. It is well known that the scope of American discovery is often significantly broader than is permitted in other jurisdictions, and we are satisfied that foreign tribunals will recognize that the final decision on the evidence to be used in litigation conducted in American courts must be made by those courts. We therefore do not believe that an American court should refuse to make use of Convention procedures because of a concern that it may ultimately find it necessary to order the production of evidence that a foreign tribunal permitted a party to withhold.

Nevertheless, we cannot accept petitioners' invitation to announce a new rule of law that would require first resort to Convention procedures whenever discovery is sought from a foreign litigant. Assuming, without deciding, that we have the lawmaking power to do so, we are convinced that such a general rule would be unwise. In many situations the Letter of Request procedure authorized by the Convention would be unduly time consuming and expensive, as well as less certain to produce needed evidence than direct use of the Federal Rules. A rule of first resort in all cases would therefore be inconsistent with the overriding interest in the "just, speedy, and inexpensive determination" of litigation in our courts....

Petitioners argue that a rule of first resort is necessary to accord respect to the sovereignty of states in which evidence is located. It is true that the process of obtaining evidence in a civil law jurisdiction is normally conducted by a judicial officer rather than by private attorneys. Petitioners contend that if performed on French soil, for example, by an unauthorized person, such evidence-gathering might violate the "judicial sovereignty" of the host nation. Because it is only through the Convention that civil law nations have given their consent to evidence-gathering activities within their borders, petitioners argue, we have a duty to apply those procedures whenever they are available....We find that argument unpersuasive. If such a duty were to be inferred from the adoption of the Convention itself, we believe it would have been described in the text of that document. Moreover, the concept of international comity requires in this context a more particularized analysis of the respective interests of the foreign nation and the requesting nation than petitioners' proposed general rule would generate. We therefore decline to hold as a blanket matter that comity requires resort to Hague Evidence Convention procedures without prior scrutiny in each case of the particular facts, sovereign interests, and likelihood that resort to those procedures will prove effective.

[...]

American courts, in supervising pretrial proceedings, should exercise special vigilance to protect foreign litigants from the danger that unnecessary, or unduly burdensome, discovery may place them in a disadvantageous position. Judicial supervision of discovery should always seek to minimize its costs and inconvenience and to prevent improper uses of discovery requests. When it is necessary to seek evidence abroad, however, the District Court must supervise pretrial proceedings particularly closely to prevent discovery abuses....Objections to "abusive" discovery that foreign litigants advance should therefore receive the most careful consideration....American courts should therefore take care to demonstrate due respect for any special problem confronted by the foreign litigant on account of its nationality or the location of its operations, and for any sovereign interest expressed by a foreign state. We do not articulate specific rules to guide this delicate task of adjudication.

VI.

In the case before us, the Magistrate and the Court of Appeals correctly refused to grant the broad protective order that petitioners requested. The Court of Appeals erred, however, in stating that the Evidence Convention does not apply to the pending discovery demands. This holding may be read as indicating that the Convention procedures are not even an option that is open to the District Court. It must be recalled, however, that the Convention's specification of duties in executing states creates corresponding rights in requesting States; holding that the Convention does not apply in this situation would deprive domestic litigants of access to evidence through treaty procedures to which the contracting States have assented. Moreover, such a rule would deny the foreign litigant a full and fair opportunity to demonstrate appropriate reasons for employing Convention procedures in the first instance for some aspects of the discovery process.

Accordingly, the judgment of the Court of Appeals is vacated, and the case is remanded for further proceedings consistent with this opinion.

It is so ordered.

Justice BLACKMUN, with whom Justice BRENNAN, Justice MARSHALL, and Justice O'CONNOR join, concurring in part and dissenting in part.

Some might well regard the Court's decision in this case as an affront to the nations that have joined the United States in ratifying the Hague Convention. . . .The Court ignores the importance of the Convention by relegating it to an "optional" status, without acknowledging the significant achievement in accommodating divergent interests that the Convention represents. Experience to date indicates that there is a large risk that the case-by-case comity analysis now to be permitted by the Court will be performed inadequately and that the somewhat unfamiliar procedures of the Convention will be invoked infrequently. I fear the Court's decision means that courts will resort unnecessarily to issuing discovery orders under the Federal Rules of Civil Procedure in a raw exercise of their jurisdictional power to the detriment of the United States national and international interests. The Court's view of this country's international obligations is particularly unfortunate in a world in which regular commercial and legal channels loom ever more crucial.

I do agree with the Court's repudiation of the positions at both extremes of the spectrum with regard to the use of the Convention. Its rejection of the view that the Convention is not "applicable" at all to this case is surely correct: the Convention clearly applied to litigants as well as to third parties, and to requests for evidence located abroad, no matter where that evidence is actually "produced." The Court also correctly rejects the far opposite position that the Convention provides the exclusive means for discovery involving signatory countries. I dissent, however, because I cannot endorse the Court's case-by-case inquiry for determining whether to use Convention procedures and its failure to provide lower courts with any meaningful guidance for carrying out that inquiry. In my view, the Convention provides effective discovery procedures that largely eliminate the conflicts between United States and foreign law on evidence gathering. I therefore would apply a general presumption that, in most cases, courts should resort first to the Convention procedures. An individualized analysis of the circumstances of a particular case is appropriate only when it appears that it would be futile to employ the Convention or when its procedures prove to be unhelpful.

I.

Even though the Convention does not expressly require discovery of materials in foreign countries to proceed exclusively according to its procedures, it cannot be viewed as merely advisory....The differences between discovery practices in the United States and those in other countries are significant....Of particular import is the fact that discovery conducted by the parties, as is common in the United States, is alien to the legal system of civil-law nations, which typically regard evidence gathering as a judicial function.

The Convention furthers important United States interests by providing channels for discovery abroad that would not be available otherwise....The Convention also serves the long-term interests of the United States in helping to further and to maintain the climate of cooperation and goodwill necessary to the functioning of the international legal and commercial systems.

[...]

Unless they had expected the Convention to provide the normal channels for discovery, other parties to the Convention would have had no incentive to agree to its terms. The civil-law nations committed themselves to employ more effective procedures for gathering evidence within their borders, even to the extent of requiring some common-law practices alien to their systems.... As a result, the primary benefit the other signatory nations would have expected in return for their concessions was that the United States would respect their territorial sovereignty by using the Convention procedures.

II.

By viewing the Convention as merely optional and leaving the decision whether to apply it to the court in each individual case, the majority ignores the policies established by the political branches when they negotiated and ratified the treaty....

It is the Executive that normally decides when a course of action is important enough to risk affronting a foreign nation or placing a strain on foreign commerce. It is the Executive, as well, that is best equipped to determine how to accommodate foreign interests along with our own.... The Convention embodies the result of the best efforts of the Executive Branch, in negotiating the treaty, and the Legislative Branch, in ratifying it, to balance competing national interests. As such, the Convention represents a political determination—one that, consistent with the principle of separation of powers, courts should not attempt to second guess.

Not only is the question of foreign discovery more appropriately considered by the Executive and Congress, but in addition, courts are generally ill equipped to assume the role of balancing the interests of foreign nations with that of our own. Although transnational litigation is increasing, relatively few judges are experienced in the area and the procedures of foreign legal systems are often poorly understood.... A pro-forum bias is likely to creep into the supposedly neutral balancing process and courts, not surprisingly, often will turn to the more familiar procedures established by their local rules. In addition, it simply is not reasonable to expect the Federal Government or the foreign state in which the discovery will take place to participate in every individual case in order to articulate the broader international and foreign interests that are relevant to the decision whether to use the Convention. Indeed, the opportunities for such participation are limited. Exacerbating these shortcomings is the limited appellate review of interlocutory discovery decisions, which prevent any effective case-by-case correction of erroneous discovery decisions.

III.

The principle of comity leads to more definite rules than the *ad hoc* approach endorsed by the majority. The Court asserts that the concept of comity requires an individualized analysis of the interests present in each particular case before a court decides whether to apply the Convention. . . .There is, however, nothing inherent in the comity principle that requires case-by-case analysis. The Court frequently has relied upon a comity analysis when it has adopted general rules to cover recurring situations in areas such as choice of forum, maritime law, and sovereign immunity, and the Court offers no reasons for abandoning that approach here.

Comity is not just a vague political concern favoring international cooperation when it is in our interest to do so. Rather it is a principle under which judicial decisions reflect the systemic value of reciprocal tolerance and goodwill. . . .

[. . .]

In most cases in which a discovery request concerns a nation that has ratified the Convention there is no need to resort to comity principles; the conflicts they are designed to resolve already have been eliminated by the agreements expressed in the treaty. . . .

[. . .]

Use of the Convention advances the sovereign interests of foreign nations because they have given *consent* to Convention procedures by ratifying them. This consent encompasses discovery techniques that would otherwise impinge on the sovereign interests of many civil-law nations. In the absence of the Convention, the informal techniques provided by Articles 15–22 of the Convention—taking evidence by a diplomatic or consular officer of the requesting state and the use of commissioners nominated by the court of the state where the action is pending—would raise sovereignty issues similar to those implicated by a direct discovery order from a foreign court. "Judicial" activities are occurring on the soil of the sovereign by agents of a foreign state. These voluntary discovery procedures are a great boon to United States litigants and are used far more frequently in practice than is compulsory discovery pursuant to letters of request.

Civil-law contracting parties have also agreed to use, and even to compel, procedures for gathering evidence that are diametrically opposed to civil-law practices. The civil-law system is inquisitional rather than adversarial and the judge normally questions the witness and prepares a written summary of the evidence. Even in common-law countries no system of evidence-gathering resembles that of the United States. Under Article 9 of the Convention, however, a foreign court must grant a request to use a "special method or procedure," which includes requests to compel attendance of witnesses abroad, to administer oaths, to produce verbatim transcripts, or to permit examination of witnesses by counsel for both parties. These methods for obtaining evidence, which largely eliminate conflicts between the discovery procedures of the United States and the laws of foreign systems, have the consent of ratifying nations. The use of these methods thus furthers foreign interests because discovery can proceed without violating the sovereignty of foreign nations.

[. . .]

In most instances, use of the Convention will serve to advance United States interests, particularly when those interests are viewed in a context larger than the immediate interest of the litigants' discovery. The approach I propose is not a rigid *per se* rule that would require first use of the Convention without regard to strong indications that no evidence would be forthcoming. All too often, however, courts have simply assumed that to resort to the Convention would be unproductive and have embarked on speculation about foreign procedures and interpretations. . . .When resort to the Convention would be futile, a court has no choice but to resort to a traditional comity analysis. But even then, an attempt to use the Convention will often be the best way to discover if it will be successful, particularly in the present state of general inexperience with the implementation of its procedures by the various contracting states. An attempt to use the Convention will open a dialogue with the authorities in the foreign state and in that way a United States court can obtain an authoritative answer as to the limits on what it can achieve with a discovery request in a particular contracting state.

[. . .]

Use of the Convention would help develop methods for transnational litigation by placing officials in a position to communicate directly about conflicts that arise during discovery, thus enabling them to promote a reduction in those conflicts. In a broader framework, courts that use the Convention will avoid foreign perceptions of unfairness that result when United States courts show insensitivity to the interests safeguarded by foreign legal regimes. Because of the position of the United States, economically, politically, and militarily, many countries may be reluctant to oppose discovery orders of United States courts. Foreign acquiescence to orders that ignore the Convention, however, is likely to carry a pricetag of accumulating resentment, with the predictable long-term political cost that cooperation will be withheld in other matters. Use of the Convention is a simple step to take toward avoiding that unnecessary and undesirable consequence.

[. . .]

* * * *

The French Blocking Statute

Law No. 80–538 dated July 16, 1980 regulates the communication of documents and information on economical, commercial or technical matters to foreign physical or juridical persons.

The "Assemblée Nationale" (House of Representatives) and the Senate have carried, The President of the Republic promulgate[s] the law which reads as follows:

Article 1—The title of the Law No.68–678 dated July 26, 1968 regarding the communication of documents and information on economical, commercial or technical matters to physical or juridical foreign persons.

Article 2—I-The article 1 of the Law No. 68–678 dated July 26, 1968, hereabove indicated is written as follows:

"Article 1—Subject to treaties or international agreements, it is forbidden to all physical persons of French nationality or usually residing in France and to all managers, representatives, agents or officials of a juridical person having its head office or an establishment in France to communicate by writing, orally or in any other form . . . to foreign public authorities, the documents or the information on economical, commercial, industrial, financial or technical matters, the communication of which can, by [their] nature, interfere with the sovereignty, the security, the essential economical interests of France or with Law and Order, specified by the administrative authority when required."

II—It is added, after the article I of the Law No. 68–678 dated July 26, 1968, hereabove indicated, an article 1A written as follows:

"Article 1A—Subject to treaties or international agreements and laws and regulations in force, it is forbidden to all persons to ask, research or communicate, by writing, orally or under any other form, documents or information on economical, commercial, industrial, financial or technical matters leading to establishing evidence for use directly or indirectly in foreign judicial or administrative proceedings."

Article 3—The article 2 of the Law No. 68–678 dated July 26, 1968, hereabove indicated is modified as follows:

"Article 2—The persons affected by articles 1 and 1A must inform, without any delay, the Minister in charge whenever they are requested in any manner to provide such information."

Article 4—The article 3 of the Law No. 69–678 dated July 26, 1968, hereabove indicated is modified as follows:

"Article 3–Without prejudice to heavier sanctions stipulated by the Law, any infraction to the present Law articles 1 and 1A provisions will be punished with two months to six month imprisonment and with a 10,000 to 120,000 French francs fine or any one of these two penalties only."

The present law will be executed as State Law.

Paris, July 16, 1980

* * * *

Professor Bermann criticized the ruling in *Aérospatiale*. *See* George Bermann, *The Hague Evidence Convention In The Supreme Court: A Critique of the Aérospatiale Decision*, 63 TUL. L. REV. 525 (1989). Stating that the "*Aérospatiale* majority has given the Convention a profile that is extremely unflattering and even caricatural," Professor Bermann concluded:

> The heart of my difficulty with the *Aérospatiale* decision, therefore, does not lie in the Court's refusal to treat the Convention as displacing the ordinarily applicable procedures or as requiring by its own terms prior resort to Convention procedures. It lies rather in the Court's rejection of what it identified as the third option, namely requiring prior resort to Convention procedures as a general rule in furtherance of traditional comity considerations. That solution had won favor not only among academic writers, but also among the lower federal courts. And in the end, it persuaded four members of the Court.
>
> A rule of prior resort does present the advantage of injecting a measures of certainty into an otherwise unguided exercise of discretion. Relying on comity to develop strong presumptions in international legal relations is, as the minority opinion notes, an established practice, whether in choice of forum, choice of law, sovereign immunity, or other matters not mentioned in the opinion. Each of these areas is now marked by a general rule chosen because it tends most to promote a cooperative international regime. There is no reason to suppose that the Convention could not serve as a useful signpost in the same direction so far as extraterritorial discovery is concerned.

63 TUL. L. REV. at 536.

What is your assessment of the assessment? Isn't this internationally-minded Court making a point about the juridical and practical quality of the Hague Evidence Convention? Why should the untenable be sustained just because it physically exists and it is all the people with political authority and responsibility could do? Is that a fair criticism of Professor Bermann's point or was he saying something else? What is your view of the dissent's position? Should the Evidence Convention rule unless its procedures are very likely to or have failed? What are the broader and long-term interests that the dissent mentions? Are the Convention procedures ever likely to be effective? Is the dissent denouncing cultural and political imperialism or is it bemoaning American superiority because of guilt feelings? How persuasive are the dissent's references to "foreign perceptions of unfairness" and the "pricetag of accumulating resentment"? Is this law or political policy?

Chapter 5

THE STATUS OF FOREIGN LAW AND FOREIGN COURT RULINGS IN U.S. LAW

Table of Sections

§ 1. PLEADING AND PROOF OF FOREIGN LAW

Choice-of-Law

Choice-of-law has always been a significant part of transborder litigation. In fact, it once was the near totality of private international law. When parties fail to choose a law governing the merits (or even sometimes when they do choose), the ruling court will provide an answer to the governing law issue by applying the jurisdiction's choice-of-law rules. The Restatement (Second) of Conflict of Laws § 188 is an example of a choice-of-law rule.

Restatement (Second) of Conflict of Laws § 188

(1) The rights and duties of the parties with respect to an issue in contract are determined by the local law of the state, which, with respect to that issue has the most significant relationship to the transaction and the parties under the principles stated in § 6.

(2) In the absence of an effective choice of law by the parties (see § 187), the contacts to be taken into account in applying the principles of § 6 to determine the law applicable to an issue include:

(a) the place of contracting,

(b) the place of negotiation of the contract,

(c) the place of performance,

(d) the location of the subject matter of the contract, and

(e) the domicile, residence, nationality, place of incorporation and place of business of the parties.

These contacts are to be evaluated according to their relative importance with respect to the particular issue.

(3) If the place of negotiating the contract and the place of performance are in the same state, the local law of this state will usually be applied, except as otherwise provided in §§ 189–199 and 203.

* * * *

When the contracting parties fail to make a choice or if the court rejects their choice, the question of determining the applicable law can consume an inordinate amount of time in litigation. Like jurisdiction, choice-of-law is a threshold issue, but it can be difficult to resolve and can be complicated. It is also a lawyer's issue, filled with the types of considerations that entice the legal imagination. It can have a significant bearing on the parties' legal rights and the outcome of litigation. The next case demonstrates this last point forcefully and with clarity.

KRISTINUS v. H. STERN COM. E. IND., S.A.

463 F.Supp. 1263 (S.D.N.Y. 1979).

LASKER, District Judge.

While visiting Rio de Janeiro in December, 1974, Rainer Kristinus, a Pennsylvania resident, purchased three gems from H. Stern Com. e. Ind. S.A. (H. Stern) for $30,467.43. According to Kristinus, a flyer advertising H. Stern's wares had been slipped under the door of his hotel room in Brazil. The flyer contained the following statement (in English) in red type:

> "Every sale carries Stern's one-year guarantee for refund, creditor exchange either here or in your own country. H. Stern Jewelers New York, (681 Fifth Avenue) are at your disposal for help and service."

Kristinus asserts that when he purchased the gems, a vice-president of H. Stern assured him that he would be able to return them for a complete refund in New York.

In January, 1975, Kristinus tendered the gems to H. Stern Jewelers, Inc. in New York City and requested a refund. His request was denied, and this suit for specific performance of the alleged oral promise to refund the purchase price followed.

H. Stern moves to dismiss the complaint on the ground that the alleged oral promise is unenforceable under the laws of Brazil, which H. Stern contends govern the transaction in question.

The provisions of Brazilian law on which H. Stern relies are Article 141 and 142 of the Brazilian Civil Code, which provide:

> "Article 141. Except in cases specifically provided for to the contrary, evidence which is solely by testimony is only admitted as to Contracts whose value does not exceed Cr $10.000,00 (ten thousand cruzeiros).
>
> Sole Paragraph. Whatever the amount of the Contract, evidence by testimony is admissible as a subsidiary to or complement of evidence in writing.
>
> Article 142. There cannot be admitted as witnesses:
>
> [. . .]
>
> IV. The person interested in the object of the litigation, as well as the ancestor and the descendant, or collateral relative, through the third degree of one of the parties, whether by blood or by affiliation."

[. . .]

In deciding choice-of-law questions, the rule in New York is that "the law of the jurisdiction having the greatest interest in the litigation will be applied and that the facts or contacts which obtain significance in defining State interests are those which relate to the purpose of the particular law in conflict." . . .

An examination of the provisions of the Brazilian Civil Code on which H. Stern relies suggests that those provisions promote two interests. First, they protect the integrity of the judicial process in Brazil against the taints of perjured and biased testimony, by 1) requiring that testimony regarding a contract be corroborated by written evidence (Article 141), and 2) barring testimony from interested parties (Article 142). This interest is not implicated in the present case, since the integrity of the Brazilian judicial process is not threatened in a suit in the United States District Court for the Southern District of New York.

Second, Article 141 protects persons who transact business in Brazil from unfounded contractual claims by requiring that such claims, to be enforceable, be supported by a writing. This interest of Brazil does have a bearing on this case, since presumably Brazil seeks to provide this protection to anyone who transacts business there, regardless of where suit on the transaction is brought. The question, then, is whether this interest is greater than any interest that New York may have in applying its own law (which we assume, for the purposes of this motion, would permit enforcement of the contract alleged by Kristinus) to the transaction involved here.

Although Kristinus is not a New York resident, New York may nonetheless assert an interest on his behalf. . . . New York's contacts with this case are 1) that H. Stern transacts business in New York through its franchisee and agent, H. Stern Jewelers, Inc., and 2) that the alleged promise that Kristinus seeks to enforce was to refund the purchase price of the gems in New York through that franchisee. New York has some interest in ensuring that persons who transact business within its borders (and thus subject themselves to some extent at least to the authority of the state) honor obligations, including contracts made elsewhere. Usually, of course, this interest must bow to the paramount interest of the state or country where the contract is made in regulating the conduct of those within its territory. When the contract is to be performed in New York, however, New York's interest is heightened, since its ability to regulate business affairs and the rights and obligations of those within its territory is then directly implicated. In such circumstances, we conclude that a New York court would decline to apply foreign law where, as here, that law would foreclose enforcement of a contract valid under New York law. In short, a New York court would not permit H. Stern of Brazil to contract in Brazil to refund Kristinus' purchase price in New York, and then rely on the laws of Brazil to avoid its obligation under the contract. . . . Accordingly, New York law should be applied. This is an equitable result, since it simply preserves the dispute between the parties for resolution on the merits.

For the reasons stated, H. Stern's motion to dismiss is denied.

Notes and Questions

You should ponder the court's reasoning for selecting the application of New York law. Do you believe that it was an objective, disinterested choice? Should it be? Does the court's determination on law applicable have any extraterritorial consequence? Is it realistic to expect a national court to apply a foreign law with the requisite knowledge and ability? How expensive and difficult do you believe it was to get to the court's level of comparative law analysis? Is a regime of universally applicable law tenable or even conceivable? Is the conflicts approach the only viable solution? Doesn't the new era warrant a new era solution?

Is the choice-of-law discussion really necessary? Wouldn't Brazilian law arguably enforce the flyer as a makeshift offer rather than an invitation to deal because of the verbal representation that later accompanied it? How would one discover what Brazilian law provides on this score? Shouldn't New York law govern simply because New York is the place of litigation? If that determination were unacceptable, shouldn't the court dismiss the case? What impact should the plaintiff's status of being a Pennsylvania resident have upon the court's choice-of-law determination?

* * * *

The solution may be to allow or to require that the parties choose the law applicable in their agreement. The materials that follow demonstrate the basic strength of the party autonomy and freedom of contract rule. Although municipal courts supervise party choice, in most circumstances, the latter controls on this issue. This feature of the law lends predictability to the transaction, but also increases the importance of and time devoted to negotiating the contract.

Restatement (Second) of Conflict of Laws § 187

(1) The law of the state chosen by the parties to govern their contractual rights and duties will be applied if the particular issue is one which the parties could have resolved by an explicit provision in their agreement directed to that issue.

(2) The law of the state chosen by the parties to govern their contractual rights and duties will be applied, even if the particular issue is one which the parties could not have resolved by an explicit provision in their agreement directed to that issue, unless either

(a) the chosen state has no substantial relationship to the parties or the transaction and there is no other reasonable basis for the parties' choice, or

(b) application of the law of the chosen state would be contrary to a fundamental policy of a state which has a materially greater interest than the chosen state in the determination of the particular issue and which, under the rule of § 188, would be the state of the applicable law in the absence of an effective choice of law by the parties.

(3) In the absence of a contrary indication of intention, the reference is to the local law of the state of the chosen law.

FARRIS ENGINEERING CORP. v. SERVICE BUREAU CORP.

406 F.2d 519 (3d Cir. 1969).

[...]

The complaint sought damages arising out of a breach of a contract for data processing services to be rendered by the defendant. The contract contained two paragraphs which are of importance here. One explicitly limited the liability of the supplier of data processing services to the amount paid by the customer for the services. The other provided that "this agreement shall be governed by the laws of New York."

The appellant makes a threshold claim that the contract is governed by New Jersey law.... New Jersey normally refers to the law of the place of contracting to determine the validity of a contractual provision.... In this case[,] New York was the place of contracting.... The New Jersey courts seem disposed to give effect to such a [choice of law] provision where the law chosen by the parties is that of a state to which the transaction is significantly related.... We add that we have found no comprehensive overriding New Jersey policy against the enforcement of the present type of contractual provision limiting liability, such as would be necessary to prevent the normal application of New Jersey conflict of law rules in this case. It follows that the validity of the challenged provision of the present contract is properly determined in accordance with New York law. And New York law treats such a contractual limitation as valid and enforceable....

* * * *

Proof of Foreign Law

Once a law is chosen (by whatever means or process), if it is a law foreign to the jurisdiction, it must be established. In effect, proving what the applicable foreign law provides is generally done through experts. Most courts do not have the linguistic, library, or resource capabilities to engage in the judicial notice of the foreign law. Each party will secure an expert on the law to testify about what provisions of the law are relevant and how they should be applied to the instant litigation. Obviously, such expert testimony will be calculated to advance the position of the party who retained the expert. The dueling between the experts may confound the court's mission of resolving the matter. The use of experts will certainly increase the costs of litigation substantially, as well as the time that must be dedicated to it. There is the further practical question of whether any expert or expert opinion can explain a foreign law or legal system sufficiently to generate a real understanding of them on the part of the court. Therefore, not only is the enterprise tainted by adversarial politics, but it also is beset by a sense of impracticality and a lack of realistic assessment. Insight into a foreign law assumes a cultural, sociological, and historical understanding.

In the federal court system, special masters have been used to deal with the foreign law aspects of a litigation. The designated special master usually has the language capability of reading the foreign statutory and decisional law and ordinarily will be an expert in the foreign legal system. The special master will be "bi-jural" in terms of professional culture. Why should such complex litigation be brought before a U.S. federal court? Unless the parties agree to translate everything themselves and/or to procure simultaneous translation and supply the court with an agreed-upon, certified foreign law expert, such suits probably should be dismissed. Such a practice would raise self-evident issues of access to and denial of justice.

The use of a special master solves some of the problems, but raises others. In particular, given the range of the special master's authority because of his language ability and cultural familiarity, the delegated agent of the court, in fact, may be exercising the court's authority and accomplishing its mandate. In effect, the special master would be performing the function of a judge without being invested as a judge. Do these circumstances point to the need for specialized courts? Are the cases too variable to accommodate all of them? Does the volume of current or potential transborder litigation justify the expenditure of resources? You should consider the range of problems and articulate a means or device for dealing with them. How would you advise clients in light of these circumstances?

In any event, the establishment of an applicable foreign law still must be addressed in the context of the existing system. There are several statutory regimes that provide rules by which to deal with the need to prove foreign law. In evaluating these regimes, you should assess how practically useful each of them is in the typical circumstances. What basic notions do they advance? What appears to be their core concerns? Do those core concerns respond to the practical problems that are likely to arise? How are they different? How are they similar? Is an ideal composite of them possible? Should proof of foreign law be a matter of fact or a matter of law? If a matter of fact, who decides it? Again, what do you tell clients in light of this consideration? Is proof of foreign law by itself sufficient to make transborder litigation untenable before municipal courts? Why?

Federal Rule of Civil Procedure 44.1

Determination of Foreign Law:

A party who intends to raise an issue concerning the law of a foreign country shall give notice in his pleadings or other reasonable written notice. The court, in determining foreign law, may consider any relevant material or source, including testimony, whether or not submitted by a party or admissible under the Federal Rules of Evidence. The court's determination shall be treated as a ruling on a question of law.

The rule clearly lays down several requirements for the litigant intending to rely on foreign law. First, notice is required. Such notice must be written and reasonable, though it need not be incorporated in the pleadings. A second clarification introduced by Rule 44.1 is that the court has the freedom to go beyond the material on foreign law presented by the parties. Thus, it may conduct its own research and consider any relevant material. Finally, the rule globally denominates the determination of an issue of foreign law as a question of law, not fact. The Advisory Committee explained the significance of this provision as follows:

> Under the third sentence, the court's determination of an issue of foreign law is to be treated as a ruling on a question of "law," not "fact," so that appellate review will not be narrowly confined by the "clearly erroneous" standard of Rule 52(a)....
>
> The new rule parallels Article IV of the Uniform Interstate and International Procedure Act, approved by the Commissioners on Uniform State Laws in 1962, except that section 4.03 of Article IV states that "[t]he court, not the jury" shall determine foreign law. The new rule does not address itself to this problem, since the rules refrain from allocating functions as between the court and the jury. See Rule 38(a). It has long been thought, however, that the jury is not the appropriate body to determine issues of foreign law.

State Statutes on Pleading and Proof of Foreign Law

Most states have either adopted some version of Rule 44.1 or enacted legislation authorizing judicial notice of foreign law. Only a few states still follow the common law fact doctrine.

New York Civil Practice Law and Rules

Rule 4511. Judicial notice of law

(a) When judicial notice shall be taken without request. Every court shall take judicial notice without request of the common law, constitutions and public statutes of the United States and of every state, territory and jurisdiction of the United States and of the official compilation of codes, rules and regulations of the state except those that relate solely to the organization or internal management of an agency of the state and of all local laws and county acts.

(b) When judicial notice may be taken without request; when it shall be taken on request. Every court may take judicial notice without request of private acts and resolutions of the Congress of the United States and of the legislature of the state; ordinances and regulations of officers, agencies or governmental subdivisions of the state or of the

United States; and the laws of foreign countries or their political subdivisions. Judicial notice shall be taken of matters specified in this subdivision if a party requests it, furnishes the court sufficient information to enable it to comply with the request, and has given each adverse party notice of his intention to request it. Notice shall be given in the pleadings or prior to the presentation of any evidence at the trial, but a court may require or permit other notice.

[. . .]

California Evidence Code

§ 452. Matters which may be judicially noticed. Judicial notice may be taken of the following matters to the extent that they are not embraced within section 451:

(a) The decisional, constitutional, and statutory law of any state of the United States and the resolutions and private acts of the Congress of the United States and of the Legislature of this state.

(b) Regulations and legislative enactments issued by or under the authority of the United States and of any state of the United States.

[. . .]

(f) The law of an organization of nations and of foreign nations and public entities in foreign nations.

[. . .]

§ 311. Procedure when foreign or sister-state law cannot be determined

If the law of an organization of nations, a foreign nation or a state other than this state, or a public entity in a foreign nation or a state other than this state, is applicable and such law cannot be determined, the court may, as the ends of justice require, either:

(a) Apply the law of this state if the court can do so consistently with the Constitution of the United States and the Constitution of this state; or

(b) Dismiss the action without prejudice or, in the case of a reviewing court, remand the case to the trial court with directions to dismiss the action without prejudice. (Stats. 1965, c. 299, § 311.)

Comment–Assembly Committee on Judiciary (1995 Main Volume)

. . . The last paragraph of Section 1875, which Section 311 supersedes, applies, "if the court is unable to determine" the applicable foreign law. Instead, Section 311 comes into operation if the applicable out-of-state law "cannot be determined." This revised language emphasizes that every effort should be made by the court to determine the applicable law before the case is otherwise disposed of under Section 311.

The reason why the court cannot determine the applicable foreign or sister-state law may be that the parties have not provided the court with sufficient information to make such determination. In such a case, the court may, of course, grant the parties additional time within which to obtain such information and make it available to the court. If they fail to obtain such information and the court is not satisfied that they made a reasonable effort to do so, the court may dismiss the action without prejudice. On the other hand, where counsel have made a reasonable effort and when all sources of information as to the applicable foreign or sister-state law are exhausted and the court cannot determine it, the court may either apply California law, within constitutional limits, or dismiss the action without prejudice.

§ 2. THE ENFORCEMENT OF FOREIGN JUDGMENTS

The question of whether and on what basis national courts should enforce foreign judgments restates in many respects the threshold question of jurisdiction. A major part of the scrutiny will focus upon whether the court of rendition had the proper authority to resolve the controversy between the parties. The question of enforcement will also be the practitioners' first concern when suit is being considered. There is no need to pursue a litigation that will not result in an enforceable judgment.

Ordinarily, foreign judicial judgments are enforced on the basis of international comity. Under modern laws, foreign judgments are no longer merely evidentiary elements that inform the domestic relitigation of the matter in the requested State. A foreign judgment results from a proceeding before a court of a foreign State and is entitled to be considered for enforcement on that basis. To maintain international harmony and judicial efficiency, the objective is enforcement, not relitigation. The enforcement of foreign judgments is a type of transborder *res judicata* and collateral estoppel.

Modern laws also generally exclude a merits review of foreign judgments for purposes of enforcement. Foreign judgments are usually assessed on a due process basis: Notice, an opportunity to be heard and to defend, and the impartial administration of justice. The judgment and the proceedings leading to it must be devoid of fraud and prejudice. At times, under the law of a number of countries, the requirement of reciprocity or "mutual guarantee" becomes a factor in the recognition and enforcement of foreign court judgments. Finally, the foreign judgment cannot violate the requested State's public policy.

Most national laws on the enforcement of foreign judgments also require that the court of rendition have had proper jurisdiction: Its jurisdiction over the defendant and the subject matter. The former usually is determined by reference to the law of the place of enforcement and the latter by the law of the place of rendition. Enforcement can also be challenged on the basis that the assertion of jurisdiction by the foreign court was contrary to the choice-of-forum clause in the parties' contract. It could also be argued that jurisdiction was improper because it was based on a form of "tag" or "transient" jurisdiction and not acceptable personal service. It could be alleged further that another venue was so clearly the best place for litigation that no other forum could assert jurisdiction—a type of reverse *forum non conveniens* argument.

Courts of enforcement in the United States will not deny effect to a foreign judgment if it contains legal or factual errors. A foreign judgment cannot be challenged on the basis that it was rendered pursuant to a trial procedure different from the one that applies in the United States. The test is conformity to the dictates of legal civilization, not to the intricacies of U.S. procedure. The default status of a foreign judgment does not create a presumption of nonenforceability. As long as the court of rendition had proper *in personam* jurisdiction over the defendant, only due process violations, public policy, fraud, or collusion can impede enforcement.

The Restatement (Third) of Foreign Relations Law (1986) describes the common law of foreign judgment enforcement:

§ 481. Recognition and Enforcement of Foreign Judgments

(1) Except as provided in § 482, a final judgment of a court of a foreign state granting or denying recovery of a sum of money, establishing or confirming the status of a person, or determining interests in property, is conclusive between the parties, and is entitled to recognition in courts in the United States.

(2) A judgment entitled to recognition under Subsection (1) may be enforced by any party or its successor or assigns against any other party, its successors or assigns, in accordance with the procedure for enforcement of judgments applicable where enforcement is sought.

§ 482. Grounds for Nonrecognition of Foreign Judgments

(1) A court in the United States may not recognize a judgment of the court of a foreign state if:

(a) the judgment was rendered under a judicial system that does not provide impartial tribunals or procedures compatible with due process of law; or

(b) the court that rendered the judgment did not have jurisdiction over the defendant in accordance with the law of the rendering state and with rules set forth in § 421 [outlining the analysis under traditional U.S. Due Process standards].

(2) A court in the United States need not recognize a judgment of a court of a foreign state if:

(a) the court that rendered the judgment did not have jurisdiction of the subject matter of the action;

(b) the defendant did not receive notice of the proceedings in sufficient time to enable him to defend;

(c) the judgment was obtained by fraud;

(d) the cause of action on which the judgment was based, or the judgment itself, is repugnant to the public policy of the United States or of the State where recognition is sought;

(e) the judgment conflicts with another final judgment that is entitled to recognition; or

(f) the proceeding in the foreign court was contrary to an agreement between the parties to submit the controversy on which the judgment is based to another forum.

In addition, there are two uniform laws on the question: The Uniform Foreign Money–Judgment Recognition Act of 1962 (Recognition Act), 13 ULA 149 (1986), and the Uniform Enforcement of Foreign Judgments Revised Act of 1964 (Enforcement Act), 13 ULA 261 (1986).

Generally, foreign money judgments are upheld and enforced in the United States. This allows U.S. business parties to engage in global commerce and promotes a worldwide rule of law. While Congress has not specifically exercised its power to facilitate the recognition and enforcement of foreign court judgments, many states have adopted the Recognition Act which specifically recognizes the validity of foreign judgments and makes streamlined procedures available to foreign plaintiffs to have the results of foreign litigation enforced swiftly, predictably, and efficiently. The minimum requirement for enforcement is that the judgment must have been obtained or rendered in compliance with the Recognition Act, which is now in force in twenty-two states. One of the main objectives of the Recognition Act was to translate common-law precedent into statutory form to convince foreign civil law courts that U.S. jurisdictions would recognize foreign judgments and that U.S. judgments, as a consequence, were entitled to the same treatment abroad. *See* Adold Homburger, *Recognition and Enforcement of Foreign Judgments: A New Yorker Reflects on Uniform Acts*, 18 AM. J. COMP. L. 367, 270, 404 (1970).

The Recognition Act applies to foreign judgments which are considered to be final, conclusive, and enforceable where rendered even though an appeal may be pending. Section 3 provides that judgments which satisfy the grounds for recognition are conclusive between the parties, and will be enforced in the same manner as a judgment from another state of the United States which is entitled to full faith and credit. The Recognition Act codifies grounds which may prevent recognition of a foreign judgment. In this connection, however, § 5(a)(3) of the Recognition Act specifies that a court may not refuse to recognize a foreign judgment for lack of personal jurisdiction if the defendant agreed to submit to the jurisdiction of the foreign court with respect to the matter involved.

The provisions of the Recognition Act apply only to the recognition of foreign judgments. These provisions do not apply to the collection of the judgment in the forum's territory. In these circumstances, resort must be had to the procedures of the Enforcement Act. The Enforcement Act primarily pertains to judgments entered by other state courts in the United States, but it also applies to judgments rendered by other courts which are entitled to full faith and credit. Judgments rendered by courts of other countries which are recognized under the Recognition Act are enforced under the Enforcement Act as judgments entitled to full faith and credit. Finally, the application of the Recognition Act and the Enforcement Act are not necessarily uniform in the various states.

In assessing the text of the Recognition Act, you should focus upon the conditions that are established for recognition and enforcement. What is meant by the term "conclusive"? How does it function in the scheme for enforcement? What State systems might be targeted by the language of § 4(a)(1)? Which law governs determinations under § 4(a)(2) and (3)? How is recognition to be distinguished from enforcement? You should read Pittman, Note, *The Public Policy Exception to the Recognition of Foreign Judgments*, 22 VAND. J. TRANSNAT'L L. 969, 970–71 (1989) ("recognition" meaning the court sees the judgment as binding whereas "enforcement" means that the requested court orders the relief granted by the court of rendition). Explain the meaning and implied content of § 4(b)(5) and (6). Notice the shifting of the burden in § 5; it establishes, in effect, a presumption of legitimate jurisdiction. Does the alteration make the rule more effective? Analyze and explain each of the grounds.

13 UNIFORM LAWS ANNOTATED 261, (1)(2) (1986)

Commissioners' Prefatory Note

In most states of the Union, the law on recognition of judgments from foreign countries is not codified. In a large number of civil law countries, grant of conclusive effect to money-judgments from foreign courts is made dependent upon reciprocity. Judgments rendered in the United States have in many instances been refused recognition abroad either because the foreign court was not satisfied that local judgments would be recognized in the American jurisdiction involved or because no certification of existence of reciprocity could be obtained from the foreign government in countries where existence of reciprocity must be certified to the courts by the government. Codification by a state of its rules on the recognition of money-judgments rendered in a foreign court will make it more likely that judgments rendered in the state will be recognized abroad.

The Act states rules that have long been applied by the majority of courts in this country. In some respects the Act may not go as far as the decision. The Act makes clear that a court is privileged to give the judgment of the court of a foreign country greater effect than it is required to do by the provisions of the Act. In codifying what bases for assumption of personal jurisdiction will be recognized, which is an area of the law still in evolution, the Act adopts the policy of listing bases accepted generally today and preserving for the courts the right to recognize still other bases. Because the Act is not selective and applied to judgments from any foreign court, the Act states that judgments rendered under a system which does not provide impartial tribunals or procedures compatible with the requirements of due process of law shall neither be recognized nor enforced.

The Act does not prescribe a uniform enforcement procedure. Instead, the Act provides that a judgment entitled to recognition will be enforceable in the same manner as the judgment of a court of a sister state which is entitled to full faith and credit.

Uniform Foreign Money-Judgments Recognition Act of 1962

§ 1. [Definitions]

As used in this Act:

(1) "foreign state" means any governmental unit other than the United States, or any state, district, commonwealth, territory, insular possession thereof, or the Panama Canal Zone, the Trust Territory of the Pacific Island, or the Ryukyu Islands;

(2) "foreign judgment" means any judgment of a foreign state granting or denying recovery of a sum of money, other than a judgment for taxes, a fine or other penalty, or a judgment for support in matrimonial or family matters.

§ 2. [Applicability]

This Act applies to any foreign judgment that is final and conclusive and enforceable where rendered even though an appeal therefrom is pending or it is subject to appeal.

§ 3. [Recognition and Enforcement]

Except as provided in section 4, a foreign judgment meeting the requirements of section 2 is conclusive between the parties to the extent that it grants or denies recovery of a sum of money. The foreign judgment is enforceable in the same manner as the judgment of a sister state which is entitled to full faith and credit.

§ 4. [Grounds for Non-recognition]

(a) A foreign judgment is not conclusive if:

(1) the judgment was rendered under a system which does not provide impartial tribunals or procedures compatible with the requirements of due process of law;

(2) the foreign court did not have personal jurisdiction over the defendant; or

(3) the foreign court did not have jurisdiction over the subject matter.

(b) A foreign judgment need not be recognized if

(1) the defendant in the proceedings in the foreign court did not receive notice of the proceedings in sufficient time to enable him to defend;

(2) the judgment was obtained by fraud;

(3) the [cause of action] or [claim for relief] on which the judgment is based is repugnant to the public policy of this state;

(4) the judgment conflicts with another final and conclusive judgment;

(5) the proceeding in the foreign court was contrary to an agreement between the parties under which the dispute in question was to be settled otherwise than by proceedings in that court; or

(6) in the case of jurisdiction based only on personal service, the foreign court was a seriously inconvenient forum for the trial of the action.

§ 5. [Personal Jurisdiction]

(a) The foreign judgment shall not be refused recognition for lack of personal jurisdiction if:

(1) the defendant was served personally in the foreign state;

(2) the defendant voluntarily appeared in the proceedings, other than for the purpose of protecting property seized or threatened with seizure in the proceedings or of contesting the jurisdiction of the court over him;

(3) the defendant prior to the commencement of the proceedings had agreed to submit to the jurisdiction of the foreign court with respect to the subject matter involved;

(4) the defendant was domiciled in the foreign state when the proceedings were instituted, or, being a corporate body had its principal place of business, was incorporated, or had otherwise acquired corporate status, in the foreign state;

(5) the defendant has a business office in the foreign state and the proceedings in the foreign court involved a [cause of action] or [claim for relief] arising out of business done by the defendant through that office in the foreign state; or

(6) the defendant operated a motor vehicle or airplane in the foreign state and the proceedings involved a [cause of action] or [claim for relief] arising out of such operation.

(b) The courts of this state may recognize other bases of jurisdiction.

§ 6. [Stay in Case of Appeal]

If the defendant satisfies the court either that an appeal is pending or that he is entitled and intends to appeal from the foreign judgment, the court may stay the proceedings until the appeal has been determined or until the expiration of a period of time sufficient to enable the defendant to prosecute the appeal.

§ 7. [Saving Clause]

This Act does not prevent the recognition of a foreign judgment in situations not covered by this Act.

§ 8. [Uniformity of Interpretation]

This Act shall be so construed as to effectuate its general purpose to make uniform the law of those states which enact it.

§ 9. [Short Title]

This Act may be cited as the Uniform Foreign Money–Judgments Recognition Act.

* * * *

Professors von Mehren and Trautman provide the following summary of the rationale underlying the enforcement of foreign judgments:

> We believe that at least five policies are important: a desire to avoid the duplication of effort and consequent waste involved in reconsidering a matter that has already been litigated; a related concern to protect the successful litigant, whether plaintiff or defendant, from harassing or evasive tactics on the part of his previously unsuccessful opponent; a policy against making the availability of local enforcement the decisive element, as a practical matter, in the plaintiff's choice of forum; and interest in fostering stability and unity in an international order in which many aspects of life are not confined to any single jurisdiction; and, in certain classes of cases, a belief that the rendering jurisdiction is a more appropriate forum than the recognizing jurisdiction, either because the former was more convenient as the predominantly concerned jurisdiction or for some other reason its views as to the merits should prevail.
>
> *See* von Mehren & Trautman, *Recognition of Foreign Adjudications: A Survey and a Suggested Approach*, 81 HARV. L. REV. 1601, 1603–04 (1968).

Notes and Questions

1. Under U.S. law, domestic or sister state judgments are enforceable on a nationwide basis under the doctrine of full faith and credit. For U.S. judgments abroad, there is no transborder equivalent of full faith and credit. The United States is not a party to any bilateral or multilateral treaty on the enforcement of foreign judgments. Agreement on a transborder regime for the enforcement of judgments has been elusive even between allied, like-minded, and similar legal systems.

2. Evaluate each of the statutory frameworks for the regulation of the enforcement of foreign judgments under U.S. and state law. Are there points

of commonality that can serve as the foundation for a general rule application? What factors seem to reappear?

3. How is the propriety of the rendering court's jurisdiction established?

4. How would you define the phrase "impartial tribunals" and the phrase "procedures compatible with the requirements of due process"? In particular, in the Recognition Act, how do you square § 4(a)(1) and § 4(b)(1)? Are they ultimately consistent?

5. Would an Islamic court qualify as an "impartial tribunal"? What about a "Truth and Reconciliation" tribunal?

6. To what extent are political considerations lurking below the surface of the stated rules?

7. What is meant by "finality"?

8. Is federal law distinct and different from state law on these matters?

9. Of the several rationales they advance for the enforcement of foreign judgments in the United States, which of von Mehren and Trautman's proposals is most persuasive and why?

The Case Law

The U.S. Constitution requires each state to give full faith and credit to judgments rendered by courts of other states. This constitutional requirement does not apply to judgments made by foreign tribunals. Nonetheless, American courts historically have recognized and enforced foreign judgments as a matter of comity to maintain appropriate international relations. The basic requirements for enforcement were specified in *Hilton v. Guyot*, 159 U.S. 113, 205–06, 16 S.Ct. 139, 40 L.Ed. 95 (1895):

> When an action is brought in a court of this country, by a citizen of a foreign country against one of our own citizens, to recover a sum of money adjudged by a court of that country to be due from the defendant to the plaintiff, and the foreign judgment appears to have been rendered by a competent court, having jurisdiction of the cause and of the parties, and upon due allegations and proofs, and opportunity to defend against them, and its proceedings are according to the course of a civilized jurisprudence, and are stated in a clear and formal record, the judgment is *prima facie* evidence, at least, of the truth of the matter adjudged; and the judgment is conclusive upon the merits tried in the foreign court, unless some special ground is shown for impeaching it as by showing that it was affected by fraud or prejudice, or that by the principles of international law, and by the comity of our own country, it is not entitled to full credit and effect.

Thus, under the common law holding of *Hilton*, foreign judgments will be enforced in American courts if (i) there is a final judgment, (ii) the foreign court had subject matter jurisdiction and jurisdiction over the parties, (iii) gave proper and timely notice of the proceedings, (iv) the defendant had the opportunity to present a defense to a regularly constituted, impartial tribunal, and (v) the proceedings were conducted in a regular manner according to accepted notions of civilized justice. It should be noted that these criteria do not permit inquiry into the merits or the correctness of the decision rendered by the foreign tribunal. While it is not entirely settled, it does appear that reciprocity is not a requirement for the recognition and enforcement of a foreign judgment under U.S. law. *See Banco Nacional de Cuba v. Sabbatino*, 376 U.S. 398, 84 S.Ct. 923, 11 L.Ed.2d 804 (1964).

HILTON v. GUYOT

159 U.S. 113, 16 S.Ct. 139, 40 L.Ed. 95 (1895).

[. . .]

International law, in its widest and most comprehensive sense—including not only questions of right between nations, governed by what has been appropriately called the law of nations; but also questions arising under what is usually called private international law, or the conflict of laws, and concerning the rights of persons within the territory and dominion of one nation, by reasons of acts, private or public, done within the dominions of another nation—is part of our law, and must be ascertained and administered by the courts of justice, as often as such questions are presented in litigation between man and man, duly submitted to their determination.

The most certain guide, no doubt, for the decision of such questions is a treaty or a statute of this country. But when, as is the case here, there is no written law upon the subject, the duty still rests upon the judicial tribunals of ascertaining and declaring what the law is, whenever it becomes necessary to do so, in order to determine the rights of parties to suits regularly brought before them. In doing this, the courts must obtain such aid as they can from judicial decisions, from the works of jurists and commentators, and from the acts and usages of civilized nations. . . .

No law has any effect, of its own force, beyond the limits of the sovereignty from which its authority is derived. The extent to which the law of one nation, as put in force within its territory, whether by executive order, by legislative act, or by judicial decree, shall be allowed to operate within the dominion of another nation, depends upon what our greatest jurists have been content to call "the comity of nations." Although the phrase has been often criticized, no satisfactory substitute has been suggested.

[. . .]

Chancellor Kent says: "The effect to be given to foreign 'comity,' in the legal sense, is neither a matter of absolute obligation, on the one hand, nor of mere courtesy and good will, upon the other. But it is the recognition which one nation allows within its territory to the legislative, executive or judicial acts of another nation, having due regard both to international duty and convenience, and to the rights of its own citizens or of other persons who are under the protection of its laws ... judgment is altogether a matter of comity, in cases where it is not regulated by treaty." 2 Kent Com. (6th ed.) 120.

In order to appreciate the weight of the various authorities cited at the bar, it is important to distinguish different kinds of judgments. Every foreign judgment, of whatever nature, in order to be entitled to any effect, must have been rendered by a court having jurisdiction of the cause, and upon regular proceedings and due notice. In alluding to different kinds of judgments, therefore, such jurisdiction, proceedings, and notice will be assumed. It will also be assumed that they are untainted by fraud....

[...]

The extraterritorial effect of judgments *in personam*, at law or in equity, may differ, according to the parties to the cause. A judgment of that kind between two citizens or residents of the country, and thereby subject to the jurisdiction, in which it is rendered, may be held conclusive as between them everywhere. So, if a foreigner invokes the jurisdiction by bringing an action against a citizen, both may be held bound by a judgment in favor of either. And if a citizen sues a foreigner, and judgment is rendered in favor of the latter, both may be held equally bound....

The effect to which a judgment, purely executory, rendered in favor of a citizen or resident of the country, in a suit there brought by him against a foreigner, may be entitled in an action thereon against the latter in his own country—as is the case now before us—presents a more difficult question, upon which there has been some diversity of opinion....

The law upon this subject, as understood in the United States, at the time of their separation from the mother country, was ... that foreign judgments were only *prima facie* evidence on the matter which they purported to decide; and that by the common law, before the American Revolution, all the courts of the several Colonies and States were deemed foreign to each other, and consequently judgments rendered by any one of them were considered as foreign judgments, and their merits reexaminable in another Colony, not only as to the jurisdiction of the court which pronounced them, but also as to the merits of the controversy, to the extent to which they were understood to be reexaminable in England....

It was because of that condition of the law, as between the American Colonies and States, that the United States, at the very beginning of their existence as a nation, ordained that full faith and credit should be given to the judgments of one of the States of the Union in the courts of another of those States.

[. . .]

The decisions of this court have clearly recognized that judgments of a foreign state are *prima facie* evidence only, and that, but for these constitutional and legislative provisions, judgments of a State of the Union, when sued upon in another State, would have no greater effect. . . .

In view of all the authorities . . . we are satisfied that, where there has been opportunity for a full and fair trial abroad before a court of competent jurisdiction, conducting the trial upon regular proceedings, after due citation or voluntary appearance of the defendant, and under a system of jurisprudence likely to secure an impartial administration of justice between the citizens of its own country and those of other countries, and there is nothing to show either prejudice in the court, or in the system of laws under which it was sitting, or fraud in procuring the judgment, or any other special reason why the comity of this nation should not allow it full effect, the merits of the case should not, in an action brought in this country upon the judgment, be tried afresh, as on a new trial or an appeal, upon the mere assertion of the party that the judgment was erroneous in law or in fact. The defendants, therefore, cannot be permitted, upon that general ground, to contest the validity or the effect of the judgment sued on.

[. . .]

It is further objected that the appearance and litigation of the defendants in the French tribunals were not voluntary, but by legal compulsion, and therefore that the French courts never acquired such jurisdiction over the defendants, that they should be held bound by the judgment. . . .

The present case is not one of a person traveling through or casually found in a foreign country. The defendants, although they were not citizens or residents of the State of New York, and their principal place of business was in the city of New York, yet had a storehouse and an agent in Paris, and were accustomed to purchase large quantities of goods there, although they did not make sales in France. Under such circumstances, evidence that their sole object in appearing and carrying on the litigation in the French courts was to prevent property, in their storehouse at Paris, belonging to them, and within the jurisdiction, but not in the custody, of those courts, from being taken in satisfaction of any judgment that might be recovered against them, would not, according to our law, show that those courts did not acquire jurisdiction of the persons of the defendants.

It is next objected that in those courts one of the plaintiffs was permitted to testify not under oath, and was not subjected to cross-examination by the opposite party, and that the defendants were, therefore, deprived of safeguards which are by our law considered essential to secure honesty and to detect fraud in a witness; and also that documents and papers were admitted in evidence, with which the defendants had no connection, and which would not be admissible under our own system of jurisprudence. But it having been shown by the plaintiffs, and hardly denied by the defendants, that the practice followed and the method of examining witnesses were according to the laws of France, we are not prepared to hold that the fact that the procedure in these respects differed from that of our own courts is, of itself, a sufficient ground for impeaching the foreign judgment.

[. . .]

It must, however, always be kept in mind that it is the paramount duty of the court, before which any suit is brought, to see to it that the parties have had a fair and impartial trial, before a final decision is rendered against either party.

When an action is brought in a court of this country, by a citizen of a foreign country against one of our own citizens, to recover a sum of money adjudged by a court of that country to be due from the defendant to the plaintiff, and the foreign judgment appears to have been rendered by a competent court, having jurisdiction of the cause and of the parties, and upon due allegations and proofs, and opportunity to defend against them, and its proceedings are according to the course of a civilized jurisprudence, and are stated in a clear and formal record, the judgment is *prima facie* evidence, at least, of the truth of the matter adjudged; and it should be held conclusive upon the merits tried in the foreign court, unless some special ground is shown for impeaching the judgment, as by showing, that it was affected by fraud or prejudice, or that, by the principles of international law, and by the comity of our own country, it should not be given full credit and effect.

[. . .]

But whether those decisions can be followed in regard to foreign judgments, consistently with our own decisions as to impeaching domestic judgments for fraud, it is unnecessary in this case to determine, because there is a distinct and independent ground upon which we are satisfied that the comity of our nation does not require us to give conclusive effect to the judgments of the courts of France; and that ground is, the want of reciprocity, on the part of France, as to the effect to be given to the judgments of this and other foreign countries. . . .

[W]hen the judgments of tribunals of foreign countries against the citizens of France are sued upon in the courts of France, the merits of the controversies upon which those judgments are based are examined anew, unless a treaty to the contrary effect exists between the Republic of France and the country in which such judgment is obtained, (which is not the case between the Republic of France and the United States,) and that the tribunals of the Republic of France give no force and effect, within the jurisdiction of that country, to the judgments duly rendered by courts of competent jurisdiction of the United States against citizens of France after proper personal service of the process of those courts has been made thereon in this country. . . .

It appears, therefore, that there is hardly a civilized nation on either continent, which, by its general law, allows conclusive effect to an executory foreign judgment for the recovery of money. In France, and in a few smaller States—Norway, Portugal, Greece, Monaco, and Haiti—the merits of the controversy are reviewed, as of course, allowing to the foreign judgment, at the most, no more effect than of being *prima facie* evidence of the justice of the claim. In the great majority of the countries on the continent of Europe—in Belgium, Holland, Denmark, Sweden, Germany, in many cantons of Switzerland, in Russia and Poland, in Rumania, in Austria and Hungary, (perhaps in Italy) and in Spain—as well as in Egypt, in Mexico, and in a great part of South America, the judgment rendered in a foreign country is allowed the same effect only as the courts of that country allow to the judgments of the country in which the judgment in question is sought to be executed.

The reasonable, if not the necessary, conclusion appears to us to be that judgments rendered in France, or in any other foreign country, by the laws of which our own judgments are reviewable upon the merits, are not entitled to full credit and conclusive effect when sued upon in this country, but are prima facie evidence only of the justice of the plaintiffs' claim.

In holding such a judgment, for want of reciprocity, not to be conclusive evidence of the merits of the claim, we do not proceed upon any theory of retaliation upon one person by reason of injustice done to another; but upon the broad ground that international law is founded upon mutuality and reciprocity, and that by the principles of international law recognized in most civilized nations, and by the comity of our own country, which it is our judicial duty to know and to declare, the judgment is not entitled to be considered conclusive. By our law, at the time of the adoption of the Constitution, a foreign judgment was considered as *prima facie* evidence, and not conclusive. There is no statute of the United States and no treaty of the United States with France, or with any other nation, which has changed that law, or has made any provision upon the subject. It is not to be supposed that, if any statute or treaty had been or should be made, it would recognize as conclusive the judgments of any country, which did not give like effect to our own judgments. In the absence of statute or treaty, it appears to us equally unwarrantable to assume that the comity of the United States requires anything more.

[. . .]

FULLER, J. dissenting;

Plaintiffs brought their action on a judgment recovered by them against the defendants in the courts of France, which courts had jurisdiction over person and subject matter, and in respect of which judgment no fraud was alleged, except in particulars contested in and considered by the French courts. The question is whether under these circumstances, and in the absence of a treaty or act of Congress, the judgment is reexaminable upon the merits. This question I regard as one to be determined by the ordinary and settled rule in respect of allowing a party, who has had an opportunity to prove his case in a competent court, to retry it on the merits, and it seems to me that the doctrine of *res judicata* applicable to domestic judgments should be applied to foreign judgments as well, and rests on the same general ground of public policy that there should be an end of litigation.

This application of the doctrine is in accordance with our own jurisprudence, and it is not necessary that we should hold it to be required by some rule of international law. The fundamental principle concerning judgments is that disputes are finally determined by them, and I am unable to perceive why a judgment *in personam* which is not open to question on the ground of want of jurisdiction, either intrinsically or over the parties, or of fraud, or on any other recognized ground of impeachment, should not be held *inter partes*, though recovered abroad, conclusive on the merits. . . .

I cannot yield my assent to the proposition that because by legislation and judicial decision in France that effect is not given to judgments recovered in this country which, according to our jurisprudence, we think should be given to judgments wherever recovered, (subject, of course, to the recognized exceptions,) therefore we should pursue the same line of conduct as respects the judgments of French tribunals. The application of the doctrine of *res judicata* does not rest in discretion; and it is for the government, and not for its courts, to adopt the principle of retorsion, if deemed under any circumstances desirable or necessary.

As the court expressly abstains from deciding whether the judgment is impeachable on the ground of fraud, I refrain from any observation on that branch of the case.

* * * *

The *Hunt* Saga testifies to a number of different features of transborder litigation and contains a virtually programmatic account of the U.S. law on the enforcement of foreign judgments. The liability exposure in this case was in the range of $34 to $45 million (USD). It was, therefore, imperative for the defendant—after failing so badly in the English courts—to create a barrier to the enforcement of the English court judgment in the United States, specifically Texas. The potential liability justified a large expenditure for legal representation and for political solutions, both of which were undertaken. High-priced legal talent cannot always change the reality of the circumstances. Studied, able arguments were made but were of no avail in the circumstances. The "last ditch" attempt came close, but failed—surprisingly—due to a lack of evidence (maybe, none could be gathered).

A number of significant rules are established as to the question of enforcement. Identify them by responding to the following questions: What role does state law play in the enforcement of foreign court judgments? Does the doctrine of full faith and credit apply? If not, why not? What presumption does the court establish in regard to judgments from so-called favored systems? When and how can the presumption be rebutted? Which countries have "favored" systems? What defenses to enforcement exist? Why should U.S. legal standards determine the jurisdiction of a foreign court? Finally, what is the status of reciprocity according to the *Hunt* court?

HUNT v. BP EXPLORATION COMPANY (LIBYA) LTD.

492 F.Supp. 885 (N.D. Tex. 1980).

[Hunt I]

[. . .]

In this diversity action, *Erie Railroad Co. v. Tompkins*, 304 U.S. 64, 58 S. Ct. 817, 82 L. Ed. 1188 (1938), requires that a federal district court apply the law of the forum state. In *Klaxon Co. v. Stentor Electric Mfg. Co.*, 313 U.S. 487, 61 S. Ct. 1020, 85 L. Ed. 1477 (1941), the Supreme Court held that *Erie* required that the conflict of laws rules to be applied in a federal court must conform to those that would be applied in the courts of the forum state.... Courts, both federal and state, in the absence of federal preemptive actions, have held that state law governs the recognition and enforcement of foreign country judgments....

[. . .]

Its requirement of reciprocity aside, *Hilton v. Guyot* has a substantial following by courts in this country with respect to the recognition and enforcement of foreign-country judgments. ...Its application is, however, unlike the relatively ministerial task of applying the constitutional requirements of full faith and credit in recognition of sister state judgments. Applying the *Hilton v. Guyot* principles of comity instead of a constitutional requirement in order to determine whether a foreign country judgment should be recognized presents difficult social and public policy judgments:

> "Comity is a recognition which one nation extends within its own territory to the legislative, executive, or judicial acts of another. It is not a rule of law, but one of practice, convenience, and expediency. Although more than mere courtesy and accommodation, comity does not achieve the force of an imperative or obligation. Rather, it is a nation's expression of understanding which demonstrates due regard both to international duty and convenience and the rights of persons protected by its own laws. Comity should be withheld only when its acceptance would be contrary or prejudicial to the interest of the nation called upon to give it effect." *Somportex Ltd. v. Philadelphia Chewing Gum Corp.*....

Where, as here, the rendering forum's system of jurisprudence has been a model for other countries in the free world, and whose judges are of unquestioned integrity independent of the political winds of the moment, the judgment rendered is entitled to a more ministerial, less technocratic, recognition decisional process. The basis elements needed to establish a *prima facie* case under a *Hilton v. Guyot* standard that conclusive effect should be given to a foreign country judgment—that the rendering court had jurisdiction over the person and subject matter, that there was timely notice and an opportunity to present a defense, that no fraud was involved, that the proceedings were according to a civilized jurisprudence—are the same for both favored and nonfavored systems.... But the elements of the *prima facie* case are more likely to be met and it is less likely that such *prima facie* cases would be rebutted for judgments from favored systems.

In this case, Hunt cannot seriously assert that there was not timely notice and opportunity to defend, that fraud was involved or that the proceedings were not rendered according to a civilized jurisprudence. The only elements of the *prima facie* case seriously challenged by Hunt are as to the rendering court's jurisdiction over him and over the subject matter.

Hunt asserts, correctly, that if the English court had no personal jurisdiction over him, the judgment should not be recognized. The record reflects, however, that the English court did have jurisdiction over Hunt, certainly as measured by British law.... [T]his Court feels that in the interest of affording United States citizens a reasonable degree of certainty as to when our own courts will, under principles of comity, enforce a judgment rendered against such citizens in foreign countries, the issue of whether the foreign country had jurisdiction over the United States national should be determined by our own standards of judicial power as promulgated by the Supreme Court under the due process clause of the Fourteenth Amendment.

[...]

Hunt ... argues that the English judgment violates the public policy of Texas and the United States and so should be denied recognition. The argument is: (1) English courts no longer accept American judgments based upon American statutes; (2) the judgment is based on an English statute which abrogated the common law of England; (3) the judgment imposes a statutory penalty in the absence of any wrongdoing by Hunt; and (4) the English judgment is in violation of American public policy because it abrogates the fundamental right to contract. These assertions do not support denial, even assuming *arguendo* that (1) is true.

Hunt's argument that an American judgment would not be recognized in England and so should not, on public policy grounds, be recognized here is in essence an assertion that reciprocity is an essential element of recognition. The court disagrees.

Though the *Hilton* case required reciprocity as a condition of recognition, American decisions since *Hilton* have moved "decisively away from the requirement of reciprocity as a condition of recognition." ... Indeed, the draftsmen of the Uniform Foreign Money Judgment Recognition Act, "consciously rejected reciprocity as a factor to [consider] in recognition of foreign money judgments...."

There is little justification for judicial imposition of a reciprocity requirement. An argument often made is that reciprocity encourages foreign courts to recognize U.S. judgments. Yet, requiring reciprocity would arbitrarily penalize "private individuals for positions taken by foreign governments and ... such a rule has little if any constructive effect, but tends instead to a general breakdown of recognition practice." ... Application of reciprocity would also reduce predictability in the recognition of foreign court judgments: The reciprocity rule is difficult to apply both because of uncertainty as to just how much foreign recognition of American judgments should be considered adequate and because courts are ill-equipped to determine foreign law.... Moreover, even if reciprocity can be used to bring pressure on foreign countries to recognize American judgments, such utilization of reciprocity would probably be more effective and appropriate as part of executive or legislative action....

[...]

Hunt's assertion that the English judgment offends both Texas and American public policy because the judgment is based on an English statute which abrogated the common law of England is without merit. Taken to its conclusion, this principle would mean that no foreign judgment could be recognized if it is based on law which is contrary to the English common law. Conformity with the common law is not an element of recognition.

Third, Hunt asserts that the judgment, based on the Act, is a form of "statutory penalty," in that Hunt was not guilty of any breach of contract "when he is not at fault." ... Hunt's "statutory penalty" argument fails. The meaning of "statutory penalty" as used here is not clear. It appears to be a characterization of the circumstances that Hunt entered into a business transaction upon an express agreement that he would not be personally liable for any breach, but finds himself held liable to the tune of some $35 million—by virtue of a British statute, and not the common law.

The Act is no more, but no less than a legislative scheme to allocate losses suffered by parties when a court discharges full performance of a contract.... [T]he statute cannot be considered penal. Indeed, the statute has distinct common law roots....

Fourth, Hunt argues that the English judgment violates Texas public policy because it permits the recovery of prejudgment interest on a sum which was uncertain until time of judgment. United States courts generally declare that to do so would contravene public policy. "Although the decisions are not entirely consistent in application, they normally will not deny recognition merely because the law or practice of the foreign country differs, even if markedly, from that of the recognition forum." ... The level of contravention would have to be high before recognition would be denied on public policy grounds....

[. . .]

Even assuming that the recovery of prejudgment interest on a sum which was uncertain until time of judgment is permitted by English law and would not be permitted in Texas, this dissimilarity with Texas law cannot be said to rise any higher than the dissimilarities found tolerable in . . . [other cases].

Finally, Hunt asserts that the English judgment is in violation of American public policy because it violates the fundamental right to contract by requiring Hunt to personally pay a judgment contrary to contractual provision. The argument is little more than a quarrel with the substantive law of England. Unless categorized as violative of good morals and natural justice . . . that quarrel reduces to an argument that preclusive effect ought to be denied. . . .

Hunt next argues that the English judgment is not entitled to recognition because it is now on appeal; and the decision of the Court of Appeal will be subject to review by the House of Lords. "It is unsettled whether an American court will apply the foreign court's rules of *res judicata* and collateral estoppel when called upon to recognize the foreign court's judgment." . . . In the absence of Texas precedent on the effect of an appeal in a foreign country judgment on its *res judicata* effect, it is doubtful that a Texas court will grant more conclusive effect to a foreign country judgment being appealed than a Texas judgment being appealed. Existing precedent on comity, the principle under which foreign country judgments are recognized, lends support to this assumption. . . .

[. . .]

In sum, it is likely that Texas courts will not permit a foreign country judgment to have *res judicata* effects until appeals have been exhausted. . . . [I]t is necessary for this court to stay the proceedings until a final determination of the proceedings in England.

Many of the reasons for recognition and enforcement of foreign country judgments are the same as for giving conclusive effect to domestic judgments: prevention of harassment of the successful party, elimination of duplicative judicial proceedings, and providing some measure of settled expectations to the parties. . . . In a domestic context, the benefits of preclusion are palpable. In our Union, since courts in each state are subject to due process limitations, are subject to the same overlap of federal laws and the Constitution, are sharing to a large extent the same body of court precedents and socioeconomic ideas and are presumptively fair and competent, the benefits of giving conclusive effect are not balanced by any recognizable costs. Giving an automatically conclusive effect—full faith and credit—to sister state judgments could be fully justified on the grounds of fairness to litigants and judicial economy; there is no reason for a second trial—the rendering forum had at least the constitutionally requisite contacts with the litigant, there is little possibility of an error in the rendering forum and the substantive policies effected by that forum are likely fully acceptable in the recognizing forum.

The benefit-cost calculation for giving an automatically conclusive effect to foreign country judgments is far less favorable. There is less expectation that the courts of a foreign country will follow procedures which would comport with our notions of due process and jurisdiction and that they will apply substantively tolerable laws. Moreover, especially if the loser in the initial litigation is American, there will be suspicions here of unfairness or fraud. The modern versions of the *Hilton v. Guyot* rule—neither pretending that the initial litigation never occurred, nor giving an automatic conclusive effect—is a natural and tempered response to the tension between the benefits and costs of giving effect to foreign country judgments. By going to the halfway house, courts can deny effect to foreign country judgments when the rendering court has acted in ways intolerable by our country's then-felt ideal of fundamental fairness.

In this case, the *Hilton v. Guyot* mode of analysis did not call for a full technocratic analysis of benefit and cost. Because this was an English judgment, in the absence of proof to the contrary, it was not necessary, for example, to gauge the fairness of the initial trial. In sum, a litigant is entitled to no more than one clean bite of one clean apple—at least at the table of our British brethren.

Proceedings in this action are stayed until the final termination of appeals in England.

HUNT v. BP EXPLORATION COMPANY (LIBYA) LTD.

580 F.Supp. 304 (N.D. Tex. 1984).

[Hunt II]

Nelson Bunker Hunt ("Hunt"), the plaintiff in this diversity case asks this court to declare that a prior English judgment adjudicating the same dispute between these parties is unenforceable, to declare further that he is not indebted to defendant BP Exploration Company (Libya) Ltd. ("BP"), and to order that BP repay him the amount it previously collected under the English judgment ($40,833,000.00 plus interest). Alternatively, Hunt seeks a declaration that, in accordance with the parties agreement, the dispute is subject to arbitration.

In a prior opinion, this court held "that the English judgment is entitled to recognition and that such recognition would bar most if not all of Hunt's claims in this litigation," but that summary judgment could not be granted BP until exhaustion of all appeals determined the scope of the bar. . . .

BP's Renewed Motion for Summary Judgment

BP renews its motion for summary judgment, stayed by the court's earlier opinion, on grounds that the English judgment, which was not modified by the appellate courts in any respects, has become final (*i.e.*, all appeals have been exhausted); that the English judgment is entitled to recognition here; and that such recognition bars all of Hunt's claims in this case. Hunt does not dispute the finality of the English judgment. He argues instead that the question of recognition is governed by the Texas Uniform Foreign Country Money–Judgment Recognition Act, Art. 23–28b–6, TEX. REV. CIV. STAT. ANN. (Vernon Supp. 1982) (the "Texas Act") and that BP has failed to conclusively establish, on its motion for summary judgment, that all conditions of that statute have been satisfied.

Hunt's response to BP's renewed motion for summary judgment presents only two issues not previously determined by this court: the question of reciprocity, *i.e.*, whether England grants recognition to American judgments, and whether the parties agreed to arbitrate, rather than litigate, their differences. These issues arise under Section 5(b)(7) and 5(b)(5), respectively, of the Texas Act.... The summary judgment record reveals no disputed material fact involved in the determination of these issues. Summary judgment is appropriate where the only issues to be decided are questions of law....

Both parties agree that this court, sitting in diversity, must apply the law of Texas, including its choice of law rules.... At the time of *Hunt I*, that is, before the Texas Act was adopted, "the law in Texas as to reciprocity [was] not clear." ... In support of this conclusion, the court noted the difficulties involved in applying reciprocity, and the institutional limitations on judicial determination of foreign law, as well as the general trend in the federal courts against requiring reciprocity.

Notwithstanding these considerations and the court's view of the direction of Texas law, the Texas legislature late chose to include lack of reciprocity as a ground for refusing to give conclusive effect to a foreign judgment....

Although the Texas Act does not apply to "a judgment rendered before the effective date of the Act," and the English judgment was rendered prior to that date, the Fifth Circuit has indicated that

> While it is true that the Act specifically states that it will not apply to judgments entered before its passage, we think that the Texas courts would nevertheless apply to the present case those provisions in the Act that incorporate the doctrine of reciprocity.... [Since] the issue of reciprocity had never been squarely addressed in recent years by the Texas judiciary, a Texas court in our position would look to the new statute in the interest of uniformity ... [rather than] carving out a new and different rule for an arbitrary set of cases.

Royal Bank of Canada v. Trantham Corp., 665 F.2d 515, 517–18 (5th Cir. 1981). The Texas legislature thus declared invalid, retrospectively, Hunt I's conclusion that the question of reciprocity need not be decided. This court must therefore apply the Texas Act, which includes a reciprocity requirement, in deciding the question of recognition.

Although Section 5(b) of the Statute calls for an exercise of discretion, this court must proceed cautiously in the absence of criteria for guidance fashioned by the Texas courts.... With only the words of the subsection as guideposts, it appears that the Legislature placed the burden of proof on the party opposing recognition of a foreign money judgment....

[...]

BP did not wait, however, for Hunt to establish lack of reciprocity. Instead, it presented the consularized affidavit of Robert Alexander MacCrindle, currently based in Paris as European Counsel to the New York firm of Shearman & Sterling. [The affidavit established that English courts would recognize and enforce a final foreign money judgment rendered.]

[...]

By contrast, Hunt has submitted neither affidavits from English counsel nor any decisions from English courts refusing recognition of a Texas judgment. Moreover, he has failed to dispute the MacCrindle affidavit. Under these circumstances, Hunt has failed both to rebut the *prima facie* case presented by BP and to carry the burden of establishing non-reciprocity imposed on him by Section 5(b)(7) of the Texas Act.

The only remaining roadblock to recognition of the English judgment is Hunt's new contention that the parties to the contract agreed to submit any disputes to arbitration rather than resolving them in court. Hunt's argument is apparently based on the discretionary portion of the Texas Act, which provides that a foreign country judgment need not be recognized if "the proceeding in the foreign country was contrary to an agreement between the parties under which the dispute in question was to be settled otherwise than by proceedings in that court." ...

Hunt's claim that this dispute should be arbitrated derives from paragraph 29 of the 1960 Operating Agreement attached to the farm-in agreement between the parties. It provides as follows:

> If any dispute arises between the parties hereto that cannot be satisfactorily settled by mutual agreement relating to anything herein contained or in connection herewith, and if either party hereto desires to submit such dispute to arbitration, it shall notify the other party in writing and name the party selected by it as an arbitrator.

This provision is clearly optional rather than mandatory; consequently, the proceeding in the English court was not contrary to an agreement between the parties that the dispute would be settled in another manner.... Each party remained free to institute court proceedings, and each chose to do so, BP in London and Hunt in Dallas. Hunt has not controverted BP's assertion that Hunt failed to give the written notice required by paragraph 29. Neither has Hunt named the party selected by him as arbitrator. By engaging strenuously in the judicial resolution of this dispute over a seven-year period, during which Hunt failed to initiate arbitration or advance the arbitration clause as a defense, Hunt waived any right he may have had to arbitration. . . .

Extent of Preclusion

In both this opinion and Hunt I, the court has carefully considered and rejected all those grounds for non-recognition of the English judgment advanced by Hunt. The conclusion follows inescapably that judgment is conclusive between the parties insofar as it granted BP recovery of the sum of money at issue here. Under Texas law, therefore, the English judgment is enforceable in the same manner as the judgment of a sister state that is entitled to full faith and credit. . . .

Yet to be considered are the dimensions of the zone of preclusion, which the court's previous decision declined to delineate. . . .This case must be compared to the English suit to determine whether all the prerequisites for application of the doctrine of *res judicata* have been fulfilled: For a prior judgment to bar a subsequent action, it is firmly established (1) that the prior judgment must have been rendered by a court of competent jurisdiction; (2) that there must have been a final judgment on the merits; (3) that the parties, or those in privity with them, must be identical in both suits; and (4) that the same cause of action must be involved in both suits.

In *Hunt I*, . . .this court concluded that the English court had both personal and subject matter jurisdiction. All appeals have been exhausted in the English forum, so that judgment on the merits is final.

BP is therefore entitled to judgment as a matter of law. Hunt's prayer for relief is DENIED in all respects and BP's for summary judgment is GRANTED.

* * * *

BRITISH MIDLAND AIRWAYS, LTD. v. INTERNATIONAL TRAVEL, INC.

497 F.2d 869 (9th Cir. 1974).

BURNS, District Judge:

This action was brought to enforce a judgment obtained in the High Court of Justice in England. The District Court found the British judgment to be valid and enforceable. We agree and affirm.

Plaintiff–Appellee, British Midland Airways Limited (BMA), a corporation organized under the laws of the United Kingdom, and Defendant–Appellant, International Travel, Inc., (International), a Washington corporation, entered into a contract on May 14, 1971, providing for an agency to arrange charter flights from the western United States and Canada to England. In Clause 12 of that contract, the parties agreed to be "governed by the laws of England" and to submit "any dispute arising (from the contract) or in relation thereto" to the High Court of

Justice in England. Approximately one year later, such a dispute did occur, and BMA sued International for breach of contract in the Queen's Bench Division of the High Court of Justice in London, seeking damages of [Eng. Pds.] 82,455.93 ($201,788.00), plus interest ($18,864.00) and costs ($1,200.00).

International's British attorneys entered an unconditional appearance (not contesting jurisdiction) to defend the lawsuit. BMA filed a motion pursuant to British Order 14, Rule 1(1), a procedure which roughly parallels our Rule 56 summary judgment procedure. Additional rules under Order 14 allow the Court to "give a defendant against whom such an application is made leave to defend the action with respect to the claim, or the part of a claim, to which the application relates either unconditionally or on such terms as to giving security or time or mode of trial or otherwise as it thinks fit." Order 14, Rule 3.

The motion was granted by a Master (a "junior" judge similar to the United States Magistrate) in August, 1972, but International was still given leave to defend if it deposited an amount equal to the prayer of the complaint with the Court. Both parties appealed this order. BMA maintained that its motion should have been granted outright (with no conditional defense allowed). International contended it should be allowed to defend without being required to make any deposit. No transcripts are made of these proceedings, but a "certificated bundle of documents" containing affidavits and other papers is filed.

The appeals were heard in November, 1972, by Justice Forbes of the High Court of Justice, Queen's Bench Division, Supreme Court of Judicature, England, who decided that International had not made a *prima facie* showing of any valid defense, with the possible exception of the claim for cancellation charges. Accordingly, the judge ordered the deposit diminished by that amount of the alleged damages, but ruled that if the money was not deposited within the month, judgment for BMA for the full claim would be entered. At this point, International could have appealed again to a higher court, but failed either to pursue this remedy or to make the deposit. Judgment was then entered for BMA in the amount originally claimed, together with interest and costs on December 14, 1972.

In February, 1973, BMA brought this action in the United States District Court for the Western District of Washington to enforce the British judgment. Based on the same material which compiled the record in the High Court of Justice, the District Court granted BMA's motion for summary judgment in August, 1973, and denied a motion for rehearing in October, 1973. International's opposition to the motion was grounded on principles of comity, namely, its claim that the action of the British courts denied it due process in (1) requiring the deposit as a prerequisite to defending the lawsuit and holding International in 'default' for its failure to comply with that order; and (2) not recording the proceedings and not allowing proof of damages to be submitted.

We find it unnecessary to decide BMA's contention that any foreign judgment is conclusive under Washington law unless the foreign court exceeded its jurisdiction. We agree in this case with the Third Circuit's view, stated in a similar British default case, that "English procedure comports with our standards of due process." ... It has long been the law that unless a foreign country's judgments are the result of outrageous departures from our own notions of "civilized jurisprudence," comity should not be refused....

United States courts which have inherited major portions of their judicial traditions and procedure from the United Kingdom are hardly in a position to call the Queen's Bench a kangaroo court. Indeed, it appears that Order 14 was the forerunner of our summary judgment rule. In fact, a rational observer could well conclude that it is superior to our own practice. The British judges afforded International ample opportunity to present affidavits and argue its case.

It was International's choice not to pursue the matter on appeal or take advantage of the conditional defense allowance. International initially agreed to be bound by British law. Where contractual parties themselves freely agree that their disputes are to be litigated in the courts of the United Kingdom, we will not disturb such a choice. We need not consider whether the result would be otherwise if between the time when the contract was signed and the litigation commenced a change occurred in the English judicial system which radically altered either the substantive rules of law or the procedure by which such were administered....

Affirmed.

Notes and Questions

1. Does the ruling create a presumption? If so, how would you articulate the presumption? What rationale justifies it? Do U.S. judgments have a similar standing in England? Should such extensions of liability always be qualified by reciprocity?

2. What type of unfairness might have rendered the English judgment unenforceable? Does England become the 51st state for the purpose of full faith and credit?

3. Do any of the differences between U.S. and English civil procedure matter? The civil jury? Damages—quantum and type? Discovery, depositions, and interrogatories? Insurance coverage? The significance of personal injury litigation in the legal system?

4. You should be aware that the United States and the United Kingdom have tried for a number of years to negotiate a bilateral treaty for the enforcement of foreign judgments. *See* Convention on the Reciprocal Recognition and Enforcement of Judgments in Civil Matters, 16 I.L.M. 71 (1977). The parties have never succeeded in reaching an agreement despite the two systems' shared history and characteristics. *See* Ch. 1(2), at 24 *supra*. Also, an effort to promulgate a transborder convention on jurisdiction and the

enforcement of foreign judgments has yet to result in a positive outcome, although numerous attempts to reach an accommodation have been made. *See* Ch. 1(2), at 24 *supra*. What do these facts say about the issue under discussion?

* * * *

Somportex reinforces and refines the presumption favoring the enforcement of English judicial judgments under U.S. law. It provides that the default status of an English court judgment has no bearing on its enforceability before a U.S. court. It appears that the courts through common law have achieved what the U.S. State Department and the British Foreign Ministry have been unable to accomplish over the years: A regime of mutuality between like-minded States on the matter of enforcement. The question remains about how strong the emerging presumption is—in what circumstances could it be defeated? A denial of justice? A breach of domestic public policy? A violation of international public policy?

SOMPORTEX LTD. v. PHILADELPHIA CHEWING GUM CORP.

453 F.2d 435 (3d Cir. 1971).

ALDISERT, Circuit Judge.

Several interesting questions are presented in this appeal from the district court's order, 318 F. Supp. 161, granting summary judgment to enforce a default judgment entered by an English court. To resolve them, a complete recitation of the procedural history of this case is necessary.

This case has its genesis in a transaction between appellant, Philadelphia Chewing Gum Corporation, and Somportex Limited, a British corporation, which was to merchandise appellant's wares in Great Britain under the trade name "Tarzan Bubble Gum." According to the facts as alleged by appellant, there was a proposal which involved the participation of Brewster Leeds and Co., Inc., and M. S. International, Inc., third-party defendants in the court below. Brewster made certain arrangements with Somportex to furnish gum manufactured by Philadelphia; M. S. International, as agent for the licensor of the trade name "Tarzan," was to furnish the African name to the American gum to be sold in England. For reasons not relevant to our limited inquiry, the transaction never reached fruition.

Somportex filed an action against Philadelphia for breach of contract in the Queen's Bench Division of the High Court of England. Notice of the issuance of a Writ of Summons was served, in accordance with the rules and with the leave of the High Court, upon Philadelphia at its registered address in Havertown, Pennsylvania, on May 15, 1967. The extraterritorial service was based on the English version of long-arm statutes utilized by many American states. Philadelphia then consulted a firm of English solicitors, who by letter of July 14, 1967, advised its Pennsylvania lawyers:

I have arranged with the Solicitors for Somportex Limited that they will let me have a copy of their Affidavit and exhibits to that Affidavit which supported their application to serve out of the Jurisdiction. Subject to the contents of the Affidavit, and any further information that can be provided by Philadelphia Chewing Gum Corporation after we have had the opportunity of seeing the Affidavit, it may be possible to make an application to the Court for an Order setting the Writ aside. But for such an application to be successful we will have to show that on the facts the matter does not fall within the provision of (f) and (g) [of the long-arm statute . . .].

In the meantime we will enter a conditional Appearance to the Writ in behalf of Philadelphia Chewing Gum Corporation in order to preserve the *status quo*.

On August 9, 1967, the English solicitors entered a "conditional appearance to the Writ" and filed a motion to set aside the Writ of Summons. At a hearing before a Master on November 13, 1967, the solicitors appeared and disclosed that Philadelphia had elected not to proceed with the summons or to contest the jurisdiction of the English Court, but instead intended to obtain leave of court to withdraw appearance of counsel. The Master then dismissed Philadelphia's summons to set aside plaintiff's Writ of Summons. Four days later, the solicitors sought to withdraw their appearance as counsel for Philadelphia, contending that it was a conditional appearance only. On November 27, 1967, after a Master granted the motion, Somportex appealed. The appeal was denied after hearing before a single judge, but the court of Appeal, reversing the decision of the Master, held that the appearance was unconditional and that the submission to the jurisdiction by Philadelphia was, therefore, effective. But the court let stand "the original order which was made by the master on Nov. 13 dismissing the application to set aside. The writ therefore will stand. On the other hand, if the American company would wish to appeal from the order of Nov. 13, I see no reason why the time should not be extended and they can argue that matter out at a later stage if they should so wish."

Thereafter, Philadelphia made a calculated decision: it decided to do nothing. It neither asked for an extension of time nor attempted in any way to proceed with an appeal from the Master's order dismissing its application to set aside the Writ. Instead, it directed its English solicitors to withdraw from the case. There being no appeal, the Master's order became final.

Somportex then filed a Statement of Claim which was duly served in accordance with English Court rules. In addition, by separate letter, it informed Philadelphia of the significance and effect of the pleading, the procedural posture of the case, and its intended course of action.

Philadelphia persisted in its course of inaction; it failed to file a defense. Somportex obtained a default judgment against it in the Queen's Bench Division of the High Court of Justice in England for the sum [Eng. Pds.] 39,562.10 (approximately $94,000). The award reflected some $45,000.00 for loss of profit; $46,000.00 for loss of good will and $2,500.00 for costs, including attorneys' fees.

Thereafter, Somportex filed a diversity action in the court below, seeking to enforce the foreign judgment, and attached to the complaint a certified transcript of the English proceeding. The district court granted two motions which gave rise to this appeal: it dismissed the third-party complaints for failure to state a proper claim under F.R.C.P. 14; and it granted plaintiff's motion for summary judgment, F.R.C.P. 56(a).

We will quickly dispose of the third-party matter. We perceive our scope of review to be limited to an inquiry whether the district court abused its discretion in refusing impleader. At issue here was not the alleged contract to peddle Tarzan chewing gum in England. Had such been the case, Philadelphia's third-party argument would have been persuasive. The complaints might have met the liability test and "transaction or occurrence" requirement of F.R.C.P. 14(a). But the transaction at issue here is not the contract; it is the English judgment. And neither third-party defendant was involved in or notified of the proceedings in the English courts. Accordingly, we find no abuse of discretion in the district court's dismissal of the third-party complaints.

Appellant presents a cluster of contentions supporting its major thesis that we should not extend hospitality to the English judgment. First, it contends, and we agree, that because our jurisdiction is based solely on diversity, "the law to be applied . . . is the law of the state," in this case, Pennsylvania law. . . .

Pennsylvania distinguishes between judgments obtained in the courts of her sister states, which are entitled to full faith and credit, and those of foreign courts, which are subject to principles of comity. . . .

Comity is a recognition which one nation extends within its own territory to the legislative, executive, or judicial acts of another. It is not a rule of law, but one of practice, convenience, and expediency. Although more than mere courtesy and accommodation, comity does not achieve the force of an imperative or obligation. Rather, it is a nation's expression of understanding which demonstrates due regard both to international duty and convenience and to the rights of persons protected by its own laws. Comity could be withheld only when its acceptance would be contrary or prejudicial to the interest of the nation called upon to give it effect. . . .

[. . .]

Appellant's contention that the district court failed to make an independent examination of the factual and legal basis of the jurisdiction of the English Court at once argues too much and says too little. The reality is that the court did examine the legal basis of asserted jurisdiction and decided the issue adversely to appellant.

[. . .]

Thus, we will not disturb the English Court's adjudication. That the English judgment was obtained by appellant's default instead of through an adversary proceeding does not dilute its efficacy. In the absence of fraud or collusion, a default judgment is as conclusive an adjudication between the parties as when rendered after answer and complete contest in the open courtroom.... The polestar is whether a reasonable method of notification is employed and reasonable opportunity to be heard is afforded to the person affected....

English law permits recovery, as compensatory damages in breach of contract, of items reflecting loss of good will and costs, including attorneys' fees. These two items formed substantial portions of the English judgment. Because they are not recoverable under Pennsylvania law, appellant would have the foreign judgment declared unenforceable because it constitutes an "action on the foreign claim [which] could not have been maintained because it is contrary to the public policy of the forum," citing Restatement, Conflict of Laws, § 445. We are satisfied with the district court's disposition of this argument:

> The Court finds that ... while Pennsylvania may not agree that these elements should be included in damages for breach of contract, the variance with Pennsylvania law is not such that the enforcement "tends clearly to injure the public health, the public morals, the public confidence in the purity of the administration of the law, or to undermine that sense of security for individual rights, whether of personal liberty or of private property, which any citizen ought to feel, is against public policy." ...
>
> *Somportex Limited v. Philadelphia Chewing Gum Corp.*, 318 F. Supp. 161, 169 (E.D.Pa. 1970).

Finally, appellant contends that since "it maintains no office or employee in England and transacts no business within the country" there were no sufficient contacts there to meet the due process tests of *International Shoe*.... It argues that, at best, "the only contact Philadelphia had with England was the negotiations allegedly conducted by an independent New York exporter by letter, telephone and telegram to sell Philadelphia's products in England." In *Hanson v. Denckla*, 357 U.S. 235, 253, 78 S.Ct. 1228, 1240, 2 L.Ed. 2d 1283 (1958), Chief Justice Warren said: "The application of [the requirement of contact] rule will vary with the quality and nature of the defendant's activity, but it is essential in each case that there be some act by which the defendant purposely avails itself of the privilege of conducting business within the forum State, thus invoking the benefits and protection of its law." We have concluded that whether the New York exporter was an independent contractor of Philadelphia's agent was a matter to be resolved by the English Court. For the purpose of the constitutional argument, we must assume the proper agency relationship. So construed, we find his activity would constitute the "quality and nature of the defendant's activity" similar to that of the defendant in *McGee v. International Life Ins. Co.*, 355 U.S. 220, 78 S.Ct. 199, 2 L.Ed. 2d 223 (1957), there held to satisfy due process requirements.

For the reasons heretofore rehearsed we will not disturb the English Court's adjudication of jurisdiction; we have deemed as irrelevant the default nature of the judgment; we have concluded that the English compensatory damage items do not offend Pennsylvania public policy; and held that the English procedure comports with our standards of due process.

. . . In sum, we are not persuaded that appellant met its burden of showing that the British "decree is so palpably tainted by fraud or prejudice as to outrage our sense of justice, or [that] the process of the foreign tribunal was invoked to achieve a result contrary to our laws of public policy or to circumvent our laws or public policy." . . .

* * * *

Summaries of Recent and Different Cases on Enforcement

BACHCHAN v. INDIA ABROAD PUBLICATIONS

154 Misc. 2d 228, 585 N.Y.S. 2d 661
(Sup. Ct. N.Y. County 1992).

India Abroad Publications, Inc. ("India Abroad") wired a news service story from England to a news service in India on January 31, 1990. The article, written by a reporter from London for India Abroad, stated that a Swedish newspaper, Dagens Nyjeter, had reported that Swiss authorities had frozen Ajitabh Bachchan's bank account. Prior to the India Abroad article, miscellaneous publications had previously linked Bachchan with a kickback scheme involving arms sales by the Swedish firm Bofars to the Indian government. The Indian news service disseminated the story to newspapers in India after receiving the wire. Not only was the story published in India, but copies were also distributed in the United Kingdom. India Abroad wired Bachchan's denial of the story three days later. Bachchan initiated suit against both Dagens Nyjeter and India Abroad. Ultimately, Dagens Nyjeter issued a formal apology, thus settling their dispute with Bachchan, explaining that sources within the Indian government had misled it. India Abroad, however, never issued an apology.

Bachchan brought suit against India Abroad for the wire service article that had been transmitted from England to India. The case was tried before the High Court of Justice in London before a jury under the English law of defamation. The English law of defamation requires only that plaintiffs prove that the defendant published a statement harmful to the reputation of the plaintiff. "Any published statement which adversely affects a person's reputation, or the respect on which that person is held, is *prima facie* defamatory." Plaintiffs' only burden is to establish that the words complained of refer to them, were published by the defendant, and bear a defamatory meaning. The defendant may raise the truth of the statement as a defense to the charge, but failure to succeed in such a defense exposes the defendant to aggravated damages.

The London jury awarded Bachchan a judgment for £40,000 in damages plus attorney's fees.

Bachchan sought enforcement of his London judgment in New York City, which was the home of India Abroad. Bachchan exercised an option granted to him by the New York version of the Recognition Act, filing a motion for summary judgment in lieu of a complaint. "Both the Recognition Act and its New York version generally consider such a judgment 'conclusive between the parties' in such an action." India Abroad challenged the motion, citing as a defense another provision of the Recognition Act found in the New York Civil Practice Law and Rules ("CPLR") section 5304 which lists grounds upon which a court need not recognize a foreign money judgment. Included as a ground justifying the dismissal of the foreign judgment is the circumstance that "the cause of action on which the judgment is based is repugnant to the public policy of this state." India Abroad argued that the English cause of action was repugnant to the public policy "embodied in the First Amendment." Bachchan countered with the argument that the public policy exception to recognition of foreign judgments was narrow, that New York entertains "causes of action" for defamation, and that the U.S. law of defamation was comparable to the English law.

The New York court rejected Bachchan's arguments. In doing so, it emphasized the differences between the English and American law of defamation. Constitutional requirements would make "the refusal to recognize the judgment 'constitutionally mandatory' "and the judgment repugnant to New York public policy. The English law of defamation differed in terms of the causes of actions and the burdens it imposed on the defendant. "English law does not distinguish between private person and those who are public figures or are involved in matters of public concern." "None are required to prove falsity of the libel or fault on the part of the defendant. No plaintiff is required to prove that a media defendant intentionally or negligently disregarded proper journalistic standards in order to prevail." Unlike the English law, American law obligates defamation plaintiffs to prove both the falsity of the contemptuous statement and the fault (to varying degrees) of the defendant.

In resolving the issue, the court stated that: "placing the burden of proving truth upon media defendants who publish speech of public concern has been held unconstitutional because fear of liability may deter such speech." The court further asserted that the " 'chilling effect' would be no different where liability results from enforcement in the United States of a foreign judgment obtained where the burden of proving truth is upon media defendants." The court resolved the issue by holding that Bachchan's failure to demonstrate falsity in England's High Court of Justice made his judgment unenforceable in New York courts. The court's major concern was the fear of compromising first amendment protections afforded to United States citizens, especially the media, and the concern that lack of such protection would inhibit free speech.

The court reasoned that first amendment protections would be seriously jeopardized by the entry of foreign libel judgments granted pursuant to standards deemed appropriate in England but considered antithetical to the protections afforded the press by the U.S. Constitution. It stated that the Constitution permitted no discretion. Concluding that enforcement would chill and jeopardize free speech in New York, the court denied Bachchan's motion for summary judgment, becoming thereby the first U.S. court to refuse to enforce an English libel judgment.

TELNIKOFF v. MATUSEVITCH

347 Md. 561, 702 A.2d 230 (1997).

Telnikoff was employed by the BBC's Russian service. He had emigrated to England from the Soviet Union. There, he had been a human rights activist. On February 13, 1984, Telnikoff published an article in the Daily Telegraph in which he discussed the Russian personnel employed by Radio Free Europe/Radio Liberty. Telnikoff insisted that the notions of "Communist" and "Russian" should be distinguished. He further maintained that "this confusion . . . manifest[ed] itself in the policy of recruitment for the Russian Service. While other services are staffed almost exclusively from those who share the ethnic origin of the people [to] whom they broadcast, the Russian Service is recruited almost entirely from Russian-speaking national minorities of the Soviet empire, and has something like 10 per cent of those who associate themselves ethnically, spiritually or religiously with Russian people. However high the standards and integrity of that majority there is no more logic in this than having a Greek service which is 90 per cent recruited from the Greek-speaking Turkish community of Cyprus."

Matusevitch, also a Russian ex-patriot employed by the United States radio station Radio Liberty in London, criticized Telnikoff's article. He published a letter entitled "Qualifications for Broadcasting to Russia," in the Daily Telegraph on February 18, 1984. Matusevitch asserted that there was a single culture in Russia, namely Russian, and that Telnikoff advocated racist policies. Matusevitch contended that "Mr. Telnikoff demands that in the interest of more effective broadcasts the management of the BBC's Russian Service should switch from professional testing to a blood test."

Telnikoff sued Matusevitch for defamation in English court. After two appeals, a jury for the High Court of Justice returned a verdict for £240,000 in favor of Telnikoff. Shortly thereafter, Telnikoff filed an enforcement action in Montgomery County, Maryland. Eventually, "Matusevitch commenced the present action by filing a complaint in the United States District Court for the District of Maryland, seeking a declaratory judgment that the English judgment was 'repugnant' to the First and Fourteenth Amendments to the United States Constitution, to Article 40 of the Maryland Declaration of the Rights, and to Maryland common law and Maryland public policy." Telnikoff counterclaimed, "seeking enforcement of his English judgment in Maryland." Upon stipulation by the parties, the case was transferred to the United States District court for the District of Columbia. On January 27, 1995, the District Court entered judgment for Matusevitch, holding "that the cause of action underlying the English libel judgment was 'repugnant to the public policy of the State' within the meaning of Maryland's Uniform Foreign Money–Judgments Recognition Act, and that recognition of the foreign judgment under principles of comity 'would be repugnant to the public policies of the State of Maryland and the United States.' " Telnikoff appealed to the United States Court of Appeals for the District of Columbia Circuit.

The Court of Appeals concluded that "the principles underlying comity, including the public policy exception, have been codified in the Maryland Uniform Foreign–Money Judgments Recognition Act, Code (1974, 1995 Repl. Vol.), §§ 10–701 *et seq.* of the Courts and Judicial Proceedings Article. Section 10–704(b)(2) of the Recognition Act specifically states that a 'foreign judgment need not be recognized if 'the 'cause of action on which the judgment is based is repugnant to the public policy of the State...' " "American and Maryland history reflects a public policy in favor of a much broader and more protective freedom of the press than ever provided for under English law." "As pointed out by this Court over one hundred years ago, the liberty of the press guaranteed by the Constitution [of Maryland] is a right belonging to every one, whether proprietor of a newspaper or not, to publish whatever he pleases, without the license, interference or control of the government, being responsible alone for the abuse of the privilege. It is a right which, from the introduction of the printing press down to the year 1694, did not in England belong to the subject. On the contrary, no one was allowed to publish any printed matter without the license and supervision of the government, and it was against such interference on the part of the government, that this provision found its way into our Bill of Rights."

"We concluded as a matter of state law that the *Gertz* principles should apply regardless of whether the alleged defamatory statement involved a subject of public concern and regardless of whether the action was against a media defendant or a non-media defendant." The court adopted the common law that "there could be no recovery without fault in any defamation action. Truth is no longer an affirmative defense to be established by the defendant, but instead the burden of proving falsity rests upon the plaintiff." The courts took pains to note that the principles governing defamation actions under English law were contrary to Maryland defamation law and to the policy of freedom of the press underlying Maryland law. Telnikoff's judgment, as a result, should be denied recognition under the principles of comity. Citing *Bachchan*, the court asserted that "recognition of English defamation judgments could well lead to wholesale circumvention of fundamental public policy in Maryland and the rest of the country." "The importance of that free flow of ideas and opinions on matters of public concern precludes Maryland recognition of Telnikoff's English libel judgment."

* * * *

Excerpts From the Bachchan *Court's Opinion*

[. . .]

Defendant argues that the defamation law of England fails to meet the constitutional standards required in the United States because plaintiff, a friend of the late prime minister of India Rajiv Ghandi and the brother and manager of a movie star and former member of Parliament, is a public figure. In *New York Times Co. v. Sullivan*, 376 U.S. 254, 279–280 (1964), the Supreme Court of the United States ruled that in order to recover damages for defamation a public official must prove by clear and convincing evidence that the defendant published the allegedly defamatory statement with " 'actual Malice'—that is, with knowledge that it was false or with reckless disregard of whether it was false or not." That burden of proof was placed on public figures who sued media defendants in *Curtis Publishing Co. v. Butts*, 388 U.S. 130 (1967).

However, it seems neither necessary nor appropriate to decide whether plaintiff, an Indian national residing in England or Switzerland, is a public figure. Instead, the procedures of the English Court will be compared to those which according to decisions of the United States Supreme Court are constitutionally mandated for suits by private persons complaining of press publications of public concern.

In *Gertz v. Robert Welch, Inc.*, 418 U.S. 323, 347 (1974), the court held that a private figure could not recover damages for defamation without showing that a media defendant was at fault, leaving the individual States to "define for themselves the appropriate standard of liability for a publisher or broadcaster of defamatory falsehood injurious to a private individual."

Reviewing the Supreme Court's decisions enunciating constitutional limitations on suits for defamation, Justice O'Connor stated in *Philadelphia Newspapers v. Hepps*, 475 U.S. 767, 775:

> One can discern in these decisions two forces that may reshape the common-law landscape to conform to the First Amendment. The first is whether the plaintiff is a public official or figure, or is instead a private figure. The second is whether the speech at issue is of public concern. When the speech is of public concern and the plaintiff is a public official or public figure, the Constitution clearly requires the plaintiff to surmount a much higher barrier before recovering damages from a media defendant than is raised by the common law. When the speech is of public concern but the plaintiff is a private figure, as in *Gertz*, the Constitution still supplants the standards of the common law, but the constitutional requirements

are, in at least some of their range, less forbidding than when the plaintiff is a public figure and the speech is of public concern.

The issue in *Hepps* was the validity under the First Amendment of the common-law presumption that a defamatory statement is false, pursuant to which the burden of proving truth is on the defendant. Finding plaintiff to be a private figure and the subject of the newspaper articles in issue to be of public concern, the Court held that, "the common-law's rule on falsity—that the defendant must bear the burden of proving truth—must. . .fall here to a constitutional requirement that the plaintiff bear the burden of showing falsity, as well as fault, before recovering damages." (475 U.S. at 776)

It is obvious that defendant's publication relates to a matter of public concern. The affidavits and documents submitted by both parties reveal that the wire service report was related to an international scandal which touched major players in Indian politics and was reported in India, Sweden, the United States, England and elsewhere in the world. Consider the revelation of Mr. Zaiwalla, who had the conduct of the action resulting in the English judgment, that it was given priority over other defamation actions waiting to be tried because "the Indian General Election was imminent and the Bofars affairs and the plaintiff's long-time family friendship with Mr. Rajiv Gandhi, the former prime minister of India ... and leader of the main opposition party ... were being used as electoral weapons in India." (Zaiwalla aff. pp. 4–5) Mr. Justice Otten, in his instructions, referred to the political context of the story by suggesting to the jury that it "ignore the complexities" of the Indian politics and political parties which were the background of the news stories. (Transcript, p. 6, Exhibit B, Handman further aff.)

Placing the burden of proving truth upon media defendants who publish speech of public concern has been held unconstitutional because fear of liability may deter such speech.

Because such a 'chilling' effect would be antithetical to the First Amendment's protection of true speech on matters of public concern, we believe that a private figure plaintiff must bear the burden of showing that the speech at issue is false before recovering damages for defamation from a media defendant. To do otherwise could 'only result in a deterrence of speech which the Constitution makes free.' (citation omitted) *Philadelphia Newspapers, Inc. v. Hepps*, *supra* at 777.

The "chilling" effect is no different where liability results from enforcement in the United States of a foreign judgment obtained where the burden of proving truth is upon media defendants. Accordingly, the failure of Bachchan to prove falsity in the High Court of Justice in England makes his judgment unenforceable here.

There is, of course, another reason why enforcement of the English judgment would violate the First Amendment: in England, plaintiff was not required to and did not meet the "less forbidding" constitutional requirement that a private figure show that a media defendant was at fault.

New York's standard for liability in actions brought by private persons against the press is set forth in *Chapadeau v. Utica Observer–Dispatch*, 38 N.Y.2d 196, 197 (1975): "[W]here the content of the article is arguably within the sphere of legitimate public concern, which is reasonably related to matters warranting public exposition, the party defamed may recover; however to warrant such recovery he must establish, by a preponderance of the evidence, that the publisher acted in a grossly irresponsible manner without due consideration for the standards of information gathering and dissemination ordinarily followed by responsible parties."

As stated above, the English courts do not require plaintiff to prove that a press defendant was at fault in any degree. Bachchan certainly did not establish, as required by *Chapadeau*, that defendant was grossly irresponsible, a difficult task, where defendant disseminates another's news report. *See Rust Communication Group v. 70 State St. Travel Service*, 122 A.D.2d 584 (N.Y. App. Div. 1986).

It is true that England and the United States share many common law principles of law. Nevertheless, a significant difference between the two jurisdictions lies in England's lack of an equivalent to the First Amendment to the United States Constitution. The protection to free speech and the press embodied in that amendment would be seriously jeopardized by the entry of foreign libel judgments granted pursuant to standards deemed appropriate in England but considered antithetical to the protections afforded the press by the U.S. Constitution.

For the above-stated reasons, the motion for summary judgment in lieu of complaint is denied.

[. . .]

Notes and Questions

1. These opinions have been roundly criticized by a number of commentators. *See, e.g.*, Minehan, *The Public Policy Exception to the Enforcement of Foreign Judgments: Necessary or Nemesis?*, 18 Loy. L.A. Int'l & Comp. L.J. 795 (1996).

2. They represent a departure from the standards that were previously articulated and that remain otherwise applicable.

3. Are these decisions insufferably bad and completely untenable? Don't they represent a brief for the unique and quintessential feature of American law and political culture? Aren't these results commanded by Constitutional rules?

4. Do the circumstances unnecessarily politicize the commercial liability problem?

5. How might all of this be made more workable?

* * * *

The Law of Enforcement in Other Countries

It is difficult to find a jurisdiction that is more liberal than the United States on the question of the enforcement of foreign judgments. Canada, England, and most Western European countries are hospitable to foreign juridical acts and readily grant enforcement orders. Many other venues—in emerging and re-emerging countries, in socialist regimes with statist economies, and for political reasons of all sorts—engage as a matter of course or periodically in protectionist practices through municipal courts that safeguard national entities from accountability. These latter policies render global trade and commerce difficult.

The resource and development disparity between North and South adds an ideological layer to the pursuit of global commerce. Southern jurisdictions sometimes claim immunity from accountability because of the inequality of benefit that diverse parties reap from the world marketplace. The rule of contract and the pursuit of commercial profit and markets benefit the stronger, more prosperous party. When national concerns are implicated and likely to lose, it is warranted and necessary to achieve justice by exempting the less fortunate from the applicable standard. The enforcement of legitimate legal determinations is cancelled out by the roving reparationist view of ideological (and financial) accountability.

It is, of course, the basic professional duty of legal counsel to apprise clients who engage in foreign investment of the risk of confiscatory State practices. In some circumstances, the risk is irreducible and irremediable. Otherwise, contracts should be written to minimize the risk and to promote indirect or direct enforcement of commercial obligations. Lawyers should explore nonjudicial recourse, the purchase of political risk insurance, the use of escrow accounts and confirmed irrevocable letters of credit, and third-party guarantees, risk distribution arrangements, and other devices to stabilize and secure obligations.

As was stated earlier, enforcement is the key consideration both at the outset and at the culmination of the transaction. The materials that follow depict the law of like-minded but different countries on the question of enforcement. They describe the complexity of national legal approaches to the question. They also testify to an emerging Western, Northern consensus on the matter. Finally, they exhibit the challenges that are associated with the transborder practice of law.

France

THOMAS E. CARBONNEAU, THE FRENCH EXEQUATUR PROCEEDINGS: THE EXORBITANT JURISDICTIONAL RULES OF ARTICLES 14 AND 15 (*CODE CIVIL*) AS OBSTACLES TO THE ENFORCEMENT OF FOREIGN JUDGMENTS IN FRANCE

2 HASTINGS INT'L & COMP. L. REV. 307 (1979).

(Reprinted with permission).

(Excerpted and footnotes omitted)

[. . .]

In the absence of an international agreement providing for the recognition and enforcement of foreign judgments, the *ordonnance d'exequatur* constitutes the legal procedure by which foreign judgments are given *force exécutoire, i.e.*, are given *res judicata* effect and rendered enforceable, in France. Unlike its United States procedural analogue, the *exequatur* proceeding is not a new plenary action, but rather represents an abbreviated procedure and can be likened to a motion: the granting of an *exequatur* is simply the recognition by a French court of the validity and enforceability in France of an already existing judgment rendered by a foreign jurisdiction. With the notable exception of foreign judgments relating to personal status matters (and despite the fact that a foreign judgment, even when it lacks an *exequatur*, may have evidentiary and other legal consequences in French proceedings), foreign judgments which have not been granted an *exequatur* are devoid of legal effect in France as a general rule. The only legal recourse left to the beneficiary of a foreign judgment who has failed to obtain an *exequatur* is to sue in France on his original cause of action.

Although specific reference is made to the *exequatur* in several provisions of the various French *Codes*, most notably in Article 2133 of the *Code Civil*, Article 546 of the old *Code de Procédure Civile*, and Article 821 of the *Nouveau Code de Procédure Civile*, the task of devising rules for its procedural and substantive application was left to the courts. According to a jurisprudence that dates back to the first half of the Nineteenth Century, a French court sitting in *exequatur* proceeding had (until 1964) the authority to engage in full review of the merits of foreign judgments, especially those involving non-status matters. It could deny enforceability to a foreign judgment if it deemed any factual or legal point to have been decided erroneously by the foreign tribunal. In the opinion of the court: "[J]udges ruling on a request for *exequatur* have general jurisdiction to review a judgment rendered by foreign judges." And in *Holker v. Parker*, an 1819 case involving the enforcement in France of a United States money judgment, the *Cour de Cassation* held that foreign judgments have no conclusive legal effect in France; the French courts could engage in general review of the merits of such judgments. Although there had been a more liberal evolution relating to the recognition and enforcement of foreign judgments involving personal status matters, the position taken by the *Cour de Cassation* in *Holker* was reaffirmed in subsequent cases involving non-status foreign judgments.

This all-encompassing discretion not only ran counter to the ostensible purpose of the *exequatur* proceeding (*i.e.*, to avoid double litigation and to prevent post-judgment forum shopping), but was also an unnecessary grant of power since the judge could invoke a number of other grounds to deny *exequatur* to a foreign judgment he considered unsuitable for enforcement in France.

In *Munzer c. dame Jacoby–Munzer*, a landmark case decided in 1964, the *Cour de Cassation* reversed the earlier jurisprudence and laid down new rules relating to the enforcement of foreign judgments in France. Before being granted an *exequatur*, a foreign judgment must satisfy all of the following requirements:

1. it must have been rendered by a competent foreign tribunal, *i.e.*, one having both domestic and international jurisdiction to hear the matter;

2. it must have been rendered according to regular procedure, *i.e.*, a procedure conforming to the requirements of basic procedural fairness;

3. the foreign tribunal must have applied the law designated by French choice of law rules as the law governing the merits of the litigation;

4. the judgment must not be tainted by fraud;

5. finally, the judgment must be enforceable in the country in which it was rendered.

In establishing the conditions for enforcement, the court also restricted the *exequatur* judge's scope of authority and explicitly prohibited the judge from engaging in a review of the merits of the foreign judgment:

> [T]his verification, which suffices to protect the legal order and French interests, the very purpose of the *exequatur* proceeding, constitutes simultaneously in all matters the expression and the limit of the supervisory function of the judge ... without having him engage in a review of the merits of the (foreign) judgment....

The court's holding relating to the review power (*pouvoir de révision*) of the *exequatur* judge represented a significant departure from former doctrine. Until *Munzer*, the *Cour d'Appel* of Paris was the only modern court to have criticized the scope of the *exequatur* judge's authority. In *Charr c. Hazim Ulusahim*, the *Cour d'Appel* held that a foreign judgment should be enforceable in France provided it did not violate procedural safeguards or French international public policy concerns (*ordre public*). It reasoned that the *pouvoir de révision* had become an anachronism since it had emerged at a time when the conditions for the granting of an *exequatur* were ill-defined. By refining the requirements and standards, contemporary jurisprudence had obviated any need for their continued application. Finally, the court pointed to the practical consideration that an accurate review of the substance of a foreign litigation might well be impossible precisely because it took place in a foreign judicial setting.

Although the *Charr* reasoning did not surface explicitly in the text of the *Munzer* decision, other cases confirmed that the substance of that decision was meant to act as an approval of the *Cour d'Appel's* reasoning in *Charr*.

The *Munzer* Doctrine in Light of EEC Developments

The EEC Convention on Jurisdiction and the Enforcement of Judgments in Civil and Commercial Matters, which came into force on February 1, 1973, embodies the *Munzer* prohibition against a substantive review of the merits of foreign judgments making the prohibition a part of the European treaty law relating to the six original Member States of the EEC community. In conformity with Article 220 of the Rome Treaty, the Convention attempts to simplify legal formalities for the recognition and enforcement of foreign judgments by providing for a set of uniform and concise rules which apply, albeit with some notable exceptions, to most civil judgments rendered by one of the Contracting States.

Article 29 of the Convention clearly proscribes a national court of a Member State from reviewing the merits of a foreign judgment in an enforcement proceeding: "Under no circumstances may a foreign judgment be reviewed as to its substance." Additionally, the Convention provides for a simplified *exequatur* proceeding: "A judgment given in a Contracting State shall be recognized in the other Contracting States without any special procedure being required." It also outlined the restrictive grounds upon which a foreign judgment can be denied recognition:

> A judgment shall not be recognized:
>
> 1. If such recognition is contrary to public policy in the state in which the recognition is sought;
>
> 2. where it was given in default of appearance, if the defendant was not duly served with the document which instituted the proceedings or notice thereof in sufficient time to enable him to arrange for his defense;
>
> 3. if the judgment [cannot be reconciled] with a judgment [rendered] in a dispute between the same parties in the State in which recognition is sought;
>
> [. . .]
>
> In its examination of the grounds of jurisdiction referred to in the foregoing paragraph [Article 27], the court or authority applied to

> shall be bound by the findings of fact on which the court of the State in which the judgment was given based its jurisdiction.
>
> Subject to the provisions of the first paragraph, the jurisdiction of the court of the State in which the judgment was given may not be reviewed; the test of public policy referred to in Article 27 (1) may not be applied to the rules relating to jurisdiction.

The chief innovation of the Convention, however, consists of the fact that, in matters involving foreign parties, the Convention premises the jurisdiction of a court in a Contracting State upon domicile rather than the nationality of the parties:

> Subject to the provisions of this Convention, persons domiciled in a Contracting State shall, whatever their nationality, be sued in the courts of that State.
>
> Persons who are not nationals of the State in which they are domiciled shall be governed by the rules of jurisdiction applicable to the nationals of that State.

The Convention thereby minimizes, if not eliminates, the obstacles to the recognition and enforcement of foreign judgments which arise from rules of exorbitant jurisdiction, such as those contained in Articles 14 and 15 of the French *Code Civil*. Articles 14 and 15 have been interpreted to give French courts exclusive jurisdiction to hear matters involving French nationals. They, therefore, can be invoked by a French judgment debtor to prevent the enforcement of a foreign money judgment in France on the ground that the foreign tribunal lacked international jurisdiction to render the judgment (the first *Munzer* requirement for the enforcement of foreign judgments in France).

To dispel any doubt on this matter, Article 3 of the Convention specifically excludes the application of Articles 14 and 15 of the French *Code Civil* against any person domiciled in a Contracting State. Article 4, however, does permit a court in a Contracting State to apply rules of exorbitant jurisdiction to a defendant who is not domiciled in the EEC Community:

> If the defendant is not domiciled in a Contracting State, the jurisdiction of the courts of each Contracting State shall . . . be determined by the law of that State.
>
> As against such a defendant, any person domiciled in a Contracting State may, whatever his nationality, avail himself in that State of the rules of jurisdiction there in force, and in particular those specified in the second paragraph of Article 3 [*i.e.*, Articles 14 and 15 of the French *Code Civil*], in the same way as the nationals of that State.

Accordingly, in an enforcement proceeding in which an Italian court rendered a default judgment against a French defendant which the Italian plaintiff seeks to have enforced in France against the assets of the judgment debtor, Articles 14 and 15 of the French *Code Civil* could not be invoked to deny recognition and enforcement of the foreign judgment in France. Yet, in a similar enforcement proceeding between a French defendant and a United States party in which the latter obtained a default judgment against the French national in a United States jurisdiction, the provisions of the Convention would be inoperative and the French exorbitant jurisdictional rules could be invoked to deny *exequatur* to the United States judgment. Arguably, Articles 14 and 15 would not be invoked against a United States party which had a subsidiary, hence a domicile, in a Member State. Article 5(5) of the Convention reads, "A person domiciled in a Contracting State may, in another Contracting State, be sued: . . . (5) as regards a dispute arising out of the operations of a branch, agency or other establishment, in the courts for the place in which the branch, agency or other establishment is situated." The notion of domicile contained in Article 5(5), however, has been interpreted by the drafters of the Convention to be applicable only when the corporate seat of the company is located in a Member State. The Convention does not define the term "corporate seat," rather, it leaves that determination to the national courts of the Contracting State. Under French rules of private international law, the corporate seat of a company is its corporate headquarters. Accordingly, in an enforcement proceeding in France, a United States company with its corporate headquarters in a United States jurisdiction would be unable to avail itself of the benefits of the Convention, despite the fact that it has a subsidiary in a Member State.

The foregoing analysis of the Convention reveals that its provisions accord with the liberal doctrine established in *Munzer* in that the Convention abolishes the prerogative of national courts of the EEC Community to engage in a substantive review of foreign judgments. It is equally evident, however, that the Convention is meant only to facilitate the free circulation of judgments which emanate from, and are to be enforced in, EEC jurisdictions. The rebuttable presumption that all judgments are to be recognized and enforced does not extend to foreign judgments rendered in non-EEC jurisdictions. By failing to extend the full faith and credit principle to all foreign judgments, the Convention and, as the following analysis reveals, the *Munzer* jurisprudence, in effect, have given new importance to the French rules of exorbitant jurisdiction.

An Analysis of the *Munzer* Requirements for the Enforcement of a Foreign Judgment in France

1. The Foreign Court Must Have Had Domestic and International Jurisdiction

Even after the *Munzer* decision, some controversy reigned over the question of whether the *exequatur* judge should review a foreign court's application of its own jurisdictional rules. Most French courts and legal scholars, however, agreed that the judgment must have been rendered by the *proper* foreign tribunal (*i.e.*, one having domestic jurisdiction to hear the action). The satisfaction of this domestic jurisdictional requirement was considered indispensable to the granting of an *exequatur*. In *Bachir c. Dame Bachir*, the *Cour de Cassation* announced that the scrutiny of the procedure followed by the foreign tribunal need not be as rigorous as it had been in the past: "[T]he *exequatur* judge must verify if the proceeding which took place before the foreign jurisdiction was regular, this requirement of regularity must be assessed solely in relation to French international public policy concerns and in respect to the right to be represented by legal counsel...." Legal scholars have applied the general substance of this holding by analogy to the domestic jurisdiction requirement, interpreting it to imply that the *exequatur* judge can no longer ascertain whether the foreign court had domestic jurisdiction to hear the matter and render judgment.

The foreign court's international jurisdiction raises a more problematic issue. As a preliminary matter, it should be noted that, although the *Munzer* decision effectively abolished the *exequatur* judge's general prerogative to engage in a reassessment of the merits of a foreign judgment, it did not abridge his authority to determine whether the foreign judgment satisfied the requirements of international regularity. Most notably, it did not abrogate his authority to determine whether the foreign tribunal had international jurisdiction to hear the matter upon which it rendered judgment. Indeed, the *exequatur* judge's discretion still is quite extensive in this area. Its legitimate exercise does not preclude a review of one or many of the legal elements touching, either directly or indirectly, upon the merits of a foreign judgment as they relate to the foreign tribunal's jurisdiction.

For example, in *Soc. Italiban c. Lux–Air*, a Lebanese and a Luxembourg airline company entered into an exclusive agency agreement containing a compromissory clause. The latter provided that any disputes arising under the contract would be submitted to a single arbitrator or, in the event that the parties failed to agree on a common arbitrator, to the Tribunal de Commerce of the Grand Duchy of Luxembourg. Alleging reasons of commercial reorganization, Lux–Air rescinded the contract unilaterally, whereupon Italiban named an arbitrator and requested that Lux–Air do likewise. In the event that Lux–Air failed to designate an arbitrator within a week, Italiban declared that it would initiate an action before the "competent tribunal." Accordingly, when Lux–Air did not name an arbitrator, Italiban brought an action before a Lebanese court. The latter rendered a default judgment against Lux–Air which Italiban sought to have enforced in France.

The *Tribunal de Grande Instance* and the *Cour d'Appel* of Paris denied the request for *exequatur* on a number of grounds, including procedural "irregularity," violation of basic defense rights, and the misinterpretation by the Lebanese tribunal of its own procedural law. On appeal before the *Cour de Cassation*, Italiban contended, *inter alia*, that the court of appeals had engaged in an impermissible review of the merits of the Lebanese judgment. Although it deemed the technical legal grounds upon which the court of appeals denied *exequatur* to be superfluous, the Supreme Court nonetheless upheld its decision, reasoning that, by virtue of the language of the compromissory clause attributing jurisdiction to a Luxembourg tribunal, the Lebanese court lacked international jurisdiction to hear the matter. By establishing a distinction between the review of the merits of a foreign judgment and the scrutiny applied to the foreign tribunal's international jurisdiction, the court minimized the doctrinal importance of the *Munzer* prohibitions against the *pouvoir de révision* of the *exequatur* judge by limiting their application to the later stages of the *exequatur* proceeding. As a consequence, to paraphrase Professor Alexandre, while the *exequatur* judge cannot review the merits of a foreign judgment once it has satisfied the requirements of international regularity, to arrive at the latter determination, he can nonetheless challenge the foreign tribunal's substantive assessment of legal issues, including the grounds upon which it premised its jurisdiction.

Under the *Munzer* conditions, the validity of the foreign tribunal's international jurisdiction is to be assessed according to the jurisdictional rules of the country in which enforcement is sought, namely France. Under the provisions of Articles 14 and 15 of the *Code Civil*, which have been construed as containing a grant of exclusive jurisdiction despite their literal language, the French courts have exclusive jurisdiction to hear matters in which the plaintiff or defendant is a French national:

> Art 14. The foreigner, whether or not residing in France, can be brought before the French tribunals, for the execution of obligations contracted by him in France with a French national; he can be brought before French tribunals, for the obligations he contracted in a foreign country with French nationals.
>
> Art 15. A French national can be brought before a French tribunal, for the obligations he contracted in a foreign country, even with a foreigner.

The exclusive jurisdiction of the French courts is premised solely upon the nationality of a French party, and is assumed regardless of the party's actual residence or domicile and despite the fact that the substance of the litigation and the conduct giving rise to it may be far removed from the French territory or juridical interests. The jurisdictional rule in Articles 14 and 15 extends not only to actions arising out of contractual disputes, as the articles specify, but also has been interpreted to cover every other type of case—for example, torts, quasi-contract and inheritance claims. The few exceptions to this general rule are: (1) actions *in rem* concerning immovable property located in a foreign country; (2) actions such as garnishment or attachment which are to take place in a foreign country; and (3) actions against foreign States acting in a sovereign capacity. The provisions of Articles 14 and 15 apply to both physical and juridical persons. Under French law, as a general rule, the nationality of a corporation is determined by its *siège social*, *i.e.*, the "seat" of its operations.

Clearly, when a party seeks to enforce a foreign judgment in France against a French national, the latter's jurisdictional privilege under Articles 14 and 15 constitutes a significant, if not an insurmountable, barrier to the granting of an *exequatur*. At first blush, Article 46 of the *Nouveau Code de Procédure Civile* appears to lessen the impact of the jurisdictional rule of Articles 14 and 15 by attributing concurrent jurisdiction to the national and foreign courts in tort or contract matters. The article includes the implicit caveat that there must be a sufficient nexus with the foreign jurisdiction:

> Art. 46. The plaintiff has the choice of bringing an action either in the place where the defendant resides or:
>
> — in contractual matters, the place of the effective delivery of the thing or the place where the services were performed;
>
> — in tort matters, the place where the tortious act took place or the place in the province in which the injury was suffered;
>
> — in matters mixed, the place where the property is located;
>
> — in matters relating to support payments or contributions to the cost of marriage, the place where the creditor resides.

Despite the apparent textual conflict between it and Article 46, the language of Article 42 of the *Nouveau Code de Procédure Civile* reinforces the jurisdictional rule of Articles 14 and15 by providing, or more precisely by having been interpreted to provide, that the French courts also have exclusive jurisdiction to hear matters in which the defendant is a French domiciliary. Article 42 of the *Nouveau Code de Procédure Civile* reads: "The jurisdiction which is territorially competent is, except where indicated otherwise, the place where the defendant resides."

The grant of overwhelming jurisdictional authority that has been read into Articles 14 and 15 nonetheless can be challenged on a semantic basis, *i.e.*, by pointing out that the literal language of Articles 14 and 15 states that a French national *can* sue or *can* be sued in French courts, not that he *must* sue or *must* be sued before them. Furthermore, the parties can waive their jurisdictional privileges by merely so stating in their agreement or by presenting evidence corroborating an intent to recognize the jurisdiction of a foreign tribunal. The French courts, however, have been, and continue to be, extremely reluctant to imply a waiver of these jurisdictional prerogatives. Finally, the *Cour de Cassation* has ruled that the French courts will apply neither Article 14 nor Article 15 *ex officio*, the French party must invoke these provisions expressly before the courts in order to avail himself of the jurisdictional prerogatives.

These arguments, however, are unavailing. In litigation, the *Cour de Cassation* has construed the substance of Articles 14 and 15 to carry a jurisdictional privilege greater than that indicated by their literal language. For example in *Consorts Sempere c. Crédit Lyonnais*, the court reversed a lower court decision granting *exequatur* to an Algerian judgment rendered against two French nationals. It reasoned that Article 14 of the *Code Civil*

> gave the French defendant the right not to be brought before any but the French tribunals ... even if the French debtor is held with

> or for another who does not have the same nationality, the jurisdiction of the French courts being premised on the French nationality of the parties or one of them....

The holding in *Sempere* affirmed the precedent set in *Dame Huret c. Sieur Huret* in which the same court ruled that the provisions of Articles 14 and 15 "excluded ... any concurrent jurisdiction by [a] ... foreign jurisdiction."

Arguments contesting the absolute jurisdictional prerogative of French nationals under Article 15 have been raised in other contexts, namely in cases involving claims against French insurance companies. Although under certain exceptional circumstances the plaintiff can contend that the French defendant's conduct amounted to an implied waiver of Article 15, the French courts have insisted that that assertion be corroborated to their satisfaction. The *Cour de Cassation*'s recent holding in *C.R.M.A. c. Consorts Duport*, to the effect that a French defendant's simple failure to appear before the foreign tribunal is not sufficient proof of an implied waiver, makes that evidentiary requirement particularly onerous, if not impossible, to satisfy.

[...]

The outcome of these cases points to an evident conclusion. Unless the French party expressly waives the provisions of Articles 14 and 15 of the *Code Civil* or those of Article 42 of the *Nouveau Code de Procédure Civile*, a foreign judgment, involving either a French national or domiciliary, very likely will be denied an *exequatur* in France on the ground that the foreign tribunal lacked international jurisdiction to hear the action. As the *Cour d'Appel* of Paris observed recently in *Dame Chartrand c. Giroux*, the French courts will recognize the jurisdiction of a foreign tribunal only when the French jurisdictional rules, as construed by the French judiciary, do not give exclusive jurisdiction to the French courts. Even in the absence of exclusive French jurisdiction, there must be a "sufficient nexus" between the litigation and the foreign jurisdiction which rendered the judgment:

> [I]n every instance in which the French rule to the conflict of jurisdiction does not attribute exclusive jurisdiction to the French courts, it suffices, for a foreign tribunal to have jurisdiction, that there be a sufficient nexus between the litigation and the country in which the action is brought, that is to say, that the choice of the forum be neither arbitrary, nor artificial, nor fraudulent.

[...]

Conclusion

The liberal development instituted by the *Munzer* decision, in terms of facilitating the recognition and enforcement of foreign judgments in France, appears to have been attained at the price of giving a new doctrinal importance to the French rules of exorbitant jurisdiction—at least for judgments rendered by non-EEC jurisdictions.... [T]he inequities which result from the continued application of these rules serve to prevent international reciprocity in a non-EEC context, and also stand as an impediment, indeed a not inconsiderable obstacle, to transnational commercial activity.

Articles 14 and 15 of the French *Code Civil* do not pose a policy dilemma. Their principal, if not their sole, justification appears to lie in an obsolete attitude of uncompromising nationalism. United States and other non-EEC parties should take notice of the reach of the French rules of exorbitant jurisdiction and insist that their French co-contractants explicitly waive any jurisdictional prerogative which attaches to their nationality as a result of these provisions. In a more optimistic vein, one would hope that the *Cour de Cassation* or the French Parliament would take an enlightened view of the systemic and practical inequities which inhere in the court's interpretation of Articles 14 and 15 and extend the principle of full faith and credit, embodied in the EEC convention, to all foreign judgments irrespective of their jurisdictional origin. Limiting the grounds for the denial of recognition and enforcement to matters of essential public policy not only would promote more secure transnational commercial activity, but also would eliminate one more frustrating technical intricacy in the international administration of justice—adding a much needed degree of basic and broadminded fairness to the resolution of international commercial disputes.

[. . .]

Notes and Questions

1. But for the Brussels and Lugano Conventions in the EU context, there is no multilateral treaty on jurisdiction and the enforcement of judgments and there are few effective bilateral agreements on the subject. *See* Chapter 1(2) *supra*. States seem to guard their prerogatives jealously in the area of transborder judicial authority. They appear to want to leave matters to common law rules and to fashion an internal consensus on the subject over time. It is a curious cottage-industry approach in the age of regional legal systems and global trade. How do you assess it? Should the two major national political parties develop a "plank" on this matter? What appearance might each piece of new lumber have?

2. The French law on enforcement is characteristic of the regulation endorsed by economically-advanced countries. From initial distrust, it proceeds to embrace a highly liberal and tolerant view of foreign court judgments. In this civil law jurisdiction, ironically, it is case law that supplies the governing rules on matters of enforcement. What is the primary contribution of the *Munzer* holding? What does it mean to require that the court of rendition have had "international" jurisdiction? How do due process considerations fit into the basic requirements? How do you assess the reference to French choice-of-law rules? What is the meaning of being enforceable in the country of rendition? Is this a statement that requires foreign judgments to get an *exequatur* in the place of rendition and enforcement—the so-called double *exequatur* requirement? As an historical aside, the phrase "double

exequatur" is said to have arisen at the time when there were two papacies—one in Rome and the other in Avignon. Courts and governments sent the same communication to both places to avoid diplomatic and political incidents. As a result, the practice of getting each communication enforced in two places arose.

3. How does the French law fit into EU regulations? Are the due process requirements and concerns similar?

4. In the non-EU context, what impact does French nationality have upon the enforcement of foreign judgments by French courts? What is meant by the phrase "rule of exorbitant jurisdiction"? In your view, why has the French Supreme Court (*Cour de Cassation*) affixed such an exaggerated construction of the nationality concept to Articles 14 and 15 of the *Code Civil*. Isn't that interpretation sectarian and, therefore, highly disruptive of transborder commercial dealings and the transborder rule of law?

5. How would you address this problem in representing a U.S. company that is looking to do business with a French enterprise?

Germany

German law provides for the recognition and enforcement of foreign judgments. Section 328 of the Code of Civil Procedure (1988) lists the grounds upon which such judgments may be rejected:

(1) Recognition of a judgment of a foreign court is excluded:

1. If the courts of a state, to which the foreign court belongs, are not competent according to German law;
2. if the defendant, who has not participated in the proceedings and raises this plea, has not been served with the written pleadings initiating the proceedings in the regular way or in a timely manner, so that he was not in a position to defend himself;
3. if the judgment is inconsistent with a judgment issued here or with an earlier foreign judgment subject to recognition or if the proceedings on which it is based are inconsistent with an earlier proceeding here which has become final;
4. if the recognition of the judgment would give rise to a result which is manifestly incompatible with the basic principles of the German law, especially when the recognition would be inconsistent with the constitution;
5. if reciprocity is not assured.

(2) The provision of no. 5 does not bar the recognition of the judgment if the judgment concerns a claim other than a money claim and under the German law no jurisdiction was established inland or if it concerns an affiliation matter (§ 640).

Reciprocity often appears in the codes of European and Latin American countries. Whether it exists can be determined by the foreign affairs ministry or by the courts or yet again by a combination of agencies and courts. The concept of reciprocity is itself susceptible to several definitions.

Notes and Questions

1. In most civil law texts and provisions, the word "competence" can be translated as "jurisdiction." The term means that the court has the right and the authority to rule.

2. You should note in § 328(1) that the propriety of the foreign court's jurisdiction is determined according to German law. This rule is not new or novel; it is simply stated here with greater clarity. Its rigorous application could lead to insurmountable conflicts between national laws and make most foreign judgments unenforceable in Germany.

3. What is the significance and consequence of default for due process requirements under the German law?

4. Discuss the effect of collateral estoppel and *res judicata* on enforcement under German law.

5. Does § 328 contain a public policy exception to enforcement? How is it stated? Is it a domestic law notion? If so, why should it apply here? In a recent case, the German Federal Court of Justice (BGH) held that the punitive damage part of a California judgment was unenforceable in Germany. When a U.S. civil judgment awards punitive damages in addition to compensatory damages, it intrudes upon the State's monopoly over punishment. It thereby violates the fundamental principles of German law. It was more, in the court's view, than a mere difference of procedure. *See* Zekoll, *The Enforceability of American Money Judgments Abroad: A Landmark Decision by the German Federal Court of Justice*, 30 COLUM. J. TRANSNAT'L L. 641 (1992). How do you assess this development? Does it have any parallels to *Bachchan* and the First Amendment freedom issue? Are both opinions equally untenable?

BRUSSELS CONVENTION ON JURISDICTION AND THE ENFORCEMENT OF JUDGMENTS IN CIVIL AND COMMERCIAL MATTERS

8 I.L.M. 229 (1969).

(excerpted)

[. . .]

Article 25

Within the meaning of this Convention, a "judgment" shall be any judgment rendered by a court or tribunal of a Contracting State, whatever such judgment may be called, such as a decree, decision, or an order or writ of execution, including the determination of costs by the clerk of the court.

Section 1

RECOGNITION

Article 26

Judgments rendered in a Contracting State shall be recognized in the other Contracting States without a special procedure being required.

In the event of a dispute, all interested parties invoking recognition on the main issue may have it declared in accordance with the procedures specified in Sections 2 and 3 of this Title that the judgment must be recognized.

If recognition is invoked incidentally before a court of a Contracting State, that court shall have jurisdiction in the matter.

Article 27

Recognition shall, however, not be accorded:

(1) If it is contrary to "public policy" in the State applied to;

(2) If the defaulting defendant was not served with the summons correctly and in good time for him to arrange for his defence;

(3) If the judgment is incompatible with a judgment rendered in a dispute between the same parties in the State applied to;

(4) If the court of the State of origin has, in rendering its judgment in settlement of a matter concerning the status or capacity of natural persons, marriage *regimes*, wills and inheritances contravened a rule of the private international law of the State applied to, unless the effect of its judgment is the same as if it had applied the provisions of the private international law of the State applied to.

Article 28

Neither shall judgments be recognized if the provisions of Sections 3, 4 and 5 of Title II have been contravened, or in the case specified in Article 59.

When the jurisdictions referred to in the foregoing paragraph are examined, the authority applied to shall be bound by the *de facto* verifications on which the court of the State of origin based its jurisdiction.

Without prejudice to the provisions of the first paragraph, the jurisdiction of the court of the State of origin may not be reviewed; the rules relating to jurisdiction do not apply to the matters of "public policy" referred to in Article 27(1).

Article 29

In no circumstances may the foreign judgment be reviewed as to the merits.

Article 30

Any court of a Contracting State before which recognition of a judgment rendered in another Contracting State is invoked may stay the judgment if an ordinary appeal has been lodged.

Section 2

Enforcement

Article 31

All judgments rendered in a Contracting State which are enforceable in that State shall be enforced in another Contracting State when the writ of execution has been issued at the request of any interested party.

Article 32

[. . .]

The competent court shall be a court in the area in which is domiciled the party against which enforcement is applied for. If the party is not domiciled in the State applied to, jurisdiction shall be determined by the place of enforcement.

Article 33

The procedure for filing the application shall be determined by the law of the State of enforcement.

The applicant must elect domicile within the area jurisdiction of the court applied to. However, if the law of the State of enforcement does not provide for election of domicile, the applicant shall nominate a representative *ad litem*.

The documents referred to in Articles 46 and 47 shall be attached to the application.

Article 34

The court applied to shall render judgment at an early date, and the party against which an enforcement is applied for shall at this stage in the proceedings not be entitled to submit comments.

The application may be dismissed only for one of the reasons specified in Articles 27 and 28.

Under no circumstances may the foreign judgment be reviewed as to the merits.

Article 35

The judgment rendered as a result of the application shall immediately be brought to the knowledge of the applicant by the clerk of the court in accordance with the procedure specified by the law of the State of enforcement.

Article 36

If enforcement is authorized, the party against which enforcement is applied for may appeal against the judgment within a period of one month of its notification.

If that party is domiciled in a Contracting State other than that in which the judgment authorizing the enforcement was rendered, the aforementioned period shall be two months and shall run from the date when the judgment was served on him in person or at his domicile. There shall be no extension of the period on the grounds of distance.

[. . .]

Article 38

Any court with which the appeal is lodged may, at the request of the party appealing, stay judgment if an ordinary appeal has been lodged against the foreign judgment in the State of origin or if the period for appealing has not expired; in the latter case, the court may allow time for appealing.

The court may also make enforcement subject to the provision of a guarantee determined by itself.

Article 39

During the period for appeal specified in Article 36, and until judgment has been rendered on the appeal, action concerning the property of the party against whom enforcement is applied for shall not exceed preservation measures.

The judgment granting enforcement shall include authorization to proceed to such measures.

[. . .]

Article 41

The judgment rendered in response to the appeal specified in Article 40 may be challenged only by an appeal for reversal (*pourvoi en cassation*) and, in the Federal Republic of Germany, by a complaint on a point of law (*Rechtsbeschwerde*).

Article 42

When the foreign judgment has ruled on a number of heads of the application and when enforcement cannot be authorized for all them, the court shall grant enforcement for one or more of them.

The applicant may request partial enforcement.

Article 43

Foreign judgments imposing a pecuniary penalty shall be enforceable in the State applied to only if the amount of the penalty has been finally determined by the courts of the State of origin.

Article 44

An applicant receiving legal aid in the State where the judgment was rendered shall also qualify for legal aid, without further examination, in the proceedings specified in Articles 32 to 35.

Article 45

No guarantee or deposit, however designated, may be required, either on the grounds of foreign origin or on the grounds of lack of domicile or residence in the country, from the party applying for enforcement in a Contracting State of a judgment rendered in another Contracting State.

[. . .]

Notes and Questions

The Brussels and Lugano Conventions establish the EU position on the enforcement of Member State judgments by other Member States. Is the Brussels Convention a modern law on the subject? What makes it so? Explain the content of Article 27(4). Is Article 29 the centerpiece provision? Why? What is the significance of domicile in the convention framework? When is appeal possible and on what grounds? When is partial enforcement possible? When is it desirable?

Japanese Law on the Enforcement of Foreign Judgments

Article 200 of the Japanese Code of Civil Procedure establishes the requirements for the enforcement of foreign judgments in Japan:

> A foreign judgment that has become final and binding [in the country of rendition] shall be valid [enforceable in Japan] only if it satisfies the following conditions:
>
> (1) the jurisdiction of the foreign [rendering] court does not violate the provisions of laws, executive orders, or treaties;
>
> (2) the Japanese national against whom the judgment was rendered duly received a summons or other public notice of the proceeding or, in the absence of receiving such notice, made a voluntary appearance;
>
> (3) the foreign judgment does not violate Japanese public policy or good morals;
>
> (4) the foreign jurisdiction in which the judgment was rendered must afford reciprocity (or mutual guarantee) to Japanese judgments.

According to the decisional law of the Japanese courts, article 200(1) requires that the foreign court's assertion of jurisdiction be valid according to Japanese law. *See* Judgment of Nov. 30, 1973 (Tokyo Dist. Ct.), *Kasai-geppo* 26, 10, 8. Article 200(2) is designed to afford the Japanese national against whom the judgment is rendered protection from abbreviated proceedings before foreign courts. *See* S. KIDANA, H. MATSUOKA, & S. WATANABE, OUTLINE OF PRIVATE INTERNATIONAL LAW (1985). The foreign court must have allowed the Japanese national a fair opportunity to defend against the lawsuit. The public policy exception to enforcement under article 200(3) applies both to the content of the foreign judgment and the proceeding that gave rise to it. Neither aspect can violate Japanese public policy. *See* Judgment of June 7, 1983 (Sup. Ct.), *Saiko-saibansyo minji hanreisyu* 37, 5, 611. The final requirement, contained in article 200(4), refers to reciprocity (or "mutual guarantee") between Japan and the foreign jurisdiction. Although the requirement of reciprocity is usually strictly applied by Japanese courts, it is sometimes difficult to ascertain whether reciprocity in fact exists and, moreover, reciprocity has little, if anything, to do with the legal validity or acceptability of the foreign judgment's content or of the foreign court's proceeding. *See* S. KIDANA, H. MATSUOKA, & S. WATANABE, *supra*, at 268. In a recent judgment, the Japanese Supreme Court diluted somewhat the demands of reciprocity under Japanese law by holding that it required that Japanese judgments of the same type as the foreign judgment should be valid in the foreign jurisdiction according to requirements that do not differ substantially from those applying in Japanese law. *See* Judgment of June 7, 1983, *supra*.

Notes and Questions

1. There is nothing new about the Japanese approach, especially when it is compared with its German counterpart, from which it likely hails. The standard elements are all present: (1) propriety under the requested State's domestic law of the assertion of jurisdiction by the court of rendition; (2) basic due process requirements; (3) public policy; and (4) reciprocity. The critical problems remain definitional, attributing content, for example, to the notion of reciprocity.

2. *A Note on Canadian Practice*: To return to the North American sector of this foreign law inquiry, Canadian courts have wholeheartedly joined the Western liberal consensus on the enforcement of foreign judgments. In *Morguard Investments Ltd. v. De Savoye*, 76 D.L.R. (4th) 256 (Can. Sup. Ct. 1990), the Supreme Court of Canada reviewed the difficulties in enforcing judgments between Canadian provinces and found that many of them had arisen due to a misapprehension regarding the real nature of the doctrine of comity of nations. Comity, the court held, was not based solely on respect for other jurisdictions, but also upon convenience, if not necessity, when legal authority was divided among a number of sovereign States.

Writing for a unanimous court of seven justices, Mr. Justice LaForest observed that the most complete formulation of the concept of comity appeared in *Hilton v. Guyot*. The judicial reason of modern times must also be grounded in the need to facilitate the flow of wealth, skills, and people across state and international boundaries in a fair an orderly manner. Against this backdrop, the Supreme Court of Canada concluded that the courts of one Canadian province should give full faith and credit, to use the language of the U.S. Constitution, to the judgments given by a court in another province or territory, as long as the court had properly, or appropriately, exercised jurisdiction in the proceeding. In fairness to a defendant, a court ought not to assume jurisdiction unless there is a real and substantial connection between the damages suffered and the jurisdiction.

In *United States of Am. v. Robert Ivey, Mazi Ind., Ltd.*, 130 D.L.R. (4th) 647, *aff'd*, 139 D.L.R. (4th) 570 (Ont. Ct. Just., Gen. Div. 1995), the court held—along with prior courts—that the *Morguard* "real and substantial connection" test applied to U.S. and other foreign court judgments that emanated from legal regimes with juridical principles and values that were compatible with the Canadian standards of justice. In a mobile global society, it is both necessary and desirable for governments and national courts to engage in mutual respect for the work product of their foreign counterparts, including substantive law and rules of procedure. It would disrupt transborder commercial activity if it were possible for a domestic resident to engage in business abroad for several years and then seek shelter behind domestic walls from accountability for that activity.

The Canadian decisional law appears to add or emphasize a factor of practicality to the enforcement of foreign judgment question. For the highest Canadian court, it would be unthinkable to withhold enforceability from a U.S. judgment because of a procedural difference or a substantive liability standard. In this sense, it creates a contrast to the German ruling on U.S. punitive damages and to the holding in *Bachchan*. The Canadian court appears to conclude that the functionality of the transborder system trumps any domestic consideration. How do you assess the comparison?

Chapter 6

AN INTRODUCTION TO INTERNATIONAL COMMERCIAL ARBITRATION (ICA)*

Table of Sections

---

* In writing the next two chapters, I have adapted materials from two of my previous books: CASES AND MATERIALS ON THE LAW AND PRACTICE OF ARBITRATION (Rev. 3d ed. 2003) and THE LAW AND PRACTICE OF ARBITRATION (2004). The adaptation of these materials is done with the permission of the publisher, Juris Publishing, Inc.

§ 1. DEFINITION OF ARBITRATION

Arbitration is a private trial procedure. It can yield binding determinations through less expensive, more efficient, expert, and fair proceedings. It can achieve finality and avoid most of the histrionics of court litigation. Arbitration, however, is not a means of accomplishing dispute resolution through party agreement. Party choice functions primarily at the outset of the process. The contracting parties confer upon the arbitrators the authority to adjudicate their disputes, *i.e.*, to render a final disposition on the matters submitted that can eventually be coercively enforced at law. Party agreement sets the process in motion, but it does not necessarily dictate the procedure or the outcome. Once the parties entrust the arbitral tribunal with the authority to rule, they relinquish control of the resolution of the dispute to the arbitrators.

Contract provides the entry into arbitration. The parties agree to submit existing or prospective disputes to arbitration. The agreement to arbitrate is the centerpiece of the process—both legally and practically. The parties have the freedom—the legal right—to engage in arbitration and to make specific provisions for the implementation and operation of their arbitration. By entering into an arbitration contract, the parties voluntarily surrender their right to judicial relief and, in effect, create a private system of adjudication that presumably is better adapted to their dispute resolution needs.

Notes and Questions

1. The agreement to submit disputes to arbitration is nothing more or less than an agreement to create a private trial conducted by a private judge. The objective appears to be to provide access to an expert decision-maker through a fair process. You should note that arbitration "can" have a number of features, not that it always "does" or "must." Because lawyers are involved in the proceedings, arbitrations can become adversarialized. Should lawyers or legally-trained parties be excluded? How would such a practice be justified? If exclusion is not possible or desirable, should advocacy be tempered otherwise as a matter of course? Should the arbitrator in each case decide representational and procedural matters? But, couldn't an *ad hoc* approach create disparities and unexpected instances of unfairness? Is referring these matters to the administering arbitral institution the answer?

2. The function of party agreement is critical to an accurate definition of arbitration. The parties agree to delegate the authority to decide disputes to the arbitrators who then take control of the process, unless the agreement provides for a non-standard arrangement. The exercise of controlling authority by the arbitrators once they are constituted as a tribunal is an aspect of the process that has recently been emphasized by the U.S. Supreme Court. *See Howsam v. Dean Witter Reynolds, Inc.*, 537 U.S. 79, 123 S.Ct. 588, 154 L.Ed.2d 491 (2002); *Green Tree Fin. Corp. v. Bazzle*, 539 U.S. 444, 123 S.Ct. 2402, 156 L.Ed.2d 414 (2003). Once a court determines that a valid agreement to arbitrate exists or—under U.S. law—duly-designated arbitrators come to the same conclusion, the arbitral tribunal generally assumes complete authority over the proceeding and the outcome. Parties should not lose sight of the "benefit of the bargain" for arbitration or, in effect, what it means to agree to arbitrate: It is to have the arbitrators decide submitted

matters. This "truth" cannot be altered except through mutual party agreement.

3. Freedom of contract is an essential facet of arbitration law. In your view, are there any limits to the parties' right to customize their reference to arbitration? Clearly, their inability to agree is a limit. Are there others? Does contract trump statute in this setting? Why and why not? Who is the law-giver in these circumstances?

4. One of the more challenging professional duties is to determine your client's actual dispute resolution needs. You need to understand your client, his/her business, and be clairvoyant about the future. How would you proceed to satisfy this duty? When would you recommend arbitration without reservation? On what basis? For what reason(s)?

§ 2. ARBITRATION AS A COMMERCIAL REMEDY

Arbitral adjudication responds well to the character of commercial disputes. First, arbitral proceedings are not open to the public and awards generally are not published. The disputes, the proceedings, and the outcome are not accessible to business associates, competitors, and clients. The recourse to arbitration, therefore, allows commercial parties to maintain at least the appearance of a competitive position despite transactional problems. Second, the parties have the right to select the arbitrators. The designated arbitrators ordinarily have considerable expertise in the field. Their commercial experience allows them to reach determinations that reflect accepted standards. By choosing to arbitrate, therefore, business parties avoid inexpert judges, legalistic solutions, and unwanted publicity.

Third, arbitral adjudication can be more flexible and less adversarial and protracted than its judicial counterpart. It can result in an economy of both time and money. The commercial experience of the arbitral tribunal lessens the significance of legal precedent, eliminates the need for complex rules of evidence, and minimizes discovery, the use of experts, and other trial procedures. These features reduce the prospect of tactical litigious warfare. Procedural informality, placing trust in the arbitrators' professional capabilities, and allowing commercial equity to trump jural considerations are the hallmarks of commercial arbitration.

In international commerce, the neutrality of arbitration as to nationality and legal tradition is a fourth factor that contributes to its "business appeal." In fact, the reference to arbitration is indispensable in multinational commercial ventures. It eliminates the conflicts associated with the assertion of national court jurisdiction, the choice of applicable law, and the enforcement of foreign judgments. Arbitration also tempers the disparities between different legal systems. In the context of transborder business, arbitration functions as a *de facto* transborder legal system, providing an adjudicatory process free of national bias, parochial laws and practices, and able to dispense sensible commercial justice.

Finally, it should be underscored that arbitration's more flexible approach to adjudication can be less destructive of business relationships. It allows the parties to continue to do business once the dispute has been resolved. By agreeing to arbitrate, the parties also surrender some of their legal rights. The bargain for expedient and less contentious adjudication carries with it the possibility that expectations of fairness will be frustrated without the possibility of correction.

Notes and Questions

1. How valuable is arbitrator expertise? Is it a remedy to all problems? Does it mean that the *status quo* is never altered or that dissenting views are never tolerated? *A contrario sensu*, does expertise always yield consistent airtight solutions? Don't the factors of judgment and choice make expert knowledge inherently unstable and prone to shifts in temperament?

2. Doesn't private adjudication exact a substantial social price? Don't societies and their members have a right to know how contractual disputes are resolved and how commercial conduct is being regulated? Is there a viable, perhaps necessary, distinction between the contractual disputes and the regulation of commercial conduct? Explain your thinking. What would you advise an international arbitrator to do if, in the course of developing the record of an international arbitration involving allegations of contract breach, she discovers a violation of the U.S. Foreign Corrupt Practices Act or the Sherman Antitrust Act or the IRS Code? To whom or to what entity, if any, does the international arbitrator owe allegiance and a professional duty?

3. What consequence if an international arbitration only offers the parties a neutral, non-national forum for adjudicating international contract claims? The arbitration is otherwise expensive, lengthy, and riddled with disagreement and counter-disagreement. Do these features make arbitration less attractive, less necessary, or illegitimate and, therefore, can either party rescind the agreement to arbitrate at will? Should an award that results from such proceedings be challengeable on the basis that the arbitral procedure didn't deliver on its promises? How would you codify that ground in statutory language?

4. How do you assess and define the neutrality factor? How significant is it as a consideration—practically, legally, or ethically? Is arbitration a transborder "one size fits all"? Is it, rather, a creative and dynamic mechanism by which to achieve the reconciliation of various national legal protocols?

5. Is peace or the preservation of business relationships a good exchange for legal rights? Is arbitration a begrudging or bad compromise? Is it forced? Is it acceptable?

§ 3. THE OPERATION OF THE ARBITRAL PROCESS

Assuming an agreement to arbitrate exists and that it is an enforceable contract, the proceedings usually take place in accordance with the rules of an administering arbitral institution. The institutional rules provide the framework for the operation of the various stages of the arbitral process: (1) the constitution of the arbitral tribunal; (2) the establishment of the submission to arbitration or the tribunal's terms of reference; (3) the selection of procedural rules for the proceedings; (4) the conduct of the proceedings; (5) the closure of the proceedings; (6) the tribunal's deliberations; and (7) the rendering of an award.

Following receipt of a "demand for arbitration," the administering arbitral institution notifies the other party of the demand and requests that the parties nominate arbitrators pursuant to their agreement. The administering institution, if necessary, can supply the parties with arbitrator lists. As a general matter, the parties select an uneven number of arbitrators to avoid a deadlock one arbitrator is usually agreed upon for smaller matters and a three-member panel presides over larger, more complex cases. When a three-member panel is chosen, each party names its arbitrator and the two party-appointed arbitrators name a third arbitrator, known as the neutral, who acts as the chair of the panel.

The received wisdom has been that party-appointed arbitrators favor the designating party's case, leaving the neutral arbitrator to cast the deciding vote. At a minimum, a party-designated arbitrator is expected to represent the appointing party's position in the tribunal's deliberations. The practice sometimes leads to "arbitrations-within-arbitrations," in which the neutral arbitrator moderates the debate between the party-appointed arbitrators who advocate on behalf of "their" party and seek to persuade the neutral to vote their way. In these circumstances, the appointment of the neutral arbitrator becomes a critical aspect of the process.

Despite their appointment by a party, party-designated arbitrators are now expected to act in a fully disinterested professional manner. Some courts disagree and hold that partisan expectations still validly accompany party appointment. Recent institutional practice, however, provides that all arbitrators—including party-appointed arbitrators—should assess the submitted matter with complete impartiality. Contemporary appointment rules further insist upon thorough disclosure and transparency by arbitrators.

Once an arbitral tribunal is constituted, the parties enter into a submission agreement. The agreement describes the matters upon which the parties disagree and establishes the arbitral tribunal's authority to rule—its jurisdictional authority. In some arbitral systems, the parties need not enter into a submission. They correspond or meet with the arbitrators and identify the matters to be arbitrated in a type of prehearing conference. In ICC practice, by contrast, the description of the parties' dispute constitutes the arbitrators' terms of reference. The terms of reference are a significant part of ICC arbitrations. The arbitral tribunal has no authority to adjudicate beyond the stipulations contained in the terms of reference (unless the parties provide otherwise). In all forms of arbitration, the arbitrators' failure to rule upon a submitted claim or a ruling on a matter not submitted can result in the nullification or setting aside of the award or part of it.

The content of the submission, of the terms of reference, or of the prehearing conference are important to the contemplated arbitration. Because they are, they can generate a great deal of representational debate. In order to maintain the functionality of arbitration, practice has rendered the definition of the terms of reference more fluid. After consultations with the parties, the arbitrators establish a general protocol of considerations that will be modified, amplified, and amended during the course of the proceedings.

Before the proceedings can begin, the designated arbitrators must accept their appointment and the statement of claims that has been submitted. The arbitrators are obligated to disclose any conflicts of interest or other matter that might impair their ability to rule in an impartial manner. The failure to disclose necessary and available information can result in the vacatur of the award on the basis of evident partiality. The arbitrators can refuse to serve on the panel or can disqualify themselves. The parties can lodge an action to disqualify an arbitrator before the administering arbitral institution or a court of law. With the acquiescence of the parties and under the direction of the administering arbitral institution, the arbitral tribunal chooses a place for the arbitration and sets a time for the initial hearing. At this stage of the process, parties submit a deposit for arbitrator and administrative fees with the administering arbitral institution.

There is generally a lag between the filing of a demand for arbitration and the constitution of the arbitral tribunal. Between the initiation of the arbitration and the investiture of the arbitrators, critical matters may arise that relate to the prospective proceedings, *e.g.*, involving the preservation of evidence, the attachment of assets, or the enforceability of the arbitration agreement itself. Delay on these matters could compromise the anticipated arbitral proceedings or render them useless. The parties or the arbitral institution should provide for the exercise of necessary procedural authority in these circumstances. The parties' agreement or the applicable institutional rules could permit the appointment of an interim or magistrate-like arbitrator or administrator who would have temporary emergency authority to rule on threshold matters and thereby give effect to the parties' agreement to arbitrate.

An arbitration can be conducted on a purely documentary basis. In an "arbitration on the documents," the parties supply the administering arbitral institution with a statement of their position and allegations, as well as their supporting evidence. The arbitral tribunal or the sole arbitrator then rules on the basis of the submitted materials. Arbitrations can also consist of a documentary record with an abbreviated hearing or of a set of elaborate hearings that include pretrial procedures and live testimonial evidence. Actual proceedings can be as varied as the type of parties involved and the circumstances of the dispute. The character of the proceeding is generally determined by the arbitration agreement or by the parties' ability to agree once a dispute arises. If no contractual disposition exists and the parties are unable to agree, the arbitral tribunal—under the supervision of the administering arbitral institution—would decide on the protocol for the arbitration.

The proceedings begin once preliminary procedural matters have been resolved. The parties' traditional expectation is to have reasonably fair and flexible proceedings. The arbitrators usually have sufficient procedural authority to thwart trial tactics that unnecessarily lengthen the proceedings. Generally, the parties want to be able to make their case. They then want the arbitral tribunal to decide the matter.

Arbitral systems ordinarily do not include a right to pretrial discovery. Parties are generally required to exchange documents and witness lists prior to the commencement of the proceedings. The arbitral tribunal has the authority to decide whether proffered evidence is relevant and to evaluate the significance of the evidence that it admits. While the arbitrating parties have the right to be heard, neither side can abuse its rights by manufacturing specious arguments, issues, and requests for evidence—thereby tactically prolonging the proceeding for litigious advantage.

During an arbitral proceeding, the parties make their case through the means described in the document and witness lists. In most arbitral systems, the parties' agreement to arbitrate implies a duty to arbitrate in good faith. Failing to respond to tribunal requests in a timely fashion, attempting to create delay by presenting too many lay or expert witnesses, pursuing the other side's witnesses too stridently, or refusing to comply with the tribunal's requests for specific documentary information—all constitute a possible breach of the obligation to arbitrate in good faith. The arbitral tribunal determines whether noncomplying conduct amounts to a breach of the good faith obligation, and the tribunal can then take the breach into account in its final award or assess penalties against the non-complying party during the proceeding.

The right to notification and equal treatment are strictly enforced in arbitral proceedings. Direct or indirect *ex parte* communications between the arbitrators and one of the parties are generally prohibited. All communications must be directed to the administering arbitral institution, which then supplies both the arbitrators and the other side with the information. During the proceeding, the tribunal can rule on jurisdictional questions (under U.S. law, if so authorized by the parties' agreement) and other matters such as the attachment of assets by rendering interim awards.

Rulings on provisional matters should be described as constituting a final determination on the issues addressed by the award. Labeling the ruling as an interim determination may lead to problems of enforcement if the requested court concludes that it can only confirm final arbitral rulings. It is well-settled that the bringing of judicial actions to secure the process or to enforce provisional or permanent measures does not constitute a breach of the agreement to arbitrate.

When the parties have presented their evidence and witnesses and established their respective positions, the arbitral tribunal closes the proceedings and adjourns to deliberate. At this stage, new information can be admitted only with the tribunal's permission. The admission of new information requires that the opposing party be given an opportunity to respond. The tribunal's deliberations are conducted in secret. A decision can be and usually is reached by simple majority vote. Especially in domestic practice, arbitral tribunals render awards without issuing an opinion explaining the reasons for the determination. The award usually follows a standard format: a statement of the facts, a description of the issues, the parties' respective positions, and a disposition of the matters submitted. The practice of not providing an opinion with domestic awards is intended to discourage judicial review. With the expansion of arbitration's jurisdictional scope, that practice may be altered. The administering arbitral institution usually provides the parties with the award within thirty days of the conclusion of the proceedings.

The rendering of an award triggers the final payment of outstanding institutional and arbitrator fees from the money placed on deposit by the parties. The administering arbitral institution may withhold the award until all fees and costs have been paid. The costs of the arbitration generally are shared equally by the parties. The arbitral tribunal, in its discretion, may allocate the costs of the arbitration among the parties. Each party is responsible for its attorney's fees, unless the agreement contains a "loser-pays-all" provision. The inclusion of such a provision may require the arbitral tribunal to reconvene and to rule upon whether there is a "loser" and, if not, how the costs should be apportioned. Alternatively, the arbitral tribunal may exercise its discretion to distribute the costs of the proceeding. The parties can comply voluntarily with the terms of the award or file an action to confirm or vacate the award. The grounds for challenging arbitral awards are few in number and focus upon narrow procedural issues. Courts rarely vacate arbitral awards.

Arbitrations can experience problems. Parties can try to thwart the process. They can challenge the arbitral tribunal's jurisdiction by alleging that the arbitration agreement is nonexistent, an invalid contract, or that it does not apply to the dispute in question. Also, a party can simply refuse to appear at the proceedings, decline to appoint an arbitrator, or ignore the directives and rules of the administering arbitral institution. In addition, a party can contest the procedures to be followed or the power of the arbitral tribunal—for example, whether the tribunal can award punitive damages, whether experts can appear and how they are to be qualified or questioned, or whether the arbitrators can order attachments during the proceedings to secure the payment of an eventual award. Further disagreement can be generated regarding matters of administrative detail such as whether the place of arbitration is equally convenient for both parties or how the costs of the arbitration and arbitrator fees are to be apportioned. Arbitration can be a better remedy, but it is hardly a panacea—let alone, a "formula for world peace."

Notes and Questions

1. The point of the foregoing description is to acquaint readers with the actual operation of arbitration proceedings. It is a "nuts and bolts" assessment that means to convey an accurate practical representation of the process. The essential phases and characteristics of the process are all described, *e.g.*, the demand for arbitration and the lack of pre-trial discovery.

2. The placid description, however, does not imply that the process is without its problems or controversies. The status of party-appointed arbitrators is one illustration. Why do you think arbitral institutions are advocating for complete neutrality on the arbitral tribunal? Isn't this an unrealistic posture to assume? Isn't it also against the self-interest of the service-providers?

3. Assuming tribunal-wide neutrality is the rule, how is it established generally and in the particularity of cases? Is disclosure the sole or primary element? What result if the parties nonetheless want their partisan arbitrators? Is this necessarily an evil?

4. The progressive elaboration of the terms of reference or submission during the course of the proceedings is an intelligent way to address the adversarial difficulty that can be encountered on this matter at the outset of the proceedings. Doesn't this approach, however, give the arbitral tribunal nearly unfettered discretion to establish the terms? In effect, the parties' adversarial relationship forces them to delegate the jurisdictional function of the terms of reference to the arbitrators. Doesn't this development make vacatur on the basis of excess of authority even more unlikely?

5. Does and should arbitral tribunals have the right to render injunctions in connection with the arbitral proceedings? Against whom? What are the arguments for and against?

6. What function would an interim or acting arbitrator fulfill? How would you provide for such an arbitrator in the agreement? What about replacement or shadow arbitrators in the event of recusation, disqualification, or incapacity in the designated tribunal? Is this also a significant concern?

7. In what, if any, circumstances would you expressly provide for the use of experts in a prospective arbitral proceeding? Would you ever stipulate that the process should include the reference to a civil jury or its equivalent? Would the use of such a mechanism render all tort disputes automatically arbitrable?

8. Does the absence of pretrial discovery mean that arbitrators decide on the basis of an inadequate record? How is information collected in an arbitration and when is it sufficient? Who makes that decision?

9. In your estimation, when should the "duty to arbitrate in good faith" be used to police arbitral proceedings and the parties' conduct in the arbitration? Can you make a specific recommendation?

10. Should dissenting opinions be allowed in arbitration? Should they be in writing and integrated into the award? What function would they serve? What about concurring opinions?

§ 4. THE RISE OF ICA

Modern-day International Commercial Arbitration (ICA) emerged in the aftermath of WWII. In all likelihood, it reflected the transborder experience of former military personnel and became part of Western efforts to advance and promote democracy and the institution of capitalism. Because it permitted engagement in international business, it maintained the unity of the free-world alliance and developed the prosperity of allied countries. ICA, however, was limited by the cold war ideology that contributed to its emergence. Worldwide East–West distrust made unfettered global commercial exchanges impossible. Ideological divisions prevented the establishment of a unitary world position on trade and commerce.

The form of arbitration that was practiced between United States commercial interests and their European continental counterparts differed significantly from arbitration in Eastern bloc countries. In the former, arbitral adjudication supplied Western merchants with a transborder means of stabilizing international contracts. Although the latter adhered to an internally unified position on arbitration in trade relations, the insularity and ideological preoccupation of these countries hardly gave their policy universal credibility. In effect, the Soviet bloc devised bureaucratic entities, known as trade commissions, to regulate commerce within the bloc. The trade commissions established arbitral systems by which to resolve the transactional disputes that arose between participants. The arbitral mechanism was of narrow scope and subservient to the reigning political ideology. Its purpose was to facilitate statist policies, not achieve commercial justice or promote free and open markets.

Two events brought about a second phase in the development of ICA: (1) The collapse of the Soviet Union and the end of the cold war (symbolized by the fall of the Berlin Wall in 1989); and (2) the eventual realization among leading international lawyers on Wall Street that transborder arbitration had replaced U.S. federal courts as the venue for international commercial litigation. ICA was also bolstered by the advent of "globalization," a reinvigorated form of international commerce done on a truly worldwide basis. The pursuit of self-interest through economic consensus and pragmatic cooperation took the place of the more destructive competition for ideological spheres of influence in the world community. In the 1990s, in fact, commerce replaced politics as the primary language of the international community.

During the 1990s, there was also an eruption of national arbitration laws throughout the globe—from Latin American countries to Germany to former Soviet bloc States and Asian jurisdictions. These laws generally reflected a favorable international consensus on ICA. Moreover, a

number of countries created arbitral centers to compete for the business of arbitration. Most jurisdictions became hospitable to arbitration. ICA was no longer relegated to the domain of the specialist or considered a renegade process. It became the symbol of and the passport to global capitalism and national commercial prosperity. The success of ICA in the transactional area led to new vistas of application. The arbitral process began to perform a new, more public-law-oriented mission. Arbitral procedure became a mechanism by which countries could "depoliticize" commercial disputes that had divisive diplomatic and political overtones.

The Iran–United States Claims Tribunal, created by the Algiers Accords, was the first significant experiment in this vein. Despite a variety of shortcomings, the Tribunal successfully provided compensation to many of the commercial interests that were affected by the Iranian Revolution. *See* C. Brower & J. Brueschke, The Iran–United States Tribunal (1998); R. Lillich, ed., The Iran–United States Tribunal 1981–1983 (1984). The arbitral framework in Chapters 19 and 20 of NAFTA reflects a more sophisticated use of arbitration in the regulatory law context. There, ICA procedure is meant to resolve trade disputes between private parties and governments and between the participating governments. NAFTA or investment arbitration gives private parties the extraordinary right to arbitrate transactional disputes about trade regulations directly with the foreign government. A less binding form of government-to-government arbitration is also contemplated under the NAFTA. *See* Jack J. Coe, Jr., *Taking Stock of NAFTA Chapter 11 in Its Tenth Year: An Interim Sketch of Selected Themes, Issues, and Methods*, 36 Vand. J. Transnat'l L. 1381 (2003); *see also http://www.natialaw.org.*

Notes and Questions

1. The makeshift political history of commercial arbitration emphasizes the progressive awakening of national societies and economies to the potential of the international marketplace. Isn't this attitude better than isolationism and the distrust of things foreign?

2. The acceptance of or participation in transborder relations, however, always entails the surrender of domestic authority and control. The European Union is the most developed form of transborder regional government; NAFTA and the WTO are much less complete examples of the same phenomenon. The European Parliament and Commission in Brussels and the European Court of Justice exercise real authority and power. They trump or dislodge domestic counterparts. Participating in NAFTA implies a willingness to accept the decisional authority of NAFTA arbitrators. Do these illustrations indicate that domestic authority has succumbed to the rule of an alien, faceless international bureaucracy? Is the progression to regional government and justice inevitable?

3. What lesson about arbitral adjudication do you draw from the use of trade commission arbitration in former Soviet States?

4. What function does a national arbitration center perform? Is it a good idea to attempt to create one? How would you proceed?

§ 5. ICA'S MIXED REGIONAL STANDING

ICA has a wide, but uneven, standing in the world community. As noted earlier, it originated in Europe and initially reflected the continental civilian procedural approach to adjudication. The International Chamber of Commerce (ICC), which is headquartered in Paris, was a significant force during the 1950s in drafting and fostering the widespread acceptance of ICA and the New York Arbitration Convention. Eisemann, *The Court of Arbitration: Outline of Its Changes from Inception to the Present Day, in* INTERNATIONAL CHAMBER OF COMMERCE 60 YEARS OF ICC ARBITRATION 391 (1984).

The French government ratified the Convention within months of its being opened for signature, attesting to the importance it attached to the international arbitration process. Moreover, French courts progressively elaborated a judicial policy that heavily favored the recourse to and the effective operation of ICA. France was the principal proponent of transborder arbitration at the outset of its contemporary development. *See, e.g.*, Carbonneau, *The Elaboration of a French Court Doctrine on International Commercial Arbitration: A Study in Liberal Civilian Judicial Creativity*, 55 TUL. L. REV.1 (1980).

Once the United States government ratified the Convention in 1970 and the United States Supreme Court began to issue rulings on transborder litigation and arbitration, the doctrinal center of gravity shifted from Europe to the United States. U.S. common law lawyer practices began to influence the process. The influence extended to the structure of arbitral proceedings, which began to mirror the basic characteristics of a U.S. adversarial trial. In effect, the coexistence of two influential centers of legal doctrine on arbitration instituted a struggle between the European civil law and the Anglo–American common law for dominance in the conduct of arbitral proceedings. This tension continues to be present in contemporary arbitral practice.

Accordingly, Northern and Western countries generally accepted ICA as necessary and professed support for the process. In recent times, ICA has become more popular in formerly inhospitable regions like Latin America. *See* Barclay, *Arbitration in Latin America*, 43 ARB. 105 (1977). Mexico is a good example. Historically, for Mexico, the settlement of boundary and other disputes through international claims commissions had made any form of international adjudicatory process suspect. The commissions were seen as mechanisms by which the United States imposed its will upon its weaker, Southern neighbor. Mexico refused, by and large, to participate in these proceedings and embraced the rationale of the Calvo Clause, providing for the national treatment of foreign investors and the exclusive reference to local remedies for the resolution of foreign investment disputes. In response to the emergence of globalization, Mexico revised its position on arbitration. *See* Siqueirois, *Mexican Arbitration: The New Statute*, 30 TEX. INT'L L.J. 227 (1995).

In 1993, Mexico became one of the first Latin American countries to adopt a modern arbitration statute. The Mexican endorsement of ICA symbolized a desire and willingness to participate in world commerce on transborder terms. A number of the other Latin Amerian countries, including Brazil (1996), Bolivia (1997), Chile (2004), Colombia (1996), Costa Rica (1997), Ecuador (1997), Guatemala (1995), Panama (1999), Peru (1995), and Venezuela (1998), followed the Mexican example.

The depth of commitment to ICA in the individual countries, however, is difficult to gauge. Uncertainty looms especially in circumstances in which the enforcement of an international arbitral award might be antagonistic to local interests or favor a national or corporate entity from a developed country. Despite the adoption of a modern statutory framework, courts in these countries might use procedural delay to thwart enforcement indirectly or invoke the public policy exception to express direct opposition. Thus far, the days of the Calvo Clause appear to be a bygone area. It is difficult to ascertain whether episodic economic decline and political instability will have a substantial impact upon the stature of ICA in the area.

ICA has a mixed standing in Asian countries, such as Japan, Singapore, the new Hong Kong, and India. *See* P. McConnaughay & T. Ginsburg, International Commercial Arbitration in Asia (2002). The Japanese endorsement of ICA has been circumspect and unenergetic. Institutional centers for the conduct of international arbitrations have existed in Japan for years, but the volume of cases has never been substantial and a strong international arbitration community has never been established. Generally, international arbitral awards are enforceable in Japan. The Japan Commercial Arbitration Association (JCAA) is one of Japan's best known arbitral institutions; established in 1953, it resolves disputes arising from international and domestic business transactions.

Japanese culture has a strong preference for negotiated dispute settlement. The bringing of public court proceedings to resolve a dispute is tantamount to public humiliation under Japanese concepts. Engaging in private forms of adjudication that have no official sanction is an even greater social affront. Unlike judges, arbitrators have no public basis for their authority to rule. The law merely tolerates their investiture by contract.

Some commentators ascribe the underdeveloped character of arbitration in Japan to the fact that few Japanese attorneys speak English. Linguistic insularity contributes to the lack of outreach. Also, the Japanese code provisions on arbitration had been dated. The Japanese Diet, however, enacted a new Japanese law on arbitration that came into force on March 1, 2004. The text of the law is a composite of a number of sources. Its content appears to be somewhat opaque. Its basic impact remains to be determined.

Singapore differs significantly from Japan in its approach to ICA. It is eager to become the Asian center for ICA. Recently, it adopted new laws that favor arbitration. There also is an administrative center for arbitration that actively supports the recourse to arbitration in Singapore and the international marketplace. *See* Morgan, *The Arbitration Act 1996 and Arbitration Law Reform in Hong Kong and Singapore: A Brave New World?*, [1997] ARB. & DISP. RESOL. L.J. 177. In seeking to assume a dominant position, however, Singapore must contend with the new Hong Kong. *See* Lin, *Enforcement of Mainland China's Arbitral Awards in the Hong Kong Special Administrative Region After 1 July 1997*, 65 ARB. 56 (1999). Prior to the historic reunification in 1999, Hong Kong was a bustling center of capitalism and could serve a meeting place for East–West business interests. Its present-day ability to act as a venue for international business and commercial adjudication is uncertain. Historically and geographically, it is an ideal setting for achieving such intermediation.

Other members of the Asian communist world seem to be embracing arbitration and international commerce. Despite long-standing difficulties, Vietnam has demonstrated a genuine willingness to comply with the *quid pro quos* of ICA. *See* Dingh, *Arbitration in Vietnam*, 11 WORLD ARB. & MED. REP. 164 (2000). In late 2001, for example, the Lam Dong People's Court confirmed an arbitral award rendered by the International Chamber of Commerce and Industry (ICCI) in Geneva, Switzerland against a Vietnamese company and in favor of a South Korean company. The arbitrators ruled that the Vietnamese company breached its contract with a South Korean company, and ordered the Vietnamese company to pay damages. The court enforced the award, holding that it "conformed to international practices, the Vietnam Trade Law, and the ordinance on international arbitration in Vietnam." The result demonstrates Vietnamese willingness to accept the discipline of the international marketplace and of the transborder rule of law.

Finally, in the last several years, India has endeavored to revise its position on ICA. Its previous reservations may have stemmed from geopolitical positioning and been grounded in political ideology. In any event, in 1996, India adopted the Arbitration and Conciliation Ordinance. The purpose of the legislation was to stabilize the arbitration system in India and to encourage foreign investment by bringing Indian laws on the settlement of disputes in line with international standards. The new ordinance made several improvements to the prior law. In particular, the parties are free to control various aspects of the arbitration process through their agreement. Among other things, the parties can make a provision for the number and selection of arbitrators, the procedure of the arbitration, the presentation of evidence, and the use of experts.

Under the ordinance, an arbitral award can be set aside if: (1) an arbitrating party is under some incapacity; (2) the agreement is null under the applicable law; (3) a party was not given proper notice of the appointment of the arbitrator or of the proceedings; (4) the award deals with a dispute outside the scope of the arbitration agreement; or (5) the composition of the arbitral tribunal or the arbitral procedure violates Indian public policy. Enforcement of a foreign award can be refused only if, in addition to the reasons for vacating a domestic award, the award has not yet become binding on the parties or the subject matter is not capable of settlement by arbitration under Indian law.

Middle Eastern Muslim countries generally do not favor ICA, seeing it as a tool of Western business interests. State ratification of major international treaties is limited or perfunctory. Positions shift, but—in the end—acquiescing to ICA represents a surrender of autonomy and values. There is reluctance to enforce international arbitral awards on any consistent or predictable basis.

Bahrain is the Arab State most adapted to the Western view of international commercial arbitration. It has adopted the UNCITRAL Model Law on International Commercial Arbitration with very few changes. There is a Bahrain Centre for International Commercial Arbitration. The Centre applies the UNCITRAL Rules on arbitration and enforces awards in accordance with the provisions of the New York Arbitration Convention. Bahrain acceded to the Convention in 1988.

Saudi Arabia is the least hospitable Arab jurisdiction on arbitration. Although it has ratified the New York Arbitration Convention, the enforcement of a foreign arbitral award in Saudi Arabia can be difficult and time-consuming. The award is enforceable only if it is accompanied by a court judgment from the State of rendition. The award must be authenticated by the Saudi Ministry of Foreign Affairs, the Saudi Ministry of Justice, and the Saudi consulate in the State of rendition. Moreover, an award not rendered in Arabic must be translated by a sworn translator before it can be submitted to the Saudi government through proper diplomatic channels. The Saudi government reserves the right to refuse enforcement of the award. Awards rendered by default against a Saudi party are unenforceable.

However well-established ICA may be in the legal civilization of the world community, it remains possible, even under Article V of the New York Arbitration Convention, to thwart the enforcement of an international arbitral award. In an unreported case, for example, a Sri Lankan court refused to enforce an LCIA arbitral award. The award on the merits appeared to be perfectly sound. It involved a straightforward ruling on a clear-cut and costly breach of contract. The procedure of rendition and the conduct of the proceedings seemed to be in full conformity with generally-accepted standards. Despite the compliance of the award to existing standards, the Sri Lankan court ruled that the award could not be enforced because it violated domestic public policy.

Such enforcement rulings constitute unfortunate and poorly-disguised attempts to protect nationals or national entities from basic contract accountability. Pervasive protectionism could foil the entire transborder arbitral process. In addition, protectionism is more likely in countries outside the Northern–Western consensus on arbitration. Opposition to ICA can be based upon factors like political ideology, disparate views of economic development, differences in religious belief, or the lack of a truly functional rule of law or national legal and political institutions.

ICA certainly cannot eradicate or even subdue all of the tensions and conflicts that exist among nations in the world community. The international practitioner must be attentive to the local variations that can exist on a given theme or problem of arbitration law. Despite the diversity of views within the family of nations, globalization has emerged and participation in international commerce is seen by most countries as a desirable objective. A system of transborder arbitration is essential to the pursuit of commerce across national boundaries. Therefore, countries at least pay lip-service to ICA; many of them are attempting to become an integral part of the process; yet others have fully acceded to its ground rules and structures and have made a commitment to its effective operation.

Notes and Questions

1. Are the European–American origins of contemporary ICA a factor that limits the process? Do its origins make the process less universal? Is it really universal or merely a regional system that functions among like-minded States?

2. Would you be confident that you could enforce an international arbitral award in Mexico? Why and why not? What if the arbitrators ruled that the Mexican defendant breached the governing American law—a statutory provision, in this case—and ordered the payment of substantial damages?

3. A few years ago, the Supreme Court of Panama ruled that the doctrine of *kompetenz-kompetenz* or jurisdiction to rule on jurisdictional challenges was unconstitutional under Panamian law. In the court's view, the exercise of these judge-like powers by arbitrators was excessive and untoward. How do you evaluate this development generally and in relation to the status of transborder arbitration in Panama?

In Costa Rica, the law requires that all international arbitrators be of Costa Rican nationality. The same rule applies in Venezuela. What is the effect of such legislative regulation? Does the requirement protect the public or only economic self-interest? Isn't this outright protectionism, unbecoming of a country like Costa Rica or Venezuela? How can such a policy be justified? Make arguments on both sides.

4. Isn't Japanese reluctance to embrace ICA likely to undermine the country's economic standing? Isn't the Japanese disposition toward arbitration surprising given Japan's maritime interests? Doesn't this factor confirm the counterproductive character of the Japanese attitude? Do you believe Singapore is a likely and better Asian center for ICA?

5. What is the international standard on the resolution of disputes? How does the most recent Indian statute on arbitration reflect that standard? Does alignment to international standards mean effectiveness of operation? What degree of confidence should alignment inspire in the practitioner?

6. Develop your understanding of the Arab reluctance to endorse ICA. How would you advise a client seeking to do business in the Middle East? What protections or guarantees might exist?

7. Assess the implications of the Sri Lankan case for the system and for your practice.

8. Some Muslim countries will not enforce an international arbitral award if the arbitral tribunal included a woman or a non-Muslim and the award was decided against a Muslim. (Research provided by Saimi A. Khattak, LL.M. [Tulane University]. *See also* SAMIR SALEH, COMMERCIAL ARBITRATION IN THE MIDDLE EAST [1984]. A Muslim judge may set aside an arbitral award if it violates the general spirit of the *Sharia* or its sources.) How does this information affect your assessment of the Arab world view of arbitration?

§ 6. ARBITRAL INSTITUTIONS

A number of traditional service providers constitute the transborder arbitration service industry. The American Arbitration Association (AAA), which has a long-standing history as a domestic provider of arbitration services, now administers international arbitrations through an international dispute resolution center in New York City. The AAA created the International Center for Dispute Resolution in June 1996. Since its inception, the Center has administered more than 1,000 cases, and its annual caseload is approaching 400 cases. There is controversy about how the Center classifies disputes as international. In 2001, the AAA opened a European Office of the International Center in Dublin, Ireland. The Irish International Centre represents the AAA's second institutional incursion into the domain of ICA. *See AAA Center Administers Its 1,000th International Case*, 10 WORLD ARB. & MED. REP. 149 (1999); *AAA Will Open International Center for Dispute Resolution in Dublin*, 12 WORLD ARB. & MED. REP. 177 (2001).

The International Chamber of Commerce (ICC), headquartered in Paris, France, is the most well-established and well-known international arbitral institution. See W. CRAIG, W. PARK, & J. PAULSSON, INTERNATIONAL CHAMBER OF COMMERCE ARBITRATION (3d ed. 1999). Despite recent attempts to lower costs, ICC administration of transborder arbitration remains expensive. Given its long-standing presence in the field, some international lawyers (with or without ties to the ICC) maintain that ICC arbitral awards have greater credibility before national courts than awards from other arbitral institutions. They believe that a stronger presumption of enforceability attaches to ICC awards on a worldwide basis. Be that as it may, the ICC has administered more than 13,000 arbitrations since the mid–1920s. It administers approximately 650 arbitrations annually and usually at least half of these arbitrations represent very significant cases in terms of the amount in dispute and the stature of the parties.

The ICC organizational structure includes a court of arbitration. The ICC Court of Arbitration consists of nearly 120 members who meet several times a month in Paris to review arbitral awards that have been drafted by ICC arbitral tribunals. The Court can criticize the arbitrators' reasoning and determination and ask that they reconsider their award or parts of it. The arbitrators nonetheless remain fully sovereign as to the decision; they can, therefore, disregard the Court's suggestions. The

Court's review is not an appellate procedure. It is intended to act as quality control and it is usually a successful process. The Court has no power over the parties or the dispute. The ICC sees the Court's review as an important factor in promoting voluntary party compliance with and, when necessary, court enforcement of ICC awards. Otherwise, the court's function is largely administrative; it addresses problems that arise in conducting ICC arbitrations.

The London Court of International Arbitration (LCIA) is also an important entity in the provision of arbitration services to international commercial parties. *See* R. Bernstein & D. Woods, eds., Handbook of Arbitration Practice (2d ed. 1993). It, too, is an experienced service provider and benefits from an impeccable professional reputation. Because it charges an hourly rate rather than a fee based on a percentage of the amount in controversy, LCIA arbitration is regarded as less expensive than ICC arbitration. The LCIA, however, does less business than the ICC—approximately 150 cases per year. Among international lawyers, LCIA arbitration has generally been perceived as English arbitration and linked to English court supervision of the merits of arbitral awards. The organization added "international" to its corporate title and created a number of regional councils throughout the world to alter this perception. That effort, however, has met with mixed results. The 1996 UK Arbitration Act, like its predecessor in 1979, improved England's standing as a venue for transborder arbitration. The further liberalization of English arbitration law accompanied by the tempering of English court supervision of awards have made LCIA arbitration more attractive to commercial parties and given the LCIA a more noticeable presence in the world marketplace of arbitration services.

Additionally, a number of national chambers of commerce administer international arbitrations. The Zurich Chamber of Commerce, for example, has its own set of arbitration rules and actively seeks to administer transborder arbitral proceedings. The Stockholm Chamber of Commerce is another case in point. During the cold war era, Sweden played a vital role in ICA by acting as the principal center for holding East–West arbitrations. Stockholm had a sophisticated bar of professionals who addressed the special problems associated with these arbitrations. When the cold war ended and China developed its own form of arbitration, the need for a venue specializing in East–West arbitrations diminished considerably. In 1999, the Swedish Parliament enacted the Swedish Arbitration Act to modernize the Swedish law of arbitration and to recast Sweden's reputation as a venue for international arbitrations. The enactment of the law demonstrated that Sweden was attempting to find its role in the refashioned international commercial order.

Notes and Questions

1. Your chief concern should center on the choice of a suitable arbitral institution for your client's arbitration. It is rare for parties to choose to participate in *ad hoc* arbitration. These arbitrations, done outside the

umbrella of institutional arbitration, demand that the parties establish and implement the rules of arbitration. It is difficult, if not impossible, to be both a participant in and a manager of a transborder arbitration. The vast majority of parties choose to have their arbitration administered by a reputable arbitral institution.

2. The ICC appears to be the primary service-providing organization in regard to transborder arbitration. The new runner-up may well be the Institute of Arbitration of the Stockholm Chamber of Commerce that is engaged in promoting a new image and in extolling its advantages. The number of arbitrations done by the AAA Center appears, to most observers, to be somewhat inflated or, at least, the amounts involved are not as significant as for ICC cases. It is also new to the international sector.

3. CIETAC arbitration is another form of institutional arbitration. It is Chinese arbitration and applies to most commercial transactions done in China involving foreign parties. In the 1990s, CIETAC arbitration became extremely popular. There were eventually almost twice as many CIETAC arbitrations as ICC arbitrations (in the range of 700 to 900). The amounts involved, however, were nowhere near as significant. For the last several years, CIETAC has been plagued by problems of corruption.

4. In light of the foregoing information base, how would you devise a protocol for selecting an institutional framework?

§ 7. BASIC CONCEPTS

(i) Freedom of Contract

The primary rule that governs the law, practice, and regulation of arbitration in the vast majority of national jurisdictions, including the United States, is the principle of freedom of contract. In *Volt Information Sciences, Inc. v. Board of Trustees of Leland Stanford Junior University*, the U.S. Supreme Court gave expression to this fundamental principle when it held that: "the FAA does not require parties to arbitrate when they have not agreed to do so ... nor does it prevent parties who do agree to arbitrate from excluding certain claims from the scope of their arbitration agreement.... It simply requires courts to enforce privately negotiated agreements to arbitrate, like other contracts, in accordance with their terms.... Arbitration under the Act is a matter of consent, not coercion, and parties are generally free to structure their arbitration agreements as they see fit...." 489 U.S. 468, 478, 479, 109 S.Ct. 1248, 103 L.Ed.2d 488 (1989).

Freedom of contract in arbitration allows the parties to write their own rules of arbitration—in effect, it permits them to have the agreement establish the law of arbitration for the particular transaction. The parties can customize the arbitral process to fit their needs, eliminate legal rules or trial techniques that might prove inconvenient or unsuitable, and maintain procedural elements they believe necessary to achieving fairness, finality, and functionality.

Courts generally uphold the parties' efforts to tailor the arbitral proceedings to their particular needs and requirements. For example, the parties might believe that compliance with formal evidentiary rules is necessary for a fair arbitral trial, or that arbitrators are bound to apply the rules of law, or that the arbitral adjudication of matters relating to trade secrets must be conducted *in camera*. Moreover, a proper hearing must include the right to pretrial discovery, to call witnesses and to question them directly, or to engage in adversarial cross-examination.

This "deregulatory" approach to arbitration enhances the position of the stronger party to the transaction. It also requires that the parties identify their adjudicatory needs ahead of time and understand how the features of arbitration respond to them. Finally, it places a "front-end load" on the parties' dealings, demanding that they spend time negotiating a workable agreement about these matters.

(ii) Arbitration Agreements

A contract for arbitration can take one of two forms: the submission or the arbitral clause. The submission is an arbitration agreement in which the parties agree that an existing dispute will be submitted to arbitration. The arbitral clause is a contract under which the parties agree to submit future disputes to arbitration. In either form, an arbitration agreement must be in writing and should satisfy the requirements for contract validity.

The arbitral clause is the most common form of arbitration agreement. It generally contains simple, straightforward, standard language providing for the resolution of disputes through arbitration: "Any dispute arising under this contract shall be submitted to arbitration under the rules of [a chosen arbitral institution]." Ordinarily, the arbitral clause is a provision within a larger contract; it, however, can be a physically separate agreement. In such instances, the main contract should provide for the incorporation of the arbitration agreement and the latter, likewise, should contain an unambiguous declaration that it is part of the main contract.

As a matter of law, the arbitral clause—whether it is a stand-alone agreement or a provision within the larger contract—is always distinct from the principal contract. The separability doctrine establishes that the arbitral clause is a distinct entity, governed by its own legal rules. It is juridically separable and autonomous. The nullity of the main contract, therefore, does not—*ipso facto*—invalidate the agreement to arbitrate. The moving party must establish that the nullity directly affects the provision for arbitration. Thereupon, the arbitrators can decide, subject to court scrutiny, whether they have a proper basis for adjudicating the matter. Separability, therefore, reduces the likelihood of delay tactics: Simply alleging the nullity of the main contract will not—on its own—foreclose the reference to arbitration by mandating court action. It also allows the arbitrators eventually to exercise their *kompetenz-kompetenz* authority.

Once a dispute arises, the parties to an arbitral clause usually enter into a submission agreement. The submission functions as the threshold step to arbitration. It establishes the matters in disagreement. In so doing, it defines the arbitrators' jurisdictional authority. The submission eventually leads to the initiation of the arbitral proceeding through the appointment of arbitrators.

A valid written agreement to arbitrate divests the courts of jurisdiction to entertain any matter covered by the agreement. The exercise of judicial authority to adjudicate disputes is extinguished even when an arbitral award is vacated or the arbitral process is functioning badly. The reference to arbitration establishes exclusive jurisdiction in the arbitral tribunal. Court assistance, however, is available throughout the arbitral process. It may become necessary, for example, to compel compliance with the agreement, appoint arbitrators, or to enforce subpoenas.

(iii) Arbitrability

Arbitrability establishes which disputes can be lawfully submitted to arbitration. A finding of inarbitrability can act as a defense to the enforcement of an arbitration agreement or arbitral award. Arbitrability limits the parties' right to engage in arbitration and the arbitrators' authority to rule. Inarbitrability can arise as a result of the subject matter of the dispute or because of contractual flaws in the arbitration agreement.

Under subject-matter inarbitrability, a dispute cannot be submitted to arbitration as a matter of law because it involves matters that are directly linked to the public interest. Only courts can rule on such issues because they are public bodies and have a public mandate. They are also publicly accountable. Matters of criminal culpability generally are deemed to be inarbitrable because of their subject matter. Therefore, allegations of bribery or criminal violations of RICO or of the tax regulations would be inarbitrable because the private commercial conduct implicates the public interest. To some extent, subject-matter inarbitrability overlaps with the public policy exception to arbitration. In both circumstances, public interest considerations prevent the recourse to arbitration.

Inarbitrability also functions on the basis of contract. In these circumstances, the matter does not involve the application of public law or the invocation of the public interest. The challenges converge on the contract of arbitration—its existence, making, or scope. The contention of contract inarbitrability can be premised upon the lack of an agreement to arbitrate, a contract deficiency in an existing agreement, or the limited scope of application of an otherwise existing and valid agreement. Without an actual, enforceable, and applicable agreement, there is no legal obligation to arbitrate. In more limited circumstances, contract inarbitrability can also arise from the improper constitution of the arbitral tribunal, *i.e.*, when the strictures of the agreement are not followed in establishing the tribunal.

(iv) The Separability Doctrine and Kompetenz–Kompetenz

These concepts protect the autonomy of the arbitral process by maintaining the arbitral tribunal's authority to rule in the face of challenges to its jurisdiction. Prior to their elaboration, a party bent on delay would allege that the principal contract was unenforceable—usually, because it violated public policy. Given that the arbitration agreement was part of the basic contract, the would-be nullity of the latter would at least temporarily incapacitate the arbitration agreement. The agreement to arbitrate was arguably void because it was a clause in an allegedly invalid contract. The claim that the main contract was invalid, in effect, removed the litigation from the purview of arbitration and gave the courts jurisdiction to decide whether an enforceable agreement to arbitrate existed. Such judicial recourse at the outset of the process at least delayed, and might perhaps impede, the agreed-upon reference to arbitration.

The separability doctrine was intended to shield the arbitral process from such maneuvers. Separability provides that the agreement to arbitrate is independent of the main contract. Therefore, allegations of contractual invalidity made against the main contract do not necessarily affect the validity of the arbitral clause. The party must establish that the alleged invalidity bears directly upon the arbitral clause itself. Separability then works in tandem with *kompetenz-kompetenz*. In fact, separability has no practical function other than to trigger the application of *kompetenz-kompetenz*. The *kompetenz-kompetenz* doctrine, or jurisdiction to rule on jurisdictional challenges, provides that the arbitral tribunal has the authority to rule on matters involving the validity or the scope of the agreement to arbitrate. The arbitral tribunal, therefore, can rule on allegations that there is a flaw in the main contract that affects the validity of the arbitral clause. The tribunal can also decide claims that the dispute in question is not covered by the arbitral clause. Its determinations on the matters are subject to judicial supervision, but usually at a later phase of the process.

(v) Enforcement of Awards

The judicial supervision of arbitral awards is limited, narrow, and restricted by statute. In most instances, it excludes the possibility of a review of the merits of awards. The parties have a right to judicial relief from the award only when it arises from flagrant and fundamental procedural deficiencies, amounting to a denial of justice. The statutory grounds for judicial supervision contemplate highly exceptional circumstances. They are intended to provide a remedy when relief is absolutely warranted and necessary. The vacatur of an award is exceedingly unlikely to occur.

Corruption is the principal basis by which courts can supervise arbitral awards: Corruption of the arbitrators, the proceedings, or of the ruling. Arbitrators cannot accept bribes or receive favors from the parties or their representatives, and they must engage in sufficient disclosure to avoid being deemed partial or giving the appearance of partiality. Real or potential conflicts must be divulged. Conflicts can emerge with the parties, the other arbitrators, or with legal counsel. Moreover, some courts and arbitral institutions require that party-appointed arbitrators meet the impartiality standards that traditionally have applied to neutral arbitrators. The practice of having partisan arbitrators who are refereed by a neutral arbitrator is being challenged and, seemingly, is in decline.

The arbitral proceedings can become corrupted when the arbitrators fail to provide the parties with a genuine opportunity to be heard. Basic procedural fairness is essential to the legitimacy of the process. Once the arbitrators have given the parties notice of the proceedings and a reasonable opportunity to present their case, the prospect of corruption of the proceedings through procedural unfairness is virtually eliminated. Courts generally hold that arbitrators have sovereign discretion in the conduct of the actual proceedings. This authority applies to all matters procedural: The hearing of witnesses; the gathering, evaluation, and introduction of evidence; the use of experts; and the need for site inspections. It is well-settled that an adversarial rule of absolute fairness need not constrain the arbitrator's exercise of authority to conduct the proceedings, to rule, or to foster the efficiency of the hearing. This abbreviated rule of due process establishes a workable balance between the rule of law, the protection of legal rights, and the need for functional adjudicatory proceedings.

Corruption can also exist in the arbitrators' execution of their mandate; namely, if they exceed their authority to rule by deciding matters not submitted to arbitration. Excess of arbitral authority is a universal basis upon which to effectuate the judicial supervision of arbitral awards. It emphasizes that the contractual character of the reference to arbitration and of the arbitrator's investiture with the authority to rule cannot be diluted or abridged. Arbitrators can only decide matters that are properly before them. A ruling on any other matter represents an exorbitant use of power and subjects the award to vacatur. The severance doctrine, however, can salvage the valid rulings in the award.

Excess of arbitral authority also exists when the arbitrators rule on the basis of a law or other predicate that the parties have ignored, not authorized, or rejected. An arbitral tribunal's failure to follow the agreed-upon content of the arbitration agreement is a classical illustration of excess of arbitrator authority. Moreover, excessiveness can result from the improper use of authority. The arbitrators' failure to be even-handed in the proceeding or to respect the basic procedural rights of the parties amounts to an excessive exercise of power. In all these circumstances, the arbitrators are abusing their rights as decision-makers.

Anglo–Saxon law uniquely permits courts to review arbitral awards on the merits. For example, the limited right of appeal in the English

Arbitration Act allows courts to reject arbitrator determinations that they believe are contrary to law. The common law grounds for vacatur in U.S. arbitration law permit the judicial review of arbitral awards: (1) on the basis of the manifestly erroneous application of law; (2) for irrational arbitrator determinations; or (3) if public policy would be violated by their enforcement. While the judicial policy favoring arbitration limits the application of these grounds, they nonetheless allow courts to scrutinize the merits of arbitral awards.

Finally, practice has created a new standard for review. Parties, in effect, have begun to incorporate a provision in agreements to arbitrate for the judicial review of arbitrators' legal rulings. The courts have given the practice a mixed reception. The "opt-in" provisions for judicial review transform the otherwise governing statutory standard into a default regime for the judicial supervision of awards. Through their agreement, the parties heighten the standard of review for purposes of their arbitration. The Fifth and Third Circuits have favored such provisions. The Second, Sixth, Seventh, Ninth, and Tenth Circuits have opposed the development, reasoning that private parties cannot create federal judicial jurisdiction by contract.

(vi) "Anational" Arbitration

In the international area, arbitration has developed in such an independent fashion that it has broken away from national law and established its own regulatory principles. The theory of "anational arbitration" provides that transborder commercial arbitrations are beyond the jurisdictional reach of national law. Whatever limitations are imposed upon domestic arbitration do not apply to international arbitral agreements, proceedings, or awards. No matter where they might be localized, transborder arbitrations are subject only to the constraints agreed upon in international conventions or, more likely, that exist as a matter of customary international arbitral practice. Courts at the place of arbitration can only render assistance to the arbitral proceedings (designate arbitrators, compel a party to arbitrate, order the production of evidence, or enforce rulings for interim relief). Courts at the place of enforcement can supervise awards only on the basis of narrow treaty grounds and usually are expected to find some means of giving effect to the presumption of enforceability. In effect, international arbitration is an autonomous, private, and self-regulating transborder system of adjudication.

In contrast, the concept of the *lex loci arbitri* (law of the place of arbitration) argues for the continued vitality of national law in the regulation of international arbitration. When the parties designate a particular country as the place of arbitration—whether by happenstance, for the sake of convenience, on the basis of personal whim, or because of the location's neutrality in relation to the parties and the transaction—they enter that State's territory and subject themselves and the arbitration to the State's sovereign authority. The local regulation of arbitration cannot be ignored or suspended for purposes of transborder arbitral proceedings. Local courts can assist the arbitration (if they are authorized to do so under national law), but they also must apply the restrictions of the local law to the arbitration if the national legislation requires them to do so. Under this view, the legality of adjudication depends upon the will of the sovereign—not the private parties' agreement. The legitimacy of an adjudicatory determination arises from the operation of law, not a contract. Territorial sovereignty authorizes national courts and laws to govern transborder arbitrations.

The exercise of national legal authority can impede transborder arbitrations in a number of ways. The national law of arbitration, for example, could require that arbitral tribunals have a particular composition or that certain trial procedures be utilized or excluded in arbitration. If the parties have agreed otherwise and are unable to modify their agreement, local courts—upon the motion of a party resisting arbitration or upon their own motion—could compel compliance with the local requirements or declare the agreement to arbitrate void and nullify the arbitration. The nullification of the arbitral agreement or award at the place of arbitration might render both the agreement and the award unenforceable in any other jurisdiction. Such a result represents a severe curtailment of the functionality of arbitration and of the parties' usually unfettered contractual right to agree to arbitrate.

There is little justification for allowing the rules of one locality to thwart a transborder arbitration on an international basis when the national jurisdiction has no interest in the arbitral proceeding or award and the arbitration is connected to it only for reasons of neutrality, convenience, or resource infrastructure. States in which awards are requested for enforcement have more reason to espouse a rigorous practice of judicial supervision of awards. Even these States, however, are likely to be excluded from the lucrative business of acting as a transborder venue for arbitrations if they develop a negative reputation for their regulation of arbitration. Transborder arbitral proceedings do not call into question domestic legality or its core objectives. The purpose of these proceedings is to achieve commercial justice among international business parties, not resolve the perplexities of civil liberties or the politics of government regulation. Moreover, the growing, if not the established, uniformity of national laws on arbitration renders the concerns that underlie the *lex loci arbitri* anodyne. It is, therefore, unlikely that these concerns will have a significant impact upon the developing world law of arbitration.

The *lex mercatoria* (or law merchant) also reinforces the anational character of international arbitration. Under the theory of the arbitral law merchant, international arbitrators not only decide international commercial disputes. In their awards, they are also creating a common law of international contracts and business transactions. Despite their lack of allegiance to a State, international arbitrators exercise sovereign lawmaking authority in their rulings. They make law as much as domestic judges or legislators. Whether published or made available privately, international arbitral awards can constitute legal precedent that binds subsequent arbitrators—provided their content reflects a consensus view within the international commercial community.

Notes and Questions

1. Freedom of contract is an efficient regulatory principle. Answering the question about what the law of arbitration provides by saying "Whatever the parties have provided" is an economical means of establishing the law generally and in specific cases. Is freedom of contract absolute, however? Can the parties reverse or disregard case law and statutes in their agreement? Can customization be taken too far, for example, by creating pathological arbitration agreements that cannot be implemented because they contradict mandatory local law, are fundamentally impractical, or simply too eccentric to be understood?

2. In domestic U.S. arbitration, the contract validity of arbitration agreements is a frequent, albeit generally unsuccessful, issue of litigation. The parties often occupy different positions of power and the stronger party often imposes arbitration upon the weaker party. This issue usually does not arise in ICA; the circumstances, parties, and transactions are different. Moreover, ICA is a virtual necessity in international business transactions. You should reflect upon the content of an international arbitration agreement. What are the essential material terms? Also think about reducing the terms to suitable language.

3. Inarbitrability acts as a defense to an alleged obligation to arbitrate. It goes to the question of whether there is a proper foundation in law or contract for the duty to arbitrate. Objections must be made in a timely fashion or a waiver of the right to object on this basis may occur. For reasons of fairness and practicality, it is unlikely that courts would rule favorably on a contract inarbitrability claim made at the end of the proceeding if it could have been brought at the outset. Arbitrators can rule on contract inarbitrability issues. Subject-matter inarbitrability—that the subject matter of a claim cannot, as a matter of law, be submitted to arbitration—can apply to both the agreement and the award. It, therefore, can be raised at any stage of the arbitral process. It is not clear whether sitting on the issue and delaying consideration preclude making the defense. Moreover, it is not certain whether arbitrators or courts or both can rule on the question. Finally, the law of the State of rendition of the award and the law of the requested State for enforcement can differ and conflict on the issue of subject-matter arbitrability. Therefore, which law is controlling, by whom, and when?

4. Does the arbitral tribunal also have the jurisdictional authority to rule on a claim that it was not constituted in the manner prescribed in the arbitration agreement? Assuming that it does and it discovers an objective, material error in its constitution, is it possible to cure the defect or must the process go back to "square one?" What is "square one," anyway? Aren't arbitrators likely to adopt a highly adaptive and pragmatic approach to these issues—a position that also upholds their financial self-interest? Is this wrong? What if the eventual court of enforcement in another country

disagrees with the arbitrators' solution to the matter? What happens then? Shouldn't this question be directed exclusively to courts because it is so fundamental, evident at the threshold, and implicates the arbitrators' self-interest directly?

5. The enforcement of awards is generally favored and strongly presumed to apply. Review ordinarily is confined to matters of procedure that are fundamental to procedural fairness and basic legal civilization. There are exceptions, one of which the Anglo–Saxon practice of merits review. The latter is unlikely to yield an untoward result, but vacatur or a refusal to enforce does occur on this basis. In exceptional circumstances, courts do infringe upon the arbitrator's decisional sovereignty because they disagree with the result reached by the arbitral adjudicator. Shouldn't these exceptions be eliminated because they contradict the general trend and are likely to expand? Why maintain this basis of scrutiny if it is so unusual and out-of-keeping with ordinary standards? Does the emergence of "opt-in" provisions indicate a decline in ICA's reputation and functionality? Doesn't the trend show a distrust of international arbitrators and their capabilities? Is it also based on an illusory view of the law? Should awards be automatically enforced everywhere?

6. The concept of "anational" arbitration is likely to create controversy. It represents, in effect, a negation of sovereign national authority and the acceptance of transnational principles as controlling. The surrender of sovereignty—no matter how necessary—is always a source of debate. Isn't ICA a *de facto* legal system and process? Is the law it generates legitimate? Does that matter if the results are enforceable? What problems might this aspect of ICA create for clients and for drafting international arbitral clauses?

§ 8. TRANSBORDER ORGANIZATIONS AND ARBITRATION

(i) World Bank Arbitration

In 1966, the Convention on the Settlement of Investment Disputes between States and Nationals of Other States (the "ICSID Convention" or "Washington Convention") established a "truly international" form of arbitration for dealing with investment disputes that arise between foreign investors and host States. International Centre for the Settlement of Investment Disputes (ICSID) arbitration addresses problems that emerge from the investment activity of foreign nationals or companies in host States. It provides a process for dealing with the commercial liability of sovereign States in the transborder commercial context. The objective underlying the creation of the Centre was two-fold: First, to relieve the President of the World Bank and his staff from intervening in investment disputes between States and foreign nationals; and, second, to establish a permanent agency that would facilitate the resolution of such disputes in order to foster greater foreign investment. Despite its close connection to the World Bank, the ICSID is "an autonomous international organization." *See* Giardina, *ICSID: A Self-Contained,*

Non–National Review System, *in* R. LILLICH & C. BROWER, eds., INTERNATIONAL ARBITRATION IN THE 21ST CENTURY: TOWARDS "JUDICIALIZATION" AND UNIFORMITY? 199 (1994). It has an Administrative Council and a Secretariat. It is funded by the World Bank. The Governor of the Bank generally chairs ICSID's Administrative Council. Annual meetings are held jointly with the Bank.

Recourse to ICSID is voluntary, but—once it is undertaken—unilateral withdraw is not possible. ICSID provides facilities for the mediation or arbitration of investment disputes between Member States and foreign nationals whose home State is a Member State. Since 1978, ICSID has offered an "Additional Facility" under which the ICSID Secretariat can administer proceedings between States and foreign investors for a dispute that falls outside the scope of the Convention. The remedial process used in the Additional Facility can be either mediation or arbitration. It can be applied to foreign investment disputes in which one of the parties does not belong to ICSID, to non-investment transborder commercial disputes that have some link to sovereign parties or matters, or to the use of fact-finding procedures.

Arbitrations need not take place at the ICSID headquarters in Washington, D.C. The Secretary–General of ICSID can also appoint arbitrators for *ad hoc* arbitral proceedings administered under the UNCITRAL Arbitration Rules. *See* Escobar, *Conducting Arbitration Proceedings Under the ICSID Convention*, *in* B. BARIN, ed., CARSWELL'S HANDBOOK OF INTERNATIONAL DISPUTE RESOLUTION RULES 206–212 (1999). The parties can freely choose the situs of their arbitration. ICSID has external venue arrangements with a number of institutions on a worldwide basis: The Permanent Court of Arbitration at The Hague; the Regional Arbitration Centres of the Asian–African Legal Consultative Committee at Cairo and Kuala Lumpur; the Australian Centre for International Commercial Arbitration in Melbourne; the Australian Commercial Disputes Centre in Sidney; the Singapore International Arbitration Centre; and the GCC Commercial Arbitration Centre in Bahrain.

ICSID arbitration clauses appear in foreign investment contracts, national investment laws (about twenty), and in several thousand bilateral investment treaties (BITs). The reference to ICSID arbitration can also be found in multilateral trade treaties: the North American Free Trade Agreement, the Energy Charter Treaty, the Cartagena Free Trade Agreement, and the Colonia Investment Protocol of Mercosur. The ICSID arbitral process is intended to be an entirely autonomous and self-contained dispute resolution mechanism. The national courts of the contracting States cannot entertain challenges to ICSID arbitral proceedings or awards; the only course of action allowed to national courts is to recognize and enforce ICSID awards. In other words, these national courts must recognize an ICSID award as binding and enforce it as if it were a final judgment of a court of the requested State. The exclusive remedial recourse against an ICSID award lies within the ICSID framework itself; an award can be subject to interpretation, revision, and annulment through an internal appellate procedure. *See, e.g.*, Pinsolle, *The Annulment of ICSID Arbitral Awards*, 1 J. World Investment 243 (2000).

Although one hundred and thirty-nine States have ratified the Convention, the utility of ICSID arbitration has historically been limited. The number of submitted cases since 1966, when the Convention entered into force, until 2001 was less than overwhelming, fewer than forty cases. Approximately twenty-six actual decisions were rendered during that period. Also, considerable controversy was generated as a result of the annulment of two ICSID awards in the mid–1980s through the internal *ad hoc* committee review procedure (*Klöckner* and *Amco Asia*). The infrequency of recourse to the ICSID process resulted from the difficulty of obtaining final and binding ICSID arbitral awards. S. Toope, Mixed International Arbitration 219–262 (1990). The finality problem had a number of aspects.

First, the annulment procedure was presumably intended as a substitute for the judicial supervision of awards that is ordinarily available before national courts. The provision for automatic enforcement of awards in the ICSID Convention eliminated the judicial supervision of ICSID awards before national courts. Accordingly, the internal appeal process was designed to act as a "safety valve" by which to block exceptionally defective rulings or procedures.

The petition for annulment is submitted to the office of the ICSID Secretary–General. The Secretary–General appoints an *ad hoc* Committee (in effect, a second arbitral tribunal) that evaluates the award in light of the objections that have been advanced. The grounds for the annulment of awards, contained in Article 52(1) of the ICSID Convention, are narrow both in scope and content. As with other statutory frameworks providing for the challenging of arbitral awards, these grounds do not constitute an "open invitation" to nullify arbitral determinations. An ICSID award can be annulled if: (1) the arbitral tribunal was improperly constituted; (2) it manifestly exceeded its powers; (3) one or some of its members were corrupt; (4) there was a serious departure from a fundamental rule of procedure; or (5) the tribunal failed to provide reasons for its determination. ICSID Convention, Art. 52(1).

The first ground (improper constitution of the tribunal) emphasizes the primacy of the parties' agreement in the conduct of arbitration. Moreover, excess of arbitral authority and corruption are standard bases for vacatur in most, if not all, statutory frameworks. The excess of authority in the ICSID provision, however, must be "manifest"—a qualification that should make a finding of excessive use of power even less likely than it usually is under national statutes. It is difficult to conceive of an arbitral procedure that would be legitimate if any of the arbitrators are found to be corrupt, although "planting" a corrupt arbitrator could become an effective means of undermining an inevitably unfavorable arbitral determination. The due process requirement in ground four also is qualified: There must be "a serious departure" from basic procedural fairness. This language, once again, emphasizes the "tolerant" character of the grounds; they are meant to sanction only grave lapses in the process. Finally, the tribunal must give explanatory reasons for its ruling. The provision reflects the fact that the rights and liability of a sovereign State are at issue and that the process should acknowledge that aspect of the litigation. Moreover, in some or many instances, the arbitral tribunal will be applying the law of the host State. Therefore, there should be a means of determining whether the tribunal did in fact apply the State law and whether it construed the law in a reasonable fashion.

Second, there is apparently no limit to the number of annulment actions a party can bring. Relatedly, the grounds for annulment are subject to a wide variety of possible interpretations. In a word, despite their restrictive character, the grounds can (and have) become a vehicle for stating a multitude of objections to the validity of an ICSID award. Therefore, ICSID awards can be readily challenged within the ICSID framework; such proceedings can be protracted and eventually lead to a reversal of the award. This prospect—needless to say—is a far cry from the "automatic enforcement" promised by the Convention.

Third, ICSID awards also can be stymied by the law of sovereign immunity from execution. Article 55 of the Convention provides that, while the ICSID framework establishes a State waiver of sovereign immunity from suit, it does not derogate "from the law in force in any Contracting State relating to immunity of that state or of any foreign state from execution." Although the ICSID Secretariat contends that no ICSID award has ever been denied enforcement on this basis, the effect of the provision is evident, and its eventual application is likely to be counterproductive to the functioning of ICSID arbitration. While such a "safety valve" may have been necessary to gain a significant number of ratifications to the Convention, it can have a substantially negative effect upon the effectiveness of ICSID arbitration.

ICSID arbitration, therefore, is not a perfect system. By acceding to the Convention, States do not surrender their most meaningful sovereign rights or political privileges. Even though ICSID provides a mechanism for resolving foreign investment disputes, it does not eliminate the State's status or power, nor does it supply an adjudicatory process that is as functional as the one that operates in the private commercial sector. In effect, the State can renege on its promise to arbitrate, render the arbitral proceedings difficult—if not impossible, and refuse to pay the award. Accordingly, ICSID arbitration is merely an indicia of possible transactional security in a global commercial context.

Several well-known cases illustrate the problems. *Klöckner GmbH v. United Republic of Cameroon*, ICSID Case No. ARB/81/2, *reprinted in* 1 J. INT'L ARB. 145 (1984), involved a joint venture between a European multinational company and the Government of Cameroon. The objective of the transaction was to build and render operational a fertilizer factory in Cameroon. Eighteen months after it was built, the factory was closed down because it was unprofitable. Pursuant to contract documents, Klöckner filed a demand for ICSID arbitration to secure the payment of the remainder of the contract price. Cameroon counterclaimed, alleging that Klöckner failed to perform all of its contract obligations.

The tribunal held that the partial payment of the contract price by Cameroon was sufficient to compensate Klöckner for its partial performance. Klöckner filed an application for annulment against the award, alleging that the decision violated at least four of the five grounds under Article 52(1) of the ICSID Convention (*i.e.*, the tribunal manifestly lacked jurisdiction, manifestly exceeded its powers, seriously strayed from a fundamental procedural rule, and did not provide reasons for its determination). The *ad hoc* Committee reviewing the award agreed with two of these arguments and annulled the award. In its view, the tribunal manifestly exceeded its powers by failing to apply the law of the State party to the arbitration under Article 42(2) of the Convention. The Committee ruled that the tribunal had applied general principles of equity rather than legal provisions and rules, and was not authorized to do so by the parties' agreement. Additionally, the Committee found that the tribunal had failed to provide explanatory reasons with the award. In the committee's view, the reasons given needed to be "sufficiently relevant"—*i.e.*, "reasonably capable of justifying the result reached by the tribunal." Reasons that were "sufficiently relevant" "are not just any reasons, purely formal or apparent, but rather reasons having some substance, allowing the reader to follow the arbitral tribunal's reasoning, on facts and on law."

The *ad hoc* Committee's decision in *Klöckner* had the effect of expanding substantially the scope and content of the grounds for annulment. In effect, it allowed the *ad hoc* Committee to disagree with the arbitral tribunal's approach to the adjudication and to substitute its judgment on that matter for that of the tribunal. Such recourse is generally not available under the New York Arbitration Convention or is not the usual practice before national courts. It makes the recourse to ICSID arbitration less attractive because the adjudicatory results can be challenged and completely undermined in a never-ending stream of challenges.

In *Amco Asia Corp. v. Republic of Indonesia*, ICSID Case No. ARB/81/1, *reprinted in* 1 INT'L ARB. REP. 601 (1986), ICSID Case No. ARB/81/1, Amco (a U.S. company) agreed to construct and manage a hotel in Jakarta for a private Indonesian company, P.T. Wisma. The latter had been organized by Indonesian military officers. Under the agreement, Amco also agreed to invest $3 million USD in Indonesia. After construction was completed, the Indonesian Government seized the hotel and terminated Amco's license. It alleged that Amco failed to fulfill its investment obligations.

After exhausting its local remedies, Amco filed a petition for arbitration under the ICSID framework as provided in the contract. Amco claimed $9 million USD in damages, but the tribunal awarded it only $3 million USD in a unanimous award. The *ad hoc* Committee partially annulled the award on the ground that the tribunal manifestly exceeded its powers (it did not apply fundamental provisions of Indonesian investment law) and for its failure to state explanatory reasons (*i.e.*, not justifying its conclusions on damages). Again, the award was invalid because the annulment tribunal disagreed with the original tribunal's approach, conception of the case, and application of law. It simply redid the litigation as it believed it should have been done at the outset. The action eventually lead to Amco's request for a second arbitration.

In recent years, ICSID has undergone a substantial revitalization as a result of the reference to ICSID arbitration in the NAFTA agreement and in bilateral investment treaties. The ICSID Secretariat reports that filings have increased astronomically over prior practice; there are some sixty pending cases. Globalization and the increased affirmative activity of States in transborder commerce have given ICSID arbitration a new stature in international commercial dispute resolution. The duration of this change and whether it will alter the decision-making process under ICSID arbitration remain to be seen. Moreover, ICSID arbitration could prove to be ineffective in resolving the problem of sovereign participation in international commerce. The expansion of foreign investment, however, may require a diminution of sovereign prerogatives and a new destiny for ICSID arbitration.

Notes and Questions

In your view, how effective is ICSID arbitration in resolving the problem of sovereign participation in international commercial relations? Doesn't sovereignty remain a blackhole that absorbs all elements of legal civilization in the context of foreign investment? What might remedy the problems? Shouldn't a unanimous ICSID award be spared internal review? When would you recommend ICSID arbitration to clients?

(ii) The UNCITRAL

The UN General Assembly established the United Nations Commission on International Trade Law (UNCITRAL) in 1966. The purpose of the Commission was to foster the adoption of uniform laws on matters of international trade so that "obstacles to the flow of trade" could be reduced or removed. *See generally* J. Lew, M. Loukas, & S. Kroll, Comparative International Commerical Arbitration (2003). The Commission has become the principal UN agency on trade law. The membership of the Commission consists of sixty Member States elected by the General Assembly. One of its six working groups focuses upon international arbitration and ADR. The Secretariat is located in Vienna, Austria, and the Commission carries out its work at annual sessions.

The Commission has been and continues to be active in the area of international commercial arbitration. In addition to the New York Arbitration Convention itself (*see* A. Van Den Berg, The New York Arbi-

TRATION CONVENTION OF 1958 [1981]), which the UNCITRAL helps to promote, there are currently four major UNCITRAL documents on international commercial arbitration and dispute resolution. First, the UNCITRAL Model Arbitration Rules, which were adopted in 1976, represent a thorough set of rules for the procedural conduct of arbitral proceedings. The Rules were meant to apply primarily in *ad hoc* arbitrations in which the parties have chosen not to have an institutional framework. The Rules, however, can also (and are) applied to arbitrations administered by arbitral institutions. The Rules were adopted by the UN General Assembly in recognition of "the value of arbitration as a method of settling disputes arising in the context of international commercial relations," and with the view that establishing "rules for *ad hoc* arbitration that are acceptable in countries with different legal, social and economic systems would significantly contribute to the development of harmonious international economic relations." *See* I. DORE, ARBITRATION AND CONCILIATION UNDER THE UNCITRAL RULES: A TEXTUAL ANALYSIS (1986); P. SANDERS, THE WORK OF UNCITRAL ON ARBITRATION AND CONCILIATION (2001). The Rules provide for the right to legal representation in the arbitral proceedings; the appointment, disqualification, and replacement of arbitrators; the equal treatment of the parties; the parties' right to a "full opportunity" to present their case; *kompetenz-kompetenz* on jurisdictional challenges; evidence-gathering; interim measures; and requirements for the form and content of the award.

Second, the UNCITRAL Model Law on International Commercial Arbitration, adopted in 1985, was intended to allow States without an arbitration law or with an antiquated law to enact a fully modern statute on the subject of international commercial arbitration. P. BINDER, INTERNATIONAL COMMERCIAL ARBITRATION IN UNCITRAL MODEL JURISDICTIONS: AN INTERNATIONAL COMPARISON OF THE UNCITRAL MODEL LAW ON INTERNATIONAL COMMERCIAL ARBITRATION (2000); A. BROCHES, COMMENTARY ON THE UNCITRAL MODEL LAW ON INTERNATIONAL COMMERCIAL ARBITRATION (1990); I. DORE, THE UNCITRAL FRAMEWORK FOR ARBITRATION IN CONTEMPORARY PERSPECTIVE (1993); H. HOLTZMANN & J. NEUHAUS, A GUIDE TO THE UNCITRAL MODEL LAW ON INTERNATIONAL COMMERCIAL ARBITRATION: LEGISLATIVE HISTORY AND COMMENTARY (1989). The Model Law reflects contemporary standards in the legal regulation of arbitration. It advances contract freedom, party autonomy, and anationalism as the primary principles of the doctrinal foundation of arbitration. The Model Law has been adopted by a number of U.S. states (*e.g.*, Georgia), in developed countries (*e.g.*, Germany), and in developing countries. It, or a variation of it, usually sets the statutory standard in arbitration. The global reference to the Model Law allows for uniformity of regulation and ready access to and understanding of the governing legal provisions by practitioners on a worldwide basis.

Third, in 1996, the UNCITRAL issued its *Notes on Organizing Arbitral Proceedings*. The *Notes* list standard matters that an arbitral tribunal should address and consider in the conduct of the arbitral proceedings. They facilitate the structuring and organization of the proceedings and allow the tribunal to prepare sufficiently for the conduct of the proceedings. The *Notes* are not binding and are intended to supplement institutional rules on arbitration. The matters listed include: selecting rules of arbitration; determining the language of the proceedings; choosing a place of arbitration; setting a schedule for deposits; establishing an agreement on confidentiality; creating a system for the submission and exchange of written submissions and documentary evidence as well as for witnesses; and establishing the process of hearings (single or multiple sessions, length, order of presentation, creating a record, and other similar matters). U.N. Doc. A/CN.9/WG.II/WP.108.

Finally, in 2002, the Commission adopted the Model Law on International Commercial Conciliation. Conciliation is transborder parlance for mediation as it is understood in the United States. By adopting the law, UNCITRAL was expanding the range of its recommended remedies for resolving international commercial conflicts. It, like so many other institutional actors, was adding mediation as a precursor to the recourse of arbitration. In doing so, it adopted an absolute privilege of confidentiality for mediation proceedings.

The Model Law on Conciliation is meant to serve as an efficient and effective dispute resolution system for business transacted across national boundaries. It is designed to encourage States to develop non-adjudicatory dispute settlement procedures. Such a practice should decrease the cost of settling disputes and increase the stability of international trade. When using the term "conciliation," the Model Law refers to any proceedings or process in which an independent and impartial person or panel of persons assists the parties to a dispute in reaching a settlement of the matter. "Alternative dispute resolution" is a term used to refer to techniques for solving disputes by conciliatory means rather than by a binding adjudicatory procedure like arbitration. Unlike arbitration, conciliation allows the parties to retain ultimate control over the process and the outcome. Each conciliation technique has different procedures for reaching a settlement between the parties.

In preparing the Model Law, the Commission espoused a broad notion of conciliation that incorporated "mediation," "alternative dispute resolution," and "neutral evaluation" and applied to a broad range of commercial disputes. Although the Model Law is designed to apply only to international and commercial cases, the enacting State can extend its scope of application to domestic commercial disputes and certain non-commercial disputes.

The Model Law is a recommendation to States to incorporate a similar legislative text into their national law. The Model Law may be modified to adapt it to the States' national judicial system and trial process. In order to achieve uniformity and certainty, States are encouraged to make as few changes as possible in incorporating the new Model Law into their legal systems. In any event, any changes should remain within the basic principles of the Model Law so that the law remains familiar to foreign parties, advisers, and conciliators.

Articles 1 through 3 of the Model Law provide background information, define conciliation, and explain its international application. Articles 4 through 9 cover the rules for regulating conciliation procedures. These procedural rules apply especially in circumstances in which parties have not adopted rules governing dispute resolution processes. They are, therefore, designed to function as default provisions. When the parties have agreed upon dispute resolution rules and procedures, the UNCITRAL rules act only as a supplement to the agreed-upon provisions. The remainder of the Model Law addresses post-conciliation issues.

Notes and Questions

The UNCITRAL does the work of uniform law. It has become an excellent source of general principles and emerging international legal standards. It is now preparing to collect the global decisional law on the New York Arbitration Convention.

What content must the Convention have? Why? Would some non-core principles be useful as well? The Convention was briefly described in the context of the enforcement of arbitral awards (*supra* ch. 6[v]) and will be described more thoroughly later (*infra* ch. 7[2]). For present purposes, assume that it is meant to codify a uniform world law on the enforcement of international arbitral awards.

What might the UNCITRAL Rules mean by "equal treatment of the parties?" Why should arbitrating parties have a "full opportunity" to make their case? Isn't a reasonable opportunity sufficient? Neither the UNCITRAL Model Law or Rules appears to address transparency in arbitration. How would you incorporate that factor? Is transborder uniformity illusory?

(iii) Investment Arbitration: WTO and the NAFTA

The GATT (now WTO), 55 U.N.T.S. 194, 33 I.L.M. 1124 (1994), and NAFTA, 32 I.L.M. 605 (1993), illustrate circumstances in which adjudicatory frameworks, akin to arbitration, are used to contain and resolve trade policy disagreements among States. Rulings from the GATT or NAFTA dispute resolution mechanisms can have a substantial impact upon government policy and the regulation of national economies. Obviously, they also affect private commercial interests. These agreements are treaty-like instruments; they are congressional-executive agreements implemented by federal statutes having the same effect as a treaty. Their purpose is to establish viable trade regimes between the contracting States in which national policy follows agreed-upon trade rules and practices.

The dispute settlement procedures seek to resolve disagreements in the implementation of the agreement, thereby avoiding a crippling of the framework through unilateral conduct and retaliation. The effectiveness of the dispute settlement provisions depends, to a large extent, upon the willingness of contracting States to forgo some aspects of their national sovereign authority and to accept rulings from the provided-for international panels as final and binding determinations. Both instruments reveal a trend among States to accept the discipline of binding adjudication in matters of trade conflicts, rather than use dispute settlement processes as a mere context for discussion and the possible adjustment of position.

The 1994 GATT, which resulted from the Uruguay Round, established a more rigorous procedure for the resolution of disputes among the contracting States. Under GATT, only a Member State is able to bring a complaint against another Member State. Private parties who believe their rights are compromised by the trade policy of a Member State must have their claim espoused by their government. Once a complaint is lodged, the Member States must pursue consultations, conciliation, or mediation before a panel can be constituted to hear the complaint. GATT '94 established the World Trade Organization (WTO) to administer the dispute settlement procedures, along with a dispute settlement body (DSB) that supervises State compliance with panel rulings and recommendations. The DSB enforces strict time limits for the implementation of panel decisions and can impose the payment of compensation for noncompliance.

Under GATT '94, Member States are no longer able to block the appointment of a panel or the enforcement of a panel decision through the GATT Council. The new GATT provides for the automatic effectiveness of panel decisions (although they have no direct effect on litigation before U.S. courts, even over the same dispute), strict and brief time limits for actions, and a limited and expedited appellate review of panel decisions. The DSB has a standing appellate body that hears party appeals against a decision on points of law. If the appellate body upholds the determination by the panel, the panel decision becomes effective within thirty days unless the membership decides by consensus not to adopt the appellate body's report. Also, States must respond to a request for consultation within ten days; a panel must complete its work within six months; and appeals are held to a three-month time limit. Finally, the selection of the three-member panels can now be drawn from a wider group of "well-qualified" individuals.

NAFTA is a regional, tri-national trade agreement that eliminates trade barriers and facilitates trade in goods and services. It contains three dispute resolution chapters that create the Free Trade Commission (FTC), which supervises dispute settlement, and that establish frameworks for processing the different types of disputes that might arise under the agreement. Chapter 11(b) provides a remedy for non-governmental parties by allowing investors to have recourse to binding international arbitration when the host State allegedly violates the equal investment provisions in NAFTA. The provision creates some innovations in arbitration. It provides for a relatively new arbitral mechanism, but also allows aggrieved investors to pursue relief for alleged violations of NAFTA under the auspices of ICSID or the UNCITRAL Model Rules of arbitration. There are a number of preconditions to the exercise of the arbitral remedy; for example, the investor must have undertaken consultations and negotiations with the State; there are a ninety-day notice requirement and a six-month "cooling-off" period; and the investor must consent to the arbitration and thereby waive other remedies. The arbitral tribunal consists of three arbitrators: Failing party agreement, the neutral is appointed by ICSID. The award is a binding determination, subject only to the means of recourse under the various conventions.

Chapter 19 covers disputes relating to national agency determinations on matters of antidumping or countervailing duties. It provides for the review of the final determinations of agencies like the U.S. International Trade Commission and the U.S. Department of Commerce. Under Chapter 19, nationals of a State party who are affected by final determinations of a trade agency of another State party may choose to forgo judicial review of the determinations in the State's national courts and avail themselves of review by a panel dispute settlement system under NAFTA. Once this procedure is invoked, review of the agency determinations and of the panel decisions by national courts is precluded. The panels consist of five members, two panelists appointed by each State and the designation of a neutral. The panel decision is binding and subject only to a form of extraordinary challenge on very narrow grounds. The recourse to a panel of experts acts as a substitute for national judicial review, and the panel must apply the same standard of review and law that would be applied by the courts of the concerned State. The panel engages in adjudicatory proceedings that involve the filing of briefs and oral arguments. The panel is obligated to rule in a timely manner. It can only affirm or remand the agency decision.

Chapter 20 establishes a mechanism for addressing State disputes under NAFTA. The disputes can involve: Allegations that State conduct violates the provisions of NAFTA, disagreements regarding the interpretation or application of NAFTA, or contentions that State practice nullifies or impairs NAFTA benefits. The panel procedure under Chapter 20 can be used as a substitute for dispute resolution under GATT. Panel procedures under Chapter 20 differ in some respects from their analogue under Chapter 19. Only State parties have standing to trigger the remedies under Chapter 20 and prior consultation between the governments must precede the invocation of Chapter 20 procedures.

The panel procedures operate according to strict time limits, for example, the panel's initial report is due within thirty days of the panel's constitution. Once the panel has heard the parties, it issues an initial report that includes recommendations for resolving the dispute. The parties have fourteen days in which to state their objections to the report. The panel considers these comments and issues a final report within thirty days. The panels have broad discretion in fashioning remedies. The parties can either accept the panel decision or agree to their own solution. There is no appeal of the panel's final rulings and recommendations. The ultimate sanction for non-compliance is the suspension of NAFTA benefits.

The practice of NAFTA arbitration, especially under Chapter 11, is just beginning—the rules and rulings thus far articulated are embryonic. There is no settled law or customary practice. Whether the existing structure of the process is adequate or sufficient to achieve the Agreement's purposes remains to be seen. *See* Alvarez, *Arbitration Under the North American Free Trade Agreement*, 16 ARB. INT'L 393 (2000); Price, *An Overview of the NAFTA Investment Chapter: Substantive Rules and Investor–State Dispute Settlement*, 27 INT'L LAW. 727 (1993). *See also* Alvarez & Park, *The New Face of Investment Arbitration: NAFTA Chapter 11*, 28 YALE J. INT'L L. 365 (2003).

It should be noted that, even though Chapter 11 refers to ICSID arbitration as a possible process of dispute resolution, neither Canada nor Mexico has ratified the ICSID Convention. Accordingly, recourse can only be had to ICSID's Additional Facility and only when the United States is directly (as the respondent State) or indirectly (through the nationality of the claimant) a party to the dispute.

Chapter 11 arbitrations are organized and conducted much like a standard international commercial arbitration. There is, however, no governing arbitral clause; arbitration takes place pursuant to the treaty. The lack of a party agreement, arguably, gives the arbitrators greater discretion in deciding preliminary and procedural matters. The process has been criticized for its lack of transparency. The parties select the arbitrators; the panel consists of two party-appointed arbitrators and a neutral. Arbitrators can address preliminary jurisdictional matters, questions of procedures, and the merits of litigation. They decide disputes on the basis of the treaty and customary international law. Claims can be barred by the three-year time limit. Agents for the non-litigating States can intervene in proceedings and make submissions on matters of interpretation and procedure. The submission of *amicus* briefs is permitted in light of the possible public impact of some rulings. Awards are enforceable under the New York Arbitration Convention. Awards can be subject to local law variations on matters of enforcement. The standard rules of sovereign immunity from suit and execution can be applied against the enforcement of NAFTA awards.

Notes and Questions

Is the WTO dispute settlement process under the DSB more effective than ICSID arbitration at curtailing sovereign prerogative? Are the frameworks at all comparable? Is the WTO in the best interest of the United States? What does it mean to say that the parties provide for dispute resolution mechanisms that are "akin to arbitration?" Who should qualify as a potential WTO or NATFA arbitrator? Isn't nationality far less important than substantive training and experience? Does investment arbitration become particularly vulnerable to an expert oligarchy? Is enforcement really guaranteed in either setting? Are States held accountable for their conduct in either framework? Do either dispute settlement apparatus violate Article III of the U.S. Constitution?

Chapter 7

CONTEMPORARY ISSUES IN TRANSBORDER ARBITRAL PRACTICE

Table of Sections

This chapter asks that you engage in a process of implementing the information in the previous chapter. Although the distinction is somewhat artificial, the materials consist of two types of problems: First, analytical problems that have arisen in the modern evolution of ICA and that have a critical standing in the area (sections 1–6); second, the salient practical problems that are associated with putting together a transborder arbitration (sections 7–10). In regard to the latter, you should refer to the circumstances of the purchase of sugar by a U.S. candy manufacturer from Brazil (described in the Introduction [5], at 13 *supra*) for a context in which to discuss the problems. No device or process will eliminate all the risks of transactions and contracts; the goal is to minimize them. The former set of problems warrants consideration because they are a means of gauging the direction and momentum of practice. They demonstrate that ICA remains a dynamic and adaptive process, capable of responding to challenges and being practically vital. The two final sections (sections 11 and 12) highlight a critical recent development and a longer range perspective on the practice of transborder arbitration.

§ 1. THE ARBITRABILITY OF REGULATORY LAW: EXPANDING THE DECISIONAL AUTHORITY OF INTERNATIONAL ARBITRATORS

SCHERK v. ALBERTO-CULVER CO.

417 U.S. 506, 94 S. Ct. 2449, 41 L.Ed. 2d 270,
reh'g denied, 419 U.S. 885, 95 S. Ct. 157, 42 L.Ed.2d 129 (1974).

(footnotes omitted)

MR. JUSTICE STEWART delivered the opinion of the Court.

Alberto–Culver Co., the respondent, is an American company incorporated in Delaware with its principal office in Illinois. It manufactures and distributes toiletries and hair products in this country and abroad. During the 1960's [,] Alberto–Culver decided to expand its overseas operations, and as part of this program it approached the petitioner Fritz Scherk, a German citizen residing at the time of trial in Switzerland. Scherk was the owner of three interrelated business entities, organized under the laws of Germany and Liechtenstein, that were engaged in the manufacture of toiletries and the licensing of trademarks for such toiletries. An initial contact with Scherk was made by a representative of Alberto–Culver in Germany in June 1967, and negotiations followed at further meetings in both Europe and the United States during 1967 and 1968. In February 1969[,] a contract was signed in Vienna, Austria, which provided for the transfer of the ownership of Scherk's enterprises to Alberto–Culver, along with all rights held by these enterprises to trademarks in cosmetic goods. The contract contained a number of express warranties whereby Scherk guaranteed the sole and unencumbered ownership of these trademarks. In addition, the contract contained an arbitration clause providing that "any controversy or claim [that] shall arise out of this agreement or the breach thereof" would be referred to arbitration before the International Chamber of Commerce in Paris, France, and that "[t]the laws of the State of Illinois, U.S.A. shall apply to and govern this agreement, its interpretation and performance."

The closing of the transaction took place in Geneva, Switzerland, in June 1969. Nearly one year later [,] Alberto–Culver allegedly discovered that the trademark rights purchased under the contract were subject to substantial encumbrances that threatened to give others superior rights to the trademarks and to restrict or preclude Alberto–Culver's use of them. Alberto–Culver thereupon tendered back to Scherk the property that had been transferred to it and offered to rescind the contract. Upon

Scherk's refusal, Alberto–Culver commenced this action for damages and other relief in a Federal District Court in Illinois, contending that Scherk's fraudulent representations concerning the status of the trademark rights constituted violations of 10(b) of the Securities Exchange Act of 1934 . . . and Rule 10b–5 promulgated thereunder. . . .

In response, Scherk filed a motion to dismiss the action for want of personal and subject-matter jurisdiction as well as on the basis of *forum non conveniens*, or, alternatively, to stay the action pending arbitration in Paris pursuant to the agreement of the parties. Alberto–Culver, in turn, opposed this motion and sought a preliminary injunction restraining the prosecution of arbitration proceedings. On December 2, 1971, the District Court denied Scherk's motion to dismiss, and, on January 14, 1972, it granted a preliminary order enjoining Scherk from proceeding with arbitration. In taking these actions the court relied entirely on this Court's decision in *Wilko v. Swan*, . . . which held that an agreement to arbitrate could not preclude a buyer of a security from seeking a judicial remedy under the Securities Act of 1933, in view of the language of 14 of that Act, barring "[a]ny condition, stipulation, or provision binding any person acquiring any security to waive compliance with any provision of this subchapter. . . ." . . . The Court of Appeals for the Seventh Circuit, with one judge dissenting [Judge, later Justice, Stevens], affirmed, upon what it considered the controlling authority of the *Wilko* decision. . . . Because of the importance of the question presented we granted Scherk's petition for a writ of *certiorari* . . .

I.

The United States Arbitration Act, . . . reversing centuries of judicial hostility to arbitration agreements, was designed to allow parties to avoid "the costliness and delays of litigation," and to place arbitration agreements "upon the same footing as other contracts. . . ." . . . Accordingly the Act provides that an arbitration agreement such as is here involved "shall be valid, irrevocable, and enforceable, save upon such grounds as exist at law or in equity for the revocation of any contract." . . . The Act also provides in [§] 3 for a stay of proceedings in a case where a court is satisfied that the issue before it is arbitrable under the agreement, and [§] 4 of the Act directs a federal court to order parties to proceed to arbitration if there has been a "failure, neglect, or refusal" of any party to honor an agreement to arbitrate.

In *Wilko v. Swan*, . . . this Court acknowledged that the Act reflects a legislative recognition of the "desirability of arbitration as an alternative to the complications of litigation," . . . but nonetheless declined to apply the Act's provisions. . . .

The Court found that "[t]wo principles, not easily reconcilable, are involved in this case." . . . On the one hand, the Arbitration Act stressed "the need for avoiding the delay and expense of litigation," . . . and directed that such agreements be "valid, irrevocable, and enforceable" in federal courts. On the other hand, the Securities Act of 1933 was "[d]esigned to protect investors" . . . by creating "a special right to recover for the misrepresentation...." ...In particular, the Court noted that [§] 14 of the Securities Act...provides:

> Any condition, stipulation, or provision binding any person acquiring any security to waive compliance with any provision of this subchapter or of the rules and regulations of the Commission shall be void.

The Court ruled that an agreement to arbitrate "is a 'stipulation,' and [that] the right to select the judicial forum is the kind of 'provision' that cannot be waived under [§] 14 of the Securities Act." ... Thus, Wilko's advance agreement to arbitrate any disputes subsequently arising out of his contract to purchase the securities was unenforceable under the terms of [§] 14 of the Securities Act of 1933.

Alberto–Culver, relying on this precedent, contends that the District Court and Court of Appeals were correct in holding that its agreement to arbitrate disputes arising under the contract with Scherk is similarly unenforceable in view of its contentions that Scherk's conduct constituted violations of the Securities Exchange Act of 1934 and the rules promulgated thereunder. For the reasons that follow, we reject this contention and hold that the provisions of the Arbitration Act cannot be ignored in this case.

At the outset, a colorable argument could be made that even the semantic reasoning of the *Wilko* opinion does not control the case before us. *Wilko* concerned a suit brought under [§] 12(2) of the Securities Act of 1933, which provides a defrauded purchaser with the "special right" of a private remedy for civil liability.... There is no statutory counterpart of [§] 12(2) in the Securities Exchange Act of 1934, and neither [§] 10(b) of that Act nor Rule 10b–5 speaks of a private remedy to redress violations of the kind alleged here. While federal case law has established that [§] 10(b) and Rule 10b–5 create an implied private cause of action...the Act itself does not establish the "special right" that the Court in *Wilko* found significant. Furthermore, while both the Securities Act of 1933 and the Securities Exchange Act of 1934 contain sections barring waiver of compliance with any "provision" of the respective Acts, certain of the "provisions" of the 1933 Act that the Court held could not be waived by Wilko's agreement to arbitrate find no counterpart in the 1934 Act. In particular, the Court in *Wilko* noted that the jurisdictional provision of the 1933 Act ... allowed a plaintiff to bring suit "in any court of competent jurisdiction—federal or state—and removal from a state court is prohibited."... The analogous provision of the 1934 Act, by contrast, provides for suit only in the federal district courts that have "exclusive jurisdiction,"... thus significantly restricting the plaintiff's choice of forum.

Accepting the premise, however, that the operative portions of the language of the 1933 Act relied upon in *Wilko* are contained in the Securities Exchange Act of 1934, the respondent's reliance on *Wilko* in this case ignores the significant and, we find, crucial differences between the agreement involved in *Wilko* and the one signed by the parties here.

Alberto–Culver's contract to purchase the business entities belonging to Scherk was a truly international agreement. Alberto–Culver is an American corporation with its principal place of business and the vast bulk of its activity in this country, while Scherk is a citizen of Germany whose companies were organized under the laws of Germany and Liechtenstein. The negotiations leading to the signing of the contract in Austria and to the closing in Switzerland took place in the United States, England, and Germany, and involved consultations with legal and trademark experts from each of those countries and from Liechtenstein. Finally, and most significantly, the subject matter of the contract concerned the sale of business enterprises organized under the laws of and primarily situated in European countries, whose activities were largely, if not entirely, directed to European markets.

Such a contract involves considerations and policies significantly different from those found controlling in *Wilko*. In *Wilko*, quite apart from the arbitration provision, there was no question but that the laws of the United States generally, and the federal securities laws in particular, would govern disputes arising out of the stock-purchase agreement. The parties, the negotiations, and the subject matter of the contract were all situated in this country, and no credible claim could have been entertained that any international conflict-of-laws problems would arise. In this case, by contrast, in the absence of the arbitration provision considerable uncertainty existed at the time of the agreement, and still exists, concerning the law applicable to the resolution of disputes arising out of the contract.

Such uncertainty will almost inevitably exist with respect to any contract touching two or more countries, each with its own substantive laws and conflict-of-laws rules. A contractual provision specifying in advance the forum in which disputes shall be litigated and the law to be applied is, therefore, an almost indispensable precondition to achievement of the orderliness and predictability essential to any international business transaction. Furthermore, such a provision obviates the danger that a dispute under the agreement might be submitted to a forum hostile to the interests of one of the parties or unfamiliar with the problem area involved.

A parochial refusal by the courts of one country to enforce an international arbitration agreement would not only frustrate these purposes, but would invite unseemly and mutually destructive jockeying by the parties to secure tactical litigation advantages. In the present case, for example, it is not inconceivable that if Scherk had anticipated that Alberto–Culver would be able in this country to enjoin resort to arbitration he might have sought an order in France or some other country enjoining Alberto–Culver from proceeding with its litigation in the United States. Whatever recognition the courts of this country might ultimately have granted to the order of the foreign court, the dicey atmosphere of such a legal no-man's-land would surely damage the fabric of international commerce and trade, and imperil the willingness and ability of businessmen to enter into international commercial agreements.

The exception to the clear provisions of the Arbitration Act carved out by *Wilko* is simply inapposite to a case such as the one before us. In *Wilko* [,] the Court reasoned that "[w]hen the security buyer, prior to any violation of the Securities Act, waives his right to sue in courts, he gives up more than would a participant in other business transactions. The security buyer has a wider choice of courts and venue. He thus surrenders one of the advantages the Act gives him...." ... In the context of an international contract, however, these advantages become chimerical since, as indicated above, an opposing party may by speedy resort to a foreign court block or hinder access to the American court of the purchaser's choice.

Two Terms ago in *The Bremen v. Zapata Off–Shore Co.*, ... we rejected the doctrine that a forum-selection clause of a contract, although voluntarily adopted by the parties, will not be respected in a suit brought in the United States "unless the selected state would provide a more convenient forum that the state in which suit is brought."... Rather, we concluded that a "forum clause should control absent a strong showing that it should be set aside."...

An agreement to arbitrate before a specified tribunal is, in effect, a specialized kind of forum-selection clause that posits not only the situs of suit but also the procedure to be used in resolving the dispute. The invalidation of such an agreement in the case before us would not only allow the respondent to repudiate its solemn promise but would, as well, reflect a "parochial concept that all disputes must be resolved under our laws and in our courts.... We cannot have trade and commerce in world markets and international waters exclusively on our terms, governed by our laws, and resolved in our courts."...

[...]

Accordingly, the judgment of the Court of Appeals is reversed and the case is remanded to that court with directions to remand to the District Court for further proceedings consistent with this opinion.

It is so ordered.

Mr. Justice Douglas, with whom Mr. Justice Brennan, Mr. Justice White, and Mr. Justice Marshall concur, dissenting.

[...]

The basic dispute between the parties concerned allegations that the trademarks which were basic assets in the transaction were encumbered and that their purchase was induced through serious instances of fraudulent representations and omissions by Scherk and his agents within the jurisdiction of the United States. If a question of trademarks were the only one involved, the principle of *The Breman v. Zapata Off–Shore Co.*...would be controlling.

We have here, however, questions under the Securities Exchange Act of 1934....

[...]

...[§] 29(b)...[of the 1934 Act provides] that "[e]very contract" made in violation of the Act "shall be void." No exception is made for contracts which have an international character.

The Securities Act of 1933...has a like provision in its [§] 14:

> Any question, stipulation, or provision binding any person acquiring any security to waive compliance with any provision of this subchapter or of the rules and regulations of the Commission shall be void.

In *Wilko v. Swan*...[t]he Court held that an agreement for arbitration was a "stipulation" within the meaning of [§] 14 which sought to "waive" compliance with the Securities Act. We accordingly held that the courts, not the arbitration tribunals, had jurisdiction over suits under that Act. The arbitration agency, we held, was bound by other standards which were not necessarily consistent with the 1933 Act....

Wilko was held by the Court of Appeals to control this case—and properly so.

[...]

It could perhaps be argued that *Wilko* does not govern because it involved a little customer pitted against a big brokerage house, while we deal here with sophisticated buyers and sellers: Scherk, a powerful German operator, and Alberto–Culver, an American business surrounded and protected by lawyers and experts. But that would miss the point of the problem. The Act does not speak in terms of "sophisticated" as opposed to "unsophisticated" people dealing in securities. The rules when the giants play are the same as when the pygmies enter the market.

If there are victims here, they are not Alberto–Culver the corporation, but the thousands of investors who are the security holders in Alberto–Culver. If there is fraud and the promissory notes are excessive, the impact is on the equity in Alberto–Culver.

Moreover, the securities market these days is not made up of a host of small people scrambling to get in and out of stocks or other securities. The markets are overshadowed by huge institutional traders. The so-called "off-shore funds," of which Scherk is a member, present perplexing problems under both the 1933 and 1934 Acts. The tendency of American investors to invest indirectly as through mutual funds may change the character of the regulation but not its need.

There has been much support for arbitration of disputes; and it may be the superior way of settling some disagreements. If A and B were quarreling over a trademark and there was an arbitration clause in the contract, the policy of Congress in implementing the United Nations Convention on the Recognition and Enforcement of Foreign Arbitral

Awards. . . would prevail. But the Act does not substitute an arbiter [sic] [arbitrator] for the settlement of disputes under the 1933 and 1934 Acts. . . .

But [§] 29(a) of the 1934 Act makes agreements to arbitrate liabilities under [§] 10 of the Act "void" and "inoperative" [under Article II(3) of the Convention]. Congress has specified a precise way whereby big and small investors will be protected and the rules under which the Alberto–Culvers of this Nation shall operate. They or their lawyers cannot waive those statutory conditions, for our corporate giants are not principalities of power but guardians of a host of wards unable to care for themselves. It is these wards that the 1934 Act tries to protect. Not a word in the Convention governing awards adopts the standards which Congress has passed to protect the investors under the 1934 Act. It is peculiarly appropriate that we adhere to *Wilko*, more so even than when *Wilko* was decided. Huge foreign investments are being made in our companies. It is important that American standards of fairness in security dealings govern the destinies of American investors until Congress changes these standards.

The Court finds it unnecessary to consider Scherk's argument that this case is distinguishable from *Wilko* in that *Wilko* involved parties of unequal bargaining strength. . . . Instead, the Court rests its conclusion on the fact that this was an "international" agreement, with an American corporation investing in the stock and property of foreign businesses, and speaks favorably of the certainty which inheres when parties specify an arbitral forum for resolution of differences in "any contract touching two or more countries."

This invocation of the "international contract" talisman might be applied to a situation where, for example, an interest in a foreign company or mutual fund was sold to an utterly unsophisticated American citizen, with material fraudulent misrepresentations made in this country. The arbitration clause could appear in the fine print of a form contract, and still be sufficient to preclude recourse to our courts, forcing the defrauded citizen to arbitration in Paris to vindicate his rights.

It has been recognized that the 1934 Act, including the protections of Rule 10b–5, applies when foreign defendants have defrauded American investors, particularly when, as alleged here, they have profited by virtue of proscribed conduct within our boundaries. This is true even when the defendant is organized under the laws of a foreign country, is conducting much of its activity outside the United States, and is therefore governed largely by foreign law. The language of [§] 29 of the 1934 Act does not immunize such international transactions, and the United Nations Convention provides that a forum court in which a suit is brought need not enforce an agreement to arbitrate which is "void" and "inoperative" as contrary to its public policy. When a foreign corporation undertakes fraudulent action which subjects it to the jurisdiction of our federal securities laws, nothing justifies the conclusion that only a diluted version of those laws protects American investors.

Section 29(a) of the 1934 Act provides that a stipulation binding one to waive compliance with "any provision" of the Act shall be void, and the Act expressly provides that the federal district courts shall have "exclusive jurisdiction" over suits brought under the Act. . . .The Court appears to attach some significance to the fact that the specific provisions of the 1933 Act involved in *Wilko* are not duplicated in the 1934 Act, which is involved in this case. While Alberto–Culver would not have the right to sue in either a state or federal forum as did the plaintiff in *Wilko*. . .the Court deprives it of its right to have its Rule 10b–5 claim heard in a federal court. We spoke at length in *Wilko* of this problem, elucidating the undesirable effects of remitting a securities plaintiff to an arbitral, rather than a judicial, forum. Here, as in *Wilko*, the allegations of fraudulent misrepresentation will involve "subjective findings on the purpose and knowledge" of the defendant, questions ill-determined by arbitrators without judicial instruction on the law. . . .An arbitral award can be made without explication of reasons and without development of a record, so that the arbitrator's conception of our statutory requirement may be absolutely incorrect yet functionally unreviewable, even when the arbitrator seeks to apply our law. We recognized in *Wilko* that there is no judicial review corresponding to review of court decisions. . . . The extensive pretrial discovery provided by the Federal Rules of Civil Procedure for actions in district court would not be available. And the wide choice of venue provided by the 1934 Act. . .would be forfeited. . . . The loss of the proper judicial forum carries with it the loss of substantial rights.

When a defendant, as alleged here, has through proscribed acts within our territory, brought itself within the ken of federal securities regulation, a fact not disputed here, those laws including the controlling principles of *Wilko*, apply whether the defendant is foreign or American, and whether or not there are transnational elements in the dealings. Those laws are rendered a chimera when foreign corporations or funds unlike domestic defendants, can nullify them by virtue of arbitration clauses, which send defrauded American investors to the uncertainty of arbitration on foreign soil, or, if those investors cannot afford to arbitrate their claims in a far-off forum, to no remedy at all.

Moreover, the international aura which the Court gives this case is ominous. We now have many multinational corporations in vast operations around the world, Europe, Latin America, the Middle East, and Asia. The investments of many American investors turn on dealings by these companies. Up to this day, it has been assumed by reason of *Wilko* that they were all protected by our various federal securities Acts. If these guarantees are to be removed, it should take a legislative enactment. I would enforce our laws as they stand, unless Congress makes an exception.

The virtue of certainty in international agreements may be important, but Congress has dictated that when there are sufficient contacts for our securities laws to apply, the policies expressed in those laws take precedence. Section 29 of the 1934 Act, which renders arbitration clauses void and inoperative, recognizes no exception for fraudulent dealings which incidentally have some international factors. The Convention makes provision for such national public policy in Art. II(3). Federal jurisdiction under the 1934 Act will attach only to some international transactions, but when it does, the protections afforded investors such as Alberto–Culver can only be full-fledged.

Notes and Questions

1. The *Scherk* opinion specifically incorporates *The Bremen* doctrine into the realm of international commercial arbitration. After all, arbitration can be and was characterized by the Court as a "super" forum-selection clause. The majority's determination that the *Wilko* ruling is either irrelevant or inapplicable to international business transactions attests to the Court's intent to restrict the extraterritorial reach of U.S. domestic law and to devise special rules for transnational litigation. The majority determination also provides a forceful illustration of the conflict that is emerging between the judicial policy on arbitration and the domain of law, in particular, sectors of regulatory activity with public importance. For example, although it is never stated in these terms, the question in *Scherk* centers upon subject-matter inarbitrability: Whether securities claims, specifically those arising under the 1934 Securities Exchange Act, can be submitted to arbitration as a matter of law. The resolution of that question also involves another vital, and equally understated, aspect of arbitration law, namely, the role of contract rights in defining arbitration's scope of application and their impact upon the legal regulation of arbitration. The decision ignores both considerations and places nearly exclusive emphasis upon the judicial policy on transnational litigation and the perceived needs of international commerce.

There is, therefore, some incongruity between the statement of policy and the analytical questions and doctrinal considerations that are raised in *Scherk*. In fact, it is possible to agree with the Court's internationalist policy (the rejection of extraterritoriality and the recognition of the need for the global regulation of commerce) and to disagree with the conclusions it reaches on the questions of law that are presented. The policy appears to be unnecessarily intolerant of legal restrictions on arbitration. While the New York Arbitration Convention obligates contracting States to enforce international arbitral awards on a nondiscriminatory basis and with only a modicum of judicial supervision, it allows them to refuse to enforce arbitral agreements and awards that pertain to an inarbitrable subject matter under their law or which violate national public policy. The balance between arbitral autonomy and national legal interests achieved in the Convention simply does not factor into the Court's reasoning and elaboration of policy. The Court's view seems to be that any legal curtailment of arbitration *per force* invites greater restrictions, leading inevitably to the collapse of world trade and financial markets. The hyperbole is manifest, but to what end is the policy exaggerated?

The Court may be concerned about the influence of its ruling upon lower federal courts or about the effect of the U.S. decisional law upon courts in other national jurisdictions. The discipline of an unequivocal policy and clear doctrine avoids the undermining reference to exceptions or the *ad hoc* invocation of *sui generis* rules. It is also possible that the Court's policy on arbitration reflects systemic concerns: The congressional ratification of the New York Arbitration Convention establishes law which the Court is obligated to enforce and to safeguard against the historical menace of judicial hostility to arbitration. None of these rationales is particularly convincing or explains how the right of arbitration acquires a constitutional status nearly equivalent to the right of freedom of political expression. Despite its many allusions to a congressional mandate, the Court's policy exceeds any legislative endorsement of arbitration and constitutes an example of how the Court fashions law on its own. There are, for example, no congressional statutes that consecrate the importance to the United States of international business transactions or transborder commerce.

The consistency and the unequivocal character of the Court's policy on international arbitration, as well as its eventual merger with the policy on domestic arbitration, perhaps can best be explained by the Court's need to manage judicial dockets and to administer the federal court system. Because transnational litigation imposes an additional and more complex burden upon the federal courts, it is critical to make arbitration agreements and awards effective to avoid placing inordinate demands upon national judicial resources. The same "managerial" rationale explains the compromise of rights that occurred in the federalization of domestic U.S. arbitration law and the extension of domestic arbitration to statutory conflicts.

Do you agree with the foregoing construction of *Scherk*? What parts of the interpretation do you or might you find problematic? Do you believe that *Scherk* is a statement of pure judicial policy? Is it also a distorted policy? Does the rights protection argument undermine the reasoning in the *Scherk* decision?

2. In the remaining notes, we will examine the more technical aspects of the decision. You should observe that, unlike some other arbitration rulings, *Scherk* emanated from a divided Court. The vote was 5 to 4. There is, therefore, considerable disagreement with the majority decision, that eventually—over time—will be reduced to isolated, single-justice dissents. The opposition comes primarily from the liberal wing of the Court (Justices Douglas, Brennan, Marshall, and—to some extent—White), although neither the majority nor dissenting opinion fits neatly into a fixed ideological pattern. In fact, with the exception of *Volt Information Sciences, Inc.*, 489 U.S. 468 (1989), none of the Court's rulings on arbitration appear to be motivated to any significant extent by its members' ideological convictions. *Scherk*, therefore, appears to be an initial step at a critical juncture in the direction of a judicial policy on arbitration that espouses most, if not all, the tenets of "anational" arbitration, but for the name.

3. The applicable arbitral clause in *Scherk* provided:

> The parties agree that if any controversy or claim shall arise out of this agreement or the breach thereof and either party shall request that the matter shall be settled by arbitration, the matter shall be settled exclusively by arbitration in accordance with the rules then obtaining of the International Chamber of Commerce, Paris, France, by a single arbitrator, if the parties shall agree upon one, or by one arbitrator

appointed by each party and a third arbitrator appointed by the other arbitrators. In case of any failure of a party to make an appointment referred to above within four weeks after notice of the controversy, such appointment shall be made by said chamber. All arbitration proceedings shall be held in Paris, France, and each party agrees to comply in all respects with any award made in any such proceeding and to the entry of a judgment in any jurisdiction upon any award rendered in such proceeding. The laws of the State of Illinois, U.S.A. shall apply to and govern this agreement, its interpretation and performance. 417 U.S. at 508 n.1.

The *Scherk* agreement should give you a sense of the content, structure, and function of an international agreement to arbitrate. In light of the circumstances of the case, do you believe the foregoing provision is an appropriate representation of the parties' dispute resolution needs and interests? Despite its length and deviation from the standard clause, it appears to leave gaps and fails to provide for many reasonably foreseeable contingencies. Can you identify and cure the agreement's deficiencies? In what respects is it a good provision for arbitration? The parties appear to have "traded-off" Paris-based ICC arbitration for the application of Illinois state law to the contract. Is the exchange equally beneficial to the parties? Does the exchange reveal that one party had the upper hand or was a more able negotiator? What comfort should Alberto–Culver derive from the application of Illinois law by ICC arbitrators? Does Illinois law include federal law? If so, which federal laws? Who decides those questions? According to the arbitration agreement, which national law of arbitration governs the arbitral proceeding? Does the phrase "if any controversy or claim shall arise out of this agreement or the breach thereof" cover claims arising under the 1934 Securities Exchange Act? Who should decide that matter? Why doesn't the Court focus upon that question?

4. Both sides of the Court view the question of *Scherk* as a conflict of statutes: Whether the obligations under the New York Arbitration Convention will prevail over the rights contained in the 1934 Act. As has just been suggested, another perspective that could have been adopted by the Court would look to whether the parties intended in their agreement to arbitrate to submit both contractual and statutory claims to arbitration. If the contract provision as such is interpreted to limit the reference to arbitration to contractual claims or if the Court determines that the reference to arbitration is always limited to contract disputes as a matter of law, the question of statutory conflict does not need to be addressed because the litigation is resolved on other, less controversial grounds.

Do you find this approach to be analytically sound? What advantages does it have over the Court's methodology and conceptualization of the case? What if the ICC arbitrators rule that the contract of arbitration does not allow them to rule on noncontractual claims or that they have no authority to rule on a dispute involving the application of the 1934 Act? Would that award be enforceable in the United States? Could Scherk seek an injunction from a U.S. federal court, or an Austrian, German, Swiss, French, or Liechtensteinian court, ordering the arbitrators to rule on the statutory cause of action? Would it be proper and lawful for the ICC arbitrators to rule that the 1934 Act has no bearing upon the controversy between Scherk and

Alberto–Culver and to dismiss that part of the cause of action? Would that award be enforceable in the United States? Could Alberto–Culver's grievance be reviewed in an enforcement proceeding?

In a footnote to his dissent, Justice Douglas observes that the choice-of-law provision may not lead the arbitrators to apply federal law. Even if it does, the arbitral tribunal may misapply or misinterpret the legislation and review of the determination would be unavailable. "Even if the arbitration court should read this clause to require application of Rule 10b–5's standards, Alberto–Culver's victory would be Pyrrhic." *See* 417 U.S. at 532 n.11. Lack of discovery would compromise Alberto–Culver's right to the redress of its grievances.

5. As was mentioned in the foregoing, the arbitrability of statutory rights is never expressly mentioned in *Scherk*, although that issue will preoccupy the Court in *Mitsubishi* ten years later. In *Scherk*, the issue never escalates beyond the applicability of domestic precedents and statutes in the context of international business transactions. The question centers upon the *Wilko* bar to arbitration in securities matters. The Court quickly determines that *Wilko* is inoperative in litigation dealing with international arbitration. It initially makes a number of technical distinctions to support its determination: *Wilko* addressed a conflict between the FAA and the 1933 Securities Act, while *Scherk* pits the codification of the New York Arbitration Convention in Title 9 against the 1934 Securities Exchange Act. Moreover, despite the enormous similarities between the statutes, "[t]here is no statutory counterpart of [§] 12(2) in the Securities Exchange Act of 1934, and neither [§] 10(b) of that Act nor Rule 10b–5 speaks of a private remedy to redress violations of the kind alleged here." While 10b–5 creates "an implied private cause of action," it "does not establish the 'special right' that the Court in *Wilko* found significant." Moreover, the Court identifies a lack of concordance between the jurisdictional "provisions" of the Acts. *See* 417 U.S. at 513–14. Accordingly, these distinctions create "a colorable argument" for sustaining the view that the *Wilko* bar to predispute "arbitration agreements in securities contracts does not apply to the international contract in *Scherk*."

How persuasive is the Court's reasoning on these points? Is the "colorable" logic of its argument persuasive? Do the Acts not provide for exclusive judicial jurisdiction in terms of the adjudication of claims arising under their provisions? In comparing section 14 of the 1933 Act and section 29(a) of the 1934 Act, the Court concludes in a footnote that "[w]hile the two sections are not identical, the variations in their wording seem irrelevant to the issue presented in this case." *See* 417 U.S. at 514 n. 7. Isn't this a more plausible account of the significance and content of the securities laws? Isn't the legislation necessary to maintain the integrity of the financial market? Also, the Court advanced a different interpretation of the provisions in the later *Rodriguez de Quijas v. Shearson/American Express, Inc.* case, 490 U.S. 477 (1989), in which it reversed *Wilko* for its would-be outdated hostility to arbitration.

6. Having established these technical distinctions, the Court turns to the elaboration of its now celebrated language on the international contract and the significance of arbitration to transborder commerce. There is no

doubt that an international commercial divorce can be acrimonious, and that the parties, in all likelihood, will have recourse to all the adversarial and conflicts devices at their disposal to hamper resolution. Arbitration does stabilize international commercial dispute resolution and allows the avoidance of jurisdictional and conflicts issues. It provides neutrality, predictability, expertise, and enforceability where organized litigious chaos would otherwise reign. You should isolate the most meaningful phrases from the majority opinion's proclamation of its internationalist policy on arbitration and international contracts. They echo the essence of the policy elaborated in *The Bremen*.

Of what analytical relevance is this eloquent language to the issue involving the applicability of national law, the provision for exclusive domestic court jurisdiction over securities disputes, and the arbitrability of statutory disputes that arise pursuant to a contract relationship? The admonition against parochialism, the need to avoid the uncertainty of resolution that proceeds from the entanglements of conflicts and forum-shopping strategies, and the rejection of extraterritoriality in transborder litigation appear to have little to do with whether securities claims arising under the 1934 Act can be submitted to arbitration. Federal statutory law is applicable because Scherk chose to engage in a business transaction with a U.S. party covered by the provisions of the statute. The facts involve not only a breach of contract, but implicate directly the regulation of commercial conduct for the benefit of society. It is not the character of the contract that is at issue, but rather how the behavior of the parties affected larger U.S. juridical interests.

The majority responds to these arguments in a footnote:

> This case . . . provides no basis for a judgment that only United States laws and United States courts should determine this controversy in the face of a solemn agreement between the parties that such controversies be resolved elsewhere. The only contact between the United States and the transaction involved here is the fact that Alberto–Culver is an American corporation and the occurrence of some—but by no means the greater part, of the pre-contract negotiations in this country. To determine that "American standards of fairness" . . . must nonetheless govern the controversy demeans the standard of justice elsewhere in the world, and unnecessarily exalts the primacy of United States law over the laws of other countries. 417 U.S. at 517 n.11.

Again, the brief against extraterritoriality is admirable, but is it germane to the issues and facts of the case? Is the ICC a sovereign national entity? Didn't the parties agree to the application of U.S. law? What other laws would be displaced by the application of U.S. law? Didn't the Congress define the scope of application of the statute in question to cover foreign commerce?

You should attempt to choose the better analysis and approach to the litigation in light of the foregoing discussion.

7. The majority uses the ratification of the New York Arbitration Convention as a justification for its policy. "Our conclusion today is confirmed by international developments and domestic legislation in the area of commercial arbitration subsequent to the *Wilko* decision. In 1970 the United States acceded to the [Convention] . . . and Congress passed Chapter 2 of the

United States Arbitration Act.... [W]e think that this country's ... ratification of the Convention ... provide[s] strongly persuasive evidence of congressional policy consistent with the decision we reach today." 417 U.S. at 520 n.15.

Do you believe that the Convention supports or dictates the result in *Scherk*? Would a different determination have contravened either the spirit or the letter of the Convention? In the same passage, the Court describes the essential purpose of the Convention: "[T]o encourage the recognition and enforcement of commercial arbitration agreements in international contracts and to unify the standards by which agreements to arbitrate are observed and arbitral awards are enforced...." *Id.* Is this an accurate appraisal? Does *Scherk* affect this objective? Might the decision undermine it?

The dissent responds to this reasoning in its own footnote: "Neither [§] 29 [of the Securities Exchange Act], nor the Convention on international arbitration, nor *The Bremen* justifies abandonment of a national public policy that securities claims be heard by a judicial forum simply because some international elements are involved in a contract." 417 U.S. at 532 n.10. Do these comments constitute an effective argument against the majority position?

8. Read the dissenting opinion carefully, identifying its basic points and the elements of its reasoning. Justice Douglas' objections to the majority's judicial policy are both useful and prophetic. They anticipate, for example, the more ambitious doctrinal content of the later Court opinion in *Mitsubishi v. Soler* (*infra*). They also clarify the legal issues and interests that are at stake in *Scherk* through the haze of the majority's high-minded rhetoric. The concept of the "international contract talisman" is a reminder of the dangers of creating legal policy without regard to substantive analytical considerations. Justice Douglas argues that the issues in *Scherk* are not a matter of contract, but rather a matter of law—that rights established by Congress are substantially compromised by the reference of disputes to arbitration. Although there may not be much sympathy for rescuing Alberto–Culver from its unfortunate circumstances, the rule of decision involves more than the immediate circumstances of the litigation. It calls into question the very "fabric" of securities regulation.

You should remember that *Scherk* begins a progression toward a more far-reaching judicial arbitral policy. The Court eventually will decide that all statutory claims arising under national law are arbitrable in transborder arbitration and that the reference to arbitration represents a mere choice of trial procedure, having no impact upon the substantive rights at issue. The integration of these internationalist doctrines into the domestic law of arbitration and the reversal of *Wilko v. Swan* also will become part of the judicial policy set in motion in *Scherk*.

MITSUBISHI MOTORS CORP. v. SOLER CHRYSLER–PLYMOUTH, INC.

473 U.S. 614, 105 S.Ct. 3346, 87 L.Ed.2d 444 (1985).

(footnotes omitted)

MR. JUSTICE BLACKMUN delivered the opinion of the Court.

The principal question presented by these cases is the arbitrability, pursuant to the Federal Arbitration Act ... and the Convention on the

Recognition and Enforcement of Foreign Arbitral Awards,...of claims arising under the Sherman Act ... and encompassed within a valid arbitration clause in an agreement embodying an international commercial transaction.

I.

Petitioner-cross-respondent Mitsubishi Motors Corporation ... is a Japanese corporation ... and has its principal place of business in Tokyo, Japan. Mitsubishi is the product of a joint venture between, on the one hand, Chrysler International, S.A. (CISA), a Swiss corporation registered in Geneva and wholly owned by Chrysler Corporation, and, on the other, Mitsubishi Heavy Industries, Inc., a Japanese corporation. The aim of the joint venture was the distribution through Chrysler dealers outside the continental United States of vehicles manufactured by Mitsubishi and bearing Chrysler and Mitsubishi trademarks. Respondent-cross-petitioner Soler Chrysler–Plymouth, Inc.... is a Puerto Rico corporation with its principal place of business in Pueblo Viejo, Guaynabo, Puerto Rico.

On October 31, 1979, Soler entered into a Distributor Agreement with CISA which provided for the sale by Soler of Mitsubishi-manufactured vehicles within a designated area, including metropolitan San Juan....On the same date, CISA, Soler, and Mitsubishi entered into a Sales Procedure Agreement ... which, referring to the Distributor Agreement, provided for the direct sale of Mitsubishi products to Soler and governed the terms and conditions of such sales.... Paragraph VI of the Sales Agreement, labeled "Arbitration of Certain Matters," provides:

> "All disputes, controversies or differences which may arise between [Mitsubishi] and [Soler] out of or in relation to Articles I–B through V of this Agreement or for the breach thereof, shall be finally settled by arbitration in Japan in accordance with the rules and regulations of the Japan Commercial Arbitration Association."...

Initially, Soler did a brisk business in Mitsubishi-manufactured vehicles....In early 1981, however, the new-car market slackened. Soler ran into serious difficulties in meeting the expected sales volume, and by the spring of 1981 it felt itself compelled to request that Mitsubishi delay or cancel shipment of several orders.... About the same time, Soler attempted to arrange for the transshipment of a quantity of its vehicles for sale in the continental United States and Latin America. Mitsubishi and CISA, however, refused permission for any such diversion, citing a variety of reasons, and no vehicles were transshipped. Attempts to work out these difficulties failed. Mitsubishi eventually withheld shipment of 966 vehicles, apparently representing orders placed for May, June, and July 1981 production, responsibility for which Soler disclaimed in February 1982....

The following month ... Mitsubishi sought an order, pursuant to 9 U.S.C. 4 and 201, to compel arbitration in accord with ... the Sales Agreement.... Shortly after filing the complaint, Mitsubishi filed a request for arbitration before the Japan Commercial Arbitration Association....

Soler denied the allegations and counterclaimed against both Mitsubishi and CISA.... In the counterclaim premised on the Sherman Act, Soler alleged that Mitsubishi and CISA had conspired to divide markets in restraint of trade. To effectuate the plan, according to Soler, Mitsubishi had refused to permit Soler to resell to buyers in North, Central, or South America vehicles it had obligated itself to purchase from Mitsubishi; had refused to ship ordered vehicles or the parts, such as heaters and defoggers, that would be necessary to permit Soler to make its vehicles suitable for resale outside Puerto Rico; and had coercively attempted to replace Soler and its other Puerto Rico distributors with a wholly owned subsidiary which would serve as the exclusive Mitsubishi distributor in Puerto Rico....

After a hearing, the District Court ordered Mitsubishi and Soler to arbitrate each of the issues raised in the complaint and in all the counterclaims save two and a portion of a third. With regard to the federal antitrust issues, it recognized that the Courts of Appeals, following *American Safety Equipment Corp. v. J.P. Maguire & Co.*, 391 F.2d 821 (2d Cir. 1968), uniformly had held that the rights conferred by the antitrust laws were " 'of a character inappropriate for enforcement by arbitration.' " ... The District Court held, however, that the international character of the Mitsubishi–Soler undertaking required enforcement of the agreement to arbitrate even as to the antitrust claims. It relied on *Scherk v. Alberto–Culver Co.*...

The United States Court of Appeals for the First Circuit affirmed in part and reversed in part. 723 F.2d 155 (1983)....

Finally, after endorsing the doctrine of *American Safety*, precluding arbitration of antitrust claims, the Court of Appeals concluded that neither this Court's decision in *Scherk* nor the Convention required abandonment of that doctrine in the face of an international transaction....Accordingly, it reversed the judgment of the District Court insofar as it had ordered submission of "Soler's antitrust claims" to arbitration....

We granted *certiorari* primarily to consider whether an American court should enforce an agreement to resolve antitrust claims by arbitration when that agreement arises from an international transaction....

II.

[...]

... [W]e find no warrant in the Arbitration Act for implying in every contract within its ken a presumption against arbitration of statutory claims. The Act's centerpiece provision makes a written agreement to arbitrate "in any maritime transaction or a contract evidencing a transaction involving commerce...valid, irrevocable, and enforceable, save upon such grounds as exist at law or in equity for the revocation of any contract."...The "liberal federal policy favoring arbitration agreements," *Moses H. Cone Memorial Hospital*,...manifested by this provision and the Act as a whole, is at bottom a policy guaranteeing the enforcement of private contractual arrangements: the Act simply "creates a body of federal substantive law establishing and regulating the duty to honor an agreement to arbitrate."...

Accordingly, the first task of a court asked to compel arbitration of a dispute is to determine whether the parties agreed to arbitrate that dispute....Thus, as with any other contract, the parties' intentions control, but those intentions are generously construed as to issues of arbitrability.

There is no reason to depart from these guidelines where a party bound by an arbitration agreement raises claims founded on statutory rights....[W]e are well past the time when judicial suspicion of the desirability of arbitration and of the competence of arbitral tribunals inhibited the development of arbitration as an alternative means of dispute resolution.... Of course, courts should remain attuned to well-supported claims that the agreement to arbitrate resulted from the sort of fraud or overwhelming economic power that would provide grounds "for the revocation of any contract." ... But, absent such compelling considerations, the Act itself provides no basis for disfavoring agreements to arbitrate statutory claims by skewing the otherwise hospitable inquiry into arbitrability.

That is not to say that all controversies implicating statutory rights are suitable for arbitration. There is no reason to distort the process of contract interpretation, however, in order to ferret out the inappropriate.... For that reason, Soler's concern for statutorily protected classes provides no reason to color the lens through which the arbitration clause is read. By agreeing to arbitrate a statutory claim, a party does not forgo the substantive rights afforded by the statute; it only submits to their resolution in an arbitral, rather than a judicial, forum. It trades the procedures and opportunity for review of the courtroom for the simplicity, informality, and expedition of arbitration. We must assume that if Congress intended the substantive protection afforded by a given statute to include protection against waiver of the right to a judicial forum, that intention will be deducible from text or legislative history....Having made the bargain to arbitrate, the party should be held to it unless Congress itself has evinced an intention to preclude a waiver of judicial remedies for the statutory rights at issue. Nothing, in the meantime, prevents a party from excluding statutory claims from the scope of an agreement to arbitrate....

[...]

III.

We now turn to consider whether Soler's antitrust claims are nonarbitrable even though it has agreed to arbitrate them. In holding that they are not, the Court of Appeals followed the decision of the Second Circuit in *American Safety Equipment Corp. v. J.P. Maguire & Co.*, 391 F.2d 821 ([2d Cir.] 1968). Notwithstanding the absence of any explicit support for such an exception in either the Sherman Act or the Federal Arbitration Act, the Second Circuit there reasoned that "the pervasive public interest in enforcement of the antitrust laws, and the nature of the claims that arise in such cases, combine to make ... antitrust claims ... inappropriate for arbitration." ... We find it unnecessary to assess the legitimacy of the *American Safety* doctrine as applied to agreements to arbitrate arising from domestic transactions. As in *Scherk v. Alberto–Culver Co.*,... we conclude that concerns of international comity, respect for the capacities of foreign and transnational tribunals, and sensitivity to the need of the international commercial system for predictability in the resolution of disputes require that we enforce the parties' agreement, even assuming that a contrary result would be forthcoming in a domestic context.

[...]

The Bremen and *Scherk* establish a strong presumption in favor of enforcement of freely negotiated contractual choice-of-forum provisions. Here, as in *Scherk*, that presumption is reinforced by the emphatic federal policy in favor of arbitral dispute resolution. And at least since this Nation's accession in 1970 to the Convention, ... that federal policy applies with special force in the field of international commerce. Thus, we must weigh the concerns of *American Safety* against a strong belief in the efficacy of arbitral procedures for the resolution of international commercial disputes and an equal commitment to the enforcement of freely negotiated choice-of-forum clauses.

At the outset, we confess to some skepticism of certain aspects of the *American Safety* doctrine. As distilled by the First Circuit, ... the doctrine comprises four ingredients. First, private parties play a pivotal role in aiding governmental enforcement of the antitrust laws by means of the private action for treble damages. Second, "the strong possibility that contracts which generate antitrust disputes may be contracts of adhesion militates against automatic forum determination by contract." Third, antitrust issues, prone to complication, require sophisticated legal and economic analysis, and thus are "ill-adapted to strengths of the arbitral process, *i.e.*, expedition, minimal requirements of written rationale, simplicity, resort to basic concepts of common sense and simple equity." Finally, just as "issues of war and peace are too important to be vested in the generals, ... decisions as to antitrust regulation of business are too important to be lodged in arbitrators chosen from the business community—particularly those from a foreign community that has had no experience with or exposure to our law and values." ...

Initially, we find the second concern unjustified. The mere appearance of an antitrust dispute does not alone warrant invalidation of the selected forum on the undemonstrated assumption that the arbitration clause is tainted. A party resisting arbitration of course may attack directly the validity of the agreement to arbitrate.... Moreover, the party may attempt to make a showing that would warrant setting aside the forum-selection clause, that the agreement was "[a]ffected by fraud, undue influence, or overweening bargaining power"; that "enforcement would be unreasonable and unjust"; or that proceedings "in the contractual forum will be so gravely difficult and inconvenient that [the resisting party] will for all practical purposes be deprived of his day in court." ... But absent such a showing—and none was attempted here—there is no basis for assuming the forum inadequate or its selection unfair.

Next, potential complexity should not suffice to ward off arbitration. We might well have some doubt that even the courts following *American Safety* subscribe fully to the view that antitrust matters are inherently insusceptible to resolution by arbitration, as these same courts have agreed that an undertaking to arbitrate antitrust claims entered into after the dispute arises is acceptable.... And the vertical restraints which most frequently give birth to antitrust claims covered by an arbitration agreement will not often occasion the monstrous proceedings that have given antitrust litigation an image of intractability. In any event, adaptability and access to expertise are hallmarks of arbitration. The anticipated subject matter of the dispute may be taken into account when the arbitrators are appointed, and arbitral rules typically provide for the participation of experts either employed by the parties or appointed by the tribunal. Moreover, it is often a judgment that streamlined proceedings and expeditious results will best serve their needs that causes parties to agree to arbitrate their disputes; it is typically a desire to keep the effort and expense required to resolve a dispute within manageable bounds that prompts them mutually to forgo access to judicial remedies. In sum, the factor of potential complexity alone does not persuade us that an arbitral tribunal could not properly handle an antitrust matter.

For similar reasons, we also reject the proposition that an arbitration panel will pose too great a danger of innate hostility to the constraints on business conduct that antitrust law imposes. International arbitrators frequently are drawn from the legal as well as the business community; where the dispute has an important legal component, the parties and the arbitral body with whose assistance they have agreed to settle their dispute can be expected to select arbitrators accordingly. We decline to indulge the presumption that the parties and arbitral body conducting a proceeding will be unable or unwilling to retain competent, conscientious, and impartial arbitrators.

We are left, then, with the core of the *American Safety* doctrine—the fundamental importance to American democratic capitalism of the regime of the antitrust laws.... Without doubt, the private cause of action plays a central role in enforcing this regime.... As the Court of Appeals pointed out:

> "A claim under the antitrust laws is not merely a private matter. The Sherman Act is designed to promote the national interest in a

> competitive economy; thus, the plaintiff asserting his rights under the Act has been likened to a private attorney-general who protects the public's interest." . . .

The treble-damages provision wielded by the private litigant is a chief tool in the antitrust enforcement scheme, posing a crucial deterrent to potential violators. . . .

The importance of the private damages remedy, however, does not compel the conclusion that it may not be sought outside an American court. Notwithstanding its important incidental policing function, the treble-damages cause of action conferred on private parties by [§] 4 of the Clayton . . . Act and pursued by Soler here by way of its third counterclaim, seeks primarily to enable an injured competitor to gain compensation for that injury.

[. . .]

There is no reason to assume at the outset of the dispute that international arbitration will not provide an adequate mechanism. To be sure, the international arbitral tribunal owes no prior allegiance to the legal norms of particular states; hence, it has no direct obligation to vindicate their statutory dictates. The tribunal, however, is bound to effectuate the intentions of the parties. Where the parties have agreed that the arbitral body is to decide a defined set of claims which includes, as in these cases, those arising from the application of American antitrust law, the tribunal therefore should be bound to decide that dispute in accord with the national law giving rise to the claim. . . .And so long as the prospective litigant effectively may vindicate its statutory cause of action in the arbitral forum, the statute will continue to serve both its remedial and deterrent function.

Having permitted the arbitration to go forward, the national courts of the United States will have the opportunity at the award-enforcement stage to ensure that the legitimate interest in the enforcement of the antitrust laws has been addressed. The Convention reserves to each signatory country the right to refuse enforcement of an award where the "recognition or enforcement of the award would be contrary to the public policy of that country." . . . While the efficacy of the arbitral process requires that substantive review at the award-enforcement stage remain minimal, it would not require intrusive inquiry to ascertain that the tribunal took cognizance of the antitrust claims and actually decided them.

As international trade has expanded in recent decades, so too has the use of international arbitration to resolve disputes arising in the course of that trade. The controversies that international arbitral institutions are called upon to resolve have increased in diversity as well as in complexity. Yet the potential of these tribunals for efficient disposition of legal disagreements arising from commercial relations has not yet been tested. If they are to take a central place in the international legal order, national courts will need to "shake off the old judicial hostility to arbitration" ... and also their customary and understandable unwillingness to cede jurisdiction of a claim arising under domestic law to a foreign or transnational tribunal. To this extent, at least, it will be necessary for national courts to subordinate domestic notions of arbitrability to the international policy favoring commercial arbitration.

Accordingly, we "require this representative of the American business community to honor its bargain" ... by holding this agreement to arbitrate "enforce[able] ... in accord with the explicit provisions of the Arbitration Act." ...

The judgment of the Court of Appeals is affirmed in part and reversed in part, and the cases are remanded for further proceedings consistent with this opinion.

It is so ordered.

JUSTICE POWELL took no part in the decision of these cases.

JUSTICE STEVENS, with whom JUSTICE BRENNAN joins, and with whom JUSTICE MARSHALL joins except as to Part II, dissenting.

[...]

... This Court's holding rests almost exclusively on the federal policy favoring arbitration of commercial disputes and vague notions of international comity arising from the fact that the automobiles involved here were manufactured in Japan. Because I am convinced that the Court of Appeals' construction of the arbitration clause is erroneous, and because I strongly disagree with this Court's interpretation of the relevant federal statutes, I respectfully dissent. In my opinion, (1) a fair construction of the language in the arbitration clause in the parties' contract does not encompass a claim that auto manufacturers entered into a conspiracy in violation of the antitrust laws; (2) an arbitration clause should not normally be construed to cover a statutory remedy that it does not expressly identify; (3) Congress did not intend § 2 of the Federal Arbitration Act to apply to antitrust claims; and (4) Congress did not intend the Convention on the Recognition and Enforcement of Foreign Arbitral Awards to apply to disputes that are not covered by the Federal Arbitration Act.

I.

On October 31, 1979, respondent, Soler Chrysler–Plymouth, Inc. (Soler), entered into a "distributor agreement" to govern the sale of Plymouth passenger cars to be manufactured by petitioner, Mitsubishi Motors Corporation of Tokyo, Japan (Mitsubishi). Mitsubishi, however, was not a party to that agreement. Rather the "purchase rights" were granted to Soler by a wholly owned subsidiary of Chrysler Corporation that is referred to as "Chrysler" in the agreement. The distributor agreement does not contain an arbitration clause. Nor does the record contain any other agreement providing for the arbitration of disputes between Soler and Chrysler.

Paragraph 26 of the distributor agreement authorizes Chrysler to have Soler's orders filled by any company affiliated with Chrysler, that company thereby becoming the "supplier" of the products covered by the agreement with Chrysler. Relying on paragraph 26 of their distributor agreement, Soler, Chrysler, and Mitsubishi entered into a separate Sales Procedure Agreement designating Mitsubishi as the supplier of the products covered by the distributor agreement. The arbitration clause the Court construes today is found in that agreement. As a matter of ordinary contract interpretation, there are at least two reasons why that clause does not apply to Soler's antitrust claim against Chrysler and Mitsubishi.

First, the clause only applies to two-party disputes between Soler and Mitsubishi. The antitrust violation alleged in Soler's counterclaim is a three-party dispute. Soler has joined both Chrysler and its associated company, Mitsubishi, as counterdefendants. The pleading expressly alleges that both of those companies are "engaged in an unlawful combination and conspiracy to restrain and divide markets in interstate and foreign commerce, in violation of the Sherman Antitrust Act and the Clayton Act." ... It is further alleged that Chrysler authorized and participated in several overt acts directed at Soler. At this stage of the case we must, of course, assume the truth of those allegations. Only by stretching the language of the arbitration clause far beyond its ordinary meaning could one possibly conclude that it encompasses this three-party dispute.

Second, the clause only applies to disputes "which may arise between MMC and BUYER out of or in relation to Articles I–B through V of this Agreement or for the breach thereof...." ... Thus, disputes relating to only 5 out of a total of 15 Articles in the Sales Procedure Agreement are arbitrable. Those five Articles cover: (I) the terms and conditions of direct sales (matters such as the scheduling of orders, deliveries, and payment); (2) technical and engineering changes; (3) compliance by Mitsubishi with customs laws and regulations, and Soler's obligation to inform Mitsubishi of relevant local laws; (4) trademarks and patent rights; and (5) Mitsubishi's right to cease production of any products. It is immediately obvious that Soler's antitrust claim did not arise out of Articles I–B through V and it is not a claim "for the breach thereof." The question is whether it is a dispute "in relation to" those Articles.

Because Mitsubishi relies on those Articles of the contract to explain some of the activities that Soler challenges in its antitrust claim, the Court of Appeals concluded that the relationship between the dispute and those Articles brought the arbitration clause into play. I find that construction of the clause wholly unpersuasive. The words "in relation to" appear between the references to claims that arise under the contract and claims for breach of the contract; I believe all three of the species of arbitrable claims must be predicated on contractual rights defined in Articles I–B through V.

The federal policy favoring arbitration cannot sustain the weight that the Court assigns to it. A clause requiring arbitration of all claims "relating to" a contract surely could not encompass a claim that the arbitration clause was itself part of a contract in restraint of trade.... Nor in my judgment should it be read to encompass a claim that relies, not on a failure to perform the contract, but on an independent violation of federal law. The matters asserted by way of defense do not control the character, or the source, of the claim that Soler has asserted. Accordingly, simply as a matter of ordinary contract interpretation, I would hold that Soler's antitrust claim is not arbitrable.

II.

Section 2 of the Federal Arbitration Act describes three kinds of arbitrable agreements. Two—those including maritime transactions and those covering the submission of an existing dispute to arbitration—are not involved in this case.... The plain language of this statute encompasses Soler's claims that arise out of its contract with Mitsubishi, but does not encompass a claim arising under federal law, or indeed one that arises under its distributor agreement with Chrysler. Nothing in the text of the 1925 Act, nor its legislative history, suggests that Congress intended to authorize the arbitration of any statutory claims.

Until today all of our cases enforcing agreements to arbitrate under the Arbitration Act have involved contract claims. In one, the party claiming a breach of contractual warranties also claimed that the breach amounted to fraud actionable under [§] 10(b) of the Securities Exchange Act of 1934. *Scherk v. Alberto–Culver Co.*.... But this is the first time the Court has considered the question whether a standard arbitration clause referring to claims arising out of or relating to a contract should be construed to cover statutory claims that have only an indirect relationship to the contract. In my opinion, neither the Congress that enacted the Arbitration Act in 1925, nor the many parties who have agreed to such standard clauses, could have anticipated the Court's answer to that question.

On several occasions we have drawn a distinction between statutory rights and contractual rights and refused to hold that an arbitration barred the assertion of a statutory right. Thus, in *Alexander v. Gardner–Denver Co.*, ... we held that the arbitration of a claim of employment discrimination would not bar an employee's statutory right to damages under Title VII of the Civil Rights Act of 1964 ... notwithstanding the strong federal policy favoring the arbitration of labor disputes.... In addition, the Court noted that the informal procedures which make arbitration so desirable in the context of contractual disputes are inadequate to develop a record for appellate review of statutory questions. Such review is essential on matters of statutory interpretation in order to assure consistent application of important public rights.

In *Barrentine v. Arkansas–Best Freight System, Inc.*, ... we reached a similar conclusion with respect to the arbitrability of an employee's claim based on the Fair Labor Standards Act, 29 U.S.C. §§ 201–219. We again noted that an arbitrator, unlike a federal judge, has no institutional obligation to enforce federal legislative policy. . . .

. . . In view of the Court's repeated recognition of the distinction between federal statutory rights and contractual rights, together with the undisputed historical fact that arbitration has functioned almost entirely in either the area of labor disputes or in "ordinary disputes between merchants as to questions of fact," . . . it is reasonable to assume that most lawyers and executives would not expect the language in the standard arbitration clause to cover federal statutory claims. Thus, in my opinion, both a fair respect for the importance of the interests that Congress has identified as worthy of federal statutory protection, and a fair appraisal of the most likely understanding of the parties who sign agreements containing standard arbitration clauses, support a presumption that such clauses do not apply to federal statutory claims.

III.

The Court has repeatedly held that a decision by Congress to create a special statutory remedy renders a private agreement to arbitrate a federal statutory claim unenforceable. Thus, . . . the express statutory remedy provided in the Ku Klux Act of 1871, the express statutory remedy in the Securities Act of 1933, the express statutory remedy in the Fair Labor Standards Act, and the express statutory remedy in Title VII of the Civil Rights Act of 1964, each provided the Court with convincing evidence that Congress did not intend the protections afforded by the statute to be administered by a private arbitrator. The reasons that motivated those decisions apply with special force to the federal policy that is protected by the antitrust laws.

. . . The Sherman and Clayton Acts reflect Congress' appraisal of the value of economic freedom; they guarantee the vitality of the entrepreneurial spirit. Questions arising under these Acts are among the most important in public law.

The unique public interest in the enforcement of the antitrust laws is repeatedly reflected in the special remedial scheme enacted by Congress. Since its enactment in 1890, the Sherman Act has provided for public enforcement through criminal as well as civil sanctions. The preeminent federal interest in effective enforcement once justified a provision for special three-judge district courts to hear antitrust claims on an expedited basis, as well as for direct appeal to this Court bypassing the courts of appeals. . . .

The special interest in encouraging private enforcement of the Sherman Act has been reflected in the statutory scheme ever since 1890. Section 7 of the original Act[ ] used the broadest possible language to describe the class of litigants who may invoke its protection. . . .

The provision for mandatory treble damages—unique in federal law when the statute was enacted—provides a special incentive to the private enforcement of the statute, as well as an especially powerful deterrent to violators. What we have described as "the public interest in vigilant enforcement of the antitrust laws through the instrumentality of the private treble-damage action" ... is buttressed by the statutory mandate that the injured party also recover costs, "including a reasonable attorney's fee." ... The interest in wide and effective enforcement has thus, for almost a century, been vindicated by enlisting the assistance of "private Attorneys General"; we have always attached special importance to their role because "[e]very violation of the antitrust laws is a blow to the free-enterprise system envisaged by Congress." ...

There are, in addition, several unusual features of the antitrust enforcement scheme that unequivocally require rejection of any thought that Congress would tolerate private arbitration of antitrust claims in lieu of the statutory remedies that it fashioned.... [A]n antitrust treble-damages case "can only be brought in a District Court of the United States." The determination that these cases are "too important to be decided otherwise than by competent tribunals" surely cannot allow private arbitrators to assume a jurisdiction that is denied to courts of the sovereign States.

[...]

In view of the history of antitrust enforcement in the United States, it is not surprising that all of the federal courts that have considered the question have uniformly and unhesitatingly concluded that agreements to arbitrate federal antitrust issues are not enforceable....

This Court would be well advised to endorse the collective wisdom of the distinguished judges of the Courts of Appeals who have unanimously concluded that the statutory remedies fashioned by Congress for the enforcement of the antitrust laws ... render an agreement to arbitrate antitrust disputes unenforceable. Arbitration awards are only reviewable for manifest disregard of the law and the rudimentary procedures which make arbitration so desirable in the context of a private dispute often mean that the record is so inadequate that the arbitrator's decision is virtually unreviewable. Despotic decisionmaking of this kind is fine for parties who are willing to agree in advance to settle for a best approximation of the correct result in order to resolve quickly and inexpensively any contractual dispute that may arise in an ongoing commercial relationship. Such informality, however, is simply unacceptable when every error may have devastating consequences for important businesses in our national economy and may undermine their ability to compete in world markets. Instead of "muffling a grievance in the cloakroom of arbitration," the public interest in free competitive markets would be better served by having the issues resolved "in the light of impartial public court adjudication." ...

IV.

The Court assumes for the purposes of its decision that the antitrust issues would not be arbitrable if this were a purely domestic dispute, ... but holds that the international character of the controversy makes it arbitrable. The holding rests on vague concerns for the international implications of its decision and a misguided application of *Scherk v. Alberto–Culver Co.* . . . .

INTERNATIONAL OBLIGATIONS OF THE UNITED STATES

[. . .]

. . . [T]he United States, as *amicus curiae*, advises the Court that the Convention "clearly contemplates" that signatory nations will enforce domestic laws prohibiting the arbitration of certain subject matters. . . . The construction is beyond doubt.

[. . .]

. . . Thus, reading Articles II and V together, the Convention provides that agreements to arbitrate disputes which are nonarbitrable under domestic law need not be honored, nor awards rendered under them enforced.

This construction is also supported by the legislative history of the Senate's advice and consent to the Convention. . . .

INTERNATIONAL COMITY

It is clear then that the international obligations of the United States permit us to honor Congress' commitment to the exclusive resolution of antitrust disputes in the federal courts. The Court today refuses to do so, offering only vague concerns for comity among nations. The courts of other nations, on the other hand, have applied the exception provided in the Convention, and refused to enforce agreements to arbitrate in specific subject matters of concern to them.

It may be that the subject-matter exception to the Convention ought to be reserved—as a matter of domestic law—for matters of the greatest public interest which involve concerns that are shared by other nations. The Sherman Act's commitment to free competitive markets is among our most important civil policies. . . . This commitment, shared by other nations which are signatory to the Convention, is hardly the sort of parochial concern that we should decline to enforce in the interest of international comity. Indeed, the branch of Government entrusted with the conduct of political relations with foreign governments has informed us that the "United States' determination that federal antitrust claims are nonarbitrable under the Convention . . . is not likely to result in either surprise or recrimination on the part of other signatories to the Convention." . . .

[. . .]

. . . [I]t is especially distressing to find that the Court is unable to perceive why the reasoning in *Scherk* is wholly inapplicable to Soler's antitrust claims against Chrysler and Mitsubishi. The merits of those claims are controlled entirely by American law. It is true that the automobiles are manufactured in Japan and that Mitsubishi is a Japanese corporation, but the same antitrust questions would be presented if Mitsubishi were owned by two American companies instead of by one American and one Japanese partner. When Mitsubishi enters the American market and plans to engage in business in that market over a period of years, it must recognize its obligation to comply with American law and to be subject to the remedial provisions of American statutes.

The federal claim that was asserted in *Scherk*, unlike Soler's antitrust claim, had not been expressly authorized by Congress. Indeed, until this Court's recent decision in *Landreth Timber Co. v. Landreth*, . . . the federal cause of action asserted by Scherk would not have been entertained in a number of Federal Circuits because it did not involve the kind of securities transaction that Congress intended to regulate when it enacted the Securities Exchange Act of 1934. The fraud claimed in Scherk was virtually identical to the breach of warranty claim; arbitration of such claims arising out of an agreement between parties of equal bargaining strength does not conflict with any significant federal policy.

In contrast, Soler's claim not only implicates our fundamental antitrust policies . . . but also should be evaluated in the light of an explicit congressional finding concerning the disparity in bargaining power between automobile manufacturers and their franchised dealers. In 1956, when Congress enacted special legislation to protect dealers from bad-faith franchise terminations, it recited its intent "to balance the power now heavily weighted in favor of automobile manufacturers." . . . The special federal interest in protecting automobile dealers from overreaching by car manufacturers, as well as the policies underlying the Sherman Act, underscore the folly of the Court's decision today.

V.

The Court's repeated incantation of the high ideals of "international arbitration" creates the impression that this case involves the fate of an institution designed to implement a formula for world peace. But just as it is improper to subordinate the public interest in enforcement of antitrust policy to the private interest in resolving commercial disputes, so is it equally unwise to allow a vision of world unity to distort the importance of the selection of the proper forum for resolving this dispute. Like any other mechanism for resolving controversies, international arbitration will only succeed if it is realistically limited to tasks it is capable of performing well, the prompt and inexpensive resolution of essentially contractual disputes between commercial partners. As for matters involving the political passions and the fundamental interests of nations, even the multilateral convention adopted under the auspices of the United Nations recognizes that private international arbitration is incapable of achieving satisfactory results.

In my opinion, the elected representatives of the American people would not have us dispatch an American citizen to a foreign land in search of an uncertain remedy for the violation of a public right that is protected by the Sherman Act. This is especially so when there has been no genuine bargaining over the terms of the submission, and the arbitration remedy provided has not even the most elementary guarantees of fair process. Consideration of a fully developed record by a jury, instructed in the law by a federal judge, and subject to appellate review, is a surer guide to the competitive character of a commercial practice than the practically unreviewable judgment of a private arbitrator.

Unlike the Congress that enacted the Sherman Act in 1890, the Court today does not seem to appreciate the value of economic freedom. I respectfully dissent.

Notes and Questions

1. The *Mitsubishi* opinion introduces a more detailed substantive focus in the Court's decisional law on international commercial arbitration. From the outset of the opinion, Justice Blackmun recognizes arbitrability as the principal question of the case. In keeping with *Scherk*, a domestic law precedent is on point and is determined to be inapplicable in the context of international commercial arbitration. Also, the decision, as in *Scherk*, includes a forceful dissent authored by a member of the Court with longstanding expertise in the area deemed arbitrable by the majority. Unlike *Scherk*, the dissent in *Mitsubishi* does not harness the allegiance of a substantial minority of the Court. Finally, the Court in *Mitsubishi* begins to commingle its rulings on domestic and international arbitration. The majority makes significant reference to the federalism trilogy in supporting its conclusions on the question of arbitrability. Although the ruling is still couched in terms of the needs of transborder commerce, a unitary policy on arbitration begins to emerge. By the time it decides *McMahon* and *Rodriguez*, the Court will have forgotten the international specialty of the rule of statutory arbitrability. There had been an expectation that *Mitsubishi* would provide the Court with the opportunity to refine and contain its judicial policy on international commerce and arbitration. That expectation, needless to say, was disappointed by the opinion.

2. From the facts recited in the opinion, how would you characterize the dispute between Soler and Mitsubishi? Is it exclusively a commercial or contractual dispute—a breach of contract and nothing more? Is it more accurate to represent the conflict as a private contractual dispute with some public law implications? When should a "mixed" dispute become inarbitrable and who should make that decision? Why not sever the private and public law claims and have separate adjudications to resolve them? Would such a procedure raise *res judicata* and collateral estoppel problems? Isn't the result in *Mitsubishi* the best solution, especially in the transborder context? Should questions pertaining to important jurisdictional matters be resolved exclusively from the perspective of practicality?

In assessing these questions, you should note that, to justify its refusal to allow Soler to transship some of the vehicles, Mitsubishi alleges that a diversion of the vehicles to Houston, Texas, for example, could have had a negative impact upon U.S.-Japan trade relations. Moreover, some vehicles were unsuitable for sale in other locales because of manufacturing specifications (*e.g.*, type of gas required, availability of heaters and defoggers) and an inability to service the vehicles in these locations. 473 U.S. at 618 n.1.

Mitsubishi's claim against Soler stated that Soler did not pay for the 966 vehicles it had ordered or for the cost of storage and financial charges. Moreover, Soler failed to fulfill warranty obligations to customers, thereby harming Mitsubishi's commercial reputation. Soler allegedly also did not obtain the agreed-upon financing. *See id.* at 619 n.2. Soler's counterclaim against Mitsubishi and CISA included a series of contract breaches (wrongful refusal to ship vehicles and parts, failure to pay for warranty work and rebates, bad faith in determining sales volume); two defamation claims; and violations of two federal and two Puerto Rican statutes. *See id.* at 619–20 nn.5–6.

In this context, you should attempt to determine whether Soler's antitrust claim constituted a legitimate cause of action under the applicable statute. Was Soler simply "blowing smoke" in an attempt to complicate the litigation and avoid the arbitral proceeding? Moreover, Soler's desire to avoid arbitration may have been linked to Mitsubishi's decision to invoke that remedy. If the antitrust allegation was indeed bogus and amounted to a dilatory tactic, would that factor explain or account for the content of the majority opinion?

3. In Part II of the majority opinion, the Court elaborates the doctrinal framework that is now generally applicable in matters of arbitration, making extensive reference to the FAA and domestic law precedent (*Moses H. Cone Memorial*, 460 U.S. 1 [1983], *Byrd*, 470 U.S. 213 [1985], *Keating*, 465 U.S. 1 [1984], *Prima Paint*, 388 U.S. 395 [1967] and even labor arbitration cases like *United Steelworkers v. Warrior & Gulf Navigation Co.*, 363 U.S. 574 [1960]). Is this an appropriate methodology? What role does freedom of contract play in the doctrine? Is it meant to eradicate judicial hostility to arbitration? Does the Court give any importance to the character and quality of the arbitration contract? Was adhesion involved in *Mitsubishi*? In your view, does the FAA foster the arbitration of statutory claims? Following *Mitsubishi*, which "controversies implicating statutory rights" cannot be submitted to arbitration?

At the end of Part II, the Court argues that the submission of claims to arbitration has no impact upon substantive rights, and that the arbitration agreement reflects a mere choice of remedy or forum of litigation. Do you agree? The Court then establishes two defenses to the arbitrability of claims based upon statutory rights: (1) an express or implied congressional provision in the statute for exclusive judicial recourse; and (2) a provision in the arbitral clause which excludes such claims from the arbitrators' jurisdiction. Given the content of the case law, is it likely that even an express congressional directive for the exclusive judicial resolution of disputes would be sufficient to defeat the recourse to arbitration? The Court could require that arbitral adjudication be specifically disallowed or that the statutory or contractual exclusion of arbitration conform to the Court's assessment of the adjudicatory viability of arbitration in the particular setting. In any event, given the current climate, it is unlikely that specific congressional proscriptions of arbitration will be forthcoming.

The Court then places the burden of defining subject-matter inarbitrability upon the parties and their lawyers. This, in effect, is the practical contribution of the *Mitsubishi* decision: To avoid surprises and potential malpractice, lawyers must advise their clients to decide whether the reference to "disputes" includes both contractual and statutory conflicts that might arise between the parties during the course of their transaction. If clients want to conserve some ability to seek judicial relief, their agreement to arbitrate must specify that the arbitral clause only provides for the arbitral adjudication of ordinary contractual disputes (such as disagreements about performance, delivery, payment, or the interpretation of the contract). The Court, in effect, anticipates the contractualist theory of arbitration in *Kaplan,* 514 U.S. 938 (1995): "Nothing ... prevents a party from excluding statutory claims from the scope of an agreement to arbitrate." *Mitsubishi*, 473 U.S. at 628. How comprehensive can the exclusion of law and of the legal process become in an arbitration agreement? Can the parties agree to eliminate all forms of judicial supervision, even those specifically mandated by the governing law? Can they agree to eliminate the inarbitrability defense and the public policy exception to enforcement for purposes of their arbitration? Why should the parties be invested with such law-making authority even for purposes of their particular transaction?

Filing a petition for bankruptcy may be the only way to defeat the presumption that statutory claims are arbitrable. Soler did participate in the arbitration, but later filed a petition for bankruptcy reorganization under Chapter 11. *See Mitsubishi*, 473 U.S. at 623 n.12. The filing of a petition for bankruptcy "halted" the arbitration. Bankruptcy reorganization is perhaps the most effective defense to the obligation to arbitrate claims that a party believes to be unwarranted. In these circumstances, the question becomes whether Soler initiated the filing simply for litigious purposes, whether the bankruptcy resulted from Mitsubishi's failure to seek accommodations within the context of the transaction and from its refusal to allow transshipment, or whether Soler—as an economic actor—simply poorly assessed its abilities, misjudged the market, and entered into a transaction that was economically misguided. The filing for bankruptcy protection confirms the evident and substantial disparity of position between the parties both within the transaction and the litigation. It also illustrates that recourse to the courts and the application of antitrust statutes might have redressed the disparity somewhat and salvaged the economic viability of the weaker party, and provided consumers with a local distributor of goods. However interpreted, the petition for bankruptcy arguably may not have constituted a mandatory barrier to the continuation of the arbitral proceedings. To preclude arbitration, the issues in the bankruptcy would have had to involve "core" matters.

4. Part III of the majority opinion recites the reasoning and doctrine previously established in *Scherk* and *The Bremen*. *See Mitsubishi*, 473 U.S. at 629–31. The Court remains committed to the elaboration of bifurcated rules on domestic and international arbitration, although its determination appears to be wavering: "We find it unnecessary [not inapposite or inapplicable] to assess the legitimacy of the *American Safety* doctrine as applied to agreements to arbitrate arising from domestic transactions." 473 U.S. at 629. The Court's ambivalence (demonstrated again by its further conditional qualification: " ... even assuming that a contrary result would be forthcoming in a domestic context") anticipates the abandonment of the bifurcated doctrine in *McMahon*, 482 U.S. 220 (1987), and *Rodriguez*, 490 U.S. 477 (1989), where the specialty of transborder circumstances, the gravamen of

the holding both in *Scherk* and *Mitsubishi*, is simply cast aside and forgotten.

The Court devotes a good deal of its considerations in Part III to eviscerating the holding and essential rationale of the *American Safety* doctrine. The Court notes the four reasons the First Circuit identified to deny submission of antitrust claims to arbitration in domestic litigation. The Court responds to the *American Safety* doctrine by a steadfast proclamation of faith in arbitration. You should evaluate *American Safety* on your own and then assess the Court's critique of the *American Safety* doctrine. Which version has the greater appeal? Wasn't the transaction in *Mitsubishi* troubled by a disparity of position between the parties and an arbitration agreement that was one-sided on its face? How sympathetic or sensitive do you think the Japanese arbitrators were to Soler's antitrust assertions?

Is the arbitral clause fair? What does it indicate about the parties' respective economic positions? What type of arbitration is provided for in the clause? The arbitral tribunal actually consisted of three Japanese lawyers: a former law school dean, a former judge, and a practicing lawyer who had some U.S. legal training and had written on Japanese antitrust law. *See Mitsubishi*, 473 U.S. at 634 n.18. Would the arbitral litigation in Japan at all resemble a trial proceeding in the United States? Do you believe that the regulatory culture and the antitrust laws in Japan bear any equivalency to their U.S. counterparts? What about the importance of private attorneys-general, treble damages, and the discovery features of the applicable U.S. statute? Isn't the Court right to focus upon the nonnational and private character of arbitration? Don't those additional features argue for the inarbitrability of statutory claims? Is the Court being flippant in its assessment of the situation? Is it at all possible that "the statute will continue to serve both its remedial and deterrent function"? *See Mitsubishi*, 473 U.S. at 637. Can there be any doubt that the reference of the antitrust claims to arbitration results in a deprivation of rights? Would the Court's reasoning be more plausible in a domestic context in which arbitrators might have the requisite adjudicatory experience and legal and cultural knowledge? Doesn't the reasoning in *Mitsubishi per force* entail a substantial diminution of the status of the antitrust legislation and of law itself? While the implied rejection of extraterritoriality is admirable, is it feasible—politically or legally—when it entails a unilateral divestiture of legal authority in circumstances in which there is no international regime of antitrust regulation to fill the void?

5. There are two technical arguments that appear at the end of Part III of the majority opinion. First, the Court states in a footnote: "[I]n the event the choice-of-forum and choice-of-law clauses operated in tandem as a prospective waiver of a party's right to pursue statutory remedies for antitrust violations, we would have little hesitation in condemning the agreement as against public policy." *Mitsubishi*, 473 U.S. at 637 n.19. Second, in the text of the opinion, the Court observes: "[T]he national courts of the United States will have the opportunity at the award-enforcement stage to ensure that the legitimate interest in the enforcement of the antitrust laws has been addressed." *Mitsubishi*, 473 U.S. at 632.

Both remarks are intended to allay fears that all legal authority in matters of antitrust has been abdicated to international arbitrators. How do you assess the meaning and significance of what the Court is saying in these two passages of the opinion? Do they constitute effective judicial supervision? Are they intended to do so? As to the first passage, how does it square with the contractualist theory of arbitration? As to the second passage, known as the "second look" doctrine, does it coincide with the obligations contained in Articles III and V of the New York Arbitration Convention? How do you evaluate the general impact of *Mitsubishi* upon the Convention? The majority states: "The utility of the Convention in promoting the process of international commercial arbitration depends upon the willingness of national courts to let go of matters they normally would think of as their own." *Mitsubishi*, 473 U.S. at 639 n.21. What does that remark signify?

§ 2. ENFORCING INTERNATIONAL ARBITRAL AWARDS: THE CRITICAL ROLE OF THE NEW YORK ARBITRATION CONVENTION

The 1958 New York Arbitration Convention was ratified by the United States in Public Law 91–368 of July 31, 1970, 84 Stat. 692. The Convention entered into force for the United States on December 29, 1970. 9 U.S.C. §§ 201–08 contains statutory provisions integrating the ratified convention into the U.S. legal system. The various sections of Title 9 deal with jurisdictional and venue questions that might arise under federal and state law in matters of international arbitration. Despite this oblique codification under Title 9, the text of the Convention constitutes the law applicable in the United States to matters of international commercial arbitration.

The New York Arbitration Convention is an exemplary treaty—a model of modern arbitration legislation. The force of its authority is based upon its codification of the international consensus on arbitration. Also, rather than attempt to regulate all aspects of the arbitral process, the New York Convention focuses directly upon two vital elements of arbitral procedure (the validity of arbitration agreements and the enforcement of arbitral awards), leaving a more comprehensive regulatory scheme to be implied from its express principles.

The Convention's objective is to unify national laws on the enforcement of international arbitral awards and to establish a transnational rule of law that favors the recourse to arbitral adjudication. For example, Article II(1) provides that the contracting States shall recognize an agreement to submit disputes to arbitration. The purpose of this provision is to eradicate systemic hostility to arbitration—hostility stemming from the view that arbitration amounts to a usurpation of judicial adjudicatory authority. Consequently, by adhering to the Convention, contracting States agree to recognize the arbitral process as a legitimate means of resolving disputes. Under Article II(3), a motion to compel arbitration can be defeated only by establishing that the arbitration agreement was null and void, inoperative, or incapable of being performed. Decisional interpretations of the Convention demonstrate that these grounds were meant to function as ordinary contract defenses to the enforcement of an agreement. Arbitration agreements, therefore, are valid contractual arrangements and do not, *per se*, violate public policy. They symbolize party use of contractual rights—rights the assertion of which can be defeated only by a deficiency in contractual intent, capacity, or language. Accordingly, courts in the contracting States are under a legal obligation to enforce arbitration agreements if they satisfy the ordinary requirements of contractual validity.

The text of the Convention proposes a unified transnational rule of law not only in regard to the validity of arbitration agreements, but also concerning the enforcement of foreign arbitral awards. The systemic viability of any nonjudicial adjudicatory process is dependent both upon the legal system's recognition of the validity of agreements to enter into such processes and its willingness to give binding effect to its determinations. The seven grounds for the judicial supervision of awards contained in Article V can be grouped into two broad categories. The first category encompasses the procedural requirements that dictate compliance with basic adjudicatory standards. The parties must have had the contractual capacity to enter into an arbitration agreement; they must have been afforded proper notice of the proceeding; the arbitrators must not have exceeded the jurisdictional authority conferred upon them by the agreement; the composition of the arbitral tribunal and the appointment of arbitrators must comply with the provisions of the agreement; and the award must have been binding in the jurisdiction in which it was rendered.

Second, national courts can deny recognition and enforcement to an international arbitral award upon the basis of two broad substantive law grounds. The dispute which the award settles must be arbitrable under the law of the requested jurisdiction; moreover, recognition and enforcement of the award must not be contrary to the requested jurisdiction's public policy. To some extent, the inarbitrability defense and public policy exception overlap. For example, as a general rule, disputes relating to the status and capacity of persons are inarbitrable. An award relating to a person's status and capacity, if recognized and enforced, would also be contrary to the public policy of the requested jurisdiction.

The Convention's truly international stature and law-making capacity are built upon two factors. First, its symbolic function of codifying an existing and emerging international consensus on arbitration. Second, its endorsement by national legal systems which seek to affirm and integrate the Convention's content and underlying intent, and thereby entrench the transnational recognition of and support for arbitration.

Traditional analysis would argue that national courts must apply the provisions of the Convention as written. Subsequent developments and schools of thought cannot repeal or amend the content of an international treaty. The Convention expressly refers to national law and its application. Therefore, the law of the place of arbitration, the parties' national law, and the law of the place of enforcement should play a significant role in validating arbitration agreements and awards. Private international adjudications are still dependent upon national legal authority. Coercive enforcement cannot be achieved without invoking the laws of the requested territorial jurisdiction.

There is, however, another view of the Convention's law-making status—one that relies upon a sense of the realities of litigation practice and which ignores, rightly or wrongly, the legal considerations of territory and hierarchy. The provisions of the Convention are not static, but rather reflect law-in-the-making. They are primarily responsive to the policy imperative that underlies the Convention. The references to the application of national law within the Convention may have been necessary to create an international movement toward ratification. Events, however, have outpaced that original purpose. International commercial arbitration has become an "anational" phenomenon. Although trans-border adjudication can acquire the force of law only through national legal authority, arbitration—once the Convention gained universal adherence—transcended the need for continued approbation of national law.

National courts and legislation, in effect, surrendered their authority to regulate arbitration and permitted it to function autonomously. As a result, factors such as the parties' national law, the law of the place of arbitration, and even the law of the place of enforcement are relevant only to the extent that they converge with the norms generated by the process of "anational" arbitration.

Moreover, the movement toward uniform national laws on arbitration has undercut much of the debate about the impact of national sovereignty and national law in the implementation of the Convention. In fact, the continuing global ratification of the Convention has reversed the traditional tendency of States to make local exceptions to an agreed-upon international regime. Moreover, States appear to be competing to enact the most liberal laws on international commercial arbitration. The UNCITRAL Model Law and Model Rules on arbitration also indicate a trend toward "anational" uniformity. Parties seeking to enforce arbitration agreements and awards, of course, are always subject to the particularities of their case and a given national law and judiciary. By and large, however, national law is no longer a constraint upon arbitration. States understand the international commercial importance of arbitration and actively promote themselves as venues for international arbitral proceedings. The "deregulatory" movement and the State acquiescence to the rise of arbitration are motivated in large measure by the desire to sell professional and infrastructure services to the international business community.

The Convention represents one of the most successful United Nations efforts at establishing a rule of law in the community of nations. The Convention has been ratified by more than one hundred countries (135 at last count) and generally receives a uniformly favorable construction in the national courts of the ratifying States. Its success reflects the breadth and depth of the world community perception that transborder commerce is vital to national interests and that arbitration is indispensable to the operation of international business. The New York Arbitration Convention replaces several prior international agreements on arbitration and is intended to function as the "universal charter" on international commercial arbitration. To some extent, the New York Arbitration Convention has superseded its own content and legislative history. It has become a juridical vehicle for the elaboration of a transborder law on international commercial arbitration.

The United States was initially reluctant to adhere to the Convention. The lack of enthusiasm reflected in part the traditional U.S. skepticism about participation in international instruments, namely, that they create an obligation to abide by non-national rules of conduct and amount to a relinquishment of national legal authority to govern. It also demonstrated the power of U.S. business interests following the Second World War; there was no need to acquiesce to a system of private international adjudicatory mechanisms when transborder contract disputes could be resolved according to our laws and before our courts. These various factors delayed United States adhesion to the emerging world community perception of the need to establish an autonomous rule of transborder commercial law and litigation.

The United States ratified the Convention in December 1970, some twelve years after the Convention had been opened for signature. Once ratification had been achieved, the United States began playing a central role, primarily through the case law of the U.S. Supreme Court, in legitimizing and promoting international commercial arbitration. In fact, ratification provided a juridical foundation upon which the Court elaborated not only a judicial doctrine on international commercial arbitration, but also a larger U.S. private international law on transborder litigation. The Court's rulings on international commercial arbitration are among the most liberal and supportive judicial pronouncements on arbitration. In fact, the U.S. law on arbitration now directs the global consensus on arbitration.

CONVENTION ON THE RECOGNITION AND ENFORCEMENT OF FOREIGN ARBITRAL AWARDS

opened for signature June 10, 1958,
21 U.S.T. 2517, T.I.A.S. No.6997, 330 U.N.T.S. 3,
codified in 9 U.S.C.A. §§ 201–08 (1970).

ARTICLE I

1. This Convention shall apply to the recognition and enforcement of arbitral awards made in the territory of a State other than the State where the recognition and enforcement of such awards are sought, and arising out of differences between persons, whether physical or legal. It shall also apply to arbitral awards not considered as domestic awards in the State where their recognition and enforcement are sought.

2. The term "arbitral awards" shall include not only awards made by arbitrators appointed for each case but also those made by permanent arbitral bodies to which the parties have submitted.

3. When signing, ratifying or acceding to this Convention, or notifying extension under article X hereof, any State may on the basis of reciprocity declare that it will apply the Convention to the recognition and enforcement of awards made only in the territory of another Contracting State. It may also declare that it will apply the Convention only to differences arising out of legal relationships, whether contractual or not, which are considered as commercial under the national law of the State making such declaration.

Article II

1. Each Contracting State shall recognize an agreement in writing under which the parties undertake to submit to arbitration all or any differences which have arisen or which may arise between them in respect of a defined legal relationship, whether contractual or not, concerning a subject matter capable of settlement by arbitration.

2. The term "agreement in writing" shall include an arbitral clause in a contract or an arbitration agreement, signed by the parties or contained in an exchange of letters or telegrams.

3. The court of a Contracting State, when seized of an action in a matter in respect of which the parties have made an agreement within the meaning of this article, shall, at the request of one of the parties, refer the parties to arbitration, unless it finds that the said agreement is null and void, inoperative or incapable of being performed.

Article III

Each Contracting State shall recognize arbitral awards as binding and enforce them in accordance with the rules of procedure of the territory where the award is relied upon, under the conditions laid down in the following articles. There shall not be imposed substantially more onerous conditions or higher fees or charges on the recognition or enforcement of arbitral awards to which this Convention applies than are imposed on the recognition or enforcement of domestic arbitral awards.

Article IV

1. To obtain the recognition and enforcement mentioned in the preceding article, the party applying for recognition and enforcement shall, at the time of the application, supply:

(a) The duly authenticated original award or a duly certified copy thereof;

(b) The original agreement referred to in article II or a duly certified copy thereof.

2. If the said award or agreement is not made in an official language of the country in which the award is relied upon, the party

applying for recognition and enforcement of the award shall produce a translation of these documents into such language. The translation shall be certified by an official or sworn translator or by a diplomatic or consular agent.

Article V

1. Recognition and enforcement of the award may be refused, at the request of the party against whom it is invoked, only if that party furnishes to the competent authority where the recognition and enforcement is sought, proof that:

(a) The parties to the agreement referred to in article II were, under the law applicable to them, under some incapacity, or the said agreement is not valid under the law to which the parties have subjected it or, failing any indication thereon, under the law of the country where the award was made; or

(b) The party against whom the award is invoked was not given proper notice of the appointment of the arbitrator or of the arbitration proceedings or was otherwise unable to present his case; or

(c) The award deals with a difference not contemplated by or not falling within the terms of the submission to arbitration, or it contains decisions on matters beyond the scope of the submission to arbitration, provided that, if the decisions on matters submitted to arbitration can be separated from those not so submitted, that part of the award which contains decisions on matters submitted to arbitration may be recognized and enforced; or

(d) The composition of the arbitral authority or the arbitral procedure was not in accordance with the agreement of the parties, or, failing such agreement, was not in accordance with the law of the country where the arbitration took place; or

(e) The award has not yet become binding on the parties, or has been set aside or suspended by a competent authority of the country in which, or under the law of which, that award was made.

2. Recognition and enforcement of an arbitral award may also be refused if the competent authority in the country where recognition and enforcement is sought finds that:

(a) The subject matter of the difference is not capable of settlement by arbitration under the law of that country; or

(b) The recognition or enforcement of the award would be contrary to the public policy of that country.

Article VI

If an application for the setting aside or suspension of the award has been made to a competent authority referred to in article V(I)(e), the authority before which the award is sought to be relied upon may, if it considers it proper, adjourn the decision on the enforcement of the award and may also, on the application of the party claiming enforcement of the award, order the other party to give suitable security.

ARTICLE VII

1. The provisions of the present Convention shall not affect the validity of multilateral or bilateral agreements concerning the recognition and enforcement of arbitral awards entered into by the Contracting States nor deprive any interested party of any right he may have to avail himself of an arbitral award in the manner and to the extent allowed by the law or the treaties of the country where such award is sought to be relied upon.

2. The Geneva Protocol on Arbitration Clauses of 1923 and the Geneva Convention on the Execution of Foreign Arbitral Awards of 1927 shall cease to have effect between Contracting States on their becoming bound and, to the extent that they become bound, by this Convention.

[. . .]

CHAPTER 2 OF THE FAA: CONVENTION ON THE RECOGNITION AND ENFORCEMENT OF FOREIGN ARBITRAL AWARDS

9 U.S.C. Ch. 2 (§§ 201–08) (2000).

§ 201. Enforcement of Convention

The Convention on the Recognition and Enforcement of Foreign Arbitral Awards of June 10, 1958, shall be enforced in United States courts in accordance with this chapter.

§ 202. Agreement or award falling under the Convention

An arbitration agreement or arbitral award arising out of a legal relationship, whether contractual or not, which is considered as commercial, including a transaction, contract, or agreement described in section 2 of this title, falls under the Convention. An agreement or award arising out of such a relationship which is entirely between citizens of the United States shall be deemed not to fall under the Convention unless that relationship involves property located abroad, envisages performance or enforcement abroad, or has some other reasonable relation with one or more foreign states. For the purpose of this section a corporation is a citizen of the United States if it is incorporated or has its principal place of business in the United States.

§ 203. Jurisdiction; amount in controversy

An action or proceeding falling under the Convention shall be deemed to arise under the laws and treaties of the United States. The district courts of the United States (including the courts enumerated in section 460 of title 28) shall have original jurisdiction over such an action or proceeding, regardless of the amount in controversy.

§ 204. Venue

An action or proceeding over which the district courts have jurisdiction pursuant to section 203 of this title may be brought in any such court in which save for the arbitration agreement an action or proceeding with respect to the controversy between the parties could be brought, or in such court for the district and division which embraces the place designated in the agreement as the place of arbitration if such place is within the United States.

§ 205. Removal of Cases from State Courts

Where the subject matter of an action or proceeding pending in a State court relates to an arbitration agreement or award falling under the Convention, the defendant or the defendants may, at any time before the trial thereof, remove such action or proceeding to the district court of the United States for the district and division embracing the place where the action or proceeding is pending. The procedure for removal of causes otherwise provided by law shall apply, except that the ground for removal provided in this section need not appear on the face of the complaint but may be shown in the petition for removal. For the purposes of Chapter 1 of this title any action or proceeding removed under this section shall be deemed to have been brought in the district court to which it is removed.

§ 206. Order to compel arbitration; appointment of arbitrators

A court having jurisdiction under this chapter may direct that arbitration be held in accordance with the agreement at any place therein provided for, whether that place is within or without the United States. Such court may also appoint arbitrators in accordance with the provisions of the agreement.

§ 207. Award of arbitrators; confirmation; jurisdiction; proceeding

Within three years after an arbitral award falling under the Convention is made, any party to the arbitration may apply to any court having jurisdiction under this chapter for an order confirming the award as against any other party to the arbitration. The court shall confirm the award unless it finds one of the grounds for refusal or deferral of recognition or enforcement of the award specified in the said Convention.

§ 208. Chapter 1; residual application

Chapter 1 applies to actions and proceedings brought under this chapter to the extent that that chapter is not in conflict with this chapter or the Convention as ratified by the United States.

Notes and Questions

1. The Convention has created an effective and functional rule of law in the international community. Its textual provisions are neither numerous

nor complex. The economy of the Convention's text is as remarkable as its international force. Of the sixteen articles that constitute the Convention, only Articles I, II, III, and V contain law-making content; other articles deal with formal procedural concerns. We now examine the salient provisions of the Convention.

Article I establishes the Convention's scope of application. You should note that the provision first establishes a territorial definition of "foreign" arbitral awards and then refers, as a secondary matter, to definitions of "nondomestic" awards under the national law of the requested States. Accordingly, a ratifying State can apply the provisions of the Convention to the enforcement of arbitral awards rendered outside its territory or which it deems as a matter of law not to be domestic awards. The Convention's proffered definition is objective (territory of rendition) and its secondary definition (national legal definitions of "foreign") is more subjective and variable. The Convention's tolerance for individual national variations on its scope of application, necessary for wide ratification, could have created problems for its subsequent uniform application.

Some States, like France, adopted a broad subject matter definition of the term "foreign" arbitral award or arbitration. Under French law, an award is foreign, international, or nondomestic whenever it implicates the interests of international commerce. Accordingly, an arbitration between two French nationals taking place in France could still be considered "foreign" despite the linkage to France because the transaction giving rise to the arbitration may have had a bearing upon or contained elements of international commerce. Prior to and under the legislation enacted in 1996, the English position on this question focused in major part upon nationality (Section 85 of the 1996 Arbitration Act). A "nondomestic" arbitral award is one which does not involve British nationality. Therefore, a commodities transaction between a U.S. and a British national, involving transport between three different countries, leading to an arbitral award might not be considered as "nondomestic" for purposes of enforcement in the United Kingdom.

The U.S. position on the Convention's scope of application intermediates between the French and English views. Under 9 U.S.C. § 202, an award has the requisite foreign character when it pertains to a transaction that involves some "reasonable" relationship or connection "with one or more foreign states." A transaction that lacks foreign nationality and that gives rise to an award will not fall under the jurisdiction of the Convention unless it has other ties to transborder commerce. U.S. law also requires that the award resolve commercial differences between the parties.

The question of the Convention's scope of application would be significant only if there were a substantial disparity between the Convention's enforcement provisions and the national provisions on the enforcement of domestic or international arbitral awards. The purpose of the Convention was to establish a hospitable regime for the enforcement of international arbitral awards in the ratifying States by exempting these awards from restrictive domestic requirements for the enforcement of arbitral awards. Allowing States to apply a narrow definition of "nondomestic" awards could have undermined the underlying intent of the Convention regime.

Modern arbitration statutes tend to minimize the difference between the enforcement of domestic and international arbitral awards, making the problem of distinguishing between domestic and "nondomestic" awards moot to some extent. In fact, it appears that, under U.S. law, it is easier to enforce a domestic award under Section Ten of the FAA (Federal Arbitration Act) than an international award under Article V of the Convention. Section Ten contains no mention of the inarbitrability defense and public policy exception to enforcement, while Article V(2)(a) & (b) includes both grounds. The equivalency of regimes and the alignment of arbitral policy have lessened the importance of the issue and transformed it primarily into a legalistic concern.

Do you agree with this assessment of the problem? Doesn't a determination that the award is domestic eliminate the application of the policy favoring the enforcement of international arbitral awards? Do all jurisdictions have an equally favorable policy on the enforcement of domestic arbitral awards? How do you know? What makes an arbitral award international or non-domestic in your view? Do you believe your definition would persuade a U.S. court or a foreign tribunal? Why do you believe the Convention has survived this knotty problem of definition?

You should also note that Article I(3) allows States to declare that their ratification of the Convention is subject to two reservations: (1) reciprocity—the Convention shall apply only to awards rendered in the territory of another ratifying State; and (2) the commercial relationships qualification—the Convention shall apply only to awards that resolve commercial disputes (as defined by national law) between the parties. The United States ratified the Convention with the two reservations. Of what significance are the two reservations? How do they protect the sovereign interests of the ratifying State? In particular, what does the commercial relationship qualification achieve? Given the depicted evolution of law under the Convention, do these reservations have any but a formalistic meaning? Finally, are there in your view other interpretative difficulties with the text of Article I that have not been identified in the discussion?

2. *Article II* establishes the legal obligations of ratifying States in regard to arbitration. By ratifying the Convention, States agree to recognize the submission and the arbitral clause as valid contractual undertakings and to enforce them as they would ordinary contracts. What specific problems of arbitration law are these obligations intended to cure? What parallel can you establish between the Convention and the FAA on this question? Article II(1), establishing the States' obligation to recognize arbitration agreements, refers at the end of its formulation to restrictions upon the States' obligation, namely, that the arbitration agreement relates to "a defined legal relationship, whether contractual or not" and to "a subject matter capable of settlement by arbitration." What do these restrictions mean, especially the latter reference to the subject matter of the contract or dispute? Do you find any parallel between the Convention and the FAA on this question? When can a ratifying State refuse to recognize an arbitration agreement as a valid "agreement in writing"?

Article II(2) defines the "in writing" requirement broadly and by reference to commercial practices rather than legal requirements. This provision reveals aspects of the underlying ideology of the Convention, namely, that it is meant to codify the dispute resolution practices of the international commercial community rather than establish a legal regime for its governance. Courts have recognized that new technological means of communication also satisfy the "in writing" requirement.

Finally, Article II(3) establishes the duty of national courts in the ratifying States to compel arbitration in the appropriate circumstances. The obligation is triggered upon the request of a contracting party when it can establish that an arbitration agreement exists. The motion can be denied only if the court finds that the agreement to arbitrate is deficient as a contract. The parallelism to the FAA is evident; both statutes require a cooperative relationship between the judicial and arbitral process. Moreover, the parties have the right to enter into arbitration agreements; that right can be defeated only when the requirements of contractual validity are not satisfied. Would the language of Article II(3) authorize a U.S. court to compel arbitration in a foreign jurisdiction between foreign nationals? How would you formulate a basis for responding to that question? Also, in this regard, what happens to the *kompetenz-kompetenz* doctrine under Article II? Doesn't the provision authorize the court to decide whether there is a contract of arbitration?

3. Having established its jurisdictional application and the State obligation to recognize and enforce arbitration agreements, the Convention then provides, in *Article III*, that contracting States also are under an obligation to recognize and enforce foreign arbitral awards. In the second sentence, the language of the provision expresses the concern that foreign arbitral awards not be subject to discriminatory treatment, that they should be treated in a manner similar to domestic arbitral awards. The content of the provision testifies to the enormous distance that has been traveled since 1958. The actual effect of the Convention has been to establish an enforcement regime that distinctly favors international, non-domestic, or foreign arbitral awards and exempts them from any rigorous domestic law scrutiny. You should also note the economy and focus of the regulatory framework; in three relatively short articles, the Convention has addressed all of the fundamental stages of the legal process regulating arbitration.

4. *Article V* is a critical provision. It outlines the grounds upon which a national court in a contracting State can deny recognition and enforcement to an international, non-domestic, or foreign arbitral award. There are five procedural grounds and two other grounds based upon substantive law considerations.

Article V(1)(e) incorporates a traditional private international law consideration into the enforcement regime under the Convention, namely, *res judicata* and the conflict of judgment. This provision puts into play the national law question and brings the text of the Convention into direct conflict with the tenets of "anational" arbitration. It provides that an award can be denied recognition or enforcement if it is not final or has been set aside by a court in another jurisdiction with contacts to the arbitration. The courts having jurisdiction to set aside an award are courts in the place of arbitration or courts in the jurisdiction the law of which governed the making of the award. This part of the provision, in effect, restates the problem of the "double exequatur" in a diluted form. Although an award need not be enforceable both at the place of rendition and at the place of enforcement, it must not have been rendered unenforceable at the place of rendition in order to be legally enforceable at the place of enforcement.

There are significant interpretative difficulties with the language of Article V(I)(e). For example, it is unclear what the wording "[t]he award has not yet become binding on the parties" actually means. Have the arbitrators failed to rule upon some submitted claims? Is it a partial award? Do damages or costs remain to be assessed? Is there something in the arbitral procedure that remains incomplete? Under French law, a domestic arbitral award has *res judicata* effect upon its rendition. Therefore, once the arbitrators have ruled, the resulting award, like a court judgment, is binding upon the parties. Appeals can delay the enforcement of a judicial judgment, but the right of appeal is very limited in arbitration and ordinarily confined to the grounds that apply in an enforcement proceeding.

It is also difficult to interpret the meaning of the binding requirement because it is linked by the disjunction "or" to the setting aside procedure. The disjunction denotes two separate rather than related actions. It seems, therefore, that, unlike the situation in French law, an award under the Convention is not legally binding until the adverse party has exercised its right to relief from the enforcement of the award either at the place of rendition, the place of the law governing the merits or the arbitration, or the place of actual enforcement. A denial of recognition or enforcement (setting aside the award) at the place of rendition or at the place of the governing law can cripple its enforceability under the Convention at the place of intended enforcement.

There is a further ambiguity in the reference to "the country ... under the law of which ... [the] award was made." The designation could mean the jurisdiction the substantive law of which was applied by the arbitrators to the merits of the dispute or the jurisdiction the arbitration law of which controlled the arbitral proceeding or, albeit more unlikely, the jurisdiction the procedural law of which controlled the proceeding. Depending upon the complexity of the parties' choice of applicable law, an award could be subject to the scrutiny of four different national courts (place of rendition, place of substantive governing law, place of governing arbitration law, place of governing trial or curial law) before any action was brought at the place of intended enforcement. Moreover, the reference to an award being "set aside or suspended" entails further problems of construction. Are the two actions equivalent or do they refer to independent means by which to challenge an award at anyone of the four possible jurisdictions?

Article V(1)(e) squarely places the enforcement of international, non-domestic, or foreign arbitral awards under the Convention into a complex choice-of-law framework. It contradicts the liberal policy on arbitration that animates the other provisions of the Convention and undermines the effort to establish a functional transborder regime for the enforcement of arbitral awards. In particular, it invites lawyers to engage in forum-shopping strategies to protect the interests of their award-averse clients by using disparate national laws to frustrate the process of international commercial accountability and justice. Article V(1)(e) is expressly at odds with the central premise of "anational" arbitration that the only national law of any consequence in an enforcement action is the law of the place of intended enforcement (where assets exist to satisfy the award). Laws or venues selected for transactional or contractual convenience should not impinge upon the legitimacy of awards. Considerations of territoriality have little relevance to modern global commerce. Moreover, the emerging view of "anational" arbitration is that the local law of the place of intended enforcement should have a bearing on the award only to the extent that it conforms with the "anational" transborder norms on arbitration.

In light of the foregoing remarks, how do you evaluate the content and implications of Article V(1)(e)? Do you believe the provision is no longer applicable law and has been written out of the Convention by subsequent events and practice? Has the would-be uniformity of national laws on arbitration made the language of ground "e" perfunctory? Are the conflict-of-law problems likely to arise in the more modern and developed climate of international commercial arbitration?

Article V(2)(a) & (b) establishes the substantive law grounds for opposing the enforcement of an award under the Convention: (1) substantive inarbitrability (ground a); and (2) public policy (ground b). Both concepts expressly rely upon the local law of the enforcement jurisdiction for their content; according to the Convention, it is the national law version of inarbitrability and public policy that governs. As noted previously, there is some unavoidable overlap between the two grounds: More than likely, a subject area will be deemed inarbitrable because its importance to the State makes it part of national public policy. The public policy exception to enforcement, however, can include matters that have no linkage to the inarbitrability defense. An award could violate local public policy for reasons of trial procedure or for its conflict with other fundamental legal norms of the jurisdiction. A vigorous application of the public policy exception to enforcement could come close in some instances to a judicial review of the merits of the award.

For example, the requested court might determine that the arbitrators misapplied a provision of law or awarded excessively generous damages and that "misconduct" violates local public policy. This is precisely what the Convention intended to eradicate: Arbitral awards are presumptively enforceable unless they represent a fundamental miscarriage of procedural justice or are juridically repugnant to the requested jurisdiction. National courts are precluded from revisiting the litigation on any other ground, especially as to the determination on the merits. Otherwise, the prospect of judicial second-guessing would rob the process of arbitral adjudication of its viability.

The deference paid to national law in Article V(2)(a) & (b) again points to the danger of acknowledging the role of national law in the regulation of international commercial arbitration and of inviting choice-of-law considerations to have a bearing upon the operation of a transborder regime for arbitration. Practice under the Convention since 1958 has largely eliminated the possibility of national law interference. In applying the Convention, national courts have responded to the underlying spirit rather than the technical letter of the Convention and Article V(2)(a) & (b). In fact, they have devised the notion of an "international" public policy that applies under Article V(2)(b) and which replaces the application of domestic notions of public policy to guard against unwarranted national law intrusion upon the transborder regime of arbitration. Also, through the efforts primarily of the U.S. Supreme Court, the inarbitrability defense has waned considerably in significance and operation. The emerging position under many national laws of arbitration is that international arbitrators have the right, if not the obligation, to rule upon disputes that involve rights created by statute rather than through contract. Both of these developments attest to the fact that, through its application before national courts, the Convention has generated legal norms that transcend the specific language of its provisions, and that it stands as the foundation of a transborder law on arbitration in constant adaptation.

In light of the foregoing remarks, can you make the case for retaining some national law reach in matters of international commercial arbitration through the inarbitrability defense or the public policy exception to enforcement? Is a more moderate position possible, desirable, or workable? Why should international arbitrators be authorized to apply national or regional regulatory law? Is there a difference between "unlimited" arbitration in the domestic and international sectors?

Finally, does Article V(1)(c), addressing excess of arbitral authority, conflict with *kompetenz-kompetenz*? Criticizing arbitrators for ruling on matters not submitted also conflicts with the modern, fluid view of the terms of reference that applies in practice. This type of discretion may be part of the arbitrator's sovereign authority.

5. 9 U.S.C. §§ 202–208 implements the Convention in U.S. law. Section 202 defines the scope of application of the Convention or its jurisdictional reach in U.S. law. The significance of the provision has already been discussed, but you should be attentive to the requirements for determining when an award becomes subject to the Convention. Given the liberal enforcement regime that generally applies to arbitral awards, however, there is no real doctrinal or practical handicap associated with the enforcement of non-Convention arbitral agreements or awards. Section 203 establishes that the application of the Convention raises federal question jurisdiction that cannot be defeated by the amount in controversy requirement. Sections 204 and 205 are largely self-explanatory. Section 206 gives U.S. courts extraterritorial powers to sustain the reference to arbitration. Does this exceed the mandate in the Convention? Is the use of this authority likely to work? Would a foreign court need to approve the order? Section 207 establishes both a three-year statute of limitation period for bringing an enforcement action under the Convention and an obligation upon courts to confirm awards that do not violate the grounds for enforcement. The three-year limit tolls from the date of the award's rendition. *See Seetransport Wiking Trader Schiffarhtsgesellschaft MBH & Co., Kommanditgesellschaft v. Navimpex Centrala Navala*, 989 F.2d 572, 580–81 (2d Cir. 1993). Section 208 is largely self-explanatory.

Case Law Developments

1. In the Matter of *Chromalloy Aeroservices*

The decision in the *Chromalloy* case addresses the question of whether a U.S. court—applying the New York Arbitration Convention—

should enforce an international arbitral award that has been set aside by a court at the place of rendition. The question involves an apparent conflict between Articles V and VII of the New York Arbitration Convention. Generally, it implicates the functioning of the process of international commercial arbitration and of the New York Arbitration Convention.

The approving view argues that *Chromalloy* adds to the autonomy of international commercial arbitration by insulating it from arbitrary national idiosyncrasies on arbitration:

> By limiting the ability of courts in the countries of origin to thwart enforcement abroad through the use of their nullification powers, the court's decision sends a message to business, governments, and arbitrators that they can rely on international arbitration for final and binding resolution of the merits of disputes.

Sampliner, *Enforcement of Foreign Arbitral Awards After Annulment in Their Country of Origin*, 11–9 Mealey's Int'l Arb. Rep. 22, 28 (1996).

The disapproving interpretation criticizes the U.S. court's disregard of treaty obligations and its creation of potential inconsistencies in enforcement:

> Enforcing set aside awards may result in the coexistence of two conflicting awards concerning the same issues between the same parties, and thus violate the intended uniformity of the Convention and damage the image of international commercial arbitration.

Gharavi, *Chromalloy: Another View*, 12–1 Mealey's Int'l Arb. Rep. 21, 23 (1997).

Another commentator sees *Chromalloy* as providing support for the position that the New York Arbitration Convention establishes a permissive set of guidelines for enforcement matters:

> . . . I propose here to demonstrate that the leading commentator on the New York Convention, Prof. van den Berg, is wrong when he contends that Article V(1)(e) of the New York Convention precludes the enforcement of an award set aside in its country of origin. The fact is that courts of a State bound by the Convention *cannot violate it by enforcing a foreign award*. Rather, a violation would occur if such a court were to *refuse* enforcement in the absence of one of the limited exceptions defined in Article V(I).
>
> This brings us to a core objective of the New York Convention: to free the international arbitral process from the domination of the law of the place of arbitration.

Paulsson, *Rediscovering the N.Y. Convention: Further Reflections on Chromalloy*, 12–4 Mealey's Int'l Arb. Rep. 20, 24 (1997).

The federal court action was echoed in at least one major European arbitration jurisdiction. The Paris Court of Appeals upheld a lower court decision granting enforcement to the *Chromalloy* award in France. *See* 12–4 Mealey's Int'l Arb. Rep. 5 (1997). The court reasoned that, under the 1982 Franco–Egyptian Treaty of Judicial Cooperation, domestic French law applied pursuant to Article VII of the New York Arbitration Convention. In matters of enforcement, French law (which does not include foreign annulment of the award as a ground for nonenforcement) is less restrictive than the Convention.

Apparently, this position is not new among French courts. According to Gharavi, "[f]or more than a decade, French courts have held that the setting aside of a foreign arbitral award in the rendering country is not a ground for refusing [the] enforc[ment] of the award in France." Gharavi, *Chromalloy, Another View*, *supra*, at 25, n.8. *See also* Gharavi, *Enforcing Set Aside Arbitral Awards: France's Controversial Steps Beyond The New York Convention*, 6 J. Transnat'l L. & Pol'y 93 (1996). In a reply to Paulsson, Gharavi states pointedly that "[t]he fact that the award was also enforced in France does not make *Chromalloy* immune from criticism." Gharavi, *The Legal Inconsistencies of Chromalloy*, 12–5 Mealey's Int'l Arb. Rep. 21, 22 (1997).

The text of the *Chromalloy* decision is reproduced below. It should be evaluated by reference generally to the basic U.S. judicial policy on arbitration and more specifically as it relates to the enforcement question. Do you find the court's reasoning persuasive? Is there no textual conflict between the various provisions of the New York Arbitration Convention? Is Paulsson's construction of the Convention plausible in light of the court's opinion? Is Gharavi's view more prudent and practical?

IN THE MATTER OF THE ARBITRATION OF CERTAIN CONTROVERSIES BETWEEN CHROMALLOY AEROSERVICES AND THE ARAB REPUBLIC OF EGYPT

939 F.Supp. 907 (D.D.C. 1996).

(Footnotes omitted)

[. . .]

II. Background

This case involves a military procurement contract between a U.S. corporation, Chromalloy Aeroservices, Inc., [(CAS)], and the Air Force of the Arab Republic of Egypt.

On June 16, 1988, Egypt and CAS entered into a contract under which CAS agreed to provide parts, maintenance, and repair for helicopters belonging to the Egyptian Air Force. On December 2, 1991, Egypt terminated the contract by notifying CAS representatives in Egypt. . . . On December 4, 1991, Egypt notified CAS headquarters in Texas of the termination. . . .On December 5, 1991, CAS notified Egypt that it rejected the cancellation of the contract "and commenced arbitration proceedings on the basis of the arbitration clause contained in Article XII and Appendix E of the Contract." . . . Egypt then drew down CAS' letters of guarantee in an amount totaling some $11,475,968. . . .

On February 23, 1992, the parties began appointing arbitrators, and shortly thereafter, commenced a lengthy arbitration....On August 24, 1994, the arbitral panel ordered Egypt to pay to CAS the sums of $272,900 plus 5 percent interest from July 15, 1991, (interest accruing until the date of payment), and $16,940,958 plus 5 percent interest from December 15, 1991, (interest accruing until the date of payment).... The panel also ordered CAS to pay to Egypt the sum of 606,920 pounds sterling, plus 5 percent interest from December 15, 1991, (interest accruing until the date of payment)....

On October 28, 1994, CAS applied to this Court for enforcement of the award. On November 13, 1994, Egypt filed an appeal with the Egyptian Court of Appeal, seeking nullification of the award. On March 1, 1995, Egypt filed a motion with this Court to adjourn CAS's [sic] [CAS'] Petition to enforce the award. On April 4, 1995, the Egyptian Court of Appeal suspended the award, and on May 5, 1995, Egypt filed a Motion in this Court to Dismiss CAS's [sic] [CAS'] petition to enforce the award. On December 5, 1995, Egypt's Court of Appeal at Cairo issued an order nullifying the award....

Egypt argues that this Court should deny CAS' Petition to Recognize and Enforce the Arbitral Award out of deference to its court.... CAS argues that this Court should confirm the award because Egypt "does not present any serious argument that its court's nullification decision is consistent with the New York Convention or United States arbitration law." ...

III. Discussion

A. Jurisdiction

[...]

CAS brings this action to confirm an arbitral award made pursuant to an agreement to arbitrate any and all disputes arising under a contract between itself and Egypt, a foreign state, concerning a subject matter capable of settlement by arbitration under U.S. law.... Enforcement of the award falls under the Convention on Recognition and Enforcement of Foreign Arbitral Awards, ("Convention"), ... which grants "[t]he district courts of the United States ... original jurisdiction over such an action or proceeding, regardless of the amount in controversy ." ...

B. Chromalloy's Petition for Enforcement

A party seeking enforcement of a foreign arbitral award must apply for an order confirming the award within three years after the award is made....The award in question was made on August 14, 1994. CAS filed a Petition to confirm the award with this Court on October 28, 1994, less than three months after the arbitral panel made the award. CAS's [sic] [CAS'] Petition includes a "duly certified copy" of the original award as required by Article IV(I)(a) of the Convention, translated by a duly sworn translator, as required by Article IV(2) of the Convention, as well as a duly certified copy of the original contract and arbitration clause, as required by Article IV(I)(b) of the Convention.... CAS's Petition is properly before this Court.

1. The Standard under the Convention

This Court must grant CAS's [sic] [CAS'] Petition to Recognize and Enforce the arbitral "award unless it finds one of the grounds for refusal ... of recognition or enforcement of the award specified in the ... Convention." ... Under the Convention, "Recognition and enforcement of the award may be refused" if Egypt furnishes to this Court "proof that ... [t]he award has ... been set aside ... by a competent authority of the country in which, or under the law of which, that award was made." ... In the present case, the award was made in Egypt, under the laws of Egypt, and has been nullified by the court designated by Egypt to review arbitral awards. Thus, the Court *may,* at its discretion, decline to enforce the award.

While Article V provides a discretionary standard, Article VII of the Convention *requires* that, "The provisions of the present Convention shall not ... deprive any interested party of any right he may have to avail himself of an arbitral award in the manner and to the extent allowed by the law ... of the count[r]y where such award is sought to be relied upon." ... In other words, under the Convention, CAS maintains all rights to the enforcement of this Arbitral Award that it would have in the absence of the Convention. Accordingly, the Court finds that, if the Convention did not exist, the Federal Arbitration Act ("FAA") would provide CAS with a legitimate claim to enforcement of this arbitral award.... Jurisdiction over Egypt in such a suit would be available under 28 U.S.C. §§ 1330 (granting jurisdiction over foreign states "as to any claim for relief *in personam* with respect to which the foreign state is not entitled to immunity ... under sections 1605–1607 of this title") and 1605(a)(2) (withholding immunity of foreign states for "an act outside ... the United States in connection with a commercial activity of the foreign state elsewhere and that act causes a direct effect in the United States").... Venue for the action would lie with this Court under 28 U.S.C. § 1391(f) & (f)(4) (granting venue in civil cases against foreign governments to the United States District Court for the District of Columbia).

2. Examination of the Award under 9 U.S.C. § 10

[...]

The Court's analysis thus far has addressed the arbitral award, and, as a matter of U.S. law, the award is proper.... The Court now considers the question of whether the decision of the Egyptian court should be recognized as a valid foreign judgment.

As the Court stated earlier, this is a case of first impression. There are no reported cases in which a court of the United States has faced a situation, under the Convention, in which the court of a foreign nation has nullified an otherwise valid arbitral award. This does not mean, however, that the Court is without guidance in this case....

In *Scherk*, the Court forced a U.S. corporation to arbitrate a dispute arising under an international contract containing an arbitration clause.... In so doing, the Court relied upon the FAA, but took the opportunity to comment upon the purposes of the newly acceded-to Convention:

> The delegates to the Convention voiced frequent concern that courts of signatory countries in which an agreement to arbitrate is sought to be enforced should not be permitted to decline enforcement of such agreements on the basis of parochial views of their desirability or in a manner that would diminish the mutually binding nature of the agreements.... [W]e think that this country's adoption and ratification of the Convention and the passage of Chapter 2 of the United States Arbitration Act provide strongly persuasive evidence of congressional policy consistent with the decision we reach today.

... The Court finds this argument equally persuasive in the present case, where Egypt seeks to repudiate its solemn promise to abide by the results of the arbitration.

C. The Decision of Egypt's Court of Appeal

1. The Contract

[...]

... Article XII of the contract requires that the parties arbitrate all disputes that arise between them under the contract. Appendix E, which defines the terms of any arbitration, forms an integral part of the contract. The contract is unitary. Appendix E to the contract defines the "Applicable Law Court of Arbitration." The clause reads, in relevant part:

> It is ... understood that both parties have irrevocably agreed to apply Egypt (sic) [Egyptian] Laws and to choose Cairo as seat of the court of arbitration.
>
> [...]
>
> The decision of the said court shall be final and binding and cannot be made subject to any appeal or other recourse....

This Court may not assume that the parties intended these two sentences to contradict one another, and must preserve the meaning of both if possible.... Egypt argues that the first quoted sentence supersedes the second, and allows an appeal to an Egyptian court. Such an interpretation, however, would vitiate the second sentence, and would ignore the plain language on the face of the contract. The Court concludes that the first sentence defines choice of law and choice of forum for the hearings of the arbitral panel. The Court further concludes that the second quoted sentence indicates the clear intent of the parties that any arbitration of a dispute arising under the contract is not to be appealed to any court. This interpretation, unlike that offered by Egypt, preserves the meaning of both sentences in a manner that is consistent with the plain language of the contract. The position of the latter sentence as the seventh and final paragraph, just before the signatures, lends credence to the view that this sentence is the final word on the arbitration question. In other words, the parties agreed to apply Egyptian Law to the arbitration, but, more important, they agreed that the arbitration ends with the decision of the arbitral panel.

2. The Decision of the Egyptian Court of Appeal

The Court has already found that the arbitral award is proper as a matter of U.S. law, and that the arbitration agreement between Egypt and CAS precluded an appeal in Egyptian courts. The Egyptian court has acted, however, and Egypt asks this Court to grant *res judicata* effect to that action.

The "requirements for enforcement of a foreign judgment ... are that there be 'due citation' [*i.e.*, proper service of process] and that the original claim not violate U.S. public policy." ... The Court uses the term 'public policy' advisedly, with a full understanding that, "[J]udges have no license to impose their own brand of justice in determining applicable public policy." ... Correctly understood, "[P]ublic policy emanates [only] from clear statutory or case law, 'not from general considerations of supposed public interest.' "...

The U.S. public policy in favor of final and binding arbitration of commercial disputes is unmistakable, and supported by treaty, by statute, and by case law. The Federal Arbitration Act "and the implementation of the Convention in the same year by amendment of the Federal Arbitration Act," demonstrate that there is an "emphatic federal policy in favor of arbitral dispute resolution," particularly "in the field of international commerce." ... A decision by this Court to recognize the decision of the Egyptian court would violate this clear U.S. public policy.

3. International Comity

"No nation is under an unremitting obligation to enforce foreign interests which are fundamentally prejudicial to those of the domestic forum."..."[C]omity never obligates a national forum to ignore 'the rights of its own citizens or of other persons who are under the protection of its laws.' " ... Egypt alleges that, "Comity is the chief doctrine of international law requiring U.S. courts to respect the decisions of competent foreign tribunals." However, comity does not and may not have the preclusive effect upon U.S. law that Egypt wishes this Court to create for it.

[...]

4. Choice of Law

Egypt argues that by choosing Egyptian law, and by choosing Cairo as the sight [sic] [site or situs] of the arbitration, CAS has for all time signed away its rights under the Convention and U.S. law. This argument is specious. When CAS agreed to the choice of law and choice of forum provisions, it waived its right to sue Egypt for breach of contract in the courts of the United States in favor of final and binding arbitration of such a dispute under the Convention. Having prevailed in the chosen forum, under the chosen law, CAS comes to this Court seeking recognition and enforcement of the award. The Convention was created for just this purpose. It is untenable to argue that by choosing arbitration under the Convention, CAS has waived rights specifically guaranteed by that same Convention.

5. Conflict between the Convention & the FAA

As a final matter, Egypt argues that, "Chromalloy's use of [A]rticle VII [to invoke the Federal Arbitration Act] contradicts the clear language of the Convention and would create an impermissible conflict under 9 U.S.C. § 208," by eliminating all consideration of Article V of the Convention.... As the Court has explained, however, Article V provides a permissive standard, under which this Court *may* refuse to enforce an award. Article VII, on the other hand, mandates that this Court *must* consider CAS' claims under applicable U.S. law.

Article VII of the Convention provides:

> The provisions of the present Convention shall not ... deprive any interested party of any right he may have to avail himself of an arbitral award in the manner and to the extend allowed by the law ... of the count[r]y where such award is sought to be relied upon.

9 U.S.C. § 201 note. Article VII does not eliminate all consideration of Article V; it merely requires that this Court protect any rights that CAS has under the domestic laws of the United States. There is no conflict between CAS' use of Article VII to invoke the FAA and the language of the Convention.

IV. CONCLUSION

The Court concludes that the award of the arbitral panel is valid as a matter of U.S. law. The Court further concludes that it need not grant *res judicata* effect to the decision of the Egyptian Court of Appeal at Cairo. Accordingly, the Court Grants Chromalloy Aeroservices' Petition to Recognize and Enforce the Arbitral Award, and Denies Egypt's Motion to Dismiss that Petition.

Notes and Questions

In related litigation, the U.S. District Court of the Southern District of New York recently refused to enforce an arbitral award rendered in Italy because the award had been nullified by an Italian court of first instance, and the nullification had been upheld by Italy's highest court. The trial court in Italy ruled that the arbitrators had exceeded their authority because they conferred a "bonus" on the petitioner that had not been authorized by the parties' contract. The petitioner sought to enforce the award in the district court in New York while his opponent challenged the award before the

Italian courts. The U.S. district court deferred judgment until the Italian trial court rendered its ruling. The district court eventually denied the petition. The court stated that a foreign court decision setting aside an award should not be ignored simply because a national court would have reached a different result with respect to the enforcement of the award under an application of domestic law. *See Spier v. Calzaturificio Tecnica, S.p.A.*, 77 F. Supp. 2d 405 (S.D.N.Y. 1999).

Martin Spier, an engineer and U.S. citizen, entered into a contract with Calzaturificio Tecnica S.p.A. (Tecnica), an Italian corporation, to provide expertise for the manufacture, by Tecnica, of various hard boots. The contract was executed in Italy and included an agreement to arbitrate any disputes arising between the two parties concerning the contract. A dispute arose between Tecnica and Spier over compensation for a line of footwear allegedly created with the help of Spier's expertise. The dispute went to arbitration. During the arbitration, the arbitrators retained a technical consultant who advised them on the disputed issue. The arbitrators declined to follow the consultant's opinion. The arbitrators awarded Spier monetary damages—an award that Spier would not have received had the arbitrators followed the consultant's opinion. Tecnica appealed the award to an Italian court. The Italian court of first instance entered judgment nullifying the award. The court of appeals of Venice affirmed the judgment, which was in turn affirmed by Italy's highest court, the Court of Cassation. In its decision, the Court of Cassation stated that the arbitrators exceeded their authority by rendering an award that was unrelated to the content of the arbitration agreement.

Spier made three arguments in favor of enforcement before the U.S. district court. First, he argued that U.S. law required enforcement. The court rejected this argument stating that, when an arbitration takes place in another State, the arbitral proceeding is subject to the laws of that State, unless otherwise provided. Spier also argued that, under Article V(1) of the Convention, a court may overturn a foreign court's denial of enforcement to an arbitration award for adequate reasons. The court found that Spier presented no adequate reason why it should overturn the Italian courts' decisions. Finally, Spier argued that, under *In re Chromalloy Aeroservices*, 939 F.Supp. 907 (D.D.C. 1996), the FAA required the U.S. policy in favor of arbitration to override the decisions of the Italian courts. The district court disagreed. *Chromalloy* was distinguishable in that, there, the Egyptian government, a party to the arbitration, had blatantly disregarded its contractual agreement not to appeal the arbitral award. No such agreement was present in the case before the court. The court noted further that, even if the decision had been subject to the laws of the United States, the result may not have been different. All three Italian courts nullified the arbitral award on the ground that, in making their decision, the arbitrators had exceeded their authority, a specific ground for vacatur under the FAA. The court, therefore, denied the petition to enforce the arbitral award.

Can *Spier* be reconciled with *Chromalloy*? What is the status of the New York Arbitration Convention's Article V grounds now? Does the court advance persuasive distinctions between the two cases? What role does the FAA play in these matters?

A COMMENT ON *YUSUF AHMED ALGHANIM & SONS v. TOYS "R" US, INC.*

126 F.3d 15 (2d Cir. 1997), *cert. denied*, 522 U.S. 1111, 118 S.Ct. 1042, 140 L.Ed.2d 107 (1998).

In *Alghanim v. Toys "R" Us*, the Second Circuit also addressed the question of the application of the FAA under the New York Arbitration Convention. The court held that the grounds under the FAA Section Ten can supplement Article V of the Convention as long as they do not conflict with the Convention. The rule of "non-conflicting overlap," however, only applies to Convention awards that are rendered abroad. For Convention awards rendered in the United States, the FAA grounds can apply to matters of enforcement in the setting aside procedure provided for in the Convention regardless of possible conflict with the other provisions of the Convention. The Second Circuit is one of the few federal courts to have interpreted the language of Article V(1)(e). Its disposition appears to conflict not only with the Convention's objectives, but also with the enforcement policy endorsed by the D.C. Circuit in *Chromalloy*.

In November 1982, Toy "R" Us entered into an agreement with Alghanim & Sons in which it granted the privately-owned Kuwaiti business a limited right to open Toys "R" Us stores and use its trademarks in Kuwait and in several other Middle Eastern countries. Pursuant to the agreement, Alghanim opened four toy stores—all of them in Kuwait and only one of which constituted a typical Toys "R" Us outlet. From 1982 to 1993, Alghanim's operation of the stores resulted in nearly $7 million in losses. In 1991 and 1992, the parties attempted to renegotiate the transaction; Alghanim wanted Toys "R" Us to assume greater responsibility for capital expenditures which Toys "R" Us was unwilling to do. In July 1992, Toys "R" Us sent Alghanim a notice of non-renewal, stating that the parties' agreement would terminate on January 31, 1993. Alghanim alleged that the notice was late and that, as a result, the term of the agreement was extended for another two years (until January 16, 1995).

After a number of unsuccessful attempts to settle their differences, the parties went to arbitration pursuant to the contract. Specifically, in December 1993, Toys "R" Us initiated an AAA arbitration, seeking a ruling that the Toys "R" Us–Alghanim agreement terminated on December 31, 1993. Alghanim counterclaimed for breach of contract. The arbitrator denied Toys "R" Us' request for a declaratory judgment and agreed with Alghanim's claim for breach of contract. After proceedings that lasted for nearly two years, the arbitrator awarded Alghanim $46 million plus interest for lost profits. The arbitrator's findings and legal conclusions were set out in an extensive opinion. The arbitration was conducted and the award rendered in New York.

Alghanim petitioned the U.S. District Court for the Southern District of New York to confirm the award under the New York Arbitration

Convention. Toys "R" Us argued that the award should be vacated under the FAA because it was irrational and in manifest disregard of the law and of the terms of the parties' agreement. The district court agreed with Toys "R" Us that the FAA was applicable and "the Convention and the FAA afford[ed] overlapping coverage." It, however, ruled that Toys "R" Us' objections to the enforcement of the award were without merit. The district court then confirmed the award.

On appeal, the Second Circuit addressed the question of the "overlapping coverage" between the New York Arbitration Convention and the FAA. First, it concluded that the Convention was clearly applicable to the enforcement of the award. The transaction giving rise to the arbitration and the award was unequivocally "non-domestic" in character (it involved parties of different nationalities and contract performance principally abroad). The statutory standard (9 U.S.C. § 202) and the interpretative decisional law among federal circuits (*Bergesen v. Joseph Muller Corp.*, 710 F.2d 928 [2d Cir. 1983] and *Jain v. de Méré*, 51 F.3d 686 [7th Cir. 1995]) made the "Convention's applicability" "clear."

Second, the Second Circuit recognized that, under U.S. law, the grounds in Article V of the Convention are the exclusive means for setting aside an international or "non-domestic" arbitral award. The FAA may supplement the Convention in such cases, but only "to the extent that [the FAA] is not in conflict with ... the Convention...." This rule of non-conflicting application applies both to the statutory and nonstatutory grounds contained in Section 10 of the FAA. According to the court, when the "application of the FAA's implied grounds" "are in conflict" with the Convention, they are "precluded." Therefore, only non-conflicting overlap is possible. The court acknowledged that this position is well-settled in the decisional law, including its own precedent (*Bergesen*, *supra* and *Parsons & Whittemore Overseas Co. Inc. v. Société Générale de L'Industrie du Papier* (RAKTA), 508 F.2d 969 [2d Cir. 1974]):

> There is now considerable case law holding that, in an action to confirm an award rendered in, or under the law of, a foreign jurisdiction, the grounds for relief enumerated in Article V of the Convention are the only grounds available for setting aside an arbitral award.

This well-settled position coincided with the purpose of the New York Arbitration Convention to establish, in all signatory States, a uniform regime for the enforcement of international or foreign arbitral awards. The nonstatutory grounds under Section Ten (irrationality, capricious and arbitrary awards, manifest disregard of the law, violations of public policy) are derived from the federal decisional law on domestic U.S. labor arbitration. They deal with the special circumstances of that form of arbitration, in which labor arbitrators interpret collective bargaining agreements and federal labor law. They have a variable status among the federal circuits, and make possible (in theory, at least) the judicial scrutiny of the merits of arbitral determinations. Although these grounds as interpreted pose little serious challenge to the enforcement of domestic arbitral awards, their particularly domestic character and their tolerance for judicial merits review make them inapposite for application in the context of international or foreign arbitral awards. On this score, the nonstatutory grounds conflict with the Convention and—according to the court's reasoning—should be preempted by the Convention's exclusive application.

Third, the Second Circuit, however, noted the special circumstances of the Toys "R" Us award, circumstances that took the case out of the scope of the foregoing framework. The arbitration took place and the award was rendered in New York. Because of its rendition in the United States, the nondomestic award in Toys "R" Us triggered the application of Article V(1)(e) of the Convention. Under the relevant language of Article V(1)(e), a Convention award can be "set aside or suspended by a competent authority of the country in which, or under the law of which, that award was made." According to the court, Article V(1)(e) allows for the application of the FAA in an action to set aside such an award:

> We read Article V(1)(e) of the Convention to allow a court in the country under whose law the arbitration was conducted to apply domestic arbitral law, in this case the FAA, to a motion to set aside or vacate that arbitral award.

The court assembled support for its position from federal decisional law, foreign state practice under the Convention, and scholarly commentators. As the court acknowledges, few—if any—other federal courts have confronted the question of Article V(1)(e) "head-on" and the court strained to find precedent for its construction of the text. It cited *Spector v. Torenberg*, 852 F. Supp. 201 (S.D.N.Y. 1994), as directly on point for the same proposition, but it also attempted to distill an alliance between its reasoning and the ruling in *Chromalloy v. Egypt*, 939 F. Supp. 907 (D.D.C. 1996). *Chromalloy*, however, seems to be directly at odds with the policy implications of the doctrine elaborated by the Second Circuit in *Toys "R" Us*. Moreover, the survey of various commentators (van den Berg, Craig, Paulsson—the leading authorities in the area) and of their reference to the practice of foreign courts was selective and failed to emphasize the problematic character of the language of Article V(1)(e) to the attainment of the Convention's objectives.

It is true, as the court states, that: "There appears to be no dispute among [scholarly commentators and 'sister signatories to the Convention'] that an action to set aside an international arbitral award, as contemplated by Article V(1)(e), is controlled by the domestic law of the rendering state." It is also accurate to observe that "many commentators and foreign courts have concluded that an action to set aside an award can be brought only under the domestic law of the arbitral forum, and can never be made under the Convention." (Referring to van den Berg and Paulsson.) Or, referring to Craig, that: "The Convention provides no restraint whatsoever on the control functions of local courts at the seat of arbitration.'' The court is entirely correct in its final conclusion on this question:

> From the plain language and history of the Convention, it is thus apparent that a party may seek to vacate or set aside an award in the state in which, or under the law of which, the award is rendered. Moreover, the language and history of the Convention make it clear that such a motion is to be governed by domestic law of the rendering state, despite the fact that the award is nondomestic within the meaning of the Convention.

The court's analysis failed to consider that most, if not all, commentators view Article V(1)(e) as a domestic law intrusion into the international regime for the enforcement of transborder arbitral awards. The availability of Article V(1)(e) makes the practice of international commercial arbitration hazardous and can render the enforcement regime of the Convention dysfunctional in some cases. Under the language of the provision, some or all of the disruptive choice-of-law problems that the Convention intended to remedy re-emerge and confound the aim of creating a unitary transborder framework for enforcement.

In one of the excerpts cited by the court, Albert Jan van den Berg—long recognized as the foremost authority on the Convention—states, in regard to Article V(1)(e), that "the grounds for refusal of enforcement under the Convention may indirectly be extended to include all kinds of particularities of the arbitration law of the country of origin. This might undermine the limitative character of the grounds for refusal listed in Article V and thus decrease the degree of uniformity existing under the Convention.'' Another commentator cited by the court, Daniel Kolkey, also focused upon the procedural perils of the provision:

> If the scope of judicial review in the rendering state extends beyond the other six defenses allowed under the New York Convention, the losing party's opportunity to avoid enforcement is automatically enhanced: The losing party can first attempt to derail the award on appeal on grounds that would not be permitted elsewhere during enforcement proceedings.

In other words, Article V(1)(e) allows a disappointed party to forum-shop and delay by triggering the application of the local law of the place of rendition. And, having the award set aside at the place of rendition can render the award unenforceable in all signatory jurisdictions. In effect, the provision can allow such a party to escape and undermine the very enforcement regime the Convention establishes.

The Second Circuit could have adopted another approach to the interpretation of Article V(1)(e) in these circumstances. The "emphatic federal policy'' on arbitration, especially as it applies to matters of international commercial arbitration, might have warranted extending the rule of nonconflicting overlap to international awards rendered domestically. For example, the application of restrictive domestic provisions could have the effect of thwarting treaty obligations. Even though the Convention itself provides for its subordination to domestic law in some matters, the court could have viewed the language of Article V(1)(e) and other similar provisions in the Convention as historical carry-overs—necessary to gain maximum State ratification at the time the Convention was opened for signature in 1958. Arguably, the role of domestic law within the Convention framework has been eclipsed by the process of ratification itself and re-evaluated by the decisional practice of national courts. In other words, uniformly favorable and consistent interpretation of the Convention by courts in signatory States—expressed in part by the emergence of the UNCITRAL Model Law and Rules on arbitration and the enactment of national laws favoring arbitration—have created international norms on arbitration that render the reference to national law irrelevant and unnecessary.

In effect, the Second Circuit could have adopted a less technical approach to the interpretation of Article V(1)(e), emphasizing the Convention's underlying policy and basic enforcement objectives. An opinion containing such reasoning could have readily been integrated into the federal decisional law on arbitration—more specifically, the decisional law on the Convention: The opinion in *Chromalloy* prepared the way for such a ruling. According to the court in *Chromalloy*, Article VII of the Convention allows a national court to apply the provisions of domestic law when the latter promote the enforcement of an award where the Convention might not do so because of Article V(1)(e). In *Toys "R" Us*, the Second Circuit interpreted the Convention without regard to the practical consequences on enforcement—seemingly, almost exclusively for the sake of doctrinal refinement.

Also, having the nonstatutory grounds supplement the provisions of the Convention for the enforcement of domestically-rendered international awards generates at least a theoretical conflict between the domestic law and the norms and objectives of the Convention. The nonstatutory grounds provide for a form of judicial review of the merits of arbitral awards—a defense to enforcement that exceeds supervision for violations of domestic public policy and for constraints of subject matter inarbitrability. It is a form of national judicial intervention that the Convention precludes in its stated grounds for review and that most threatens the autonomy of international arbitration. Arguably, even the English statutory position on the judicial supervision of the merits of awards in a non-Convention setting is more restrictive of national court authority than the standard adopted by the Second Circuit. It also is justified by a more reasoned appraisal of its need and role.

Finally, the court applies the nonstatutory grounds to the facts of the case and "swiftly" concludes that none of the arguments advanced on that basis by Toys "R" Us even remotely warrants the vacatur of the award. As is characteristic of domestic litigation, the court invokes the policy of deferential judicial review and finds that the arbitrator's determinations are well within the bounds of the required legality and rationality. For example, the court states at one point that the "[i]nterpretation of these contract terms is within the province of the arbitrator and will not be overruled simply because we disagree with that interpretation." The complex doctrinal reasoning applying to Article V(1)(e) appears to have been elaborated to reach the conclusion that the application of domestic rules of enforcement would be inconsequential. It may be invigorating for courts to discuss standard of review questions in both the domestic and international setting, but the point of the exercise in *Toys "R" Us*, unlike *Chromalloy*, remains elusive.

In the final analysis, the Second Circuit may have missed an opportunity to provide doctrinal leadership on the question of domestic law and the setting aside procedure referred to in Article V of the Convention. If the court had held that domestic enforcement norms are inapposite under the Convention regardless of the award's place of rendition, it could have reinforced the autonomy of the international arbitral process and perhaps made the setting aside procedure less likely of success in other signatory jurisdictions. In so doing, the court could have further suggested that Article V(1)(e) only allows fundamental domestic juridical norms to be invoked. In any event, by integrating domestic provisions into the Convention regime, the Second Circuit dilutes and confuses the governing international standard, creates additional potential problems for enforcement, and makes a cohesive interpretation of the federal decisional law on the Convention more difficult. Despite the latitude it took with regard to the Convention and its technical language, *Chromalloy* appeared at least to articulate a coherent and comprehensible policy on the enforcement question.

Notes and Questions

Do you agree with the various evaluations of the case law that are advanced? Is there exaggeration and misassessment? The New York Arbitration Convention appears to be a patchwork of outmoded text and decisional additions that demand a complete overhaul of the treaty. How would you rewrite the Convention in light of the passage of time and these emerging difficulties?

§ 3. THE ROLE OF COURTS IN ICA: THE ASSERTION OF EXORBITANT JUDICIAL JURISDICTION

A recent case attests to the continuing vitality of the forces of liberalism and creativity in the French law of arbitration. In *NIOC v. Israel*, Decision of March 29, 2001, Cr. d'Appel, Paris, [2002] REV. ARB. 427, the Paris Court of Appeal ruled that, under French law, a national court (French or otherwise) could assist an international arbitration, provided there was some minimal connection between the arbitration and the national jurisdiction. In effect, the court held that, under French law, national courts owed a fiduciary obligation to all international arbitrations to render necessary assistance in the conduct of the proceeding to avoid a denial of justice.

In *NIOC v. Israel*, the requested assistance was the designation of an arbitrator. The Iranian party filed an action before a French court, requesting the court to appoint an arbitrator for Israel. Israel had failed to name its arbitrator in an arbitration involving a dispute between it and the National Iranian Oil Company over a gas pipeline project that the parties had entered into in 1968. Subsequently, Israeli courts had declared Iran to be an enemy of the State of Israel, making it legally impossible for Israel to participate in the anticipated arbitration to resolve the dispute. The connection to France was a reference in the 1968 contract to the ICC, which is headquartered in Paris. The parties had agreed that, in the event they could not name arbitrators, the ICC was authorized to do so in their place. The court deemed this connection sufficient to authorize the application of the French law and French court jurisdiction.

Notes and Questions

1. It is difficult to assess the basic character of the French court's extraordinary ruling. It could be seen as the judicial expression of a political policy that favors Arab interests over Israeli interests. It could also be seen as creative decisional law done to further the development of ICA. Which construction appeals to or convinces you? Why?

2. Is the ruling a good illustration of "anational" arbitration? How?

3. Can the ruling ever be enforced? Is it, therefore, purely symbolic?

4. Could other national courts use this case to contend that they have "universal suppletive judicial jurisdiction" in matters of ICA? What does that phrase mean?

5. Should your arbitration agreement take this case into account? Could a French or other national court "visit" you on the basis of extravagant extraterritorialism?

6. The French ruling parallels Section Two of the 1996 UK Arbitration Act, under which English courts have extraterritorial jurisdiction to assist arbitral proceedings that are localized elsewhere or which have yet to be localized. Such authority, however, may not be exercised if the intervention of an English court would be deemed (by the requested court) to be "inappropriate." Moreover, in U.S. law, under the Federal Arbitration Act § 206, a U.S. district court can "direct that arbitration be held in accordance with the agreement at any place therein provided for, whether that place is within or without the United States."

7. Do the legal references in the foregoing note change your evaluation of the French judicial ruling? Why? Do they increase your apprehension? Why? How would you characterize the role of judicial extraterritorialism in aid of arbitration in ICA? What is the objective and the purpose?

§ 4. THE ENGLISH STATUTORY LAW ON ARBITRATION

The UK Arbitration Act 1996 represents a modern formulation of national law on arbitration. It merits serious attention because of its substantive innovations as well as for its codification of various transborder consensus positions on arbitration. In fact, the Arbitration Act 1996 is a remarkable arbitration statute. It is, in many respects, a better model law than the UNCITRAL framework. The legislation represents a comprehensive and well-articulated statement of modern arbitration rules and principles. Compared to its predecessors, the statute is also eminently readable and accessible because of the clarity of its language. The 1996 Act contains 110 provisions that address in a logical progression the regulatory and practical problems that can arise during the various stages of the arbitral process. It codifies the contemporary principles and practices and is informed by a keen sense of the realities of arbitral practice.

The statutory provisions read as a hybrid of standard legislative enactments and institutional rules on arbitration. The fundamental precepts of the "world law" on arbitration (party autonomy, the contractual validity of arbitration agreements, judicial assistance and cooperation, limited scrutiny of awards, the requirement of basic procedural fairness, and the need for finality and arbitral autonomy) are present throughout the statutory provisions. These principles are not new to English arbitration law, but the clarity of the codification and the cohesion of expression in the 1996 Act give them a renewed vitality.

The legislation contains its own far-reaching concepts. In some respects, it is also a "tough" arbitration statute. It intends to foster compliance with the agreement to arbitrate and privileges the functionality of the arbitral process. The statute retains the procedure for "appeal to the court on a question of law arising out of an award," but recourse to that procedure is subject to a number of restrictions. The possibility of having arbitral awards subject to judicial supervision on the merits remains the most perplexing aspect of English arbitration law. Its practical consequences, however, are likely to be exceedingly limited and, given the deregulatory movement in regard to arbitration, may provide an example in the future of how potential excesses can be curbed.

Relatedly, the statute is less limpid about the place and standing of international commercial arbitration within its regulatory scheme. It still employs a nationality-based definition of international or non-domestic arbitration and allows "exclusion agreements" as long as the New York Arbitration Convention or other treaties do not govern enforcement. The treatment of international arbitration is less unified and suffers from the complication of internal and external cross-references. These attributes confuse rather than clarify. Given the significance of London as an international center for maritime, insurance, and other forms of transborder commercial arbitration, a more transparent set of regulatory provisions should have been articulated.

The goal underlying the enactment was to modernize the English law of arbitration by codifying recent English case rulings that favored arbitration and to make the principles of party autonomy in arbitration and the practice of judicial assistance of and support for the arbitral process key features of the law. There were also concerns that the law should be readily accessible and comprehensible. Giving the statutory law these characteristics would maintain England's, especially London's, competitive advantage in the arbitration service industry. Accordingly, the 1996 legislation "gives maximum scope for the parties to an arbitration to decide for themselves how the arbitration should be handled. The provisions of the [legislation] come into play to support the arbitration only when the parties have not decided what should happen.... [T]he decision of the parties to choose a private tribunal ... must be respected. The powers of the arbitrators have therefore been strengthened and the role of the courts is limited to those occasions when it is obvious that either the arbitral process needs assistance or that there has been or is likely to be a clear denial of justice."

The materials that follow reproduce significant provisions in the statute. You should assess each provision and provide an accounting of its content and role in the regulation of arbitration. Why is the provision good or bad? What impact does it have upon your understanding of arbitration? How might it affect your representation of clients?

The 1996 UK Arbitration Act

Introductory

1. General Principles

The provisions of this Part are founded on the following principles and shall be construed accordingly—

(a) the object of arbitration is to obtain the fair resolution of disputes by an impartial tribunal without unnecessary delay or expense;

(b) the parties should be free to agree how their disputes are resolved, subject only to such safeguards as are necessary in the public interest;

(c) in matters governed by this Part the court should not intervene except as provided by this Part.

2. Scope of application of provisions

(1) The provisions of this Part apply where the seat of the arbitration is in England and Wales or Northern Ireland.

(2) The following sections apply even if the seat of the arbitration is outside England and Wales or Northern Ireland or no seat has been designated or determined—

(a) sections 9 to II (stay of legal proceedings, & c), and

(b) section 66 (enforcement of arbitral awards).

(3) The powers conferred by the following sections apply even if the seat of the arbitration is outside England and Wales or Northern Ireland or no seat has been designated or determined—

(a) section 43 (securing the attendance of witnesses), and

(b) section 44 (court powers exercisable in support of arbitral proceedings);

but the court may refuse to exercise any such power if, in the opinion of the court, the fact that the seat of the arbitration is outside England and Wales or Northern Ireland, or that when designated or determined the seat is likely to be outside England and Wales or Northern Ireland, makes it inappropriate to do so.

(4) The court may exercise a power conferred by any provision of this Part not mentioned in subsection (2) or (3) for the purpose of supporting the arbitral process where—

(a) no seat of the arbitration has been designated or determined, and

(b) by reason of a connection with England and Wales or Northern Ireland the court is satisfied that it is appropriate to do so.

(5) Section 7 (separability of arbitration agreement) and section 8 (death of a party) apply where the law applicable to the arbitration agreement is the law of England and Wales or Northern Ireland even if the seat of the arbitration is outside England and Wales or Northern Ireland or has not been designated or determined.

[. . .]

7. Separability of arbitration agreement

Unless otherwise agreed by the parties, an arbitration agreement which forms or was intended to form part of another agreement (whether or not in writing) shall not be regarded as invalid, non-existent or ineffective because that other agreement is invalid, or did not come into existence or has become ineffective, and it shall for that purpose be treated as a distinct agreement.

[. . .]

29. Immunity of arbitrator

(1) An arbitrator is not liable for anything done or omitted in the discharge or purported discharge of his functions as arbitrator unless the act or omission is shown to have been in bad faith.

(2) Subsection (1) applies to an employee or agent of an arbitrator as it applies to the arbitrator himself.

(3) This section does not affect any liability incurred by an arbitrator by reason of his resigning (but see section 25).

Jurisdiction of the arbitral tribunal

30. Competence of tribunal to rule on its own jurisdiction

(1) Unless otherwise agreed by the parties, the arbitral tribunal may rule on its own substantive jurisdiction, that is, as to—

(a) whether there is a valid arbitration agreement,

(b) whether the tribunal is properly constituted, and

(c) what matters have been submitted to arbitration in accordance with the arbitration agreement.

(2) Any such ruling may be challenged by any available arbitral process of appeal or review or in accordance with the provisions of this Part.

31. Objection to substantive jurisdiction of tribunal

(1) An objection that the arbitral tribunal lacks substantive jurisdiction at the outset of the proceedings must be raised by a party not later than the time he takes the first step in the proceedings to contest the merits of any matter in relation to which he challenges the tribunal's jurisdiction.

A party is not precluded from raising such an objection by the fact that he has appointed or participated in the appointment of an arbitrator.

(2) Any objection during the course of the arbitral proceedings that the arbitral tribunal is exceeding its substantive jurisdiction must be made as soon as possible after the matter alleged to be beyond its jurisdiction is raised.

(3) The arbitral tribunal may admit an objection later than the time specified in subsection (1) or (2) if it considers the delay justified.

(4) Where an objection is duly taken to the tribunal's substantive jurisdiction and the tribunal has power to rule on its own jurisdiction, it may—

(a) rule on the matter in an award as to jurisdiction, or

(b) deal with the objection in its award on the merits.

If the parties agree which of these courses the tribunal should take, the tribunal shall proceed accordingly.

(5) The tribunal may in any case, and shall if the parties so agree, stay proceedings whilst an application is made to the court under section 32 (determination of preliminary point of jurisdiction).

32. Determination of preliminary point of jurisdiction

(1) The court may, on the application of a party to arbitral proceedings (upon notice to the other parties), determine any question as to the substantive jurisdiction of the tribunal.

A party may lose the right to object (see section 73).

(2) An application under this section shall not be considered unless—

(a) it is made with the agreement in writing of all the other parties to the proceedings, or

(b) it is made with the permission of the tribunal and the court is satisfied—

(i) that the determination of the question is likely to produce substantial savings in costs,

(ii) that the application was made without delay, and

(iii) that there is good reason why the matter should be decided by the court.

(3) An application under this section, unless made with the agreement of all the other parties to the proceedings, shall state the grounds on which it is said that the matter should be decided by the court.

(4) Unless otherwise agreed by the parties, the arbitral tribunal may continue the arbitral proceedings and make an award while an application to the court under this section is pending.

(5) Unless the court gives leave, no appeal lies from a decision of the court whether the conditions specified in subsection (2) are met.

(6) The decision of the court on the question of jurisdiction shall be treated as a judgment of the court for the purposes of an appeal.

But no appeal lies without the leave of the court which shall not be given unless the court considers that the question involves a point of law which is one of general importance or is one which for some other special reason should be considered by the Court of Appeal.

The arbitral proceedings

33. General duty of the tribunal

(1) The Tribunal shall—

(a) act fairly and impartially as between the parties, giving each party a reasonable opportunity of putting his case and dealing with that of his opponent, and

(b) adopt procedures suitable to the circumstances of the particular case, avoiding unnecessary delay or expense, so as to provide a fair means for the resolution of the matters falling to be determined.

(2) The tribunal shall comply with that general duty in conducting the arbitral proceedings, in its decisions on matters of procedure and evidence and in the exercise of all other powers conferred on it.

[...]

45. Determination of preliminary point of law

(1) Unless otherwise agreed by the parties, the court may on the application of a party to arbitral proceedings (upon notice to the other parties) determine any question of law arising in the course of the proceedings which the court is satisfied substantially affects the rights of one or more of the parties.

An agreement to dispense with reasons for the tribunal's award shall be considered an agreement to exclude the court's jurisdiction under this section.

(2) An application under this section shall not be considered unless—

(a) it is made with the agreement of all the other parties to the proceedings, or

(b) it is made with the permission of the tribunal and the court is satisfied—

(i) that the determination of the question is likely to produce substantial savings in costs, and

(ii) that the application was made without delay.

(3) The application shall identify the question of law to be determined and, unless made with the agreement of all the other parties to the proceedings, shall state the grounds on which it is said that the question should be decided by the court.

(4) Unless otherwise agreed by the parties, the arbitral tribunal may continue the arbitral proceedings and make an award while an application to the court under this section is pending.

(5) Unless the court gives leave, no appeal lies from a decision of the court whether the conditions specified in subsection (2) are met.

(6) The decision of the court on the question of law shall be treated as a judgment of the court for the purposes of an appeal.

But no appeal lies without the leave of the court which shall not be given unless the court considers that the question is one of general importance, or is one which for some other special reason should be considered by the Court of Appeal.

The award

46. Rules applicable to substance of dispute

(1) The arbitral tribunal shall decide the dispute—

(a) in accordance with the law chosen by the parties as applicable to the substance of the dispute, or

(b) if the parties so agree, in accordance with such other considerations as are agreed by them or determined by the tribunal.

(2) For this purpose the choice of the laws of a country shall be understood to refer to the substantive laws of that country and not its conflict of law rules.

(3) If or to the extent that there is no such choice or agreement, the tribunal shall apply the law determined by the conflict of laws rules which it considers applicable.

§ 5. INSTITUTIONAL ARBITRATION: THE EXAMPLE OF CIETAC

Arbitration in China is governed by the 1995 Arbitration Law and the 1991 Civil Procedure Law. The Arbitration Law of China was created to ensure fair and timely arbitration of disputes relating to economic matters. China maintains a bifurcated approach to foreign-related and domestic arbitration cases, applying distinct sets of rules and procedures for conducting arbitration proceedings and enforcing awards under each category. China's courts commonly consider a case foreign-related only in circumstances in which at least one party to the dispute is registered in a foreign jurisdiction or is a foreign national; the subject matter of the transaction is foreign; or the legal relationship was made, amended, or terminated outside China. Cases involving only Chinese-registered parties and transactions located in China are considered domestic. When hearing an action for the enforcement of a domestic arbitral award, the People's Court can review both the arbitral procedure and the substance of the award. The Law of Civil Procedure provides that the award shall be denied enforcement if the People's Court determines that the main evidence was insufficient to support the allegations made on the record. In effect, this basis for review allows the People's Court to conduct a *de novo* review of the arbitral proceeding and the award, and can lead to conflicting determinations.

Foreign-related arbitration is limited to economic, trade, transportation, and maritime disputes. The State Council issued a notice in 1996 expressly authorizing domestic arbitration commissions to administer foreign-related cases. No foreign-related case may be arbitrated without a valid arbitration agreement. If a party challenges the validity of the arbitration agreement, both the People's Court and the Arbitration Commission have jurisdiction to rule on the validity of the agreement. If both the People's Court and the Arbitration Commission are asked to rule, the ruling by the People's Court will be given effect. This applies only to arbitrations taking place in China. If the arbitration is before a Foreign Arbitration Commission, and both that commission and the People's Court are requested to rule on the validity of the arbitration agreement, the ruling by the People's Court will be given effect only if Chinese law governs the arbitration.

Article 259 of the Civil Procedure Law empowers the Intermediate People's Court located within the jurisdiction of the defendant's residence or where the property associated with the contract is located to hear petitions for the enforcement of arbitral awards issued by a "foreign affairs arbitration organization" of China. In general, enforcement of foreign-related and foreign arbitral awards depends upon a determination that no procedural irregularities occurred in the arbitral process. In contrast to the practice in domestic arbitration, the rules do not provide for a merits review of awards. In cases in which the Intermediate People's Court refuses to enforce an award, it must submit a report to the Supreme Court of China before it issues its determination. This procedure is intended to reduce the possibility that Chinese courts will favor and protect the interests of nationals.

In China, international arbitrations or arbitrations with a foreign element are administered almost exclusively by two arbitral institutions. The China Maritime Arbitration Commission (CMAC) administers the

arbitration of maritime disputes. The China International Economic Trade and Arbitration Commission (CIETAC) administers the arbitration of disputes that arise from foreign-related economic and trade activity. In the 1980s, foreign firms lacked confidence in Chinese arbitral proceedings and in their ability to enforce arbitral awards in China. That attitude has now been substantially modified. CIETAC has become one of the world's busiest arbitral institutions, and both CIETAC and CMAC enjoy reputations as fair venues for arbitration.

CIETAC is headquartered in Beijing and maintains two sub-commissions—one in Shenzhen, and the other in Shanghai. The three entities function as a single arbitral organization, using the same arbitration rules and maintaining the same lists of arbitrators. In recent years, CIETAC has had a huge volume of business, administering in excess of 700 arbitrations annually. In fact, in 1998, the number of CIETAC arbitrations was greater than the number of ICC arbitrations. In May 1998, CIETAC was authorized to modify its rules and to extend its jurisdiction to disputes involving foreign-invested enterprises (PIEs). Previously, PlEs were obligated to go before domestic arbitration commissions—a less attractive remedy for foreign investors.

According to Article 2 of its Arbitration Rules, CIETAC has jurisdiction over: (1) international or foreign-related disputes; (2) disputes pertaining to the Hong Kong SAR, Macao, or Taiwan regions; (3) disputes between enterprises which engage in foreign investment or disputes between an enterprise which engages in foreign investment and another Chinese entity (physical or legal person or economic organization); (4) disputes arising from project financing, invitations for tender, bidding, construction, and other activities conducted by Chinese entities (physical or legal person or economic organization) for utilizing capital, technology, or services from foreign countries, international organizations, or from the Hong Kong SAR, Macao, and Taiwan regions; and (5) disputes that may be taken cognizance of by the Arbitration Commission pursuant to special provisions of or special authorization by the law or administrative regulations of the People's Republic of China. Under Article 7, the CIETAC Arbitration rules will apply if the parties agree to submit their dispute to CIETAC. Other arbitration rules can apply if the parties so agree, provided the Arbitration Commission acquiesces in their choice.

Under Chinese law, an arbitration agreement must be entered into by parties able to contract; the agreement must be in writing and must contain language that codifies the parties' intent to arbitrate disputes. The agreement must also designate the administering Arbitration Commission and describe the matters the parties have agreed to submit to arbitration. The subject matter of submitted disputes must be legally capable of resolution by arbitration. CIETAC recommends the following model clause for incorporation into foreign business contracts: "Any dispute arising from or in connection with this contract shall be submitted to the China International Economic and Trade Arbitration Commission for arbitration which shall be conducted in accordance with the

Commission's arbitration rules in effect at the time the demand for arbitration is made. The award shall be final and binding upon both [or all contracting] parties."

The demand for arbitration is submitted to the CIETAC Secretariat. It should contain a copy of the relevant arbitration agreement, a written request for arbitration, the names and addresses of the parties, a statement of the facts and evidence upon which the claim is based, and payment in advance of the fee for arbitration. The demand and any counterclaims must be signed by the party or its representative. The fee—which is payable by the claimant upon filing for arbitration and by the respondent when making a counterclaim—is based upon the Commission's Arbitration Fee Schedule. That fee schedule is based on a percentage of the amount in controversy.

For claims of one million yuan or less, the amount of the fee is 4% of the amount claimed (the minimum fee being 20,000 yuan). (The exchange rate between the Chinese yuan and the U.S. dollar is approximately 8.3 yuan to the dollar. Here, 20,000 yuan is about $2420[U.S.]). For claims between one and five million yuan, 40,000 yuan plus 3% of the amount over one million yuan. For claims in the range of five to ten million yuan, 160,000 yuan plus 2% of the amount over five million yuan. For claims between ten to fifty million yuan, 260,000 yuan plus 1% of the amount over ten million yuan. For claims exceeding fifty million yuan, 660,000 yuan plus 0.5% of the amount over fifty million yuan. When the amount in dispute cannot be determined at the time of the demand or other special circumstances exist, the Secretariat of the Commission or of the two Sub–Commissions shall determine the amount of the arbitration fee. The arbitral tribunal can reallocate the arbitration fee among the parties when it renders the award. It can also order the losing party to pay part of the winning party's other costs incurred in connection with the arbitration. That amount cannot exceed 10% of the total amount awarded to the winning party. In addition, there is also a registration fee due at the time of the demand. This fee is set at 10,000 yuan (or $1200 [U.S.]) and covers processing costs associated with the application and the adjudication.

The parties must choose arbitrators from the Commission's Panel of Arbitrators. CIETAC has more than 400 arbitrators on its lists; they come from more than twenty-five different countries. The arbitrators consist of Chinese and foreign nationals who are selected for their expert knowledge and practical experience in various relevant fields (*e.g.*, science, technology, trade, economics, and law). CIETAC arbitration can either be done through a single arbitrator procedure or a tribunal of three arbitrators. Single-arbitrator proceedings usually involve less than 500,000 yuan ($60,000 [U.S.]) and are conducted according to a summary procedure. Larger cases are heard by a panel of three members according to a regular procedure.

A number of time limits apply to the submission of briefs, documents, evidence, and counterclaims. An arbitration can be conducted solely on the basis of submitted documents. Usually, the arbitral tribunal, however, will hold oral hearings. The applicable procedure reflects what the parties have agreed in their contract or (failing such provision) what the arbitral tribunal decides. The tribunal's basic responsibility is to conduct flexible and fair hearings that allow for the timely resolution of disputes. Hearings are held where the action is filed—either Beijing, Shenzhen, or Shanghai. Proceedings can be conducted elsewhere (in or outside China) with the permission of the Secretary–General of the Commission.

The parties are responsible for establishing their claims with sufficient evidence. Seven forms of evidence are admissible: physical evidence, documentary evidence, statements by the parties and witnesses, photographs, video or audio tapes, expert reports, and on-site inspection reports. The arbitral tribunal can investigate and gather evidence on its own initiative. The tribunal can appoint experts and conduct on-site inspections, if it deems such measures to be necessary.

The tribunal must render an award within nine months from the date of its constitution. When the arbitration is conducted on the basis of a summary procedure, the tribunal must render an award either within thirty days of the oral hearing or (if there is no oral hearing) within ninety days from the date of its constitution. In special circumstances, these time limits can be extended by the Secretary–General of the Commission at the request of the tribunal. Awards are rendered by a majority. When a majority cannot be established, the opinion of the presiding arbitrator becomes the award. The tribunal must provide reasons with the award, unless it is an award on agreed terms or the parties agree that reasons need not be given. The tribunal can render interim awards.

According to Article 260 of China's Civil Procedure Law, a court (usually an Intermediate People's Court) can refuse enforcement to a foreign-related arbitral award on the following grounds: (1) there is no agreement to arbitrate; (2) the party against whom enforcement is sought was not notified of the arbitral proceeding or was otherwise unable to present his case for reasons beyond his/her control; (3) the constitution of the arbitral tribunal or the conduct of the arbitral proceeding was not in conformity with the rules of arbitration; or (4) the rulings in the award exceed the scope of the arbitration agreement or are beyond the authority of the arbitral institution. An award can also be set aside if the court determines that it violates the public interest. The time limit for setting aside an award is six months from the date the award is delivered to the parties. Studies indicate that Chinese courts are likely to enforce CIETAC arbitral awards. The legal grounds for refusing to enforce awards, including the public interest defense, are rarely invoked successfully. The vast majority of awards that are denied enforcement are deemed to be unenforceable because there are no assets against which to enforce the award.

In 1998, revisions to the CIETAC rules made it clear that the principle of party autonomy was central to the Commission's regulatory framework. If the parties agreed upon different arbitral rules and those rules were approved by CIETAC, they could be substituted for CIETAC's rules in a CIETAC-administered arbitration.

Finally, in foreign-related arbitration in China, arbitration can be combined with and supplemented by conciliation (or mediation). This is a rather unique and fundamental part of Chinese arbitration law and practice. When the arbitrating parties agree to attempt a conciliation of their dispute, the CIETAC rules allow the arbitral tribunal to conciliate the matter. If the tribunal is successful, it can render an award on agreed terms. If the attempt at conciliation fails, the arbitration resumes. The conciliation terminates when one of the parties so requests or the tribunal believes that further efforts in that regard will be unavailing. Statements or proposals made in conciliation cannot be used in a subsequent arbitral or judicial proceeding. About 30% of the international cases accepted by CIETAC are resolved through conciliation/mediation.

[Research provided by Guangyu Cai, Guiqin Fan, Siyang Liao, LL.M.s (Tulane University).]

Notes and Questions

1. Recently, CIETAC Arbitration has been criticized and declined because of allegations of corruption among arbitrators. Despite the efforts to legitimate CIETAC Arbitration, the volume of cases plummeted when this development manifested itself.

2. It is difficult to avoid CIETAC Arbitration if your client is doing business in China. Does the foregoing description inspire confidence in the process and the likelihood of enforcement? How would you describe the Chinese options for dispute resolution to your client?

3. What alternatives might exist to CIETAC Arbitration? How would you respond to the question in your agreement?

4. Are sovereignty, bureaucracy, and politics the real problems here?

§ 6. INVESTMENT ARBITRATION

STAFF & LEWIS, *ARBITRATION UNDER NAFTA CHAPTER 11: PAST, PRESENT, AND FUTURE,*

25 Houston J. Int'l L. 301, 308–326 (2003).

(Reprinted with permission).

(footnotes omitted)

[. . .]

4. Investor–State Disputes Under Chapter 11—A Controversial Past

Chapter 11 permits foreign investors to invoke binding international arbitration against [a] signatory state that violates the investment provisions of NAFTA. Although other countries have attempted to secure similar protections under the Organisation for Economic Co-operation and Development (OECD), currently NAFTA is the only international agreement that provides these protections. Section A of Chapter 11 (section A), designed to deter "illegal takings of U.S. and Canadian businesses by the Mexican government," protects the rights of foreign investors from government action by signatory states. Specifically, foreign investors are protected from signatory states' measures. Section A affords four basic protections to foreign investors: parity with investors in the signatory state; freedom from performance requirements; free investment-related funds transfers; and expropriation only in accordance with the international law.

Section B of Chapter 11 (section B) establishes a procedure for binding international arbitration between a signatory state and a foreign investor. The adoption of section B "represents the first time Mexico has entered into an international agreement providing for investor-state arbitration."

> Under other multilateral trade regimes, including GATT, companies that suffer damages due to the actions of a foreign government have no right of private action against the host state; their only remedy is to persuade their home state to pursue a trade complaint on their behalf. Where this remedy is unavailable or inadequate (which is almost invariably the case), the investor's only option is to pursue its complaint under the sometimes inhospitable judicial system of the host country.

Section B allows foreign investors to use international arbitration to resolve a dispute when a foreign investor alleges that foreign investors' investment has been damaged by a signatory state's violation of section A. The foreign investor has three years from when the foreign investor acquires knowledge of the alleged section A violation to notify the signatory state of the foreign investor's intent to submit a claim. Before filing a claim, the foreign investor and signatory state (the disputing parties) are required to attempt settlement. If the disputing parties fail to settle, and the foreign investor wants to pursue arbitration, the foreign investor must notify the signatory state within ninety days of submitting the claim. After following these procedures, the foreign investor may submit the claim to arbitration no earlier than six months after the alleged violation. Arbitration fora available to the foreign investor are:

> (a) the ICSID Convention..., provided that both the disputing Party and the Party of the investor are parties to the Convention;
>
> (b) the Additional Facility Rules of ICSID, provided that either the disputing Party or the Party of the investor, but not both, is a party to the ICSID Convention; or
>
> (c) the UNCITRAL...Arbitration Rules.

The United States is the only signatory state that is a party to the ICSID Convention; therefore, Chapter 11 disputes by foreign investors cannot be heard under this convention. However, claims brought by American investors or claims against the United States may be brought under the ICSID Additional Facility Rules or UNCITRAL. The Additional Facility Rules are only available for investment disputes between signatory states and foreign investors. Specifically, the Additional Facility Rules apply in the following situations:

(i) conciliation or arbitration proceedings for the settlement of investment disputes arising between parties one of which is not a Contracting State or a national of a Contracting state;

(ii) conciliation or arbitration proceedings between parties at least one of [whom] is a Contracting State or a national of a contracting State for the settlement of disputes that do not directly arise out of an investment; and

(iii) fact-finding proceedings.

While there are other international arbitration fora, the available rules for arbitration under Chapter 11 are limited to the three enumerated in the chapter. . . .

Remedies available under Chapter 11 arbitrations include: monetary damages and applicable interest, however, no punitive damages are allowed; restitution of property; and costs in accordance with the selected arbitration rules. According to published arbitration awards, arbitrators have used discretion assessing costs. The *Waste Management* tribunal decided not to award costs because it did not find evidence of bad faith or recklessness. [*Waste Mgmt., Inc. v. United Mexican States*, Case No. ARB (AF)/98/2 (ICSID AF June 2, 2000)]. The *Azinian* tribunal cited their reasons for declining to award costs as: the novelty of the dispute resolution mechanism, the efficiency of the Claimant's presentation, the Respondent's incorrect objection to lack of notice invited litigation, and the tribunal['s] lack of power to punish the bad actors. [*Azinian v. United Mexican States*, Case No. ARB (AF)/97/2 (ICSID AF No. 1, 1999)].

The final arbitration is only binding on the parties to the arbitration. However, each signatory state is required to provide for the enforcement "of an award in its territory." After the award is rendered and a time period has elapsed, "a disputing party shall abide by and comply with an award without delay."

A foreign investor may seek enforcement of a Chapter 11 award under the Convention on the Settlement of Investment Disputes Between States and Nationals of Other States, the United Nations Convention on the Recognition and Enforcement of Foreign Arbitral Awards (New York Convention), or the Inter–American Convention on International Commercial Arbitration (Inter–American Convention). NAFTA specifically provides that a Chapter 11 claim is "considered to arise out of a commercial relationship or transaction for purposes of Article I of the New York Convention and Article I of the Inter–American Convention."

If a signatory state fails to abide by a Chapter 11 award, the foreign investor's signatory state may request that a Chapter 20 arbitral panel review the signatory state's failure. This review determines whether the signatory state's failure is inconsistent with its obligations under NAFTA and the arbitral panel may recommend that the signatory state comply with the Chapter 11 award. Thus, failure to comply with a final Chapter 11 arbitration award may result in [the] suspension of NAFTA benefits to the non-complying signatory state. Because Chapter 20 applies only between signatory states, the foreign investor's signatory state must take action to compel performance of the arbitration award. Furthermore,

> Chapter 20 panels have no power to actually overturn United States law. Rather, the panels issue reports that allow the United States to decide what course of action to take in the event a given law is found to violate NAFTA.... Failure to alter a law to conform to NAFTA gives the injured nation the right to unilaterally impose trade sanctions on the United States.... Of course, in the absence of this arrangement, the governments of Canada and Mexico would be free to set tariff levels at whatever point they see fit.

Chapter 11 awards may be published under the following circumstances:

> Where Canada is the disputing Party, either Canada or a disputing investor that is a party to the arbitration may make an award public. Where Mexico is the disputing Party, the applicable arbitration rules apply to the publication of an award. Where the United States is the disputing Party, either the United States or a disputing investor that is a party to the arbitration may make an award public.

However, there is no mechanism to force publication or compilation of awards. This discretionary publication of arbitration awards has prompted criticism and debate. Such criticism prompted the Free Trade Commission to adopt the Notes of Interpretation, clarifying, among other things, the Commission's position on publishing awards.

III. Chapter 11 Cases: Past and Present

Despite the debate over the Chapter 11 cases, a review of published cases does not provide support to Chapter 11 champions or critics, due to the paucity of published cases. The arbitration fora allowed by NAFTA provide for confidentiality, because they were designed for private commercial dispute resolution. Although the United Nations maintains a system for the compilation of UNCITRAL decisions and awards, it is difficult to collect the decisions and awards[:]

> The accessibility of arbitral awards varies considerably and is, as a rule, rather limited. Often, their availability is restricted by requirements of confidentiality. Their accessibility may also be restricted by

the general usage of an arbitral institution. . . .Thus, arbitral awards are included in the collection only in so far as they come to the attention of national correspondents and in the form in which they are made available to them.

However, electronic media sources help to disseminate Chapter 11 decisions. Presently, twenty-eight Chapter 11 actions have been publicly noticed. . . .

Cases under Chapter 11 are unique. The publicly available cases range from a challenge to a multimillion-dollar punitive damage judgment in Mississippi against a foreign investor to a claim that certain Mexican criminal prosecutions violate Chapter 11.

While arbitration is touted as bringing predictability to international disputes, the public history of Chapter 11 refutes this claim. A great deal is known about several of the cases, while little or nothing is known about many of them. In some cases, claimants fail to file Notices of Arbitration after filing Notices of Intent. In at least two cases, the Notice of Intent was withdrawn. Three cases filed against Mexico had three different results. *Metalclad* was decided in favor of the foreign investor. [*Metalclad Corp. v. United Mexican States*, ICSID Case No. ARB (AF)/97/1 (ICSID AF Sept. 2, 2000)]. *Waste Management* was dismissed on jurisdictional grounds. *Azinian* was decided in favor of Mexico. Two final tribunal awards were submitted for review to Canadian courts.

Of the twenty-eight cases, fifteen (fifty-four percent) were initiated after the year 2000. Of the fifteen, two have been withdrawn, one has resulted in a final award, and the remaining twelve appear to be in the early procedural stages.

[. . .]

Critics in the United States and Canada complain the loudest that Chapter 11 threatens sovereignty, arguing that Chapter 11 actions threaten present signatory state regulations and chill future signatory state regulatory initiatives. . . . U.S. and Canadian investors have brought the majority of Chapter 11 cases. Five cases brought under Chapter 11 exemplify this perceived threat to sovereignty.

A. *Ethyl Corp. v. Canada*

Ethyl Corporation (Ethyl), a U.S. corporation that produces methylcyclopentadienyl manganese tricarbonyl (MMT), filed a notice of intent to submit a Chapter 11 claim against Canada. [*Ethyl Corp. v. Canada* (UNCITRAL Sept. 10, 1996) (notice of intent).] Ethyl claimed that a proposed Canadian ban on the import and interprovincial trade of MMT amounted to an expropriation that merited compensation under Chapter 11. The case settled after the tribunal dismissed Canada's request to deny the claim on procedural grounds. The *Ethyl* settlement required Canada to pay Ethyl thirteen million U.S. dollars, to amend the proposed ban, and to state that there was a lack of scientific evidence to support the proposed ban. The *Ethyl* settlement has been characterized as "tak[ing] environmental regulations out of the hands of governments and giv[ing] ultimate control to NAFTA investors." However, one commentator noted that the issue was not the validity of the environmental regulation but its discriminatory application. Yet another commentator concluded that "the Ethyl claim may stand for the inability of Parties to enact environmental regulations indirectly, through trade restrictions, though perhaps the environmental regulations would be defensible if enacted directly." Finally, another commentator stated:

> In essence, Ethyl was able to intimidate Canadian lawmakers into rescinding a valid environmental regulation, which resulted in the Canadian taxpayer "paying off the polluter" for importing a dangerous chemical. The use of Chapter 11 to lobby against valid environmental legislation in this case set a major precedent for the cases to follow.

B. Metalclad Corp. v. United Mexican States

In *Metalclad*, the U.S. investor contended that the state government of San Luis Potosi (SLP) unlawfully refused Metalclad permission to reopen a waste disposal facility. Metalclad had purchased COTERIN, a Mexican corporation, which owned a development site for a waste disposal facility in SLP. Federal environmental officials issued a construction permit to Metalclad. However, municipal officials refused to issue a municipal construction permit. Metalclad proceeded to develop the waste disposal facility, based solely on Federal authority. Before Metalclad opened the waste disposal facility, the governor of SLP declared the area, including the waste disposal facility, a "Natural Area for the protection of rare cactus," barring the opening of the waste disposal facility.

Metalclad brought a Chapter 11 action against Mexico. The tribunal ordered Mexico to reimburse Metalclad for its investment in the waste disposal facility. The tribunal based its decision on the inconsistency in construction permit grants and the environmental decree. Because the denial was inconsistent with the NAFTA objective of "transparency," the tribunal found the denial of construction permits violated article 1105. With respect to the environmental decree, the tribunal found that Mexico's action was an expropriation that violated article 1110.

Mexico appealed to the Supreme Court of British Columbia. On appeal, Justice David Tysoe upheld the award. [(2001) 89 B.C. L.R. 3d 359.] Although Justice Tysoe found no violation of article 1105, he found the environmental decree to be an expropriation under article 1110, independent of the tribunal's considerations of transparency. Because of this ruling, Mexico settled the claim.

Chapter 11 critics cite *Metalclad* as an example of Chapter 11's interference with state sovereignty, particularly with respect to environmental regulation. However, one critic notes that *Metalclad* may merely question which level of government has the ability to impose environmental regulations.

C. S.D. Myers v. Canada

In another illustrative case, S.D. Myers (SDM), a U.S. company, brought a Chapter 11 action against Canada. [*S.D. Myers v. Canada* (UNCITRAL, July 21, 1998, Nov. 13, 2000, Oct. 21, 2002), (Notice of Intent) (first partial award) (second partial award)]. SDM challenged Canada's prohibition on polychlorinated biphenyls (PCB) export. Canada argued that SDM was not a foreign investor within the meaning of Chapter 11. The tribunal issued a final award in favor of SDM, finding that Canada had acted in a discriminatory manner and that Canada's action violated the minimum standard of treatment under international law with respect to SDM's foreign investment. The tribunal awarded SDM over six million Canadian dollars plus interest in damages. After considering several factors, the tribunal awarded SDM $350,000 (Canadian) for arbitration costs and $500,000 (Canadian), plus interest for legal representation and assistance costs.

Critics of Chapter 11 contend that *S.D. Myers* stands for the proposition that "corporate rights of foreign investors must be the chief policy concern of public officials crafting a domestic regulatory policy." Others suggest that the case was merely a discriminatory application of a regulation to a foreign investor in violation of Chapter 11.

Commentators also cite *S.D. Myers* as broadening the definition of investment in Chapter 11. This broadening creates new opportunities for challenges to signatory state regulations. Although some commentators consider *S.D. Myers* a threat to sovereignty, at least one commentator asserts that *S.D. Myers* may bolster sovereignty. There may now be a defense for signatory states to Chapter 11 claims based on the legitimacy of a signatory state's environmental interests in the challenged measure.

D. Methanex Corp. v. United States

Methanex, a Canadian corporation, brought a Chapter 11 claim against the United States seeking $970 million (U.S.) in damages. [*Methanex Corp. v. United States* (UNCITRAL July 2, 1999) (Notice of intent)]. Methanex's claims were prompted by a California decision to phase out the gasoline additive methyl tertiary-butyl ether (MTBE). Methanex was a supplier of methanol, an ingredient used in the production of MTBE. Methanex alleged that California's action breached articles 1105 and 1110. The tribunal dismissed Methanex's claims for lack of jurisdiction, but left the door open for Methanex to try again with a fresh pleading.

Methanex filed a fresh statement of claim alleging violations of articles 1102, 1105, and 1110. In the introduction to their fresh statement, Methanex notes that they [were] not trying to "expand international guarantees in a way that would threaten nations' or states' ability to enact or enforce valid and non[-]discriminatory environmental laws[,]" rather Methanex claim[ed] that "California's unlawful protectionism comports exactly with the investment guarantees Chapter 11 was meant to provide." . . .

E. Loewen Group, Inc. v. United States

The issue in *Loewen* [was] whether a Mississippi state court action expropriated the Loewen Group's (Loewen) assets in violation of NAFTA Chapter 11. [*Loewen Group, Inc. v. United States*, ICSID Case No. ARB (AF)/98/3 (ICSID AF July 29, 1998)]. In a state court suit, brought by Loewen's former business partner, the jury returned a verdict against Loewen for $260 million (U.S.) in actual damages and four hundred million U.S. dollars in punitive damages. [*Dockins v. Allred*, 755 So. 2d 389 (Miss. 1999)]. Mississippi state law requires an appeal bond of 125 percent of the judgment, which Loewen was unable to afford. Loewen settled the suit and then sued the United States government under NAFTA Chapter 11 for $725 million (U.S.). The tribunal entered an award on jurisdiction on January 5, 2001. . . .

Loewen has been the subject of great public outcry in the United States because it is a perceived assault on the U.S. legal system and the sanctity of jury decisions. A thorough analysis of *Loewen* suggests that the case should be reviewed dispassionately. An exceptionally thorough analysis of every step of *Loewen* while in the Mississippi courts caused Lucien J. Dhooge to conclude:

> The scant evidence presented during the punitive damages phase of the trial is further demonstrative of the lack of a rational basis for the jury's award. The enormous size of the award in relation to [the plaintiff's] actual injuries and economic loss, previous awards in the state and the financial condition of Loewen lead to the conclusion that it was an unconstitutional, albeit perhaps unintentional, attempt to redistribute wealth amongst the parties. . . .
>
> . . . .
>
> . . . Given the inconsistency of the punitive damages awarded in the *O'Keefe* litigation [the Mississippi case against Loewen] with applicable American, Canadian and international standards, it may be concluded that it constituted an uncompensated expropriation pursuant to Article 1110 of NAFTA. Although not a direct taking, the Mississippi judiciary's acquiescence in a biased process that resulted in an excessive verdict, denied Loewen meaningful substantive review of such verdict and ultimately compelled a financially devastating settlement is without doubt an indirect measure tantamount to expropriation. The biased nature of the proceedings as evidenced by the repeated emphasis upon nationality, race and wealth do not support the existence of a legitimate public purpose underlying this expropriation.

Another commentator points out: "If Loewen is successful in its claim against the United States, investors would be encouraged to try to circumvent domestic law by filing NAFTA claims challenging the state, local, and federal court systems, where U.S. citizens and businesses must abide by U.S. court rulings." Therefore, cases such as *Loewen* are seen by some as a threat to signatory state sovereignty, and damages awarded in Chapter 11 cases are unfairly shifted to the signatory state taxpayers.

[. . .]

Notes and Questions

1. The reading is an objective summary of the workings of NAFTA under Chapter 11. After the public murmurings and outcries, all of the controversial cases, especially *Methanex* and *Loewen*, were basically dismissed on jurisdictional grounds. NAFTA arbitrators had originally used an aggressive concept of expropriation under the NAFTA, but—in the end—backed away from championing the concept and commercial accountability for State domestic political conduct. Isn't the inescapable conclusion that NAFTA arbitrators are not independent of external influence and that the NAFTA process is not independent of political pressure? Should they be? Doesn't the "pull back" demonstrate that NAFTA not only lost its promise, but also its basic function and integrity?

2. Why is there a continued and persistent brief for transparency in the NAFTA process? The same criticism is made of WTO. Is confidentiality essential to the functioning of the NAFTA process? Would transparency detract from the arbitrators' independence? How useful or effective is transparency likely to be? Do you believe the would-be lack of access is deliberate and calculated? Who would benefit from such a policy?

3. The critique of NAFTA arbitration appears to be grounded in considerations of politics and the management of power. The detractors believe that a victory for corporate interests over collectivist regulatory designs is always bad and indicates that the system does not operate properly (as they believe it should). Moreover, governments should be entitled to enact whatever measures they believe are desirable and should not be held accountable for the commercial impact of these measures. "Green" is always better than civilization and certainly better than crass mercantilism. Is this ideological unilateralism sensible? Is the diatribe a proper foundation for action?

4. Shouldn't the NAFTA process be allowed to evolve and develop as a process on its own? Shouldn't a great deal of attention be devoted to selecting arbitrators, developing and publicizing the case law, and making NAFTA mechanisms a part of public education?

5. Wasn't the behavior of the California legislature and the Mississippi jury indefensible? Don't both measures at least subject foreign companies to highly particularized and surprising local practices? Were the arbitrators wrong initially to perceive the conduct as grossly unfair to commercial activity? Should the making of all legal rules conform to the New England town meeting model of decision-making? Don't expertise and experience provide better points of reference for economic, trade, and adjudicatory issues?

6. How would you cure the problems with NAFTA arbitration?

§ 7. THE CONTRACT OF ARBITRATION

This section and the next two address the process of establishing an international commercial arbitration. The principal stages of that process are: (1) the writing of the agreement; (2) the selection of an arbitrator; and (3) the procedural provision for a proceeding. The latter two stages arise out of or are at least prepared by the first. These are the practical aspects of arbitration. They, however, deserve and demand serious reflection and professional analysis. It may be more productive and enjoyable to act out the content of these stages to get a sense of how difficult it is to negotiate with parties who have a different self-interest and perception of reality (known in divorce circles as the marriage dynamic). A simulated negotiation on these matters, both within your firm and with the other side, should also convey an understanding of how truly difficult it is to memorialize agreement into language. Finally, if you do engage in a law firm production, you need to be mindful of the necessity of economy and focus. Each segment must be circumscribed and fit into and work with the totality. You also may have an audience acting as spectator. Preliminary "break out" groups could constitute the preparatory phase and eventually lead to an enactment of the negotiations. The fact pattern, as noted earlier, is the one that relates to the purchase of sugar in Brazil in the Introduction (4), at 11. You should be aware that the facts can be, and are likely to be, modified as the process progresses and can include undisclosed information relating to the position of one of sides. The reality of actual cases also develops as time progresses; this is what discovery and record-building mean.

(i)

The contract of arbitration must have a basic legal and substantive content. It must state that the parties agree to arbitrate and that they understand that arbitration represents a surrender of judicial remedies. A valid contract of arbitration that covers the dispute in question obligates the parties to arbitrate and divests the courts of jurisdiction (except to assist the arbitration or enforce the award). The decisional law indicates that the term "dispute" should be defined with some limited specificity. The U.S. federal law does provide that a broad reference to disputes is all-inclusive: The term includes both contractual and statutory (or regulatory) disputes. Under the tolerant and supportive U.S. federal law, however, the authority to rule on jurisdictional challenges must be expressly delegated to the arbitrators (*Kaplan*, 514 U.S. 938 [1995]). U.S. law may not have any bearing upon an agreement for international commercial arbitration, but careful lawyering may be a better approach than trusting circumstances not to produce difficulties.

Accordingly, a standard provision on the scope of the reference to arbitration might read: "Any dispute arising under this contract, including but not limited to contractual, statutory, regulatory, or jurisdictional disputes, shall be submitted to arbitration." The clause describes the comprehensive reach of the parties' agreement to arbitrate. It could be made more precise by incorporating illustrations of what is meant by a particular category of disputes—for example, contractual disputes include but are not limited to breach, inadequate performance, or a failure to pay or to deliver in a reasonably timely or stipulated manner. There also may be questions about the phrase "under this contract." Does it include an alleged breach of a subcontract that one of the contracting parties entered into in order to satisfy its obligations under the principal contract? Assume that the contracting party is the disgruntled party in the subcontracting circumstances. The simple doctrinal answer to this question is that the subcontracting party allegedly in breach is not a party to the principal contract and is, therefore, not bound by its arbitral provision. The general language of the phrase, nevertheless, can invite and tolerate maneuvering by parties anxious to postpone the day of reckoning. It might be useful to state that the arbitration agreement only applies to disputes between "the contracting parties" or "the parties directly involved in or implicated by the contract...."

Any question raised in this regard would be decided by the arbitrators—at least, under American concepts (*Bazzle*, 539 U.S. 444 [2003], and *Howsam*, 537 U.S. 79 [2002]), but also under the law of most jurisdictions given the decisional range of *kompetenz-kompetenz*. The objective, therefore, is not primarily to avoid a negative result, but rather to minimize the delay that can proceed from an adversarial litigious posture. The risk of obfuscation on this point may be so small that it is not worth the time and effort to negotiate the matter. Moreover, putting an unfamiliar or unrefined phrase in the clause could create trouble where none might have existed. It also can make the agreement less susceptible of efficacious implementation.

(ii)

A modern agreement to arbitrate might in reality be a dispute resolution provision. In this framework, arbitration could be a remedy of last resort. The dispute resolution clause might state that the parties and their representatives will undertake to negotiate any differences that might emerge. If the party negotiations do not result in a settlement within a specified time, the parties agree to engage in mediation pursuant to the UNCITRAL Model Law on Conciliation as administered by the Stockholm Chamber of Commerce. If no mediated settlement is reached within thirty days, either party can submit a demand for arbitration. Arbitration shall constitute a final and binding remedy. The parties agree to abide by the arbitral tribunal's award. The agreement to arbitrate, however, does not preclude the parties from seeking judicial assistance in aid of arbitration or from seeking vacatur or confirmation of the award before a competent court of law.

This aspect of the contract of arbitration raises a number of considerations. First, the rationale for the tripartite remedial approach is to encourage inexpensive, quick, and responsive solutions to the problems of implementing the transaction. As soon as a third-party becomes involved—either as a mediator or as an adjudicator, the dispute takes on a more formal and remote character. The parties no longer have direct or unimpeded access to the problem. They must contend with the mediator's perspective and advice. They are free to reject them, unlike the arbitrator's conclusion. Party negotiations are the most basic response—and also the most adapted and knowledgeable, in some respects. It might behoove the parties to make a commitment to this form of dispute resolution at the outset in the contract.

Second, the nonadjudicatory stages of the dispute resolution framework are subject to a time limit rule. The latter serves to discipline the use of negotiated relief—to avoid having the discussion of issues and the submission of settlement proposals become a means for creating delay and increased expense. The party who is advantaged by and seeks solely an adjudicated outcome in contravention of the terms established at the outset of the agreement can take advantage of the time-limit rule to foreclose other forms of relief. Should that circumstance, if indeed it can be established, result in a claim for bad faith conduct before the arbitrators? Should such a claim be available only if the agreement acknowledges it? What result if the arbitrators on their own want to consider it or believe that it should apply? The parties may also want to limit the duration of any arbitration. In this case, they should subscribe to "fast-track" arbitration or to a customized version of it.

Third, the use of mediation pursuant to two different institutional protocols can become confusing and riddled with conflicts. In fact, the first reference is statutory and not institutional at all except for the source of the law. The availability of the UNCITRAL Model Law on Conciliation, in fact, may depend upon whether an implicated jurisdiction has adopted the model law as its own. Assuming it has or that affected jurisdictions allow party choice to trump local law, the model law regulates the relationship between a legal system and mediation activities. It does not constitute a set of rules on mediation procedure. Therefore, the parties may have intended to be governed in their mediation efforts by the latest legislation on mediation, but their implementation of that intent may have been off-center or somewhat misguided.

Moreover, it is uncertain whether the Stockholm Chamber of Commerce has rules on mediation, and—if it does, whether they are in agreement with the substance of the uniform law. The parties need to engage in some amount of due diligence. Also, it is unclear whether the reference to mediation needs to be legalized by referring to rules and institutions. The appointment of a mediator may be all that is necessary on this score. Mediation is a form of structured negotiation, not a trial mechanism. The parties appoint an individual mediator with a particular mediation style and personality. It may be more pertinent to state rules for the selection of a mediator than anything else. Whether and how many candidates will be interviewed? Whether a third-party should appoint the mediator? In addition, there should be some indication of whether mediators can also function as arbitrators or vice versa. Do the parties intend for mediation/arbitration or arbitration/mediation procedures to apply?

Four, the parties need to understand the significance of providing for a hierarchy of remedies. Once a dispute materializes, they are bound—subject to mutual rescission—to the agreed-upon terms. A number of recent courts have held that preliminary resort to other dispute resolution techniques is a necessary condition precedent to arbitration, if the agreement so provides.

Finally, the last part of the clause contains "recital" language. The content of this part of the clause, however, is more standard than it is perfunctory. In fact, it addresses significant issues in the process, but that have been so commonplace that practice has settled upon a formulaic means of dealing with them. Therefore, the parties accept arbitration as their exclusive remedy for dispute resolution and further agree that the arbitrator's determination shall be final. The fact of agreement to arbitration does not preclude the parties from seeking judicial assistance during the arbitration or challenging the award through a vacatur action.

Despite its standard character, the language does not convey its meaning readily or in a transparent manner. The recital tends to be approximative and murky. Language that is more straightforward might read: "The contracting parties agree that, once negotiation remedies have failed, the recourse to arbitration shall be the exclusive means of dispute resolution. Accordingly, they agree to arbitrate disputes and to accept the arbitral award as a final and binding determination of their disputes. Nonetheless, the parties further agree that, despite their recourse to binding arbitration, they may seek the assistance of courts in implementing the arbitral agreement or proceedings and may bring an action to confirm or vacate or otherwise challenge the award or the arbitrators."

(iii)

Selecting an administrative format for the arbitration also is an important part of an arbitration agreement. *Ad hoc* arbitrations do take place especially under the UNCITRAL Rules of arbitration, but they are not the common practice. The responsibility of establishing and managing an arbitration, as well as participating in it, usually would be overwhelming to commercial parties and their representatives. It is much easier to designate an administering arbitral institution and to let it handle the management of the process for a fee. The institutions are professional organizations with substantial experience in these matters. The considerations should focus upon choosing between the various organizations. On this matter, costs can be a significant factor.

§ 8. CHOOSING AND EMPOWERING INTERNATIONAL ARBITRATORS

Selecting the arbitrators is a critical facet of the arbitral process. The designated arbitrators must be experienced and capable of exercising sound professional judgment. They should be experts in the area.

They also must be capable of working well together. These objectives may require the party representatives to engage in a substantial amount of due diligence. There is a Roster of International Arbitrators and a Martindale & Hubbell directory of professionals in the ADR area. Personal contacts can be instrumental in identifying the proper arbitrator.

Once a group of suitable individuals has been identified, each of them should be asked to submit a dossier of prior arbitral rulings and a list of other pertinent qualifications. The appointing party should have a sense of how the perspective arbitrators approach a decisional mandate, whether they can cooperate with others in performing adjudicatory functions, and how they are likely to rule on a given subject area. The latter does not compromise impartiality. It would be foolhardy for a party not to appoint an arbitrator who has an affinity for the positions that support its interests. This procedure is distinguishable from the process of interviewing prospective arbitrators and asking them how they would rule and whether they would defend the appointing party's position on the tribunal. Any extensive interviewing of candidates is suspect. Independent due diligence in addition to a brief telephone or email discussion is the better, more professional, and legitimate approach.

Further, the parties could agree in the arbitration agreement that the designated arbitrators must share certain characteristics. For example, the parties may stipulate that any arbitrator must be fluent in a particular language, have formal training in a particular legal system or in a professional specialty, be familiar with a specific culture(s), or have no financial exposure in particular types of companies. They may also agree that any tribunal would include partisan arbitrators who need not be as impartial as the neutral arbitrator. Finally, a protocol for arbitrator disclosure could be established in the arbitration agreement.

A final consideration could be a statement of the arbitrators' adjudicatory powers. The parties should agree on whether the arbitrators can award damages beyond ordinary compensatory damages: attorney's fees, punitive damages, treble damages, or pre-and post-award interest. Also, are there ceilings on the amount of damages? In addition, do the arbitrators have unlimited authority to decide procedural matters? As long as there is a collegial majority, the arbitral tribunal can decide on the use of experts, the questioning of witnesses, the place and length of the proceedings, the form of the award, and other related matters. The parties can impose restrictions on the arbitrators' discretion. They could require, for example, that all witnesses be heard live and be subject to cross-examination.

§ 9. THE ARBITRAL TRIAL

Finally, a contemporary agreement to arbitrate can establish the core features of the arbitral trial. There are a number of critical concerns about any international arbitral proceeding: Whether the arbitrators function as referees or primary decision-makers; whether documentary discovery and other record-building devices are available; the admission and evaluation of evidence; how witnesses are to perform; and the content of the award. As to the latter, the traditional question has involved determining whether the arbitrators are required to provide reasons for their determination and, if so, how extensive they need to be. The more modern question relates to the provision of a standard of review for the award at the place of rendition or enforcement. Can the parties "opt-in" to a review of the merits of the award?

There may be other essential aspects of the arbitration agreement and process: Confidentiality, language, replacing arbitrators, payment of fees, law applicable to the arbitration agreement and the arbitration proceedings, and the joinder of parties. Governing law considerations can become particularly complex. Different laws can apply to the parties, the contract, the arbitration agreement, the arbitration proceeding, and the award. Complicated provisions can be pathological. Many of these topics are regulated by arbitral institutional rules. You may believe, however, that they warrant special treatment. It is now up to you to decide.

§ 10. ANTI–SUIT INJUNCTIONS AND INTERNATIONAL ARBITRAL PROCEEDINGS

An emerging potential problem of international arbitral practice is whether U.S. or other national courts have the authority to issue anti-suit injunctions to litigants prohibiting them from participating in an international arbitral proceeding. The prospect of the exercise of such judicial power appears objectionable on a number of grounds: First, such a judicial practice seemingly violates the "emphatic federal policy" in favor of arbitration—in particular, the policy's strong endorsement of ICA. The use of court power in these circumstances clearly infringes upon the autonomy and independence of arbitration. Second, in light of the decisional law that renders international judicial assistance under § 1782 unavailable to international arbitrators (presumably for the reason of the public-private boundary), it is inconsistent then to use public judicial power to contravene lawful recourse to arbitration. To attack ICA openly on this basis clearly frustrates the would-be policy in favor of arbitration. Finally, it creates the standard problem of comity (at least indirectly) by commanding the imposition of national jurisdictional rules on a non-national entity. An ICA tribunal is not a national public law entity in the sense of a court, but judicial interference strikes it more than in an offensive manner. It calls its very legitimacy and effectiveness into question.

According to Professor Bachand of the McGill Law Faculty, English courts have enjoined arbitral proceedings from continuing when they believed that the proceedings were defective—because the arbitrator was seemingly partial, where the arbitration agreement was defective as a contract, when a party repudiated the contract of arbitration, or in instances in which the parties had mutually rescinded the agreement to arbitrate. Professor Bachand further asserts that courts in both the

United States and Canada believe that their "injunctive powers allow them to issue orders enjoining ongoing arbitral proceedings." *See* Frédéric Bachand, *The UNCITRAL Model Law's Take on Anti–Suit Injunctions*, *in* E. Gaillard & Y. Banifatemi, eds., The Use of Anti-Suit Injunctions in International Arbitration (2004) (forthcoming).

The issue joins the arbitral considerations with the jurisdictional matters that we considered earlier in regard to municipal courts. It also transforms the concept of judicial deference to and helpful assistance to ICA proceedings into a type of interference. Courts assume the authority to regulate and police the propriety of arbitral proceedings. Is there any way to assess this development positively and to encourage it? Doesn't it undermine the entire architecture of the modern world judicial and legislative consensus on ICA? Does the emerging practice service any necessary policy objective? Does it respond or resolve an existing or possible problem? Is it nothing other than a power play? Is it likely to be exercised only in cases in which such an injunction is the only possible resolution? Who makes that determination? On what basis?

§ 11. ARBITRATOR IMPARTIALITY: THE *IBA GUIDELINES*

On May 22, 2004, the Council of the International Bar Association approved the *IBA Guidelines On Conflicts Of Interest In International Arbitration*. The *Guidelines* reflect more than two years of discussions and dialogue with leading authorities around the world. They seek to establish workable standards by which to define and guarantee arbitrator impartiality. The *Guidelines* contain seven General Standards that can govern the appointment and retention of international arbitrators. The Standards focus upon disclosure and independence. Arbitrators have a duty of disclosure as to prior relationships between themselves and their organization and the parties and the subject matter of the disputes. Arbitrating parties also must disclose prior or current relationships with any of the arbitrators.

Moreover, to implement the directives in the General Standards, the *Guidelines* have three color-coded categories of circumstances that carry a recommended level of disclosure. The "red list" describes two types of circumstances: (1) instances of conflicts which should preclude the designated arbitrator from accepting the appointment; and (2) conflicts that must be disclosed fully, but which can be accepted by the appointing party once it has a full knowledge and understanding of them. In the latter circumstance, the designation of the arbitrator can remain effective. So-called nonwaivable conflicts could be the ownership of stock in one of the companies to the dispute. Financial self-interest always clouds judgment and makes it impossible to reach a disinterested conclusion. The would-be waivable conflicts might include ownership of mutual fund shares in companies of the type to which the implicated companies belong. The provision of legal representation to affiliated companies in the past by members of the large law firm to which the prospective arbitrator belongs may also be a "forgivable" conflict that can be repaired by full disclosure. Transparency as to the members of the arbitral tribunal—their experience, judgment, and professional leanings—is the critical factor and basic objective.

The "orange list" of conflicts represents grey-area circumstances. The failure to disclose such conflicting activities can taint the appointment with the possibility of bias—for example, working within the recent past for an affiliate of one of the parties on an unrelated matter. The connection is remote and indirect, but it nonetheless exists. Its discovery later by one of the parties could impair or prevent the enforcement of the award. Finally, the "green list" of circumstances attempts to prevent "over" disclosure. It contains a list of matters that do not need to be disclosed—for example, another lawyer in another office of the arbitrator's law firm represented another company against an affiliate of one of the parties. The arbitrator was not involved in the representation. Too much disclosure can create delay and invite challenges on specious grounds. The *Guidelines* are meant to guide parties and practitioners and to generate a uniform and efficient transborder approach to establishing arbitrator neutrality.

IBA GUIDELINES ON CONFLICTS OF INTEREST IN INTERNATIONAL ARBITRATION

[. . .]

Introduction

1. Problems of conflicts of interest increasingly challenge international arbitration. Arbitrators are often unsure about what facts need to be disclosed, and they may make different choices about disclosures than other arbitrators in the same situation. The growth of international business and the manner in which it is conducted, including interlocking corporate relationships and larger international law firms, have caused more disclosures and have created more difficult conflict of interest issues to determine. Reluctant parties have more opportunities to use challenges of arbitrators to delay arbitrations or to deny the opposing party the arbitrator of its choice. Disclosure of any relationship, no matter how minor or serious, has too often led to objections, challenge[,] and withdrawal or removal of the arbitrator.

2. Thus, parties, arbitrators, institutions[,] and courts face complex decisions about what to disclose and what standards to apply. In addition, institutions and courts face difficult decisions if an objection or a challenge is made after a disclosure. There is a tension between, on the one hand, the parties' right to disclosure of situations that may reasonably call into question an arbitrator's impartiality or independence and their right to a fair hearing and, on the other hand, the parties' right to select arbitrators of their choosing. Even though laws and arbitration rules provide some standards, there is a lack of detail in their guidance and of uniformity in their application. As a result, quite often members

of the international arbitration community apply different standards in making decisions concerning disclosure, objections[,] and challenges.

[. . .]

PART I: General Standards Regarding Impartiality, Independence[,] and Disclosure

(1) General Principle

Every arbitrator shall be impartial and independent of the parties at the time of accepting an appointment to serve and shall remain so during the entire arbitration proceeding until the final award has been rendered or the proceeding has otherwise finally terminated.

[. . .]

(2) Conflicts of Interest

(a) *An arbitrator shall decline to accept an appointment or, if the arbitration has already been commenced, refuse to continue to act as an arbitrator if he or she has any doubts as to his or her ability to be impartial or independent.*

(b) *The same principle applies if facts or circumstances exist, or have arisen since the appointment, that, from a reasonable third person's point of view having knowledge of the relevant facts, give rise to justifiable doubts as to the arbitrator's impartiality or independence, unless the parties have accepted the arbitrator in accordance with the requirements set out in General Standard(4).*

(c) *Doubts are justifiable if a reasonable and informed third party would reach the conclusion that there was a likelihood that the arbitrator may be influenced by factors other than the merits of the case as presented by the parties in reaching his or her decision.*

(d) *Justifiable doubts necessarily exist as to the arbitrator's impartiality or independence if there is an identity between a party and the arbitrator, if the arbitrator is a legal representative of a legal entity that is a party in the arbitration, or if the arbitrator has a significant financial or personal interest in the matter at stake.*

[. . .]

(3) Disclosure by the Arbitrator

(a) *If facts or circumstances exist that may, in the eyes of the parties, give rise to doubts as to the arbitrator's impartiality or independence, the arbitrator shall disclose such facts or circumstances to the parties, the arbitration institution or other appointing authority (if any, and if so required by the applicable institutional rules) and to the co-arbitrators, if any, prior to accepting his or her appointment or, if thereafter, as soon as he or she learns about them.*

(b) *It follows from General Standards 1 and 2(a) that an arbitrator who has made a disclosure considers himself or herself to be impartial and independent of the parties despite the disclosed facts and therefore capable of performing his or her duties as arbitrator. Otherwise, he or she would have declined the nomination or appointment at the outset or resigned.*

(c) *Any doubt as to whether an arbitrator should disclose certain facts or circumstances should be resolved in favor of disclosure.*

(d) *When considering whether or not facts or circumstances exist that should be disclosed, the arbitrator shall not take into account whether the arbitration proceeding is at the beginning or at a later stage.*

[. . .]

(4) Waiver by the Parties

(a) *If, within 30 days after the receipt of any disclosure by the arbitrator or after a party learns of facts or circumstances that could constitute a potential conflict of interest for an arbitrator, a party does not raise an express objection with regard to that arbitrator, subject to paragraphs (b) and (c) of this General Standard, the party is deemed to have waived any potential conflict of interest by the arbitrator based on such facts or circumstances and may not raise any objection to such facts or circumstances at a later stage.*

(b) *However, if facts or circumstances exist as described in General Standard 2(d), any waiver by a party or any agreement by the parties to have such a person serve as arbitrator shall be regarded as invalid.*

(c) *A person should not serve as an arbitrator when a conflict of interest, such as those exemplified in the waivable Red List, exists. Nevertheless, such a person may accept appointment as arbitrator or continue to act as an arbitrator, if the following conditions are met:*

(i) *All parties, all arbitrators and the arbitration institution or other appointing authority (if any) must have full knowledge of the conflict of interest; and*

(ii) *All parties must expressly agree that such person may serve as arbitrator despite the conflict of interest.*

(d) *An arbitrator may assist the parties in reaching a settlement of the dispute at any stage of the proceedings. However, before doing so, the arbitrator should receive an express agreement by the parties that acting in such a manner shall not disqualify the arbitrator from continuing to serve as arbitrator. Such express agreement shall be considered to be an effective waiver of any potential conflict of interest that may arise from the arbitrator's participation in such process or from information that the arbitrator may learn in the process. If the assistance by the arbitrator does not lead to final settlement of the case, the parties remain bound by their waiver. However, consistent with General Standard 2(a) and notwithstanding such agreement, the arbitrator shall resign if, as a consequence of his or her involvement in the settlement process, the arbitrator develops doubts as to his or her ability to remain impartial or independent in the future course of the arbitration proceedings.*

[. . .]

(5) Scope

These Guidelines apply equally to tribunal chairs, sole arbitrators[,] and party-appointed arbitrators. These Guidelines do not apply to non-neutral arbitrators, who do not have an obligation to be independent and impartial, as may be permitted by some arbitration rules or national laws.

[. . .]

(6) Relationships

(a) *When considering the relevance of facts or circumstances to determine whether a potential conflict of interest exists or whether disclosure should be made, the activities of an arbitrator's law firm, if any, should be reasonably considered in each individual case. Therefore, the fact that the activities of the arbitrator's firm involve one of the parties shall not automatically constitute a source of such conflict or a reason for disclosure.*

(b) *Similarly, if one of the parties is a legal entity which is a member of a group with which the arbitrator's firm has an involvement, such facts or circumstances should be reasonably considered in each individual case. Therefore, this fact alone shall not automatically constitute a source of a conflict of interest or a reason for disclosure.*

(c) *If one of the parties is a legal entity, the managers, directors[,] and members of a supervisory board of such legal entity and any person having a similar controlling influence on the legal entity shall be considered to be the equivalent of the legal entity.*

[. . .]

(7) Duty of Arbitrator and Parties

(a) *A party shall inform an arbitrator, the Arbitral Tribunal, the other parties[,] and the arbitration institution or other appointing authority (if any) about any direct or indirect relationship between it (or another company of the same group of companies) and the arbitrator. The party shall do so on its own initiative before the beginning of the proceeding or as soon as it becomes aware of such relationship.*

(b) *In order to comply with General Standard 7(a), a party shall provide any information already available to it and shall perform a reasonable search of publicly available information.*

(c) *An arbitrator is under a duty to make reasonable enquiries to investigate any potential conflict of interest, as well as any facts or circumstances that may cause his or her impartiality or independence to be questioned. Failure to disclose a potential conflict is not excused by lack of knowledge if the arbitrator makes no reasonable attempt to investigate.*

[. . .]

PART II: Practical Application Of The General Standards

[. . .]

1. Non–Waivable Red List

1.1. There is an identity between a party and the arbitrator, or the arbitrator is a legal representative of an entity that is a party in the arbitration.

1.2. The arbitrator is a manager, director[,] or member of the supervisory board, or has a similar controlling influence in one of the parties.

1.3. The arbitrator has a significant financial interest in one of the parties or the outcome of the case.

1.4. The arbitrator regularly advises the appointing party or an affiliate of the appointing party, and the arbitrator or his or her firm derives a significant financial income therefrom.

2. Waivable Red List

2.1. Relationship of the arbitrator to the dispute

2.1.1 The arbitrator has given legal advice or provided an expert opinion on the dispute to a party or an affiliate of one of the parties.

2.1.2 The arbitrator has previous involvement in the case.

2.2. Arbitrator's direct or indirect interest in the dispute

2.2.1 The arbitrator holds shares, either directly or indirectly, in one of the parties or an affiliate of one of the parties that is privately held.

2.2.2 A close family member[1] of the arbitrator has a significant financial interest in the outcome of the dispute.

2.2.3 The arbitrator or a close family member of the arbitrator has a close relationship with a third party who may be liable to recourse on the part of the unsuccessful party in the dispute.

2.3. Arbitrator's relationship with the parties or counsel

2.3.1 The arbitrator currently represents or advises one of the parties or an affiliate of one of the parties.

2.3.2 The arbitrator currently represents the lawyer or law firm acting as counsel for one of the parties.

2.3.3 The arbitrator is a lawyer in the same law firm as the counsel to one of the parties.

1. Throughout the Application Lists, the term "close family member" refers to a spouse, sibling, child, parent[,] or life partner.

2.3.4 The arbitrator is a manager, director[,] or member of the supervisory board, or has a similar controlling influence, in an affiliate[2] of one of the parties if the affiliate is directly involved in the matters in dispute in the arbitration.

2.3.5 The arbitrator's law firm had a previous but terminated involvement in the case without the arbitrator being involved himself or herself.

2.3.6 The arbitrator's law firm currently has a significant commercial relationship with one of the parties or an affiliate of one of the parties.

2.3.7 The arbitrator regularly advises the appointing party or an affiliate of the appointing party, but neither the arbitrator nor his or her firm derives a significant financial income therefrom.

2.3.8 The arbitrator has a close family relationship with one of the parties or with a manager, director[,] or member of the supervisory board or any person having a similar controlling influence in one of the parties or an affiliate of one of the parties or with a counsel representing a party.

2.3.9 A close family member of the arbitrator has a significant financial interest in one of the parties or an affiliate of one of the parties.

3. Orange List

3.1. Previous services for one of the parties or other involvement in the case

3.1.1 The arbitrator has within the past three years served as counsel for one of the parties or an affiliate of one of the parties or has previously advised or been consulted by the party or an affiliate of the party making the appointment in an unrelated matter, but the arbitrator and the party or the affiliate of the party have no ongoing relationship.

3.1.2 The arbitrator has within the past three years served as counsel against one of the parties or an affiliate of one of the parties in an unrelated matter.

3.1.3 The arbitrator has within the past three years been appointed as arbitrator on two or more occasions by one of the parties or an affiliate of one of the parties.[3]

2. Throughout the Application Lists, the term "affiliate" encompasses all companies in one group of companies including the parent company.

3. It may be the practice in certain kinds of arbitration, such as maritime or commodities arbitration, to draw arbitrators from a small, specialized pool. If in

3.1.4 The arbitrator's law firm has within the past three years acted for one of the parties or an affiliate of one of the parties in an unrelated matter without the involvement of the arbitrator.

3.1.5 The arbitrator currently serves, or has served within the past three years, as arbitrator in another arbitration on a related issue involving one of the parties or an affiliate of one of the parties.

3.2. Current services for one of the parties

3.2.1 The arbitrator's law firm is currently rendering services to one of the parties or to an affiliate of one of the parties without creating a significant commercial relationship and without the involvement of the arbitrator.

3.2.2 A law firm that shares revenues or fees with the arbitrator's law firm renders services to one of the parties or an affiliate of one of the parties before the arbitral tribunal.

3.2.3 The arbitrator or his or her firm represents a party or an affiliate to the arbitration on a regular basis but is not involved in the current dispute.

3.3 Relationship between an arbitrator and another arbitrator or counsel.

3.3.1 The arbitrator and another arbitrator are lawyers in the same law firm.

3.3.2 The arbitrator and another arbitrator or the counsel for one of the parties are members of the same barristers' chambers.[4]

3.3.3 The arbitrator was within the past three years a partner of, or otherwise affiliated with, another arbitrator or any of the counsel in the same arbitration.

3.3.4 A lawyer in the arbitrator's law firm is an arbitrator in another dispute involving the same party or parties or an affiliate of one of the parties.

3.3.5 A close family member of the arbitrator is a partner or employee of the law firm representing one of the parties, but is not assisting with the dispute.

3.3.6 A close personal friendship exists between an arbitrator and a counsel of one party, as demonstrated

such fields it is the custom and practice for parties frequently to appoint the same arbitrator in different cases, no disclosure of this fact is required where all parties in the arbitration should be familiar with such custom and practice.

4. Issues concerning special considerations involving barristers in England are discussed in the Background Information issued by the Working Group.

by the fact that the arbitrator and the counsel regularly spend considerable time together unrelated to professional work commitments or the activities of professional associations or social organizations.

3.3.7 The arbitrator has within the past three years received more than three appointments by the same counsel or the same law firm.

3.4. Relationship between arbitrator and party and others involved in the arbitration.

3.4.1 The arbitrator's law firm is currently acting adverse to one of the parties or an affiliate of one of the parties.

3.4.2 The arbitrator had been associated within the past three years with a party or an affiliate of one of the parties in a professional capacity, such as a former employee or partner.

3.4.3 A close personal friendship exists between an arbitrator and a manager or director or a member of the supervisory board or any person having a similar controlling influence in one of the parties or an affiliate of one of the parties or a witness or expert, as demonstrated by the fact that the arbitrator and such director, manager, other person, witness or expert regularly spend considerable time together unrelated to professional work commitments or the activities of professional associations or social organizations.

3.4.4 If the arbitrator is a former judge, he or she has within the past three years heard a significant case involving one of the parties.

3.5 Other circumstances

3.5.1 The arbitrator holds shares, either directly or indirectly, which by reason of number or denomination constitute a material holding in one of the parties or an affiliate of one of the parties that is publicly listed.

3.5.2 The arbitrator has publicly advocated a specific position regarding the case that is being arbitrated, whether in a published paper or speech or otherwise.

3.5.3 The arbitrator holds one position in an arbitration institution with appointing authority over the dispute.

3.5.4 The arbitrator is a manager, director[,] or member of the supervisory board, or has a similar controlling influence, in an affiliate of one of the parties, where the affiliate is not directly involved in the matters in dispute in the arbitration.

4. Green List

4.1 Previously expressed legal opinions

4.1.1 The arbitrator has previously published a general opinion (such as in a law review article or public lecture) concerning an issue which also arises in the arbitration (but this opinion is not focused on the case that is being arbitrated).

4.2 Previous services against one party

4.2.1 The arbitrator's law firm has acted against one of the parties or an affiliate of one of the parties in an unrelated matter without the involvement of the arbitrator.

4.3 Current services for one of the parties

4.3.1 A firm in association or in alliance with the arbitrator's law firm, but which does not share fees or other revenues with the arbitrator's law firm, renders services to one of the parties or an affiliate of one of the parties in an unrelated matter.

4.4 Contacts with another arbitrator or with counsel for one of the parties

4.4.1 The arbitrator has a relationship with another arbitrator or with the counsel for one of the parties through membership in the same professional association or social organization.

4.4.2 The arbitrator and counsel for one of the parties or another arbitrator have previously served together as arbitrators or as co-counsel.

4.5 Contacts between the arbitrator and one of the parties

4.5.1 The arbitrator has had an initial contact with the appointing party or an affiliate of the appointing party (or the respective counsels) prior to appointment, if this contact is limited to the arbitrator's availability and qualifications to serve or to the names of possible candidates for a chairperson and did not address the merits or procedural aspects of the dispute.

4.5.2 The arbitrator holds an insignificant amount of shares in one of the parties or an affiliate of one of the parties, which is publicly listed.

4.5.3 The arbitrator and a manager, director[,] or member of the supervisory board, or any person having a similar controlling influence, in one of the parties or an affiliate of one of the parties, have worked together as joint experts or in another professional capacity, including as arbitrators in the same case.

[. . .]

Notes and Questions

1. There is no doubt that arbitrator impartiality is a serious practical problem. The arbitral tribunal's failure to be impartial can result in the vacatur of the award under either domestic law or international standards. It also creates a practical threshold problem of how to address the neutrality issue in the appointment of arbitrators. The answer has generally been through the disclosure of information by the arbitrator to the appointing party, the other party, the other arbitrators, and the administering institution. The parties and their counsel generally owed a duty of similar disclosure.

Tribunal-wide neutrality was not always the controlling ethic. In U.S. domestic law, in fact, some courts (for example, the U.S. Court of Appeals for the Seventh Circuit) still accept and expect to see "partisan" arbitrators on a three-member tribunals. The demand for arbitrator neutrality and/or disclosure has been much greater in transborder arbitration. Neutrality and impartiality standards were once directed principally at the third arbitrator. The party-appointed arbitrators were expected at least to lean in the direction of the appointing party's position. That system of weighting the arbitral tribunal is currently being challenged vigorously by arbitral institutions and other groups. The trend is not in response to any actual abuse or an Enron-like situation, but rather—it seems—to anticipate and disarm prospective criticisms about the legitimacy and authority of the process.

It is to this situation that the *IBA Guidelines* are intended to respond in a timely manner. The *Guidelines* are not meant to be a final proclamation on the matter; rather, they seek to generate a discussion and to outline possible solutions. A progressive application of the *Guidelines* over time, it is hoped, will create eventually an acceptable uniform transborder practice in the area.

2. Is the IBA approach the best strategy for accomplishing this goal? Is the objective of achieving neutrality illusory? Isn't the achievable objective professionalism? Aren't dispositions the most critical factor to appointment? Is any party to a dispute involving $50 million USD likely to appoint an "unknown" to be its arbitrator? If all arbitrators are really neutral, why have three of them? Do disclosures guarantee or speak to neutrality? Don't they simply reveal and make the process (more) transparent? The fact of conflict or of some conflict does not necessarily invalidate the appointment. Who decides whether a disclosed conflict is enough to engender disqualification? The appointing party? The other party? The arbitrators? The implicated arbitrator? The administering institution? A court? Aren't such circumstances likely to adversarialize the process even more? Is all of this necessary? A good idea?

3. Doesn't the "Introduction" to the *Guidelines* point to insurmountable obstacles to implementing a transborder regime on this matter? Isn't the

issue a Pandora's box of irreconcilable conflicts? Is the attempt to legitimate the process only achievable through adversarialization which, in the end, will discredit the process much more and will actually harm it? Are these concerns mere theory and, like an anticipatory breach of contract, purely speculative? Does the quest for tribunal-wide neutrality represent an example of fixing something that isn't broken? Can the more complicated process of ICA no longer rely on individual trust and professional integrity?

4. In Part I, the *General Principle*, it is difficult, if not impossible, to disagree with the aspiration of impartiality and independence. The challenge is determining what these terms mean in actual circumstances in which a party initially communicates with a prospective arbitrator and conducts a preliminary interview. Would establishing a rule of a single *ex parte* communication at the outset of the matter for conveying objective information about the dispute and the offer to serve as an arbitrator resolve the problem and clarify the meaning of impartiality and independence? The rule would need to be uniformly enforced by arbitrators. What do you think?

5. In Part I, *Conflicts of Interest*, the concept that is critical to the regulation of arbitrator neutrality is "justifiable doubts." How are such doubts likely to arise? Could a party "corrupt" the other side's arbitrator by an improper *ex parte* communication? Doesn't an attempt to disqualify an arbitrator, if unsuccessful, create "justifiable doubts" as to that arbitrator's ability to assess neutrally the challenging party's case? Therefore, the lodging of a challenge to an arbitrator could automatically lead to a disqualification for "justifiable doubts." How could it be otherwise? It also appears that General Standards (2) is dependent upon arbitrators' self-policing. Does that feature of the rule inspire credibility? Ground (d) seems to clarify the basis for "justifiable doubts." Isn't the statement self-evident? Does the statement add anything to the cause of protecting arbitration's legitimacy? There is no indication that these standards have not been applied or are not respected by international arbitrators.

6. In Part I, *Disclosure by the Arbitrator*, the standard stated in 3(a) for arbitrator disclosure is contrasted in the Working Group's commentary to the standard adopted in 2(b) regarding disqualification. The Working Group describes one as "objective" and the other as "subjective." Can you ascribe correctly the adjectives to the provisions? Explain your attributions. Why are disclosure and disqualification treated differently? Is the distinction between "objective" and "subjective" helpful in implementing and interpreting the procedures? Is all of this still based upon the arbitrator's judgment? Do you think that disclosures and disqualification should incorporate national standards? Those of the arbitrator? Those of the parties? Is arbitrator disclosure an admission of a conflict of interest? Does it create "justifiable doubts"? Who is the final judge of this matter? Does General Standard (3) encourage "over" disclose? What does the latter mean and what consequences does it have on the arbitral process? What meaning do you attribute to (3)(d)? Isn't the provision impractical? Doesn't it invite abuse and opportunistic undermining of the process?

7. In Part I, *Waiver by the Parties*, General Standard (4) places some limits on the ability of the parties to require arbitrator disclosure or seek the disqualification of arbitrators. Objections must be expressly stated within a

reasonable time after discovery. Otherwise, the basis for challenge is waived. The quest for impeccable integrity and neutrality must yield to the efficacy of the process. The evident interpretative problem here relates to the definition of "express objection" or when a party learns of facts or circumstances. The tolling period is thirty days generally.

Does 4(b) unreasonably or unlawfully restrict the arbitrating parties' freedom of contract? If duress or incapacity cannot be established, why can't the parties mutually agree to any requirement or arbitrator. Is there a national law and public policy involved in such circumstances? Is the party agreement to this effect invalid according to IBA law? Can NGOs make law and issue regulations? What result if the designated arbitral tribunal rules that it has contractual and legal authority to rule? What result if that ruling is confirmed by a national court? Wouldn't this provision be more effective as an institutional arbitral rule chosen by the parties?

As to 4(c), what sanction can be used to enforce the content of the provision? Professional or monetary? Black-listing? Medieval forms of public humiliation? Isn't this provision, like the others, an aspiration? Shouldn't it, therefore, be written to persuade and convince, rather than as a rule? Does it contradict 4(b)? Is there a distinction based upon waivable and nonwaivable requirements? Isn't the framework already too complex to use? What if 4(c)(i) is satisfied, but not 4(c)(ii)?

Section 4(d) is probably the most controversial aspect of the General Standards, in some respects. It implicitly acknowledges that a mixing of remedial approaches is not only advisable, but also should be given specific protections. The protection relates nearly exclusively to maintaining the arbitrator's ability to function as an arbitrator after acting as a mediator. This is a very narrow professional perspective and approach. It is now well-settled that communications made in mediation are fully privileged. If an adjudicator attempts or is asked to mediate the dispute and then resumes his/her previous role, discovery is no longer the same because the adjudicator has acquired privileged knowledge outside the process of adjudication. The mixing of remedies, in effect, makes both of them less effective and fair. The parties may get a diluted form of mediation and are not able to have the full benefits of arbitral adjudication. Rather than protect the arbitrator's ability to serve as an arbitrator, the directive should protect the parties by mandating that they receive an objective evaluation of arb/med and med/arb as remedial processes.

8. In General Standard (5) does the tolerance of non-conforming parallel regimes dilute considerably the effect and credibility of the *Guidelines*? Is there a better accommodation that could be made? Which source of regulations has the better view of arbitrators? Explain. Assess the various categories of arbitrators that are referred to in (5). Should chairs have no additional requirements as to neutrality and disclosure? Doesn't the broad rule extinguish the distinctions and the need for tribunals?

9. In part I, *Relationships*, the IBA Working Group addresses "[t]he growing size of law firms" and the variability of "individual corporate structure arrangements" and their impact upon "maintaining confidence in the impartiality and independence of international arbitration." [*Explanation to General Standard 6.*] What basic rules are established? Is party choice

as to the selection of arbitrators protected? If the designated arbitrator is a member of a law firm, how should "the nature, timing, and scope" of the law firm's work affect arbitrator disclosure and disqualification? What is meant by the phrase "legal entity"? Why is it used? What is the equivalency language in (c) all about?

10. In Part I, *Duty of Arbitrator and Parties*, General Standard (7) addresses the need to disclose prior relationships and the obligation to engage in "reasonable" due diligence in this matter. What is the purpose of the rule? Does it establish a reasonable balance? What is the incentive for enforcement? How does it fit into the general framework?

11. You should assess the lists in Part II. Are they helpful or useful? Do they provide "guidance"? Are they an example of over zealous, rather mechanical regulation? How would they influence your representation of clients or the drafting of contracts for arbitration and to hire arbitrators?

12. Markham Ball, a distinguished international lawyer and arbitrator, presently the Director of the ADR Center of the International Law Institute and Adjunct Professor at the Georgetown University Law Center, has written an extensive assessment of the *IBA Guidelines*. *See* Markham Ball, *Probity Deconstructed—How Helpful, Really, are the New International Bar Association Guidelines on Conflicts of Interest in International Arbitration?*, 15 World Arb. & Mediation Rep. 333, 340 (2004). Mr. Ball reaches the following conclusion:

> The *Guidelines* make an important contribution toward the analysis and solution of the problems they address. The Working Group's detailed examination and debate of both principle and practice illuminate the complexity of the issues and the often conflicting considerations that must be brought to bear in addressing them. The *Guidelines* will be of significant assistance to arbitrators, arbitration lawyers, and institutions, and probably also to many courts and legislators as well, in the future. As the introduction to the *Guidelines* states quite candidly, however, the IBA and the Working Group that drafted the *Guidelines* view them "as a beginning, rather than an end, of the process."[5]
>
> To the extent the *Guidelines* are an attempt to bring certainty and international uniformity to the treatment of arbitrator conflicts of interest, they succeed only somewhat. The Working Group's studies confirm that laws and practices now differ substantially in many respects from country to country. The elucidation and homogenization of these laws and practices will come about only over time, through developments in one case and one country after another. In this process, the *Guidelines* provide helpful analysis and valuable suggestions. Beyond that, however, they cannot and do not go.
>
> To a common law lawyer, and probably to most lawyers, it can come as neither a surprise nor a disappointment to learn that there is, and can be, no final, complete and definitive rulebook, or that the governing rules now differ in different countries. The common law is quite used to solving cases one at a time, in one jurisdiction at a time, balancing one interest against another, and to seeing rules evolve case by case. Most

5. *Id.* at 3.

lawyers will be quite comfortable with the notion that, after all the debate and illumination, the decision in the next case that arises must be based, not only on general rules, but also on common sense, good judgment and the rule of reason in applying those rules. It should come as no surprise that, for the foreseeable future, the answer to a conflict of interest question in a difficult case will remain to a large extent a "judgment call."

Do you share this assessment? Are the problems addressed by the *Guidelines* "essentially insoluble"? Won't the truly difficult cases exceed the guidance proffered by the IBA rules? Is there any "pre-fab" framework for addressing such cases? Are the *Guidelines*' focus upon the tendency to "over" disclosure and the attempt to deal rationally with disclosure in the context of "mega" international law firms their true contribution to the discussion of the neutrality and impartiality issues? Mr. Ball also asserts that the disqualification of international arbitrators is "relatively rare." *Id.* at 334. When disqualification occurs, however, it is highly disruptive in terms of delay and complication and may even lead to the vacatur or nonenforcement of the award. Are the *Guidelines* too much too soon? Won't they reduce the pool of qualified arbitrators? Do you have a better test or framework for disclosure?

13. As a point of information and comparison, you should note and consider that the ABA (American Bar Association) and the AAA (American Arbitration Association) published a new Code of Ethics for Arbitrators in 2004. It replaces the 1977 Code. Prior to the new code, the presumption had been that a party-appointed arbitrator was a non-neutral. The new code reverses the presumption: All arbitrators, including party-appointed arbitrators, are presumed to be neutral. There are exceptions to the rule—for example, in cases in which the parties agree that party-appointed arbitrators are non-neutral. According to a distinguished practitioner: "From my perspective, a non-neutral arbitrator, party-appointed or otherwise, makes no sense whatsoever. The effective result of non-neutrals is that each party is essentially paying for two advocates—one who presents their case in that role, and the other who sits as their advocate on the arbitral tribunal." Arkin, *Neutrality of Dispute Resolvers in International Commercial Dispute Resolution*, 15 WORLD ARB. & MEDIATION REP. 270 (2004). What do you think?

§ 12. CULTURAL PREDICTABILITY IN INTERNATIONAL ARBITRATION

by

Lawrence W. Newman and *David Zaslowsky*
Partners, Litigation Department, Baker & McKenzie (New York)
(reprinted with permission).
[Previously published in the New York Law Journal, May 25, 2004, and the Baker & McKenzie
International Litigation and Arbitration Newsletter.]

In today's world it is probably fair to say that a majority of important international contracts—whether they are for joint ventures, concession agreements, major projects or major investments—have clauses providing for [the] resolution of disputes through arbitration. These provisions ordinarily bind the parties to arbitrate in accordance with the rules of such well-known international arbitral institutions as the International Chamber of Commerce or the International Centre for Dispute Resolution of the American Arbitration Association.

International arbitration gives business[] [managers] peace of mind in that parties from faraway countries will not be able to drag them into courts where procedures are alien and where impartiality is frequently uncertain, especially for outsiders. Likewise, an agreement to arbitrate avoids the risk of having the parties race to their favorite courthouse. These benefits of arbitration stem, in no small measure, from the widespread acceptance, in over 140 countries, of the United Nations Convention on the Recognition and Enforcement of Foreign Arbitral Awards (the U.N. Convention). The Convention requires signatory countries to refer disputes covered by arbitration clauses to arbitration in accordance with the parties' agreement.

(i) Procedural Predictability

Are the business[] [managers] obtaining the kind of predictability of dispute resolution that they think they are? The answer is, frequently, only to a limited extent, especially if the parties and the arbitrators are from different legal cultures. One of the reasons is that, although the rules of the international arbitral institutions provide certainty in some areas, in other areas they are not specific about the ways in which arbitral proceedings are to be conducted. One example relates to the extent of discovery that will be permitted. More subtle examples are the emphasis that will be placed in the hearings on oral testimony, cross-examination[,] and the maintenance of a verbatim transcript of proceedings.

In major international arbitrations, there is ordinarily a preliminary conference among the parties and the arbitrators in which various matters concerning the future course of the proceedings are discussed and decided. Prior to such a meeting, the parties can, and should, try to agree between themselves on as much as they can concerning the procedures to govern the case. Often, at this stage, however, the parties are antagonistic and not in a mood to agree. (Frequently, they have even been unable to agree on the chair[] of the arbitration panel, leaving the selection to the arbitral institution.) In the face of the parties' inability to agree on such important matters as discovery and other procedures of the case, the way in which the proceedings will be conducted will be up to the tribunal, and particularly its chair[], who has, under international arbitration practice, enormous control over the procedural aspects of the arbitration.

Chair[s] of arbitration panels come from many countries, with different legal cultures, and therefore have different views as to the ways in which evidence should be presented in adversarial proceedings. Thus, in court and arbitration proceedings in France and other Continental European countries, greater emphasis is placed on documentary evidence than on the testimony of witnesses, which is regarded as a less reliable form of proof. Oral testimony from parties is either discounted or not permitted because it is presumed to be unreliable as coming from a biased participant. [Because] oral testimony is of lesser importance, cross-examination of witnesses is correspondingly less significant. This relative lack of importance is emphasized by a practice that is often followed by European arbitration chair[s] of not having a verbatim transcript (court reporters are rare in Continental Europe) but, rather, of summarizing, in a relatively short memorandum, the essence of a witness's testimony. That document is prepared immediately after the witness finishes testifying and is then signed by the witness, making the statement another in the series of documents that are the record that is considered by the tribunal.

The approach described above, which is taken by many—but not necessarily all—European arbitrators, is frequently not understood by non-European parties when they enter into their contract with an arbitration clause. A party hoping to present part of its case through the cross-examination of representatives of the other side may therefore be disappointed when it finds that the chair[] does not want to hear that witness—perhaps because his written witness statement is already before the arbitral panel or because he places little credence on oral testimony by a person whom he regards as an obviously biased participant in the proceeding. Such a chair[] may permit, at best, only a limited period of time for cross-examination, with the result that cross-examination will not play an important role in the way in which the case is presented and regarded by the arbitral tribunal.

This Continental European approach of relying on documentary proof and distrusting oral evidence is accompanied by a strong antipathy for discovery. [Because] most arbitration disputes revolve around contracts, it is likely that there is often not a strong practical need for disclosure by the parties of correspondence between them. There is, however, likely to be additional documentary material (including, today, e-mail) that is relevant to the dispute that is exclusively in the hands of one of the parties. One example would be documents concerning a party's dealings with third parties such as its subcontractors or licensees. Another would be communications between one of the contracting parties and a third party that is not supposed to be dealing with that contracting party, which might be the most relevant evidence to a particular claim. In the absence of discovery of this kind and also in the absence of the production of internal documents—also anathema under Continental-European practice—there is far less material for use in cross-examining witnesses—as well as, of course, less evidence on the merits of the case to be considered by the arbitrators.

In the United States, on the other hand, lawyers are accustomed to having access to a plethora of documents created or held by the other side. Even in arbitration proceedings, it is not unheard of for there to be pre-hearing depositions of witnesses in cases in which the parties and arbitrators are American. In England, it is *de rigueur* for the parties to an arbitration to exchange documents relevant to the issues in the case, although arbitrators in England do not ordinarily permit depositions to be taken of witnesses who will testify at trial or in hearings, which is similar to the practice in English court proceedings.

(ii) Arbitration Hearings

Thus, whether a chair[] is from England, the United States[,] or Continental Europe can make a huge difference in the way in which arbitral proceedings are conducted, and thus, quite possibly, the outcome of the proceedings. A chair[] from a third-world country might introduce still further unexpected issues. Parties seeking predictability with respect to the way in which proceedings are being conducted can try to obtain it by making detailed arrangements in their arbitration clauses. However, such detailed clauses require that the parties have sufficient foresight and arbitration experience to think, at the time of the negotiation of a complex deal, of the details of how a dispute (which they may well think will never arise) might be conducted.

In actuality, detailed arbitration clauses are rare, and the reason for that is easily understood. Dispute resolution clauses ordinarily play a minor role in the negotiation of important business transactions. They are among those clauses found near the back of the contract and not given much attention by those concentrating on the "business" aspects of the agreement. Moreover, lawyers whose experience is in transactions and not in dispute resolution often negotiate them. The result is that the parties, rather than wrangle over details regarding dispute resolution clauses that might never be invoked, often settle for "plain vanilla" arbitration clauses that simply refer to the application of the rules of a specified arbitral institution.

An example of how arbitration clauses can be applied in unexpected ways with respect to the culture of an arbitration proceeding [is to be gained from experience.] The arbitration clause in [a] joint venture contract called for arbitration in London under the rules of the International Chamber of Commerce (ICC). We expected that, if the ICC had to make the appointment of the chair[], it would appoint an Englishman, who would have certain attitudes toward the conduct of the proceedings and discovery. When the parties could not agree on a chair[], the ICC surprised us by appointing a German chair[]. His ideas, which he imposed on the parties—concerning whether or not there should be discovery and how the proceedings should be conducted—were far removed from what we, on our side, thought would be applied by an English chair[] sitting in London.

Compounding the problem of cultural unpredictability is the attitude of some arbitrators that the parties are best off having a strong chair[] to tell them what to do. Cases that have both arbitrators with strong feelings about how the matter should be conducted and experienced lawyers with their own ideas about proper procedure raise the issue of "whose arbitration is it anyway?" From the point of view of the arbitrators, they have been selected to determine the dispute and, therefore, they believe that they have the right to decide on all issues that are not in the arbitration agreement or in the rules of the arbitration institution. From the parties' perspective, an arbitration proceeding is created under an agreement between the parties and they therefore should, if they reach agreement about certain procedures, have the right to control the case. Indeed, the parties can, if they wish, agree to terminate the arbitration panel and create another one, should the arbitrators not follow their collective wishes. Of course, such steps are seldom taken because the parties cannot agree or because of the additional cost and time involved in constituting an entirely new panel.

(iii) Reducing Procedural Unpredictability

What can be done to assure a greater level of predictability in international arbitration than is now generally obtained? One possibility is for there to be a code of procedure for arbitration, which sets forth rules regarding such issues as discovery and the conduct of hearings. That is not, however, realistic because the very existence of the different cultures would make it impossible to develop a single procedure applicable to all cases.

Another possibility may lie in the provision by the major arbitral institutions of options in connection with their model arbitration clauses that the parties can consider when making use of those model clauses in their contracts. For example, institutions could provide the texts of certain supplementary provisions with respect to how the arbitration will be conducted that the parties could, if they wish, add to the standard arbitration clauses. Option "A," for example, could provide for arbitration in the Continental European fashion, with little or no discovery, no transcription of hearings[,] and similar limitations on oral evidence. Option "B" could be what is generally regarded as the American approach, with greater opportunity for discovery, oral transcription of the hearings through a verbatim transcript[,] and ample time provided for cross-examination. Option "C" could be what one might call the English approach of permitting discovery but not going as far in this regard as the American approach. The optional provisions could be brief, with the institutions' rules or other literature explaining their content more fully.

Parties negotiating contracts could take these optional procedural regimes into consideration and add one of them, should they wish to do so, to their arbitration clause. That provision would be binding on the arbitrators and on the parties unless the parties chose to change it. As a result, arbitrators from cultures different from those of the parties would be obliged to follow what the parties had agreed to with respect to how the proceedings would be conducted. With such optional supplements to arbitration clauses, business[] [managers] would be able to secure greater predictability, not only in knowing that their disputes will be arbitrated, but also in how the arbitration [would] be conducted.

Notes and Questions

1. Do the authors—who have very considerable transborder litigation experience—argue that legal cultural differences are irreconcilable and always conflictual?

2. Which of the three legal traditions has the best trial format? Why? What's wrong with the others?

3. How do you evaluate the proposed three options? Should all arbitral institutions integrate them into their rules?

4. Is diverse uniformity the answer? Why?

5. How would you deal with these issues in your model international agreement to arbitrate?

Index

References are to Pages

†